D1756411

This book is a collection of papers, including three not previously published, by one of the leading philosophers in epistemology. It defends a well-groundedness account of justification and knowledge in a way that transcends the stereotypes of two of the most widely misunderstood positions in philosophy – foundationalism and coherentism. Robert Audi constructs a distinctively moderate, internalist foundationalism that incorporates major virtues of both coherentism and reliabilism. He also develops important distinctions, crucial for any epistemology, between positive and negative epistemic dependence, substantively and conceptually naturalistic theories, dispositional beliefs and dispositions to believe, and several forms of internalism. These contrasts are applied not only to rational belief but also to rational action and rational desire. The result is an integration of theoretical and practical reason that exhibits both as having a common structure and a basis in human experience.

In its detailed, cumulative treatment of many of the central topics in epistemology, the book will interest teachers and students in the theory of knowledge. However, by offering a theory of rationality – including practical rationality – as well as an account of justification and knowledge, it will also interest readers in ethical theory, philosophy of action, and philosophy of the social sciences.

The structure of justification

The structure
of justification

ROBERT AUDI

UNIVERSITY OF NEBRASKA – LINCOLN

CAMBRIDGE
UNIVERSITY PRESS

Published by the Press Syndicate of the University of Cambridge
The Pitt Building, Trumpington Street, Cambridge CB2 1RP
40 West 20th Street, New York, NY 10011–4211, USA
10 Stamford Road, Oakleigh, Melbourne 3166, Australia

First published 1993

Printed in the United States of America

Library of Congress Cataloging-in-Publication Data
Audi, Robert, 1941–
The structure of justification / Robert Audi.
p. cm.
Includes bibliographical references and index.
ISBN 0-521-44064-5. – ISBN 0-521-44612-0 (pbk.)
1. Justification (Theory of knowledge). 2. Knowledge, Theory of.
I. Title.
BD212.A83 1993
121'.6 – dc20   92–37498
CIP

A catalog record for this book is available from the British Library.

ISBN 0-521-44064-5 hardback
ISBN 0-521-44612-0 paperback

To my children

Contents

Contents

Preface and acknowledgments

This book brings together most of my epistemological papers published in the past fifteen years. There are also three prepared specially for this volume, including the introductory essay, which presents an overview of my position in epistemology. I offer the papers in the hope that they will repay reading or rereading, and that the whole is more than the sum of the parts. Within each of the book's four parts, the order of the papers is chronological. This is also their natural order. Many of the papers develop points, problems, or arguments introduced in their predecessors. Inevitably, then, there is some overlap. I believe, however, that any inconvenience to readers who, for this reason, choose to speed through certain parts will be outweighed by the gain in continuity and in the level of detail with which some of the recurring problems are treated. I should add that in one sense this book represents work in progress: My epistemological position is still very much in development.

For permission to use the previously published papers – in which only minor revisions have been made – I thank the editors of the following journals, listed with the relevant chapters: Chapter 1, *The Monist* (62, 4, 1978, 592–610); Chapter 2, *The Canadian Journal of Philosophy* (XII, 1, 1982, 163–182); Chapter 3, *Synthese* (55, 1, 1983, 119–139; Copyright © 1983 by D. Reidel Publishing Co., Dordrecht, Holland, and Boston, U.S.A.; reprinted by permission of Kluwer Academic Publishers); Chapter 5, *The Canadian Journal of Philosophy* (IV, 2, 1974, 253–267); Chapter 6, *Midwest Studies in Philosophy* (V, 1980, 75–95); Chapter 7, *The Journal of Philosophy* (LXXX, 7, 1983, 398–415); Chapter 8, *Philosophical Topics* (XIV, 1, 1986, 27–65); Chapter 9, *The Journal of Philosophical Research* (XVI, 1991, 473–492); Chapter 10, *Philosophy and Phenomenological Research* (XLIX, 1, 1988, 1–

29); Chapter 11, *American Philosophical Quarterly* (26, 4, 1989, 309–320); Chapter 13, *Social Theory and Practice* (9, 2–3, 1983, 311–334); Chapter 14, *Synthese* (65, 2, 1985, 159–184; reprinted by permission of Kluwer Academic Publishers); and Chapter 15, *Proceedings and Addresses of the American Philosophical Association* (62, 1, 1988, 227–256). This chapter was prepared as a presidential address to the American Philosophical Association and given at its Central Division Meeting in April 1988.

I wish it were possible to name all of the philosophers – and students of philosophy – from whom I have learned some of what went into these papers. They include authors of papers presented to the American Philosophical Association, at conferences, in the Department of Philosophy at the University of Nebraska, and in the National Endowment for the Humanities Summer Seminars and Summer Institute I directed during the 1980s. They also include many of the authors referred to in the papers – and many not referred to only because of space constraints. I particularly thank William P. Alston, Albert Casullo, Roderick M. Chisholm, Richard A. Foley, Paul K. Moser, Alvin Plantinga, and Ernest Sosa for critical comments and stimulating epistemological conversations over many years. In recent years, I have fruitfully discussed issues in epistemology with, and benefited from reading, Frederick R. Adams, Robert Almeder, John A. Barker, John B. Bender, Laurence BonJour, Panayot Butchvarov, the late Hector-Neri Castañeda, Wayne A. Davis, Michael DePaul, Fred Dretske, Susan Feagin, Richard Feldman, Richard Fumerton, Carl Ginet, Alan H. Goldman, Alvin I. Goldman, Gilbert Harman, John Heil, Risto Hilpinen, Jaegwon Kim, Peter D. Klein, Jonathan Kvanvig, Keith Lehrer, James Montmarquet, George S. Pappas, John R. Perry, Louis P. Pojman, Lawrence Powers, Philip L. Quinn, William L. Rowe, Frederick Schmitt, Robert Shope, Eleonore Stump, Donna Summerfield, Marshall Swain, James Van Cleve, Jonathan Vogel, and Nicholas Wolterstorff.

Overview

The grounds of justification
and the epistemic structure
of rationality

This book presents my overall conception of justification, a related view of knowledge, and detailed positions on a number of the major issues in epistemology. These issues include the debates between foundationalism and coherentism, internalism and externalism, naturalism and normativism, rationalism and empiricism, skepticism and common sense, and causal versus acausal accounts of the relation between justifying grounds and the beliefs they warrant. The book also connects theoretical reason, which is the chief focus of epistemology, with practical reason, which is a central element in the foundations of ethics.

This essay introduces the chapters, interconnects them, and, in some cases, extends what they say. For the most part, they exhibit a series of developing and mutually supporting epistemological positions. This is one reason for their chronological placement in each of the four parts. I will indicate, quite briefly, some of the developmental lines and many of the connections. In places, moreover, I make points not in the chapters themselves, sometimes by way of clarification and in other cases by replying to some criticism I have not previously answered.[1]

1. Not all of my epistemological papers are included, and there is much in my *Belief, Justification, and Knowledge* (Belmont, Cal.: Wadsworth, 1988) that is not included, particularly the chapters on the four classical basic sources of that triad: perception, memory, introspection, and reason. I have omitted, e.g., "Justification, Deductive Closure, and Reasons to Believe," *Dialogue* XXX (1991); "Moral Epistemology and the Supervenience of Ethical Concepts," *Southern Journal of Philosophy* XXIX Supplement (1991); "Scientific Objectivity and the Evaluation of Hypotheses," in Merrilee H. Salmon, ed., *The Philosophy of Logical Mechanism* (Dordrecht and Boston: Kluwer, 1989); "Foundationalism, Coherentism, and Epistemological Dogmatism" (though Chapter 4 incorporates its main points); "Believing and Affirming," *Mind* XCI (1982); and "Epistemic Disavowals and Self-Deception," *The Personalist* 57 (1976).

Parts I through III are squarely in epistemology; Part IV carries the general epistemological position into action theory in particular and the theory of rationality in general. There are at least two reasons for this. First, the kind of account of justification I offer has broad features that make it readily extendable from belief to action and the non-cognitive propositional attitudes. Indeed, I suggest that an account of justification for beliefs that is not to a significant degree extendable is likely to be deficient even in the cognitive domain. Second, I have tried to produce an account of justified belief that is realistic from the point of view of what belief *is*, understood from the perspective of psychology and the philosophy of mind. Beyond this, I am convinced that there are important analogies, both structural and normative, between action and belief and between belief and the conative propositional attitudes, especially desire and intention – the conative attitudes most important for understanding practical rationality. Some of these analogies run through all four parts.

I. THE FOUNDATIONALISM–
COHERENTISM CONTROVERSY

Despite its venerable age, foundationalism is one of the most widely misunderstood positions in philosophy. Coherentism is only slightly better understood. A major purpose of this section – and, indeed, of the book as a whole – is to transcend stereotypes of both. Foundationalism need not be understood along Aristotelian, Cartesian, or classical empiricist lines, any more than coherentism must be taken to be a kind of idealism. Both are rooted partly in these traditions, but each has outgrown its initial confines. Moreover, each is best understood in the context of the associated psychology of the epistemic agent. This is where the first chapter begins.

THE PSYCHOLOGICAL STRUCTURE OF COGNITION

If knowledge is constituted by a kind of belief – or indeed of any psychological materials – then a person who has it must have at least one belief (or other psychological element) for each item of knowledge. "Psychological Foundationalism" (Chapter 1) explores how we must be structured psychologically if foundationalism gives a correct account of our knowledge. The chapter does the same sort of work for coherentism and thereby provides a comparison of the two theories that differs from the comparisons standard in epistemology. On the assumption that a good epistemological theory should not imply an implausible psychological one, this proves instructive.

Foundationalism *as such*, taken as common to the various theorists who hold it, is above all a structural view. It says that a person's knowledge (or justified belief) has a foundational structure, but not what sorts of content the constitutive cognitions must have. In outline, the idea is that if one has any knowledge or justified belief, then, first, one has at least some knowledge or justified belief that is foundational, in the sense that it is not (inferentially) based on any further knowledge or belief and, second, any other knowledge or justified belief one has in some way rests on one or more of these foundational elements. This view does not imply that such foundational beliefs are, e.g., epistemically certain, or not themselves *grounded* in something else, such as perceptual experience. Thus, it is left open that, psychologically, the presence of these elements can be explained, and, epistemically, an answer can often be given to the question of what justifies them. What is ruled out is simply that they are justified, *inferentially*, by other beliefs. If they were, those beliefs would raise the same question, and we would either have to posit foundational ones or suppose – what psychological foundationalism argues is at best unlikely – that our cognitive systems contain inferential circles or infinite regresses.

This brings us to the question of psychological coherentism. For epistemological coherentism, inferential justification is crucial. Knowledge and justified belief possess their epistemic credentials by virtue of their relations to other cognitions; and the paradigms of such inferential relations are those connecting the belief of the conclusion of a good argument with the belief(s) of its premise(s). But what kind of psychology does this give us? On the plausible assumption that I have a finite set of beliefs,[2] I cannot have beliefs of premises for my premises, and beliefs of premises for those in turn, ad infinitum. It might seem that a solution would be *circular*

---

2. An assumption for which I have argued in "Believing and Affirming," *Mind* XCI (1982).

epistemic chains, finite sets of beliefs the first of which is (inferentially) based on the second, the second of which is based on the third, and so on until we come full circle, with the *n*th belief being based on the original one. This, however, does not make good psychological sense. One problem is that we do not seem to have any such chains, especially for our justified beliefs or our knowledge. But there is an *internal* and conceptual problem (one that to my knowledge is first introduced into the literature in this essay). On the plausible assumption – defended especially in Chapters 2, 7, and 14 – that if my belief that *p* is based on my belief that *q*, there is a partial causal sustaining relation between the latter belief and the former, we get a prima facie incoherence. For imagine the inferential circle again. Causation seems to be carried all the way through: if my belief that *p* is based on my belief that *q* and the latter belief is based on my belief that *r*, and this belief in turn on my belief that *p*, it seems that the belief that *p* sustains the belief that *r*, the belief that *r* sustains the belief that *q*, the belief that *q* sustains the belief that *p* – and hence the belief that *p* sustains itself, by virtue of the transitivity of the (partial) sustaining relation. Leaving aside the problem of how a belief can derive any justification from a chain going from it back to itself – something that sounds like the "self-justification" foundationalists have been accused of relying on – it is doubtful that anything *can* causally sustain itself.

Chapter 1 also explores other psychological models of coherence but notes that they raise serious difficulties. I conclude that, viewed psychologically, foundationalism can be seen not to suffer from a number of the difficulties brought against it, whereas coherentism, in one major form, has a serious internal problem. The kind of justificatory circle it would rely on cannot be virtuous.

THE FOUNDATIONALISM–COHERENTISM CONTRAST IN THE THEORY OF VALUE

The conclusion just stated is developed further in later chapters, beginning with "Axiological Foundationalism" (Chapter 2). Let me explain. Justified belief is only one among many normative domains. Our values – in the psychological sense of *valuations* – may also admit of justification (and rationality). Once it is realized that, understood generically, foundationalism and coherentism are mainly structural positions, we can see that the contrast between them should also arise in the domain of value. I do not mean the domain of intrinsic value – of objective value as a property of, say, enjoyable experiences. We *can* talk of foundationalism here, as we can speak of it for truths: the idea would be that just as some truths might be foundations of others, certain things of value, for instance pleasures, might be the basis of other valuable things. The chapter bears on these objective structures, but the issue is valuations taken as propositional attitudes analogous to beliefs. I note that valuations may be called sound when the thing valued really has intrinsic value, just as a belief is called true when its propositional object is true; but my concern is neutral with respect to such objectivism, just as psychological foundationalism is neutral with respect to skepticism. The foundations–coherence problem arises whether or not skepticism is correct.

The starting point of the axiological foundationalism constructed here is an analogy between non-inferential belief – the kind that is a candidate for foundational status – and intrinsic valuation: valuing something for its own sake, and not (wholly) on the basis of something further. The latter, instrumental valuation depends for its justification on its relation to the valuation(s) it is based on, much as an inferentially justified belief depends for its justification on the belief(s) it is based on. In both cases, two points are crucial. First, for the superstructure element to be justified, the foundational element must be also; second, the former must be suitably related to the latter, e.g. by an instrumental relation between valuations, as where my believing a film would please my daughter justifies my valuing the film on the basis of an intrinsic valuation of pleasing her. Plainly, then, we can formulate various foundationalist and coherentist theses for valuations as for beliefs.

A moderate version of axiological foundationalism would represent our cognitive structure as two-tiered. If we have any justified valuations, then, first, we have some directly justified ones (e.g., justified intrinsic valuations of enjoyable activities), and, second, any other justified valuations we have are based on one or more of these, say through being produced by one of the latter by our rationally believing that if we realize the object of one of these superstructure valuations (getting the film), we will thereby realize the object of some foundational one (pleasing the child).

In the case of coherentism, there is again the self-sustenance problem: the difficulty of representing a finite set of elements as cohering in a way that produces justification but does not imply that some element in part causally sustains itself. Can we formulate coherentism so as to avoid the problem? One major suggestion is that the coherentist can, in the interest of psychological realism, allow that some elements are *psychologically* foundational but deny that they are justificationally so. This applies to valuations as well as to beliefs and other propositional attitudes. Axiological coherentism, then, would be to the effect that, first, any justified valuation derives its justification from a justificatory relation to one or more other valuations with which it coheres and, second, if any justified valuation is psychologically direct (roughly, intrinsic as opposed to instrumental) and so not based wholly on another such element, the agent has available some further element that can be appealed to as providing a coherence justification for the direct valuation.

This avoids the self-sustenance problem, but at least two others remain. First, the formulation will apply to many foundational valuations (perhaps even to all in certain kinds of people); for assuming that foundationalism is committed only to unmoved movers and not to unmovable movers, it is left open that one can, if one wishes (e.g., in replying to skeptical queries), appeal to yet deeper foundations in shoring up those one has at a given time. Second, without a causal requirement on justificatory relations, we cannot adequately distinguish justification from *rationalization*. If, for instance, I do not value the film (in part) *because* I believe it will please my daughter, that instrumental belief may merely rationalize my valuing it – which is certainly what we would say it does if we found out that the reason for which I value the film is that I myself believe it will give *me* pleasure. Granting that I *have* an altruistic justification *for* valuing it, what justifies my valuing *of* it, if anything does, is egoistic. This issue is not fully resolved here and is dealt with in more detail in Chapters 7 and 14.

Before concluding this section, I want to sketch an interesting objection I have encountered more than once but have not answered in print.[3] A coherentist wishing to vindicate circular epistemic chains might claim that partial sustaining relations are *not* irreflexive: a thing can in part sustain itself. For consider the sticks of a tepee. One leans on another, which in turn leans on it, so by the transitivity of causal sustenance the first stick partly sustains itself. Now there is no need to deny that such a structure is in

---

3. Laurence BonJour is one of the people to mention this objection to me.

some sense "self-sustaining"; it is not, e.g., bolstered by stones at its base. But the example needs analysis. If we reflect on the physical forces, we can see that there really is no sustaining *simpliciter;* rather, each stick exerts a force *in a direction.* Indeed, one cannot properly describe the forces exerted without specifying their direction. As I see it, then, the first stick bears to the second a relation like *sustaining northwardly;* the second bears to the first a relation like *sustaining southwardly.* Each of these relations is transitive and irreflexive; but because they are different relations, there is no question of literal self-sustenance. What we have is a balance of opposite forces between the sticks, with each placed in the ground, and the ground sustaining the entire structure – a foundational picture. The self-sustenance turns out to rest squarely on the ground. One might say that the cognitive case lacks any analogy to the physical case of indexed forces: Among cognitions there is only sustaining simpliciter, which is not irreflexive. But there is an analogy. For one thing, a foundational belief sustains a belief based on it with respect to argumentative opposition to the latter, because it supplies a premise for support against the relevant objections, and with respect to conviction, because (other things equal) it adds to the strength of the belief it sustains. Thus, invoking a finer conception of sustenance in defense of the objection to circular (causal) coherence accounts does not undermine its use in the foundationalist framework. We can index the relevant forces there, too, and refine our cognitive psychology in doing so.[4]

The chapter closes with a sketch of what axiological foundationalism might actually look like in an Aristotelian interpretation, based on the *Nichomachean Ethics.* First, we take the valuation of one's own happiness as psychologically foundational – and presumably justified. Then other justified valuations can be seen to be based on it by virtue of *valuational chains,* the analogue of inferential chains of beliefs. This view need not be näively monistic

---

4. Other models may seem more appropriate to coherentism, e.g. an *agglutinative model* such as a geodesic dome floating in empty space. Each part cleaves to its neighbors, to which it is bolted; but the relation of cleaving is symmetric, and there is no gravitational force sustaining the dome. One trouble is that this leaves unclear how justification is supposed to come in. What, e.g., is the counterpart of inferential relations, which are crucial for both coherence and justification and are, in their psychological realizations in our belief system, causal and hence (I argue) asymmetrical? More must be said, but these points suggest that models of this sort do not circumvent the self-sustenance problem.

about valuation, since there are so many kinds of happiness; nor need it be psychologically näive, since things can be justifiedly valued for their contribution to happiness even if only indirectly, say where one values exercise as a means to relaxation, and that as a means to health and health as a means to happiness, but does not connect exercise directly with happiness.[5] The valuation of happiness is then the ultimate normative foundation of one's valuing of exercise but not its immediate motivating basis.

TWO TYPES OF EPISTEMIC DEPENDENCE

A major source of support for coherentism comes from the sense that whereas foundationalism cannot account for the apparent dependence of all justified beliefs on other beliefs, coherentism makes this dependence expectable. The most salient cases are inferential beliefs. These typically depend for their justification on beliefs they are based on.[6] But the latter are not the problem: it is *non*-inferential beliefs that anti-foundationalists have thought foundationalism must take to be "independent" of others, including beliefs the person *would* form upon gathering new evidence. This, however, is a mistake. A foundationalist need not posit any indefeasibly justified beliefs, and moderate foundationalists countenance at most a few such (e.g. beliefs of simple logical truths). Their point is not that other beliefs are *irrelevant:* some might strengthen, others destroy, the justification of foundational beliefs. The point is that the *source* of the justification of foundationally justified beliefs is not other beliefs.[7] How, then, could foundationalism be so misunderstood?

---

5. Aristotle has been criticized on this point – undeservedly, I think, for reasons given in my *Practical Reasoning* (London and New York: Routledge, 1989), ch. 1.
6. Typically, because a belief could be directly justified, e.g. through perception, yet based on inferences, say from testimony. Directness of the justification does not entail directness of the belief. Note that direct justification does not imply *self*-justification – a notion foundationalists need countenance, if at all, only for very special cases, such as beliefs of luminously self-evident propositions.
7. Except in special cases, most notably that in which one non-inferentially believes that, e.g., one believes people are fascinating. But here the basis belief does not express a "premise." This is belief on a ground of a kind that is the right sort to express a premise but does not function epistemically to supply one.

It has apparently been easy for some philosophers to miss a distinction between positive and negative epistemic dependence. This distinction is perhaps the central contribution of Chapter 3, "Foundationalism, Epistemic Dependence, and Defeasibility." Consider an analogy. One's safety on a walk in Washington Square depends, in a positive way, on what is happening there – or relevantly near there – not on the absence of ruffians who are several miles away stalking Central Park but could have been on the Square. Yet, in a negative way, it also depends on them, for if they had been on the Square instead, one would have been in danger. The crucial epistemic difference is between dependence on one's *source* of justification, such as visual experience, and dependence on the absence of defeaters, e.g. reasons to think one has been merely hallucinating. The first is a kind of derivational dependence and looks backward (or downward) to a source of justification; the second is a kind of vulnerability and looks forward (or upward) to a threat. Positive dependence is on something present; negative dependence is on something absent.

Preoccupation with skepticism tends to invite conflation of positive dependence with negative dependence – defeasibility. For skepticism makes us tend to think of our beliefs as under attack; even perceptual beliefs may thus seem unjustified unless supported by other justified beliefs to the effect that there is no defeater. It is as if I could not be safe in an environment, even when it is free of hazards, without being justified in believing that none of the *potential* attackers will enter it to assail me. The stronger the skepticism, the greater the dependence on such beliefs; the greater the fear of injury, the greater the need for assurance that potential – or even just possible – attackers are far away.

The overall conclusion, then, is that a foundationalist need only claim that basic beliefs are justified independently of others in the sense that they do not positively depend on them. Any sensible foundationalist will grant that they typically exhibit negative dependence on other beliefs – at least hypothetical beliefs – because this is implicit in their defeasibility through the discovery of counterevidence. If one thinks that coherentism is implied by taking seriously the kind of *in*coherence that is a major source of defeasibility, one will tend to think that foundationalism cannot do justice to the epistemic role of incoherence. There is also a danger of misunderstanding coherentism as well; for (as Chapter 4 brings out) coherence is not the mere absence of incoherence, and a view that gives incoherence a significant place in understanding justification need no more be coherentist than anti-foundationalist.

Chapter 3 closes with two points. First, contrary to what many have thought, reliabilism can be foundationalist. Defeat of justification by the occurrence of "relevant alternatives" – e.g. defeat of my justification for believing I see Joan when I discover that she has a twin I did not know about and cannot visually distinguish from the woman I take to be Joan – is a special case of negative epistemic dependence, not a concession to coherentism. Moreover – and this is the second main distinction the chapter introduces – it is essential to differentiate between two kinds of naturalism in epistemology: *substantive naturalism,* which (as in the case of Quine) treats all the truths of epistemology as empirical, roughly as truths of psychology; and *conceptual naturalism,* which simply uses no irreducibly normative concepts, such as justification understood in terms of *permissible* believing. Neither reliabilism nor any foundationalist theory need be substantively naturalistic, and I leave open whether the foundationalism sketched in the chapter is conceptually naturalistic.

MODERATE FOUNDATIONALISM, HOLISTIC COHERENTISM, AND THE REGRESS PROBLEM

A major point emerging in the first three chapters is that when coherentism is formulated so that it avoids the problem of self-sustenance, and when foundationalism is understood so that it accommodates the kind of epistemic dependence of foundational beliefs that is really a kind of defeasibility, then the contrast between the two positions is less sharp. The contrast becomes still less pronounced when we realize that epistemic as well as psychological considerations favor a holistic coherentism over a linear one: one in which justification emerges from coherent patterns and not only from inferential chains, certainly not from circular ones. The main business of Chapter 4, which addresses the foundationalism–coherentism controversy, is, first, to articulate the epistemic regress problem in a way that brings out its role in motivating both foundationalism and coherentism; second, to formulate both of those positions in plausible forms likely to be acceptable to many of their respective proponents; third, to assess the controversy between them in that light; and fourth, to appraise the vulnerability of each to the charge of dogmatism.

Despite the frequency with which philosophers refer to the epistemic regress problem and the associated regress argument, both have been commonly formulated without sufficient clarity. It is especially important to formulate the regress argument clearly because, both historically and philosophically, it is a major ground for foundationalism, and – as many have not realized – that general epistemological position, as opposed to some particular philosopher's formulation of it, should not be taken to be stronger than a plausible regress argument warrants. If anything can, as it were, functionally define foundationalism, it is the role of providing an appropriate solution to the regress problem.

Chapter 4 begins by distinguishing between two forms of the regress problem: a *structural* form and a *dialectical* one. I argue that the primary issue is the status of beliefs, not of moves in a dialectic – especially one with the skeptic. If we think of the regress as constituted by skeptical charges and replies to them, followed by countercharges and rejoinders, we never get a good picture of actual belief and knowledge. For one thing, dialogue *creates* new beliefs, and the premises one holds at the end of a discussion are often far more extensive than (and in some cases inconsistent with) those on which one's position initially rested. For another, if our task is to stop the regress in a dialectic, we easily slide into making second-order claims, such as that we know that we have hands.[8] For the skeptic is challenging us to show that we know something, and a proper reply will ascribe knowledge and hence will have second-order content. But such second-order claims presuppose epistemic concepts and may, for other reasons as well, be unjustified even if we *have* first-order justification, say for believing we have hands.

I prefer, then, to work mainly with the structural form of the regress problem, which concerns stopping the apparent regress of

8. The allusion is to G. E. Moore's citing his hands as paradigms of things he knows to exist. For statements of some of his views see his *Philosophical Papers* (London: George Allen and Unwin, 1959), esp. "A Proof of the External World" (1939) and "A Defence of Common Sense" (1925). For an interesting discussion of Moore's position see Norman Malcolm, "Moore and Ordinary Language," in P. A. Schilpp, ed., *The Philosophy of G. E. Moore* (Evanston: Open Court, 1942) and "Moore and Wittgenstein on the Sense of 'I Know,' " in Malcolm's *Thought and Knowledge* (Ithaca and London: Cornell University Press, 1977).

cognitive justifiers, not of *justificatory claims*. For both knowledge and justification, I formulate regress arguments that lead to moderate versions of foundationalism, versions that allow coherence to play a role in justification so long as foundationally justified beliefs would remain justified if (other things remaining equal) any justification they receive from coherence were eliminated. Opposite this, I articulate coherentism simply as the view that if one has any justified beliefs, they are justified by virtue of coherence with further beliefs one holds, and they would remain justified even if any justification they receive from other sources were eliminated. Thus, foundationalism allows coherence a role in explicating justification, and coherentism allows foundations a role in that same task.

In the light of an extended illustration of holistic coherentism, Chapter 4 goes on to show that if the issue is whether we may have second-order justification – a problem that the dialectical form of the regress problem brings to the fore – then foundationalists should grant that coherence may play a further role. For surely to show that I have justified beliefs (or knowledge) I must rely on other beliefs, such as beliefs of epistemic principles, that will (if I succeed) cohere with the beliefs they are used to defend. Evidential support relations, after all, are paradigms of coherent relations among beliefs. On the other hand, it is suggested that wherever coherence appears to yield justification, we can *also* find the materials for a foundationalist justification. The coherent set of beliefs surrounding my justified belief that there is daylight outside will include some that can be attributed to my perceptual experience, which even coherentists typically admit is causally responsible for the justified belief. The suggestion is that *both* coherence and justification may be grounded in the same foundational sources.

This view is entirely consistent with coherence's being a necessary condition for justification; this may be one reason coherentists have apparently not seen the need to refute the view. But the view allows that coherence be what I call a *consequential necessary condition*, as opposed to a *constitutive necessary condition*. In the former case, coherence is necessary as a result of its production by foundationalist elements; in the latter case, which coherentists endorse, coherence is what produces justification. If coherence is a truly constitutive necessary condition, it is also a *basic source* of justification, i.e. one whose justificatory power is not derivative from that of any other source. This is how coherentists have tended to construe coherence. It could, however, be something else: a *conditionally basic source*. Suppose that once some degree of justification arises from some other source, coherence can raise its level; this would mean that it can produce justification, but not without the person's already having some as raw material. I do not see that a foundationalism which accounts for coherence as a consequence of basic sources such as sensory experience need grant it this conditionally generative role. Still, such a role could be granted without abandoning the heart of foundationalism as most plausibly developed: the idea that justification always depends on, and "essentially" derives from, the basic sources in experience and reason.

Once it is clear how much of the coherentist position foundationalism can accommodate – and in particular that it can take *incoherence* seriously as a defeater, without treating positive coherence as a basic source of justification – it is not difficult to see that a moderate foundationalism need be in no way dogmatic. Even if, in debate, I appeal to a foundational belief, I may be prepared both to admit that it could be false and to try to find a yet more plausible proposition that I already believe, or can reasonably come to believe, which supports it – as where I may appeal to how things (visually) appear to me to justify my observational, and initially foundational, belief that it is daylight. On the other hand, coherentism, although it does not invite dogmatism, is not immune to it. As a coherentist, I could perfectly well have an inflated and rigid view of the strength of my own evidence. This might even be easy, depending on how readily I find – or arrive at through an evidential search – an impressive body of supporting beliefs.

Foundationalism, then, is not the rigid, incorrigibilist, atomistic view some have thought it to be. It can be moderate, fallibilist, common-sensical, and psychologically realistic. It can also provide a role for coherence in understanding justification and, in some contexts, in generating it. All of these points are expanded in the remaining chapters. If they are granted, then the myth of the demise of foundationalism will be exposed as just that. Rightly understood, moderate foundationalism has the main virtues of coherentism and none of its severe defects. If it countenances, at any given time, unmoved movers, it need not posit unmovable movers; and the very foundations that support the superstructure may be corrected from above.

II. KNOWLEDGE AND JUSTIFICATION

Until quite recently, nearly all epistemologists believed that knowledge entails justification, and this is still the majority view. Moreover, even if the entailment does not hold, at least the typical cases of knowledge represent justified belief, and certainly, other things being equal, when justification accrues to a true belief, the belief either becomes knowledge or comes closer to that status. Quite naturally, then, justification and knowledge are treated together; and although Part I concerns justification more than knowledge, much of what is said there about justification also applies to knowledge. They are similarly grounded, structurally parallel, and often psychologically coincident. The five chapters in Part II amply illustrate all these points, but they do not provide a full-scale analysis of knowledge or even of justification, about which they say more. My aim has been to develop a theory of the nature and scope of justification and knowledge, as opposed to an account of them in the form of a detailed set of necessary and sufficient conditions. There are, however, *conceptions* of both operating in these pages, and through them one could, I hope, advance to a detailed analysis. Let me briefly state these conceptions before proceeding to a discussion of the chapters themselves.

It should be plain that the broad conception of justification with which I have been working is *a well-groundedness view*. A justified belief is one that is well-grounded; the paradigms of basic grounds are sensory experience, introspection (or consciousness, at least), memory, and reason (including intuition and reflection); and the paradigm of non-basic grounding is inferential grounding. Both types of grounding require some kind of causal sustenance. This thesis is defended, for the inferential case, in a number of places and, for the non-inferential case, it is suggested as plausible in, e.g., Chapter 8. Both kinds are also defeasible. Not all grounding, then, is good. I do not claim that there can be no other basic sources (or even that there are none), a topic briefly addressed in Chapter 10; and I explicitly allow for the possibility of other non-basic sources, e.g. coherence.

If we are to understand knowledge, we must enhance the account of justification by adding both to the grounding dimension – the epistemic side – and to the ontic one, because truth is required. On my parallel conception of knowledge, then, it is *appropriately grounded true belief*, i.e., true belief based in the right way on the

14

right kind of ground.[9] Appropriate grounding here is not equivalent to justificatorily good grounding; for one thing, I could fail to
know I will lose a sweepstakes with a billion tickets of which I hold
just one, without there being any defect in my justification. It is
simply the wrong kind to ground knowledge. It may also turn out
that one need not be justified at all.[10] But there surely must *be* a
ground of a belief constituting knowledge; the belief cannot be, for
instance, just a lucky guess. Many of the chapters in Part II, especially 6 and 7, bear on what sorts of grounds are appropriate.
Some of the difficulties concern the kind of inferential relation that
inferential knowledge must have to its "premise" belief(s). Others
concern defeat by relevant alternatives, as in the identical-twin case
mentioned previously. And even if there is no doubt about a causal
sustaining requirement, there can be problems about the right kind
of causal chain.

THE BASTION OF PRIVILEGED ACCESS

Historically, epistemologists have tended to regard self-knowledge
as the best grounded kind of (empirical) knowledge and even to
think that the *only* non-inferential knowledge of mental events and
states belongs to the person in whom they occur. In Chapter 5,
"The Limits of Self-knowledge," I critically appraise these and other
strands in the doctrine of privileged access. The chapter begins by
distinguishing between various kinds of epistemic-status claims
about beliefs concerning one's present mental life, particularly incorrigibility, indubitability, and infallibility. The other direction is
also considered, starting with the mental and looking at beliefs
about it. Are mental events or states "self-intimating," in the sense
that the person automatically knows or justifiedly believes that they
are present? Both directions are considered from the point of view
of a distinction between dispositional and occurrent mental states.
Two kinds of example are used to cut the thesis of privileged

---

9. I suggested and developed this conception in ch. 7 of *Belief, Justification, and
Knowledge*. James E. Taylor plausibly argues that it *is* an analysis and that
greater detail will inevitably lead to error. See "Conceptual Analysis and the
Essence of Knowledge," forthcoming in *American Philosophical Quarterly*.
10. That knowledge is possible without justified belief is briefly argued in Chapter 10. On this point my views have changed over a period of years, though
there is little of importance to my earlier work that needs revision in the light
of the change.

access down to a reasonable size: self-deception and the possibility of electroencephalographic or other scientific data about mental states. It is argued that (a) one could falsely believe that one is in a particular occurrent mental state and (b) given the reasons for which this is so, one might even fail to be justified in believing that one is. This conclusion allows, however, that normally one's beliefs about one's current mental life are non-inferentially justified. This result is altogether in line with moderate foundationalism: on the one hand, introspection is a good source of justified foundational beliefs; on the other, even when introspective, they are not in general infallible or even incorrigibly (roughly, indefeasibly) justified, and so not candidates for the dogmatic convictions that coherentists have thought foundationalists must take to be "independent" of other beliefs.

The possibility of ignorance of what is going on in one's mind is also considered, and related considerations are brought against the view that we are omniscient about our current mental life. The chapter does not show, however, that we can fail to believe, of some present occurrent mental state, that it is there, under *some* description. In the light of more recent work, including some reflected in Chapters 4 and 9, I would now add that one could fail to believe that one is in an occurrent mental state one is in fact in – not because one is wrong about what state one is in or has an ill-grounded belief that one is in it, but because one simply has not *formed* a belief to the effect that one is in it. One might instead have only a *disposition to believe* this (among other propositions made obvious by the experience in question). This account of the situation (as Chapter 9 shows) leaves what we might call our evidence base equally strong – because we *can* form as many justified beliefs as, on a sensible view of privileged access, we are entitled to hold – yet the account is psychologically more realistic in that it does not posit so many actual beliefs, as opposed to dispositions to form them. There would, after all, be a huge number. For a single visual image of printed paper I would believe that I see something white, that it looks flat, that it has black print, that it is steady, and so on.[11]

11. It is a difficult question just why we form the beliefs we do in response to experience and just how many we tend to form. I give a detailed account of such issues in "Dispositional Beliefs and Dispositions to Believe," in progress.

Overview

The past quarter-century has been plagued by the notoriously knotty problem of what must be added to justified true belief to make it knowledge.[12] Chapter 6, "Defeated Knowledge, Reliability, and Justification," addresses this problem. Its main work is to compare the resources of leading reliabilist and leading justificationist theories, conceived as efforts to solve this problem and explicate knowledge. Since direct (non-inferential) and indirect (inferential) beliefs raise somewhat different problems, the chapter considers these theories in relation to each kind of belief separately, as well as how the distinction between the two kinds of belief is to be drawn.

None of the theories considered seems entirely satisfactory, and the chapter proposes two principles to extend our understanding of the more basic, direct cases. These principles emphasize several variables as bearing on the epistemic status of a direct belief, such as one based on perception: (i) the acuteness of the senses relevant to forming, sustaining, and confirming the belief; (ii) the normality of their operation at the time; (iii) the appropriateness of the perceptual circumstances to the content of the belief; (iv) the normality of the perceiver's responses to the sense(s); and (v) the absence of a justified belief – or of justification *for* believing – that one or more of (i)–(iv) fails to hold. The general idea is that we obtain perceptual knowledge only if we have the power to discriminate the relevant fact; we do not lack the power at the time; the circumstances do not undermine the power (as where an identical twin is brought in to confuse us); we do not "misread" the data; and we are not justified in believing that one of these defeaters is present. In terms of my overall epistemology, these conditions help us understand the *way* in which true belief must be grounded in order to constitute knowledge.

The chapter has one other major purpose: to explore whether reliabilist accounts, which are avowedly naturalistic, can account for knowledge without invoking any normative notion, such as that of being justified, understood in terms of a normative concept like good evidence (in one sense of 'good'). Consider a representa-

12. Edmund Gettier's "Is Justified True Belief Knowledge?" *Analysis* 23 (1963) launched this discussion. The view that justification is not *necessary* did not come to the fore as an alternative until much later.

tive problem: determining when an alternative is relevant. Given that I cannot tell Joan from her twin, how likely must it be, for instance, that I saw the twin instead of Joan before we must say that a justified true belief that I saw Joan fails to be knowledge? If the answer depends on how great a likelihood of my having seen Joan gives me (normatively) *good enough* justification, then the reliability account is apparently not purely naturalistic. Questions like this, concerning buried normativity in reliabilist accounts, still appear unresolved; but I do not claim that they cannot be resolved.

THE STRUCTURE OF JUSTIFICATORY CONNECTIONS

Our discourse about justification and knowledge is pervaded by causal locutions. We speak of justification *on the basis* of what we have discovered, of being warranted on testimonial *grounds*, of knowing *because of* what we have seen. Foundationalism would lead one to expect causal connections between one's grounds and what they justify; coherentism – apart from the problem of self-sustenance – would at least make this seem a natural expectation: causal as well as epistemic support is easily thought to come from the beliefs whose cohering with a given belief justifies it. The task of Chapter 7, "The Causal Structure of Indirect Justification," is to show that an indirectly (i.e., inferentially) justified belief must be at least in part causally sustained by any belief that (inferentially) justifies it.

To focus the issue, I distinguish *personal justification* – that of a person's belief that *p* – from *impersonal justification* – that of the proposition that *p*, or of "the belief that *p*" in the abstract, say the belief that there are human beings elsewhere in the galaxy. Propositional justification may also be person-relative, as where *p* is justified *for* Gail. This may be so whether she believes it or not, just as one may be justified in an action, such as returning a purchase, whether one performs it or not. The issue in Chapter 7 is justification of actual beliefs – commonly called *doxastic* justification, or simply *belief* justification. Its thesis is that inferentially justified beliefs are at least partly sustained by the belief(s) that justify them, and that the counterpart view applies to inferential knowledge.

One reason to hold this thesis is that it explains the dual force of questions like "Why do you believe?" and "How do you know?" The former sounds clearly causal yet is usually meant to evoke a justification; the latter sounds clearly epistemic but is normally asked with a presupposition that a way in which one knows that *p* will be a cause of one's believing it. But there are other considerations, some of which are apparent in an example in which one *has* evidence that is causally irrelevant to what one believes, as in the case of a superstitious lawyer – Ken, let us say – who, on the basis of tarot cards, believes a client innocent, but also has excellent (non-sustaining) evidence usable in court.[13] I grant that the proposition in question is justified *for him*. This implies that Ken is justified *in* believing it, i.e., has justification to believe it, where that is understood as we do my being justified in believing the conclusion of an obviously valid syllogism whose premises I justifiedly believe, but whose conclusion I have not yet drawn, having not put the premises together (this can easily happen when one comes to believe each premise at a different time). But the issue is justified *belief*, not simply having justification *to* believe; and to say that Ken's belief is justified by the cards implies that even though what justifies him might as easily (and for all he is warranted in believing) have pointed to the opposite, false conclusion, he is still justified by it. One is also committed to saying that he is justified by evidence even though it is only good fortune that he has any tendency to form a belief that is in accordance with it (because the cards might as easily have steered him to a different conclusion). Parallel points about knowledge seem even more at odds with the view that if his belief is true, then he knows his client is innocent. When we know something, e.g., what grounds our knowledge is not such that it might as easily have indicated a falsehood.

In addition to developing these considerations, the chapter goes on to distinguish between justification and rationalization and argues that what the lawyer has is above all a rationalization. We *can* narrow our conception of rationalization and say that he is not producing one because, e.g., he sees the force of his evidence; but there is no good reason to do so apart from the case, and my account provides more than one way to explain where his justification *does* lie – above all, in the proposition's being justified for him. There *is* a justification that he has; but he uses it as a rationalization for

13. This case is from Keith Lehrer and has been discussed considerably since my paper, often in in relation to the paper. See, e.g., Jonathan Kvanvig, *The Intellectual Virtues and the Life of the Mind* (Savage, Md.: Rowman and Littlefield, 1991).

19

a belief that is ill grounded. The belief, then, is not justified. It is not connected with the reality in virtue of which its propositional object is warranted for him, and it does not count toward his knowing. He is lucky that the cards are right, in a way we are not lucky when, through good evidence, we know.

REASONS AND THEIR ROLE IN INFERENTIAL JUSTIFICATION

Inferential justification has been invoked in many contexts by philosophers, but epistemologists have not adequately clarified it. I take it to be justification by one or more reasons. There are many kinds of reasons and many ways a belief may be related to the reasons that do, or might, justify it. There are *reasons to believe p,* as where evidence for it is waiting to be discovered in the library; *reasons for me to believe p,* as where, given what I already know, something I remember can be brought forward that, in the light of some reflection by me, can establish *p;* there are *reasons one has to believe p,* as where I believe something that is a good premise for *p;* there are *reasons why one believes p* – explaining reasons—and there are *reasons for which one believes p,* which are both reasons one has and explaining reasons. Chapter 8, "Belief, Reason, and Inference," provides an account of inferential belief taken as belief based on one or more others that express a reason for which one believes.

Inferential belief, so conceived, is not equivalent to belief based on inference, i.e., arising (in the normal way) from or sustained by a process of passing from one or more propositions (premises) to another. An inferential belief may be based on another belief without such argumental mediation; on the basis of believing that the trees are swaying, I may believe that the wind is blowing, without mentally passing from the former as premise to the latter as conclusion. Beliefs of the former kind are *episodically inferential;* the latter are, by virtue of their grounding in some other belief(s), *structurally inferential.* Both are cases of believing for a reason, which is the central concern of the chapter.

The notion of believing for a reason turns out to be enormously hard to capture. There is little doubt that the basis belief – the one expressing the reason on which an inferential belief is based – plays an explanatory role. But there is considerable disagreement over whether the person must have a connecting belief: one linking the reason or premise to p. To get a minimal condition, I propose a variety of belief-types as candidates to express the connection. The weakest may be *de re*, i.e. beliefs *of* something, including an abstract item, to the effect that it has a property; and these beliefs do not require conceptualizing the thing in question in any particular way. Consider a belief *of* a connecting relation like entailment: one might simply believe this relation to hold between the reason and p. One way to see the plausibility of this – and here I go beyond the chapter – is to suppose that when we learn to appreciate, say, valid syllogisms, we grasp the relation of entailment between premises and conclusion *before* we develop the concept of entailment and can thereby believe *that* the premises entail the conclusion.

The connecting belief requirement is *not* the requirement that the principle of inference governing the connection be a premise; it is rather that there be a kind of cognitive appreciation of the relation between the premise and what it grounds that is necessary for the justificatory success of the relation. That the connecting requirement be weak is important for still another reason (only implicit in the chapter). There is a sense in which one can believe for (and even be justified by) an "unconscious" reason, one that, apart from special circumstances such as the help of another person, one cannot come to know one has *as* a reason. Even if I cannot come to know that I believe I will die of cancer, I can take this proposition to imply another I believe, such as that I had better get my affairs in order.[14] Indeed, because the unconsciousness is epistemically conceived and not ontically understood in terms of a mental location that precludes entering consciousness, there is no bar even to the belief's being manifested in consciousness: I may entertain the proposition that I will die of cancer but treat it as if I did not believe it or even knew it to be false.

Once the connecting requirement is accepted, it will seem reasonable to argue that the connecting belief must, like the basis belief, play some role in explaining why the person holds the belief that p. The person must also have a non-inferential disposition to attribute the belief that p to its ground, but we are fallible here and may wrongly think that some other belief is the ground – this is

---

14. In accounting for self-deception I have discussed the relevant notion of an unconscious element. See, e.g., my "Self-Deception, Rationalization, and Reasons for Acting," in Brian McLaughlin and Amelie O. Rorty, eds., *Perspectives on Self-Deception* (Berkeley and Los Angeles: University of California Press, 1988).

especially likely if the grounding belief is unconscious. Finally, the causal chain linking the basis and connecting beliefs to the belief that *p* must be of the right sort: non-wayward. The chapter develops a rough but principled way to rule out the wrong kinds of chain.

From the point of view of a well-groundedness conception of justification, it is important that inferential belief be adequately understood; for it is, on any plausible view of justification, the main case of *indirect grounding*. Roughly, my thesis is that a belief is well-grounded by virtue of an inferential connection with a foundational belief only if it is *based on* that belief in the sense I have indicated. Indeed, the chapter suggests that similar conditions – apart from the connecting belief condition – are needed to account for the way in which foundational beliefs are based on experience or reason (pages 269–70). These points apply to knowledge as well as to justification.

HAVING JUSTIFICATION

I have already distinguished between having justification and "using" it, as where one actually has a belief based on the justifying elements, as opposed to simply being aware of them and ready to use them as a rationalization. The same distinction applies to grounds, evidence, warrant, and other justificatory notions. It turns out, however, that there are many ways of having justification. Chapter 9, "Structural Justification," concentrates on a way of having it that is more "implicit" than in the most commonly discussed cases. In the latter cases, one has justification (or evidence or the like) when either one has a belief which expresses it, or one is in a sensory or other state that constitutes it, as where one has a visual impression of print, which is one's ground for believing that there is black ink before one. By contrast, it might be only on the basis of various remembered items that I have a justification for believing something; I must reflect at some length on these items in order to become justified in the way most commonly associated with the term. This might apply to the authorship of an article: only if I think back over a number of related ones and eliminate various authors can I become warranted in believing that it was X who wrote it; but because I need only reflect, and need not go "outside" for new grounds like reference books, the justification resides in my cognitive structure, and I may be said to have it.

In outline, the basic idea is this. Suppose we call the kind of justification residing in beliefs or experiences, when they function as grounds, *situational*. It is present in one's epistemic situation, doxastically or experientially, but need not be accompanied by the beliefs for which it provides grounds. The propositions in question, then, are *justified for* one. We can then say that, where reflection, for instance on what one believes or remembers, would lead one to have situational justification for *p*, one has structural justification for it. It is structural because it is implicit in one's cognitive makeup, but it is pre-situational. The proposition is not already justified for one but is *justifiable* for one – by one's doing the reflection that brings the materials from their implicit place in the structure to the focus of attention. From there one is in a position to form, though one need not form, a justified belief *on* the grounds now in focus.

Structural justification can be realized in situational justification, and eventually in justified belief, in a number of ways. There are many justificatory paths from the potential grounds to either of these other kinds of justification. Much of the chapter is an account of these paths, and of the obstacles that can arise along the way and defeat one's would-be situational justification. Even apart from developing into situational justification, structural justification has epistemologically significant properties. It can justify other dispositions of the person; it can, e.g., figure in descriptions of a person's cognitive structure.

This chapter considers knowledge as well as justification – and formulates a new epistemological problem. Recall that I conceive knowledge as appropriately grounded true belief. It is important to add that we often speak of knowledge even when there is at the time no actual belief to constitute it. Consider talk of how much is known about a subject, or about the vast extent of human knowledge, or about how much some expert knows about a topic. Some of these locutions seem to cover propositions accessible only in the relevant literature and not in anyone's memory; others apply to propositions that the relevant people are only *disposed* to believe but would not believe unless there was an occasion to form the beliefs in question. If, e.g., we encountered the relevant literature, either we would acquire the knowledge in question or there would at least be a justificatory path from our situation as readers to such knowledge. Thus, at the time the knowledge in question is said to exist, there is no corresponding belief (nor, in some cases, need there ever have been). I call this *virtual knowledge* to emphasize how close it is to knowledge in the most common sense; some of it – the kind for which no person has situational or structural justification, as in the case of one's believing true premises adequate to warrant a proposition one does not believe – might also be called *impersonal knowledge*. Virtual knowledge is *not* a challenge to the view, for which I have argued,[15] that when one's knowledge that *p* is constituted by an affirmative cognitive attitude, one believes *p*. But the phenomenon is a challenge to the standard view that knowing a proposition entails believing it. If this view is to be defended, the distinctions made here must be accommodated.

The notion of structural justification also turns out to be fruitful in other philosophical areas. There is structural justification for acting, wanting, intending, valuing, and so on. Like other important notions in epistemology, structural justification occurs in the domain of practical rationality. This confirms the wide applicability of the well-groundedness conception of justification. That applicability will be illustrated in other ways in Part III and, in Part IV, developed in detail for the domain of practical reason.

III. EPISTEMIC PRINCIPLES AND SKEPTICISM

Skepticism comes in many forms. Skeptics have different targets, such as knowledge or justification or rationality. They have different strategies, ranging from pressing the question of how one knows, to presenting systematic arguments against the commonsense view that there is a great deal we know. Even when they merely challenge us to show that we know, they usually presuppose various epistemic principles. If, for instance, we offer non-entailing grounds for a statement, they may ask how we can claim to know something on grounds that, even if true, do not preclude the falsity of what we are supposed to know on the basis of them. The associated principle is something like this: one can know that *p* on the basis of *q* only if *q* entails *p*.[16] It is quite appropriate, then, to consider skepticism in the context of some major epistemic principles. To reply to skeptics, it may be essential to refute or at least

---

15. For some arguments to show that knowing of the usual sort entails belief, see ch. 7 of *Belief, Justification, and Knowledge*.
16. In ch. 9 of *Belief, Justification, and Knowledge* I call this the entailment principle and critically assess it.

to cast in doubt the epistemic principles they rely on; indeed, these and self-evident truths are the most a careful skeptic can be compelled to assert. If, beyond showing that skeptical arguments fail, we want to establish that there *is* knowledge or justified belief, we are likely to need epistemic principles. Perhaps I may, e.g., simply wave my hands and thereby show that I know something; but if I want to offer a positive argument and not just a vivid paradigm, I apparently need some general premise. The most likely route to this end, and possibly the only route that will impress those of a skeptical cast of mind, is one using principles expressing a sufficient condition for knowledge or justified belief and showing that some of our beliefs satisfy that condition.

In considering skepticism, then, we should distinguish between *rebutting* it, which is showing that skeptical arguments do not establish that we have no knowledge or justified belief, and *refuting* it, which is showing the positive result that we do have knowledge or justified belief. It is the latter that especially requires epistemic principles. More than rebuttal, it also raises the question of the epistemic status of the principles themselves. Unless they are self-evident – perhaps even luminously so – skeptics will insist on an argument for them and will tend to require that *it* in turn be a self-evidently valid demonstration from self-evident beginnings.[17] Considering the importance of the status of these principles, epistemologists have discussed it less than one might suppose. The chapters in Part III are an attempt to focus this issue and develop a moderate rationalist account of epistemic principles that both explains how they are justified and takes us some distance toward a positive refutation of skepticism.

THE TWO FACES OF JUSTIFICATION

We are asked to justify a claim (especially) when there is doubt whether it is true; in giving our justification we adduce one or more of our grounds. Often, the justification we cite is a proposition we

---

17. Chapter 12 discusses types of self-evidence. The point here, however, simply requires distinguishing between propositions that, though their truth does not leap to the eye, can be readily seen to be true on the basis of understanding them – which does not entail that a skeptic cannot (perhaps plausibly) resist accepting them – and those whose truth, like that of identity propositions, leaps out at one so clearly that anyone who denies them ceases to seem a serious opponent.

believe or a state we are in, such as a visual awareness of the relevant evidence; but if it is not, it is at least traceable to something internal. The request for justification typically looks outward from the belief queried to what it represents; the answer typically looks – or can be traced – inward for support. These are the two faces of justification: it looks outward to the world beyond the belief, and inward for the justifying grounds.

I have spoken of a request for justification and an answer to it. Here 'justification' denotes a *process*. We may also ask whether someone *has* justification for a belief; and there the term designates a *property*. There are still the same two faces, however; for even in the latter case the justifiers succeed only if they show or at least support the truth of the belief, and they remain something that belongs to the subject. Philosophers have not always noticed this process-property duality of 'justification', and there have been some confusions (as noted in Chapter 4). Once the duality is re-alized, however, we have an interesting problem: how to account for the relation between the property and the process.

Chapter 10, "Justification, Truth, and Reliability," deals with both faces of justification and with the relation – indeed, the *in-tegration* – between the process of justification and the property it concerns. The initial focus of the chapter is the external face: the connection between justification and truth. Reliabilism is viewed as accounting for this connection by treating justification as objec-tively pointing toward truth. If justified beliefs are those produced or sustained by reliable processes – those that produce true beliefs at least most of the time – then justification probabilistically implies truth. Internalist theories of justification, by contrast, cannot make this move. On any plausible internalist view – as we become pain-fully aware in studying the possibility that a Cartesian demon sys-tematically deceives us – it is conceivable that most of our justified beliefs are false.

By way of developing a theory of how justification is connected with truth, the chapter sets out a series of epistemic principles for non-inferential belief: principles concerning justification arising in the four traditionally basic areas, perception, introspection, mem-ory, and reason. One such principle is to the effect that if one has a sensory impression of something's having a property, say of this paper's being white, and on the basis of that impression believes that it has that property, then one's belief is prima facie justified.

Principles of this sort are acceptable to both reliabilists and internalists. But each gives a different account of their epistemic status. Here I set out and briefly defend the view that such principles are a priori, and much of the chapter is concerned with working out a conception of justification that goes with this view.

I argue that if we retain a realist conception of the external world, then we cannot plausibly maintain *both* that these epistemic principles are a priori (and presumably necessary) and that justification entails an *objective* probability of truth. For one thing, we cannot know a priori that in most of the relevantly similar possible situations we are not, e.g., deceived by hallucinations. Nonetheless, we can hold that justification, both as process and as property, has a teleological connection with truth: the aim of the process of justification is to show truth (or at least an objective probability of it), and the properties which ground justified belief can be seen, a priori, to be bases that it is reasonable to cite in trying to achieve this aim. Truth is not a construct from justified belief; but the justifiedness of our epistemically reasonable attempts to show truth is explicable in terms of, and may indeed be largely constructable from, such epistemic principles. Justified beliefs are those that accord with them; reasonable processes of justification are the kind that, given the principles, yield justified beliefs.

Where does this leave us with respect to the place of reliability in justification? There is every reason to think that what, a priori, can be seen to justify – such as sensory experience – is, empirically, a reliable indicator of truth. Indeed, the *concept* of justification can evolve, in the sense that what we regard as a sufficiently reliable indicator of truth can become a conceptual criterion of justification.[18] We take the internal face of justification to be dominant but allow its complexion to change with sufficiently strong and pervasive indications of external success or failure. The view developed, then, is normative as opposed to naturalistic (at least if the most plausible naturalism is a version of reliability theory), and teleological – a *teleological normativism*.

Although internalist, this view is not deontological. In this re-

---

18. If we think of concepts as unchanging abstract entities, the more accurate way to put this is in terms of the present concept of justification being replaced by a similar one. We thus have *conceptual evolution* as evolution in the concepts we *have*, as opposed to *evolution of concepts*, as change in one or more concepts.

spect it differs from most other internalist views, especially in the foundationalist tradition.[19] One good effect of this kind of internalism is to make it clear that an induced belief which one can do nothing to remove no matter how hard one tries is not thereby justified; it is *excusable*, but not well-grounded or justified. On the deontological view that justification accrues to beliefs the holding of which violates no epistemic duties, such an entrenched belief must be considered justified. But a belief that cannot be uprooted is not thereby well-grounded or justified. It may be indelibly stamped on the brain, yet cut off from experience and reason.

We can now see how the internalism developed here may deal with skepticism. It is as well off as any plausible view in rebutting the skeptic. But when it comes to the task of refutation, it may be better off than the leading alternatives, at least as regards showing that we have justified beliefs. For we can bring a priori epistemic principles together with introspectively known facts about, e.g., our sensory states, and conclude, by self-evidently valid reasoning, that we have justification for beliefs about the external world. I can use the principle stated previously, for instance, to show that I am justified in believing that there is printing in front of me. By contrast, reliabilism as usually construed does not sanction a priori epistemic principles and so cannot claim their self-evidence in arguing against the skeptic. More serious still, the only empirical reasons one can have for believing these principles can be seen to support them only if the principles themselves are presupposed. One's justification for believing perceptual sources of belief to be reliable, for instance, depends on using perception to check on the beliefs so grounded. Only through relying on the senses can we determine that most of our sensorily grounded beliefs are true.

To be sure, because knowledge implies truth, we cannot, from epistemic principles and evidential facts accessible from an internal

19. Descartes comes readily to mind and, in this century, Chisholm's is the leading deontological view. For a short statement of his most relevant views see "A Version of Foundationalism," *Midwest Studies of Philosophy* V (1980). For other internalisms see Keith Lehrer, *Knowledge* (Oxford: Oxford University Press, 1974); Carl Ginet, *Knowledge, Perception, and Memory* (Dordrecht and Boston: D. Reidel, 1975); and Paul K. Moser, *Knowledge and Evidence* (Cambridge and New York: Cambridge University Press, 1989). For intensive critical discussion of coherentist internalisms (with responses by BonJour and Lehrer) see John Bender, *The Current Status of the Coherence Theory* (Dordrecht and Boston: Kluwer, 1989); and for both exposition and (often sympathetic) criticism of internalism see William P. Alston, *Epistemic Justification* (Ithaca and London: Cornell University Press, 1989).

point of view, provide entailing grounds for the conclusion that we have knowledge of the external world. But if, as seems plausible, non-entailing grounds *can* show something, we may still establish that we have knowledge. There may, after all, be inductive as well as deductive routes to showing such epistemic conclusions.

From what I have said about knowledge, one might think that I am taking it to be external in having content that is (apart from self-referential cases) external to the belief and often to the believer, but *evidentially internal*, in the sense that its grounds are entirely internal. This is not so; my view allows that one may know something even without having internally accessible grounds for it. The idea is that whereas justified belief is belief that is *normatively acceptable*, knowledge is belief that is *externally successful*, not just in being true but in having grounds that objectively count toward truth. Knowledge is achievable through internally accessible grounds of precisely the kinds that yield justification – so much so that one might think knowledge entails having internal grounds – but it seems to me to differ from justification, evidentially as well as ontologically, more than is generally realized by epistemologists.

In describing the prospects for refuting skepticism about justification, I noted that we can apparently show that we *have* justification for beliefs about the external world. As stressed in Chapter 7, however, having justification for a belief does not entail that the belief is justified. Chapter 10 thus introduces a further skeptical problem: what if a Cartesian demon severs the causal connection between our justifying grounds and the beliefs that would normally rest on them? We cannot know a priori that the relevant sustaining relations hold. If there is no way out, then the outlined strategy of refutation will show only that we have justification *for* beliefs about the external world, not that our actual *beliefs* about it are justified. This problem is addressed in more detail in Chapter 11, to which I now turn.

GROUNDS, GROUNDING, AND SECOND-ORDER JUSTIFICATION

It is probably no accident that internalists have tended not to endorse causal requirements on justified beliefs. It is true that if, like many internalists, one's main focus in the theory of justification is a proposition's being justified for a person, or someone's being justified in believing a proposition,[20] one may not think of the causal side of the picture. For these locutions do not even entail believing p, much less the belief's being based on the justifying grounds. But if one is convinced that being justified in holding a belief requires introspective access to what justifies it, one may think that since the existence of causal connections can be known only inductively, they cannot be necessary for justification. It may seem, then, that we must give up either internalism or causal requirements on justification.

This is the problem addressed by Chapter 11, "Causalist Internalism." It begins with a characterization of internalism, formulates the problem of access to causal conditions of justification, and proceeds to show how a distinction between first- and second-order internalism can pave the way for a causalist version of the theory. The strategy is to stress that above all internalism requires that one have internal access (roughly, access by reflection) to *what* justifies, to justifying grounds; it need not require such access to *how* what justifies does so, e.g. (in part) by sustaining the justified belief (or even to the fact that it justifies). A second-order internalism, by contrast, requires that the subject have internal access both to what justifies and to principles and facts concerning how it does so, in such a way that one could be justified in believing, for each first-order justified belief one has, that it is justified. Once it is seen that we can *be* justified without being able to show that we are, it becomes evident that there is no need for a first-order internalist to hold the second-order view, as one would have to do if one held that being justified in believing p implied also being justified in the second-order belief that one is justified in believing that p. Thus, by distinguishing between grounds of justification and other conditions for it, including the causal condition, and by showing that first-order internalism does not require its second-order counterpart, I establish that a causalist internalism is possible.

The chapter also distinguishes showing that one is justified from simply *giving* one's justification (a topic addressed further in Chapter 12 in connection with kinds of showing). Internalism *does* imply that (for people with sufficient sophistication to understand requests for justification) if one justifiedly believes p,

---

20. This applies to Chisholm and to a huge number of epistemologists, especially those writing in England and America from the 1950s into the 1970s.

then one can give one's justification; for one has access to some relevant ground and can offer it. Because giving a justification shows it in the sense of *displaying* it, and because this is often sufficient to show by implication that one is justified, it is easy to see how internalists might think that *being* justified entails being able to show that one is, where this has the more usual philosophical sense of showing, *by argument* – presumably argument appealing to epistemic principles – that one is justified. Thus, the distinction between giving and (argumentally) showing enables us to preserve the internalist idea that when you are justified, you can give your justification. It also preserves the idea, suggested in Chapter 10, that having the property of justification equips one to engage in the process of justification, and yet it shows how an internalist may hold an adequately robust causal requirement on justified belief.

There is, however, one advantage of internalism that is not obviously preserved by this strategy: its capacity to help us answer skepticism by positive refutation, which requires showing, and thereby (normally) becoming justified in believing, second-order epistemic claims such as that we justifiedly believe it is daylight.[21] Moreover, even apart from skepticism epistemologists have traditionally sought to ascertain the *scope* of our knowledge and justified belief. We may want, then, an epistemology that accounts for second-order justification (and knowledge).

In this vein, I take up the question of whether we might have appropriate access to the relevant causal conditions of justification. Chapter 8 argues that when one belief is inferentially based on a second, the agent has a non-inferential disposition to attribute the former to the latter, i.e., a disposition to make this attribution directly, rather than on the basis of one or more premises. Here it is argued, in addition, that there is no reason to think we are generally wrong about such matters. We are fallible about what our beliefs are based on, but in general the relevant causal relations between grounds and what they justify give us a tendency to recognize those relations when we carefully consider the matter. The relevant grounds are, then, accessible to reflection; and if the skeptic cannot argue in general from the fallibility of a belief to its lack of justification, we may suppose that there is justification for many

---

21. Normally, because it is possible – say for an unlucky lawyer – to show something without intending to and without grasping the process in such a way as to derive justification for the conclusion it shows.

internally grounded second-order beliefs attributing beliefs to other (premise) beliefs, or to experiential or reflectional states, as their grounds. Second-order as well as first-order internalism may thus be sound.

SKEPTICISM, FOUNDATIONALISM, AND NATURALIZED EPISTEMOLOGY

What perhaps above all makes Cartesian skepticism so powerful to philosophical minds is the thought that it is apparently possible for everything to seem to one just as it does, even if one is a lone ego merely hallucinating an external world. Anyone who prefers to think of the possibility of being a brain in a vat may; but this is a quite different possibility, because it implies that there is a physical world and may suggest, what is not self-evident, that a person could not exist without some physical embodiment.[22] Now a main plank in the Cartesian case (though I am not sure the principle is found in this form in Descartes' writings) is the idea that if one is justified in believing p, then one is justified in believing any proposition that self-evidently follows from p – call this the *transmission principle.* From the proposition that there is paper before me it self-evidently follows that no Cartesian demon is causing me to believe falsely that there is; so if I am justified in believing (even if I do not believe) that there is, then I am justified in believing that there is no such demon. But how could I be, since if there were one, my experience would be precisely what it is now? The assessment of this principle is thus crucial for appraising Cartesian skepticism – and, I think, much skepticism in general.

"The Old Skepticism, the New Foundationalism, and Naturalized Epistemology," Chapter 12, attacks this principle. In addition to proposing a plausible counterexample, I distinguish the principle from weaker principles from which it has not been generally separated. My suggestion is that the weaker ones give us all we need to understand how justification *is* transmitted over entailments, e.g. from a belief that p to a belief of a proposition self-evidently entailed by p. But these weaker principles deny skeptics what they need to mount demon or "envatment" arguments.

22. There is much literature aimed at suggesting that one could not possibly be a brain in a vat. I have found it generally unconvincing.

The chapter goes on to distinguish Cartesian foundationalism from mine: a foundationalism fallibilistic about the status of foundations, contextualist about their contents, inductivist about transmission of justification and knowledge, first order, and (moderately) holistic about justification in general. This foundationalism is also internalist about the grounds of justification and rationalist about the status of epistemic principles. Using this theory as a point of departure, I consider some different ways in which one might show that skepticism is wrong. The most interesting of these, dialectical showing, uses an epistemic principle as a major premise. I formulate such a principle governing the generation of perceptual justification, argue for its a priori status, and conclude that there is reason to think that it is possible to refute skepticism about the justification of certain beliefs concerning the external world. Here, more than in Chapter 10, I compare the anti-skeptical resources of this internalist view with those of reliabilism, the most plausible naturalistic epistemology. I show how reliabilism makes room for second-order knowledge that we have knowledge and justified beliefs about the external world, but (as already noted) I argue that, without a kind of circularity that is at best philosophically problematic, it cannot establish that we do.

At this point in the book, through Chapters 1–12, several tasks have been accomplished. The foundationalism–coherentism controversy has been clarified, and foundationalism has been shown to be a plausible position quite different from what one would expect from the stereotypic portraits of it as a rigid and monolithic conception of belief and knowledge. A moderate, internalist version of foundationalism has been developed, using a well-groundedness conception of justification and knowledge. In developing the conception, I trace both justification and knowledge to basic sources in experience and reason; and the theory explicates the inferential relation by which justification extends from foundations to superstructure. Both coherentism and reliabilism are criticized, but many of their virtues are built into the internalist foundationalism that is developed. Coherence, for instance, is accounted for in terms of the same elements that produce justification; reliability is accommodated as a de facto, though not a constitutive, property of the processes that produce justification. In the course of this theorizing, moreover, a number of distinctions are made that are useful in any epistemology: between, for instance, causal and epistemic dependence, positive and negative epistemic dependence, substantively and conceptually naturalistic epistemologies, dispositional beliefs and dispositions to believe, personal and impersonal justification, being justified in believing and justifiedly believing; between episodically and structurally inferential beliefs, the process and the property of justification, structural justification and several other kinds, justification and excusability, first- and second-order internalism, giving a justification and showing that one is justified, and rebutting and refuting skepticism. Distinctions are also made among kinds of showing, of reasons, of epistemic principles, and of skepticism on one side and dogmatism on the other. A number of the contrasts just listed are reflected in the theory of rationality, not only as applied to rational belief – which one would expect to be largely parallel to justified belief – but also as applied to rational action and rationality in the non-cognitive propositional attitudes. This brings us to the chapters on rationality.

IV. RATIONALITY

It might seem unnecessary for a book in epistemology to contain a major section on rationality. For it might seem that 'rational belief' is just a synonym for 'justified belief.' I think it is not, though I will not argue that here.[23] A more important reason for considering rationality is the conviction that normative concepts and properties are grounded in non-normative ones and that, if any view, whether foundationalist or coherentist, or internalist or externalist, accounts for justification, it may well apply to other normative notions as well. Rationality, then, may serve as a test case for the theory of justification. Beyond that, we may learn more about justification by considering rationality. Even apart from this, it speaks well for an epistemology if it can illuminate rationality. Ideally, we should achieve a unified theory of both theoretical and practical reason. The remaining chapters outline this project in some detail.

23. I have, however, argued for it in "Faith, Belief, and Rationality," *Philosophical Perspectives* V (1991).

MODERATE FOUNDATIONALISM AS A FRAMEWORK
FOR UNDERSTANDING RATIONALITY

The epistemic analogue of rationality as applied to non-cognitive propositional attitudes is justification, not knowledge. There may *be* an analogue of knowledge for these attitudes. For instance, although desires and intentions are not true or false, there are ways in which they may achieve a counterpart of the external success that, in Chapter 10, is said to characterize knowledge. This external, practical, and sometimes behavioral success is addressed in Chapter 15. Here the task is to see how far the well-groundedness conception of justification takes us in understanding rationality in general. The main issue is the territory of practical attitudes.

This problem is pursued in Chapter 13, "An Epistemic Conception of Rationality," particularly in relation to desire. I begin with some points only foreshadowed there. Skepticism can be directed against practical reason as well as against theoretical reason. The (global) skeptic about the latter claims that we have no justified beliefs; the (global) skeptic about the former maintains that we have no rational *intrinsic* desires. Skepticism may allow, however, that *relative* to an intrinsic desire, say wanting to play bridge for its own sake, an action like inviting friends to one's home may be instrumentally rational provided (for one thing) that one believes issuing the invitation will contribute to playing bridge. On this view our rational actions are roughly those designed to achieve a basic end.[24]

Epistemic skeptics can make a parallel move and countenance relative justification of beliefs, but they usually do not. Here I think we may learn something epistemologically significant from the study of practical reason. It might seem that if, in a relative sense – viz., instrumentally – an action can be rational when based on a non-rational intrinsic desire, then, in a relative sense, a belief can be justified even if inferentially based on a non-justified non-inferential belief. But this may not be so. First, the skeptic may not grant that we are justified in believing *any* principles of inference – and would certainly reject any that are non-deductive. This presents a difficulty for the theoretical case that does not clearly afflict

---

24. I ignore here the possibility that one overlooks an action one has temporarily forgotten is a *better* means. The point is that a skeptic about practical reason need not put *rationality* constraints on the instrumental beliefs, even if only a restricted range of them will serve.

the practical case: the latter concerns, after all, action itself and not practical inference, construed as a cognitive process appropriate to (but not necessary for) action; thus, there is no need for a principle of inference.[25] Second, a non-justified belief is a poor foundation,[26] whereas an intrinsic desire may be *non*-rational, as opposed to irrational, simply because it does not admit of rationality: there is no standard of rationality that condemns it. Skeptics about practical reason are unlikely to call an intrinsic desire irrational unless it is internally inconsistent or has other properties not belonging to our normal basic desires; they may also allow (though they need not) that an instrumental belief can render an action guided by it rational even if the belief itself is not rational, since they may take practical rationality to be of a sort not undermined by lack of epistemic rationality. Thus, the skeptic about theoretical reason can, like Hume, be a practical skeptic only about intrinsic desires. Actions and instrumental desires can be rational, at least in a relative sense.

It turns out, then, that the practical skeptic who is not also a epistemic skeptic can quite plausibly allow instrumental rationality. And it is this kind of skepticism that is addressed in Part IV. Moreover, though I argue against it (especially in Chapter 15), for purposes of developing a non-skeptical account of practical reason I here simply assume that it can be answered. On this basis, I suggest how intrinsic desires, the practical analogue of non-inferential beliefs, may be rationally grounded. I distinguish two main cases: those in which one wants something for (on the basis of) properties in virtue of which it is (or it is at least reasonable to take it to be) *desirable*, and cases in which one wants something because one *believes* it has such a property. The first case is experiential grounding, the second cognitive grounding.

If we can go this far, we have an analogue of foundational justification in epistemology: justification of desires grounded in experience – or at least grounded both non-inferentially and in something different from them, namely beliefs. Because beliefs admit of justification and rationality, this grounding, though not properly speaking inferential, is less basic than grounding in ex-

---

25. On some views all intentional action stems from practical inference; for discussion of the issue that supports the assumption made here, see my *Practical Reasoning* (London and New York: Routledge, 1989), esp. chs. 4 and 5.
26. In Chapter 4, I consider whether justification can emerge from a set of non-justified (but not unjustified) foundational beliefs and conclude that this is doubtful; certainly the skeptic would disallow it.

perience. My suggestion is that if it cannot be rational to want something for a property intrinsic to it, it cannot be rational to want it because one believes it has that property. How could one rationally want it on the basis of believing it has an intrinsic property – conceived as a desirability characteristic – if it could not be rational to want it for that property? The belief is, as it were, just an articulation of the desirability characteristic. This suggests that cognitive grounding of an intrinsic desire is itself to some degree experientially groundable. For if it is rational to want a thing for an intrinsic property, it is reasonable to expect that one could, through reflection on the nature and grounds of this desire, acquire justification for the corresponding evaluative belief: that the thing in question is desirable on account of that property.

From here it is easy to see how the general conception of practical rationality should go. Just as actions can be rational when suitably grounded in desires, e.g. instrumentally, desires can be rationally grounded in a similarly inferential way: when, for instance, satisfying an instrumental desire is rationally believed to be the best means to satisfying a rational intrinsic one. Notice that there is a connecting belief, as in the theoretical case. We have, then, an analogue of epistemic principles: generation principles that tell us when an intrinsic desire is (non-instrumentally) rational; and transmission principles that tell us how an instrumental desire, or an action, must be based on a rational intrinsic desire in order to be rational on that ground. Similar points apply to intention and to other propositional attitudes. There is also defeasibility, as in the case of justified belief. Even if I have a good reason to do something, if I justifiedly believe that doing it will have dire consequences that outweigh the good it will bring, the rationality of the action is defeated.

The success of this well-groundedness conception of practical rationality does not depend on an internalist version of foundationalism. The analogue of reliabilism would simply take it that an intrinsic desire is rational when it is produced or sustained by a process which, suitably often, yields desires that are – let us say – sound. The point is that there will be some external standard that does for rational desire what truth does for justified belief. Because there is so much controversy about external standards of value – about whether, e.g., anything is objectively desirable or valuable – reliabilism is more limited than internalism in providing a framework for conceiving practical rationality. But of course it is limited in the theoretical domain as well: if the external world is illusory, we not only do not have knowledge of it but also lack (genuine) justified beliefs about it.[27]

The epistemic analogy bears further fruits. The maximization of expected utility view of rational action can be seen as a counterpart of epistemological coherentism; and other views of rationality can be seen as either qualified versions of coherentism or procedurally constrained forms of foundationalism.[28] There are also points about the psychology of both action and the conative propositional attitudes that emerge from pursuit of the analogy. For instance, like theoretical ones, practical inferential relations can be structural or episodic. On balance, the well-groundedness conception of practical rationality seems not only significantly parallel to its epistemic namesake but also plausible.

RATIONALITY: ABSTRACT AND CONCRETE

The study of rationality from an epistemic point of view is doubly motivated: by a conviction that epistemology and the theory of rationality can each be advanced in the light of the other, and by a desire for a comprehensive account of rationality applicable to all the domains in which it occurs. Chapter 13 develops a number of analogies between well-groundedness as understood in Parts I through III and rationality, and it presents an account of rationality modeled on my epistemological account of justification. One important point that surfaces in Chapter 13 (and before), however, is only sketched there: the analogy between, on the one hand, a justified belief and one merely rationalizable by what justifies it and, on the other hand, a rational action or rational non-cognitive attitude and one rationalizable by the elements in virtue of which it is rational. The general issue here is that of causal conditions for *any* behavior or attitude with a positive normative status. Chapter 14, "Rationalization and Rationality," addresses this larger issue and reinforces the case made in Parts II and III for causal conditions on justified belief.

27. We can have what Goldman calls weak justification, but not the strong kind we normally think we have. See his "Strong and Weak Justification," *Philosophical Perspectives* II (1988).
28. Here I have in mind particularly R. B. Brandt's conception of rationality, which is critically assessed in Chapter 13.

It is in the domain of action that the notion of rationalization originally took shape and became a useful descriptive and evaluative category. This chapter provides an account of such behavioral rationalizations. The rough idea is that one rationalizes an action by giving an account of it that represents it as rational in terms of one or more reasons but does not explain why one performed it – for the reasons are not explanatory.[29] They are at most – if normatively successful – justificatory. I distinguish first-person from second- and third-person rationalizations, and partial from full rationalizations – because one may give an account that is *partly* explanatory and partly a rationalization. I generalize the account to the propositional attitudes. And I argue that *types* as well as *tokens,* say actions or beliefs in the abstract as opposed to specific instances of them, can be rationalized. We may, for instance, rationalize a military strategy we are only considering – this hypothetical strategy is an act-type. The belief that we should use it may therefore also be said to be rationalized, even if the belief (type) is only being considered for adoption and no one holds it, i.e., this belief-type is not instantiated. Similarly, the *proposition* that we should use it may also be rationalized, in essentially the same way a proposition can be shown to be justified: either relative to a particular person or in some other way.

In the light of this account of the kinds and pervasiveness of rationalizations, I argue that just as *having* a justification for a proposition one believes does not entail justifiedly believing it, the rationalizability of an action or propositional attitude does not entail that, if one performs the action or holds the attitude, one does so rationally. We get no support from a foundation we have available if we build on another instead. Some of the arguments used in Chapter 7 ("The Casual Structure of Indirect Justification") are relevant here; but in part because belief is not the dominant focus in this chapter, other arguments play a larger role.

One important argument concerns the connection between rationality and reasoning. A merely rationalized action, for instance, is not placed in the context of a practical argument that underlies it: the practical argument that does – corresponding to the real,

---

29. In "Actions, Reasons and Causes," *Journal of Philosophy* LX (1963) Donald Davidson uses 'rationalize' for the relation wants and beliefs normally bear to the actions they explain. The explanatory condition here does not accord with the standard use, and I note Davidson's broad construal simply to avoid its confusion with mine.

explaining reasons for the action – is *not* sufficient to render the action rational. That argument does not even render the action-type in question rational, because an action that is *merely* rationalized is not one whose explaining elements *also* render it prima facie rational. For instance, where the agent uses a rationalization – e.g. "I wanted him to learn a valuable lesson" – out of embarrassment about the real, normatively inadequate reasons – say wanting to hurt him as a competitor – the real reasons do not render the action rational because of their normative inadequacy, and the rationalizing elements do not do so because of their explanatory inadequacy. On the other hand, the explaining reasons may, e.g., be selfish but perfectly good from the point of view of rationality; in that case the action is not merely rationalized. The thrust of these points is that a good reason not to take rationalizability to entail rationality is that doing so cuts rationality off from its connection with reasoning. It may be objected that I am simply assuming that this connection is causal, but that is not so; a number of considerations suggest the causal view. One is indicated by a second line of argument, to which I now turn.

Moral philosophers from Aristotle to Hume, Kant, and Mill have made distinctions akin to Kant's famous contrast between actions merely in conformity with duty and actions done from duty.[30] My main thesis in this chapter can be partially put in these terms. An action or propositional attitude that is merely rationalizable is only in accordance with reason, not rational. Again, anti-causalist philosophers may object that there is causal and non-causal rationality, and they are simply different. My response is this. If performing rational actions and having rational propositional attitudes is to count as it does toward the rationality of persons, then the causal requirement is needed. What is produced by factors, such as superstition or luck, that are not grounds or elements of our rationality does not evidence it. Furthermore, agents are morally virtuous only if they act (in an adequate proportion of cases) from motives grounded in their virtues; epistemic virtue has a similar relation to beliefs, and only a causal theory can give a good account of the integration between normatively desirable traits and the concrete phenomena, such as actions and beliefs, that are essentially related to them.[31]

30. For Aristotle, Hume, and Kant this point is documented in chs. 1–3 of my
Practical Reasoning.
31. For a different view of epistemic virtue see Ernest Sosa, "Knowledge and In-

As Chapter 14 argues, it is generally not normal, and certainly not characteristic of rational persons, to have, and realize one has, reasons for an action one performs, or for an attitude one holds, and yet not do the deed or hold the attitude in part *for* that reason. More important, an action or attitude merely *aligned* with reasons one has, i.e., abstractly but not causally supported by them, and performed or held for an inadequate reason, does not count toward one's rationality. If one acts (in a significant way) for no reason, or only for a bad one, this tends to count *against* one's rationality. Granting that even the mere having of good reasons counts to some degree toward one's rationality, the action does not; and indeed the having of reasons that do not emerge as causal factors in an action or attitude for which they are reasons is a negative mark. Other things being equal, a person in whom this happens lacks rational *integration*. Given these and the many other relevant points tending in the same direction, the causal thesis seems superior to its alternative. This is particularly so if the needed causal requirement is consistent with internalism. I might add that the relevant causal connections need not be deterministic; hence, if rationality is thought to be incompatible with determinism (perhaps on the ground that what one cannot help doing or believing is not a candidate for rationality), it is not reasonable to deny the causal thesis on that count either.

THE INTEGRATION OF THEORETICAL AND PRACTICAL REASON

The domain of practical reason is that of action and the practical attitudes, most notably desire and intention, which express reasons for action. In Chapters 13 and 14, the epistemology of Parts I through III is brought to bear in constructing a general conception of rationality that encompasses both the theoretical and the practical. The closing chapter, "The Architecture of Reason," brings these results together, extends them, places them in historical perspective, and draws out some of their implications for ethics.

The chapter also makes some broadly epistemological advances over earlier chapters. Instrumentalism in the practical sphere is

tellectual Virtue," *The Monist* 68 (1985); Kvanvig, op. cit., and James Montmarquet's *Epistemic Virtue and Doxastic Responsibility*, forthcoming from Rowman and Littlefield.

shown to be a kind of *functionalism about rationality;* the central idea is that the function of reason is to serve desire, and rational elements need have no instrinsic content or basis or, in the case of actions, be of any intrinsic type. Moreover, the instrumentalist view, though it may be considered coherentist (on grounds introduced in Chapter 13), is quite readily understood as a subjective foundationalism: the intrinsic desires one happens to have are the foundations from which we are to judge the rationality of one's actions and other desires. A further epistemological development is best understood in the context of a major point about the foundations of practical reason. A central thesis of Chapter 15 is that although rationality is best conceived along internalist lines, it is not properly taken to be egoistic. The foundational desires of a rational person, particularly early in life, may be for internal states, such as pleasure and the elimination of pain; but these desires are not for these things *as* one's own: what is desirable about escaping the clutches of the blackberry bushes a child is trapped in is getting rid of the pain, not eliminating the pain *as* its own. Dislike of pain is psychologically more primitive than one's self-concept. I know who I am more by what I like and dislike than the other way around; and I can know what I like and dislike even if I do not know who I am.

Just as we must not conclude, from the perennial dialectic with skepticism, in which we speak of our beliefs and knowledge in second-order discourse, that the crucial issue is the status of second-order statements about justification and knowledge, we must not conclude, from the need to speak of goods and evils in our own experience in discussing what is or is not intrinsically good, that the actual goods and evils we seek are essentially self-referential. If the most primitive cases of desirability are encountered in our own experience, they are *in* us, but it does not follow that the desired objects are wanted *for* us in any sense that implies the lesser desirability of similar phenomena, such as pleasure, and relief from pain, in others.

The epistemological analogy is this. The primitive justificatory experiences are in us and warrant such foundational beliefs as that there is white here; the belief that *I see* white is far more sophisticated, embodying both a self-concept and a conception of seeing. My thesis, then, is that just as the internal grounds of foundationally justified beliefs are impersonal, the internal grounds of rational intrinsic desires are impersonal: the goodness of my experience of

42

music is in principle as realizable in your experience as is the sensory whiteness that grounds my belief that there is something white here. It is rational to want the experience of hearing the music for *what* it is, not *whose* it is; it is rational to believe there is white here because of *what* I experience, not because *I* experience it. My experience is ontically essential to the concrete existence of what I experience; but that does not make the concept of the former epistemically essential to the basis of my justification or rationality. That concept *is* essential to *showing* that I am justified or rational; but we must not allow our felt need to answer skepticism to prejudice our conception of the basic data. What is necessary to describing the foundations of rationality in second-order discourse must not be taken to be essential to their existence or to their role in grounding the elements they render rational.

If the foundations of practical rationality are impersonal for the reasons I offer, then the way is open to argue for the reasonableness of certain moral principles, above all those that take every person to be capable of realizing intrinsic value – the chief inspiration of utilitarianism – and those that take persons to be importantly alike in virtue of having similar capacities for such realization – a major inspiration supporting deontologism, though its proponents tend to countenance more kinds of value than utilitarians do. This line of argument does not presuppose that there is any specific kind of thing which it is rational for everyone to desire. But it does seem that pleasure and the elimination of pain are two such things.

I conclude this commentary on Chapter 15 with three points. First, the account of practical rationality does not entail *realism*. There need not actually be anything intrinsically good in order for the account of rationality to succeed. This is one advantage of internalism. Second, just as epistemological internalism does not force us to be skeptics about the external world, its practical counterpart does not force us to be valuational skeptics. In this way, as well as in relation to rationality conceived internally, the view can be objective: just as there can really exist rational and irrational beliefs, judged by intersubjective standards, and rational beliefs can be true, we can rationally or irrationally value things, and some things we rationally value may really be intrinsically valuable. Third, internalism roots normativity in us, but it does not make our opinion about what is rational or irrational supreme: we may fail not only by our own lights, but in terms of standards, such as epistemic principles, whose scope ranges over the entire inner domain but whose status is determined by impersonal uses of reason.

Having stressed the unity and objectivity of theoretical and practical reason, I want to close with still another rejection of dogmatism, which is sometimes felt to be inevitable in positions affirming the objectivity of questions of value. Objectivity does not imply infallibility, or even a tendency to achieve rationality that entitles one to self-confidence. Mistakes are easy and pervasive in any normal life; vigilance and self-correction are essential for the nurturance and growth of rationality. Moreover, the various qualities of experience in virtue of which beliefs and desires are rational, however repeatable they may be from person to person, are distributed differently among us and have different effects in different people. We who are physically and psychologically normal *can* see and hear much the same things; but what we actually *do* see and hear is very different. We can all enjoy the simple pleasures of a cool swim on a hot summer day and the richer pleasures of a great symphony; but we experience them, and respond to them, differently, and what gives one person pleasure may leave another pained or indifferent. In this respect the content of people's rational intrinsic desires is divergent. Even if both of them want enjoyment in general – which is not a requirement on rational persons even if they must want specific pleasures – *the* pleasures in the two cases constitute different goods.

The upshot of these points is that although the theory of rationality developed here suggests intellectual, motivational, and valuational overlap between persons, it also suggests substantial and enduring differences. The more divergent our worlds and our experiences therein, the more we should differ in all these respects. But if rationality depends on the way in which our behavior and attitudes are grounded, and if the fundamental grounds, though individually in us, are collectively spread among us, communication is possible, the scope and justification of our beliefs can be extended and shared, and our differences in matters of value can often be reconciled.

The overall position of the book, then, is at once objectivist and pluralist; it is a moderately foundationalist, internalist theory of justification, and it embodies a parallel, partly externalist conception of knowledge. Both justification and knowledge are conceived as well-grounded belief, but the grounding can be external in the case of knowledge. This much is epistemologically neutral with respect to empiricism and rationalism, and ontologically neutral with respect to realism about justification and other normative properties. But I have argued for a moderate rationalism in epistemology, and I am inclined toward a version of realism about justification and rationality. Quite apart from how these two issues are decided, my position can succeed in most of its major aims: to unite a causalist, fallibilist foundationalism with a nondeontological internalism, thereby realizing many of the virtues of coherentism without lapsing into a mere blend of foundationalism and coherentism; to account for the scope of our knowledge and justification in a way that helps to vindicate common sense against skepticism; and to provide an integration of theoretical and practical reason that exhibits both as having a common structure and a similar basis in human experience.[32]

32. This essay has benefited from comments by William Alston, John Heil, Paul Moser, Allison Nespor, and Louis Pojman.

PART I

THE FOUNDATIONALISM–COHERENTISM CONTROVERSY

Chapter 1

Psychological foundationalism

Epistemological foundationalism is best conceived as a thesis about the structure of a body of knowledge. Although its major proponents have been non-skeptics, the thesis may be construed as neutral with respect to skepticism. A modest version of epistemological foundationalism so construed might be formulated as the view that necessarily, (a) if one has any knowledge, one has some direct knowledge, i.e., knowledge not based on other knowledge or beliefs one has, and (b) any further knowledge one has is at least in part based on one's direct knowledge. Now suppose we make four plausible assumptions which most foundationalists would accept: (i) each of us (normal adults) has (propositional) knowledge, (ii) knowing entails believing, (iii) we each have at least some direct knowledge constituted by beliefs *not* based on other beliefs of ours, and (iv) if a person has direct knowledge *on* which other knowledge is based, at least some of the beliefs constituting the former are not based on other beliefs of his. Given (i)–(iv), epistemological foundationalism apparently entails some form of what I shall call *psychological foundationalism*. In its simplest form, this is the view that the structure of a person's body of beliefs is foundational in the strong sense that some of his beliefs are not based on others, and any other beliefs he has are based on the former.[1]

Psychological foundationalism is empirical, but it should interest

---

1. The reason for (iii) is that it seems possible for knowledge to be direct even though the *belief* constituting it is based on another belief, provided what *justifies* the former is not any other belief. Thus, without (iii) one's having direct knowledge would not entail one's having direct belief. Without (iv), one's having indirect knowledge would not entail one's having foundational belief, i.e., direct belief on which at least one other belief is based. Regarding (i), I am taking the question whether people have knowledge to be empirical. This may be controversial, but nothing important in this paper turns on it.

philosophers as well as psychologists. For one thing, since most epistemological foundationalists would hold (i)–(iv), they may not ignore evidence against psychological foundationalism, at least in certain restricted forms, e.g. one requiring only the subset of one's beliefs constituting knowledge to have some kind of foundational structure. It goes without saying that at least "cognitive psychologists" are interested in issues about the structure of our belief systems.[2] Other ways in which psychological foundationalism should interest both philosophers and psychologists should emerge later.

Psychological foundationalism has never (so far as I know) been explicitly formulated, nor can one easily formulate it in adequate detail just by systematically altering some available version of epistemological foundationalism. The latter view has itself rarely been expressed except in outline,[3] and even a quite explicit version of epistemological foundationalism will, as we shall see, leave its proponent considerable freedom in choosing a psychological foundationalist counterpart. I shall thus begin by pointing out some major dimensions in which psychological foundationalist theories may vary. Section II will then formulate a range of these theories. Section III will discuss an epistemologically interesting and, I hope, psychologically plausible version of psychological foundationalism, contrasting it with a form of psychological coherentism. And the last section will show how the preceding discussion bears on both epistemology and the psychology of cognition.

I

The architectural metaphor associated with foundationalism is worth developing. For many of the questions that one can ask about buildings have interesting cognitive counterparts. Among these questions are what sorts of materials are suitable for foun-

---

2. See, e.g., Joseph R. Royce, "Cognition and Knowledge: Psychological Epistemology," in E. C. Carterette and M. P. Friedman, eds., *Handbook of Perception*, vol. I (New York and London: Academic Press, 1974).
3. This point applies especially to the question of what causal relations might hold between foundational beliefs and beliefs based on them. The most detailed treatment of this I know of is D. M. Armstrong's in *Belief, Truth and Knowledge* (Cambridge: Cambridge University Press, 1973), esp. chs. 12 and 14. I hope, however, to bring out several aspects of psychological foundationalism on which his study has at least no very specific bearing.

dations, what kinds of structures are usable in a foundation, how foundational elements are related to one another, and how they are related to the ground they rest on. Regarding the relation of a building's foundations to its superstructure, we may ask how the latter is supported by the foundations, how a change in one or more foundational elements may change the superstructure, whether changes in the foundations may be made from the superstructure or only from the foundation itself or the ground below, and how, if at all, the superstructure can be extended without a change in the foundations.

If we think of a body of beliefs as divided into foundational beliefs and superstructure beliefs in some way based on them, we can readily discern the counterpart questions for cognitive structure. These questions suggest at least a good many of the major respects in which psychological (or epistemological) foundationalist theories may vary. Let me illustrate, exhibiting first some variables concerning the relations among foundational beliefs, and then some variables concerning the relation between foundational and superstructure beliefs.

First, foundational theories may differ in what sorts of beliefs they take as suitable for foundations. A strong theory might countenance only beliefs about one's immediate experience, and "logically intuitive" beliefs. On a modest theory, certain beliefs about material objects and certain confident beliefs about one's past, such as that one has seen a sunset, might be foundations. Second, foundational theories may differ in the structures they attribute to sets of foundational beliefs. One theory might affirm what we might call causal contiguity, i.e., that each such belief receives some causal support from at least one other. The idea is like that of every foundation stone touching and gaining some support from at least one other. As the analogy suggests, causal contiguity would not entail that any foundational belief be based on any other such belief. The point is that because of the support of contiguous foundational beliefs, a foundational belief would (other things being equal) be less easily eliminated than otherwise by whatever can eliminate such beliefs. On a weaker theory, a foundational belief might or might not derive causal support from any other belief. Third, foundationalist theories may differ in the interactions they postulate among foundational beliefs. One theory might deny that any foundational belief is ever causally sufficient for bringing another into existence or sustaining it; a different theory might permit this.

Fourth, such theories may differ in how they hold foundational beliefs to be related to whatever they suppose brings these beliefs into existence or sustains them. A theory might hold that each foundational belief is brought into existence at least in part by some form of non-cognitive direct awareness, whereas another theory might posit quite different sources; e.g., perceptual sensations not construed as objects of awareness, or "absorption" in socialization, or certain stimulations of the brain.

Concerning the relation of foundational to superstructure beliefs, foundationalists may vary, first, in the ways they take foundational beliefs to generate or sustain superstructure beliefs. A strong theory might hold that every superstructure belief is brought into existence and sustained by exactly one (possibly conjunctive) foundational belief, whereas a weaker theory might allow a superstructure belief to be brought into existence or sustained by a set of foundational beliefs, no one of which is sufficient to sustain it. Second, foundationalist theories may differ regarding the effect, on superstructure beliefs, of a change in one or more foundational beliefs. One theory might hold, e.g., that the loss of any foundational belief always eliminates at least one superstructure belief; another might allow superstructure beliefs to be overdetermined, in the sense that two or more causally independent foundational beliefs may each be sufficient to sustain it. Third, such theories may differ in the role, if any, they give to foundational beliefs, superstructure beliefs, or non-cognitive variables in changing the set of foundational beliefs. A strong theory might maintain that no set of superstructure beliefs, say that p and that q, can displace a foundational belief, say that r, unless by virtue of the causal power it derives from some other foundational belief(s), on which it is based; e.g., if the beliefs that p and q displace the belief that r, because S has come to believe that p and q are each inconsistent with r, S would have to be such that he *would* have given up p and q rather than r if it were not for the support his beliefs that p and q receive from some foundational belief(s) other than r. By contrast, a weaker theory might allow the beliefs that p and q to displace the belief that r in such a way that they would have done so even if not supported by any foundational belief, provided certain other conditions are met (perhaps including their being supported by other superstructure beliefs with which they in some sense "cohere"). Fourth, foundationalist theories may differ in the number and kind of superstructure beliefs they take to be capable of addition to the cognitive system without a change in its foundations. A theory might hold that, for any finite set of foundational beliefs, there is a limit to the number of superstructure beliefs which can be non-trivially added[4] without a change in the foundations, and that only certain patterns of inference may serve to make such additions. A weaker theory might countenance certain "rich" finite sets of foundational beliefs such that there is in principle no limit to the extension of the superstructure; and it might allow some extensions to take place by non-inferential processes.

To suggest the range of possible foundationalist theories, I have chosen examples quite far apart on the relevant dimensions. I believe the weaker theories suggested are epistemologically more interesting and psychologically more plausible. Both points will find some support in what follows.

II

With Section I in mind, we are ready to construct some definite formulations of psychological foundationalism. We should begin with two very general points. First, since psychologists are so often at pains to account for cognitive differences among people and changes within a given person's belief system, we may safely ignore formulations which require either that there be a particular set of beliefs which all persons have, at least at some time, as their foundational beliefs, or that there be, for any given person, some one set of foundational beliefs for all times. The theory should be relativized to both persons and times. Second, while it seems psychologically possible for one to have only direct beliefs, i.e., beliefs not based on one or more others, it appears that nobody is like this, and it is a relatively uninteresting case. I shall thus construe psychological foundationalism only as a thesis about people with both direct beliefs and beliefs based on them.

But what is it for one belief to be *based* on another? The question is important because this relation is crucial for understanding how, at least according to epistemological foundationalism, superstruc-

4. Consider S's belief that the moon is over 200,000 miles from the earth. S might trivially add at least a finite number of beliefs: that it is over 199,999 miles away, that it is over 199,998 miles away, etc. By contrast, a belief of a law of nature would in general not be a trivial addition. I cannot define 'triviality' here, but the example suggests what the issue is.

ture beliefs are related to foundational beliefs. There is wide agreement that S's belief that p, is based (wholly) on his belief that q, if
and only if q is the *reason for which* he believes p. This notion of an
"operative" reason is hard to explicate, and few philosophers have
proposed accounts of it.[5] I cannot offer an account here, but the
following points will help us considerably.

First, S's belief that p, is based (at least in part) on his belief that
q, only if the latter plays some role in causally sustaining the former.[6] Second, because of its connection with knowledge and justification, the basis relation is (in a very wide sense) epistemic.
Imagine that S and S' have the same (good) evidence, q, for p. S
believes p solely on the basis of q; S' believes p solely on the basis
of r, which is not good evidence. This difference could explain
why, though they *have* the same evidence for p, S knows it and S'
does not, and S but not S' is justified in believing it. The basis
relation is thus (broadly) epistemic in part because whether a belief
has it to some belief(s) of evidence propositions may determine
whether the belief constitutes knowledge or is even justified. Third,
if S justifiably believes q, and his belief that p is wholly based on
the former belief, then (a) he is disposed to adduce q in trying to
justify his belief that p, and (b) when certain conditions are met
(such as his not inferring p from q by a principle he should see is
invalid), his belief that p is justified by his belief that q. Fourth, the
basis relation apparently holds only if either (i) S believes something to the effect that, or at least *takes* it that (if this is not a species
of believing), q supports p (e.g., entails or confirms it); or (ii) the
belief that q, produces or sustains the belief that p by a certain sort
of process, e.g. one which is reliable in that it guarantees that if
q is true, p is also. Since (i) and (ii) can each help to explain how
the basis relation may transmit justification and knowledge from
S's belief that q to his belief that p, taking either to be necessary

---

5. A notable exception is D. M. Armstrong. Much of what I say about what it is
   for one belief to be based on another is consistent with his views in *Belief,
   Truth and Knowledge*, chs. 13 and 14; but he might well reject what I call (below) the connecting belief requirement.
6. One might wish to deny that beliefs can be causes or effects, and I shall not
   assume that strictly speaking they can be. But scarcely anyone would deny
   that the events of adopting or acquiring a belief might cause adopting or rejecting another, or that one's having a belief might partially *explain* why one
   has (or lacks) another belief. Using these terms in place of talk of one belief's
   causing another, together with terminology involving counterfactuals, I could
   avoid talk of causal relations among beliefs. But it is more convenient to use
   causal parlance.

for it partially explains why it is epistemic. (i) and (ii) are compatible, and some psychological foundationalists might take both to be necessary. To simplify matters, I shall tentatively take (i) but not (ii) to be necessary for the basis relation.

Thus, I shall take it to be necessary, though not sufficient, for S's belief that p to be based, at t, at least in part on his belief that q, that at t (a) the latter at least in part brings about or sustains the former (call this *the causal requirement*); (b) S is disposed to adduce q in trying to justify his belief that p (call this the *subjective justification requirement*); and (c) S believes something to the effect that q supports p (call this *the connecting belief requirement*). Beliefs not based at least in part on one or more others I call *epistemically direct*.

Reflection will show that the basis relation thus construed is not transitive. S may, for instance, believe that r supports (say, inductively confirms) q and that q supports p, yet not believe that r supports p. Then, even if his belief that p is based on his belief that q and the latter is based on his belief that r, his belief that p is not based on his belief that r. Still, because his belief that p is "grounded on" his belief that r by an unbroken chain of basis relations, and as a result receives some causal support from his belief that r, it is natural to say that the former is *indirectly based* on the latter. It will help us to adopt this term for cases in which, though such a chain exists between one of S's beliefs and another, the former is not (directly) based on the latter.

In the light of this discussion of the basis relation, we can see that there will be differences between psychological foundational theories in respect of the kind of support relation in which they take foundational beliefs to stand to superstructure beliefs. A theory might hold that foundational beliefs support superstructure beliefs by simply causing, or playing a role in causally sustaining, the latter. The support relation could also be taken to be non-causal, e.g. purely epistemic. Thus, one could hold that while foundational beliefs need have no causal relation to superstructure beliefs, the latter are supported by the former in a purely justificatory way; e.g., in such a way that if S were asked to justify one of the latter, he would tend to do so by adducing at least one of the former. Similarly, but less likely, one might hold that S would be disposed to explain each of the latter by appeal to at least one of the former; and there are other possibilities.

We can thus imagine at least three main kinds of theory. On a purely causal theory, some of S's beliefs are not caused or sustained by others, but are psychologically "primitive," as Russell put it,[7] and S's other beliefs are causally sustained by these. A non-causal theory would posit a different kind of support relation, such as a (subjective) justificatory relation. And a theory employing the basis relation, which is the support relation perhaps most commonly used in epistemology, would combine elements of the other two types of theory. The following illustrate each of the above kinds of theory:

I. *Causal Psychological Foundationalism:* For any person, S, and any time, t, the body of S's beliefs at t has a foundational structure such that (1) some of S's beliefs are causally direct, in the sense that they are not caused or causally sustained by any other beliefs of his; and (2) each of S's other beliefs is caused or causally sustained by a set of the former.

II. *Non-Causal Psychological Foundationalism:* for any S and any t, the body of S's beliefs at t has a foundational structure in which (1) some of S's beliefs are non-causally direct, i.e., he is not disposed to justify (explain, etc.) them by appeal to any other beliefs of his; (2) the rest of his beliefs are supported by the former in the sense that he is disposed to justify (explain, etc.) each of them by appeal to some set of the former; and (3) if any beliefs in the first set cause or causally sustain any in the second, their doing so is not a necessary condition for (2).

III. *Epistemic Psychological Foundationalism:* For any S and any t, the body of S's beliefs at t has a foundational structure such that (1) some of his beliefs are epistemically direct; and (2) the others are directly or indirectly based on the former.

Of these, II seems least plausible from a psychological point of view. III has the greatest epistemological interest. Moreover, typically anyone satisfying it will also satisfy something similar to II, and III will, I think, turn out no less plausible psychologically than I Indeed, where S's only causally direct beliefs are epistemically direct, III entails I Thus, I shall concentrate on developing III A number of the developments will clearly apply to II; hence much of our discussion may be brought to bear on II by anyone who finds II plausible.

7. See, e.g., *An Inquiry into Meaning and Truth* (London: Allen and Unwin, 1940; and Harmondsworth, Middlesex: Penguin Books, 1962), ch. 10. Maintaining that an epistemological premise must also be a "psychological premiss," Russell defines the latter as "a belief not caused by any other belief or beliefs."

Let us start with some general points about III. It allows that support relations between foundational and superstructure beliefs be one-one, one-many, many-one, or many-many. Indeed, whatever the support relation foundationalists choose from among the kinds we have considered, they may allow that a superstructure belief be supported by just one foundational belief; that many of the former might be supported by one of the latter; that a single superstructure belief might be supported by many foundational beliefs; and of course that many of the former might each be supported by many of the latter. Regarding *preservation* of the structure, various principles seem plausible; but we would expect cognitive psychologists to suppose that, within limits, memory may preserve not only foundational and superstructure beliefs, but also the relations of support holding between them. We may also expect a psychological foundationalist to try to account for *extension* of the structure. This presumably requires countenancing at least two sorts of belief-generating processes, both of which a proponent of III would be likely to consider important: inference, which produces beliefs from beliefs; and those "processes," like introspection, perceptual experience, and logical intuition, which originate beliefs, producing them (including foundational beliefs), from other things.

So far we have considered some broad features which a psychological foundationalist might attribute to the relation between foundational and superstructure beliefs, and some ways he might regard the entire body of beliefs as preserved and extended. We must also consider how he might regard foundational beliefs as alterable by various elements in the body of beliefs. Since there is reason to think that "dissonance"[8] is a source of cognitive adjustments, we might expect psychological foundationalists to allow that a foundational belief may be uprooted or modified in at least several kinds of dissonant circumstances. For instance, S might come to believe (a), of two of his foundational beliefs,[9] that they are incom-

---

8. I have in mind here such support as the theory of cognitive dissonance has received. That the dissonance I cite would be considered such by dissonance theorists is apparent in Leon Festinger, *A Theory of Cognitive Dissonance* (Stanford: Stanford University Press, 1957), ch. 1. Some confirmation of the theory is reported there and in a number of later works; e.g., Arthur R. Cohen, *Attitude Change and Social Influence* (New York: Basic Books, 1964).

9. His belief might also be to the effect that the *propositions* in question are incompatible, provided he is in some sense aware that he believes them. Moreover, S's believing, *of* two of his foundational beliefs, that they are

patible; (b), of a foundational and a superstructure belief, that they are incompatible; or (c), of a set of foundational beliefs and a set of at least one such belief and at least one superstructure belief, that the former is incompatible with the latter. Parallel cases might arise with 'not both true' or 'probably incompatible' in place of 'incompatible'.

But how, it might be asked, can a superstructure belief "outweigh" a foundational one? Again, the architectural metaphor is helpful: just as one can replace a foundation stone from above, so a superstructure belief adequately supported from below may be sufficiently strong to displace a foundational belief. It is a more difficult question whether all of the strength by which a superstructure belief may displace a foundational belief must come from one or more other foundational beliefs. The question presupposes, of course, that the notion of belief strength is at least ordinal. Let us assume so.[10] Then the crucial question is whether a superstructure belief can acquire strength from some other source than the foundational belief(s) it is based on. There is no psychological reason why not. Indeed, surely *S*'s *wanting* to believe that *p*, can strengthen his belief that *p*; and perhaps certain patterns of superstructure beliefs can give to at least some of the beliefs in the pattern some strength which is not derived from their foundations.

There is reason to think, then, that a psychological foundationalist might hold that a superstructure belief (say, that the EEG machine indicates one does not have a headache) could outweigh a foundational belief (say, that one does have a headache), even when the latter has at least as much strength as the former derives from the foundational belief(s) on which it is based. Whether he would also think that none of the strength by which a superstructure belief might outweigh a foundational belief need come from foundational beliefs is a further question I shall not try to answer. But there is no obvious psychological impossibility in this, and psychologists impressed with the influence of motivation on cognition will be disposed to allow it.

Before we express psychological foundationalism in more detail,

incompatible, does not entail his believing *that* two of his foundational beliefs are incompatible, nor even that *S* has a concept of a foundational belief.

10. Surely one "measure" of comparative belief strength is *S*'s sincere report on which of the two beliefs in question is stronger. A second is which he would give up if he believed them incompatible, wanted on balance to have a consistent set of beliefs, and behaved accordingly.

we should consider more closely the causal support relations that may hold between foundational and superstructure beliefs. At least the following seem psychologically quite possible: (a) a foundational belief might be causally sufficient for a superstructure belief; (b) the former might be causally necessary for the latter, where some set of foundational beliefs *is* sufficient: (c) a set of foundational beliefs might each causally contribute to sustaining a superstructure belief, where no one is a necessary condition, but the whole set is sufficient and any subset with *more* than one (more than two, three, etc.) members is necessary; (d) a foundational belief may contribute, whether as a necessary or sufficient condition or neither, to supporting a superstructure belief, *together with* a different kind of supporting element, e.g. a desire to hold the superstructure belief; and (e) various combinations of (a)–(d) may occur with respect to a single superstructure belief, including combinations which render it causally overdetermined.

Since we are developing an epistemic foundationalism, each relation cited will have an epistemic as well as a causal element. Tentatively, I am conceiving the main epistemic element as a connecting belief. Such beliefs connect a foundational belief with any superstructure belief that is (even in part) directly based on it. Connecting beliefs may take a variety of forms. Where S's belief that q is foundational with respect to his belief that p, the simplest case is a connecting belief that if q then p, e.g. that if there is a noise coming from over there then there is an object over there. But the connecting belief might be that q entails p, that q makes p probable, or that q justifies one in believing that p. Connecting beliefs may or may not require that S understand some logical or epistemic notion, such as entailment or justification.

Some connecting beliefs must presumably be direct: vertical foundation blocks, as it were. For if every connecting belief were indirect, each would be based on another belief, and that relation would require a further connecting belief, and so on. The regress is prima facie vicious (nor, as I shall later suggest, can it be replaced by a virtuous circle). Granted, the assumption that epistemic psychological foundationalism should posit connecting beliefs to ground superstructure beliefs on foundational beliefs is not obviously true. Here I shall make just two points in favor of this assumption.

First, without connecting beliefs it is not at all obvious how superstructure beliefs can be epistemically, rather than merely causally, grounded on foundational beliefs. If, e.g., S has no connecting belief, such as that if there is a noise over there then there is an object over there, his (direct) belief that there is a noise there can *cause* him to believe that there is an object there, but (in my terminology) the latter belief cannot be *based* on the former. However, where *both* the former and the connecting belief play a certain role[11] in sustaining the latter, it is so based. Second, where this basis relation holds, the foundational beliefs can be seen to support and, in some cases, systematize the superstructure beliefs in ways that may not apply if one postulates a causal connecting requirement in place of the connecting belief requirement. S may, e.g., be disposed to justify, explain, and interrelate a diverse set of his superstructure beliefs by tracing them, via his connecting beliefs, back to a small set of foundational beliefs. A theory that allows this might appeal to psychologists, especially if they conceive normal persons as motivated not only to avoid dissonance but to achieve consonance. For one natural route to consonance would seem to be systematizing and justifying many or most of one's beliefs by taking them to be justified by others of one's beliefs that are (subjectively) self-evident or not in need of justification; and presumably such a process could be at least largely unconscious. Moreover, particularly if the psychologist counts logically intuitive beliefs among the foundational ones, he would have no difficulty assuming that some connecting beliefs are foundational. I shall return to this question.

There are many other variables which a psychological foundationalist might want to take into account. But using those considered in this section we can give a definite shape to epistemic psychological foundationalism, which I shall express as a quite modest thesis:

IV. *Modest Psychological Foundationalism:* For any S and any t, the body of S's beliefs at t has a foundational structure such that (1) at least some of S's beliefs are foundational, these being a proper subset of his epistemically direct beliefs;[12] (2) every superstructure

11. It is notoriously difficult to say what constitues a suitable role here. Not just any causally sustaining relation will serve. For discussion of this problem, see Armstrong's *Belief, Truth and Knowledge,* ch. 14; and Chapter 8, this volume.
12. Why a proper subset? In my terminology, a belief is foundational only if it is direct and one or more other beliefs are based on it, though any direct belief is potentially foundational. Now given that, as explained above, some connecting beliefs are direct, if each had another belief based on it, *another* con-

belief, i.e., every belief based on some other, is directly or indirectly based, at least in part, on one or more foundational beliefs; (3) any belief in the structure or any basis relation holding among its beliefs can be preserved by memory; (4) the body of beliefs is alterable by inference or by perceptual experiences, introspection, or logical intuition; and (5) the foundations may be modified either as in (4) or by dissonance.

As pointed out above, support relations between foundational beliefs and superstructure beliefs may be one-one, one-many, many-one, or many-many. Moreover, a foundational belief may be (a) causally sufficient for a superstructure belief, (b) only causally necessary for it, or (c) not necessary or sufficient for it but only a causally contributing factor, where the other contributors may or may not be beliefs at all. And regarding dissonance that alters the foundations, a proponent of IV would probably include dissonance arising (usually with the acquisition of some new belief) between (i) two or more foundational beliefs, (ii) a foundational belief and a set of beliefs containing at least one foundational and at least one superstructure belief, and (iii) a foundational belief and one or more superstructure beliefs. He would be likely to hold, but need not hold, that some of the causal power by which a set of superstructure beliefs overrides a foundational belief is derived from one or more foundational beliefs.

Our discussion in this section and Section II indicates some ways in which IV might be qualified. But it is sufficiently plausible as it stands to be worth exploring both as a psychological thesis and in relation to epistemological foundationalism. The next section examines IV more closely.

III

Is it empirically possible that something like IV applies to normal persons? Let us see how that might be. First, recall that unlike some versions of epistemological foundationalism IV does not require that foundational beliefs be of any particular high epistemological status. The foundations may consist of a great many perceptual, introspective, and logically intuitive beliefs, as well as

necting belief would be required. The result would be a prima facie vicious regress.

a huge number of beliefs about the past, preserved by memory, such as that one recently heard noises and that one has often seen sunsets. At least from a psychological point of view, a belief that is based on others at one time may become foundational later when those beliefs are forgotten. This makes it possible in principle for the set of psychologically foundational beliefs to be as diverse as the set of superstructure beliefs. One's belief that one was born on a certain date, e.g., is presumably first based on believing (say) that one's parents said so (the connecting belief being that if they said so it is true); but eventually one might just directly believe one was born on that date.

As this example suggests, a psychological foundationalist will likely hold that there are many connecting beliefs among a person's foundational beliefs. Some of these should correspond to simple logical truths, such as those of first-order logic. Some would doubtless correspond to inductive principles, e.g. that if things of kind K (say, cats) always have behaved a certain way, they will in the future. And some may be idiosyncratic, such as the belief that if Sam advises one to do something, one shouldn't. (This would be unlikely to be initially direct, but it could become direct.)

According to IV., then, one can have a huge variety of foundational beliefs; and these can include both empirical and a priori connecting beliefs, any of which may serve, subjectively, to license inferences. In the light of this, how plausible is it to regard each of a person's beliefs that are based on one or more others as ultimately based, at least indirectly, on some set of his foundational beliefs? In exploring this, it is essential to keep in mind that IV. does not require each superstructure belief to be directly based on one or more foundational beliefs. Even if S infers q from r and p from q, his belief that p need not be directly based on his belief that r, since he may not believe anything to the effect that if r then p (or probably p). But even here S's belief that p will typically be indirectly based on, and causally sustained by, his belief that r (via the latter's causally sustaining his belief that q); and his belief that p will typically be directly based on his belief that q, which in turn will typically be directly based on his belief that r. Hence his belief that p has a (relative) epistemic foundation and, if we consider only beliefs, an ultimate causal foundation.

If IV is true, there will also be (epistemically) direct beliefs on which no other belief is based. Psychologically, these are potential foundations, since another belief could be based on them. From the point of view of cognitive unity, they may seem to jut out from the belief system, as it were, being contiguous with nothing in it above or below. But they may at least be laterally contiguous with other beliefs in the system, in the minimal sense that they may have a close relation to some of them in respect to subject matter. In any case, neither the psychological nor the epistemological foundationalist need consider it a problem that there are direct beliefs on which no others are based.

On the other hand, there is no obvious psychological reason why the vast *majority* of one's indirect beliefs might not be directly based, at least in part, on a set of one's foundational beliefs. Consider S's belief that a bus just went by. Assuming he did not see it, might he not believe it went by, because he believes that (i) there were certain characteristic motor sounds and (ii) if those sounds occurred, then a bus passed? His belief that (i), might be direct, though he may have originally believed that these sounds were motor sounds on the basis of believing that they came from a bus and that if they came from a bus they were bus motor sounds. S's belief that (ii), might be indirect, and (inductively) based on his once indirect but now direct belief that whenever he has heard those sounds a bus has passed. This belief, in turn, might have been originally based on several "instantial" beliefs, each to the effect that after those sounds occurred a bus went by.

The process by which such general beliefs arise from several instantial beliefs could have various forms. For instance, S might, by some generalizing causal mechanism, simply acquire the general belief from them, without the mediation of any other belief of his; or he might infer its propositional object from the instantial propositions together with the proposition that he has never heard those sounds without a bus going by; or the instantial beliefs might give rise to the general belief in such a way that it is (directly) based on them even though S could not be plausibly said to have drawn an inference. In the first case, the general belief is at least causally grounded on the instantial beliefs; in the other two it would be based on them in the sense I have associated with IV. In the second and third cases, then, S's belief that a bus just went by is directly based at least in part on his foundational beliefs.

It will be apparent that I am not taking S's belief that p being based on his belief that q, to entail his ever inferring p from q. It certainly seems that in our example S's belief need not be based on inference at all: S just "heard the bus go by." But there is much disagreement about what constitutes inference. Some would insist on at least an unconscious inference here.[13] Let us bypass the issue of what constitutes inference. Fortunately, psychological foundationalism is neutral with respect to whether the basis relation is necessarily inferential. Nothing in the position requires appealing to unconscious inference in examples like the above, though the psychological foundationalist could posit unconscious inferences here and indeed allow at least some foundational beliefs to be unconscious in a fairly strong sense. If he does posit unconscious inferences here, he need not construe them as processes with any manifestations in consciousness – a point not entailed by an inference itself being unconscious.

Even if a foundationalist holds that S's belief that p is directly based on his belief that q, only if S at least unconsciously infers p from q, he need not hold this for a belief's being *indirectly* based on another. This greatly reduces the number of inferences that would have to be posited by an "inferentialist" interpretation of IV. It should also be emphasized that IV. entails no specific theory of concept formation or of cognitive development.

Modest psychological foundationalism can be better understood if we ask whether IV might be acceptable to epistemological foundationalists. Consider a Cartesian rationalist. Clearly if S is to have knowledge, Descartes would restrict the content of S's foundational beliefs to propositions which are certain for S, and require that the propositional objects of any superstructure beliefs constituting knowledge be deducible from the propositional objects of the foundational beliefs.[14] But Descartes would not have to reject IV as a psychological thesis; he would merely require that an ideal knower instantiate it in certain restricted ways. The same appears to hold for at least some empiricist foundationalists. Consider Russell:

13. Gilbert Harman, e.g., probably would. See *Thought* (Princeton: Princeton University Press, 1973), esp. chs. 10–12. For a somewhat more psychologically oriented discussion bearing on this issue, see Eric Bush, "Perceptual Evidence and Perceptual Inference," *Behaviorism* 5 (1977).
14. See, e.g., the discussion of Rule III in his *Rules for the Direction of the Mind*, trans. by E. S. Haldane and G. R. T. Ross (Cambridge: Cambridge University Press, 1931), where he says, of intuition and deduction as routes to knowledge, that "the mind should admit no others," and that "the first principles are given by intuition alone, while, on the contrary, the remote conclusions are furnished only by deduction."

The first thing that appears when we begin to analyse our common knowledge is that some of it is derivative, while some is primitive; that is to say, there is some that we only believe because of something else from which it has been inferred in some sense, though not necessarily in a strict logical sense, while other parts are believed on their own accounts, without the support of any outside evidence. It is obvious that the senses give knowledge of the latter kind: the immediate facts perceived by sight or touch or hearing do not need to be proved by argument, but are completely self-evident.[15]

Russell differs from Descartes both in what propositions he regards as suitable objects for foundational beliefs and in allowing derivative knowledge to be inductively grounded on primitive knowledge. But Russell's concept of the structure of beliefs in a typical knower seems at least as clearly compatible with IV. as does Descartes's.

Reflection will show that IV or something close to it could be congenial to a number of other foundationalist epistemologies. But what, we may ask, would a psychological coherentism look like? Minimally, it must deny that in every person there are, at a given time, psychologically foundational beliefs. This has important implications. For if it is so, coherentists cannot plausibly construe the psychological coherence of a person's body of beliefs in the most natural way, involving each belief's deriving some causal support from at least one other. For suppose that each of S's beliefs is in some degree caused or causally sustained by another. If the number of S's beliefs is finite, then some belief would in some degree have to cause or causally sustain itself, given the transitivity of these causal relations. To allow this or give up transitivity would seem unreasonable. Nor would it seem psychologically plausible to posit an infinite set of beliefs, particularly of the kind in question.[16] One

15. *Our Knowledge of the External World*, 2nd ed. (New York: W. W. Norton and Co., 1929; and Mentor Books: New York, 1960), p. 58.
16. If the connecting belief requirement is correct, S would have to have infinitely many such beliefs. It is not at all plausible to suppose that any person has even the requisite number of concepts, much less also an infinite chain of beliefs of this sort; but even apart from the connecting belief requirement it seems psychologically implausible to attribute to S infinite sets of beliefs of the interrelated sorts coherentists would posit.

can imagine arguments to the effect that causal sustaining relations are not transitive or not irreflexive, but I am not aware of any sound case for this. Indeed, philosophers have very widely assumed that causal relations are transitive and irreflexive, though perhaps epistemological coherentists would have argued strongly against at least one of these requirements had they seen the difficulty I am raising. Whatever the status of the requirements, I shall assume that psychologists, like other scientists, would not wish to give up either one.

What one would expect is that the psychological coherentist might, like some epistemological coherentists,[17] employ, in place of the basis relation, a non-causal support relation in at least some cases. Then every belief of S's could be plausibly held to be in some way supported by at least one other. In outline, the theory might be roughly this:

V. *Psychological Coherentism:* For any S and any t, the body of S's beliefs at t has a coherent structure such that, for each of his beliefs, (1) there is some set of his other beliefs by which it is supported, in the minimal sense that S is disposed to justify or explain or ground the belief by appeal to one or more members of this set; and (2) in at least some instances this relation holds without the relevant set of supporting beliefs causing or causally sustaining the belief(s) it supports.

The support relation indicated in (1) is not the only kind that is not essentially causal; but it is perhaps as plausible a candidate as any, and we may leave this problem aside.

A more important problem is to interpret V. so that it is inconsistent with IV. If we do not restrict the support relation specified in V, V is consistent with IV, since even foundational beliefs may be such that under certain conditions, say when S is asked to justify them, he might be disposed to adduce others of his beliefs in their support. For his doing so does not imply their being based on these other beliefs. To rule this out V might require something like this: that even *apart* from S's being motivated to justify or explain or ground a belief of his, it is in some way supported by one or more other beliefs of his, in a sense which implies an appropriate disposition on his part, yet entails no causal relation. But what could

17. See, e.g., Keith Lehrer, *Knowledge* (Oxford: Oxford University Press, 1974), pp. 122–26.

this sense be? It will not do to say that he must have tried to relate each of his beliefs to some other, though a coherentist could hold that most of one's beliefs arise from others by inference or some other causal process, possibly of a kind of proponent of IV would envisage between foundational and superstructure beliefs. The point is that each of a person's beliefs receives some support from some other(s), and not *all* of these relations can be causal. Yet even when they are not causal, they must be more than the disposition to cite other beliefs *given* such prodding as is implied in a request for justification. For if that is all we require, then one could have this disposition toward one's foundational beliefs. How to tighten the requirement enough without making it too strong is not at all clear. I think, then, that the relevant support relation turns out to be at best hard to specify.

One might conclude from this that IV is too weak to capture the idea of a foundational belief, and that this is why it seems hard to find a plausible coherentist foil. But surely the idea of a foundation is essentially that of something on which other things rest; and this is quite consistent with the idea of bringing in other materials, possibly of the same sort, to strengthen it. *S*'s beliefs of a set of theorems might be based on his beliefs of the relevant axioms without his supposing that no other propositions can support the axioms. *S* might even be aware of such propositions, but find them less intuitive than the axioms; his beliefs of the axioms might not then be even in part based on his beliefs of the other propositions, though he would be quite willing to cite them in justifying the axioms to someone else.

Moreover, if, as seems reasonable, we call epistemological theories foundational in good part because they respond to the epistemic regress argument by positing directly justified beliefs, parallel considerations argue that IV is not too weak to be a psychological counterpart of epistemological foundationalism. Indeed, a psychological version of the regress argument seems quite plausible. Suppose, e.g., the psychologist thinks that one cannot have an infinite set of beliefs, each based on another, and that since the only plausible basis relations are transitive and irreflexive there cannot be a virtuous circle. IV seems adequately strong. Perhaps psychological coherentism can be made more plausible than V makes it appear, but if so I do not think it is by strengthening psychological foundationalism to make the contrast easier to draw. However this may be, we need not decide what is the most plausible version of psychological coherentism to bring out some important implications of IV.

IV

Our study of psychological foundationalism, as represented by IV, enables us to see a number of epistemologically interesting points about belief systems with a foundational structure. For instance, foundational beliefs (1) need not be of any particular high epistemological status, e.g. infallible, indubitable, or incorrigible; (2) need not have any particular kind of content; (3) need not remain the same over time and can be altered both "from below" (e.g., by new experiences) and "from above" (at least by superstructure beliefs whose causal power is in part independent of foundational beliefs); (4) need not have any particular relation to each other, so that they may be in various ways either mutually supporting or unrelated; (5) need not stand to superstructure beliefs in any one kind of relation, but may support them in a variety of ways; (6) need not be limited to small numbers, however appealing this limitation might be from the point of view of elegance or systematization; (7) need not be psychologically certain (though one would expect most of them to be at least somewhat confident); and (8) need not be such that S cannot be disposed to justify them by appeal to others of his beliefs, or to seek new beliefs for this purpose. If they are in a sense unmoved movers, they are nevertheless not unmovable movers.

The importance of these points for the psychology of cognition may not be readily apparent, but we may say at least this. Psychological foundationalism of the sort we have discussed bears not only on the general question of cognitive structure, but on the genesis of beliefs, both from other beliefs and from non-beliefs; on the ways in which beliefs and processes involving them change other beliefs; on the respects in which beliefs support or conflict with one another; on the nature of perception, introspection, intuition, and memory; and on the analysis of cognitive integration, i.e., the psychological unity and interrelatedness of a belief system. Given the importance which many psychological theories attribute to beliefs in the explanation of behavior, psychological foundationalism may also bear significantly on that important task. I might add that it has the advantage of being largely neutral with respect to many psychological issues, such as language acquisition, personality development, and habit formation. As a structural theory, it also has a partial counterpart in non-cognitive psychologies. It would appear, e.g., that a Skinnerian could distinguish operant behavioral patterns based on others from those that are not, and he might also describe analogues of inference to account for the development of one operant pattern from another.[18]

The epistemological bearing of our discussion may be more apparent. As it turns out, at least the majority of (1)–(8) correspond to criticisms of epistemological foundationalism. That view has been said, e.g., to require infallible beliefs as foundations, and to allow a foundational belief to be overridden only by at least one other such belief.[19] We must therefore ask whether a plausible version of epistemological foundationalism could, like IV, be consistent with (1)–(8). I believe that a modest foundationalism may accommodate them all.[20] For the minimum epistemic requirement on foundational beliefs seems to be some kind of direct justification; and we can take the foundational beliefs required by IV to have this, i.e., to be justified other than by virtue of being based on other beliefs, without giving up any essential part of a foundationalist theory.[21]

Supposing, however, that a belief may be immediately justified without being, say, incorrigible, can there be enough such beliefs to account for all the derivative knowledge one might reasonably countenance? I cannot try to answer this fully, but at least two relevant points are suggested by our discussion of IV. First, there is good reason to think that often what psychologists would take

18. For some reasons why something like this might hold for Skinner, if only because he is at many points covertly relying on the notions of believing and wanting, see my "B. F. Skinner on Freedom, Dignity, and the Explanation of Behavior," *Behaviorism* IV, 2 (1976).

19. E.g., by Lehrer in *Knowledge*. See esp. p. 76. This book also expresses most of the other criticisms I have mentioned.

20. For characterizations of some forms of modest foundationalism see William P. Alston, "Two Types of Foundationalism," *Journal of Philosophy* LXXIII, (1976) 7, and "Has Foundationalism been Refuted?" *Philosophical Studies* 29, (1976), 5; Mark Pastin, "C. I. Lewis's Radical Foundationalism" *Noûs*, IX, (1975), 4, and "Modest Foundationalism and Self-Warrant," *American Philosophical Quarterly Monograph Series*, No. 9 (1975); James W. Cornman, "Foundational and Nonfoundational Theories of Empirical Justification," *American Philosophical Quarterly* 14 (1977); and Anthony Quinton, "The Foundations of Knowledge," in Bernard Williams and Alan Montifiore, eds., *British Analytical Philosophy* (London: Routledge and Kegan Paul, 1966).

21. This point is supported, at least indirectly, by all the papers cited in n20.

to be the genesis of a psychologically foundational belief is the sort of thing which many epistemologists would regard as accounting for the direct justification of an epistemologically foundational belief. For instance, where the psychologist would explain why S believes he sees red, in part in terms of S's actually perceiving a red surface, many epistemologists would say that normally[22] a direct belief with this kind of genesis is immediately justified. Second, where the psychologist explains why S has a direct belief about the past, in terms of preservation by memory processes, most epistemologists would say that if the belief so preserved was originally justified, then (other things remaining equal) it still is. Thus, if I have been right about what the psychologist might well consider the main kinds of psychologically foundational beliefs, it would seem that the epistemologist could plausibly regard a quite substantial number of these beliefs as directly justified.

There remains the question of whether, given a foundation of directly justified beliefs constituting knowledge, their justification can be transmitted to enough of the superstructure to account for all our indirect knowledge. Recall that there are at least three ways in which the psychological foundationalist may be expected to regard a superstructure belief as developing from one or more foundational beliefs: (a) by inference; (b) via a connecting belief, though without inference, at least as that term is usually understood; and (c) by causal processes involving neither inference nor a connecting belief. Superstructure beliefs can also arise from other superstructure beliefs in these ways. Now given certain restrictions, all these processes can be plausibly argued to transmit both justification and knowledge from the generating beliefs to those they support. Consider our case of the derivative belief that a bus has passed. This belief would presumably represent knowledge if the beliefs it is based on do. This example, as I have interpreted it, illustrates (b). Cases illustrating (a) and (c) are not difficult to construct, and there may be other kinds of prima facie knowledge-preserving generation of beliefs from other beliefs. These considerations about the transmission of justification and knowledge, together with the points I have made about the justification of foundational beliefs, give us good reason to consider it prima facie possible that a foundationalist theory can account for our indirect knowledge.

---

22. Normally rather than always because not just any explainability relation will do here. There is no easy way to specify the appropriate relation.

In the light of this section, I think we can also conclude not only that psychological foundationalism holds psychological interest and may deserve more attention than psychologists have given it (if they have given it any),[23] but that insofar as IV is a good model for epistemological foundationalism, a modest version of that theory may avoid a number of the major criticisms commonly brought against it. Nothing I have shown implies that none of the major criticisms will in the end be decisive. But it should at least be clearer along what lines some of them might be met. It should also be clearer what sorts of psychological commitments the epistemological foundationalist must make. Our results suggest that there is some reason to think people's belief systems might have a kind of foundational structure. We have at least found no psychological reasons to think we could not be structured as the epistemological foundationalist would have us believe. Whether we are more likely to be so structured than to have the kind of structure the coherentist would attribute to us, whatever that may be, is a question that requires both psychological investigation and further philosophical analysis.[24]

23. There are, to be sure, statements by psychologists which suggest a foundationalist conception of the cognitive system or part of it. Jerome D. Frank, e.g., says that "Ultimately, all belief systems rest on value premises that for the believer are not open to question...." See "Nature and Functions of Belief Systems: Humanism and Transcendental Religion," *American Psychologist* 32 (1977), p. 555. But this is offered in a context which suggests that Frank does not have in mind any detailed formulation of foundationalism. The paragraph in question, however, does make it appear that something like IV. might be attractive to him.

24. I have benefited very substantially from William P. Alston's comments on an earlier version of this paper and from a number of his writings. I also want to thank Laurence BonJour, Eric Kraemer, and Martin Perlmutter for helpful comments.

Chapter 2

Axiological foundationalism

INTRODUCTION

Epistemological foundationalism has typically been thought to hold that in order to account for human knowledge we must countenance the direct justification of some specific kind of beliefs, such as one's beliefs to the effect that one is having a certain sensation. How else, it may be thought, can one analyse justification without confronting an infinite regress or a vicious circle? I believe that this conception of foundationalism has been so influential that most foundationalists and nearly all their critics have failed to appreciate that foundationalism may be plausibly construed as a thesis mainly about the *structure* of a body of justified beliefs. Central to the thesis, so interpreted, is that one's justified beliefs divide into foundations and superstructure; but no particular content on the part of either set of beliefs need be required. This latitude regarding content is altogether appropriate; for if we use, as a guide to understanding foundationalism, the famous regress argument, from which the thesis derives much of its plausibility, then the only foundations required by the thesis are beliefs whose justification does not depend on that of other beliefs. Precisely what beliefs these are is a controversial matter on which foundationalists may differ.

Once we construe foundationalism as mainly a structural thesis, it becomes reasonable to ask whether its plausibility rests on structural properties of justification that are exhibited in any domain whose elements admit of justification. If it does rest on such properties, then a counterpart of epistemological foundationalism should apply to, among other things, the justification of a person's values. This possibility has rarely been explored, however.[1] It is well worth examining, and this paper will introduce and assess a foundationalist theory of the justification of values. Many of the ideas to be developed are quite parallel to points that apply to epistemological foundationalism and should clarify that thesis as well; but the latter points have not yet appeared in the literature,[2] and the former in any case deserve separate treatment.

The sense of 'value' that concerns me is the one in which people are said to value something, e.g. their friends. Since 'value' is also used to designate the actual value (worth) of things, I shall often use 'valuation' for values and valuing in the psychological sense. Fortunately, we need not here analyze what it is for someone to value something. For if foundationalism is chiefly a structural thesis of the kind I shall specify, it is consistent with what seem the most plausible accounts of the nature of valuing. I shall assume the following points, however. First, valuing is like believing in being intentional; e.g., a person, S, might value continuing the services of his favorite mechanic without valuing continuing the services of the man who ruined his seatcovers, even though (unbeknownst to S) the mechanic *is* this man. Second, values are analogous to beliefs in being appropriately called justified or unjustified, and in being capable of justification by virtue of being *based on* other valuations. To say that this basis relation obtains between two valuations of S's is, roughly, to say that one is (or at least expresses) the reason, or at least one of the reasons, for which S holds the other; and just as one's belief that p, may be justified by virtue of being based on one's belief that q, when q is an adequate reason for p, one's valuing ϕ – e.g., controversy – may be justified by virtue of being based on one's valuing ψ – e.g., truth. Valuing is also significantly like wanting. For instance, it seems to have the same sorts of objects (which I shall take to be states of affairs); and

1. A notable exception is Mark Pastin, who has connected foundationalism with value theory. See "The Reconstruction of Value," *Canadian Journal of Philosophy*, 5 (1975). Some of the literature on intrinsic value also bears on the topic of this paper, though less specifically. See, e.g., G. E. Moore, *Ethics* (Oxford: Oxford University Press 1912); G. H. von Wright, *The Varieties of Goodness* (London and New York: Routledge & Kegan Paul 1963); and Monroe C. Beardsley, "Intrinsic Value," *Philosophy and Phenomenological Research*, 26 (1965).
2. Some of these points are made in Chapter 1, this volume; but the points are not developed at length there, since the paper's main concern is the implications of epistemological foundationalism and coherentism for cognitive psychology.

values, like wants, can motivate and explain actions. It may indeed seem that valuing *is* a kind of wanting. No major claim in this paper is inconsistent with this possibility, and Section V will consider the significance of some similar reducibility theses.

I. FOUNDATIONALISM IN THE THEORY OF VALUE

If epistemological foundationalism is true, there can be directly justified beliefs. Roughly, I take these to be beliefs justified independently of being based on one or more others. Let us suppose, then, that if axiological foundationalism is true, there can be directly justified values, i.e., values justified independently of being based on one or more others. This would not preclude their being justified by *non*-values. It has been plausibly maintained that some directly justified beliefs – e.g., that one seems to see red before one – are justified not by other beliefs but by the facts they express,[3] say that one does seem to see red. Similarly, perhaps one's valuing something, e.g. one's self-expression, could be justified by non-valuations, say by one's satisfying experiences of expressing oneself, or by a belief one holds, say that it is desirable for people to express themselves.[4] However, an axiological foundationalist need not accept these suggestions. He is committed to the view that directly justified values are not justified by virtue of being based on other values, but he has much latitude concerning what non-valuational justifier(s), if any, to regard as the ground on which directly justified values "rest." To be sure, if he takes them to be grounded on beliefs, then his theory is different from most versions

3. See Roderick M. Chisholm, *Theory of Knowledge,* 2nd. edn. (Englewood Cliffs, N.J.: Prentice Hall 1966), 18–24. He does not use directly justified here, but seems to have a species of directly justified beliefs in mind. As the examples I have given suggest, direct justification need not be self-justification.
4. One might object that such a belief *is* a valuation. Motivational internalists would be especially likely to think this, since they could easily take such beliefs to have motivating force, as values do and beliefs – according to motivational externalists – do not. I have argued against internalism in "Weakness of Will and Practical Judgment," *Noûs* 13 (1979); but even if internalism is true, foundationalists may simply appeal to a different kind of non-valuational justifier than I am suggesting. Indeed, even if all values are analyzable into beliefs of some sort – which seems highly unlikely if my case against internalism is sound – the foundationalist could at least equally well make his case. He would in fact be making it on ground more familiar to him. I shall return to this issue in Section VIII.

74

of epistemological foundationalism in that the foundational elements are grounded on something which itself admits of justification. But a crucial analogy remains: in neither case would the foundational elements stand in need of justification from, or necessarily derive any from, elements of the same kind.

Let us now try to formulate axiological foundationalism. Consider first a strong thesis:

(1) *Strong Axiological Foundationalism:* For any person, S, and any time, t, if, at t, S has any justified values, then, at t, (i) S has some directly justified values, and (ii) all other justified values of S's derive all of their justification from some set of the former.

Note that (1) does not entail that every directly justified value is foundational. This is appropriate, for a value is plausibly called foundational only if at least one other value is based on it. But any directly justified value could be foundational, since another value could be based on it.

To understand axiological foundationalism fully, we must consider the relation between a directly justified value and an intrinsic value, i.e., a valuing of something "for its own sake." One might expect a directly justified value to be a justified intrinsic value, since if S values something other than for its own sake, e.g. as a means, he could apparently be justified in valuing it only on the basis of its relation to whatever else it is for which he values it. I believe, however, that once the problematic notion of valuing something for its own sake – intrinsically – is clearly understood, it will be apparent that the notion of a directly justified value is not equivalent to that of a justified purely intrinsic value. Consider what intrinsic valuing is. I suggest that, roughly speaking, S values ϕ purely intrinsically if and only if (a) he values it, and (b) if there is any ψ which he values, such that he believes that ϕ in some way does (or that it might) contribute to ψ, then it is not, even in part, *for* that reason that S values ϕ.[5] This allows that S value ψ and

---

5. This entails, but is not equivalent to the proposition that S values ϕ in such a way that, other things equal, he *would* value it, at the time in question, even if there should be no ψ such that he values ψ and believes something to the effect that ϕ does (or that it might) contribute to ψ. One reason this sentence is so guarded is that even where S values ϕ purely intrinsically, his ceasing to believe that it is a means to ψ might just happen to cause him to cease valuing it at all. We might also want to speak, in the formulations in the text, of valuing *or* wanting ψ. Another problem is whether, instead of requiring only that ψ be a different state of affairs from ϕ, we should require that it be separable,

75

believe that φ is a means to ψ or that it contributes to ψ in some non-instrumental way. But where he values φ purely intrinsically this belief and valuing cannot be reasons *for which* he values φ. It is important to recognize, however, that a valuing can be only *partly* intrinsic. One may, as the next paragraph will show, value φ partly 'for its own sake' and partly as a means to ψ.

We can now see why a directly justified value need not be purely intrinsic. Imagine that Sue enjoys listening to music for its own sake, yet believes it relaxes her and values relaxation. If her valuing of listening to music is at least in part based on her valuing of relaxation, the former valuation is not purely intrinsic. However, if she truly and justifiably believes that her listening to music is enjoyable, this may justify her valuing it, and it may do so quite independently of any beliefs she may have to the effect that the listening is a means to something else. Suppose, moreover, that this belief is also causally sufficient, in the circumstances, for her retaining the valuation. Imagine, however, that Sue is neither correct nor even justified in believing that listening to music relaxes her. We may surely conclude that her valuing of relaxation is not what justifies her in valuing listening to music. Yet this conclusion would not prevent the latter value from being justified by her belief that listening to music is enjoyable for her. We would then have what at first glance may appear impossible: a value that is directly justified, since what justifies it is not its being based on any other value of hers, yet not purely intrinsic, since it is partly based on another. Doubtless an axiological foundationalist would hold that typically a directly justified value is a purely intrinsic one; but a purely intrinsic value's being justified is at best a sufficient condition for its direct justification. Thus, axiological foundationalism does not entail that directly justified valuations are purely intrinsic.

There is, however, at least one respect in which (1) is a stronger thesis than a foundationalist might wish to hold. In line with some modest versions of epistemological foundationalism,[6] he might re-

---

i.e., capable of existing apart from φ. Consider, e.g., the pleasure of an activity. This is presumably distinct but not separable from it. If Sue values playing the piano because she values the pleasure of it, does she values the former intrinsically? It may be reasonable to say so, unless (perhaps) she *believes* this pleasure is separable from the playing. These are difficult problems, but for our purposes the formulation in the text will do.

6. See, e.g., William P. Alston, "Has Foundationalism been Refuted," *Philosophical Studies*, 29 (1976), and "Two Types of Foundationalism," *Journal of Philosophy*, 73 (1976); Mark Pastin, "C. I. Lewis's Radical Foundationalism," *Noûs*, 9

quire only that justified superstructure values derive some of their justification from foundational values. Perhaps the fact that a group of superstructure values somehow 'cohere' could add to each some degree of justification not derived from their foundations. I shall not try to show how this might be so, though if it can be so, that would be important to the overall issue of the justification of values. What I shall do instead is examine a thesis which is consistent with this, but does not presuppose it and seems equally in the spirit of the foundationalist conception of justification. The thesis is

(2) *Modest Axiological Foundationalism:* For any S and any t, if, at t, S has any justified values, then, at t, (i) S has some directly justified values, and (ii) all other justified values of S's derive enough of their justification from some set of the former so that they would remain justified even if any other sources of their justification were eliminated.

Although quite modest, (2) is not minimal. One could move closer to a minimal thesis by weakening (ii) so that it allows valuations of S's which are not directly justified to be, like S's directly justified valuations, necessary conditions for the justification of his superstructure valuations. It might be desirable to weaken (ii) in that way; but (2) as it stands seems more in the spirit of foundationalism, historically understood, and will serve our purposes as it is.

II. COHERENTISM IN THE THEORY
OF VALUE

Before we try to evaluate (2), we should formulate a plausible coherentist foil. Here the bearing of epistemological models is less clear than in the case of axiological foundationalism. This is partly because the notion of coherence has been construed in widely differing ways and often used without explication. For our purposes, the best course is to formulate axiological coherentism broadly enough to avoid favoring any one plausible epistemological model over its competitors.

Perhaps the most generic thesis of coherentism is that justifi-

(1975); and James W. Cornman, "Foundational versus Nonfoundational Theories of Empirical Justification," *American Philosophical Quarterly*, 14 (1977). Cornman argues that both Quine and Sellars are, despite appearances, probably modest foundationalists; see especially 296–7.

cation is a function of relations among justified elements, or among them and other sorts of things. Coherentists have generally taken it to follow that nothing is directly justified. It is not obvious what relations might generate coherence among values, but the following are plausible examples: the fulfilment of one value (i.e., the realization of the state of affairs that is its object) being necessary (or alternatively, sufficient) for that of another; the fulfilment of one being *believed* by S to be necessary (sufficient) for that of a second; and the fulfillment of one value's explaining that of another. Thus, Sue's valuation of her practicing regularly might cohere with her valuation of her achieving virtuosity, because she believes the former to be necessary for the latter (a subjective relation), or because the former explains the latter (an objective relation). Given these points, we would expect an axiological coherentist to hold that each justified value is justified at least in part by its relation to one or more other values. A strong version of the theory will take justified values to derive all their justification from such relations; a weaker version will take such relations to be only necessary for the justification of values.

If there are many relations which might generate coherence, a further question arises. Is there at least one justificatory relation, i.e., a relation generating some justification, in which every justified value stands to at least one other value, or would a coherentist hold only that for every justified value there is some justificatory relation or other which it has to one or more other values? We shall need to discuss both interpretations, but we can best see the implications of axiological coherentism if we start with the simpler view based on the former. This view is also favored by a plausible presumption – to be explored later – namely, that if two values stand in any of the relevant justificatory relations, they must also stand in the generic relation, *being to some degree justified by*. This justificatory relation would then hold between any justified value and at least one other value.

Presumably, then, a coherentist theory of the justification of values will embody at least three ideas. First, each justified element stands in some justificatory relation to at least one other. Second, each justified element must belong, together with at least one other to which it stands in a justificatory relation, to a *coherent* set of elements. (This need not be taken to be entailed by the first requirement, since we need not assume that just any two elements standing in a justificatory relation constitute a coherent set.) Third, it is (conceptually) necessary for the justification of an element that it belong to such a set.

Let us initially construe axiological coherentism, then, as follows:

(3) *Axiological Coherentism:* For any *S* and any *t*, if, at *t*, *S* has any justified values, then, at *t*, there is some justificatory relation *R* such that (i) each justified value of *S*'s stands in *R* to one or more other values of his; (ii) each justified value of *S*'s belongs, with at least one other value of his to which it stands in *R*, to some coherent set of his values; and (iii) each of *S*'s justified values is such that a necessary condition for its justification is that it belongs to at least one such set.

This reflects a number of ideas associated with epistemological coherentism: that a justified belief does not stand alone; that its justification depends on its coherence with other beliefs; and that, as the cognitive counterpart of clause (iii) implies, there are no directly justified beliefs.

III. AXIOLOGICAL COHERENTISM AND THE REGRESS PROBLEM

A good way to understand what coherentism commits us to is to ask how a proponent of (3) might deal with the valuational parallel of the epistemic regress problem. How might he account for the justification of values without encountering either a vicious regress or a vicious circle? Some of the difficulties that confront coherentist attempts to solve the regress problem in epistemology are well known,[7] as are some confronting foundationalist attempts to solve it. I shall not discuss difficulties of these sorts. Important as these issues are, I want to focus on a problem which has not generally been discussed, if noticed at all.[8] The problem concerns not the difficulty of circular justification but the difficulty of what might be called *circular causation*. Let me explain.

Consider first what justificatory relations a coherentist can plau-

---

7. See, e.g., Ernest Sosa, "The Foundations of Foundationalism," *Noûs* 14 (1980); and Laurence Bonjour, "The Coherence Theory of Empirical Knowledge," *Philosophical Studies*, 30 (1976). The latter devotes considerable attention to problems facing foundationalism as well.
8. The problem is shown to occur in the domain of motivation, in my paper "The Structure of Motivation," *Pacific Philosophical Quarterly*, 61 (1980).

sibly take 'R' to represent. The most natural candidate is the relation which holds between one of S's values and another when the latter is (or expresses) at least part of his *reason* for the former and, given certain further conditions, justifies the former. In such cases we may say that the former value is based on the latter (at least in part). If we take R to be this basis relation, then we capture the coherentist idea that justification is always based on reasons; it is never direct. Moreover, the basis relation may be quite plausibly held to generate both coherence and justification. Clearly, S's valuing ϕ on the basis of his valuing ψ can both bring the former value into coherence with the latter and justify the former. Other relations might also be thought to do the job of R in the theory, but I do not think that an equally plausible candidate has been suggested.

Now supposing that R is the basis relation, we naturally want to know what are some of the important properties of the relation. This is a difficult question, as is its counterpart for beliefs, or other items that can stand in the relation.[9] But the following, at least, seems uncontroversial and is, for our purposes, the central point: just as one's belief that p, is not based on one's belief that q, unless the latter belief in some way *sustains* the former, so one's valuing ϕ is not based on one's valuing ψ unless a similar relation holds. Intuitively, unless one values ϕ at least partly *because* one values ψ, one's valuing ϕ is not based on one's valuing ψ.

A second central question is whether, if S's valuing ϕ is justified by virtue of being based on another value of his, the latter must itself be justified. It seems clear that, just as a belief whose justification depends on its being based on another belief is not justified unless the latter, "premise" belief is justified, a value which depends for its justification on its being based on one or more other values is not justified unless at least one value on which it is based is justified. If S is not justified in valuing his "conversations" with his plants, then he presumably cannot be justified, on the basis of that valuation, in valuing the potion he gives them to facilitate their talking to him. If the principle in question is not self-evident, the coherentist, at least, has a powerful reason to accept it. For to countenance non-justified justifiers would be like countenancing foundationalists' grounds, such as the facts on which directly jus-

9. D. M. Armstrong has recognized the difficulty of the question for beliefs and plausibly answered it. See his *Belief, Truth and Knowledge* (Cambridge: Cambridge University Press 1973), chs. 13 and 14. Some further aspects of the question are discussed in Chapter 1, this volume.

tified beliefs have been held to rest: these grounds are privileged elements which confer justification without themselves having it. Even if no one non-justified value could ground the direct justification of a value based on it, a suitable set of them surely could. It appears, then, that the coherentist must assume that each justified value is based at least partly on some other justified value.

If these considerations are correct, a serious problem arises. For suppose that (a) R is the basis relation; (b) R is transitive; and (c) every justified value stands in R to some other justified valuation. If we add to this – what is highly plausible – that (d) S has a finite number of valuations, or at least of justified ones, it follows that some of S's values are at least partly based on, and hence at least in part sustained by, themselves. But it does not seem at all plausible to say what this commits one to: that one can value ϕ at least partly because one values ϕ, that one's valuing ϕ can at least partly explain itself, and that one's valuing ϕ can at least partly sustain itself. It is unlikely that even coherentists would wish to say such things, and I believe that in any event we have yet to be given a cogent argument for any of them.

Thus, given what seems the most natural interpretation of (3), a virtuous circle appears unavailable to the coherentist, and he faces a problem of self-sustenance, as we might call it (or, less neutrally, a bootstraps problem, since a value's sustaining itself seems somewhat like pulling oneself up by one's bootstraps). Coherentists might try to work out an innocuous infinite regress; but they have not taken this move to be plausible in epistemology, and they would probably find it implausible here for similar reasons. They might also deny that the relevant sustaining relations are transitive and irreflexive; but in part because these relations seem, in a wide sense, causal, that move appears unlikely to succeed.[10]

IV. SOME PLAUSIBLE RESPONSES TO THE PROBLEM OF SELF-SUSTENANCE

Coherentism is certainly not without resources for dealing with the problem of self-sustenance, and there is much to learn from exploring these resources. That will be the task of this section.

10. There are prima facie plausible objections to taking these relations to be transitive and irreflexive. I believe they can be answered, but it would require too much space to take them up here.

First, we should ask whether coherentists might avoid the problem of self-sustenance by taking 'R' to represent a relation other than the basis relation. What is perhaps the most likely alternative is suggested by Keith Lehrer's view that a belief of S's can be justified by a set of his other beliefs even if none of the latter bears to the former any sustaining or explanatory relation.[11] The corresponding position in value theory may be defended by urging a distinction between what a value is based on and what its justification is based on. It may then be argued that even if S's valuing φ is not based on his valuing ψ, the *justification* of his valuing φ may be based on his valuing ψ. For instance, even if S does not value reading poetry in part *because* he believes it develops his imagination, if he justifiably believes that his reading poetry does so, justifiably values developing his imagination, and is disposed to cite his valuing development of his imagination in trying to justify his valuation of reading poetry, these facts may be held to justify this valuation. Roughly, then, a coherentist might maintain the following:

> *Condition C:* If S justifiably values ψ, is disposed to cite his valuing ψ in justifying his valuing φ, and justifiably believes φ to have an appropriate relation (say, being a means) to ψ, then S's valuing ψ justifies his valuing φ.

It is important to notice that a *foundational* valuation could be justified in the way C indicates; indeed, all one's foundational valuations as these might be construed by a modest foundationalism could be so justified. Thus, a coherentist's adopting C and eliminating the sustaining requirement on indirect justification – the requirement that one of S's values is justified by a set of his other values only if the latter plays some role in sustaining the former – would considerably diminish the contrast between coherentism and modest foundationalism. (3) would no longer entail, e.g., that there are no directly justified values, as the phrase is used by foundationalists. For suppose that (2) is true and that S has a directly justified value, i.e., one not justified by virtue of being based on any other value of his. It does not follow that S cannot *have* other values which, say under pressure to justify the

---

11. See Keith Lehrer, *Knowledge* (Oxford: Clarendon Press 1974) 122–6. Lehrer argues plausibly against the sustaining requirement for beliefs. I cannot discuss his arguments here, but what I shall say in defending the sustaining requirement for values seems equally applicable to beliefs.

value in question, he would appeal to in justifying it in precisely the way C indicates. Imagine that S formed these other values after adopting (or simply forming) the foundational one. Suppose also that the soundness of the latter is more intuitive to him: axiomatic, as it were. Thirdly, imagine that although he thinks the former are reasons for the latter, they play no role in sustaining it, and it is not even in part *for* the reasons they express that he holds it. His foundational value is thus not based on these other values; yet when the need arises he is disposed to use the latter to justify the former. Foundationalism may be committed to unmoved movers, but it is not committed to unmovable movers.

A coherentist could reasonably respond as follows. He might first grant that there may be values not based on others in any sense implying a sustaining relation. Call these *psychologically direct*, since they are not *held* on the basis of any other value(s). He might also hold that these may be justified in the way indicated by C. Yet he would deny that their being both justified and psychologically direct entails their being *directly* justified. For on his view they are justified *by* one or more other values. Thus, the coherentist and the foundationalist would differ at least in this: even if what the latter calls a foundational value is such that S *could* have another value which justifies the former in the way indicated by C, foundationalists would deny, and coherentists would affirm, that a psychologically direct value is justified only if it meets this condition (or some other condition making the justification indirect).

Let us explore this. Must we have, for each of our justified psychologically direct values, at least one other justified value that we could use to try to justify the former in the way C indicates? Suppose Sam has a justified psychologically direct valuation of his own happiness. Need there be something else he justifiably values which he justifiably believes to have the appropriate relation to his own happiness? He might justifiably believe that his own happiness will make his children happy. This and his justifiably valuing their happiness would, by C, justify his valuing his own happiness. But *must* Sam meet such conditions to have a justified psychologically direct valuation of his own happiness? It seems doubtful.

A likely alternative to C might be the following disjunctive requirement:

Condition C': A psychologically direct value of S's is justified if and only if S either has a set of values that justify it

in the way indicated by Condition C, or has such a set
available to him, in the sense that if he undertook to justify
the psychologically direct value, he would acquire such a
set by, e.g., reflecting on what he already values.

This is similar to the idea, stressed by some defenders of epistemological coherentism, that an observational belief is justified only
if an appropriate justificatory argument for it is available to S,[12]
i.e., such that he can marshal it if a need arises. On this view,
justification depends on one's ability to produce justificatory argument; it need not require already believing potential premises
in such arguments.

C' may not be too restrictive to provide a possible account of the
justification of all the psychologically direct valuations plausibly
called justified; but unlike C it might also apply to all the values a
modest foundationalist would likely regard as foundational, e.g.
to S's psychologically direct valuation of listening to music. C'
would therefore take the coherentist uncomfortably close to modest
foundationalism, at least in leaving coherentism consistent with
the existence of what the foundationalist considers directly justified
values. Coherentists and foundationalists would still disagree,
however, about whether C' expresses a sufficient condition for the
justification of a psychologically direct valuation. Foundationalists
would deny that it is sufficient, because a value could then be
justified without its justification's depending on any directly justified value: even if S had no directly justified values, he could
have values justified by the kind of coherence one might argue is
implicit in their satisfying C'. Moreover, foundationalists are likely
to hold the sustaining requirement, which also implies the insuf-
ficiency of C and C'. They are likely to see the requirement as part
of the most plausible way of grounding justified superstructure
values on foundational ones. For given the sustaining requirement,
justified superstructure elements have to be grounded on foundational elements by ultimately being at least partly based on them.
This is just the way foundationalists have tended to conceive the

12. For instance, Laurence BonJour holds that "it is not necessary that the belief
    orginate via inference, however tacit or even unconscious; but it must be the
    case that a tacit grasp of the *availability* of the inference is the basis for the
    continuing acceptance of the belief and for the conviction that it is war-
    ranted." Note, however, that Bonjour seems to be endorsing a sustaining re-
    quirement. See BonJour, 296.

relation of superstructure elements to foundational ones.[13] The sustaining requirement seems independently plausible, however. The next section will examine some of the considerations that support it and weigh again᠌᠌ C and C'.

V. TWO CONCEPTS OF JUSTIFICATION

Consider first an example in which the sustaining requirement is not satisfied. Suppose that Joe is a philosopher who values argument as a regular part of his conversations. Imagine that a friend of pacific temperament tells Joe that he thinks it is unreasonable to value argument so much and goes on to ask Joe what he takes to justify his valuing it. Joe might reply by pointing out that argument clarifies issues. If he justifiably believes this and justifiably values such clarification, it might seem that his valuing argument is thereby justified, even if his valuing clarifying issues is not even part of the reason why (or of what sustains) his valuing argument. But while this description would satisfy C' it allows that (a) the reason *why* Joe values argument is that he believes it enables him to put down others, and as this implies, (b) that it is not even in part because he values clarifying issues that he values argument. In both cases (a) and (b) his valuation of clarifying issues is not part of his reason *for* valuing argument; the reason for which he values it is that it enables him to put others down. Surely we would not here regard his valuing the clarification of issues and believing that argument does this as justifying him in valuing argument. Indeed, even if we do not imagine, as in (a), Joe's having reprehensible reasons for valuing argument, his purported justification of his valuing it seems to fail. For he has given us only a reason for valuing argument, not *his* reason (if he has one) for valuing it; and because his valuing the clarification of issues is no part the reason why he values argument, he is so disposed that even if he did not value the former, he would still (other things equal) value the latter. He would indeed value it just as much as he now does.

13. This appears to hold for Bertrand Russell, who says, of our "common knowledge," that "some of it is derivative, while some is primitive; that is to say, there is some that we only believe *because* of something else from which it has been inferred . . . while other parts are believed on their own accounts" (emphasis added). See *Our Knowledge of the External World*, 2nd edn. (New York; 1929), 58. Rationalist foundationalists may of course maintain the same structural thesis, and I believe Descartes held a similar one.

The example reflects an important distinction which is often not observed: the distinction between *justification of a person in valuing* φ and *justification of valuing* φ. The first represents a kind of subjective justification, the second a kind of objective justification. *That* argument clarifies issues may justify a valuation of argument; for it is a reason (an objective reason) to value it. Now if Joe values such clarification and believes that argument yields it, he *has* a reason for valuing argument. But it does not follow that, if he values argument, it is *for* a reason at all. By contrast, if it is for the above reason that he values argument, then by that fact he may be justified in valuing it. His merely having a valuation of argument that *is* justified by a good reason he has is consistent with his valuing argument wholly for reasons that would make it irrational for him to value it, e.g. that it makes him wave his hands. His valuing argument *for* a good reason rules this out.

The distinctions just drawn are apparently crucial to another which seems as important in the domain of valuation as in those of action and belief: the distinction between reasons and rationalizations. For one kind of rationalization occurs where S offers a reason for valuing something yet not *his* reason for valuing it, thereby failing to explain or justify his valuation. A coherentist might reply that the distinction between reasons and rationalization applies only to explanatory reasons (reasons *why*), not to justificatory reasons (reasons *for*). But explanation and justification surely cannot be separated in this way. It is no accident that, like "Why did you do it?" and "Why do you believe it?," "Why do you value it?" can be a request for justification as well as for explanation, and even in the former case is not regarded as correctly answered unless the reason given is taken to provide at least a partial explanation of the value in question.

It might also be replied that S rationalizes, in trying to justify his valuing φ by citing his valuing ψ, only when he in fact does not value ψ or does not believe anything to the effect that his realizing ψ would contribute to his realizing φ. Some cases like this may perhaps be rationalizations, but to take this condition as necessary appears unreasonable. For central to the notion of rationalization is a contrast between rationalization and justification. Now in cases like that of Joe's attempt to justify his valuing argument, we have not only a failure of justification but something else characteristic of rationalization; the reason he offers as justification is not his reason *for* what he offers it to justify. This fact is important in

86

evaluating him, particularly from the points of view of rationality and morality. For if, in (say) doing A or valuing ϕ, he is not even in part actuated by the reason he offers, the possibility is open that he *is* actuated by reasons on the basis of which a rational person would *not* act or adopt a value. Indeed, to believe that a reason justifies one's doing or valuing something and at the same time to do or value it without being to any degree actuated by the reason seems in itself to represent, at least in cases of the sort we are considering, some deficiency in rationality. There is certainly more to be said about these issues, but I believe the above considerations strongly support the view that an adequate distinction between a person's justifying and only rationalizing his valuations requires taking the justificatory relation R to involve some sort of sustaining and explanatory connection.[14]

VI. ALTERNATIVE VERSIONS OF AXIOLOGICAL COHERENTISM

If the problem of self-sustenance is as serious as it seems and cannot be avoided in the ways just examined, we must reconsider whether axiological coherentism should be taken to hold that there is any one justificatory relation which every justified value has to at least one other value. Perhaps the existence of justified values requires only that each such value bear some suitable relation or other to some other value(s). Imagine a set of three such that the first is based on the second and the second on the third, while the third is simply such that fulfilling it is a means to fulfilling the first. Here, the coherentist might argue, we need not say that any of the values is at least in part based on itself, and so the problem of self-sustenance is averted.

One trouble with this proposal, however, is that if the relevant relations confer justification at all, then if one of them holds be-

---

14. D. M. Armstrong also suggests that we need a sustaining requirement to distinguish reasons from rationalizations; but he requires that in rationalizing (with respect to belief) S must desire that p be true, and this desire must be the sustaining cause of S's taking q to support p, where, even though S's belief that q, does not even partly sustain his belief that p, q is the reason S would *offer* to justify his belief that p. I do not impose an analogous requirement on 'valuational rationalization,' but I believe requirements to this effect, even if not necessary for rationalization, do hold for the paradigm (and Freudian) cases. See *Belief, Truth and Knowledge*, esp. pp. 95–6.

tween two sets of valuations this would seem to imply that one set is to some degree justified by the other. Now if it is true, as argued above, that the relation *being to some degree justified by* itself implies a sustaining relation, then the problem of self-sustenance recurs.

Moreover, if the relation, *being to some degree justified by*, is, as it appears on the face of it to be, transitive, then a second and rather embarrassing problem arises for the coherentist. For if each of S's finite set of justified values bears this relation to at least one other value in this set, it follows that each is at least in part justified by itself – i.e., is partially self-justified. Surely coherentists would not wish to be committed to countenancing even partial self-justification. They have traditionally denied that self-justification is possible; and even partial self-justification, which entails (though it is not equivalent to) direct justification, might very well give a modest foundationalist enough to construct a viable theory. Even if no single partially self-justified valuation could render a superstructure valuation justified, a suitable set of self-justified valuations working together presumably could. It may be that the coherentist can show that *being to some degree justified by* is not transitive. The issue is too large to pursue here. It is enough to have suggested that coherentists owe us a solution.

There is at least one other possibility we must consider. One might hold that each justified value is so simply by virtue of membership in a suitable coherent set of values. Surely each of S's justified values could stand in this relation to such a set without there being any single justificatory relation which each justified value bears to at least one other justified value. But this move apparently fails under scrutiny. For it is by no means clear that a value could be justified by virtue of membership in a set of values unless they provided reason(s) for it, in a sense implying its being *based on* that set or some subset of the relevant values. The grounds for saying this are at least those supporting the view that a value of S's is justified by another of his values only if the former is at least in part sustained by the latter. Again, the coherentist seems to be caught between undermining the distinction between rationalization and justification and, on the other hand, embracing partial self-sustenance and partial self-justification.

As a way out, a coherentist might construe justification as a global property of systems of value and simply give up talking of any single value's being justified or unjustified. This conception is certainly vague, but it seems intelligible. It is likely, however, that coherentists would regard adopting it as a high price to pay for a theory of the justification of values;[15] and the price is especially high if modest foundationalism is a plausible alternative.

In raising these difficulties for axiological coherentism, I am not claiming to have refuted it, nor have I established axiological foundationalism. I do believe, however, that a proponent of (3) or of any plausible form of axiological coherentism must at least acknowledge a serious problem which positions like (2) need not face: if justificatory relations are construed in the most natural way, coherentists seem unable to deal with the regress of justification; and if they avoid this difficulty by adopting what seems the most plausible alternative construal of such relations, they apparently undermine the distinction between rationalizing, and really justifying, one's valuing something. There may be an adequate solution to these problems, but if there is it is certainly not apparent from the development of coherentist theories to date.

VII. A EUDAEMONISTIC INTERPRETATION OF AXIOLOGICAL FOUNDATIONALISM

If axiological coherentism encounters the difficulties raised above, we would do well to examine axiological foundationalism further to see whether it faces equally serious problems. Let us first ask what the value system of a person would have to be like for it to satisfy (2). As a philosophical thesis, (2) could be true even if no actual person instantiates it. But its interest would be greater if it could be plausibly held to apply to persons as they are; and if it does not seem applicable to persons as we know them, we shall at least have more reason to try to solve the problems confronting coherentist theories.

We might start by disposing of some baggage which a modest axiological foundationalism need not carry. First, foundational values need not be 'incorrigible' – such that no one could warrantedly override S's justification for them – nor of any similar highly priv-

---

15. Lehrer, e.g., takes a coherentist theory of (epistemic) justification to be in part an account of what it is for a particular belief to be justified. See, e.g., Lehrer, 154. He would presumably hold a parallel view regarding valuation.

ileged justificatory status. Second, although they cannot be justified by virtue of being based on other values of his, he need not regard them as beyond justification by reasons; and they can be such that S is disposed to try to justify them by appeal to other values of his and will try to do so on appropriate occasions. Third, S's foundational values may even be such that he is quite open to looking critically at one or more of them; and as this suggests, S need not be psychologically certain of the value of their objects. Fourth, S's foundational values may be changed by his experiences, e.g. disappointing experiences of the sort of thing valued. His experiences may 'directly' cause changes in his foundational values; or he may, by reflecting on his experiences or his values, adopt beliefs or desires that affect his foundational values.[16]

A number of value theorists could hold something like (2) consistently with their overall theories of value. But let us just consider Aristotle. In places he may be plausibly read as holding that (a) we all desire our own happiness for its own sake, (b) whatever else one desires is directly or indirectly desired at least partly for its contribution to one's happiness (where this may include conceiving such things as parts of, or partly constitutive of, one's happiness), and (c) one may also desire other things for their own sake provided they are, to some degree, also directly desired for their contribution to one's happiness.[17] Perhaps he meant, in part (or at least believed), that we all *value* our happiness. Perhaps he also believed that it is solely one's happiness that one values *only* intrinsically, and that everything else we value is valued by us directly or indirectly at least partly because we believe that it does (or that it might) contribute to our happiness. The force of 'indirectly' is to suggest that Aristotle need not be read as holding that all one's intentional actions are *aimed* at least in part at contributing to one's happiness, or that everything else one values is valued directly for its (believed) contribution to one's happiness. At most he seems to imply that intentional actions are connected with happiness by what might be called a *purposive chain:* the last link is one's desire for one's happiness; each previous link is a desire

---

16. These points go a significant distance toward avoiding important objections to foundationalist theories, such as those raised by Lehrer (op. cit.) and those which may be drawn from some of Wittgenstein's work. For detailed discussion of some of the latter, see Roger A. Shiner, "Wittgenstein and the Foundations of Knowledge," *Proceedings of the Aristotelian Society*, 78 (1977–8).
17. See, e.g., *Nicomachean Ethics* 1097a30-1097b1-20.

connected to the next by a belief to the effect that realizing the former will (might) realize the latter; and every intentional action is aimed at realizing *some* desire in the chain. Similarly, he might suppose values to be connected with happiness by a counterpart chain: the last link is one's valuing one's happiness; and each previous link is a value connected to the next by a belief to the effect that satisfying the value constituting the former will (or that it may) satisfy the next value.

Now consider two questions. (i) Might we be directly justified in valuing our own happiness (purely intrinsically, let us assume)? And (ii) could all our justified (purely) extrinsic values be based at least in part on a directly justified valuing of our happiness? To (i) one is inclined to answer, "Of course." Indeed, there is a plausible conception of happiness for which to value one's own happiness purely for its own sake seems a constitutive condition of rationality. If the value is rational in this way, it is presumably justified; if it is also intrinsic, it is *directly* justified. One might value one's happiness too much, e.g. so much that one reduces it by overexerting oneself in quest of it; but that is consistent with what I am suggesting. Regarding (ii), though I would not claim that anyone's extrinsic values are all based on his intrinsic valuation of happiness, this seems possible. He would of course have many values which are based only very indirectly on the latter, but that is consistent with (2). Now consider the justified extrinsic values of someone who realizes the possibility just sketched. These could be connected with his valuation of happiness by justified true instrumental beliefs. Thus, one might value controversy because one believes it contributes to discovering truth, and value discovering truth because one believes it will contribute to one's happiness, where both beliefs are justified and true. If the foundational value (whose object is happiness) is directly justified and these extrinsic values are grounded on it by such valuational chains, it is at least plausible to hold that the extrinsic values may be justified in a way appropriate to modest foundationalism.

VIII. CONCLUSION

In concluding, it is important to stress that axiological foundationalism is neutral regarding a wide variety of plausible accounts of what it is to value something. If, e.g., valuing is roughly a kind of wanting, as it might seem to be in the light of some accounts of wanting, the structure of a body of justified values could still be foundational in essentially the way I have sketched. If, on the other hand, to value φ is just to believe that φ is (in some way) good, the same point applies.

If, however, valuing φ is believing that φ is good, it might be thought that this paper accomplishes much less than it appears to, since axiological foundationalism might then seem a consequence of epistemological foundationalism, rather than a (perhaps unexpected) counterpart of it. But it would not be a consequence. For while epistemological foundationalism entails that the body of S's justified beliefs has a foundational structure, it does not entail that the particular subgroup one might identify with justified valuations has a foundational structure, much less one of the *sort* required by (2). That is, it does not entail what might be called the (limited) *autonomy of valuation*, i.e., that every justified value is either directly so or justified *by other values*. (2) requires S to have foundational justifying elements which are *themselves* values; epistemological foundationalism would not imply, even conjoined with the view that values are beliefs, that any of the beliefs which justify superstructure values are also (directly justified) values. Other sorts of beliefs besides those identified with directly justified values might be taken to justify those beliefs identified with indirectly justified values. I grant, however, that if values are beliefs, axiological foundationalism differs less from epistemological foundationalism than otherwise. But the reducibility thesis has not been established, and the burden of making it plausible seems to lie with those inclined to hold it.

If values are not beliefs, it may yet be true that S is justified in valuing φ, if and only if S is justified in believing that φ is (say) good. If this equivalence should be a necessary truth, then again axiological foundationalism could be argued to differ less from epistemological foundationalism than it appears to. For it might then seem that a body of S's justified valuations must have a foundational structure if the corresponding body of justified beliefs has one. This is not so, however. Even if (a) S's values are justified if and only if S is justified in believing the valued entities to be good, and (b) these beliefs are part of a foundational structure, axiological foundationalism does not follow. Indeed, (a) and (b) are consistent with axiological coherentism. Even if we add that each of S's justified values is justified *by* the corresponding belief, i.e., the belief that the valued object is good, the body of these values might not divide into superstructure and foundations at all. For each value, not needing to derive its justification from being based on any other value, might simply not be based on any other. We would then have at best a limiting case of foundationalism in which there is no superstructure and all the justified elements are directly justified.

In any case, the equivalence thesis is not particularly plausible. It would seem, e.g., that *S*'s satisfying experience of something might justify him in valuing it without justifying him in believing it to be good, in any sense of 'good' strong enough to protect the equivalence thesis from trivialization. But this is not the place to assess that thesis; it is enough to have suggested that even if it and certain other sorts of reducibility theses are true, axiological foundationalism remains at least a significant extension of epistemological foundationalism.

There is certainly more to be said about the justification of a person's values, but it should now be clear how a foundationalist theory of justification can be brought to bear on values, and what would be its primary commitments in the domain of valuation. Perhaps, moreover, the points developed in this paper give some support to a modest axiological foundationalism. The thesis does not require a version of incorrigibility for values, does not impose any particular content on a body of justified values, and does not represent a person's value system as static, nor its foundations as immune from revision in the light of experience. More positively, the thesis enables us to give a clear account of how superstructure values may be justified by foundational values, while allowing that the latter may themselves be justified by non-values; it provides a natural way of accounting for the unity of a person's value system, since foundational values can, somewhat like axioms in a theory, systematize and interrelate superstructure values; and it gives a good explanation of why we tend to justify some of our values by appeal to others, whereas we tend to take other values we have for granted or to justify them by appeal to non-values. Axiological foundationalism may indeed be as plausible as its epistemological counterpart. But whether or not that is so, it is fruitful to view foundationalism as a general thesis about justification, applicable not only to beliefs, but to values and other psychological elements that admit of justification. The same may be said for coherentism, of course. To have brought the two together in a domain in which neither has been adequately studied is, I hope, an advance toward their assessment.[18]

18. For helpful criticism of earlier versions of this paper I am especially grateful to William Alston, Carl Ginet, and Warren S. Quinn, who was the commentator on the version read at the 1978 Western Division Meetings of the American Philosophical Association. I have also profited from comments by a number of friends and colleagues, particularly Albert Casullo, Hardy E. Jones, Raimo Tuomela, and James Van Cleve.

Chapter 3

Foundationalism, epistemic dependence, and defeasibility

Epistemic justification is usually understood in relation to one or the other of two long-established competing types of theory of the justification of beliefs. The controversy between these two kinds of theory – foundationalist and coherentist theories – has recently been sharpened, and epistemologists on each side have made concessions to the other. Perhaps the best known position reflecting an effort to give the opposing side its due is modest foundationalism.[1] This view is called modest for at least two reasons: as compared with traditional foundationalist theories, such as Cartesianism, it makes weaker claims about the status of foundational beliefs; and, secondly, it employs weaker criteria of *epistemic dependence*, i.e. (roughly), the sort of relation that holds between one belief and another (or between a belief and something else) when the former depends on the latter either for its status as knowledge or for whatever justification it has. This second point about modest foundationalism bears particularly on its interpretation of two important variables: the degree to which justified superstructure beliefs must depend for their justification on foundational beliefs, and the sense in which justification of the latter is independent of their relation to other beliefs. The primary aim of this chapter is to clarify some of the problems and concepts that are crucial for understanding how a modest foundational theory of justification may conceive, and is likely to conceive, epistemic dependence. The notion of epistemic dependence will not be analyzed, however, nor applied directly to knowledge. My aim is just to lay some groundwork for an analysis of epistemic dependence and to clarify

1. For an idea of the content and range of modest foundationalist theories of epistemic justification, see Armstrong (1973), Pollock (1974), Pastin (1975), Alston (1976b), and Audi (1978).

95

the controversy between foundationalist and coherentist theories of epistemic justification.

My point of departure is Hilary Kornblith's far-reaching paper "Beyond Foundationalism and the Coherence Theory" (1980). Section 1 will set out his critique of modest foundationalism and his suggested thesis aimed at combining what is salvageable in foundationalism with what is correct in coherentism. Section 2 will explore epistemic dependence in relation to reasons. In Section 3, epistemic dependence will be distinguished from defeasibility, and in the light of that distinction the relation between foundationalism and skepticism will be examined. Section 4 will explore the relation of both foundationalism and coherentism to reliabilism in the theory of justification; and the final section will address the sense in which a reliabilist theory may be considered naturalistic.

1. FOUNDATIONALISM AND THE JUSTIFICATION OF BELIEFS

It is widely thought that, despite differences among them, foundationalist theories of justification maintain that any justified non-foundational beliefs of a person (S) depend for their justification on his foundational beliefs. There has been considerable discussion of the relation that must obtain between the propositional objects of foundational beliefs and those of superstructure beliefs if the foundational beliefs are to justify the latter ones. Some philosophers have at times failed to distinguish justificatory relations between the relevant sets of propositions and justificatory relations between the relevant sets of beliefs.[2] This might be partly because

2. Russell, e.g., describes an "epistemological premiss" as in part "a logical premiss," i.e., one of a set of premises from which [propositions], in "any systematic body of propositions," one can "deduce the remainder" (1940, p. 24), and in part a "psychological premiss," i.e., "a *belief* which is not caused by any other belief" and so not "inferred" (p. 125, emphasis added). A few pages later he describes basic propositions as a "subset of epistemological premisses" (p. 130). The latter "must be known independently of inference from other propositions" (p. 131); and from the latter the rest of what one believes "must be in some sense inferred" (p. 127). He later proposes "a logical definition. We can consider the whole body of empirical knowledge, and define 'basic propositions' as those logically indemonstrable propositions which are themselves empirical" (p. 132). In these chapters Russell not only sometimes conflates beliefs with propositions, but fails to distinguish justificatory relations between beliefs – as where one is inferentially produced by another which expresses good evidence for it – from justificatory relations – e.g., logi-

'belief' may be readily used to refer to either propositions or beliefs of them. In any case, a number of recent writers, including both foundationalists and coherentists, have focused on the relation between justified beliefs and beliefs that justify them. Kornblith is among these, and a main thesis of his paper is that both foundationalists and coherentists ignore the psychological relations among beliefs in a way that vitiates their account of epistemic justification.

The approach to epistemic justification which Kornblith favors is "a psychological approach to questions about knowledge and justification . . . the naturalized epistemology of W. V. Quine [1969] and Alvin Goldman [1976]" (1980, p. 598). However, "The standard account of what it is to be justified in believing a proposition is an apsychological account," as is the view underlying it, the "arguments-on-paper-thesis." This is "the view that a person has a justified belief that a particular proposition is true just in case that proposition appears on the list of propositions that person believes, and either it requires no argument, or a good argument can be given for it which takes as premises certain other propositions on the list" (Kornblith, 1980, p. 599). One reason Kornblith calls this the standard view is that he thinks both foundationalists and coherentists hold it. They simply "provide us with rival accounts of what it is to be a 'good argument'."

What is wrong with the arguments-on-paper thesis? Consider Alfred, who justifiably believes that *p* and that if *p* then *q*. Kornblith takes the thesis to entail that Alfred is also justified in believing *q*. But suppose that Alfred distrusts modus ponens, and believes *q* just because he likes the sound of some sentence expressing it.

cal connections – between propositions. At one point Pollock (1974) also fails to make this distinction (though no serious confusion in his overall presentation seems to result). Just after mentioning the supposition that "all other [non-incorrigible] *beliefs* are supposed to be grounded on these incorrigible *beliefs*" (p. 23, emphasis added), he says: "This generates a sort of pyramidal theory . . . the propositions that a particular person knows to be true can be arranged into a pyramidal structure such that: (1) the propositions in the lowest tier are justifiably believed without requiring an independent reason . . . and (2) each proposition in the higher tiers of the pyramid is justified on the basis of *epistemologically basic*" ones (p. 24). He then explicates the relation between epistemologically basic *beliefs* and those justified by them, with no explanation of how that relation is connected with the pyramidal theory (p. 33). See also Will (1974), who speaks of foundationalist theories both as concerning relations of "claims" (e.g., pp. 106–7 and 188–9), where beliefs or other "cognitions" seem intended, and in terms of "items, bound together more or less tightly by relations of necessity and probability" (p. 218), where propositional relations seem intended.

Here Alfred is surely not justified in believing q. The reason is that justification is not simply a matter of relations between the relevant *propositions:* "Alfred is justified in believing that q only if his belief that q *depends on* his beliefs that p, and that if p, then q," where "if one belief depends on another, the former must be *causally* dependent on the latter" (1980, p. 602).

On the basis of the claim that (a) a set of beliefs can justify a further belief only if the latter depends on the former, and (b) the relevant dependence is causal, Kornblith appeals to the epistemic regress argument to show that if there are any justified beliefs, there are terminal beliefs. To this extent, foundationalists have been correct. But it is essential to see that the terminal beliefs to which the regress argument leads us need not be incorrigible, i.e., such that "they are known if they are believed" (1980, p. 600). A terminal belief is simply "justified, though not justified in virtue of its dependence on any other beliefs" (1980, p. 603).

A key premise in Kornblith's case for the corrigibility of terminal beliefs emerges from his reflections about Joe and Moe. Both see an apple before them; both believe there is one before them; and both these beliefs result from the same sort of causal connections with the apple. But Joe also believes that he is so myopic that if he were looking at an artificial apple he would still take it to be real; thus, his belief that there is an apple before him is not justified. Moe has no such background belief and may be quite justified in believing that there is an apple before him. What this shows is that "A belief's justificatory status is thus a function of (at least) the process responsible for its presence, as well as the background beliefs had by the agent at the time" (1980, p. 606).

There is another controversial conclusion Kornblith draws from considerations about the relation of background beliefs to the justification of terminating beliefs, namely, that modest foundationalists are mistaken in holding that "some beliefs, though not incorrigible, are justified independently of their relations to other beliefs." For

> as long as a belief is not incorrigible, its justificatory status will vary not only with changes in the process responsible for its presence but also with changes in background beliefs that would make that process inadequate for justification. *All nonincorrigible beliefs are thus justified, in part, in virtue of their relations to other beliefs.* (1980, p. 606)

This argument enables us to see why Kornblith rejects modest foundationalism in favor of the view that, while foundationalists have been right in holding that "the structure of belief dependence is hierarchical; that some beliefs, though justified, are not dependent on others," coherentists have been right in contending that "no belief is justified independently of its relations to other beliefs" (1980, p. 606).

2. EPISTEMIC DEPENDENCE, CAUSAL DEPENDENCE, AND REASONS

The thesis that both foundationalists and coherentists have held an apsychological view of the justification of beliefs is an important claim. So is the thesis that the epistemic dependence of one belief on a second entails causal dependence of the first on the second. This section will clarify both of the theses and Kornblith's case for them.

We might begin with Kornblith's critique of the arguments-on-paper thesis. If the thesis is that S's belief that p, is justified if and only if either no argument for p is needed or there are *some* other propositions S believes such that the argument from them to p is a good one – which is apparently how Kornblith is taking the thesis – then I agree that it is false. In stating the thesis, however, he speaks of a good argument which takes as premises "certain" other propositions one believes. This would allow a proponent to restrict what constitutes *appropriate* premises, e.g. to those that are (i) believed by S to support p, or (ii) such that there is a sound rule of inference which S takes to warrant his believing p on the relevant premises, or (iii) at least such that he *not* believe, of all the rules he can grasp that do warrant the inference, that they are wrong. One might, of course, impose many other restrictions. But these have some plausibility and any of them would undermine Kornblith's counterexample to the thesis. For that example depends on Alfred's distrust of modus ponens, and this distrust makes it at best doubtful whether his belief that q would be justified by any of the above restricted versions of the arguments-on-paper thesis.

Let us also ask what might warrant the positive claim that "Alfred is justified in believing q only if his belief that q *depends* on his beliefs that p, and if p then q." This principle would be the most likely explanation of why Alfred is not justified in believing q, were it not for Alfred's distrust of modus ponens. For that seems an equally good explanation and it does not require this causal dependence assumption. If, however, we imagine a more guarded version of the arguments-on-paper thesis, one on which Alfred would have to believe the propositions that p, and that if p then q, to *warrant* his inferring q from them, then I find no argument in Kornblith's paper for the claim that Alfred's justification requires belief dependence. One is left wondering whether there may not be some form of the arguments-on-paper thesis that is quite defensible.

It is well worth exploring why any version of the arguments-on-paper thesis might be thought plausible. Consider first a view which philosophers have frequently held, and quite often presupposed: that if S's belief that p is not directly justified, then it is justified if and only if S has good reason for believing it. But what is it to have a good reason for believing p?

To answer this question clearly, we must carefully distinguish various kinds of reasons. There are at least four kinds that are epistemologically significant: reasons to believe, reasons one has for believing, reasons for which one believes, and reasons why one believes. We might briefly characterize them as follows. (1) A proposition, q, is a *reason to believe* a proposition, p, if and only if q bears some warranting relation to p, e.g. is an adequate ground on which to base a belief that p (the relevant kinds of warranting relations are difficult to specify, and need not be sorted out for our purposes here). (2) By contrast, typically, a *reason which S has for believing p* is another proposition, q, such that (a) S believes q, and (b) q is a reason to believe p. But there seem to be some uses of expressions of the form of 'S's reason for believing p' in which S may only take q (wrongly) to be a reason to believe p: here we might speak of having a bad reason for believing p. (There may be other uses of 'has a reason for believing', but the first use specified seems the most common.) (3) On the other hand, if q is *a reason for which S believes p*, then (at least normally) all the following conditions hold: (a) S believes that p and that q; (b) S believes p at least partly because he believes q; and (c) either q is a reason to believe p or S takes it to bear some warranting relation to p. (The converse of this conditional may also hold normally, but it does not hold unqualifiedly.) (4) Unlike (1)–(3), the notion of a *reason why S believes p* is not in any obvious way epistemic: a reason why S believes p is simply something that explains, at least in part, why S actually believes *p*, where the force of 'actually' is to rule out nonoperative factors that overdetermine the belief in the sense that they would operate to produce or sustain the belief if a certain condition were realized. Clearly, then, a reason for which *S* believes is a reason why he believes, whereas a reason he has for believing need not be.

In the light of these distinctions, we can see that it is not easy to specify what constitutes having a good reason to believe *p*. An initially plausible answer is that *S* has a good reason to believe *p*, if and only if there *is* some good reason, *q*, to believe that *p*, and *S* believes *q*. If we also assume that *q* is a good reason for believing *p*, if and only if the argument with *q* (which may be a conjunction) as premise and *p* as conclusion is a good one, we can express a view at least nearly equivalent to the arguments-on-paper thesis in terms of reasons. This view is that *S*'s belief that *p*, is justified if and only if either *p* is such that *S* needs no reason for (justifiably) believing it, or *S* has at least one good reason for believing it. To be sure, one might want to hold that unless *S* in some sense takes *q* to support *p*, *q* is not a good reason *S* has to believe *p*. There are also other conditions one might plausibly impose. My concern here, however, is not to explicate the elusive notion of *S*'s having a good reason to believe *p*, but to indicate a possible construal of the notion on which the arguments-on-paper thesis – and other apsychological accounts of epistemic dependence – can be seen to be plausible.

A further advantage of putting the arguments-on-paper thesis in terms of reasons is that we can also use that terminology to express the contrasting view held by Kornblith and others. Recall Alfred. He *has* a reason for believing *q*, namely that *p*, and if *p* then *q*. But this is not a reason for which he believes *q*. He believes *q* because he likes the sound of some sentence expressing *q*. Now as I read Kornblith, he appears to hold that *S*'s belief that *p* is justified by a reason, *q*, which *S* has for believing *p*, only if *q* is a reason *for* which *S* believes *p*. Clearly, where *q* is a reason *S* has for believing *p*, it can also be a reason for which *S* believes *p*, only if *S*'s belief that *q*, plays some kind of causal role in sustaining (or bringing about) *S*'s belief that *p*. On the view we are considering, then, a necessary condition for *inferential epistemic dependence*, i.e., the common kind normally exhibited by *S*'s belief that *p* being justified solely by his belief that *q*, is a causal connection between the two beliefs. We might call this necessary condition claim the thesis of the causal character of inferential epistemic dependence, provided we do not take 'inferential' to imply that *S* has actually inferred *p* from *q* in the full-blooded sense of 'infer.'[3]

Two clarifications are in order immediately. First, this thesis says nothing about whether, if justified foundational beliefs are dependent on anything else (e.g., on experiences) for their justification, they must stand in a causal relation to whatever that is. This is a further issue and quite beyond the scope of our discussion. Second, while the thesis entails that inferential epistemic dependence is a partly causal relation, it does not entail the *causal dependence* of *S*'s belief that *p* on *S*'s belief that *q*. Kornblith may not have noticed this point. In any case, he maintains (though his overall position does not require it) that inferential epistemic dependence entails causal dependence. Specifically, he holds that a belief justified by others must causally depend on them (1980, p. 602). This seems too strong. *S* might believe that *p* for two independent reasons, *r* and *t*, each such that (a) it fully justifies *p*, and (b) *S*'s believing it plays an actual role in sustaining his belief that *p* sufficient to sustain that belief should the other justifying belief be eliminated.

The above distinctions among kinds of reasons not only help us to sort out different epistemic dependency claims, they also make it easy to see still other reasons why one might accept the arguments-on-paper thesis or other noncausal accounts of epistemic dependence. For if one is, like many epistemologists, construing the justification of one belief by another in terms of reasons for believing, one can easily fail to note that some of these are, and some are not, reasons *for* which *S* believes. Consider a common kind of case in which we want to know whether someone justifiably believes *p*. We might naturally ask "his reasons for believing *p*." Since this phrase applies *both* to reasons for which one believes *p* and to reasons one merely has for believing *p*, its use in such cases contributes to a tendency to overlook the distinction between reasons *S* simply has to believe *p*, and reasons for which he believes *p*. So does the fact that in trying to justify their beliefs people invoke both reasons for which they hold the beliefs and, if less commonly, reasons they merely have for the beliefs. There are many other points to be made in explaining how the distinction may be over-

3. Philosophers have used 'infer' quite variously, but they usually do not construe inferential knowledge or inferentially justified belief as necessarily arrived at by a process of passing from one or more actually entertained premises to a conclusion.

looked or wrongly appraised; but rather than pursue that I want now to consider further the plausibility both of the arguments-on-paper thesis and of the view that inferential epistemic dependence is causal.

This latter, causal dependency thesis seems to me very plausible. But I do not believe Kornblith's paper (or others so far published) provides any cogent argument for it. I am convinced, moreover, that it is difficult to find arguments for it which are not subject to quite plausible objections.[4] Certainly Lehrer's gypsy lawyer is an obstacle to the view (1974, pp. 122–26). The arguments-on-paper thesis, on the other hand, is much less difficult to assess. One serious objection to it emerges from cases in which *S* has good reasons for believing *p* and good reasons for disbelieving it. *S* might believe two sets of propositions, one constituting premises in a good argument for *p*, the other constituting premises of a good argument for not-*p*. Surely proponents of the sort of anti-causalist view the arguments-on-paper theorist represents should account for this possibility, even if they allow that *S* might be justified both in believing and in disbelieving *p*. One would at least expect an anti-causal theorist to require that *S*'s reasons for believing *p* are not *defeated* by reasons *S* has for believing not-*p*.

A subtler difficulty is this. Suppose *q* entails *p*, and the argument from *q* to *p* is a good one. Is *S*'s believing *q* sufficient for having a good reason to believe *p*? What if *S* cannot see that *q* even supports *p*? What if *S* rejects every sound principle of inference he can grasp by virtue of which an inference of *p* from *q* can be warranted? And suppose *S* is patently unjustified in believing *q*. It is not clear whether, under one or more of these conditions, *q* would be a reason *S* has for believing *p*. But it does seem clear that Kornblith takes the arguments-on-paper thesis to entail that even if such conditions were to hold, *S* may still be justified, by *q*, in *S*'s belief that *p*. Thus, if it turns out that when one or more of them does hold, *q* is not a reason *S* has to believe *p*, Kornblith's construction of the arguments-on-paper thesis cannot, after all, be represented in terms of reasons in the way I suggested, namely, as the view that *S*'s belief that *p* is justified if and only if *p* is such that either *S* needs no reason for (justifiably) believing it, or *S* has at least one

4. For an indication of the scope of the issue see, e.g., Pappas (1979) and Swain (1981, pp. 89–92).

good reason for believing it. Either way, however, the above considerations (among others) strongly suggest that the thesis is mistaken.

If the reasons just brought out do, as I believe they do, warrant rejecting the thesis, we might ask whether it has indeed been held by all the prominent epistemologists on the impressive list Kornblith gives. I think not. Indeed, as I read most of these writers, they are not expressing the arguments-on-paper thesis in the passages Kornblith cites.[5] Perhaps he has taken such passages to imply it because they all *seem* anti-causalist, in making justification sound like a matter of relations between the justified proposition and others that are both potential "premises" for it and believed by S. I have stressed, however, that so construing justification for believing does not, by itself, commit one to the arguments-on-paper thesis.

Moreover, the arguments-on-paper thesis concerns the justification of actual beliefs. The views just referred to, however, concern either the notion of a proposition's being justified for a person or the closely related notion of what one is justified *in believing*, where one can be justified in believing p without actually believing it. It appears, e.g., that p can be nondefectively evident for S, in Chisholm's sense, without S's believing p; and presumably if p is nondefectively evident for S, S is justified in believing it. Firth, in one text cited by Kornblith, explicitly takes, as his main focus relative to justification, S's being justified in believing, where "we may assert without self-contradiction that someone is justified in believing a statement that he in fact does not believe" (1964). And Lehrer, especially in the part of *Knowledge* cited by Kornblith, is talking chiefly about what it is for S to be justified *in believing p*.

It is, to be sure, natural to suppose that a philosopher who holds that under certain conditions S is justified in believing p will also hold that if, under these conditions, S does believe p, S's belief that p is justified. But once we take seriously the reasons *for* which S believes p as factors in the justification of the belief, we are

---

5. The list cites Ayer, Chisholm, Cornman, Firth, Ginet, Lehrer, Lewis, Neurath, Pastin, Pollock, Russell, Sellars, and Sosa. In the cited passage from Chisholm (1977), however, the most relevant item I find is the definition of a proposition's being nondefectively evident for S (p. 107); and the most relevant claim of Lehrer's (1974) on the cited page seems to be that "complete justification requires coherence within a system of beliefs" (p. 17). These passages do not express the arguments-on-paper thesis, nor do the apparently relevant ones by several of the other writers mentioned.

unlikely to infer, from *S*'s being justified *in* believing *p* by a reason (or other factor), that if *S* does believe *p*, this belief is justified. *S* might, e.g., come to believe it for *other* reasons, including bad ones. Thus, even if Chisholm, Firth, Lehrer, and others do hold the counterpart of the arguments-on-paper thesis for being justified in believing, they need not hold the thesis itself, which concerns justified beliefs actually held. I see no good reason to think them committed to either of these views, however; nor does either view seem part of "the standard account of what it is to be justified in believing a proposition."[6]

An even more important issue connected with the arguments-on-paper thesis is whether it or anything like it is essential to either foundationalism or coherentism. Kornblith suggests this, e.g. in saying that "foundationalism and the coherence theory share a common false presupposition . . . in their anti-psychological approach to epistemological questions" (1980, p. 598), while also maintaining that "Foundationalism and the coherence theory of justification provide us with rival accounts of what it is to be a 'good argument' " (1980, p. 600). Whatever Kornblith's view here, it is noteworthy that the pages he cites in Chisholm, Firth, Lehrer, and others, do not support an attribution to them of the arguments-on-paper thesis. Moreover, the works cited include *both* representative foundationalist views, such as Chisholm's, and representative coherentist views, such as Lehrer's. In any case, nothing essential either to foundationalism or to coherentism seems to entail the arguments-on-paper thesis. Some of the reasons why this is so will be apparent in the next section.

3. DEFEASIBILITY AND EPISTEMIC DEPENDENCE

To understand foundationalism one must be clear about the epistemic status of the foundational beliefs. It should go without saying that foundationalists construe these beliefs as not *based*, epistemically, on other beliefs. This idea needs explication, but given its expressions in the literature one might reasonably infer, as Kornblith and others have, that foundational beliefs are epis-

6. Russell seems clearly to reject the arguments-on-paper thesis, at least in (1940). Recall his requirement (quoted in note 2) that an epistemological premise be a psychological premise.

temically independent of other beliefs. We are now in a good position to explore how strong a notion of epistemic independence is required by modest foundationalism. In particular, in what way must foundational beliefs be independent of other beliefs if their justification is to be independent of the latter beliefs?

A good way to approach this question is through examining a direction in Kornblith's paper which is quite representative of recent criticism of foundationalist theories of epistemic justification. A major thrust in the paper is his attack on the view, which he calls "modest foundationalism," that "some beliefs, though not incorrigible, are justified independently of their relations to other beliefs." This independence formulation and similar expressions have been used to characterize modest foundationalism, though perhaps more often by its critics than by its proponents.[7] In any event, it has generally not been noticed that the key sentence is ambiguous. It might be reasonably taken to mean roughly

(1) There are times at which S can have at least one justified corrigible belief whose justification does not, at these times, depend on, in the sense that it derives from, the justification of any other belief(s) S has at these times.

But there is at least one other possible interpretation, namely

(2) There are some justified corrigible beliefs which would (other things equal) remain justified regardless of other beliefs S forms.

(1) concerns justification at a time – momentary justification, we might say. (2) concerns corrigible justification at any time S may hold the relevant belief – omnitemporal justification, we might say: *de facto* justification of the belief at any time S holds it. A closely related distinction holds between the thesis that there are (or may be) beliefs whose justification is nonderivative, i.e.,

(3) There are (or may be) some beliefs whose justification does not derive from that of any other belief(s) of the person in question,

and the thesis that the justification of some beliefs is indefeasible, i.e.,

---

7. BonJour (1978), e.g., says that "the central thesis of epistemological foundationalism . . . is the claim that certain empirical beliefs possess a degree of epistemic justification or warrant which does not depend, inferentially or otherwise, on the justification of other empirical beliefs" (p. 1).

(4) There are (or may be) some beliefs that are necessarily justified, in the sense that their justification cannot be overriden.

Now clearly Kornblith's argument is directed against (2). His crucial premise is that as long as a belief is corrigible – hence not of necessity omnitemporally justified – "its justificatory status will vary not only with changes in the process responsible for its presence but also with changes in background beliefs." As I understand this, it is a plausible (though by no means uncontroversial) ground for rejecting (2). But it does nothing to undermine (1). For suppose that, at *t*, *S* has a justified belief that *p* whose justification does not, at *t*, derive from that of other beliefs. It does not follow that *S* could not later acquire, or indeed could not *have had* at *t*, beliefs such that either (a) they undermine the justification of *S*'s belief that *p* or (b) this justification comes to depend on these new beliefs being justified.

The importance of the ambiguity for the major issue before us should now be plain: if modest foundationalism is not committed to (2) but only to (1), then Kornblith's argument here does nothing to undermine modest foundationalism. Surely the theory is not committed to (2). Far from it. The contrast between (1) and (2) nicely parallels one contrast between modest and immodest foundationalism. The latter view places much stronger restrictions on the sorts of beliefs suitable for foundational material, and these beliefs are omnitemporally and, in some cases, even indefeasibly, justified: at any time *S* has such a belief it is justified. Modest foundationalists, by contrast, need only find good candidates for nonderivative, corrigible justification: the relevant beliefs may apparently have a far wider range of types of content, and certainly they need not be infallible, indubitable, or immune from revision in the light of new beliefs.

That modest foundationalism may be so interpreted is supported by the relevant literature, e.g. Armstrong (1973), Pastin (1975), and Alston (1976a and 1976b). But let me offer an important reason for interpreting it as I am. A major motivating argument supporting foundationalism is the regress argument. What the argument above all attempts to show is that if *S* has any justified beliefs, some of his beliefs are nonderivatively justified. Showing this does not require appeal to omnitemporal justification; it does not even require that all nonderivatively justified beliefs be true, or that a belief nonderivatively justified at one time cannot be derivatively justified at another. If the regress argument does not require appeal to omnitemporal justification, why should we require it of modest foundationalism? The theory takes justification to require that at any given time there are unmoved movers, but it does not tie justification to the possibility of unmovable movers.

A natural reply is that if a justification of a belief of S's can be defeated by S's adopting certain other beliefs, then it depends on other beliefs at least in the negative sense that their presence could destroy it. But compare this with saying that when one takes a walk in Washington Square, one's safety depends on one's not being harmed by certain ruffians who are several miles away stalking Central Park, but could have been stalking Washington Square. This is not obviously false, and if one has very high standards for applying the term 'safety', one may accept it. But it is perfectly reasonable to say that one's safety on a walk in Washington Square depends simply on what is happening there – or relevantly near there – at the time. A skeptic about safety, however, is likely to take the stronger view.

Similarly, a skeptic or a foundationalist preoccupied with vindicating, to the skeptic, our view that we have solidly justified beliefs may well grant that a belief whose justification is defeasible through the acquisition of other beliefs depends on them for its justification, and hence suppose that the only nonderivative justification is indefeasible. But modest foundationalists, perhaps largely because they do not adhere to the very high minimal standard of justification characteristic of much skepticism, reject this notion of dependency. One might insist that independence must be taken to imply indefeasibility; but in that case it will simply not be true that modest foundationalism embodies the claim that some corrigible beliefs are justified "independently" of their relations to other beliefs.

It is important to be clear about the relation between foundationalism – whether as a theory of knowledge or of justification – and skepticism. Both foundationalism and coherentism are best understood as theses about the *structure*, not the content, of a body of knowledge or justified beliefs. Granted, foundationalists have traditionally considered only certain types of beliefs adequate for a foundational role, but their main arguments for foundationalism itself – most notably the regress argument – have not required highly specific restrictions on the appropriate sorts of beliefs for foundations.[8] Moreover, neither foundationalism nor coherentism need be taken to entail that there *is* any knowledge or justified belief: as theses of analytical epistemology, they simply tell us what structure a body of beliefs must have if it is to contain knowledge or justified belief. Both theses are *neutral* with respect to skepticism, as is a pure analysis of knowledge. There is thus no good reason why a foundationalist must adhere to a standard of epistemic dependence which assimilates a belief's epistemic independence from other (actual or possible) beliefs to its indefeasible justification with respect to them, in the sense that *S*'s holding them (or justifiably holding them) would undermine its justification. Thus, a modest foundationalist might agree with the skeptic that we do not know certain skeptical hypotheses to be false, but deny that our justification for believing propositions whose falsity is entailed by the skeptical hypothesis requires knowing (or being justified in believing) the hypotheses to be false.[9] Moreover, a modest foundationalist need not even hold that there is any knowledge, or at least any empirical knowledge, if we judge by the high standard of justification endorsed by many skeptics. What standard of justification is required for justified belief or for knowledge is an independent matter.

Let us grant, however, that foundationalists might, when they turn to the question whether there *are* justified beliefs, want to use a standard of justification which makes it plausible to say there are. This suggests that they have good reason not to assimilate epistemic independence to indefeasibility, e.g. not to suppose that if *S*'s justification for believing *p* would be defeated by his coming to believe *q*, then his belief that *p* epistemically depends on his not believing *q*. But the matter is more complicated. For the foundationalist, like most epistemologists, wants to be able to *show* that skepticism is false. Now even a skeptic as thoroughgoing as Hume might allow that we may show something if it self-evidently follows from self-evident propositions and such first-person mental-state ascriptions as that I am thinking. For even Humean skeptics apparently consider assertions of these two sorts of propositions war-

---

8. This is shown by, e.g., Alston (1976a and 1976b). Other reasons for the point are expressed in Armstrong (1973), Pollock (1974), Pastin (1975), and Audi (1978, 1982).
9. Dretske (1970) defends this denial (though not in the context of defending foundationalism).

ranted without argument. This provides motivation to hold that such ascriptions are self-evidently and indefeasibly justified. For if they are, then even by Humean standards, whenever I am thinking, I can show that I know something. Global skepticism would then be refuted.

It seems clear that such a victory would be Pyrrhic; for by these standards it is doubtful that we can show that we know anything about the external world. But this problem has not stifled the tendency just described. That, I believe, is partly because, in their zeal to refute the skeptic, epistemologists have often failed to distinguish being justified (or knowing) from showing that one is justified (or knows).[10] Once this distinction is made, it is plain that the anti-skeptical foundationalist has good reason not to assimilate epistemic independence to indefeasibility. To do so gives the skeptic a much stronger position. The logical independence of foundationalism as a thesis about the structure of knowledge or justified belief, and skepticism as a thesis about the extent of knowledge or justified belief, remains. But so far as a desire to combat skepticism is relevant to interpreting foundationalism, it suggests a modest notion of epistemic dependence as the most likely sort to go into a plausible foundationalism.

The distinction between momentary and omnitemporal justification leads us to see a perhaps unexpected way in which coherentism may also be misconstrued. Reiterating that "coherence theorists have argued that no belief is justified independently of its relations to other beliefs," Kornblith says that this claim is "vindicated by the account" he offers. But, as he himself suggests earlier in the paper (1980, pp. 600–601), coherentists deny that there are any nonderivatively justified beliefs, even momentarily. When they maintain that no belief is justified independently of its relations to other beliefs they are expressing *this* denial, not merely denying that there are omnitemporally justified beliefs. Hence, to account for the latter denial is not to account for the coherentist's overall thesis that no belief is "independently" justified. It is true that a coherentist can allow the existence of *psychologically foundational beliefs*, i.e., beliefs not based on one or

10. Alston (1976a, 1976b, and 1980) has shown that a confusion of these two things is common and has argued that much criticism of foundationalism is traceable to it. For further discussion of skepticism relevant to the issues here described see Rescher (1980) and Klein (1981).

more others.[11] Sellars, e.g., makes this clear. For instance, regarding the thought "*Here* is a red apple," which is the "conceptual core" of the experience of seeing there is a red apple in front of one, he says that

> to say that this visual thinking-out-loud that something is
> the case is epistemically *justified* or *reasonable* or *has authority*
> is clearly *not* to say that Jones has correctly inferred from
> certain premises, which he has good reason to believe, that
> there is a red apple in front of him. For we are dealing
> with a *paradigm* case of non-inferential belief. (Sellars, 1975,
> Part 1, paragraph 34)

But the justification of such beliefs will be a matter of their relations to one or more other beliefs, as Sellars also contends.[12]

The upshot of this is that, for the coherentist, it is never reliable production alone that justifies a belief, but, minimally, reliable production in the context of coherence with one or more other beliefs, or perhaps a suitable relation to a potential justificatory argument.[13] Thus, for the coherentist, epistemic dependence, while it need not be causal, apparently is always *cognitive*, in the sense that a justified belief that *p* must depend for its justification on some relation to either one or more justified beliefs or one or more potential beliefs, say of propositions suitable to provide a satisfactory argument for *p*.

Our conclusion in this section, then, is that foundationalism is not committed either to an account of epistemic dependence which cuts it off from some kind of causal dependence or to the indefeasible justification of foundational beliefs, or anything close to the view Kornblith calls the arguments-on-paper thesis. The same holds for coherentist theories of justification, though for reasons that have not been widely recognized it is more natural for coherentists than for foundationalists to deny that epistemic depen-

---

11. It is difficult to explicate the notion of a psychologically foundational belief. For a partial account, with discussion of the contrast between foundational and coherentist approaches to understanding a person's *belief* structure, see Audi (1978).
12. For discussion and development of this view of Sellars, see BonJour (1976), Delaney (1978), and Aune (1981).
13. The most explicit account of this view I know is probably that of BonJour (1976). See esp. pp. 291–94.

dence entails causal dependence.[14] Neither type of theory is intrinsically apsychological, and both can be combined with many different accounts of epistemic dependence. The central difference is not over the possibility of indefeasible justification; it is over whether justification may be nonderivative in a sense implying that some beliefs have some degree of justification not based on coherence with one or more others.

4. FOUNDATIONALISM AND RELIABILITY

The last major topic I want to discuss is the relations of foundationalism and coherentism to reliabilism. Is there any reason why a foundationalist cannot be a reliabilist? Kornblith argues that since, on the reliabilist view of justification, "in order to be justified a belief must be produced by a process that tends to produce true beliefs in relevant counterfactual situations, and relevance is always determined, in part, by an agent's beliefs," it follows that "no belief is justified independently of its relations with other beliefs" (1980, p. 611), a conclusion inconsistent with foundationalism. I have argued, however, that modest foundationalism entails only a weak version of this independence thesis; and clearly that version is consistent with reliabilism. A reliabilist's terminal beliefs may surely be a foundationalist's nonderivatively but defeasibly justified foundational beliefs.

Moreover, it is at least very natural for a reliabilist to be a modest foundationalist. For one thing, as a theory of justification reliabilism gives a good account of how beliefs can be nonderivatively yet defeasibly justified, as where the initial justification of certain kinds of perceptual beliefs is later undermined by credible testimony that one is hallucinating. Furthermore, the application of reliabilism to persons as they are even suggests that there are nonderivatively justified beliefs and that, at any given time, these are crucial to the justification of empirical beliefs whose justification is derivative.

It is worth adding that it seems at least very *un*natural for a reliabilist to be a coherentist. For one thing, reliabilism is to at least some degree externalist, since it takes some beliefs to be justified by factors external to the belief system. Coherentism at least tends

14. This idea is defended at length in Audi (1982).

to take justification to be internal to belief systems. Granted, a strong foundationalist who holds that foundational beliefs are necessarily self-justified might be an internalist, but internalism is not essential to foundationalism.

5. CONCLUSION

In concluding, I want to make a few quite general points. The first is about the nature of epistemology and epistemological theories. The others concern more specific issues we have been examining.

Recent literature contains many discussions of the relation between epistemology and psychology. Goldman (1967) went so far as to say, of his causal theory of knowing, "The analysis presented here flies in the face of a well-established tradition in epistemology, the view that epistemological questions are questions of logic or justification, not causal or genetic questions."[15] And Kornblith, criticizing the tendency to divorce epistemological from psychological questions, calls his approach "psychological" and naturalistic. So far as I can see, however, statements like these fail to take account of two important distinctions.

The first is the distinction between construing an epistemological theory as *conceptually naturalistic,* in the sense that it uses only nonnormative concepts, and, on the other hand, construing it as *substantively naturalistic,* in the sense that its principles, or at least its major principles, are factual and thus in a certain sense empirical. Reliabilism, in its usual forms, is intended to be conceptually naturalistic. But to say that epistemological questions are not to be divorced from psychological ones strongly suggests that the former are also empirical. A reliabilist theory of justification (or knowledge) is not committed to this.

The second distinction apparently overlooked by Kornblith and others is between *epistemological questions* – questions of philosophical epistemology – and *epistemic questions* – those essentially involving epistemic concepts, such as knowledge or justified belief. Certainly the former involve the use and explication of psychological concepts. But this does not entail that they are empirical. Some

15. Goldman (1967, p. 372). Goldman adds in the next sentence, however, that "the question of what the correct analysis is of '*S* knows that *p*' is not a causal question." This is an important qualification.

epistemic questions, however, such as whether we have justified beliefs about our childhoods, are empirical, since, for one thing, an affirmative answer implies that there are people, that they have beliefs, and that some of their beliefs have a causal connection with the past. Of course, if one holds, as Quine apparently does on metaphilosophical grounds, that there is no clear distinction between questions of epistemology and those of psychology (1969), one will maintain that epistemology is substantively naturalistic. But this may not be inferred from its being conceptually naturalistic, and neither a reliabilist nor, indeed, a foundationalist or coherentist need hold it.

I do not in the least deny that answering epistemological questions requires *using* psychological concepts, including some, such as belief dependence, sometimes taken by philosophers to be of little or no epistemological importance. I believe, moreover, that epistemologists have been too heavily occupied in recent decades with explicating such notions as a proposition's being justified for a person, notions which tend to be analyzed with little or no reference to the psychological states and processes of the subject (other than beliefs themselves). Such notions are important. I believe, however, that a sound theory of knowledge or of the justification of actual beliefs must pay close attention to such partly psychological concepts as that of a reason for which a person believes. But if I have been right, neither foundationalists nor coherentists need deny this.

We may conclude, then, that a foundational theory of justification may be not only reliabilist but also naturalistic, either conceptually or substantively. Moreover, there is no reason why a foundationalist need use apsychological criteria of epistemic dependence or criteria of such strength that only indefeasible justification can be nonderivative. It remains a problem for foundationalists to explicate epistemic dependence fully and to show that there are justified beliefs not epistemically dependent on other beliefs. But we have at least seen that modest foundationalism can be readily combined with a causal notion of epistemic dependence, and that it does not require indefeasible justification on the part of foundational beliefs.[16]

16. This paper grew out of one given at a symposium with Hilary Kornblith at the Eastern Division Meetings of the American Philosophical Association in December, 1980. (An abstract of the paper, entitled "Foundationalism and Epistemic Dependence," appeared in *The Journal of Philosophy* 77 (1980, 612–

REFERENCES

Amstrong, D. M.: 1973, *Belief, Truth and Knowledge,* Cambridge University Press, Cambridge.

Alston, W. P.: 1976a, "Has foundationalism been refuted?", *Philosophical Studies* 29, 287–305.

Alston, W. P.: 1976b, "Two types of foundationalism," *The Journal of Philosophy* 73, 165–84.

Alston, W. P.: 1980, "Level confusions in epistemology," *Midwest Studies in Philosophy* 5.

Audi, R.: 1978, "Psychological foundationalism," *The Monist* 62, 592–610.

Audi, R.: 1982, "Axiological foundationalism," *Canadian Journal of Philosophy* 10, 163–83.

BonJour, L.: 1976, "The coherence theory of empirical knowledge," *Philosophical Studies* 30, 281–312.

BonJour, L.: 1978, "Can empirical knowledge have a foundation?" *American Philosophical Quarterly* 15, 1–13.

Chisholm, R. M.: 1977, *Theory of Knowledge,* Prentice-Hall, Englewood Cliffs.

Delaney, C. F.: 1978, "Basic propositions, empiricism, and science," in J. C. Pitt (ed.) *The Philosophy of Wilfrid Sellars: Queries and Extensions,* D. Reidel, Dordrecht, 41–55.

Dretske, F. I.: 1974, "Epistemic operators," *The Journal of Philosophy* 71, 1007–23.

Firth, R.: 1964, "Coherence, certainty, and epistemic priority," *The Journal of Philosophy* 61, 545–57.

Goldman, A. I.: 1967, "A causal theory of knowing," *The Journal of Philosophy* 64, 357–72.

Goldman, A. I.: 1976, "Discrimination and perceptual knowledge," *The Journal of Philosophy* 73, 771–91.

Klein, P.: 1981, *Certainty: A Refutation of Scepticism,* University of Minnesota Press, Minneapolis.

Kornblith, H.: 1980, "Beyond foundationalism and the coherence theory," *The Journal of Philosophy* 77, 597–611.

Lehrer, K.: 1974, *Knowledge,* Oxford University Press, Oxford.

Pappas, G.: 1979, "Basing relations," in G. Pappas (ed.), *Justification and Knowledge,* D. Reidel, Dordrecht, 51–63.

13). I benefited from the discussion with Kornblith and others at the symposium, and am grateful for written comments by John Heil and Hardy E. Jones.

Pastin, M.: 1975, "Modest foundationalism and self-warrant," *American Philosophical Quarterly Monograph Series* 9, 147–49.

Pollock, J.: 1974, *Knowledge and Justification*, Princeton University Press, Princeton.

Quine, W. V.: 1969, "Epistemology naturalized," in his *Ontological Relativity and Other Essays*, Columbia University Press, New York, pp. 69–90.

Rescher, N.: 1980, *Skepticism*, Basil Blackwell, Oxford.

Russell, B.: 1940, *An Inquiry into Meaning and Truth*, Allen and Unwin, London.

Sellars, W.: 1975, "The structure of knowledge," in Hector-Neri Castañeda (ed.), *Action, Knowledge, and Reality: Essays in Honor of Wilfrid Sellars*, Bobbs-Merrill, Indianapolis.

Swain, M.: 1981, *Reasons and Knowledge*, Cornell University Press, Ithaca.

Will, F. L.: 1974, *Induction and Justification*, Cornell University Press, 1974.

Chapter 4

The foundationalism–coherentism controversy: hardened stereotypes and overlapping theories

Foundationalism and coherentism each contain significant episte-mological truths.[1] Both positions are, moreover, intellectually in-fluential even outside epistemology. But most philosophers defending either position have been mainly concerned to argue for their view and to demolish the other, which they have often in-terpreted through just one leading proponent. It is not surprising, then, that philosophers in each tradition often feel misunderstood by those in the other. The lack of clarity – and unwarranted ster-eotyping – about both foundationalism and coherentism go beyond what one would expect from terminological and philosophical di-versity: there are genuine obscurities and misconceptions. Because both positions, and especially foundationalism, are responses to the epistemic regress problem, I want to start with that. Once it is seen that this perennial conundrum can take two quite different

1. For recent statements of foundationalism see, e.g., R. M. Chisholm, *Theory of Knowledge* (Englewood Cliffs, N.J.: Prentice-Hall, 1977 and 1989), and, espe-cially, "A Version of Foundationalism," *Midwest Studies in Philosophy* V (1980); William P. Alston, "Two Types of Foundationalism," *The Journal of Philosophy* LXXXIII, 7 (1976); Paul K. Moser, *Empirical Justification* (Dordrecht and Boston: D. Reidel, 1985); and Richard Foley, *The Theory of Epistemic Rationality* (Cam-bridge, Mass.: Harvard University Press, 1987); and Chapter 1, this volume. For detailed statements of coherentism see, e.g., Wilfrid Sellars, "Givenness and Explanatory Coherence," *The Journal of Philosophy* LXX (1973); Keith Leh-rer, *Knowledge* (Oxford: Oxford University Press, 1974); Gilbert Harman, *Thought* (Princeton, N.J.: Princeton University Press, 1975); and Laurence Bon-Jour, *The Structure of Empirical Knowledge* (Cambridge, Mass.: Harvard Univer-sity Press, 1985). For useful discussions of the controversy between foun-dationalism and coherentism, see C. F. Delaney, "Foundations of Empirical Knowledge – Again," *The New Scholasticism* L, 1 (1976), which defends a kind of foundationalism; and Brand Blanshard, "Coherence and Correspondence," in *Philosophical Interrogations*, edited by Sydney and Beatrice Rome (New York: Holt, Rinehart & Winston, 1964), which defends his earlier views against ob-jections by critics quoted in the same chapter.

forms, both foundationalism and coherentism can be better understood.

I. TWO CONCEPTIONS OF THE EPISTEMIC REGRESS PROBLEM

It is widely agreed that the epistemic regress argument gives crucial support to foundationalism. Even coherentists, who reject the argument, grant that the regress problem which generates it is important in motivating their views.[2] There are at least two major contexts – often not distinguished – in which the regress problem arises. Central to one is pursuit of the question of how one knows or is justified in believing some particular thing, most typically a proposition about the external world, e.g. that one saw a bear in the woods. This context is often colored by conceiving such questions as skeptical challenges, and this is the conception of them most important for our purposes. The challenges are often spearheaded by "How do you know?" Central to the other main context in which the regress problem arises are questions about what *grounds* knowledge or justification, or a belief taken to be justified or to constitute knowledge, where there is no skeptical purpose, or at least no philosophically skeptical one. Other terms may be used in framing these questions. People interested in such grounds may, for instance, want to know the source, basis, reasons, evidence, or rationale for a belief. We must consider the regress problem raised in both ways. I begin with the former.

Suppose I am asked how I know that *p*, say that there are books in my study. The skeptic, for instance, issues the question as a challenge. I might reply by citing a ground of the belief in question, say *q*: I have a clear recollection of books in my study. The skeptic then challenges the apparent presupposition that I know the ground to hold; after all, if I do have a ground, it seems natural to think that I should be able (at least on reflection) not just to produce it, but also to justify it: how else can I be entitled to take it as a ground? Thus, if "How do you know?" is motivated by a skeptical interest in knowledge, the question of how I know is

2. BonJour, e.g., says that the regress problem is "perhaps the most crucial in the entire theory of knowledge" (op. cit., p. 18); and he considers it the chief motivation for foundationalism (p. 17) and regards the failure of foundationalism as "the main motivation for a coherence theory" (p. 149).

likely to be reiterated, at least if my ground, q, is not self-evident; for unless q is self-evident, and in that sense a self-certifying basis for p, the questioner – particularly if skeptical – will accept my citing q as answering "How do you know that p?", only on the assumption that I *also* know that q. How far can this questioning reasonably go?

For epistemologists, the problem posed by "How do you know?" and "What justifies you?" is to answer such questions without making one or another apparently inevitable move that ultimately undermines the possibility of knowledge or even of justification. Initially, there seem to be three unpleasant options. The first is to rotate regressively in a vicious circle, say from p to q as a ground for p, then to r as a ground for q, and then back to p as a ground for r. The second option is to fall into a vicious regress: from p to q as a ground for p, then to r as a ground for q, then to s as a ground for r, and so on to infinity. The third option is to stop at a purported ground, say s, that does not constitute knowledge or even justified belief; but the trouble with this is that if one neither knows nor justifiedly believes s, it is at best difficult to see how citing s can answer the question of how one knows that p. The fourth option is to stop with something that is known or justifiedly believed, say r, but *not* known on the basis of any further knowledge or justified belief. Here the problem as many see it is that r, not being believed on any further ground, serves as just an arbitrary way of stopping the regress and is only capriciously taken to be known or justifiedly believed. Thus, *citing r* as a final answer to the chain of queries seems dogmatic. I want to call this difficulty – how to answer, dialectically, questions about how one knows, or about what justifies one – the *dialectical form of the regress problem.*[3]

3. Chisholm seems to raise the problem in this way when he says, "If we try Socratically to formulate our justification for any particular claim to know ('My justification for thinking that I know that A is the fact that B'), and if we are relentless in our inquiry ('and my justification for thinking that I know that B is the fact that C'), we will arrive, sooner or later, at a kind of stopping place ('but my justification for thinking that I know that N is simply the fact that N'). An example of N might be the fact that I seem to remember having been here before or that something now looks blue to me" (*Theory of Knowledge*, 1966, p. 2); cf. the 2nd ed., 1977, esp. pp. 19–20. In these and other passages Chisholm seems to be thinking of the regress problem dialectically and taking a foundational belief to be second order. To be sure, he is talking about justification of any "claim to know"; but this and similar locutions – such as "knowledge claim" – have often been taken to apply to expressions of first-order knowledge, as where one says that it is raining, on the basis of perceptions which one would normally take to yield knowledge that it is.

Imagine, by contrast, that we consider either the entire body of a person's apparent knowledge, as Aristotle seems to have done,[4] or a representative item of apparent knowledge, say my belief that there are books in my study, and ask on what this apparent knowledge is grounded (or based) and whether, if it is grounded on some further belief, *all* our knowledge or justified belief could be so grounded. We are now asking a structural question about knowledge, not requesting a verbal response in defense of a claim to it. No dialectic need even be imagined; we are considering a person's overall knowledge, or some presumably representative item of it, and asking how that body of knowledge is structured or how that item of knowledge is grounded. Again we get a regress problem: how to specify one's grounds without vicious circularity or regress or, on the other hand, stopping with a belief that does not constitute knowledge (or is not justified) or seems only capriciously regarded as knowledge. Call this search for appropriate grounds of knowledge the *structural form of the regress problem*.

To see how the two forms of the regress problem differ, we can think of them as arising from different ways of asking "How do you know?" It can be asked with *skeptical force,* as a challenge to people who either claim to know something or (more commonly) presuppose that some belief they confidently hold represents knowledge. Here the question is roughly equivalent to "Show me that you know." It can also be asked with *informational force,* as where someone simply wants to know by what route, such as observation or testimony, one came to know something. Here the question is roughly equivalent to "How is it that you know?" The skeptical form of the question does *not* presuppose that the person in question really has any knowledge, and, asked in this noncommittal way, the question tends to generate the dialectical form of the regress. The informational form of the question typically *does* presuppose that the person knows the proposition in question. It is easy to assume that it does not matter in which way we formulate the problem. But it does matter, for at least four reasons.

Knowing versus showing that one knows. First, the dialectical form

---

4. See *Posterior Analytics*, Bk 3. Having opened Bk. 1 with the statement that "All instruction given or received by way of argument proceeds from pre-existent knowledge" (71a1–2), and thereby established a concern with the structure and presuppositions of knowledge, Aristotle formulated the regress argument as a response to the question of what is required for the existence of (what he called scientific) knowledge (72b4–24). (The translation is by W. D. Ross.)

of the regress problem invites us to think that an adequate answer to "How do you know?" *shows* that we know. This is so particularly in the context of a concern to reply to skepticism. For the skeptic is not interested in the information most commonly sought when people ask how someone knows, say information about the origin of the belief, e.g. in first-hand observation as opposed to testimony. It is, however, far from clear that an adequate answer to the how-question must be an adequate answer to the show-question. If I tell you how I know there were injuries in the accident by citing the testimony of a credible witness who saw it, you may be satisfied; but I have not shown that I know (as I might by taking you to the scene), and the skeptic who, with the force of a challenge, asks how I know will not be satisfied. I have answered the informational form of the question, but not the skeptical form.

First-order versus second-order knowledge. Second, when the regress problem is dialectically formulated, any full non-skeptical answer to "How do you know that *p*?" will tend to imply an epistemic self-ascription, say "I know that *q*"; thus, my answer is admissible only if I both have the concept of knowledge – since I would otherwise not understand what I am attributing to myself – *and* am at least dialectically warranted in asserting that I do know that *q*. If you ask, informationally, how I know that there were injuries, I simply say (for instance) that I heard it from Janet, who saw them. But if you ask, skeptically, how I know it, I will realize that you will not accept evidence I merely *have*, but only evidence I *know*; and I will thus tend to say something to the effect that I *know* that Janet saw the injuries. Since this in effect claims knowledge of knowledge, it succeeds only if I meet the second-order standard for having knowledge that I know she saw this. If, however, the regress problem is structurally formulated, it is sufficient for its solution that there *be* propositions which, whether or not I believe them *prior* to being questioned, are both warranted for me (reasonable for me *to* believe) and together justify the proposition originally in question. For this to be true of me, I need only meet a first-order standard, e.g. by remembering the accident, and thereby be justified in believing that there were injuries.

Having, giving, and showing a solution. Third, and largely implicit in the first two points, the two formulations of the regress problem differ as to what must hold in order for there to *be*, and for S to *give*, an adequate answer to "How do you know?" or "What justifies you?" On the structural formulation, if there *are* warranted propositions of the kind just described, as where I am warranted in believing that there were injuries, the problem (as applied to *p*, the proposition in question) *has* a solution; and if I *cite* them in answering "How do you know that *p*?" I *give* a solution to the problem. The problem has a solution because of the mere existence of propositions warranted for me; and the solution is given, and the problem thus actually solved, by my simply affirming those propositions in answering "How do you know?" By contrast, when the problem is dialectically formulated, it is taken to have a solution only if there not only *are* such propositions, but I can show by *argument* that there are; and to give a solution I must not merely cite these propositions but also show that they are justified and that they in turn justify *p*. Thus, I cannot adequately say how I know there are books in my study by citing my recollection of them unless I can show by argument that it is both warranted and justifies concluding that there are indeed books there. Raising the structural form of the problem presupposes only that if I know that *p*, I have grounds of this knowledge that are expressible in propositions warranted for me; it does not presuppose that I can formulate the grounds or show that they imply knowledge. The structural form thus encourages us to conceive solutions as *propositional*, in the sense that they depend on the evidential propositions warranted for me; the dialectical form encourages conceiving solutions, as *argumental*, because they depend on what *arguments* about the evidence are accessible to me. I must be able to enter the dialectic with good arguments for *p*, not simply to be warranted in believing evidence propositions that justify *p*.

The process of justification versus the property of justification. Fourth, a dialectical formulation, at least as applied to justification (and so, often, to knowledge as at least commonly embodying justification), tends to focus our attention on the *process* of justification, i.e., of justifying a proposition, though the initial question concerns whether the relevant belief has the *property* of justification, i.e., of being justified. The skeptical forms of the questions "How do you know?" and "What justifies you?" tend to start a process of argument; "Show me that you know" demands a response, and what is expected is a process of justifying the belief that *p*. The informational form of those questions tends to direct one to cite a ground, such as clear recollection, and the knowledge or (property of) justification in question may be simply taken to be based on this ground. "By what route (or on what basis) do you know?"

need not start a process (though it may). It implies that providing a good ground – one in virtue of which the belief that *p* has the property of being justified – will fully answer the question. Granted, the epistemologist pursuing the regress problem in either form must use second-order formulations (though in different ways); still, the criteria for knowledge and justified belief tend to differ depending on which approach is dominant in determining those criteria.

If I am correct in thinking that the dialectical and structural formulations of the regress problem are significantly different, which of them is preferable in appraising the foundationalism–coherentism controversy? One consideration is neutrality; we should try to avoid bias toward any particular epistemological theory. The dialectical formulation, however, favors coherentism, or at least non-foundationalism. Let me explain.

Foundationalists typically posit beliefs that are grounded in experience or reason and are direct – and so not grounded through other, mediating beliefs – in two senses. First, they are *psychologically direct:* non-inferential (in the most common sense of that term), and thus not held on the basis of (hence through) some further belief. Second, they are *epistemically direct:* they do not depend (inferentially) for their status as knowledge, or for any justification they have, on other beliefs, justification, or knowledge. The first kind of direct belief has no psychological intermediary of the relevant kind, such as belief. The second kind has no evidential intermediary, such as knowledge of a premise for the belief in question. Roughly, epistemically direct beliefs are not inferentially *based on* other beliefs or knowledge, and this point holds whether or not there is any actual *process* of inference.[5] Now imagine that, in dealing with the dialectical form of the regress problem, say in answering the question of how I know I have reading material for tonight, I cite, as an appropriate ground, my knowing that there are books in my study. In choosing this as an example of knowledge, I express a belief that I do in fact know that there are books in the study. But am I warranted in this *second-order* belief, as I appear to be warranted simply in believing that there *are* books in the study (the former belief is construed as second-order on the assumption that knowing entails believing, and the belief that one

---

5. In Chapter 8, this volume, I present a detailed account of what it is for one belief to be based on another in the relevant (broadly inferential) sense.

knows is thus in some sense a belief about another belief)? Clearly it is far less plausible to claim that my second-order belief that I *know* there are books in my study is epistemically direct than to claim this status for my *perceptual* belief that there *are* books in it; for the latter seems non-inferentially based on my seeing them, whereas the former seems inferential, e.g. based on beliefs about epistemic status. Thus, foundationalists are less likely to seem able to answer the dialectical formulation of the problem, since doing that requires positing direct second-order knowledge (or at least direct, second-order justified belief).

In short, the dialectical form of the problem seems to require foundationalists to posit foundations of a higher order, and a greater degree of complexity, than they are generally prepared to posit. The same point emerges if we note that "How do you know?" can be repeated, and in some fashion answered, indefinitely. Indeed, because this question (or a similar one) is central to the dialectical formulation, that formulation tends to be inimical to foundationalism, which posits at least one kind of natural place to stop the regress: a place at which, even if a skeptical challenge *can* be adequately answered, having an answer to it is not necessary for having knowledge or justified belief.

It might seem, on the other hand, that the structural formulation, which stresses our actual cognitive makeup, is inimical toward coherentism, or at least non-foundationalism. For given our knowledge of cognitive psychology it is difficult to see how a normal person might *have* anything approaching an infinite chain of beliefs constituting knowings; hence, an infinite chain of answers to "How do you know?" seems out of the question. But this only cuts against an infinite regress approach in epistemology, not against any finitistic coherentism, which seems the only kind ever plausibly defended. Indeed, even assuming – as coherentists may grant – that much of our knowledge in fact arises, non-inferentially, from experiential states like seeing, the structural formulation of the problem allows *both* that, as foundationalists typically claim, there is non-inferential knowledge, and that, as coherentists typically claim, non-inferential beliefs are dialectically defensible indefinitely and (when true) capable of constituting knowledge only by virtue of coherence. The structural formulation may not demand that such defenses be available indefinitely; but it also does not preclude this nor even limit the mode of defense to circular reasoning.

I believe, then, that the structural formulation is not significantly biased against coherentism. Nor is it biased in favor of internalism over externalism about justification, where internalism is roughly the view that what justifies a belief, such as a visual impression, is internal in the sense that one can become (in some way) aware of it through reflection or introspection (internal processes), and externalism denies that what justifies a belief is always accessible to one in this sense. The dialectical formulation, by contrast, tends to favor internalism, since it invites us to see the regress problem as solved in terms of what propositions warranted for one are *also* accessible to one in answering "How do you know that *p*?" If the structural formulation is biased against internalism or coherentism, I am not aware of good reasons to think so, and I will work with it here.

II. THE EPISTEMIC REGRESS ARGUMENT

If we formulate the regress problem structurally, then a natural way to state the famous epistemic regress argument is along these lines. First, suppose I have knowledge, even if only of something so simple as there being a patter outside my window. Could all my knowledge be inferential? Imagine that this is possible by virtue of an infinite epistemic regress – roughly, an infinite series of knowings, each based (inferentially) on the next. Just assume that a belief constituting inferential knowledge is based on knowledge of some other proposition, or at least on a further belief of another proposition; the further knowledge or belief might be based on knowledge of, or belief about, something still further, and so on. Call this sequence an *epistemic chain;* it is simply a chain of beliefs, with at least the first constituting knowledge, and each belief linked to the previous one by being based on it. A standard view is that there are just four kinds: an epistemic chain might be infinite or circular, hence in either case unending and in that sense regressive, third, it might terminate with a belief that is not knowledge; and fourth, it might terminate with a belief constituting direct knowledge. The epistemic regress problem is above all to assess these chains as possible sources (or at least carriers) of knowledge or justification.

The foundationalist response to the regress problem is to offer a regress argument favoring the fourth possibility as the only genuine one. The argument can be best formulated along these lines:

1. If one has any knowledge, it occurs in an epistemic chain (possibly including the special case of a single link, such as a perceptual or a priori belief, which constitutes knowledge by virtue of being anchored directly in experience or reason);
2. the only possible kinds of epistemic chains are the four mutually exclusive kinds just sketched;
3. knowledge can occur only in the last kind of chain; hence,
4. if one has any knowledge, one has some direct knowledge.[6]

Some preliminary clarification is in order before we appraise this argument.

First, the conclusion, being conditional, does not presuppose that there *is* any knowledge. This preserves the argument's neutrality with respect to skepticism, as is appropriate since the issue concerns *conceptual* requirements for the possession of knowledge. The argument would have existential import, and so would not be purely conceptual, if it presupposed that there *is* knowledge and hence that at least one knower exists. Second, I take (1) to imply that inferential knowledge depends on at least one epistemic chain for its status *as* knowledge. I thus take the argument to imply the further conclusion that any inferential knowledge one has exhibits (inferential) *epistemic dependence* on some appropriate inferential connection, via some epistemic chain, to some non-inferential knowledge one has. Thus, the argument would show not only that if there is inferential knowledge, there *is* non-inferential knowledge, but also that if there is inferential knowledge, that very knowledge is *traceable* to some non-inferential knowledge as its foundation.

The second point suggests a third. If two epistemic chains should *intersect*, as where a belief that *p* is both foundationally grounded in experience and part of a circular chain, then if the belief is knowledge, that knowledge *occurs in* only the former chain, though the knowledge qua *belief* belongs to both chains. Knowledge, then, does not occur in a chain merely because the belief constituting it

6. The locus classicus of this argument is the *Posterior Analytics*, Bk. II. But while Aristotle's version agrees with the one given here insofar as his main conclusion is that "not all knowledge is demonstrative," he also says, "since the regress must end in immediate truths, those truths must be indemonstrable" (72b19–24), whereas I hold that direct knowledge does *not* require indemonstrability. There might be appropriate premises; S's foundational belief is simply not based on them (I also question the validity of the inference in the second quotation, but I suspect that Aristotle had independent grounds for its conclusion).

does. Fourth, the argument concerns the structure, not the content, of a body of knowledge and of its constituent epistemic chains. The argument may thus be used regardless of what purported items of knowledge one applies it to in any particular person. The argument does not presuppose that in order to have knowledge, there are specific things one must believe, or that a body of knowledge must have some particular content.

A similar argument applies to justification. We simply speak of *justificatory chains* and proceed in a parallel way, substituting justification for knowledge. The conclusion would be that if there are any justified beliefs, there are some non-inferentially justified beliefs, and that if one has any inferentially justified belief, it exhibits (inferential) *justificatory dependence* on an epistemic chain appropriately linking it to some non-inferentially justified belief one has, that is, to a foundational belief. In discussing foundationalism, I shall often focus on justification.

Full-scale assessment of the regress argument is impossible here. I shall simply comment on some important aspects of it to provide a better understanding of foundationalism and of some major objections to it.

Appeal to infinite epistemic chains has seldom seemed to philosophers to be promising. Let me suggest one reason to doubt that human beings are even capable of having infinite sets of beliefs. Consider the claim that we can have an infinite set of arithmetical beliefs, say that 2 is twice 1, that 4 is twice 2, etc. Surely for a finite mind there will be some point or other at which the relevant proposition cannot be grasped. The required formulation (or entertaining of the proposition) would, on the way "toward" infinity, become too lengthy to permit understanding it. Thus, even if we could read or entertain it part by part, when we got to the end we would be unable to remember enough of the first part to grasp and thereby believe what the formulation expresses. Granted, we could believe that the formulation just read expresses *a* truth; but this is not sufficient for believing *the truth* that it expresses. That truth is a specific mathematical statement; believing, of a formulation we cannot even get before our minds, or remember, in toto, that it expresses *some* mathematical truth is not sufficient for believing, or even grasping, the true statement in question. Since we cannot understand the formulation as a whole, we cannot grasp that truth; and what we cannot grasp, we cannot believe. I doubt that any other lines of argument show that we can have infinite sets of beliefs; nor, if we can, is it clear how infinite epistemic chains could account for any of our knowledge. I thus propose to consider only the other kinds of chain.

The possibility of a circular epistemic chain as a basis of knowledge has been taken much more seriously. The standard objection has been that such circularity is vicious, because one would ultimately have to know something on the basis of itself – say p on the basis of q, q on the basis of r, and r on the basis of p. A standard reply has been that if the circle is wide enough and its content sufficiently rich and coherent, the circularity is innocuous. I bypass this difficult matter, since I believe that coherentism as most plausibly formulated does not depend on circular chains.[7]

The third alternative, namely that an epistemic chain terminates in a belief which is not knowledge, has been at best rarely affirmed; and there is little plausibility in the hypothesis that knowledge can originate through a belief of a proposition S does not know. If there are exceptions, it is where, although I do not know that p, I am justified, to *some* extent, in believing that p, as in making a reasonable estimate that there are at least thirty books on a certain shelf. Here is a different case. Suppose it vaguely seems to me that I hear strains of music. If, on the basis of the resulting, somewhat justified belief that there is music playing, I believe that my daughter has come home, and she has, do I know this? The answer is not clear. But this apparent indeterminacy would not help anyone who claims that knowledge can arise from belief which does not constitute knowledge. For it is equally unclear, and for the same sort of reason, whether my belief that there is music playing is *sufficiently* reasonable – say, in terms of how good my perceptual grounds are – to give me knowledge that music is playing. The stronger our tendency to say that I know she is home, the stronger our inclination to say that I do after all know that there are strains of music in the air. Notice something else. In the only cases where the third kind of chain seems likely to ground knowledge (or justification), there is a degree – apparently a substantial degree – of justification. If there can be an epistemic chain which ends with belief that is not knowledge only because it ends, in this way, with justification, then we are apparently in the general vicinity of knowledge. We seem to be at most a few degrees of justification

7. For some major difficulties faced by circular versions see the Overview and Chapter 1, this volume.

away. Knowledge is not emerging from nothing, as it were – the picture originally evoked by the third kind of epistemic chain – but from something characteristically much like it: justified true belief. There would thus be a foundation after all: not bedrock, but perhaps ground that is nonetheless firm enough to yield a foundation we can build upon.

The fourth possibility is that epistemic chains which originate with knowledge end in non-inferential knowledge: knowledge not inferentially based on further knowledge (or further justified belief). That knowledge, in turn, is apparently grounded in experience, say in my auditory impression of music or in my intuitive sense that if A is one mile from B, then B is one mile from A. This non-inferential grounding of my knowledge can explain how that knowledge is (epistemically) direct. It arises, non-inferentially – and so without any intermediary premise that must be known along the way – from (I shall assume) one of the four classical kinds of foundational material, namely, perception, memory, introspection, and reason.

Such direct grounding in experience also seems to explain why a belief so grounded may be expected to be *true;* for experience seems to connect the beliefs it grounds to the reality they are apparently about, in such a way that what is believed concerning that reality tends to be the case. For empirical beliefs at least, this point seems to explain best why we have those beliefs. Let me illustrate all this. Normally, when I know that there is music playing, it is just because I hear it, and not on the basis of some further belief of mine; hence, the chain grounding my knowledge that my daughter has come home is anchored in my auditory perception, which in turn reflects the musical reality represented by my knowledge that there is music playing. This reality explains both my perception and, by explaining that, indirectly explains my believing the proposition I know on the basis of this perception – that my daughter is home.

The non-inferentially grounded epistemic chains in question may differ in many ways. They differ *compositionally,* in the sorts of beliefs constituting them, and *causally,* in the kind of causal relation holding between one belief and its successor. This relation, for instance, may or may not involve the predecessor belief's being necessary or sufficient for its successor: perhaps, on grounds other than the music, I would have believed my daughter was home; and perhaps not, depending on how many indications of her presence are accessible to me. Such chains also differ *structurally*, in the kind of *epistemic transmission* they exhibit; it may be deductive, as where I infer a theorem from an axiom by rigorous rules of deductive inference, or inductive, as where I infer from the good performance of a knife that others of that kind will also cut well; or the transmission of knowledge or justification may combine deductive and inductive elements. Epistemic chains also differ *foundationally*, in their ultimate grounds, the anchors of the chains; the grounds may, as illustrated, be perceptual or rational, and they may vary in justificational strength.

Different proponents of the fourth possibility have held various views about the character of the *foundational knowledge*, i.e., the beliefs constituting the knowledge that makes up the final link and anchors the chain in experience or reason. Some, including Descartes, have thought that the appropriate beliefs must be infallible, or at least indefeasibly justified.[8] But in fact all that the fourth possibility requires is *non-inferential knowledge*, knowledge not (inferentially) based on other knowledge (or other justified belief). Non-inferential knowledge need not be of self-evident propositions, nor constituted by indefeasibly justified belief, the kind whose justification cannot be defeated. The case of introspective beliefs, which are paradigms of those that are non-inferentially justified, supports this view, and we shall see other reasons to hold it.

III. FALLIBILIST FOUNDATIONALISM

The foundationalism with which the regress argument concludes is quite generic and leaves much to be determined, such as how *well* justified foundational beliefs must be if they are to justify a superstructure belief based on them. In assessing the foundationalist–coherentist controversy, then, we need a more detailed formulation. The task of this section is to develop one. I start with a concrete example.

As I sit reading on a quiet summer evening, I sometimes hear a distinctive patter outside my open window. I immediately believe

8. In Meditation I, e.g., Descartes says that "reason already persuades me that I ought no less carefully to withhold my assent from matters which are not entirely certain and indubitable than from those which appear to me manifestly to be false" (from the Haldane and Ross translation).

that it is raining. It may then occur to me that if I do not bring in the lawn chairs, the cushions will be soaked. But this I do not believe immediately, even if the thought strikes me in an instant; I believe it on the basis of my prior belief that it is raining. The first belief is perceptual, being grounded directly in what I hear. The second is inferential, being grounded not in what I perceive but in what I believe. My belief that it is raining expresses a premise for my belief that the cushions will be soaked. There are many beliefs of both kinds. Perception is a major source of beliefs; and, from beliefs we have through perception, many others arise inferentially. The latter, inferential beliefs are then based on the former, perceptual beliefs. When I see a headlight beam cross my window and immediately believe, perceptually, that a car's light is moving out there, I may, on the basis of that belief, come to believe, inferentially, that someone has entered my driveway. From this proposition in turn I might infer that my doorbell is about to ring; and from that I might infer still further propositions. Assuming that knowledge implies belief, the same point holds for knowledge: much of it is perceptually grounded, and much of it is inferential.[9] There is no definite limit on how many inferences one may draw in such a chain, and people differ in how many they tend to draw. Could it be, however, that despite the apparent obviousness of these points, there really *is* no non-inferential knowledge or belief, even in perceptual cases? If inference can take us forward indefinitely beyond perceptual beliefs, why may it not take us backward indefinitely from them? To see how this might be thought to occur, we must consider more systematically how beliefs arise, what justifies them, and when they are sufficiently well grounded to constitute knowledge.

Imagine that when the rain began I had not trusted my ears. I might then have believed just the weaker proposition that there was a pattering sound and only on that basis, and after considering the situation, come to believe that it was raining. We need not stop here, however. For suppose I do not trust my sense of hearing. I might then believe merely that it *seems* to me that there is a patter, and only on that basis believe that there is such a sound. But surely this cannot go much further, and in fact there is no need to go

---

9. That knowing a proposition implies believing it is not uncontroversial, but most epistemologists accept the implication. For defense of the implication see, e.g., Harman, op. cit., and my *Belief, Justification, and Knowledge* (Belmont, Calif.: Wadsworth, 1988).

even this far. Still, what theoretical reason is there to stop? It is not as if we had to articulate all our beliefs. Little of what we believe is at any one time before our minds being inwardly voiced. Indeed, perhaps we can have infinitely many beliefs, as some think we do.[10] But, as I have already suggested, it is simply not clear that a person's cognitive system can sustain an infinite set of beliefs, and much the same can be said regarding a circular cognitive chain.

Even if there could be infinite or circular belief chains, foundationalists hold that they cannot be sources of knowledge or justification. The underlying idea is in part this. If knowledge or justified belief arises through inference, it requires belief of at least one premise; and that belief could produce knowledge or justified belief of a proposition inferred from the premise only if the premise belief is itself an instance of knowledge or is at least justified. But if the premise belief is justified, it must be so by virtue of *something* – otherwise it would be self-justified, and hence one kind of foundational belief after all. If, however, experience cannot do the justificatory work, then the belief must derive its justification from yet another set of premises, and the problem arises all over again: what justifies that set? In the light of such points, the foundationalist concludes that if any of our beliefs are justified or constitute knowledge, then some of our beliefs are justified, or constitute knowledge, simply because they arise (in a certain way) from experience or reflection (including intuition as a special case of reflection). Indeed, if we construe experience broadly enough to include logical reflection and rational intuition, then experience may be described as the one overall source. In either case, there appear to be at least four basic sources of knowledge and justified belief: perception; consciousness, which grounds, e.g., my knowledge that I am thinking about the structure of justification; reflection, which is, for instance, the basis of my justified belief that if A is older than B and B is older than C, then A is older than C; and memory: I can be justified in believing that, say, I left a light on simply by virtue of the sense of recalling my having done so.[11]

10. See, e.g., Richard Foley, "Justified Inconsistent Beliefs," *American Philosophical Quarterly* 16 (1979). I have criticized the infinite-belief view in "Believing and Affirming," *Mind* XCI (1982).

11. It should be noted that memory is different from the other three in this: it is apparently not a *basic* source of knowledge, as it is of justification; i.e., one cannot know something from memory unless one has *come* to know it in some other mode, e.g. through perception. This is discussed in ch. 2 of my

Particularly in the perceptual cases, some foundationalists tend to see experience as a mirror of nature.[12] This seems to some foundationalists a good, if limited, metaphor because it suggests at least two important points: first, that some experiences are *produced* by external states of the world, somewhat as light produces mirror images; and second, that (normally) the experiences in some way *match* their causes, for instance in the color and shape one senses in one's visual field.[13] If one wants to focus on individual perceptual beliefs, one might think of a thermometer model; it suggests both the causal connections just sketched, but also, perhaps even more than the mirror metaphor, *reliable* responses to the external world.[14] From this causal–responsiveness perspective, it is at best unnatural to regard perceptual beliefs as inferential. They are not formed by inference from anything else believed but directly reflect the objects and events that cause them.

The most plausible kind of foundationalism will be fallibilist (moderate) in at least the following respects – and I shall concentrate on foundationalism about justification, though much that is said will also hold for foundationalism about knowledge. First, as a purely philosophical thesis about the *structure* of justification, foundationalism should be neutral with respect to skepticism and should not entail that there *are* justified beliefs. Second, if it is

Belief, Justification, and Knowledge. Cf. Carl Ginet, *Knowledge, Perception, and Memory* (Dordrecht and Boston: D. Reidel, 1973).

12. The view that such experience is a mirror of nature is criticized at length by Richard Rorty in *Philosophy and the Mirror of Nature* (Princeton, N.J.: Princeton University Press, 1979). He has in mind, however, a Cartesian version of foundationalism, which is not the only kind and implies features of the "mirror" that are not entailed by the metaphor used here.

13. This does not entail that there are *objects* in the visual field which have their own phenomenal colors and shapes; the point is only that there is some sense in which experiences *characterized by* color and shape (however that is to be analyzed) represent the colors and shapes apparently instantiated in the external world.

14. This metaphor comes from D. M. Armstrong. See esp. *Belief, Truth, and Knowledge* (Cambridge: Cambridge University Press, 1973). His theory of justification and knowledge is reliabilist, in taking both to be analyzable in terms of their being produced or sustained by reliable processes (such as tactile belief-production), those that (normally) yield true beliefs more often than false. Foundationalism may, but need not, be reliabilist; and this chapter is intended to be neutral with respect to the choice between reliabilist and internalist views. Internalism is sketched in Chapter 10, this volume, and I address the controversy between the two views in both Chapters 11 and 12. For further discussion see Paul K. Moser, *Knowledge and Evidence* (Cambridge and New York: Cambridge University Press, 1989), and R. M. Chisholm, *Theory of Knowledge*, 3rd ed. (Englewood Cliffs, N.J.: Prentice-Hall, 1989).

fallibilistic, it must allow that a justified belief, even a foundational one, be false. To require here justification of a kind that entails truth is to require that justified foundational beliefs be infallible. Third, superstructure beliefs may be only inductively, hence fallibly, justified by foundational ones and thus (unless they are necessary truths) can be false even when the latter are true. Just as one's warranted beliefs may be fallible, one's inferences may be, also, leading from truth to falsity. If the proposition is sufficiently supported by evidence one justifiedly believes, one may justifiedly hold it on the basis of that evidence, even if one could turn out to be in error. Fourth, a fallibilist foundationalism must allow for *discovering* error or lack of justification, in foundational as well as in superstructure beliefs. Foundational beliefs may be discovered to conflict either with other such beliefs or with sufficiently well-supported superstructure beliefs.

These four points are quite appropriate to the inspiration of the theory as expressed in the regress argument: it requires epistemic unmoved movers, but not unmovable movers. Solid ground is enough, even if bedrock is better. There are also different kinds of bedrock, and not all of them have the invulnerability apparently belonging to beliefs of luminously self-evident truths of logic. Even foundationalism as applied to knowledge can be fallibilistic; for granting that false propositions cannot be known, foundationalism about knowledge does not entail that one's *grounds* for knowledge (at any level) are indefeasible. Perceptual grounds, e.g., may be overridden; and one can fail (or cease) to know a proposition not because it is (or is discovered to be) false, but because one ceases to be justified in believing it.

I take *fallibilist foundationalism*, as applied to justification, to be the inductivist thesis that

> I. For any S and any t, (1) the structure of S's body of justified beliefs is, at t, foundational in the sense that any inferential (hence non-foundational) justified beliefs S has depend for their justification on one or more non-inferential (thus in a sense foundational) justified beliefs of S's; (2) the justification of S's foundational beliefs is at least typically defeasible; (3) the inferential transmission of justification need not be deductive; and (4) non-foundationally justified beliefs need not derive *all* of their justification from foundational ones, but only enough so

that they would remain justified if (other things remaining equal) any other justification they have (say, from coherence) were eliminated.[15]

This is fallibilist in at least three ways. Foundational beliefs may turn out to be unjustified or false or both; superstructure beliefs may be only inductively, hence fallibly, justified by foundational ones and hence can be false even when the latter are true; and possibility of *discovering* error or lack of justification, even in foundational beliefs, is left open: they may be found to conflict either with other such beliefs or with sufficiently well-supported superstructure beliefs. Even foundationalism as applied to knowledge can forswear infallibility. For although false beliefs cannot be knowledge, what is known can be both contingent – and so might have been false – *and* based on defeasible grounds – and so might cease to be known. We can lose knowledge when our grounds for it are defeated by counterevidence. Even introspective grounds are overridable (as argued in Chapter 5); hence, even self-knowledge is defeasible.

Since I am particularly concerned to clarify foundationalism in contrast to coherentism, I want to focus on the roles fallibilist foundationalism allows for coherence (conceived in any plausible way) in relation to justification. There are at least two important roles coherence may apparently play.

The first role fallibilist foundationalism allows for coherence – or at least for incoherence – is negative. Incoherence may defeat justification or knowledge, even the justification of a directly justified, hence foundational, belief (or one constituting knowledge), as where my justification for believing I am hallucinating books prevents me from knowing, or remaining justified in believing, certain propositions incoherent with it, say that the books in my study are before me. If this is not ultimately a role for coherence itself – which is the opposite and not merely the absence of incoherence – it *is* a role crucial for explaining points stressed by coherentism. Coherentists have not taken account of the point that incoherence is not merely the absence of coherence and cannot be explicated simply through analyzing coherence, nor accounted for as an epistemic

---

15. Clause (4) requires 'other-things-equal' because removal of justification from one source can affect justification from another even without being a basis of the latter justification; and the *level* of justification in question I take to be (as in the counterpart formulation of coherentism) approximately that appropriate to knowledge. The formulation should hold, however, for any given level.

standard only by a coherentist theory (a point to which I shall return); but they have rightly noted, for instance, such things as the defeasibility of the justification of a memorial belief owing to its incoherence with perceptual beliefs, as where one takes oneself to remember an oak tree in a certain spot, yet, standing near the very spot, can find no trace of one. Because fallibilist foundationalism does not require indefeasible justification on the part of the relevant memory belief, there is no anomaly in its defeat by perceptual evidence.

Second, fallibilist foundationalism can employ an *independence principle,* one of a family of principles commonly emphasized by coherentists, though foundationalists need not attribute its truth to coherence. This principle says that the larger the number of independent mutually coherent factors one believes to support the truth of a proposition, the better one's justification for believing it (other things being equal). The principle can explain, e.g., why my justification for believing, from what I hear, that my daughter has come home increases as I acquire new beliefs supporting that conclusion, say that there is a smell of popcorn. For I now have a confirmatory belief which comes through a different sense (smell) and does not depend for its justification on my other evidence beliefs.

Similar principles consistent with foundationalism can accommodate other cases in which coherence apparently enhances justification, for instance where a proposition's explaining, and thereby cohering with, something one justifiably believes, tends to confer some justification on that proposition. Suppose I check three suitcases at the ticket counter. Imagine that as I await them at the baggage terminal I glimpse two on the conveyor at a distance and tentatively believe that they are mine. The propositions that (a) the first is mine, (b) the second is, and (c) these two are side by side – which I am fully justified in believing because I can clearly see how close they are to each other – would be explained by the hypothesis that my three suitcases are now coming off together; and that hypothesis, in turn, derives some justification from its explaining what I already believe. When I believe the further proposition, independent of (a)–(c), that my third suitcase is coming just behind the second, the level of my justification for the hypothesis rises.

Fallibilist foundationalism thus allows for coherence to play a significant though restricted role in explicating justification, and it provides a major place for incoherence in this task. But there remains a strong contrast between the two accounts of justification, as we shall soon see.

IV. HOLISTIC COHERENTISM

The notion of coherence is frequently appealed to in epistemological and other contexts, but it is infrequently explicated. Despite the efforts that have been made to clarify coherence, explaining what it is remains difficult.[16] It is not mere consistency, though *in*consistency is the clearest case of incoherence. Whatever coherence is, it is a cognitively *internal* relation, in the sense that it is a matter of how one's beliefs (or other cognitive items) are related *to one another*, not to anything outside one's system of beliefs, such as one's perceptual experience. Coherence is sometimes connected with explanation; it is widely believed that propositions which stand in an explanatory relation cohere with one another and that this coherence counts toward that of a person's beliefs of the propositions in question. If the wilting of the leaves is explained by billowing smoke from a chemical fire, then presumably the proposition expressing the first event coheres with the proposition expressing the second (even if the coherence is not obvious and is relative to the context). Probability is also relevant: if the probability of one proposition you believe is raised by that of a second you believe, this at least counts toward the coherence of the first of the beliefs with the second. The relevant notions of explanation and probability are themselves philosophically problematic, but our intuitive grasp of them can still help us understand coherence.

In the light of these points, let us try to formulate a plausible version of coherentism as applied to justification. The central coherentist idea concerning justification is that a belief is justified by its coherence with other beliefs one holds. The unit of coherence may be as large as one's entire set of beliefs, though some may be more significant in producing the coherence than others, say because of differing degrees of their closeness in subject matter to the belief in question. This conception of coherentism would be accepted by a proponent of the circular view, but the thesis I want

16. For references to the main contemporary accounts, especially those by Lehrer and BonJour, see John B. Bender, *The Current Status of the Coherence Theory* (Dordrecht and Boston: Kluwer, 1989).

to explore differs from that view in not being *linear:* it does not take justification for believing that *p*, or knowledge that *p*, to emerge from an inferential line running from premises for *p* to that proposition as a conclusion from them, and from other premises to the first set of premises, and so on until we return to the original proposition as a premise. On the circular view, no matter how wide the circle or how rich its constituent beliefs, there is a line from any one belief in a circular epistemic chain to any other. In practice I may never trace the entire line, as by inferring one thing I know from a second, the second from a third, and so on until I reinfer the first. Still, on this view there is such a line for every belief constituting knowledge.

Coherentism need not, however, be linear, and I believe that the most plausible versions are instead holistic.[17] A moderate version of *holistic coherentism* might be expressed as follows:

II. For any *S* and any *t*, if *S* has any justified beliefs at *t*, then, at *t*, (1) they are each justified by virtue of their coherence with one or more others of *S*'s beliefs; and (2) they would remain justified even if (other things remaining equal) any justification they derive from sources other than coherence were eliminated.

The holism required is minimal, since the unit of coherence may be as small as one pair of beliefs – though it may also be as large as the entire system of *S*'s beliefs (including the belief whose justification is in question, since we may take such partial "self-coherence" as a limiting case). But the formulation also applies to the more typical cases of holistic coherentism; in these cases a justified belief coheres with a substantial number of other beliefs, but not necessarily with all of one's beliefs. Some beliefs, like those expressing basic principles of one's thinking, can be justified only by coherence with a large and diverse group of related beliefs. Coherentist theories differ concerning the sense (if any) in which the set of beliefs whose coherence determines the justification of some belief belonging to it must be a "system."

To illustrate holistic coherentism, consider a question that evokes

---

17. This applies to Sellars, Lehrer, and BonJour and is evident in the works cited in note 1. Their coherentist positions are not linear. For a statement of an internal difficulty besetting linear coherentism and probably also the most plausible versions of holistic coherentism, see the Overview and Chapters 1 and 2, this volume.

a justification. Ken wonders how, from my closed study, I know (or why I believe) that my daughter is home. I say that there is music playing in the house. He next wants to know how I can recognize my daughter's music from behind my closed doors. I reply that what I hear is the wrong sort of thing to come from any nearby house. He then asks how I know that it is not from a passing car. I say that the volume is too steady. He now wonders whether I can distinguish, with my door closed, my daughter's vocal music from the singing of a neighbor in her yard. I reply that I hear an accompaniment. In giving each justification I apparently go only one step along the inferential line: initially, for instance, just to my belief that there is music playing in the house. For my belief that my daughter is home *is* based on this belief about the music. After that, I do not even mention anything that this belief, in turn, is based on; rather, I defend my beliefs as appropriate, in terms of an entire pattern of interrelated beliefs I hold. And I may appeal to many different parts of the pattern. For coherentism, then, beliefs representing knowledge do not lie at one end of a grounded chain; they fit a coherent pattern and are justified through their fitting it in an appropriate way.

Consider a variant of the case. Suppose I had seemed to hear music of neither the kind my daughter plays nor the kind the neighbors play nor the sort I expect from passing cars. The proposition that this is what I hear does not cohere well with my belief that the music is played by my daughter. Suddenly I recall that she was bringing a friend, and I remember that her friend likes such music. I might now be justified in believing that my daughter is home. When I finally hear her voice, I know that she is. The crucial thing here is how, initially, a kind of *incoherence* prevents justification of my belief that she is home, and how, as relevant pieces of the pattern develop, I become justified in believing, and (presumably) come to know, that she is. Arriving at a justified belief, on this view, is more like answering a question by looking up diverse information that suggests the answer than like deducing a theorem from axioms.

Examples like this show how a holistic coherentism can respond to the regress argument *without* embracing the possibility of an epistemic circle (though its proponents need not reject that either). It may deny that there are only the four kinds of possible epistemic chains I have specified. There is apparently another possibility, not generally noted: that the chain terminates with belief which is *psychologically direct* but *epistemically indirect* or, if we are talking of coherentism about justification, *justificationally indirect*. Hence, the last link is, as belief, direct, since it is non-inferential; yet, as knowledge, it is *indirect*, not in the usual sense that it is inferential but rather in the broad sense that the belief constitutes knowledge only by virtue of receiving support from other knowledge or belief. Thus, my belief that there is music playing is psychologically direct because it is simply grounded, causally, in my hearing and is not (inferentially) based on any other belief; yet my *knowledge* that there is music is not epistemically direct. It is epistemically, but not inferentially, based on the coherence of my belief that there is music with my other beliefs, presumably including many that constitute knowledge themselves. It is thus knowledge *through*, though not by inference from, other knowledge – or at least through justified beliefs; hence it is epistemically indirect and thus non-foundational.

There is another way to see how this attack on the regress argument is constructed. The coherentist grants that the belief element *in* my knowledge is non-inferentially grounded in perception and is in that sense direct; but the claim is that the belief constitutes knowledge only by virtue of coherence with my other beliefs. The strategy, then – call it the *wedge strategy* – is to sever the connection foundationalism usually posits between the psychological and the epistemic. In the common cases, foundationalists tend to hold, the basis of one's *knowledge* that *p*, say a perceptual experience, is also the basis of one's belief that *p*; similarly, for justified belief, the basis of its justification is usually also that of the belief itself. For the coherentist using the wedge strategy, the epistemic ground of a belief need not be a psychological ground. Knowledge and justification are a matter of how well the system of beliefs hangs together, not of how well grounded the beliefs are – and they may indeed hang: one could have a body of justified beliefs, at least some of them constituting knowledge, even if *none* of them is justified by a belief or experience in which it is psychologically grounded.

In a sense, of course, coherentism does posit a *kind* of foundation for justification and knowledge: namely, coherence. But so long as coherentists deny that justification and knowledge can be *non-inferentially* grounded in experience or reason, this point alone simply shows that they take justification and knowledge to be based on something (to be supervenient properties, as some would put it). Justification and knowledge are still grounded in the coherence of elements which themselves admit of justification and derive their justification (or status as knowledge) from coherence with other such items rather than from grounding in elements like sensory impressions (say of music), which, though not themselves justified or unjustified, confer justification on beliefs they ground.

Apparently, then, the circularity objection to coherentism can be met by construing the thesis holistically and countenancing psychologically direct beliefs. One could insist that if a non-inferential, thus psychologically direct, belief constitutes knowledge, it *must* be direct knowledge. But the coherentist would reply that in that case there will be two kinds of direct knowledge: the kind the foundationalist posits, which derives from grounding in a basic experiential or rational source, and the kind the coherentist posits, which derives from coherence with other beliefs and not from being based on those sources. This is surely a plausible response.

Is the holistic coherentist trying to have it both ways? Not necessarily. Holistic coherentism can grant that a variant of the regress argument holds for belief, since the only kind of inferential belief chain that it is psychologically realistic to attribute to us is the kind terminating in direct (non-inferential) belief. But even on the assumption that knowledge is constituted by (certain kinds of) beliefs, it does not follow that direct belief which constitutes knowledge is also direct *knowledge*. Epistemic dependence, on this view, does not imply inferential or psychological dependence; hence, a non-inferential belief can depend for its status as knowledge on other beliefs. Thus, the coherentist may grant a kind of *psychological foundationalism* – which says (in part) that if we have any beliefs at all, we have some direct (non-inferential) ones – yet deny epistemological foundationalism, which requires that there be knowledge which is epistemically (and normally also psychologically) direct, if there is any knowledge at all. Holistic coherentism may grant experience and reason the status of psychological foundations of our belief systems, but it denies that they are the basic sources of justification or knowledge.

V. FOUNDATIONALISM, COHERENTISM, AND DEFEASIBILITY

Drawing on our results above, this section considers how fallibilist foundationalism and holistic coherentism differ and, related to that, how the controversy is sometimes obscured by failure to take account of the differences.

There is one kind of case that seems both to favor foundationalism and to show something about justification that coherentism in any form misses. It might seem that coherence theories of justification are decisively refuted by the possibility of S's having, if just momentarily, only a single belief which is nonetheless justified, say that there is music playing. For this belief would be justified without cohering with any others S has. But could one have just a single belief? Could I, for instance, believe that there is music playing yet not believe, say, that there are (or could be) musical instruments, melodies, and chords? It is not clear that I could; and foundationalism does not assume this possibility, though the theory may easily be wrongly criticized for implying it. Foundationalism is in fact consistent with *one* kind of coherentism – *conceptual coherentism.* This is a coherence theory of the acquisition of concepts which says that a person acquires concepts, say of musical pieces, only in relation to one another and must acquire an entire family of related concepts in order to acquire any concept.

It remains questionable, however, whether my justification for believing that there is music playing ultimately *derives* from the coherence of the belief with others, i.e., whether coherence is even partly the basis of my justification in holding this belief.[18] Let us first note an important point. Suppose the belief turns out to be *in*coherent with a second, such as my belief that I am standing before the phonograph playing the music yet see no movement of its turntable; now the belief may *cease* to be justified, since if I really hear the phonograph, I should see its turntable moving. But this shows only that the belief's justification is *defeasible* – liable to being either overridden (roughly, outweighed) or undermined – should sufficiently serious incoherence arise. It does not show that the justification derives from coherence. In this case the justification of my belief grounded in hearing may be overridden. My better-justified beliefs, including the belief that a phonograph with a motionless turntable cannot play, may make it more reasonable for me to believe that there is *not* music playing in the house.

The example raises another question regarding the possibility

18. With this question in mind, it is interesting to read Donald Davidson, "A Coherence Theory of Truth and Knowledge," in Dieter Hendrich, ed., *Kant oder Hegel* (Stuttgart, 1976). Cf. Jaegwon Kim, "What Is 'Naturalized Epistemology'?" *Philosophical Perspectives* 2 (1988).

that coherence is the source of my justification, as opposed to incoherence's constraining it. Could incoherence override the justification of my belief if I were not *independently* justified in believing that a proposition incoherent with certain other ones is, or probably is, false, e.g. in believing that if I do not see the turntable moving, then I do not hear music from the phonograph? For if I lacked such independent justification, should I not suspend judgment on, or even reject, the other propositions and retain my original belief? And aren't the relevant other beliefs or propositions – those that can override or defeat my justification – precisely the kind for which, directly or inferentially, we have some degree of justification through the experiential and rational sources, such as visual perception of a stockstill turntable? Note that the example shows that these beliefs or propositions need not be a priori; thus it is not open to coherentists to claim that only the a priori is an exception to the thesis that justification is determined by coherence.

A similar question arises regarding the crucial principles themselves. Could incoherence play the defeating role it does if we did not have a kind of foundational justification for principles to the effect that certain kinds of evidences or beliefs override certain other kinds? More generally, can we *use*, or even benefit from, considerations of coherence in acquiring justification, or in correcting mistaken presuppositions of justification, if we do not bring to the various coherent or incoherent patterns principles not derived from those very patterns? If, without such principles to serve as justified standards that guide belief formation and belief revision, we can become justified by coherence, then coherence would seem to be playing the kind of generative role that foundational sources are held to play in producing justification. One could become justified in believing that *p* by virtue of coherence even if one had no justified principles by which one could, for instance, inferentially connect the justified belief that *p* with others that cohere with it.

There is a second case, in which one's justification is simply undermined: one ceases to be justified in believing the proposition in question, though one does not become justified in believing it false. Suppose I seem to see a black cat, yet there no longer appears to be one there if I move five feet to my left. This experience could justify my believing, and lead me to believe, that I might be hallucinating. This belief in turn is to a degree incoherent with, and undermines the justification of, my visual belief that the cat is there, though it does not by itself justify my believing that there is *not* a cat there. Again, however, I am apparently justified, independently of coherence, in believing a proposition relevant to my overall justification for an apparently foundational perceptual belief: namely, the proposition that my seeing the cat there is incoherent with my merely hallucinating it there. The same seems to hold for the proposition that my seeing the cat there coheres with my feeling fur if I extend my hand to the feline focal point of my visual field. Considerations like these suggest that coherence has the role it does in justification only because *some* beliefs are justified independently of it.

Both examples illustrate an important distinction that is often missed.[19] It is between defeasibility and epistemic dependence or, alternatively, between *negative epistemic dependence,* which is a form of defeasibility, and *positive epistemic dependence,* the kind beliefs bear to the source(s) from which they *derive* any justification they have or, if they represent knowledge, their status as knowledge. The defeasibility of a belief's justification by incoherence does not imply that, as coherentists hold, its justification positively depends on coherence. If my garden is my source of food, I (positively) depend on it. The fact that people could poison the soil does not make their non-malevolence part of my food *source* or imply a (positive) dependence on them, such as I have on the sunshine. Moreover, it is the sunshine that (with rainfall and other conditions) explains both my having the food and the amount I have. The non-malevolence is necessary for, but does not explain, this; it alone, under the relevant conditions of potential for growth, does not even tend to produce food.

So it is with perceptual experience as a source of justification. Foundationalists need not deny that a belief's justification negatively depends on something else, for as we have seen they need not claim that justification must be indefeasible. It may arise, unaided by coherence, from a source like perception; yet it remains defeasible from various quarters – including conflicting perceptions. Negative dependence, however, does not imply positive dependence. The former is determined by the absence of something – defeaters; the latter is determined by the presence of something

---

19. This distinction seems to have been often missed, e.g. in Hilary Kornblith, "Beyond Foundationalism and the Coherence Theory," *Journal of Philosophy* LXXVII (1980), as I have argued (especially in relation to Kornblith's paper) in Chapter 3.

– justifiers. Justification can be defeasible by incoherence and thus overridden or undermined should incoherence arise, without owing its existence to coherence. Fallibilist foundationalism is not, then, a blend of coherentism, and it remains open just what positive role, if any, it must assign to coherence in explicating justification.

There is a further point that fallibilist foundationalism should stress, and in appraising the point we learn more about both coherentism and justification. If I set out to *show* that my belief is justified – as the dialectical formulation of the regress problem invites one to think stopping the regress of justification requires – I do have to cite propositions that cohere with the one to be shown to be justified for me, say that there is music in my house. In some cases, these are not even propositions one already believes. Often, in defending the original belief, one forms new beliefs, such as the belief one acquires, in moving one's head, that one can vividly see the changes in perspective that go with seeing a black cat. More important, these beliefs are highly appropriate to the *process* of self-consciously justifying one's belief; and the result of that process is twofold: forming the second-order belief that the original belief is justified and showing that the latter is justified. Thus, coherence is important in showing that a belief is justified. In *that* limited sense coherence is a pervasive element in justification: it is pervasive in the process of *justifying,* especially when that is construed as showing that one has justification.

Why, however, should the second-order beliefs appropriate to *showing* that a belief is justified be necessary for its *being* justified? They need not be. Indeed, why should one's simply having a justified belief imply even that one could be justified in holding the second-order beliefs appropriate to showing that it is justified? It would seem that just as a little child can be of good character even if unable to defend its character against attack, one can have a justified belief even if, in response to someone who doubts this, one could not show that one does. Supposing I have the sophistication to form a second-order belief that my belief that there is a cat before me is justified, the latter belief can be justified so long as the former is *true;* and it can be *true* that my belief about the cat is justified even if I am not justified in holding it or am unable to show that it is true. Justifying a second-order belief is a sophisticated process. The process is particularly sophisticated if the second-order belief concerns a special property like the justification of the original belief. Simply being justified in a belief about, say, the sounds around one is a much simpler matter. But confusion is easy here, particularly if the governing context is an imagined dialectic with a skeptic. Take, for instance, the question of how a simple perceptual belief "is justified." The very phrase is ambiguous. The question could be "By what process, say of reasoning, has the belief been (or might it be) justified?" or, on the other hand, "In virtue of what is the belief justified?" These are very different questions. The first invites us to conceive justification as a process of which the belief is a beneficiary, the second to conceive it as a property that a belief has, whether in virtue of its content, its genesis, or others of its characteristics or relations. Both aspects of the notion are important, but unfortunately much of our talk about justification makes it easy to run them together. A justified belief could be one that *has* justification or one that *has been* justified; and a request for someone's justification could be a request for a list of justifying factors or for a recounting of the process by which the person justified the belief.

Once we forswear the mistakes just pointed out, what argument is left to show the (positive) dependence of perceptual justification on coherence? I doubt that any plausible one remains, though given how hard it is to discern what coherence is, we cannot be confident that no plausible argument is forthcoming. Granted, one could point to the oddity of saying things like, "I am justified in believing that there is music playing, but I cannot justify this belief." Why is this odd if not because, when I have a justified belief, I can give a justification for it by appeal to beliefs that cohere with it? But consider this. Typically, in asserting something, say that there were lawsuits arising from an accident, I imply that, in some way or other, I *can* justify what I say, especially if the belief I express is, like this one, not plausibly thought to be grounded in a basic source such as perception. In the quoted sentence I deny that I can justify what I claim. The foundationalist must explain why that is odd, given that I can be justified in believing propositions even when I cannot show that I am (and may not even believe I am). The main point needed to explain this is that it is apparently my *asserting* that my belief is justified, rather than its being so, that gives the appearance that I must be able to give a justification of the belief. Compare "*She* is justified in believing that there is music playing, but (being an intuitive and unphilosophical kind of person) she cannot justify that proposition." This has no disturbing oddity, because the person said to have justification is not the one claiming it. Since she might be shocked to be asked to justify the proposition and might not know how to justify it, this statement might be true of her. We must not stop here, however. There are at least two further points.

First, there is quite a difference between *showing* that one is justified and simply *giving* a justification. I can give my justification for believing that there is music simply by indicating that I hear it. But this does not show that I am justified, at least in the sense of 'show' usual in epistemology. That task requires not just exhibiting what justifies one but also indicating conditions for being justified *and* showing that one meets them. It is one thing to cite a justifier, such as a clear perception; it is quite another to show that it meets a sufficiently high standard to *be* a justifier of the belief it grounds. Certainly skeptics – and probably most coherentists as well – have in mind something more like the latter process when they ask for a justification. Similarly – and this is the second point – where a regress of justification is, for fallibilist foundationalism, stopped by giving a (genuine) justification for the proposition in question, and the regress problem can be considered soluble because such stopping is possible, the skeptic will not countenance any stopping place, and certainly not any solution, that is not dialectically defended by argument showing that one is justified.[20]

To be sure, it may be that at least typically when we do have a justified belief we can give a justification for it. When I justifiedly believe that there is music playing, I surely can give a justification: that I hear it. But I need not *believe* that I hear it *before* the question of justification arises. That question leads me to focus on my circumstances, in which I first had a belief solely about the music. I also had a *disposition*, based on my auditory experience, to form the belief that *I hear* the music, and this is largely why, in the course of justifying that belief, I then *form* the further belief that I do hear it. But a disposition to believe something does not imply an actual belief of it, not even a dispositional one, as opposed to one manifesting itself in consciousness. If I am talking loudly and excitedly in a restaurant, I may be disposed to believe this – so much so that if I merely think of the proposition that I am talking loudly, I will form the belief that I am and lower my voice. But this disposition does not imply that I *already* believe that proposition – if I did, I

---

20. The prospects for offering skeptics a plausible argument along these lines are discussed in detail in Chapter 12, this volume.

would not be talking loudly in the first place. In the musical case, I tend to form the belief that I hear the music if, as I hear it, the question of whether I hear it arises; yet I need not have subliminally believed this already. The justification I offer, then, is not by appeal to coherence with other beliefs I already had – such as that I saw the turntable moving – but by reference to what has traditionally been considered a basic source of both justification and knowledge: perception. It is thus precisely the kind of justification that foundationalists are likely to consider appropriate for a non-inferential belief. Indeed, one consideration favoring foundationalism about both justification and knowledge, at least as an account of our everyday epistemic practices, including much scientific practice, is that typically we cease to offer justification or to defend a knowledge claim precisely when we reach a basic source.

VI. COHERENCE, FOUNDATIONS, AND JUSTIFICATION

There is far more to say in clarifying both foundationalism and coherentism. But if what I have said so far is correct, then we can at least understand their basic thrusts. We can also see how coherentism may respond to the regress argument – in part by distinguishing psychological from epistemic directness. And we can see how foundationalism may reply to the charge that, once made moderate enough to be plausible, it depends on coherence criteria rather than on grounding in experience and reason. The response is in part to distinguish negative from positive epistemic dependence and to argue that foundationalism does not make justification depend positively on coherence, but only negatively on (avoiding) incoherence.

One may still wonder, however, whether fallibilist foundationalism concedes enough to coherentism. Granted that it need not restrict the role of coherence any more than is required by the regress argument, it still denies that coherence is (independently) necessary for justification. As most plausibly developed, fallibilist foundationalism also denies that coherence is a *basic* (non-derivative) source of justification – or at least that if it is, it can produce *enough* justification to render a belief unqualifiedly justified or (given truth and certain other conditions) to make it knowledge. A single drop of even the purest water will not quench a thirst.

The moderate holistic coherentism formulated above is parallel in this: while it may grant foundationalism its typical psychological picture of how belief systems are structured, it denies that foundational justification is (independently) necessary for justification and that it is a basic source of justification, except possibly of degrees of justification too slight for knowledge or unqualifiedly justified belief.

The issue here is the difference in the two conceptions of justification. Broadly, foundationalists tend to hold that justification belongs to a belief, whether inferentially or directly, by virtue of its grounding in experience or reason; coherentists tend to hold that justification belongs to a belief by virtue of its coherence with one or more other beliefs. This is apparently a difference concerning basic sources. To be sure, my formulation may make coherentism sound foundationalistic, because justification is grounded not in an inferential relation to premises but in coherence itself, which sounds parallel to experience or reason. But note three contrasts with foundationalism: (1) the source of coherence is *cognitive*, because the coherence is an internal property of the belief system, whereas foundationalism makes no such restriction; (2) coherence is an inferential or at least epistemic generator, in the sense that it arises, with or without one's having inferential beliefs, from relations among beliefs or their propositional objects, e.g. from entailment, inductive support, or explanation of one belief or proposition by another, whereas experiential sources and (for pure coherentists) even rational sources are a non-inferential generator of belief (these sources can produce and thereby explain belief, but they do not, according to coherentism, justify it); and (3) S has *inferential access* to the coherence-making relations: S can wield them in inferentially justifying the belief that p, whereas foundationalism does not require such access to its basic sources. Still, I want to pursue just how deep the difference between foundationalism and coherentism is; for once foundationalism is moderately expressed and grants the truth of conceptual coherentism, and once coherentism is (plausibly) construed as consistent with psychological foundationalism, it may appear that the views differ far less than the prevailing stereotypes would have us think.

It should help if we first contrast fallibilist foundationalism with *strong foundationalism* and compare their relation to coherentism. If we use Descartes' version as a model, strong foundationalism is deductivist, takes foundational beliefs as indefeasibly justified, and allows coherence at most a limited generative role. To meet these conditions, it may reduce the basic sources of justification to reason and some form of introspection. Moreover, being committed to the indefeasibility of foundational justification, it would not grant that incoherence can defeat such justification. It would also concede to coherentists, and hence to any independence principle they countenance, at most a minimal positive role, say by insisting that if a belief is supported by two or more independent cohering sources, its justification is increased at most "additively," that is, only by combining the justification transmitted separately from each relevant basic source.

By contrast, what fallibilist foundationalism denies regarding coherence is only that it is a basic (hence sufficient) source of justification. Thus, coherence by itself does not ground justification, and hence the independence principle does not apply to sources that have *no* justification; at most, the principle allows coherence to raise the level of justification originally drawn from other sources to a level higher than it would reach if those sources did not mutually cohere. Similarly, if inference is a basic source of coherence (as some coherentists seem to believe), it is not a basic source of justification. It may enhance justification, as where one strengthens one's justification for believing someone's testimony by inferring the same point from someone else's. But inference *alone* does not generate justification. Suppose I believe several propositions without a shred of evidence and merely through wishful thinking. I might infer any number of others; yet even if by good luck I arrive at a highly coherent set of beliefs, I do not automatically gain justification for believing any of them. If I am floating in mid-ocean, strengthening my boat with added nails and planks may make it hang together more tightly and thereby make me feel secure; but if nothing indicates my location, there is no reason to expect this work to get me any closer to shore. Coherence may, to be sure, enable me to draw a beautiful map; but if there are no experiences I may rely on to connect it with reality, I may follow it forever to no avail. Even to be justified in *believing* that it will correspond with reality, I must have some experiential source to work from.

A natural coherentist reply is that when we consider examples of justified belief, not only do we always find some coherence, we also apparently find the right sort to account for the justification. This reply is especially plausible if – as I suggest is reasonable – coherentism as usually formulated is modified to include, in the coherence base, *dispositions to believe.* Consider my belief that music is playing. It coheres both with my beliefs about what records are in the house, what music my daughter prefers, my auditory capacities, etc., *and* with many of my dispositions to believe, say to form the belief that no one else in the house would play that music. Since such dispositions can themselves be well grounded, say in perception, or poorly grounded, e.g. in prejudice, they admit of justification and, when they produce beliefs, can lead to reasonable inferences. These dispositions are thus appropriate for the coherence base, and including them among generators of coherence is particularly useful in freeing coherentism from implausibly positing all the beliefs needed for the justificational capacities it tends to take to underlie justified belief. We need not "store" beliefs of all the propositions needed for our own system of justified belief; the disposition to believe them is enough. Given this broad conception of coherence, it is surely plausible to take coherence as at least necessary for justified belief. And it might be argued that its justification is based on coherence, not on grounding in experience.

Let us grant both that the musical case does exhibit a high degree of coherence among my beliefs and dispositions to believe and even that the coherence is necessary for the justification of my belief. It does not follow that the justification is based on the coherence. Coherence could still be at best a *consequential necessary condition* for justification, one that holds as a result of the justification itself or what that is based on, as opposed to a *constitutive necessary condition*, one that either expresses part of what it *is* for a belief to be justified or constitutes a basic source of it. The relation of coherence to the properties producing it might be analogous to that of heat to friction: a necessary product of it, but not part of what constitutes it.

If coherence is a constitutive necessary condition for justification, and especially if it is a basic source of it, we might expect to find cases in which the experiential and rational sources are absent, yet there is sufficient coherence for justified belief. But this is precisely what we do not easily find, if we ever find it. If I discover a set of my beliefs that intuitively cohere very well yet receive no support from what I believe (or at least am disposed to believe) on the basis of experience or reason, I am not inclined to attribute justification to any of them. To be sure, if the unit of coherence is large enough to include my actual beliefs, then because I have so many that *are* grounded in experience or reason (indeed, few that are not), I will almost certainly not in fact have any beliefs that, intuitively, seem justified yet are not coherent with some of my beliefs so grounded. This complicates assessment of the role of coherence in justification. But we can certainly imagine beings (or ourselves) artificially endowed with coherent sets of beliefs *not* grounded in experience or reason; and when we do, it appears that coherence does not automatically confer justification.

One might conclude, then, that it is more nearly true that coherence is based on justification (or whatever confers justification) than that the latter is based on the former. Further, the data we have so far considered can be explained on the hypothesis that both coherence among beliefs and their justification rest on the beliefs' being grounded (in an appropriate way) in the basic sources. For particularly if a coherence theory of the acquisition of concepts is true, one perhaps cannot have a belief justified by a basic source without having beliefs – or at least dispositions to believe – related in an intimate (and intuitively coherence-generating) way to that belief. One certainly cannot have a justified belief unless no incoherence defeats its justification. Given these two points, it is to be expected that on a fallibilist foundationalism, justification will normally imply coherence, both in the positive sense involving mutual support and in the weak sense of the absence of potential incoherence. There is some reason to think, then, that coherence is not a basic source of justification and is at most a consequentially necessary condition for it.

There is at least one more possibility to be considered, however: that *given* justification from foundational sources, coherence can generate more justification than S would have from those sources alone. If so, we might call coherence a *conditionally basic* source, in that, where there is already some justification from other sources, it can produce new justification. This bears on interpreting the independence principle. It is widely agreed that our justification increases markedly when we take into account independent sources of evidence, as where I confirm that there is music playing by moving closer to enhance my auditory impression and by visually confirming that a phonograph is playing. Perhaps what explains the dramatic increase in my overall justification here is not just "additivity" of foundational justification but also coherence as a further source of justification.

There is plausibility in this reasoning, but it is not cogent. For one thing, there really are no such additive quantities of justification. Perhaps we simply combine degrees of justification, so far as we can, on analogy with combinations of independent probabilities. Thus, the probability of at least one heads on two fair coin tosses is not $1/2 + 1/2$ (the two independent probabilities), which would give the event a probability of 1 and make it a certainty; the probability is $3/4$, i.e., 1 minus the probability of two tails, which is $1/4$. Insofar as degrees of justification are quantifiable, they combine similarly. Moreover, the relevant probability rules do not seem to depend on coherence; they seem to be justifiable by *a priori* reasoning in the way beliefs grounded in reason are commonly thought to be justifiable, and they appear to be among the principles one must *presuppose* if one is to give an account of how coherence contributes to justification. The (limited) analogy between probability and justification, then, does not favor coherentism and may well favor foundationalism.

There remains a contrast between, say, having six independent credible witnesses tell me that p on separate occasions which I do not connect with one another, and having them do so on a single occasion when I can note the coherence of their stories. In the first case, while my isolated beliefs cohere, I have no belief that they do, nor even a sense of their collective weight. This is not, to be sure, a case of six increments of isolated foundational justification versus a case of six cohering items of evidence. Both cases exhibit coherence; but in the second there is an additional belief (or justified disposition to believe): *that* six independent witnesses agree. Foundationalists as well as coherentists can plausibly explain how this additional belief increases the justification one has in the first case. It would be premature, then, to take cases like this to show that coherence is even a conditionally basic source of justification. It may only reflect other sources of justification, rather than contribute any.

VII. EPISTEMOLOGICAL DOGMATISM AND THE SOURCES OF JUSTIFICATION

Of the problems that remain for understanding the foundationalism–coherentism controversy, the one most readily clarified by the results of this chapter, is the dogmatism objection. This might be expressed as follows. If one can have knowledge or justified belief without being able to show that one does, and even without a premise from which to derive it, then the way is open to claim just about anything one likes, defending it by cavalierly noting that one can be justified without being able to show that one is. Given the conception of the foundationalism–coherentism controversy developed here, we can perhaps throw some new light on how the charge of dogmatism is relevant to each position.

The notion of dogmatism is not easy to characterize, and there have apparently been few detailed discussions of it in recent epistemological literature.[21] My focus will be dogmatism as an epistemological attitude or stance, not as a trait of personality. I am mainly interested in what it is to hold a belief dogmatically. This is probably the basic notion in any case: a general dogmatic attitude, like the personality trait of dogmatism, is surely in some way a matter of having or tending to have dogmatically held beliefs.[22]

It will be useful to start with some contrasts. Dogmatism in relation to a belief is not equivalent to stubbornness in holding it; for even if a dogmatically held belief cannot be easily given up, one could be stubborn in holding a belief simply from attachment to it, and without the required disposition to defend it or regard it as better grounded than alternatives. For similar reasons, psychological certainty in holding a belief does not entail dogmatism. Indeed, even if one is both psychologically certain of a simple logical truth *and* disposed to reject denials of it with confidence and to suspect even well-developed arguments against it as sophistical, one does not qualify as dogmatic. The content of one's view is important: even moderate insistence on a reasonably disputed matter may bespeak dogmatism; stubborn adherence to the self-evident need not. An attitude that would be dogmatic in holding one belief may not be so in holding another.

Dogmatic people are often closed-minded, and dogmatically held beliefs are often closed-mindedly maintained; but a belief held closed-mindedly need not be held dogmatically: it may be maintained with a guilty realization that emotionally one simply cannot stand to listen to challenges of it, and with an awareness that it might be mistaken. Moreover, although people who hold beliefs

---

21. One exception is David Shatz's "Foundationalism, Coherentism, and the Levels Gambit," *Synthese* 55, 1 (1983).
22. This suggestion may be controversial: an epistemic virtue theorist might argue that the trait is most basic and colors the attitude, and that these together are the basis for classifying beliefs as held dogmatically or otherwise. Most of my points will be neutral with respect to this priority issue.

dogmatically are often intellectually pugnacious in defending them, or even in trying to win converts, such pugnacity is not sufficient for dogmatism. Intellectual pugnacity is consistent with a keen awareness that one might be mistaken, and it may be accompanied by open-minded argumentation for one's view. Nor need a dogmatically held belief generate such pugnacity; I might be indisposed to argue, whether from confidence that I know or from temperament, and my dogmatism might surface only when I am challenged.

One thing all of these possible conceptions of dogmatism have in common is lack of a second-order component. But that component may well be necessary for a dogmatic attitude, at least of the full-blooded kind. Typically, a dogmatically held belief is maintained with a conviction (often unjustified) to the effect that one is right, e.g. that one knows, is amply justified, is properly certain, or can just see the truth of the proposition in question. Such a second-order belief is not, however, sufficient for a dogmatic attitude. This is shown by certain cases of believing simple logical truths. These can be held both with such a second-order belief and in the stubborn way typical of a dogmatic attitude yet not bespeak a dogmatic attitude. It might be held that in this case they would at least be held *dogmatically;* but if the imagined tenacity is toward, say, the principle that if a = b, and b = c, then a = c, one could not properly call the attitude dogmatic, and we might better speak of maintaining the belief steadfastly rather than dogmatically.

It might be argued, however, that even if the only examples of dogmatism so far illustrated are the second-order ones, there are still two kinds of dogmatism: first- and second-order. It may be enough, for instance, that one be *disposed* to have a certain belief, usually an unwarrantedly positive one, about the status of one's belief that *p.* Imagine that Tom thinks that Mozart is a far greater composer than Haydn, asserts it without giving any argument, and sloughs off arguments to the contrary. If he does not believe, but is disposed to believe on considering the matter, that his belief is, say, obviously correct, then he may qualify as dogmatically holding it. Here, then, there is no actual second-order attitude, but only a disposition to form one upon considering the status of one's belief. I want to grant that this kind of first-order pattern may qualify as dogmatism; but the account of it remains a second-order one, and it still seems that the other first-order cases we have considered, such as mere stubbornness in believing, are not cases of dogmatism. They may exhibit believing dogmatically, but that does not entail dogmatism as an epistemic attitude or trait of character, any more than doing something lovingly entails a loving attitude, or being a loving person. It appears, then, that at least the clear cases of dogmatically holding beliefs imply either second-order attitudes or certain dispositions to form them.

There may be no simple, illuminating way to characterize dogmatism with respect to a belief that *p;* but if there is, the following elements should be reflected at least as typical conditions and should provide the materials needed in appraising the foundationalism–coherentism controversy: (1) confidence that *p,* and significantly greater confidence than one's evidence or grounds warrant; (2) unjustified resistance to taking plausible objections seriously when they are intelligibly posed to one; (3) a willingness, or at least a tendency, to assert the proposition flat-out even in the presence of presumptive reasons to question it, including simply the conflicting views of one or more persons whom *S* sees or should see to be competent concerning the subject matter; and (4) a (second-order) belief, or disposition to believe, that one's belief is clearly true (or certainly true). Note, however, that (i) excessive confidence can come from mere foolhardiness and can be quite unstable; (ii) resistance to plausible objections may be due to intellectual laziness; (iii) a tendency to assert something flat-out can derive from mere bluntness; and (iv) a belief that one is right might arise not from dogmatism but merely from conceit, intellectual mistake (such as a facile anti-skepticism), or sheer error. Notice also that the notion of dogmatism is not just psychological, but also epistemic.

Of the four elements highly characteristic of dogmatism, the last may have the best claim to be an unqualifiedly necessary condition, and perhaps one or more of the others is necessary. The four are probably jointly sufficient; but this is not self-evident, and I certainly doubt that we can find any simple condition that is nontrivially sufficient, such as believing that one knows, or is justified in believing, that *p* (which one does believe), while also believing one has no reasons for believing that *p.*[23] This condition is not sufficient because it could stem from a certain view of knowledge and reasons, say a view on which one never has reasons (as op-

---

23. Shatz, op. cit., p. 107, attributes a similar suggestion to me (from correspondence), and it is appropriate to suggest here why I do not mean to endorse it.

posed to a basis) for believing simple, self-evident propositions. The condition also seems insufficient because it could be satisfied by a person who lacks the first three of the typical conditions just specified.

Let us work with the full-blooded conception of a dogmatically held belief summarized by conditions (1)–(4). What, then, may we say about the standard charge that foundationalism is dogmatic, in a sense implying that it invites proponents to hold certain beliefs dogmatically? This charge has been leveled on a number of occasions,[24] and some plausible replies have been made.[25] Given the earlier sections of this chapter, it should be plain that the charge is more likely to seem cogent if foundationalism is conceived as answering the dialectical regress problem, as it has apparently been taken to do by, e.g., Chisholm.[26] For in this case a (doxastic) stopping place in the regress generated by 'How do you know that *p*?' will coincide with the assertion of a second-order belief, such as that I know that *q*, e.g. that there is a window before me; and since knowledge claims are commonly justifiable by evidence, flatly stopping the regress in this way will seem dogmatic. Even if such a claim is justified by one's citing a non-doxastic state of affairs, such as a visual experience of a window, one is still asserting the existence of this state of affairs and hence apparently expressing knowledge: making what seems a tacit claim *to* it, though not actually claiming to *have* it.

We can formulate various second-order foundationalisms, for instance one which says that if *S* knows anything, then there is something that *S* directly knows *S* knows. But a foundationalist need not hold such a view, nor would one who does be committed to maintaining that many kinds of belief constitute such knowable

24. The dogmatism charge has been brought by, e.g., Bruce Aune in *Knowledge, Mind and Nature* (New York: Random House, 1967), pp. 41–3, and, by implication, by James Cornman and Keith Lehrer in *Philosophical Problems and Arguments,* 2nd ed. (New York: Macmillan, 1974), pp. 60–1. Alston goes so far as to say that "It is the aversion to dogmatism, to the apparent arbitrariness of putative foundations, that leads many philosophers to embrace some form of coherence or contextualist theory..." (op. cit., pp. 182–3).

25. See Alston, op. cit., for a reply (which supports mine) to the dogmatism charge.

26. A formulation of the regress problem by Chisholm is cited in note 3. For a contrasting formulation see Anthony Quinton, *The Nature of Things* (London: Routledge & Kegan Paul 1973), p. 119. Quinton, it is interesting to note, is sympathetic to the kind of moderate foundationalism that would serve as an answer to the problem in his formulation.

foundations, i.e., are knowledge one can know one has, or that every epistemic chain terminates in them. In any event, moderate foundationalists will be disinclined to hold a second-order foundationalism, even if they think that we do in fact have some second-order knowledge. For one thing, if foundational beliefs are only defeasibly justified, it is likely to be quite difficult to know that they are justified, because this requires warrant for attributing certain grounds to the belief and may also require justification for believing that certain defeaters are absent. This is not to deny that there are kinds of knowledge which one may, without having evidence for this, warrantedly and non-dogmatically say one has, for instance where the first-order knowledge is of a simple self-evident proposition. My point is that foundationalism as such, at least in moderate versions, need not make such second-order knowledge (or justification) a condition for the existence of knowledge (or justification) in general.[27]

If we raise the regress problem in the structural form, there is much less temptation to consider foundationalism dogmatic. For there is no presumption that, with respect to anything I know, I non-inferentially know that I know it (and similarly for justification). Granted, on the assumption that by and large I am entitled, without offering evidence, to assert what I directly know, it may seem that even moderate foundationalism justifies me in holding – and expressing – beliefs dogmatically. But this is a mistake. There is considerable difference between what I know or justifiably believe and what I may warrantedly assert without evidence. It is, e.g., apparently consistent with knowing that *p*, say that there is music playing, that I have some reason to doubt that *p*; I might certainly have reason to think others doubt it and that they should not be spoken to as if their objections could not matter. Thus, I might know, through my own good hearing, that *p*, yet be unwarranted in saying that I know it, and warranted, with only mod-

---

27. It is natural to read Descartes as holding a second-order foundationalism; but if he did, he was at least not committed to it by even his strong foundationalism. That requires indefeasible foundations, but it is his commitment to vindicating knowledge in the face of skepticism that apparently commits him to our having second-order knowledge. Similar points hold for Aristotle, who indeed may have taken our second-order knowledge to be at least limited; he said, e.g., "It is hard to be sure whether one knows or not; for it is hard to be sure whether one's knowledge is based on the basic truths appropriate to each attribute – the differentia of true knowledge" (*Posterior Analytics* 76a26–28).

erate confidence, even in saying simply that it is true. Here 'It is true' would *express*, but not *claim*, my knowledge; 'I know it' explicitly claims knowledge and normally implies that I have justification for beliefs about my objective grounds, not just about my own cognitive and perceptual state.

Nothing said here implies that one *cannot* be justified in believing what one holds dogmatically. That one's attitude *in* holding that p is not justified does not imply that one's holding that p is itself not justified. It might be possible, for all I have said, that in certain cases one might even be justified, overall, in taking a dogmatic attitude toward certain propositions. This will depend on, among other things, the plausibility of the proposition in question and the level of justification one has for believing that one is right. But typically, dogmatic attitudes are not justified, and moderate foundationalism, far from implying otherwise, can readily explain this.

Furthermore, once the defeasibility of foundational beliefs is appreciated, then even if one does think that one may assert the propositions in question without offering evidence, one will not take the attitudes or other stances required for holding a belief dogmatically. As the example of my belief about the music illustrates, most of the time one is likely to be open to counterargument and may indeed tend to be no more confident than one's grounds warrant. To be sure, fallibilism alone, even when grounded in a proper appreciation of defeasibility, does not preclude dogmatism regarding many of one's beliefs. But it helps toward this end, and it is natural for moderate foundationalists to hold a fallibilistic outlook on their beliefs, especially their empirical beliefs, and to bear it in mind in framing an overall conception of human experience.

If foundationalism has been uncritically thought to encourage dogmatism, coherentism has often been taken to foster intellectual openness. But this second stereotypic conception may be no better warranted than the first. Much depends, of course, on the kind of coherentism and on the temperament of its proponent. Let us consider these points in turn.

What makes coherentism seem to foster tolerance is precisely what leads us to wonder how it can account for knowledge (at least without a coherence theory of truth). For as coherentists widely grant, there are indefinitely many coherent systems of beliefs people might in principle have; hence, to suppose that mine embodies knowledge and thus truth, or even justification and thus a presumption of truth, while yours does not, is prima facie unwarranted. But the moment the view is developed to yield a plausible account of knowledge of the world (an external notion), say by requiring a role for observation beliefs and other cognitively spontaneous beliefs, as some coherents do, or by requiring beliefs accepted on the basis of a desire to believe truth and avoid error, as others do,[28] it becomes easy to think – and one can be warranted in thinking – that one's beliefs are more likely to constitute knowledge, or to be justified, than someone else's, especially if the other person(s) holds views incompatible with one's own. Indeed, while coherentism makes it easy to see how counterargument can be launched from a wide range of opposing viewpoints, it also provides less in the way of foundational appeals by which debates may be settled – and pretentions quashed. Is one likely to be less dogmatic where one thinks one can always encounter reasoned opposition from someone with a different coherent belief system, right or wrong, than where one believes one can be decisively shown to be mistaken by appeal to foundational sources of knowledge and justification? The answer is not clear; in any given case it will depend on a number of variables, including the temperament of the subject and the propositions in question. And could not my confidence that, using one or another coherent resource, I can always continue to argue for my view generate overconfidence just as much as my thinking that I (defeasibly) know something through experience or reason? Indeed, if coherence is as vague a notion as it seems, it seems quite possible both to exaggerate the extent of its support for one's own beliefs and underestimate the degree of coherence supporting an opposing belief. It turns out that coherentism can also produce dogmatism, even if its proponents have tended to be less inclined toward it than some foundationalists.

If there has been such a lesser inclination, it may be due to temperament, including perhaps a greater sympathy with skepticism, as much as to theoretical commitments. In any case, whether one dogmatically holds certain of one's beliefs surely does depend significantly on whether one is dogmatic in temperament or in certain segments of one's outlook. It may be that the tendency to seek justification in large patterns runs stronger in coherentists than in foundationalists, and that the latter tend more than the former to seek it instead in chains of argument or of inference. If

28. I have in mind, for the observation requirement, BonJour, op. cit., and, for the motivational requirement, Keith Lehrer, e.g. in *Knowledge*.

so, this could explain a systematic difference in the degree of dogmatism found in the two traditions. But these tendencies are only contingently connected with the respective theories. Foundationalism can account for the justificatory importance of large patterns, and coherentists commonly conceive argument and inference as prime sources of coherence. One can also wax dogmatic in insisting that a pattern is decisive in justification, as one can dogmatically assert that a single perceptual belief is incontrovertibly veridical.

One source of the charge of dogmatism, at least as advanced by philosophers, is of course the sense that skepticism is being flatly denied. Moreover, the skeptic in us tends to think that any confident assertion of a non–self-evident, non-introspective proposition is dogmatic. On this score, foundationalism is again likely to seem dogmatic if it is conceived as an answer to the dialectical regress formulation. For it may then seem to beg the question against skepticism. But again, foundationalism is not committed to the existence of any knowledge or justified belief; and even a foundationalist who maintains that there is some need not hold that we directly know that there is. Granted, foundationalists are more likely to say, at some point or other, that skepticism is just wrong than are coherentists, who (theoretically) can always trace new justificatory paths through the fabric of their beliefs. But if this is true, it has limited force: perhaps in some such cases foundationalists would be warranted in a way that precludes being dogmatic, and perhaps coherentists are in effect repeating themselves in a way consistent with dogmatic reassertion of the point at issue.

It turns out, then, that fallibilist foundationalism is not damaged by the dogmatism objection and coherentism is not immune to it. Far from being dogmatic, fallibilist foundationalism implies that even where one has a justified belief one cannot show to be justified, one may (and at least normally can) *give* a justification for it. As to coherentism, it, too, may be a refuge for dogmatists, at least those clever enough to find a coherent pattern by which to rationalize the beliefs they dogmatically hold.

CONCLUSION

The foundationalism–coherentism controversy cannot be settled in a single essay. But we can now appreciate some often neglected dimensions of the issue. One dimension is the formulation of the regress problem itself; another is the distinction between defeasibility and epistemic dependence; still another is that between consequential and constitutive necessary conditions; and yet another is between an unqualifiedly and a conditionally basic source. Even if coherence is neither a constitutive necessary condition for justification nor even a conditionally basic source of it, there is still reason to consider it important for justification. It may even be a *mark* of justification, a common effect of the same causes as it were, or a virtue with the same foundations. Coherence is certainly significant as suggesting a negative constraint on justification; for incoherence is a paradigm of what defeats justification.

I have argued at length for the importance of the regress problem. It matters considerably whether we conceive the problem dialectically or structurally, at least insofar as we cast foundationalism and coherentism in terms of their capacity to solve it. Indeed, while both coherentism and foundationalism can be made plausible on either conception, coherentism is perhaps best understood as a response to the problem *in* some dialectical formulation, and foundationalism is perhaps best understood as a response to it in some structural form. Taking account of both formulations of the regress problem, I have suggested plausible versions of both foundationalism and coherentism. Neither has been established, though fallibilist foundationalism has emerged as the more plausible of the two. In clarifying them, I have stressed a number of distinctions: between the process and the property of justification, between dispositional beliefs and dispositions to believe, between epistemically and psychologically foundational beliefs, between defeasibility and epistemic dependence, between constitutive and consequential necessary conditions for justification, and between unqualified and conditionally basic sources of it. Against this background, we can see how fallibilist foundationalism avoids some of the objections commonly thought to refute foundationalism, including its alleged failure to account for the defeasibility of most and perhaps all of our justification, and for the role of coherence in justification. Indeed, fallibilist foundationalism can even account for coherence as a mark of justification; the chief tension between the two theories concerns not whether coherence is necessary for justification, but whether it is a basic source of it.

It is appropriate in closing to summarize some of the very general considerations supporting a fallibilist foundationalism, since that is a position which some have apparently neglected – or supposed to be a contradiction in terms – and others have not distinguished from coherentism. First, the theory provides a plausible and reasonably straightforward solution to the regress problem. It selects what seems the best option among the four and does not interpret that option in a way that makes knowledge or justification either impossible, as the skeptic would have it, or too easy to achieve, as they would be if they required no grounds at all or only grounds obtainable without the effort of observing, thinking, or otherwise taking account of experience. Second, in working from the experiential and rational sources it takes as epistemically basic, fallibilist foundationalism (in its most plausible versions) accords with reflective common sense: the sorts of beliefs it takes as non-inferentially justified, or as constituting non-inferential knowledge, are pretty much those that, on reflection, we think people are justified in holding, or in supposing to be knowledge, without any more than the evidence of the senses or of intuition. Third, fallibilist foundationalism is psychologically plausible, in two major ways: the account it suggests of the experiential and inferential genesis of many of our beliefs apparently fits what is known about their origins and development; and, far from positing infinite or circular belief chains, whose psychology is at least puzzling, it allows a fairly simple account of the structure of cognition. Beliefs arise both from experience and from inference; some serve to unify others, especially those based on them; and their relative strengths, their changes, and their mutual interactions are all explicable within the moderate foundationalist assumptions suggested. Fourth, the theory serves to integrate our epistemology with our psychology and even biology, particularly in the crucial case of perceptual beliefs. What causally explains why we hold them – sensory experience – is also what justifies them.

From an evolutionary point of view, moreover, many of the kinds of beliefs that the theory (in its most plausible versions) takes to be non-inferentially justified – introspective and memorial beliefs as well as perceptual ones – are plainly essential to survival. We may need a map, and not merely a mirror, of the world to navigate it; but if experience does not generally mirror reality, we are in no position to move to the abstract level on which we can draw a good map. If a mirror without a map is insufficiently discriminating, a map without a mirror is insufficiently reliable. Experience that does not produce beliefs cannot guide us; beliefs not grounded in experience cannot be expected to be true.

Finally, contrary to the dogmatism charge, the theory helps to explain cognitive pluralism. Given that different people have different experiences, and that anyone's experiences change over time, people should be expected to differ from one another in their non-inferentially justified beliefs and, in their own case, across time; and given that logic does not dictate what is to be inferred from one's premises, people should be expected to differ considerably in their inferential beliefs as well. Logic does, to be sure, tell us what *may* be inferred; but it neither forces inferences nor, when we draw them, selects which among the permissible ones we will make. Particularly in the case of inductive inference, say where we infer a hypothesis as the best explanation of some puzzling event, our imagination comes into play; and even if we were to build from the same foundations as our neighbors, we would often produce quite different superstructures.

A properly qualified foundationalism, then, has much to recommend it and exhibits many of the virtues that have been commonly thought to be characteristic only of coherentist theories. Fallibilist foundationalism can account for the main connections between coherence and justification, and it can provide principles of justification to explain how justification that can be plausibly attributed to coherence can also be traced – by sufficiently complex and sometimes inductive paths – to basic sources in experience and reason.[29]

29. This chapter draws substantially on my "Foundationalism, Coherentism, and Epistemological Dogmatism," *Philosophical Perspectives* 2 (1988), 407–59 (edited by James E. Tomberlin). I thank Louis P. Pojman for many helpful comments on an earlier draft of much of the material and for permission to use selected passages from my two chapters in his book *The Theory of Knowledge: Contemporary Readings* (Belmont, Calif.: Wadsworth, 1992).

PART II

KNOWLEDGE AND JUSTIFICATION

Chapter 5

The limits of self-knowledge

Hume maintained that "since all actions and sensations of the mind are known to us by consciousness, they must necessarily appear in every particular what they are, and be what they appear."[1] Descartes maintained a very similar doctrine,[2] and Locke and Berkeley held at least part of the doctrine.[3] I shall not try to set out precisely what any of these philosophers thought about self-knowledge; I cite them simply as proponents of the general view which I shall be examining in this paper: namely, that each of us has a special epistemic authority about his own mental life. This view is still widely held,[4] particularly in the form of the thesis that one's sincere avowals of current mental states are incorrigible, i.e., such that, necessarily, no one ever has overriding reason to think them false.

It is important to distinguish the doctrine of incorrigibility from the doctrines of infallibility and indubitability.[5] As I construe these terms, to say that sincere first-person, present-tense reports of

1. *A Treatise of Human Nature*, ed. L. A. Selby-Bigge (Oxford, 1888), p. 190.
2. In *Meditation II* Descartes says such things as that the proposition that it seems to me that I see light "cannot be false"; and that "I see clearly that there is nothing which is easier for me to know than my mind." See *The Philosophical Works of Descartes*, trans. E. S. Haldane and G. R. T. Ross (Cambridge, 1931).
3. See, e.g., Locke's *Essay*, Bk. Four, ch. II, Section 1; and Berkeley's *Principles*, Section 22.
4. Among the recent proponents of incorrigibility are Norman Malcolm, e.g., in *Knowledge and Certainty* (Englewood Cliffs, 1964), pp. 84 and 93; George Nakhnikian, "Incorrigibility," *Philosophical Quarterly*, XVIII (1968), e.g., p. 207; and U. T. Place, "The Infallibility of Our Knowledge of Our Own Beliefs," *Analysis*, XXXI (1971).
5. These and other modes of privileged access are lucidly distinguished by William P. Alston in "Varieties of Privileged Access," *American Philosophical Quarterly*, VIII (1971). For the most part my definitions of the relevant epistemic terms are close to Alston's.

mental states are infallible is to say that necessarily, if the subject (S) makes such a report, then it is true; and to say that these reports are indubitable is to say that necessarily, if S makes such a report, then no one ever has good grounds for doubting it. Like incorrigibilists, proponents of these stronger theses assume that no one except S can enjoy such epistemic authority concerning S's mental states.

One reason for distinguishing these three doctrines of epistemic privilege is that we can then see clearly that attacks, such as those by Sellars[6] and Aune,[7] on the idea that empirical knowledge rests on indubitable foundations, need not apply to incorrigibility. Indeed, at least one writer who rejects this foundations picture, *viz.* Richard Rorty, has defended a kind of incorrigibility;[8] and there are others who defend incorrigibility but do not seem to hold the foundations view.[9] One can also hold a qualified foundations view, such as Quinton[10] suggests, without accepting incorrigibility. But since infallibility and indubitability each entail – though neither is entailed by – incorrigibility, if the latter doctrine is false, so are the other two. For these reasons, and because incorrigibility is more often defended than infallibility or indubitability, I shall concentrate on incorrigibility.

The doctrine of incorrigibility has been ably attacked in recent years.[11] But the arguments so far brought against it seem either

---

6. See, e.g., "Empiricism and the Philosophy of Mind," in Herbert Feigl and Michael Scriven (eds.), *Minnesota Studies in the Philosophy of Science*, Vol. I (Minneapolis, 1956).
7. See *Knowledge, Mind and Nature* (New York, 1967).
8. See "Incorrigibility as the Mark of the Mental," *Journal of Philosophy*, LXVII (1970).
9. See Place, *op. cit.*
10. Anthony Quinton, "The Foundations of Knowledge," in Bernard Williams and Alan Montifiore (eds.), *British Analytical Philosophy* (London, 1966).
11. The most plausible attack I know of is by D. M. Armstrong in "Is Introspective Knowledge Incorrigible?" *Philosophical Review*, LXXII (1963), reproduced, in essentials, in his *A Materialist Theory of the Mind* (London, 1968). J. L. Austin has also criticized the doctrine of incorrigibility; but I believe he does not show that anyone *other* than S could have overriding reason to deny a sincere occurrent MSR (mental state report). He shows only the weaker point that various considerations might make it unreasonable for S not to retract such a report. Since this still leaves S in a position of ultimate authority, some incorrigibilists might allow it. See, e.g., *Sense and Sensibilia* (Oxford, 1962), pp. 42, 112, and 114. It appears that A. J. Ayer's criticisms of infallibility (which he calls incorrigibility) in *The Problem of Knowledge* (Harmondsworth, Middlesex, 1956) also show at most that S might have overriding reason to retract a sincere occurrent mental state report. See esp. pp. 65–66.

unsound or inadequately defended. In particular, philosophers who have used possible neurophysiological evidence against the doctrine have not noticed certain weaknesses in their arguments. Moreover, neurophysiological considerations have been overemphasized at the expense of other points that are at least as important. Thirdly, attacks on incorrigibility have largely neglected the positive task of setting out the analogies and disanalogies between our knowledge of our own mental states and our knowledge of the mental states of others. This paper will attempt to fill these gaps.

I

Let us first focus the issue. Typically, what has been thought incorrigible is sincere first-person, present-tense reports of the existence – not so much the properties – of mental states (sincere MSRs). 'I am in pain' (but not 'My afterimage is octagonal') would be a typical example. The mental phenomena most often thought to be the subject of incorrigible reports are sensations (pains, afterimages, ringing in the ears); mental events (silent utterances, resolutions, sudden thoughts); and mental processes (chains of inferences, deliberations, silent soliloquies). Since it is natural to think of these as occurrences, I shall for convenience call them occurrent states and contrast them with dispositional mental states, e.g. wants and intentions. At least a good part of the distinction between dispositional and occurrent properties seems to be this: the former, including dispositional mental states, are such that a substance can have them even if, for the entire period it has them, they do not manifest themselves; whereas occurrent properties, including occurrent mental states, are such that during at least a substantial part of the time a substance has them it must do or undergo or experience something such that its doing, undergoing, or experiencing this is at least partly constitutive of what it is for a substance to have the property in question. S may, e.g., intend to do A, without ever having thoughts about doing A; but S cannot have an afterimage without experiencing something, and experiencing whatever this is is at least partly constitutive of having an afterimage. However, to say that pains, afterimages, etc. are occurrent is not to say they are "self-presenting," i.e., such that if they are present then S directly knows they are. A mental state's

169

being occurrent entails only that S is experiencing, doing, or undergoing *something;* and, as I hope to show, such constitutive manifestations, as we might call them, need not carry an unmistakable label saying what kind of state they (in part) constitute. Let me add, however, that even if the suggested contrast between dispositional and occurrent properties is quite inadequate to capture the distinction between them, the epistemological issues that concern us can be adequately dealt with by simply confronting the thesis of incorrigibility with various examples. For there is wide agreement that pains and visual sensations are representative of the mental phenomena to which it is intended to apply; and even the incorrigibilist would agree that the thesis stands or falls depending on whether it holds for phenomena of this sort.

Now although incorrigibility has been defended for reports of certain dispositional mental states,[12] recent defenses of it are usually restricted to occurrent mental states. I shall thus concentrate on the latter. It is also desirable to simplify the discussion by obviating questions about errors which arise in sincere MSRs because of such things as slips of the tongue and poor wording. I shall thus construe incorrigibility as applicable primarily to beliefs and only derivatively to avowals: specifically, as the thesis that necessarily, for any subject, S, and any occurrent mental state, M, if S believes he is now in M then no one ever has overriding reason to think S is not in M. Let us call such beliefs first-person, present-tense, occurrent mental state beliefs (MSBs), where 'occurrent' applies not to these beliefs, but to the states they are about. I shall suppose that there is overriding reason to believe a proposition false if and only if there are good grounds for believing it false, and the grounds for believing it false are better than any grounds there are for believing it to be true. Some philosophers would deny that we can speak of a person as *believing* such things as that he is in pain. But this view has been discredited by critics,[13] and if my main arguments are sound, that will show that it is intelligible to speak of beliefs of the kind here referred to.

Imagine that S is a fourteen-year-old boy who has an intense fear of heights and is asked to climb a mountain with his fellow campers. As preparations are being made, he complains of a pain

---

12. For example, by U. T. Place, *op. cit.*
13. See, e.g., Richard Rorty, "Wittgenstein, Privileged Access, and Incommunicability," *American Philosophical Quarterly*, VII (1970). Cf. D. W. Hamlyn, *The Theory of Knowledge* (New York, 1970), esp. pp. 225–232.

in his left knee and limps conspicuously. Now suppose that he is excused from the hike and that immediately after the hikers leave he goes to the tennis courts and, with no visible difficulty, plays. Asked whether his knee still hurts, he says that it does but that he is playing in spite of it. Assume that everything in his manner and in the tone of his complaint suggests sincerity, and that he is known to be scrupulously honest and to have often told the truth knowing it was to his disadvantage. Granted, S's desire for an excuse *could* have temporarily caused a pain in his knee which might then have diminished. But suppose that when S is asked whether the pain is better he says no – something he might well say just a few minutes after the hikers leave. Let us also assume that the knee is not tender to the touch, that a medical inspection shows no abnormality, that S's history has been one of fine physical health, and that there has been no injury to the knee or surrounding area.[14]

One may now say that S's enthusiasm for tennis has overshadowed the pain, which is nevertheless present. This seems possible, though it is not at all likely for a pain in the knee sufficient to have caused a conspicuous limp. But suppose we know that S hates to entertain the thought that he is afraid to do things boys can normally do easily, has a very strong need to feel masculine, and believes that to carry on despite pain is a mark of true masculinity. Assume too that very similar situations have occurred before, sometimes with others of S's limbs, but always without medically ascertainable causes of pain, and always at the right moment to avoid mountain hikes – or cave explorations, which also frighten S. We now have a good understanding of how it would be psychologically comforting to S to believe he has a pain in his knee; and we have medical and strong behavioral evidence that he does not have pain there. The question we must ask is whether it is possible that, though S believes, and desperately needs to believe, that he has a pain in his left knee, he has no pain at all.

Note first that here there is a conflict among our criteria for a

---

14. Armstrong has proposed a similar example. But it is sketchy and lacks cogency. He says only this:

> I say, perfectly sincerely, that my hand hurts. But my behavior seems no more than a perfunctory imitation of a man with a hurt hand. I wring the hand briefly, but the next moment I behave as if it were not hurt at all. Perhaps I only think I am in pain? (*A Materialist Theory of the Mind*, p. 110)

pain in the knee, not just ordinary evidence against S's avowal; and the preponderance of "criterial weight" is against the avowal, while there is also excellent reason to suppose the avowal sincere. In the light of this, I am inclined to say both that it is possible that S's belief that he is in pain is false, and that we could have overriding reason to say it is false. The plausibility of this conclusion is strengthened when we reflect on the not uncommon practice of regarding with incredulity certain complaints of pain by neurotic invalids who crave attention, or spoiled children who are being ignored. [15] The complaints in question are not regarded as insincere, particularly since in such cases there is often *some* slight discomfort; but when such people's behavior fails to cohere with the supposition that they are in pain and is at the same time readily interpretable as meant, however subliminally, to get attention, it seems quite proper to disbelieve at least some of their perfectly sincere complaints of pain. It is true that in such cases the complaint is not made reflectively on the basis of careful introspection. But if we accept – as I believe we should – the possibility of reasonably overriding some sincere MSR's of the sort described, then it seems at least as reasonable to suppose we could do the same with the greater evidence available in the case of the adolescent boy, whose reports of pain are reflective and might even be based on careful introspection.

In any case, the argument can be carried further. It seems possible that, for persons, every mental state is uniquely correlated with some neurophysiological condition and that such correlations could be discovered using electroencephalographic (EEG) equipment. An EEG machine could then be used to check on the sincerity and truth of MSRs; indeed, this would be possible even if only a suitable subset of mental states were uniquely correlated with brain states. In the case of S, if the machine could be employed quickly and without interfering with whatever states it is meant to ascertain, then we might see whether, during the tennis game, it shows the appropriate neural patterns for a belief that one has a pain in the left knee, and the absence of the patterns appropriate to having such a pain. To be sure, S might be neurally abnormal; but this could be ruled out by testing him when there is no question of either insincerity or error in the MSRs being verified.

15. I am grateful to John King-Farlow for pointing out examples of this sort to me.

This kind of EEG argument has been advanced by a number of philosophers.[16] To its proponents and many others it seems so obviously cogent that serious difficulties have been overlooked. One problem is how physiologists could discover correlates of beliefs that one is in pain which are *different* from the correlates of being in pain, unless they *assume,* and indeed correctly assume, that believing one is in pain does not entail being in pain. The incorrigibilist would charge that an EEG argument which assumes this begs the question against the thesis of infallibility, which most incorrigibilists would not give up without argument, even though they need not hold it. This charge seems perfectly warranted, unless infallibility has been discredited independently of the EEG argument or physiologists can find cases of pains that S does not believe he has. I shall not make either assumption, since a case against incorrigibility can be stronger if it does not presuppose either. But how can an EEG argument avoid these assumptions?

Suppose that physiologists first establish neural correlates of clearly corrigible beliefs. They might then be able to say what sorts of neural conditions are correlated with beliefs in general. They might also be able to compare these conditions with those that obtain when S (a) orally or (b) silently affirms a proposition without believing it. This would make it possible to see what correlates are associated with avowals that do express belief, in *addition* to the correlates of avowals that do not. Now physiologists might assume that in fact occurrent MSBs are always true. But they might note that the correlates of such beliefs differ from those of S's affirming the relevant propositions *without* believing them, in ways in which other belief correlates do not differ from the correlates of S's affirmations of the propositions in question without believing them. This is to be expected. For believing that one is, say, in pain, differs from merely affirming it, not just in the way assenting in general differs from mere affirming, but also in implying (typically, at least) the truth of the proposition believed. Since the truth of a proposition ascribing a mental state to S should be reflected in S's EEG patterns, the physiologist could reasonably hypothesize that

16. See Armstrong's *A Materialist Theory of the Mind,* pp. 108–109; Paul E. Meehl, "The Compleat Autocerebroscopist," in Paul K. Feyerabend and Grover Maxwell (eds.), *Mind, Matter, and Method* (Minneapolis, 1966); and Gregory Sheridan, "The Electroencephalogram Argument Against Incorrigibility," *American Philosophical Quarterly,* VIII (1971).

even if believing one is in pain entails being in pain, the extra elements in the correlates of such beliefs represent the pain whose existence the beliefs entail.

We can now formulate a new EEG argument. What could be discovered is that (i) *S* does not have the *usual* correlates of a belief that one has a pain in one's left knee; but (ii) *S* is in a neural state which differs from the state correlated with affirming that one has a pain in one's left knee, when one does not believe this, just in the way the state correlated with believing that, say, there are tigers in India, differs from the state correlated with affirming this without believing it; (iii) there is no activity in the circuits that carry impulses from pain receptors in the left knee to the part of *S*'s brain whose states are correlated with beliefs; and (iv) *S* satisfies none of the neural conditions we always find accompanying insincere avowals. (i)–(iv) would not *prove* that *S* falsely believes he has a pain in his left knee; but taken together with the behavioral and medical evidence cited already, they make this conclusion very plausible. Moreover, this EEG argument nowhere presupposes the falsity of the thesis of infallibility or that of incorrigibility. It simply points to a possible case in which, *given* the kind of behavioral and medical evidence already cited, it would be reasonable to abandon infallibility and even incorrigibility.

There is, however, another important objection to the EEG argument. It has been argued that because the required correlations must be established by appeal to the kinds of reports whose incorrigibility they are used to undermine, they could never outweigh the authority of the reports.[17] If you can discover the correlates of pain beliefs only by having *S* tell you he is in pain, you cannot use these correlations to override such reports. At least two points should be made in reply to this argument.

First, it is not valid. For even if we *discover* a law (or lawlike correlation) by using certain data, if the law *explains* much more than the data on which it was initially based, it may be legitimately used to correct reports of data of that kind. Nor need we even assume that *all* the initial data reports were correct. Suppose we

---

17. Harold Morick makes a stronger claim: the EEG argument "points to the fact that one can deny ultimate epistemic authority to a man's avowal *only if* one has granted this authority to other avowals." See "Is Ultimate Epistemic Authority a Distinguishing Characteristic of the Psychological?" *American Philosophical Quarterly*, VI (1969). My reply to the weaker thesis should show why this claim is too strong.

use mercury thermometers to establish that (and how much) gases expand when heated. We may then be able to construct a gas thermometer. Now suppose the gas thermometer correlates very highly with different mercury thermometers, measures temperatures below the freezing point of mercury and above its boiling point, and proves superior to mercury thermometers in making predictions, on the basis of gas thermometer readings, of processes that seem regular, e.g. the amount of expansion of metals when heated. Would it not now make perfectly good sense to correct a deviant reading of one of our original mercury thermometers by appeal to the gas thermometer? The situation is crucially analogous to the EEG case. Once the relevant correlations are established, (1) they might be checked against other MSRs than those used in discovering them; (2) they might be found to hold for psychological and bodily states clearly not the subject of incorrigible belief, e.g. attitudes, certain emotions, and certain bodily malfunctions that S himself can discover only by medical techniques; and (3) the correlations might yield better predictions of behavior than sincere reports of the same states. For instance, predictions of behavior based on the neural correlates of certain of S's wants and beliefs might tend to be more accurate than predictions based on sincere avowals of these same wants and beliefs; and this might also apply to predictions based on avowals of occurrent mental states, e.g., resolutions. Granted, temperature and pain differ significantly; e.g., one might argue that temperature is purely dispositional. But even so, my argument would hold with *rise* in temperature substituted for temperature. Moreover, the point of the argument is mainly the negative one of showing the falsity of the assumption, crucial for the validity of the objection, that if one kind of correlate of a thing (EEG reports) is discovered through another kind of correlate (where the latter, e.g. verbal reports, may have "criterial" status), then reports of the former kind can never outweigh reports of the latter kind.

My second point is that the premise of the argument is not unqualifiedly true. The relevant correlations *need* not be discovered solely or even mainly through the kind of reports whose incorrigibility is at issue. For instance, (a) there are obvious ways to create pains; (b) the sensory imagery of normal persons nearly always corresponds to what they are exposed to, e.g. bright yellow light; (c) hunger and thirst can be produced by deprivation of food and water; and (d) when people are speaking or reading, it is very probable that their thoughts correspond in some way to the relevant words. Not that the neural correlates of speaking certain words should be the same as those of uttering the same words silently; but one would expect some overlap between the two sets of correlates, and someone might systematically compare the correlates of passages "thought out" in various ways, e.g. read aloud, read silently, and recited from memory.

It thus appears that EEG techniques could be used to verify or disconfirm occurrent MSBs. If so – and, I am inclined to think, even if not – there may in special cases be overriding reason to reject such beliefs. I have not discussed many kinds of occurrent states, but I think the above considerations apply to the other cases. Consider, e.g., *S*'s believing he seems to see yellow, or believing he seems to taste something burned. Motivational factors can create a tendency to err here just as in the case of the knee; and certainly EEG techniques would be equally relevant to verifying reports of these and other occurrent states.

It is important to add, however, that nothing I have said implies that sincere MSRs are not in general extremely reliable. They surely are. Typically, it would be absurd to question a sincere MSR, or to ask someone whether he is sure he is (say) in pain, or how he knows it. Nor do we normally need to have evidence to be able to say what mental states we are in. But all this also typically applies to reports that, e.g., one is writing at a desk. It plainly does not follow that such reports are incorrigible.

On the other hand, for many psychological states, including some – such as wants and beliefs – which have been included in the domain of incorrigibility, there are cases in which the reliability of sincere MSRs drops dramatically. Take, e.g., some people's conviction (firm belief) that they believe all human beings should be treated equally. One reason for these gradations in reliability is the scope of the phenomena to be known. Wants and beliefs, e.g., especially the kind one is likely to be deluded in ascribing to oneself, are long-standing compared with the short segments of occurrent mental states that are the subject of occurrent MSRs. Furthermore, (a) dispositional mental states can be present without manifesting themselves, whereas occurrent mental states cannot; (b) typically the former have a wider variety of manifestations than the latter; and (c) behavior that really manifests one kind of disposition, e.g. a desire for revenge, can easily appear to be due to another disposition, e.g. fond possessiveness. This kind of confusion is much less likely with occurrent mental states. These are among the reasons why occurrent MSBs are far less likely to be false than dispositional MSBs.

II

Even if all of the foregoing is accepted, we should consider a qualified thesis of incorrigibility. Rorty holds that "There are no accepted procedures by applying which it would be rational to come to believe that not-p, given S's belief that p,"[18] where p is the object of an occurrent MSB. Since this thesis is relative to our present knowledge, its plausibility depends on the acceptability of arguments against incorrigibility such as those appealing to motivational influences on S. For the relevant EEG techniques are at best a thing of the future. But suppose there are no currently *accepted* procedures for rationally rejecting occurrent MSBs. As Rorty realizes, that is a very weak claim, since there may be procedures for doing this which it is even *now* rational to employ, though none is "accepted." Thus, the most his thesis implies is epistemic privilege dependent on the extent of our neuropsychological knowledge. This is of limited significance compared to the doctrine that incorrigibility is inherent in the logic of occurrent mental concepts.

However, in the light of Rorty's thesis that a kind of incorrigibility is the mark of the mental, there is an important further move the incorrigibilist may make. It is natural for philosophers who rely heavily on the notion of a criterion – as many incorrigibilists do[19] – to suppose that if a new procedure is allowed, even if only with collateral evidence, to override one of the criteria of application of a concept, then whether we realize it or not, we have adopted a different concept. Thus, it might be held that if EEG considerations could outweigh a sincere MSR, then we are operating with a new concept of a mental state.

Now if occurrent mental states were exhaustively definable in terms of S's tending to make sincere avowals of them, this would

18. Rorty, "Incorrigibility as the Mark of the Mental," p. 417.
19. For example, Norman Malcolm in, among other writings, "Wittgenstein's *Philosophical investigations*," *Philosophical Review*, LXIII (1954); perhaps Sydney Shoemaker, *Self-Knowledge and Self-Identity* (Ithaca, 1963); and perhaps Rorty in his defense of incorrigibility.

be true. But they are surely not so definable. For one thing, if we are to speak of criteria at all, S's avowals of occurrent mental states are not the only criterion for such states. For instance, certain physical stimuli, such as pinpricks and exposure to bright yellow lights, are among the criteria for applying 'is in pain' and 'has a sensation of yellow' to perceptually normal persons exposed to these stimuli in certain ways. That there are such non-verbal criteria must not be overlooked. The incorrigibilist may contend that if EEG data can outweigh sincere MSRs, then such data must have *acquired* criterial status. But we must distinguish between a "criterial relation" and a strong evidential one. The distinction is not sharp; but clearly, from the fact that, taken together with other information – indeed "criterial" information – in cases like our pain example, EEG data can outweigh a sincere MSR, it does not follow that part of the meaning of the relevant mental words must be given in terms of the correlated EEG data. For instance, no one need use such data to teach or even explain the meanings of psychological terms, and (let us hope!) such data would not be widely used in ascertaining people's mental states. With the establishment of a comprehensive neuropsychological theory, we *could* come to count EEG readings among our criteria for the application of mental terms. But this is not implied by allowing such readings, together with behavioral indications, to outweigh sincere MSRs in *some* cases.

III

If our beliefs about what occurrent mental states we are in are corrigible, the question naturally arises of how these beliefs differ in epistemic status from beliefs to the effect that these same states exist in others. A number of important contrasts remain, and they bring out truths underlying incorrigibilism.

Note first that our knowledge of our present occurrent mental states is normally direct, i.e., not based on other knowledge or other beliefs. By this I mean that there is no other knowledge or belief on the part of S which constitutes a reason of his such that it is at least in part for this reason that he believes the proposition in question. (He may *have* some other knowledge or belief that *could* justify him in believing it and could become a reason of his for believing it, provided the former *is* not a reason of his for believing the proposition.) It is possible, however, that S's believing that, say, he has a yellow patch in his visual field, might be based in part on his knowledge that this proposition is supported by EEG data he is hearing over a speaker. But apart from such rare "over-determined" knowledge and a few similar cases, self-knowledge in the domain of occurrent mental states is always direct. This obviously does not hold for our beliefs about others' mental states, occurrent or dispositional.

Our occurrent MSBs are also normally far more reliable than our beliefs ascribing occurrent mental states to others. (I say 'normally' to allow for special cases in which there is good reason, such as we have seen, to expect error.) This greater reliability exists in part because, other things being equal, direct beliefs are more reliable than indirect; and this is in part because the former are not liable to error due to the falsity of a belief on which they are based, a fact which may have led some philosophers to think, wrongly, that direct beliefs must be incorrigible.[20] Moreover, normally MSBs arise in a rather direct way from the states they are about. MSBs are thus normally at least in part effects of the very states whose presence they "report." That we suppose this helps to explain why we take sincere MSRs as excellent evidence of the states they report. On both counts, our knowledge of our own occurrent (and even of most of our dispositional) mental states contrasts with our beliefs about these states in others: the latter beliefs are not direct; nor do they arise from the states they are about in the usually inevitable and normally direct way in which our own MSBs arise from the states they are about. This is not to imply that we normally have reasons for our MSBs or that we need reasons for them. "Causes" of a belief need not be reasons for it.

If the sincere utterance of MSRs is normally excellent evidence for their truth, one might well conclude that MSBs are always warranted. If so, they differ in another important respect from the counterpart beliefs about others. Since one may be warranted in believing something false, and since the conditions under which an occurrent MSB may be false are very special and occur at best rarely, it is quite plausible to hold that at least *occurrent* MSBs are always warranted. This seems to be as a matter of fact virtually always true. But suppose S is often mistaken about certain of his

20. See, e.g., Charles Pailthorp, "Is Immediate Knowledge Reason Based?" *Mind*, LXXVII (1969), p. 555.

present occurrent mental states, e.g. his pains, though his behavior in general shows that he fully understands pain vocabulary. Need all *his* beliefs ascribing pains to himself be warranted? Surely not. This possibility shows that "self-warrant" is not a *necessary* epistemic characteristic of occurrent MSBs. *A fortiori*, it is not a necessary epistemic characteristic of dispositional MSBs. Thus, even in respect of self-warrant we cannot draw an unqualified contrast between our beliefs about ourselves and their counterparts regarding others.

Perhaps, however, there is an unqualified contrast in respect of what Alston calls autonomy,[21] where to say that a domain of knowledge or belief is autonomous for persons in a certain privileged position is to say that their beliefs about that domain are such that necessarily, *if* they are true they are warranted. Our question, then, is whether every *true* MSB must be warranted. The answer will be negative if it is possible for S to believe truly that he is in a certain occurrent mental state, but believe this for the wrong reason(s). This might seem impossible because normally S believes such propositions only directly and hence not *for* any reason. But S's believing that, say, he has a pain in his left knee *could* be based on an EEG reading. Suppose further that, because he should realize that his machine is unreliable, the reading does not warrant him in believing he has a pain in his left knee. But, one may object, if he does have such a pain, how could he not also believe this directly, in which case his belief would be warranted? Suppose he had previously found himself apparently mistaken, in very similar circumstances, about there being a pain in that knee. Then, prior to his EEG reading, he might justifiably suspend judgment. Hence he would not believe directly, and would not be warranted in directly believing, that he has a pain in his left knee. But neither would he be warranted in believing this indirectly; for he believes it *only* because of his reading of a machine which he ought to see is unreliable. Thus, a true occurrent MSB might not be warranted, and hence the domain of occurrent MSBs is not unqualifiedly autonomous. *A fortiori*, the domain of dispositional MSBs is not autonomous.

So far, we have been concerned to see how sharp a contrast can be drawn between our beliefs about our current mental states and our beliefs about the mental states of others. But we have yet to

---

21. Alston, *op. cit.*, p. 234.

ask whether, as some philosophers have thought, occurrent mental states are "self-intimating" (Ryle's term); i.e., such that they cannot be present without S's knowing this. (Note that since neither believing nor knowing is an occurrent state, this thesis of "omniscience" does not lead to an infinite regress.) If our earlier discussion is correct, it refutes this thesis and with it another part of the general doctrine of privileged access. For it seemed that S could indeed be in an occurrent mental state (pain) without justifiably believing and hence without knowing that he is. We did not show, however, that S could be in such a state without *believing* he is. Thus, perhaps a significant part of the doctrine of omniscience holds. Let us explore this.

It could be argued that one can have, say, pains and yellow afterimages only if one feels pain and seems to see yellow, and that these feelings and "percepts" entail, respectively, believing that one has pain (in the area in which one feels it) and believing that one seems to see yellow. There may be no such entailment; but that there is not does not follow from our conclusion that S can believe he is in such states without being in them. For no part of the doctrine of omniscience entails infallibility or even incorrigibility. Moreover, suppose we countenance unconscious beliefs, as we surely should, i.e., beliefs S can come to know or believe he has, only with the help of another person or by some special self-scrutiny. Then, even if S can, say, feel pain without consciously believing that he has it, he might unconsciously believe this. That would explain how he could feel pain, "know" that he has it, yet sincerely deny that he has it. One may object that the belief component of genuine knowledge cannot be unconscious. But suppose S justifiably and truly believes, though unconsciously, that he cannot have the affection of a certain attractive but aloof female acquaintance. Can we not say that he unconsciously *knows* this, particularly if, despite limping protestations that he can win her affection, he acts as if he knew better? Now if the belief component of knowledge can be unconscious, perhaps our case against the autonomy of self-knowledge does not refute the doctrine of omniscience. For it could be contended that if S is, say, in pain and does not consciously believe he is, he cannot help unconsciously believing he is and is warranted in thus believing it. It would be desirable, then, to have a further argument against omniscience.

Even if the thesis of omniscience is not refuted by my argument against autonomy, why must we say that, if S is in an occurrent mental state and does not consciously believe he is, he must unconsciously believe he is? It seems possible for S to have a pain in his knee, or a yellow afterimage, yet believe that he has a peculiar but not painful sensation in his knee, or that he sees only a patch of medium grey. For one thing, as most people's experience and reflection confirms, 'pain', 'hunger', and at least most other sensation terms are both vague and open-textured: vague because there are sensations, such as certain tingles, to which competent speakers are unsure whether to apply 'pain'; and open-textured because there are surely possible sensations, producible by electrical stimulation of the brain, to which competent speakers *would* be unsure whether to apply 'pain.'[22] Secondly, we could have good evidence, both neurophysiological and behavioral, for saying that S is in a given occurrent mental state yet does not believe he is. S might satisfy the EEG tests for pain or for a yellow afterimage, but not those for believing, consciously or unconsciously, that one has them; and there might also be EEG evidence of a breakdown in the circuitry carrying "sensory data" to the "cognitive center." Furthermore, S might carry himself as though his knee hurt (though saying only that it feels weak) and might jerk it away from pressure; and S might match the afterimage with yellow on a color chart, but call that yellow grey. In both cases the occurrent states would exist in S's "consciousness," but not in the normal way which makes it evident to S *what* state he is in. One may protest that S has lost his grasp of 'yellow' and 'grey'. Perhaps. But that would not preclude his *having* a yellow afterimage; and it would support the conclusion that it is false that he believes he seems to see yellow. Note also that newborns can have pain and, presumably, yellow afterimages. But can they, as the thesis of omniscience implies, *believe* that they have pain, or yellow afterimages? This is doubtful. On balance, then, it appears that the realm of occurrent mental states is not only not a domain of incorrigibility, but not one of omniscience either.

---

22. For discussion of the distinction between vagueness and open texture see Friedrich Waismann, "Verifiability," in Antony Flew (ed.), *Logic and Language*, First Series (Oxford, 1951), esp. pp. 120–121; and William P. Alston, *Philosophy of Language* (Englewood Cliffs, 1964), ch. V. For arguments intended to show that 'pain' and other sensation terms are open-textured see John King-Farlow, "Postscript to Mr. Aune on a Wittgensteinian Dogma," *Philosophical Studies*, VIII (1962), pp. 62–65.

IV

We have seen that *normally* first-person, present-tense, occurrent mental state beliefs are direct, far more reliable than the counterpart beliefs about others, excellent evidence for the presence of the states they "report," warranted, and autonomous. Moreover, normally the phenomena such beliefs are about constitute a domain of omniscience for the subject. There are thus sound though not unqualified epistemic contrasts underlying the doctrine of privileged access. These contrasts are strong enough to explain the facts that make the thesis of incorrigibility plausible, e.g. the fact that typically it is absurd to say of a person that he is mistaken in saying he is in pain. But the realm of present occurrent mental states is not a domain of omniscience for the subject; and the thesis of incorrigibility, which is central to the doctrine of privileged access, is surely false. Our beliefs about ourselves differ from our beliefs about others in very important respects; but they are like our beliefs about others in being fallible, dubitable, corrigible, and testable.

This should not be an unwelcome conclusion. It does imply that incorrigibility is not the mark of the mental, and indeed it casts doubt on the entire project of defining the mental in terms of epistemic privilege. But it leaves open the possibility of defining the mental in other plausible ways, e.g. perhaps in terms of intentionality; and it accommodates the underlying truths that make the doctrine of privileged access plausible and important. A further compensation for giving up incorrigibility is that once we reject the unqualified traditional contrasts between self-knowledge and our knowledge of others, and appreciate their important similarities, we undermine at least one assumption that supports skepticism about other minds. If none of our beliefs about ourselves is incorrigible, this deprives the skeptic of the high epistemic standard which he supposes can be met by empirical beliefs only if they are about ourselves, and through which he attacks the warrant of our admittedly less secure beliefs about the mental lives of others. At the same time, if even our occurrent MSBs may sometimes be justifiably overridden by other persons, this strongly argues, though it does not conclusively show, that our criteria for the application of mental terms are such that we can *know* both that there are other minds and many facts about them. The skeptic may object that my attack on incorrigibility presupposes that there are other minds. But it does not. If one conceives my arguments in the first person, all I presuppose is that there could be others and that they could have the sorts of reasons I have specified for thinking certain MSB's mistaken. The skeptic may further object that, by assuming there are behavioral criteria for applying mental terms, I have in another way trivially undermined skepticism about other minds. But this would hold only if I had assumed that certain behavior *entails* the existence of mental states. This I have not done and do not think reasonable. I have assumed only *some* conceptual connection between behavior and the mental: a connection weak enough so that, even if incorrigibilists accept it, they can consistently regard skepticism about other minds as a coherent and, in some forms, plausible position.

Quite apart from the problem of other minds, construed as the problem of whether one can know that there are other minds and at least some facts about them, there remain difficult and important questions about the epistemology of psychological concepts. Here it has been possible to treat only a few of these questions. But if I have been right, our treatment of such questions is at least freed of any commitment to an unnecessarily narrow doctrine of privileged access. We need not bridge a chasm between the assumed incorrigibility of our beliefs about our own mental lives and the obvious corrigibility of our beliefs about the mental lives of others; we can construe self-knowledge as in principle very significantly like other knowledge; and we are rid of a major obstacle to developing a unified theory of empirical knowledge.[23]

23. In writing this paper I have profited from discussions with Martin Perlmutter and Hardy E. Jones, and from comments by readers for the *Canadian Journal of Philosophy*.

Chapter 6

Defeated knowledge, reliability, and justification

Philosophers generally agree that knowledge is not merely justified true belief. But they do not agree on what kind of account of knowledge can best distinguish it from mere justified true belief. A major question dividing them is whether the distinction should be made on the basis of the kind of justification S has for believing p, or on the basis of apparently non-normative concepts such as that of the reliability of the belief, construed in terms of the likelihood that beliefs of the kind in question will be true. I shall call the first sort of approach to the analysis of knowledge *justificationist* and the second sort of approach *naturalistic.*[1] Epistemologists using both approaches have recently been occupied with problems posed by certain examples of what is sometimes called "defeated knowledge."[2] This might be characterized as justified true belief that would be knowledge if it were not undermined by one or another kind of untoward circumstance. A good account of the nature of knowledge must of course do more than rule out defeating circumstances. But this task appears to be one of the most difficult problems confronting epistemology, and many instances of defeated knowledge are challenging test cases for an account of knowledge.

1. If the apparent distinction between normative and non-normative concepts cannot be sustained, then the contrast between naturalistic and justificationist approaches must be drawn differently. I believe this could be done, but I cannot go into the matter here.
2. See, e.g., Marshall Swain, "Reasons, Causes, and Knowledge," *Journal of Philosophy* 75, no. 5 (1978):229–49; Alvin I. Goldman, "Discrimination and Perceptual Knowledge," *Journal of Philosophy* 73, no. 20 (1976):771–91; Gilbert Harman, *Thought* (Princeton, 1973); John Barker, "What You Don't Know Won't Hurt You?" *American Philosophical Quarterly* 13, no. 4 (1976):303–8; and Peter Klein, "Knowledge, Causality, and Defeasibility," *Journal of Philosophy* 73, no. 20 (1976):792–812.

I will begin by exploring some recent theories that deal with defeated knowledge. I shall then propose an alternative account of some representative examples of defeated knowledge. No attempt will be made to develop an analysis of knowledge in general; the account proposed is meant only to enhance our understanding, from a justificationist point of view, of defeated knowledge, and to help us determine whether reliability accounts of defeated knowledge, which seem to be the most plausible kind of naturalistic account, are superior to justificationist accounts of defeated knowledge. As I am conceiving a reliability account, it is one that explains the defeat of would-be knowledge that p by showing that S's belief that p is in some way inadequately reliable. By contrast, justificationist accounts explain defeated knowledge in terms of the kind of justification S has for believing p. Only a few current positions can be considered here, and some kinds of defeated knowledge will not be discussed. But the reliability and justificationist views to be studied are, I hope, sufficiently representative to warrant the conclusions I shall draw.

1. RELIABILITY THEORIES

Among the very best reliability theories yet developed is Alvin Goldman's account of non-inferential perceptual knowledge. Our problem can be readily seen through an example from his important paper, "Discrimination and Perceptual Knowledge":

> Suppose we are told that, unknown to Henry, the district he has just entered is full of papier-mâché facsimiles of barns. These facsimiles look from the road exactly like barns, but are really just façades, without back walls or interiors. . . . Having just entered the district, Henry has not encountered any facsimiles; the object he sees is a genuine barn. But if the object on that site were a facsimile, Henry would mistake it for a barn. Given this new information, we would be strongly inclined to withdraw the claim [which we would allow in a normal rural setting] that Henry *knows* the object is a barn.[3]

3. Goldman, "Discrimination and Perceptual Knowledge," p. 776. Some of the ideas in this paper of Goldman's are discussed or developed in his more recent "What Is Justified Belief?" in George S. Pappas, ed., *Justification and*

Henry has a justified true belief that is not knowledge; but it is hard to explain why it is not. Goldman himself points out that his previous account of empirical knowledge, a causal analysis, cannot explain this: "Henry's belief that the object is a barn is caused by the presence of the barn; indeed, the process is a perceptual one"[4] of just the kind that occurs when we *do* acquire perceptual knowledge by observation.

Facts that are simply about the perceiver may also defeat would-be knowledge. Suppose that unbeknownst to *S*, he has been *hallucinating* barns while driving along. Imagine that he feels normal, that the hallucinatory "barns" "look" to him like real ones, and that he has no reason to suspect anything is wrong. He may then come to a real barn, see it, and justifiably believe that it is a barn. Yet he does not *know* that it is. The reasons are similar to the reasons why Henry does not know. For instance, just as Henry would have taken a facsimile to be a barn had there been one before him. *S* would have believed there was a barn before him if he had hallucinated one instead of seeing one.

How is an analysis of knowledge to rule out such defeaters? Let us first consider Goldman's treatment of the problem. What he proposes as an explanation of why Henry's would-be knowledge is defeated is roughly this: *S* has non-inferential perceptual knowledge, of *a*, that it is *F*, only if there is no relevant perceptually equivalent state of affairs (such as would obtain if Henry viewed a barn facsimile) in which *S falsely* believes, of the perceptual counterpart of *a* (e.g., the facsimile), that it is *F*.[5] This explains why Henry lacks knowledge, because the fact that there are barn facsimiles all around Henry and he *would* believe, of any one of them, that it is a barn makes the state of affairs, Henry's viewing a fac-

---

Knowledge (Dordrecht and Boston, 1979). In what follows I try to take some account of Goldman's later paper, particularly in constructing naturalistic interpretations of some justificationist terms. But to discuss that paper seriously would take considerable space and is not required by my purposes here.

4. *Ibid.*, p. 773.

5. *Ibid.*, esp. pp. 785–86. Intuitively, a state of affairs, e.g. *S*'s perceiving *b*, is perceptually equivalent to the state of affairs, *S*'s perceiving *a*, provided *S* cannot perceptually distinguish between the two. Goldman actually offers conditions necessary *and* sufficient for *S*'s having non-inferential knowledge, of *a*, that it is *F*; but only the condition cited in the text need concern us here. Goldman also formulates his conditions for *de re* belief, whereas, for the most part, I shall speak of Henry's (*de dicto*) belief that *a* is a barn. This distinction is important, but for our purposes the more convenient *de dicto* locutions are adequate.

simile from the same angle in the same light, etc., a *relevant* perceptual equivalent. It defeats his would-be knowledge because he cannot perceptually discriminate (under the same conditions of observation) a facsimile from the barn he actually sees. Goldman does not try to specify what makes an alternative relevant, apparently in part because no prima facie satisfactory account of the notion occurs to him.

One may wonder how Goldman would deal with the hallucination possibility I have raised. It seems clear that because S's barn hallucinations are occurring frequently as he drives along and in each case he mistakenly believes he sees a barn, their occurrence is also relevant to his belief that *a* is a barn, and defeats his would-be knowledge that it is. However, there is presumably no object, a hallucinatory barn, such that S might believe falsely, of it, that it is a barn. Hence the barn hallucinations do not provide perceptually equivalent states of affairs in Goldman's sense. What Goldman suggests is that there must be "neither a relevant perceptual equivalent of the indicated sort (using our present definition of perceptual equivalence) *nor* a relevant alternative situation in which an equivalent percept occurs and prompts a *de dicto* belief that something has F, but where there is nothing that *perceptually* causes this percept and nothing *of which* F is believed to hold."[6] This explains why S's belief that *a* is a barn is unreliable. For even though there is nothing in the circumstances which he would mistakenly take to be a barn, there are relevant circumstances in which, given the same sensory evidence, he would mistakenly take it that there is a barn before him.

Before considering some justificationist proposals that also deal with the case, let us examine another important naturalistic position, namely, Armstrong's. His account is more general than Goldman's and seems to have an advantage in having fewer problematic expressions (such as 'relevant alternative').

Armstrong's reliability account of non-inferential knowledge would deal with Goldman's barn case through Armstrong's requirement that if S non-inferentially knows that *a* is F, then S has a property H, where "there is a law-like connection in nature" such that for any *x* and any *y*, if *x* has H and believes *y* has F, *y* does have F.[7] It might seem that this requirement would not rule out

6. *Ibid.*, p. 789.
7. D. M. Armstrong, *Belief, Truth, and Knowledge* (Cambridge, 1973), p. 182.

Henry's knowing that *a* is a barn. For it may appear that Henry has such a property and would thus have to be said to know that *a* is a barn.[8] He might have a "nomic" property (e.g., being affected in a certain way by light rays from a certain sort of object) such that if *anyone* who has that property believes the object in question to be a barn, then it is one. However, Armstrong would probably reply that there is no difference between the way one is visually affected by a barn and the way one is visually affected from the same distance and angle by a mere barn wall artificially supported from behind, since the same sorts of light rays reach one in the same way. Hence there is unlikely to be a suitable *H*.

This is a plausible response. It also suggests something important about Armstrong's theory: even when *S* does (visually) know that there is a barn before him, Armstrong should take *S*'s knowledge to be indirect, i.e., to be based on some other knowledge or belief of *S*'s, such as the belief that there is a woody-looking barnlike surface before him. However, it appears that Armstrong would take *S*'s knowledge that *a* is a woody-looking surface to be direct.[9] This raises no obstacle to dealing with the case of Henry; but one can still imagine defeating conditions for justified true belief of this sort, and it is doubtful that Armstrong's account can rule out all of them. Take the hallucination example, and suppose *S*'s would-be direct knowledge is the justified true belief that there is a woody-looking surface before him shaped like a barn wall. Surely his belief could be "perceptually caused" in the normal way by the barn surface *S* sees, i.e., caused in the way ordinary objects like tables and chairs cause us to believe they are before us when we perceive them in normal light. Moreover, there might be a suitable *H* in virtue of which his belief is *reliable*. Yet the belief is not knowledge.

To be sure, Armstrong puts important restrictions on *H*. The one relevant here is that *H* be such that there is a real possibility of the situation covered by the law like connection recurring.[10] But surely there is a real possibility of many situations in which a person

8. Goldman seems to think that Armstrong's account, at least in its earlier form in *A Materialist Theory of the Mind* (London, 1968), pp. 189–93, cannot deal with such cases. But Goldman's reason for saying this is apparently different from the one suggested here; see "Discrimination and Perceptual Knowledge," esp. p. 779.
9. Armstrong, *Belief, Truth, and Knowledge*, pp. 163–65. Armstrong suggests, e.g., that when we have ordinary perceptual knowledge of a dog, "the presence of a *whole* dog is inferred from more elementary information" (p. 165).
10. *Ibid.*, p. 173.

has the relevant property, e.g. being visually affected in a certain way by light rays of a certain character. One might now object that we still do not have a sufficiently specific H, since light rays from a woody-looking surface would affect one no differently than light rays from, e.g., a machine that produces optical illusions or from something that appears qualitatively very similar to a woody-looking surface yet is not a physical surface at all, or at least not an ordinary one (perhaps a laser photograph could fit this description). But if this is so, it would not be congenial to Armstrong. For he would then probably have to say that by sight one cannot directly know even that there is a physical surface before one. (For this strong a belief would not be reliable on the basis of the relevant H.) He would probably not wish to say this, and in any case the hallucination possibility we are imagining would defeat this would-be knowledge as well. Perhaps there are minor revisions that would enable Armstrong's account to deal with these problems, but I cannot explore that possibility here. I am more concerned with the view as representative of a plausible reliability theory than with its correctness. The same holds for my concern with justificationist theories, which are the subject of the next section.

2. JUSTIFICATIONIST THEORIES

We have seen how some plausible naturalistic views bear on certain cases of defeated knowledge. Let us consider how some justificationist accounts of knowledge might treat the same examples.

It will be instructive to begin with an attractively simple theory suggested by John Barker: a justified true belief that p constitutes knowledge "if and only if what isn't known won't hurt, i.e., if and only if there is some way that any other true proposition besides p could come to be known without destruction of the original justification for believing p."[11] This condition does not seem to be met in any case we have examined. For instance, apparently S cannot come to know that there are facsimiles around him which he cannot tell from real barns, without destroying his *original* justification for believing the object he sees is a barn. This justification might be, e.g., that a looks to S like a barn or that a *barn* "perceptually causes" S to believe that he sees a barn. Whatever the justification, it will

11. Barker, "What You Don't Know Won't Hurt You?" p. 303.

have to be buttressed with new information if S is to remain justified in his original belief. Similarly, in our hallucination case, if S is to know that *a* is a barn, after he discovers he has been hallucinating barns, S's belief that *a* is a barn will have to be based at least in part on something new, say a justified belief that he is not now hallucinating a barn.

Barker's necessary condition claim is plausible, perhaps even so obviously true as to be uncontroversial. For if S knows that *p*, one way in which he could come to know any potentially defeating propositions is in the context of also coming to know *how* he knows that *p*. Surely he could come to know how he does, in a manner that enables him to explain away any would-be defeaters.

On the other hand, consider justified true belief that is not defeated knowledge but simply not justified in the right sort of way to qualify as knowledge. Some cases of this kind seem to undermine Barker's sufficient condition claim. Suppose, e.g., that S has a justified true belief that he will lose in a lottery in which he has one out of the 1,000 tickets. Is there not some way he could come to know any other true proposition without destroying his original justification for believing he will lose? It would seem so. Granted, if he comes to know a true causal account of why his ticket will not be selected, then he no longer *needs* his original justification in terms of the probability that he will win in a fair lottery of the relevant sort. But surely this justification is not destroyed by his discovery of the different (and superior) one. Barker's proposal does, however, seem to give us a useful partial characterization of defeated knowledge. For no defeated knowledge seems to satisfy his condition, and defeated knowledge is often clearly such that S's justification would be undermined by discovering certain things of which he is ignorant.

We can learn much from considering how an elaborate recent theory by Marshall Swain could deal with our examples. For Swain, Henry would not know that *a* is a barn because there is a "significant alternative," C^*, to the actual causal chain, $X \rightarrow Y$, that links the state of affairs, *a*'s being a barn, to Henry's belief that *a* is one. Swain gives only a sufficient condition for C^*'s being a significant alternative, namely, that

(a) it is objectively likely that C^* should have occurred rather than $X \rightarrow Y$; and

(b), if C^* had occurred instead of $X \rightarrow Y$, then there would have been an event or state of affairs U in C^* such that S would not have been justified in believing that h [e.g., that a is a barn] if S were justified in believing that U occurred.[12]

The idea, as applied to Henry, is this. It is objectively likely that a facsimile should have caused his percepts. If it had, there would have been a state of affairs, e.g. the facsimile's causing Henry to seem to see a barn before him, such that if he were justified in believing that this occurred, he would not be justified in believing that a is a barn. Regarding our hallucination case, S's hallucinating would also be a significant alternative to his seeing a barn. It is objectively likely; and had it occurred, there would have been a state of affairs, e.g. the hallucination's causing him to seem to see a barn, that satisfies (b).

Consider another kind of example, one in which S has a justified true perceptual belief that fails to be knowledge because of some oddity in the causal chain from the relevant state of affairs to the belief. Thus,

> Suppose Milton is in a museum looking at a glass box that
> contains a vase. Entirely unknown to him, the surface of
> the box is actually a cleverly constructed television screen.
> For someone looking at the glass box, the visual appear-
> ances are precisely what they would be if the surface of the
> box were clear glass and the vase were being directly ob-
> served. Moreover, suppose that the vase whose image is
> being televised is the vase that is actually in the box. Mil-
> ton comes to believe that the vase is in the box on the basis
> of reasons R, and his believing for these reasons is justi-
> fied. But he does not know that the vase is in there.[13]

Swain deals with this by requiring that a belief constituting knowledge cannot depend on a defective causal chain:

> Where S justifiably believes that h on the basis of R, causal
> chain, $X \rightarrow Y$ is defective with respect to this justified belief
> *if* (a) there is some event or state of affairs U in $X \rightarrow Y$ such
> that S would be justified in believing that U did not occur,
> and (b) it is essential to S's justifiably believing that h on

12. Swain, "Reasons, Causes, and Knowledge," p. 240.
13. *Ibid.*, p. 233.

the basis of R that S would be justified in believing that U did not occur.[14]

Applying this to Milton, we are to assume that the case is very uncommon and that in part for this reason Milton satisfies (a). Presumably (b) holds of him too.

Goldman deals with a similar case – in which S sees a candle before him through a complex system of mirrors whose existence he does not even suspect – by appealing to the notion of a relevant alternative: S does not know that there is a candle before him, since there is a relevant alternative in which, through similar mirrors, he would falsely believe this.[15] Swain, too, can deal with the case. Just as Goldman construes as a relevant alternative S's being appeared to in the same way though the proposition in question is false, Swain can take such states of affairs as significant alternatives even if they are not objectively likely.

3. AN ALTERNATIVE ACCOUNT OF
DEFEATED PERCEPTUAL KNOWLEDGE

In this section, I want to propose a justificationist account of defeated perceptual knowledge. The account is much less broad than Swain's, which applies to non-perceptual as well as to perceptual beliefs; and although it is broader than Goldman's in applying to indirect perceptual beliefs, I do not offer a sufficient condition for any kind of perceptual knowledge, as he does for non-inferential perceptual knowledge. My concern is restricted to defeated knowledge, and there may be kinds of defeated perceptual knowledge not ruled out by the principles I propose.

A major difference between my account and Swain's is that mine makes essential use of the distinction between direct and indirect knowledge and beliefs, whereas for him both are instances of what he calls believing on the basis of a reason. One way of expressing this distinction is to say that S's knowledge or belief that p is direct if and only if it is not *based on* any other knowledge or belief of S's, i.e., roughly, no other belief of his constitutes (or expresses) a

---

14. *Ibid.*, p. 238.
15. Goldman, "Discrimination and Perceptual Knowledge," pp. 787–88. (The example is from a paper of Swain's.)

reason of his for which he believes p.[16] If S's knowledge that p is based on his knowledge that q, which is his reason for p, then he knows p *indirectly*. Such knowledge has been called inferential; but though all inferential knowledge is indirect, I shall not take S's indirectly knowing that p to entail S's having inferred p from anything else, at least not if inferring is taken, as it usually is, to imply a process of drawing a conclusion from a set of propositions one is in some sense entertaining. Some knowledge and beliefs which it is natural to call perceptual are indirect, and I want to begin by considering a case of defeated knowledge constituted by an indirect belief.

INDIRECT PERCEPTUAL BELIEFS

Imagine that S enters an office building and walks down a long corridor toward the person he is going to see. As he passes an open door, he hears the familiar sounds of a typewriter. They strike him as having the muffled quality of sounds produced by the IBM Selectric, and he takes it that a Selectric is being used inside. Let us assume that he is correct in this and that his experience with Selectrics and other typewriters is such that he is also justified in his belief that a Selectric is being used in the room he is passing. Now imagine that all the other offices S will pass on the corridor are experimenting with a new Japanese product which few people, even in the typewriter business, have heard about: the Sonilectric. It works much like the Selectric and sounds so much like it that had S passed one of the other doors he would have believed the Selectric was being used in the room in question. The case is like Henry's in that S's would-be knowledge is defeated by the proximity of relevant circumstances in which he would form a false belief. But it may differ from that of Henry; for here, supposing that we have a perceptual belief, we clearly do not have a direct one, since S's belief that a Selectric is being used is based on his belief that the sounds in question are Selectric sounds.

16. It is very difficult to explicate the notion of one belief's being based on another, and few philosophers have offered detailed accounts of the notion. One plausible account is Armstrong's; see *Belief, Truth, and Knowledge*, esp. chap. 14. The notion is also discussed extensively by George S. Pappas in "Basing Relations," in Pappas, op. cit., and at some length in my "Psychological Foundationalism" (Chapter 1, this volume). For the purposes of this paper, the brief characterization in the text will serve.

How should we deal with the case? Since Goldman would presumably not regard S's belief as non-inferential, his account would not apply to it (though, as I shall later suggest, it is easy to see how the account might be extended to deal with the example). For Swain, the defeat of S's knowledge can be explained by pointing out that in the circumstances there is a significant alternative to the actual causal chain from the Selectric to S's belief that a Selectric is being used. For it seems objectively likely that S should have heard a Sonilectric instead, and if he did he would have believed that a Selectric was being used.

I want to suggest a different way of explaining why S's knowledge is defeated here. I shall first propose an epistemic principle that seems to hold for indirect knowledge in general and then proceed to apply it to our example:

> P: If, at *t*, S's belief that *p* is essentially based on his belief that *q*, then, at *t*, S knows that *p*, only if, at *t*, (i) *q* is true; (ii) S justifiably believes *q*; (iii) there is a warranting relation, *R*, that S justifiably takes *q* to have to *p*; and (iv) *q* does, in the circumstance S is in at *t*, warrant *p*.[17]

I am using 'warranting relation' broadly and construing (iii) as satisfiable by both *de dicto* and *de re* beliefs. Clause (iii) thus encompasses S's believing that if *q* then *p*, believing that *q* entails *p*, believing that *q* is good evidence for *p*, believing that *q* indicates *p*, taking (or believing, if taking is not a kind of believing) *q* to justify (warrant, show, etc.) *p*, and so on. Since some of these beliefs can be held by a person who has no epistemic concepts, S can satisfy (iii) without having them. Regarding S's belief that *p* being based on his belief that *q*, this relation may hold even if he does not realize it, nor ever entertain *q*, nor ever entertain the proposition that he takes *q* to support *p*, nor ever infer (in any conscious way, at least) *p* from *q*. Moreover, even if S's belief that

---

17. A more complicated principle is required to deal with cases in which S's belief that *p* is based on one or more of his other beliefs, where none of this set is a necessary condition for his believing *p*. At least conditions (i) and (iii), moreover, are controversial. Condition (i) might be held to be too strong because *q* could be a conjunction with one false conjunct whose *other* conjuncts warrant *p* sufficiently to enable S to know it despite the error. Condition (iii) would be denied by most reliability theorists, on the ground that if (iv) holds (iii) need not. If the first objection is correct, P can, I believe, accommodate it with minor revision. If the second objection is correct, a more significant change in P would be needed. I am not at all sure that the second objection can be met, but in any case little in this chapter turns on clause (iii).

p is also based on his believing some proposition other than *q*, I shall say it is *essentially* based on his belief that *q*, only if, other things remaining equal, *S* would not believe *p* if he did not believe *q*. With these qualifications, P seems quite plausible.

Let us now consider some applications of P. First, in our typewriter example it seems plain that *S* does not satisfy clause (iv): *in the circumstances*, that the sounds he hears have the muffled quality of sounds produced by the Selectric does not warrant (for *S*) the proposition that a Selectric is being used. For all around him are non-Selectrics producing sounds with the muffled quality he believes he hears. Consider also the example in which *S* sees a candle through a complicated system of mirrors. On the (perhaps dubious) assumption that *S*'s belief that there is a candle before him is indirect, P implies that it will constitute knowledge only if this proposition is warranted by some other proposition *S* believes, presumably one roughly to the effect that there is before him a flame-like area at the top of a waxy-looking cylinder. Now in the circumstances this proposition does not warrant the proposition that there is a candle before him. There may be several ways to explain why not. One is that under the circumstances the former is not a *reliable* indication of the latter. Another is that if *S* realized that the circumstances in question obtained, he would not be *justified* in believing the latter on the basis of the former. I shall return to this contrast.

One may now wonder whether the case of Henry can also be dealt with by using P. This question is difficult to answer. For one thing, it requires determining whether, in the sort of circumstances imagined, Henry's belief, through sight, that *a* is a barn, is *indirect*, i.e., based on at least one other belief of his. If the belief is direct, then P does not apply to it. The question whether or not such beliefs are direct is important not only for determining the scope of P and similar principles but also for assessing coherentist theories of knowledge. For on the plausible (though by no means self-evident) supposition that if a direct belief constitutes knowledge, it constitutes *direct* knowledge, coherentists will have to construe all empirical knowledge, at least, as constituted by indirect belief. (For as usually understood, coherentists deny that there is any direct empirical knowledge, and sometimes that there is any direct *a priori* knowledge.) It is thus of considerable interest whether perceptual beliefs like Henry's are, despite appearances, indirect. If so, P might be able to explain why Henry does not have knowledge and indeed why many other apparently direct justified true perceptual beliefs fail to constitute knowledge. If not, coherentists would have to undertake the difficult task of showing at least how indirect empirical knowledge may be constituted by direct belief.[18]

Once we take seriously the question whether Henry's belief is indirect, we are confronted with another difficult question. Since it is through sight that he believes that *a* is a barn, we need to ask whether he *directly sees* that this is so. As I am using this term here, *S* directly sees that *a* is *F*, if and only if he sees that *a* is *F*, and does not see this on the basis of seeing that something else is the case. At least typically, if *S* sees that *a* is *F*, on the basis of seeing that *p*, then his belief that *a* is *F* is based on his belief that *p*; but I shall leave it open whether the former *entails* the latter.

We are now in a position to take up the question whether Henry's belief that *a* is a barn is indirect. No doubt knowledge through (or at least in part through) sight, that *a* is a barn, could be indirect. For instance, if Henry is at a considerable distance from *a* and must struggle to discern its features, in the light of which he concludes that *a* is a barn, his knowledge that it is will be based on other knowledge of his. But Goldman seems to have in mind a case in which one sees all the typical features and straightaway believes the object to be a barn. Let us explore how one might in this sort of case argue that the belief is nonetheless indirect. I shall consider several of the reasons that suggest this.

First, let us ask whether, in the situation we are imagining, where there are no facsimiles or other defeaters, *S* would directly see that *a* is a barn. Might it not be the case that what *S* directly sees to be the case is simply that there is a roughly rectangular, woody-looking surface before him? This would explain why what he *sees* to be the case seems to be the same even if there is only a (very faithful) facsimile before him, and it would *suggest* that *S*'s belief that there is a barn before him is based on his belief that there is such a surface there.

Another consideration emerges if we imagine *S* looking attentively at (say) a barn in normal light, at first believing it to be a barn and then strongly suspecting, on the basis of the false testimony of a friend beside him, that it is a facsimile. Suppose that

18. Lehrer, at least, has tried to do something that appears to give some support to this, in connection with his example of the gypsy lawyer. See Keith Lehrer, *Knowledge* (Oxford, 1974), pp. 122–26. In Chapters 1, 2, and 7, this volume, I have tried to indicate some difficulties raised by this move.

there are no facsimiles and, for the sake of argument, that S does at first directly see that the structure is a barn. How are we to explain his no longer seeing that it is when he is still looking at it under the same perceptual conditions? S's sensory state, as well as the objects and surfaces he sees, are the same. Perhaps what explains why he does not see that it is a barn after the testimony is that his suspicion prevents him from *taking* what he sees to be the side of a barn. On this view, there is no change in what he directly sees to be the case; the change is in what he believes ("sees") on the basis of what he directly sees to be the case. Thus, suppose that another observer, with the same sensory acuity and repertoire of concepts, looks unsuspectingly at the same barn. One might then plausibly argue as follows. What each directly sees to be the case is the same as what the other directly sees to be so. The first does not directly see that a is a barn (nor see that this is so at all, since he does not believe it); hence the second does not directly see this either.

A third consideration arises if we imagine that someone who knows about a barn facsimile nearby tells S about it and asks him how he knows a is a barn. If S's confidence is not easily shaken and he replies without seeking evidence beyond what he has, he might say, "Clearly, that [pointing toward the barn] is the surface of a barn," or "It looks just like a barn seen from this angle – that wall can't possibly be papier-mâché," or "It has exactly the shape and texture of a barn seen from here." Must we suppose that S has *adopted* these beliefs only in response to the questioning and then based his belief that a is a barn on them? Perhaps he is making *explicit* the basis on which he took a to be a barn. By contrast, imagine asking an ordinary person (in daylight) how he knows that a (which he sees) is a red (or a woody-looking) surface. Unless he is philosophically sophisticated, he is unlikely to have any grounds to cite, at least none which constitute his reason(s) for believing that the thing in question is a red surface. For he presumably takes himself simply to see that it is. He may realize, at this point anyway, that he could be hallucinating. But if so, it would not follow that his belief that the surface in question is red was based on his having believed he was not hallucinating. The latter belief is adopted *after* S begins to wonder about his justification for believing he sees something red, whereas it seems arguable that, even before being asked how he knows there is a barn before him, S believes there is a woody-looking surface before him. It is not that such perceptual beliefs as that there is a red surface before one could not be indirect. But ordinarily they do not seem so, whereas beliefs to the effect that something is a barn (car, dog, person) can be plausibly argued to be.

These considerations lend some plausibility to the view that in the kinds of cases we are examining, one's knowledge, through sight, that *a* is a barn, is indirect. But they are quite inconclusive. Granting a difference between what is required to know that there is a woody-looking surface before one and what is required to know that there is a barn before one, nothing said above shows that in order to know the latter one must believe (or know) that there is a woody-looking surface before one (or have other grounds or believe or know any item of evidence). Moreover, though it is plausible to suppose that what *S* directly sees to be the case is the same whether he sees that *a* is a barn or mistakenly takes a facsimile to be a barn, it is also arguable that since seeing that *a* is *F* entails knowing that it is, and *S* does not know the facsimile is a barn, *this* difference explains why *S* directly sees that *a* is a barn, yet does not directly see the same thing to be so when he views a facsimile and mistakenly believes it to be a barn. Similarly, since seeing that *a* is *F* apparently entails believing that it is, we can explain why *S* ceases to see that *a* is a barn when he comes to suspect it is a facsimile, by maintaining that he is now refusing to believe what he seems to (and previously did) see directly – namely, that *a* is a barn. We need not explain this by saying that what he seems to see directly he in fact saw only on the basis of something else he saw to be so. To be sure, these replies are not themselves conclusive. But they are sufficiently cogent to make it unreasonable to assume that P can account for cases like that of Henry (who, if his belief that *a* is a barn is indirect, would fail to satisfy clause (iv) of P). In any event, there certainly are cases of defeated knowledge constituted by direct beliefs, and the principle I shall propose to deal with these can also explain why, assuming that Henry's belief that *a* is a barn is direct, he does not know that *a* is a barn.

DIRECT PERCEPTUAL BELIEFS

Let us consider a case of defeated knowledge constituted by direct belief. Suppose *S* has only the modest justified true belief that over there is a woody-looking surface, but does not *know* this because he has, without even suspecting it, been hallucinating such surfaces and would have had the same belief had he at the time hallucinated the kind of surface he now sees. Presumably, S's belief here is *direct*, so P does not apply. We thus need a different way of explaining why the belief is not knowledge.

One direction a justificationist can take here is that of a coherence theory of justification, on which there is no direct knowledge or directly justified belief. Harman,[19] e.g., could use P or something like it after all. However, justificationists, like naturalists, need not be coherentists, any more than they need be foundationalists. How should a justificationist who is not a coherentist construe the case? A Cartesian strategy would be to deny that even S's belief that *a* is a barn surface is direct, and to argue that it is based on, say, a belief that there appears to S to be a barn surface there. Then P again applies: given the hallucinations, S is mistaken (or not justified) in taking the proposition that there appears to him to be a barn surface there, to warrant the proposition that there is one there.

This strategy is not without plausibility, and it brings out that P is neutral between theories of perception that deny we have direct knowledge of the physical world and direct realist views that affirm this. But wherever one might locate direct belief in perceptual experience, there remains the problem of how to explain its defeat – unless, of course, we hold that certain beliefs, such as appearance-beliefs, are *necessarily* knowledge and hence indefeasible. I prefer not to be forced to take that view,[20] and in any case it would be desirable to show that a justificationist need not hold it nor choose between coherentism and retreating inward for direct knowledge.

We may make some headway if we think of perceptual knowledge as a function of success in several interrelated dimensions. If we can locate defeaters in terms of these, we may get a better understanding of defeated direct perceptual beliefs. One important dimension seems to be S's *perceptual capacity* relative to the belief and the circumstances. Are his eyes or ears, e.g., good enough to enable him to know what he believes on the basis of their input? Second, there is *perceptual normality*. If S's senses malfunction, e.g. in such a way that there are gaps in his hearing, then he may be unable to know that Beethoven's "Appassionata" is being played,

19. See Harman, *Thought*, esp. chaps. 9–11.
20. In "The Limits of Self-Knowledge" (Chapter 5, this volume), I have argued that the view is mistaken.

even though he would ordinarily recognize it and hears very clearly the parts he does hear. Third, *perceptual circumstances* are crucial. The presence of mirrors, e.g., can produce false visual beliefs, and background noise can produce false beliefs about what someone has said to one. Fourth, since perceptual knowledge requires responding to input from the senses, there is the dimension of *cognitive responses to one's senses.* *S*'s perceptual beliefs must be in some sense appropriate to his perceptual state. When, for instance, he has a clear impression of both color and shape before him, he must not believe that there is merely a color before him. There may well be further dimensions of perceptual knowledge to be emphasized, and one could make important distinctions within these four categories. But if we take the above as a point of departure, at least the following conditions for direct perceptual knowledge are suggested:

(a) *S*'s senses must (as Goldman's case of Henry shows) be sufficiently acute, relative to the proposition in question and the circumstances in which he believes it, to distinguish the relevant sort of object or property from things he might confuse it with in the circumstances. *S* must not, e.g., claim to discern precisely the shape of a distant object if he is so far away that its edges look highly blurred. Similarly, given Henry's circumstances, his vision is insufficiently acute to record differences in appearance between a barn and a facsimile.

(b) The sense(s) through which *S* believes *p* must be normal. For instance, if *S* has a loud (illusory) ringing in his ears at the pitch of A 440, he may be quite unable to certify the corresponding note on a piano as in tune even if he has "absolute pitch." Similarly, his senses must not be playing tricks on him, as with certain optical illusions or the hallucinations described above. (In the case of a hallucinatory perceptual belief, I shall speak of the sense(s) *appropriate* to the belief rather than a belief *through* a sense. For although the sense of sight [say] is appropriate [or relevant] to a belief arising from a visual hallucination, S does not, or at any rate need not, "see" the thing in question through sight.)

(c) *S*'s perceptual circumstances must be appropriate for the belief in question. For instance, where the belief is to the effect that *a* is (say) red, the lighting must not make it appear to have a color it does not have; and where the belief concerns the shape of something, *S*'s orientation to it must not be inappropriate for judging its shape.

(d) *S*'s cognitive responses to his sense impressions must be normal, so that he is not, e.g., failing to believe *a* is red when his seeing it is producing the usual sensations of red, nor confusing two things – say, horses and cows – when he knows them perfectly well and is having the normal perceptual sensations of them. (It would be difficult to ascertain that the states of affairs described here have occurred, but doing so nevertheless seems quite possible.)

I am not in the least suggesting that *S* must believe (a) through (d) in order to have direct perceptual knowledge. My suggestion is only that he must be such that he either is not unjustified in believing (a) through (d), or would not be unjustified in believing them, if he did believe them. More positively, I am inclined to think that (a) through (d) are a *presumption* of our ascribing perceptual knowledge to *S*. In calling them a presumption I mean, not that we ascribe perceptual knowledge to *S* in a given case only if we believe he satisfies them in that case, but (in part) that if we consider any of them *false* in a given case, then we deny that *S* knows *p*.[21]

The counterpart conceptual claim, which seems equally plausible, is that a direct, justified true perceptual belief of *S*'s represents knowledge only if this presumption is true of it. The plausibility of this claim can be seen by imagining someone *denying* that, e.g., *S*'s vision being abnormal is a reason to question his claim (from a distance) to have visual knowledge that *a* is a barn. Similarly, imagine someone's denying that *S*'s being unjustified in trusting his vision is a reason to question this claim. Such denials would be prima facie ground for thinking that the person did not share our concept of perceptual knowledge. To be sure, *S*'s vision may be subnormal, yet still perfectly adequate to give him knowledge, at the distance in question, that *a* is a barn. Similarly, *S*'s being color-blind may not bear on his ability to acquire visual knowledge that a car is passing. Moreover, auditory hallucinations that give

21. Cp. Barker's similar notion of a presupposition of *S*'s; "What You Don't Know Won't Hurt You?" p. 305.

S false beliefs may not affect any of his visual beliefs. Nor need colored light or even an opaque (but snug) wrapping affect one's judgment of shape. Some abnormalities are not relevant to the question whether, in the circumstances, *S*'s belief that *p* represents knowledge. The notions we need are (at least) those expressed in (a) through (d): the notion of the acuity of *S*'s senses, relative to the proposition in question and to the circumstances in which *S* believes it; and the notions of *S*'s senses, his cognitive responses to his sense impressions, and his perceptual circumstances being relevantly normal with respect to a perceptual belief. I shall have to leave these notions of relevant normality rather vague; but explicating some such notions seems a problem for any theory of perceptual knowledge, and nothing I say should turn on their vagueness.

As in other cases, we can imagine both justificationist and reliability accounts of relevance. For instance, a reliability theorist might argue that *S*'s senses, or *S*'s perceptual circumstances, are not relevantly normal if they render the belief in question unreliable. And a justificationist might argue that they are not relevantly normal if they are such that if *S* believed that the circumstances obtained, or that his senses had the abnormality in question, then he would no longer be justified in believing that *p*. I shall return to this problem. But let us first consider how, using the presumption I have formulated, a justificationist account of defeated knowledge might deal with some of the cases we have discussed.

The epistemic principle corresponding to the presumption I am exploring might be formulated along the following lines:

Q: *S*'s direct perceptual belief that *p* constitutes, at *t*, direct perceptual knowledge that *p*, only if, at *t*, and with respect to the direct perceptual belief that *p*, (i) the sense (or combination of senses) through which *S* believes (or appropriate to *S*'s believing) that *p* is sufficiently acute to enable *S* to distinguish the object or property in question from things *S* might confuse it with in the circumstances; (ii) this sense or combination of senses is not relevantly abnormal; (iii) *S*'s perceptual circumstances are appropriate; (iv) *S*'s responses to his sense impressions are not relevantly abnormal; and (v) *S* does not unjustifiably believe, or would not be unjustified if, in the perceptual situation he is in at *t*, he did believe, any of (i), (ii), (iii), and (iv).²²

In our example, S is hallucinating barn surfaces without knowing it, in such a way that, since clause (ii) is not satisfied, the presumption Q expresses is false. Q thus provides a prima facie explanation of why S's direct justified true belief that *a* is a woody-looking surface is defeated.

Let us now consider a case in which clauses (i) through (iv) are satisfied, but S is unjustified in believing them, so that clause (v) is not satisfied. Suppose S's senses return to normal, though no one yet knows this; and imagine that S has not realized he has been hallucinating, but *should* have realized it because credible witnesses have told him so. Let us assume that he argues against their testimony plausibly, but inconclusively. We might suppose that he has good reasons to believe his senses are normal, yet is not justified in believing this because his reasons are still not good enough to warrant his rejecting the testimony. He might nevertheless be justified in believing that *a* is a barn, at least where the testimony of his senses to this effect is vivid and steady. For given his firm belief, based on good reasons, that his senses are (relevantly) normal, one can hardly fault him for accepting their vivid steady testimony. It seems, however, that his justified true belief that *a* is a barn is not *knowledge*. The reason is apparently that he is *unjustified* in believing the (true) presumption that his senses are normal.

This sort of example is important for justifications. If there were no such cases, the presumption they appeal to in dealing with defeated direct knowledge might be held to require no use of the notion of justification. That would not imply that all defeated knowledge could be accounted for on non-justificationist lines, but

---

22. Q requires several comments. If perceptual knowledge of objects is in some (or all) cases direct, Q would still apply to it. Q does not require that any particular kind of perceptual knowledge be direct or indirect. With minor revisions, it would apparently hold for indirect knowledge also. Regarding (v), I shall take it to be satisfiable by appropriate *de re* beliefs, e.g. by S's believing his senses *to be* normal. The reference in (ii) to a combination of senses is meant to accommodate cases in which, e.g., S acquires perceptual knowledge, from a distance, that *a* is a horse, only by virtue of jointly seeing the appropriate shape and hearing the appropriate hoof sounds. Concerning (ii), the notion of a perceptual circumstance is somewhat vague; but no point in this paper will turn on its vagueness.

it would weaken their case for the view that defeated knowledge is best understood on a justificationist theory.

We should also consider how Q might apply to cases like that of Henry if the relevant belief is construed as direct. Suppose that Henry's belief that a is a barn is not based on any other belief of his. Notice first that the presence of barn facsimiles is a feature of Henry's circumstances. Similarly, if we imagine him observing a candle through a system of mirrors, as described above, their presence would also be what I am calling a circumstance. Now with respect to the circumstances involving the facsimiles, his senses will not be sufficiently acute. He would confuse facsimiles with barns at the distance in question. Thus, by clause (i) of Q, Henry's belief does not constitute knowledge. Regarding the example involving the mirrors, his perceptual circumstances are not appropriate to the belief in question. Judging location through a complicated system of mirrors of the sort imagined is somewhat like judging color in red light. Here, then, Henry would not satisfy (iii) of Q.

These conditions, like (ii) and (iv), are related to, and to some extent unified by, the idea of justification at least in the following way: if Henry *believed* that his circumstances were as they are in relation to the beliefs in question, he would not be justified in holding them. More generally, it is at least often the case that what undermines S's would-be knowledge without undermining his justification *would* undermine his justification if he believed it. And this makes it natural to say, though it does not require us to say, that much defeated knowledge is defeated because S's *justification* is in some way insecure or defective.

4. RELIABILITY AND JUSTIFICATIONIST THEORIES COMPARED

We have seen how some representative naturalistic and some representative justificationist principles can deal with certain cases of defeated knowledge. I now want to consider some of the relative merits of these approaches to defeated knowledge, focusing mainly on Goldman's position and the justificationist proposal employing principles P and Q.

One thing the positions have in common is neutrality with respect to skepticism. Neither approach favors skepticism or rules it out. Skeptics might accept Goldman's view and then take S's (apparent) knowledge that a is a barn to be defeated by even the mere possibility of a barn facsimile which S cannot visually distinguish from a real barn. They might also accept P and then construe the mere possibility of such facsimiles as showing that S is mistaken (or unjustified) in taking the proposition that over there is a barnlike surface, to warrant the proposition that the object over there is a barn, so that he fails to satisfy (iv) of P. Moreover, though neither of the approaches favors skepticism, both make it easy to see how skepticism can be plausible.

What is the reason for these and other similarities between the approaches? Could it be in part that our intuitions about what alternatives are relevant to indirect justified true perceptual beliefs are based on our intuitions about what alternatives would either (a) undermine S's *justification* for taking some proposition to warrant the proposition about the object (e.g., that it is a Selectric), or (b) falsify the proposition that the former does warrant the latter? Similarly, regarding direct justified true perceptual beliefs, are our intuitions about what alternatives are relevant to whether the belief is knowledge based on our intuitions about the satisfaction of Q or something like it? Since 'relevant alternatives' is an undefined term of art, these questions are problematic. But given the possible justificationist explanations of defeated knowledge we have considered, some burden of showing that the answers are negative, or at least that the terms can be explicated without tacit reliance on justificationist notions, seems to rest on those who hold that the notion of a relevant alternative can be naturalistically analyzed.

Let us suppose, however, that an adequate non-justificationist account of relevant alternatives can be given. Would this be a better account than any justificationist account? This is a large question. I shall simply ask whether there are cases of defeated knowledge which a highly plausible naturalistic account like Goldman's does not explain in as theoretically satisfactory a way as some justificationist accounts. There may be such cases. Consider one of Goldman's own examples involving identical twins:

> Suppose Sam's "schemata" of Judy and Trudy have hitherto been indistinct, so Judy-caused percepts sometimes elicit Judy-beliefs and sometimes Trudy-beliefs, and similarly for Trudy-caused percepts. Today Sam falls down and hits his head. As a consequence a new feature is "added"

to his Judy-schema, a mole-associated feature. From now
on he will believe someone to be Judy only if he has the
sort of percept that would be caused by a Judy-like person
with a mole over the left eye. Sam is unaware that this
change has taken place and will remain unaware of it, since
he isn't conscious of the cues he uses. Until today, neither
Judy nor Trudy has had a left-eyebrow mole; but today
Judy happens to develop such a mole.[23]

To rule out Sam's knowing the twin with the mole to be Judy,
Goldman adds to his account of non-inferential perceptual knowledge the condition that "S's propensity to form an F-belief as a
result of percept P has an appropriate genesis."[24]

Goldman does not offer an account of an appropriate genesis.
Perhaps a plausible naturalistic account can be given, but apparently none has been developed to date. Let me suggest, however,
that some justificationist conceptions of knowledge enable us to
account for the case reasonably well. Consider several variants
of it.

Suppose first that Sam knows at the time of the accident that he
has been unable to tell Judy from Trudy. Then, even after the
accident he is not justified in believing, of Judy with the mole, that
she is Judy (assuming he has not forgotten his previous inability
to tell them apart). This shows that even very high reliability does
not entail justification.

Suppose, on the other hand, that Sam has seen only Judy and
has not the slightest inkling that Trudy exists. Then, when he sees
Judy, he presumably is justified in believing her to be Judy. Again
there are two cases. First, there is the sort of case Goldman seems
to be imagining: Sam directly believes her to be Judy; and although
this is in part because the relevant percept has the mole feature,
no inference occurs. Alternatively, Sam may indirectly believe her
to be Judy on the basis of taking her to have the mole feature. The
latter case could well occur if Sam has come to believe, just after
the accident, that he will have to identify Judy at a masquerade
party where her face will be heavily made up. Because of the
accident, he believes that she has a mole, and when he sees her
he takes her to be Judy, believing this, not directly, but on the
basis of seeing (and believing) her to have the mole.

23. Goldman, "Discrimination and Perceptual Knowledge," p. 789.
24. *Ibid.*, p. 789.

In the case involving direct justified belief, we have defeated knowledge. Yet Sam's belief is perfectly reliable; and he has the relevant discriminative powers. Why is it not knowledge? Q would explain this as follows. First, surely Sam's cognitive responses to his senses are abnormal, with respect to a direct perceptual belief that *a* is *F*, when an essential part of what causes the belief is the sort of feature of the *a*-percept which the mole-feature represents. For one thing, it has not been acquired through any perceptual experience, on Sam's part, of *a*. Nor has the property in question been otherwise appropriately associated with *a*, e.g. through someone's telling Sam that *a* has the feature. Intuitively, the idea is that a new feature of one's *a*-percept does not normally become a necessary or sufficient condition for one's perceptually believing *a* to be *F* unless one has *associated* the feature with *F* or with at least one other *a*-feature in virtue of which one takes *a* to be *F*. This certainly seems to hold when we can say that *S* knows *a* to be *F* *by* the feature in question. One could account for this idea by saying that only by some such association would one's belief that *a* is *F*, if based on this feature, be *reliable,* or by saying that only by some such association could one be justified, by virtue of this feature, in taking *a* to be *F*.

Our construal involving indirect belief does not embody defeated knowledge, since Sam is not justified in believing, of the woman with the mole, that she is Judy. On the other hand, P can explain why in this case he would not know that she is Judy, even if this belief were not only justified but also reliable and backed by adequate discriminative capacities. For Sam is not justified in believing that only a Judy-like person with a mole is Judy; nor is he justified even in taking the mole to be evidence that its bearer is Judy.

Let us see whether Swain's justificationist account of knowledge can also deal with the mole example, construed in any of the ways I have sketched. There are at least two ways Swain might proceed. First, the causal chain from the mole state of affairs to Sam's belief, of Judy, that she is Judy, might be defective in Swain's sense. For perhaps Sam would be (a) justified in believing, say, that the state of affairs, an accidentally acquired neural property's causing him to be such that he will perceptually take a Judy-like person to be Judy only if she has a mole, did not occur, and (b) justified in believing, of Judy, that she is Judy, only if he would be justified in believing that this state of affairs did *not* occur. It is not clear to me whether Sam satisfies these conditions. For one thing, is it essential to Sam's justification for believing the woman with the mole to be Judy that he would be justified in believing that no such intermediary occurred? And under what conditions would he have to be justified in believing this? Under conditions as they are at the time, if he believed this I suppose he would be justified.

Imagine, however, that someone has told Sam of the strange accident and given him reasons to believe it occurred which he should accept but stubbornly rejects. Now Sam would not be justified in believing that the relevant state of affairs did not occur. He would then apparently not satisfy the condition of Swain's which might otherwise rule out Sam's knowing. Swain would need, I think, to appeal to another of his conditions. Perhaps the state of affairs, Trudy-with-a-mole, would qualify as a significant alternative to the one actually obtaining. To be sure, this state of affairs does not seem objectively likely. However, Swain says, of the objective likelihood of an alternative, only that it is "not *clear* that the objective likelihood of an alternative is necessary for its significance."[25] Since Trudy-with-a-mole apparently might be a significant alternative even if its objective likelihood is small, and since Swain's account can deal with the example just sketched only by construing this state of affairs as a significant alternative, it would seem that Swain should not take objective likelihood to be necessary for significance, even though this leaves his account less definite. Thus interpreted, the account can deal with this and similar examples.

The last few paragraphs have described how a hard case might be treated using (a) Goldman's reliability account of non-inferential perceptual knowledge, (b) principles P and Q, and (c) some of Swain's principles. With this case the latter two sets of principles seem to provide more understanding of why the subject lacks knowledge. I now want to take up a further question that is suggested by this apparent finding: Can the (partial) account of defeated knowledge provided by P and Q give us a reasonable way of characterizing a relevant alternative with respect to perceptual beliefs? Could it be that whenever we find a relevant alternative in such cases, S fails to satisfy P or Q, and that whenever S fails to satisfy P or Q with respect to a justified true perceptual belief, we have defeated knowledge? If this hypothesis is true, P and Q

25. See Swain, "Reasons, Causes, and Knowledge," p. 240.

209

may be taken to give some account of the notion of a relevant alternative for perceptual beliefs. I am not sure that they do, and if they do they are admittedly not much less vague than that notion as introduced by Goldman; but the above hypothesis is to some degree confirmed by the fairly wide range of examples we have considered.

Similarly, P and Q appear capable of enhancing our understanding of what Swain calls a significant alternative. For one thing, they help us see what *sorts* of things make alternatives significant. Roughly, significant alternatives are states of affairs such that (a) they might have occurred instead of certain states of affairs that did occur in the actual causal chain terminating with *S*'s belief that *p*, and (b) *S* would not be justified in believing that *p* if he were justified in believing one (or more) of the former states of affairs to have occurred. If principle Q is correct, then among the former (the defeating states) are states of affairs involving deficiencies in perceptual capacity relative to the belief that *p*; perceptual abnormalities; untoward perceptual circumstances; and abnormal responses to one's sense impressions. It would be easy to exaggerate the degree to which our understanding of these notions is independent of examples like those we have been working with; but this seems true of all the plausible theories currently in the literature, and if so then even a tentative categorization like the one embodied in Q is worth taking seriously.

It may be objected, however, that P and Q readily lend themselves to a reliability interpretation, so that if they do give an account of relevant alternatives it need not be justificationist. Consider P first. It might be argued, with respect to the justificationist clauses, that in place of (ii) one could put '*S*'s belief that *q* is reliable', that one could eliminate (iii), and that in place of (iv) one could put 'in the circumstances *S* is in at *t*, *q* is a reliable indication of *p*'. Regarding Q, it might be held that for '*S* unjustifiably believes, or would be unjustified in believing' one could substitute '*S* has an unreliable belief, or would have an unreliable belief'. Would P and Q lose any of their explanatory power if we made these substitutions? To argue that each of the substitutions would produce a significant loss would require a long discussion. I shall make just one point about each principle.

First, it seems doubtful that the notion of warranting in P can be naturalistically analyzed. We might, at least in certain cases, give a naturalistic *explanation* of why a belief is warranted, but that is a different matter. One might try to produce a naturalistic analysis by explicating 'q is a reliable indication of p' as equivalent to 'q strictly implies or inductively supports p'. But not just any degree or kind of inductive support will do. The support must be *adequate;* and it is not clear that such adequacy can be explicated independently of justificationist notions. One reason for saying this emerges if we ask how reliable a belief has to be to count as knowledge. Consider Henry. Suppose he can, in the relevant kind of situation, distinguish barns from facsimiles 95 percent of the time. Have we any way of saying whether this is good enough for knowledge without simply relying on our intuitions about knowledge or justification? Could it be that our intuitions about adequate reliability are guided by, or even dependent on, our sense of (1) whether in the circumstances Henry's discriminative powers are such that for him the proposition that over there is a woody-looking barnlike surface *warrants* the proposition that *that* (the thing that has the surface) is a barn, or (2) whether, if he realized there were facsimiles that he could not visually distinguish from barns at the relevant distance, he would, in the circumstances, be *justified* in taking the former proposition to warrant the latter? One might avoid this move by requiring, as Dretske does, that knowledge be based on "conclusive reasons."[26] For then only completely reliable beliefs would qualify. But it is surely not clear that knowledge does require conclusive reasons.[27]

Similar considerations apply to the proposed reliability construal of Q. When we ask what constitutes, e.g., an unreliable belief that one's senses are relevantly normal, it looks as if we do not have a plausible way of answering except through our intuitions about knowledge or justification. Indeed, the crucial question seems to be whether, in the circumstances, S's senses are reliable enough so that, if he knew their acuity relative to the belief that p, he would still be justified in believing that p. Thus, where S is normal but knows he has been hallucinating barns, it is only when his belief that his senses are back to normal is justified, or reliable *enough* to be justified, that he can again know an object before him to be a barn. His belief need not be completely reliable, in the sense that

---

26. See Fred Dretske, "Conclusive Reasons," *Australasian Journal of Philosophy* 49 (1971): 1–22.
27. Some of these difficulties are brought out by George S. Pappas and Marshall Swain in "Some Conclusive Reasons against 'Conclusive Reasons'," *Australasian Journal of Philosophy* 51 (1973):72–76.

in the circumstances his being mistaken would be a physical impossibility; and surely, for him to know that there is a barn before him, his senses need not be so acute that, taking his acuity together with the circumstances he is in, it is physically impossible that this belief be mistaken. But it appears that the right sort of reliability may be in some way a function of S's justification for one or another belief or proposition.

One might at this point object that our intuitions about when q warrants (or justifies) p, or about when S is justified in taking q to warrant (or justify) p, are no *less* dependent on our intuitions about whether S knows that p than are our intuitions about whether S's belief that p is adequately reliable to constitute knowledge that p. But I do not think that is so. Surely one thing shown by many cases of defeated knowledge is that it *can* be quite clear that S is justified, even "fully" ("completely") justified, in the ordinary sense of this phrase, in believing that p, or in believing both that q and that q warrants p, when it is also clear that S does not know that p. Perhaps, then, justificationist accounts of defeated knowledge have greater conceptual independence of the notion of knowledge than those reliability accounts – the most plausible, I think – which do not require conclusive reasons. I cannot claim to have shown this, but given the present tendency (as I see it) to prefer reliability theories, it would be enough to have shown that the view is plausible.

Nothing I have said implies that a naturalistic or, in particular, a reliability account of knowledge cannot succeed. My negative purpose has been simply to show that, contrary to the impression many epistemologists seem to have, it is by no means clear that such accounts are superior to justificationist accounts, at least as regards explaining defeated knowledge. This conclusion would gain support if it should turn out that a reliability account – and perhaps most other plausible naturalistic accounts – of defeated knowledge can succeed only by taking knowledge to require conclusive reasons. For in that case, the positions in question face all the problems confronting the conclusive reasons thesis.

My positive aim has been to argue that principles P and Q (or something close to them) provide a useful account of some important cases of defeated knowledge. They are also meant to support my negative aim and to complement Swain's principles. To be sure, both P and Q need further clarification and further study;

but that assessment seems to apply to a significant degree to all the currently available plausible accounts of defeated knowledge.

There are kinds of defeated knowledge we have not considered. Nor have we considered justificationist or naturalistic accounts of knowledge in general. But with respect to some important cases of defeated knowledge, we have seen that some justificationist accounts apparently can succeed reasonably well. And I have suggested that our intuitions about what alternatives are relevant might be based on our intuitions about whether certain beliefs are justified or on whether certain justificationist principles are satisfied. Although my arguments by no means show that no naturalistic account of relevance can be given, they do indicate the need for an explication of the notion along naturalistic lines. This is a significant point. It tends to offset what naturalists can gain by pointing out that their vocabulary is already required by the sciences, whereas justificationists need at least one normative notion. It remains to be seen which approach can give a better overall account of knowledge. But if my main points are correct, it appears that at least in dealing with some special problems of defeated knowledge, a justificationist position embodying something like principles P and Q can provide at least as good an account as the currently leading naturalistic theories.[28]

28. An earlier version of this chapter was given at the University of Minnesota, Morris, and I profited from discussing it with the faculty and students there. I have also benefited from discussion with Alvin Goldman at the time he presented "Discrimination and Perceptual Knowledge" at the University of Nebraska, and that paper did much to generate my interest in doing this one. For helpful comments on earlier versions of this paper, I am also grateful to William Alston, Panayot Butchvarov, George Pappas, Mark Pastin, Thomas Vinci, and Howard Wettstein.

Chapter 7

The causal structure
of indirect justification

People often have reasons for what they believe, and frequently a belief is justified by a reason the believer has for holding it. Ann's reason for believing that there has been little rain might be that the grass is dry, and this reason might justify her belief that there has been little rain. Clearly this sort of justification requires that she also believe the proposition constituting her reason. It is in part her believing it that makes it *her* reason. Moreover, since it is in some sense *through* her evidential belief, as we might call it, that her belief justified by a reason is justified, it is natural to speak of the latter belief as indirectly justified. More explicitly, let us call S's belief that p indirectly justified if and only if it is justified by one or more reasons S has for believing p. Using this terminology, we can now formulate a major problem. How must an indirectly justified belief be related to the evidential belief(s) by which it is justified? The problem is very large. This paper is addressed to only part of it, namely the question whether, if S's belief that p is indirectly justified by one or more of S's other beliefs, there must be some kind of (causal) sustaining relation between the latter belief(s) and the former. This question is important in understanding how psychological and causal concepts are related to epistemic concepts, in distinguishing justification from rationalization, in assessing the analogy between justified belief and justified action, and in other ways that will soon be apparent.

The causal structure of indirect justification

I. THE SUSTAINING REQUIREMENT OF INDIRECT JUSTIFICATION

Our central question is whether, if S's belief that p is indirectly justified by one or more of S's other beliefs, then it is at least in part causally sustained by the belief(s) in question.[1] We might call an affirmative answer the *sustaining requirement on indirect justification* (hereinafter simply the sustaining requirement). A number of epistemologists have regarded it, or something very nearly equivalent, as a necessary condition on indirect justification,[2] but so far as I know neither the grounds for affirming it nor its connections with other epistemological topics have been adequately brought out. This section will begin to fill that gap.

We might start with a sketch of what it is for one of S's beliefs, say, that p, to be at least in part sustained by another of his beliefs, say, that q. In the simplest case in which S's believing q sustains his belief that p, his believing q explains why he believes p. Ann's believing that the grass is dry might both sustain and (hence) explain why she believes there has been little rain. As this example illustrates, a sustaining relation entails a kind of explanatory one (and may perhaps be equivalent to it, though I shall not assume the converse entailment). There are also cases in which S's belief that q is only a partial sustainer of his belief that p. Suppose, e.g., that the former belief is not adequate to sustain his belief that p (for instance, because he takes q to be, by itself, insufficient evidence for p), and that S believes p for a second reason as well, in such a way that while his two evidential beliefs together sustain (and explain) his belief that p, each by itself only partly sustains and partly explains it. There is a third case, however, in which S

---

1. To ask whether indirect justification requires a sustaining relation is not to ask whether reasons are causes. For one thing, I am construing reasons as propositions, which seem the wrong sort of things to be causes. (I am not ruling out a non-propositional, e.g. sentential, construal of reasons; but I doubt that this would make it more plausible to call them causes.)
2. Russell held, in at least one work, that all our inferentially justified beliefs are held "because of" epistemological premises, where "an epistemological premiss" must be "a psychological premiss," i.e., "a belief which is not caused by any other belief." See *An Inquiry into Meaning and Truth* (London: Allen and Unwin, 1940), Introduction, p. 15, and chs. 9–11, esp. pp. 124–125, 129, and 130–131. D. M. Armstrong also holds something at least close to the sustaining requirement; see, e.g., *Belief, Truth and Knowledge* (Cambridge: Cambridge University Press, 1973), pp. 151 and 209–210. Alvin I. Goldman maintains a version of the requirement in "What is Justified Belief?," in George S. Pappas, ed., *Justification and Knowledge* (Dordrecht: D. Reidel, 1979), pp. 8–9.

believes p for two independent reasons, where he takes each to be sufficient grounds for p, and each evidential belief may, by itself, be truly said to sustain and to explain S's believing p. Each would thus be part of what explains this, but not a merely partial explainer. The third case represents a kind of overdetermination, but none of the three exhibits a non-sustaining, non-explanatory relation that has been called pseudo-overdetermination. This fourth case might be exhibited by a belief of Ann's, say that Joe said there had been little rain, if, while it did not to any degree sustain her belief that there has been little rain, it *would* sustain it if her belief that the grass is dry did not do so. One difference between the two kinds of overdetermination concerns explanation: Ann's belief that Joe said there has been little rain is not part of what explains why she believes this. A related difference is that the strength of her belief that there has been little rain does not in part derive from her believing that Joe said so.

One might compare the respects in which pillars may sustain a balcony: any one might be necessary or sufficient or both; and each may be neither necessary nor sufficient, but contribute to some degree to sustaining the balcony. There may also be unstressed pillars, like ornamental pilasters whose tops barely touch the balcony, which, we might say, pseudo-sustain its weight. None of this characterizes the relevant sustaining relations fully, but nothing in our discussion will hinge on what remains unspecified. Let us turn, then, to the initial case for the sustaining requirement.

Consider contexts in which we ask someone what justifies him in believing something. Suppose Joe says that he believes Sue is a good teacher. Ann, who knows Joe has not observed Sue teaching, might reply, "I don't see what justifies you in believing that." He might respond: "Having seen her present her ideas to non-students, I think she has a lot to say and says it well." Here Joe surely implies that he believes Sue is a good teacher, in part *because* he believes what he cites as justifying that belief.

To see the point better, contrast a question Ann implicitly asks, namely whether *Joe's* belief that Sue is a good teacher is justified, with a question to which it is easily assimilated, namely whether there *is* evidence to justify *the belief* that she is. Joe has this belief, but one might ask whether there is enough evidence to justify it, even if – as when a new teacher is being reviewed by superiors who have suspended judgment – no one presently holds the belief. The contrast is between what I shall call *personal justification*, that of a particular person's belief of a specific proposition, and *impersonal justification*, that of a belief in the abstract, whether or not anyone holds it, or of a proposition, such as the proposition that every even number is the sum of two primes. The distinction applies to both justification as a status of beliefs – justifiedness – and justification as a process, but only the former will concern us directly. Impersonal justification is often expressed by phrases of the form of 'the justification of the belief that p', or, especially, of the form of 'the justification of the statement that p'. In so speaking we need not have in mind any particular believer of p, nor even assume that anyone holds or has stated it. (Indeed, what justifies in this sense need not itself be believed.) A jury, for instance, might regard its task as deciding whether to adopt the belief that S is innocent or the belief that he is guilty, and might compare possible justifications of each. Such parlance does not presuppose that anyone holds either belief. It might sometimes be preferable to speak of what *would* justify one or the other belief, or *does* justify one or the other statement, but the former terminology is not improper and we should account for it.

To make clear that Ann's concern is personal justification, assume that she already believes Sue is a good teacher, but has been impressed with the meager justification of many people's beliefs about teaching, and wonders whether Joe's belief is justified. Then, if she discovers that Joe believes what he does about Sue solely because of her student teaching evaluation scores, Ann would reject his reply to her. Her interest is in whether *his* belief is justified, not in whether there *is* a justification for what he believes; and if what he adduces as justifying his belief in no way sustains it, then (other things equal) he would hold it even if he had not seen Sue present her ideas. Thus, he would be offering, as what justifies a belief of his, reasons which do not move him. Call these *nonsustaining*, since S's believing the relevant propositions does not sustain the belief(s) which (to some degree) those propositions evidentially support. It is quite unclear, as we shall see, that a nonsustaining reason can justify the belief in question.

Some of what has been said also applies where someone asks "How do you know?," intending to determine whether the addressee has adequate reasons to qualify as knowing, and not merely how it happened that he *came* to know, e.g. who told him. If S answers "How do you know Black Beauty will lose the race?" with "He's no match for Wild Stallion," it is at least normally presupposed by the questioner and S alike that it is at least in part because S believes Black Beauty is no match for Wild Stallion, that S believes Black Beauty will lose. To see this, imagine that S has another reason, e.g. that Black Beauty's jockey has been bribed, and that it is entirely S's believing *this* that sustains his belief that Black Beauty will lose. Here, if S cites the superiority of Wild Stallion, he is apparently not explaining how he knows. He is not citing *a way in which he knows,* but rather *a way of knowing* (thus a way he or others *might* know). For one thing, if a reason r adequately explains how S knows that p, then, other things equal, on the basis of r he will still know p even if he gives up any other reason he has for believing p. But that may well not be so here. Since S's belief that Black Beauty is no match for Wild Stallion plays no role in sustaining his belief that the former will lose, he might well not believe Black Beauty will lose, and hence might well not know it, if (other things equal) he had no other reason to believe it.[3]

There is some ground for concluding, then, that if r is a reason of S's by virtue of which he knows that p, his belief of p must be to some degree sustained by his belief that r. Why should there not also be a sustaining relation between an evidential belief and a belief justified by it? Granted a belief may be both amply justified by another, and true, without constituting knowledge. But I am aware of no such cases in which the causal relation (or lack of it) between the evidential belief and the justified true belief which fails to constitute knowledge is significantly different from what it is where the evidential belief is so related to the true belief it justifies that the latter does constitute knowledge. This surely applies, e.g., to a justified true belief that one's ticket will lose in a 10,000-ticket lottery, where what justifies this is one's belief that one's chance of winning is only .0001. The same apparently holds for the sorts of cases offered by Gettier, and where a justified true belief is not knowledge because S lacks appropriate discriminative capacities. There is thus some reason to suppose that indirectly justified belief is like indirect knowledge at least in this: just as an evidential belief that q, in virtue of which one knows p, at least partly sustains one's belief that p, so an evidential belief that q, in virtue of which one justifiably believes p, at least partly sustains one's belief that p. (Perhaps not all indirectly justified beliefs are naturally said to be

3. I am assuming that S's knowing that p entails his believing p, but I cannot argue for this here. I am also assuming that S's belief that Black Beauty will lose is the sort he would not hold except *for some* reason.

justified by evidence, but I am using 'evidential' in a broad sense in which, if q is a reason to believe p, then S's belief that q, is evidential with respect to his belief that p.)

Notice, however, a prima facie disanalogy between knowledge and justified belief. Suppose S knows that p wholly on the basis of his belief that q, where q is a fully sustaining reason, and his only sustaining reason, for believing p, yet S has a non-sustaining good reason, r, for believing p. Then, whereas S might well cease to know that p if he ceased to believe q – since he might well then cease to believe p – he would (other things equal) still have an adequate reason, r, *for* believing p, and would hence remain, in an important sense, justified in believing p. For one can be justified in believing p even if one does not believe it. Consider a case of gathering evidence for a hypothesis on which one has been suspending judgment. One might reach a point where one can truly say, "Surely we are now justified in believing it." This can be true of investigators even if they cautiously continue to withhold belief. But the possibility of being justified in believing p by non-sustaining evidence beliefs is not strictly relevant to our concern: indirect justification of S's (actual) belief that p. It may appear relevant because 'S is justified in believing p' has at least two uses: it can mean (i) p is justified for S, i.e. (roughly), under the circumstances, if S should hold, in a suitable relation to the justifying factor(s), the belief that p, this belief would be justified; or (ii) S's belief that p is justified. (i) concerns the epistemic status of a proposition relative to a person; (ii) concerns the epistemic status of a particular belief. It is the latter notion which is in question here. (It also seems to be the latter kind of justification which, under appropriate conditions, makes true belief knowledge.)

So far, then, we have seen no good reason not to make the natural assumption that an evidential belief bears to a belief it justifies the same sort of sustaining relation whether or not the latter represents knowledge. We can see another dimension of the problem by comparing 'Why do you believe that p?' with 'How do you know that p?' We can ask either question intending to request an explanation or intending to request a justification (or intending both). Why is it that, like 'How do you know that?', 'Why do you believe that?' can serve both purposes at once? And why is it that, ordinarily, when we ask this we expect to get at least what S takes to be both a justification and an explanation? If one asks, "Why do you believe he is seriously ill?" and receives a normal reply like "He is much too weak to have an ordinary flu," one assumes both that S takes this to justify believing him seriously ill and that S offers it as at least partially explaining why he believes him seriously ill. A further reason to think we ordinarily make both assumptions is the clear relevance of two sorts of rejoinder: (a) That does not justify believing him seriously ill – lots of merely incapacitating viruses do that; and (b) That isn't *why* you believe it – you're hiding what the doctor told you.

It appears, then, that (typically) questions of the form of 'Why do you believe p?' are asked with the presupposition that a correct answer will indicate both what S takes to be an explanation of why he believes p and something he takes to justify him in his believing p. Call this *the dual force thesis*. How should we explain why these queries have this dual force? The best explanation seems to be, in part,[4] that (within a certain range of circumstances) our use of the relevant terms presupposes that when, in answering the relevant queries, S takes an evidence belief of his, say that q, to justify (or to explain) his belief that p, he will also typically take his believing q to explain (or to justify) his believing p. This does not entail that the sustaining requirement is presupposed; for that concerns actual (objective) justification, and the relevant point here concerns what S takes to justify his belief. But if the uses in question did not generally presuppose that S's belief that q, justifies his belief that p, only if the former belief at least partly sustains the latter, why would we typically expect people, in answering 'Why do you believe p?' asked to elicit (indirect) justification, to adduce only beliefs they take to be at least part of what explains why they believe p? Presumably, if our use of the relevant terms did not presuppose the sustaining requirement, we would not have a general justification-requesting query to which the *only* correct answers, when the question is asked to elicit (indirect) justification of the belief that p, conform (and often seem in some sense designed to conform) to the sustaining requirement.

To be sure, nothing said here proves the sustaining requirement or even the dual force thesis. But taken together with the other points in this section, the indicated facts about our use of 'Why do you believe that?' strongly suggest that the requirement is both

4. One reason this explanation is partial is that it does not apply where S answers by adducing not a belief but, e.g., an experience, say his seeing something. There is reason to think that a sustaining requirement holds there too, but that issue is not of direct concern here.

true and important for understanding the notion of justification. The next section will support this view further by explicating and assessing some objections to the requirement.

II. THE CASE AGAINST THE SUSTAINING REQUIREMENT

The most detailed case against the sustaining requirement seems to be Keith Lehrer's. His strategy is to propose a counterexample involving a gypsy lawyer whose client has been accused of eight murders and whose

> cards tell him that his client is innocent of the eighth murder though guilty of the others. He never doubts the cards. His conviction of innocence leads him to reconsider the evidence. He discovers a complicated though valid line of reasoning from the evidence to the conclusion that the client did not commit the eighth murder . . . He freely admits, however, that the evidence which he claims shows that he knows his client to be innocent of that crime is not what convinced him of the innocence of his client, and, indeed, would not convince him now were he not already convinced by the cards . . . His conviction could not be increased by his consideration of the evidence because he was already completely convinced. On the other hand, were his faith in the cards to collapse, then emotional factors which influence others would sway him too. Therefore the evidence which completely justifies his belief does not explain why he believes as he does, his faith in the cards explains that, and the evidence in no way supports . . . or partially explains why he believes as he does.[5]

Lehrer is careful not to say that the gypsy's belief about the eighth murder is based on the evidence beliefs. Instead Lehrer speaks of *the justification* of a belief being based on evidence.[6] He denies that the gypsy's belief about the eighth murder is based on, or even in part sustained by, his evidence beliefs. Certainly he would deny that it need be in part sustained by them to be justified by them.

5. Keith Lehrer, *Knowledge* (Oxford: Oxford University Press, 1974), pp. 124–125.
6. *Ibid.*, pp. 122–123.

Let us call the latter view the *divergence thesis,* since it asserts the possibility of a divergence between a belief's justifying another and its sustaining it.

One might well question whether, as the gypsy is described, his evidence beliefs would not to *any* degree sustain the belief they are said to justify. But let us grant this for the sake of argument. Do we now have a counterexample to the sustaining requirement? Recall first the distinction between personal and impersonal justification. When Lehrer says such things as "If one statement or belief justifies another, then the former is evidence for the latter,"[7] he may have in mind the impersonal notion of what justifies *a* belief that p (or the belief that p). This contrasts with what justifies a particular person's belief that p, i.e., as I shall sometimes put it, justifies a person *in his belief that p,* where S is justified in his belief that p, if and only if he *justifiably believes p.* (I think these locutions are standardly used equivalently, but in any event nothing important will turn on my so using them here.) The contrast is roughly between the belief that p being justifiable (whether or not it is held) and a person's justifiably believing that p.

Granted, what (impersonally) justifies the belief that p *would,* other things equal, justify S *in his belief* that p should S believe p on that basis. This fact may help to explain why the distinction is easily overlooked. It may seem, e.g., that one may argue as follows for the divergence thesis:

> Since (1) the justification of the belief that p is q, which is good evidence for p, and (2) S believes q, and sees its full evidential bearing on p, (3) S *has* good evidence for p. Hence, (4) S has a justification for the belief that p. Thus, (5) if S believes p, then even if his believing p is not to any degree sustained by his believing q, he justifiably believes p, and the (or a) justification of this belief is based on his belief that q.

---

7. *Ibid.,* p. 122. Lehrer also says: "It is how a man knows that is explained by evidence. Why he believes what he does may be explained by anything whatever. Therefore, a justification of a belief that is known to be true is based on certain evidence if and only if his having that evidence explains how he knows the belief is true" (pp. 125–126). Clearly Lehrer is using 'justification of a belief' and 'a belief that is known to be true' as if he meant, by 'belief', 'proposition', and were speaking of impersonal justification; but the context requires that we take his main concern to be personal justification.

One trouble with this argument is that from *there being* a justification, *q*, which S "has" in the relevant sense, for *the* belief that *p* (which S holds), one may not infer that S *justifiably believes p*, without begging the question against the sustaining requirement. Lehrer may not be committed to this argument. But once the above distinctions are observed, the argument ceases to appear clearly valid, and the proposed counterexample is less plausible. The remainder of this section will suggest both why this argument is invalid, at least in the step from (4) to (5), and how the sustaining requirement can be plausibly held, even if the case of the gypsy is acknowledged to show something important about justification.

Let us first consider some consequences of Lehrer's interpretation of the example. Recall the assumption that the cards are not actually relevant to *p*. Thus, even though S (here the gypsy) has (objectively) good evidence for *p*, given a contrary verdict from the cards he would (other things equal) have had the false belief that not-*p*. Second, given his faith in the cards, he would have believed *p* even if it had been false, indeed, even if, on the basis of the cards, it had not been rendered so much as objectively *likely* (to any degree) to be true, i.e., very roughly, likely to some degree given the actual facts relevant to *p* (I leave open how relevance is to be specified). Third, S would have believed *other* falsehoods about the crime, had the cards pointed to them, e.g. that the client's spouse committed it. These points, especially the second, strongly suggest that S does not justifiably believe *p*. It is, after all, simply good fortune (because the cards happened to be right) that S did not believe something false in place of *p*. Surely if one's belief that *p* is justified by good evidence, it cannot be simply good fortune that one did not believe something false instead.

I take this suggestion to be plausible in itself. But it is also supported by important general considerations. Think of the relation between justification and truth. There is an important (and widely recognized) connection between impersonal justification and truth; e.g., where *p* (or the belief that *p*) is justified by good evidence, *q*, then, in virtue of *q*, *p* (or the belief that *p*) is at least likely to be true. But there is also an important (and far less widely recognized) connection between personal justification and truth. The latter connection is our main concern here. In the most common cases where S's belief that *p* is justified by good evidence, *q*, S would not have believed *p* if *p* were not true or at least objectively likely to be true. For here S would not have believed *p* if he had not believed *q*, in virtue of which – since *q* is (objectively) good evidence for *p* – *p* is at least objectively likely. There is, I suggest, a measure of protection from believing falsehoods which justification by good evidence provides. This point may in part explain the plausibility of the idea that if *S* justifiably believes *p*, *S* is *reliable* regarding *p*, in a sense implying that if, in certain counterfactual situations, he should form a belief regarding *p*, the belief would be true.[8] If this idea is correct, justifiably believing implies not merely being *de facto* right or *de facto* likely to be right about *p*, but having the sort of ground that makes one right or likely to be right about *p* in a certain range of circumstances. By contrast, in the (presumably not unlikely) case of the cards' bearing false witness, the gypsy would be wrong about *p*.

There is a second, related connection between personal justification and truth. So far, we have seen that where *S* justifiably believes *p* by virtue of good evidence, *q*, he would not (other things equal) believe *p* if he did not believe *q*, and hence if *p* were not at least objectively likely to be true. But it is, I think, also true, in such cases of evidential justification, that *S*'s forming (or holding) the belief that *q* is (causally) *sufficient* to produce (or sustain) in him at least a tendency to form (or hold) the belief that *p*. Often his forming (or holding) the belief that *q* will be, in the circumstances, fully sufficient for, and will explain, his forming (or holding) the belief that *p*, as Ann's believing that the grass is dry might be sufficient for, and explain, her belief that there has been little rain. Thus, where *S* is indirectly justified, by his belief that *q*, in his belief that *p*, not only would he not (other things equal) have believed *p* if it were not at least objectively likely; his belief that *q* also gives him at least some tendency to believe *p*. The two points differ at least in this: *S* could be such that he would not believe *p* if it were not likely, even if he had no tendency whatever to believe *p*. The first point is roughly that indirect justification in one's belief that *p*, *by* good evidence, provides a measure of protection from believing *p* should *p* be *false*. The second point is roughly that such indirect justification embodies a positive tendency to believe *p*, and

8. For plausible reliability theories regarding justification or knowledge see Armstrong, *op. cit.*, and Goldman, *op. cit.*, and "Discrimination and Perceptual Knowledge," *Journal of Philosophy*, LXXIII, 20 (1976). Some reliability theorists affirm the sustaining requirement; but perhaps a reliability theorist need not hold it, and affirming it does not commit one to a reliability theory of knowledge or justification.

hence – since p is supported by good evidence – to believe something at least likely to be *true*. We have seen how the first point applies to the gypsy. Let us now apply the second point to him.

First, it is absolutely essential that we distinguish between (a) the evidence he has for believing the client is innocent guaranteeing that this *proposition* is true or objectively likely, and (b) what justifies his belief of this truth guaranteeing that he will (or has some tendency to) believe it. Since his evidence is good, (a) clearly holds. Our question concerns his *belief*. The point here is that because his evidence beliefs play no sustaining role with respect to his belief that the client is innocent, it is simply good fortune that he holds it: *relative* to his evidence beliefs, his holding it (rather than no beliefs, or a false one, on the subject) is lucky. Happily, the cards cause him to believe a true proposition for which he has evidence. But if S is justified, by good evidence, in his belief that p, his evidence belief surely cannot function in him so that, as far as it is concerned, he just happens to believe p (because of the cards). If S's belief that Jack is innocent is justified by S's beliefs about Jack's whereabouts, then given these evidence beliefs it is to be *expected* that S believe Jack is innocent, rather than, say, suspending judgment, or believing something else, about Jack. Surely the justification of a belief by good evidence is such that when S has this kind of justified belief it is not simply good fortune that he *believes* what is true (or at least objectively likely). It may, of course, be good fortune that *what* S believes (or knows) is true, e.g. that a person S believes to have survived a fall did survive it. But that is a quite different matter.

The sustaining requirement helps us in understanding both of the connections we have noted between personal justification and truth. Indeed, it is not clear that they can be plausibly explained without it. Let us consider the connections in turn.

Take first the point that indirect justification (by good evidence) provides a measure of protection from false belief. It is easiest to see this in what seems the most common case of indirect justification, where the relevant sustaining relation between S's belief that q (his evidential belief) and his belief that p is strong enough for the former to be necessary for the latter. For there he would not have believed p if (other things equal) he had not believed q, which is good evidence for p, and hence would not have believed p if it were not true or at least objectively likely. But even where such a necessary condition relation does not hold, by virtue of even a partial sustaining relation S would be less likely to have believed p if (other things equal) he had not believed q. For something which at least in part explained why he believed p, would have been absent. Not even this applies to the gypsy; he would have been as likely to believe the cards even if he had not had evidence. I suspect, however, that a set of evidential beliefs (objectively) justifies S's belief that p, only if some subset of them is (a) necessary for his believing p and (b) expresses adequate ground for it. The sustaining requirement does not entail this; but while I am defending only the modest interpretation of it given in Section I, I believe it is highly plausible with this (or a similar) necessary condition relation built in.

Now consider the point that where S is indirectly justified in his belief that p, by good evidence q, he has at least some tendency to believe something true. This connection is clearest in those (very common) cases where S's belief that q is sufficient for his belief that p. To be sure, the sustaining requirement does not entail that the set of evidence beliefs is *sufficient* for S's believing p. But I am taking the relevant sustaining connection to be strong enough to imply that, given his evidence belief(s), S at least tends to believe p. Without this implication there could surely be no causal sustaining relation. This is why, on the sustaining requirement, when, by virtue of believing q, S justifiably believes p, then *given* his belief that q, it is at least not merely good fortune (and certainly not simply accidental) that S believes p, as it is with the gypsy. It is merely good fortune, given the gypsy's evidence beliefs, that he believes the client innocent; for those beliefs exercise no influence on him, and the cards, which wholly produce his belief, only happen to point to innocence.

In the light of these points about the relation between justification and truth, I suggest that it is natural to conceive beliefs justified by evidence as appropriate *responses* (in a causal sense) to evidence beliefs. Moreover, while I have been trying to show the importance of distinguishing (non-causal) justificatory relations between propositions and (causal) justificatory relations between beliefs, there is a significant analogy. I think we not only conceive evidence for p as intrinsically connected (by implicative or probabilistic support) with the truth of p; we also conceive being justified, by evidence, in one's belief that p, as intrinsically connected (by some degree of causal support) with believing truth. The second point is crucial for the gypsy case. If one's belief is justified by evidence, it cannot be simply good fortune – as it is with him – that one believes a truth. If our question concerning the gypsy were about conditions for the relevant proposition's being justified for him, we would have a sufficient condition. But the issue is conditions for justified belief, and that is a quite different matter. What is (indirectly) justified *for* us is, as it were, a matter of evidential resources we can command. What we justifiably believe (by virtue of evidence) is causally grounded in evidence we have already in some sense commanded.

My conclusion in this section, then, is that the gypsy case is not a counterexample to the sustaining requirement. I have of course not considered every potentially plausible objection to the requirement,[9] but I have tried to indicate how the most plausible ones can be met. I have also argued positively for the requirement, and while I do not claim to have established it I believe we have seen some good reasons for accepting it. The next section will provide further support for it.

III. PERSONAL JUSTIFICATION, IMPERSONAL JUSTIFICATION, AND RATIONALIZATION

To reveal the breadth and importance of the distinction between personal and impersonal justification, let us first note its application to actions. Consider physicians deliberating about whether to use a strong medicine. Suppose it becomes clear that using it is justified. Still, if someone gives it to the patient for the wrong reasons (or for none), *he* does not justifiably give it, and is indeed reprehensible

9. Marshall Swain has argued that if the gypsy's evidence beliefs pseudo-overdetermine his belief that *p*, they may justify it. The idea is roughly that he may justifiably believe *p*, even if the evidence beliefs do not to any degree sustain this belief, provided that, should he cease to believe in the cards, then if he continued to believe *p*, it would *now* be because of the evidence beliefs. See *Reasons and Knowledge* (Ithaca: Cornell University Press, 1981), pp. 91–92. This is plausible; for we may apparently say that his evidence beliefs are sufficiently strong to sustain his belief that *p*. I cannot discuss this case in detail, but note that, as in Lehrer's example, the gypsy would still have believed *p* even if it had not been true or likely to be true; and given the merely potential causal role of his evidence beliefs in relation to his belief that *p*, it is simply good fortune that he believes *p*, rather than something false. Another plausible attempt to give a counterexample to the sustaining requirement is made by George Pappas in "Basing Relations," in Pappas, *op. cit.* What I have said about the gypsy can, I think, also be applied to Pappas's example.

for giving it. It is one thing for *what S does* to be justified; it is quite another for *S* to *do it justifiably*. The former is a kind of impersonal justification, the latter a kind of personal justification. The first is justification of a type, the second of a token. This distinction parallels that between the personal and impersonal justification of beliefs: between *S*'s justifiably believing *p*, and justification of the belief that *p*. For instance, that the forecasters predict rain may justify *the* belief that it will rain (roughly, the type, believing that it will rain); but if *S* believes, for bad reasons (or none), that it will rain, then (normally) he does not justifiably believe this.[10] Just as, from an action *A* being justified in a situation, and *S*'s *A*-ing in that situation, it does not follow that *S* justifiably (or non-reprehensibly) *A*'s, it does not follow, from *the* belief that *p* being justified and *S*'s believing *p*, that *S* justifiably (or non-reprehensibly) believes *p*.

The distinction between personal and impersonal justification, construed as I have suggested, enables us both to give an alternative positive characterization of the gypsy and to show how that characterization is related to the sustaining requirement. Imagine that on a sunny day we ask *S* what justifies his belief that it will rain at night, and suppose he cites the weather report, though he knows his belief is sustained only by his meteorological intuition. Now suppose that the forecast changes and that we discover he still holds his belief. We might ask why he has not changed his expectation. If he said that while the weather report was his evidence, his belief in no way depended on it, we would certainly conclude that he had been at least misleading. The weather report was not "his evidence" in the usual way, and I suggest that it is natural to say that he used it to *rationalize* his belief. It is true that

10. It should be noted that phrases like 'justification of the belief that *p*' may express a notion distinct from, though closely related to, that of the impersonal justification of a belief, namely *propositional justification*. If (the type) believing that *p* – say, that other galaxies are inhabited – is justified, so is the proposition that *p* (in each case the justification is relative to certain justificatory elements). But the converse may not hold. What I am calling propositional justification differs from what Roderick Firth calls by that name: a proposition's being justified *for a person* (something we might call *person-relative* propositional justification). See Firth's "Are Epistemic Concepts Reducible to Ethical Concepts?," in A. I. Goldman and J. Kim, eds., *Values and Morals* (Dordrecht: D. Reidel, 1978). In "What is Justified Belief?" Goldman has termed something at least close to what I would call person-relative propositional justification, "*ex ante*": "Here we say of the *person*, independent of his doxastic state vis-à-vis *p*, that *p* is (or isn't) suitable for him to believe" (p. 21). This paper was written before I read these articles; but both helped me in developing it, and both contain points which support some of mine.

the distinction between rationalization and justification is not commonly applied to beliefs, but it is surely applicable to beliefs as well as actions.[11] Just as a physician who gives a drug for a bad reason might rationalize his having given it by citing a good but non-motivating reason he had for giving it, S might rationalize his belief that it will rain by citing a good but non-sustaining reason he had for believing this (i.e., adducing a non-sustaining evidential belief). In both cases a good reason is cited; in neither is it the "real" reason, and hence it is not casually operative as a reason *for* which the person acts or believes. In both cases the reason may provide impersonal justification: of the giving of the drug, and of the belief that it will rain. But it does not follow that the physician justifiably gives the drug, or that S justifiably believes it will rain.

The point here is not that S's rationalizing his belief that p, entails that he does *not* justifiably believe p. One can rationalize a belief one justifiably holds. But giving a rationalization of one's belief – in what seems a (or the) central use of 'rationalization' in reference to belief – still contrasts markedly with citing something that justifies the belief, and it appears to be only through the sustaining requirement that we can account for this contrast. For what above all distinguishes good reasons that simply rationalize S's belief that p, from good reasons that justify it is that the latter, but not the former, are sustaining reasons. This point applies, of course, to particular beliefs (tokens); the contrast is thus between rationalization and personal justification. There is, however, a kind of rationalization that may suffice for impersonal justification. Let me explain.

The sort of rationalization we have so far examined might be called *belief rationalization*. It occurs (roughly speaking) where (i) S cites q to justify or to explain his belief that p, (ii) S believes q, (iii) S takes q to support p, yet (iv) S's believing q does not to any degree sustain his believing p. There is, however, at least one other important kind of rationalization we should consider. It occurs (roughly speaking) where S tries to make a proposition (or a belief-type) seem reasonable, by providing a purported justification of it. We might call this *propositional rationalization*. S may give such a

11. Armstrong has pointed this out and has argued that "A causal account of what it is for a man to have a reason for believing something enables a persuasive account to be given of the distinction between such reasons and mere rationalizations," *op. cit.*, p. 95. He does not, however, argue directly that the distinction can be made only causally.

rationalization of *p* – say, of a principle being considered for adoption – whether or not he (or anyone else) believes *p*. A propositional rationalization may succeed in impersonally justifying *p* (or the belief that *p*) if, in giving it, *S* offers good evidence, say *q*, for *p*; but if my main points have been essentially sound, then even if *S* believes both *q* and *p*, it would not follow that *S justifiably believes p*. For one thing, *S* might still believe *p* for a bad reason.

These two kinds of rationalization are alike in having a capacity to provide impersonal justification and thereby show that *the* belief that *p* is justified. They are also alike in that neither entails the existence of personal justification. In giving a belief rationalization *S* (by definition) does not give a sustaining ("real") reason for the belief he rationalizes. This is why such rationalizations contrast with explanations. In offering a propositional rationalization of *p*, *S* need not believe *p*, and, if he does, need not give a sustaining (or an explaining) reason for his belief of it. He may in fact believe it for bad reasons. For particular beliefs, then, as for particular actions, rationalizability does not entail rationality.

It is no accident that I contrast rationalization – particularly belief rationalization – with both explanation and (personal) justification. For belief rationalizations, like rationalizations of particular actions, are, I think, to be understood in part as defective attempts (whether actual or potential) to answer 'Why do you believe that?' That a failure to answer it (adequately) may result either from a failure to explain, or from a failure to justify, a particular belief, suggests that rationalization is appropriately contrasted with both justification and explanation. The sustaining requirement enables us to explain this contrast. For it ties (indirect) justification and explanation together: a belief that does not at least partly explain another belief cannot justify it. Here the epistemic order intersects the causal order.

On the basis of what we have seen regarding justification and rationalization, we can now positively characterize the gypsy in a way that accounts for the example's apparent success against the sustaining requirement. We may say not only that the gypsy is justified *in* believing his client is innocent of the eighth murder, but that he can rationalize this proposition, in a non-pejorative sense implying that he can also justify *the* belief that his client is innocent. But here we must be careful: just as we must not assimilate rationality to rationalizability, we must not assimilate justifiedness to justifiability. What the gypsy can do is justify *believing* the proposition (and I think we may thus also say that he can justify the proposition); he may even be said to be *able to justify* his belief that the client is innocent of the murder. But these points do not entail that he justifiably believes the client is innocent. His belief is not justified and is not, I think, a candidate for knowledge.

IV. CONCLUSION

On the view set forth in this paper, it is important that we be aware of ambiguities in terms concerning justification, being justified in believing, justification of belief, justification of belief by reasons, reasons for belief, and related topics. All these phrases can be used to express either personal or impersonal justification. It is crucial for understanding justification that these two notions, which have sometimes been conflated, be clearly distinguished. Personal justification contrasts with impersonal justification in at least three ways. First, its instantiation requires the existence of at least one believer. Second, when personal justification is indirect (and for purposes of this paper we need not assume it is ever direct), it is unlike impersonal justification in entailing a sustaining relation to at least one evidential belief. Third, whereas impersonal justification of a (or the) belief that p entails that p is (propositionally) justified, S's justifiably believing p does not entail that p is justified, since, for one thing (though we have not considered such cases), S may justifiably but mistakenly believe that his reasons for p are adequate. Rationalization may provide impersonal justification, but it is not sufficient for personal justification. I have thus contrasted the rationalizability of a person's belief with its justifiedness, and I have argued that the sustaining requirement enables us to give a good account of – and may indeed be required to explain – this contrast.

We may plausibly conclude, then, that the sustaining requirement is sound, and that indirectly justified beliefs stand in causal as well as epistemic relations to the beliefs by which they are justified. This conclusion is important not only for all the reasons we have seen, but because (as I have elsewhere argued[12]) it bears directly on the controversy between foundationalist and coher-

---

12. In "Axiological Foundationalism" (Chapter 2, this volume). (The main argument cannot be set out briefly enough to state here.)

entist theories of justification and knowledge. Moreover, if knowing that p entails having a justified belief that p, then a counterpart requirement holds for indirect knowledge.[13]

Our topic has been the justification of beliefs, but the idea of indirect justification can be applied, in a quite parallel way, to other propositional attitudes. In closing, I want to suggest that our results seem generalizable to these other cases.[14] If so, a counterpart of the sustaining requirement holds for desires justified on the basis of other desires, values justified on the basis of other values, and so on. What accounts for these parallels, I believe, is that justification by reasons has a common structure in all the domains in which it occurs. I hope that this paper takes us part of the way toward understanding that structure.[15]

13. It is interesting to note that Lehrer no longer holds that knowing entails believing. See his "Self-Profile," in R. Bogdan, ed., *Keith Lehrer* (Dordrecht: D. Reidel, 1981), in which he proposes to substitute acceptance for belief in his account of knowledge (pp. 79–80). I believe the distinction between personal and impersonal justification will apply to acceptance rather as it does to belief, but the question cannot be pursued now.

14. I have argued for this generalizability to values, in "Axiological Foundationalism (Chapter 2, this volume), and for the generalizability to wants, in "The Structure of Motivation," *Pacific Philosophical Quarterly*, 61, 3 (1980).

15. This paper was first presented to a National Endowment for the Humanities Summer Seminar for College Teachers (on Reasons, Justification, and Knowledge) which I directed in 1981. I benefited much from discussions in the seminar and from presenting a later version at the 1981 plenary session of the Iowa Philosphical Society and at the University of Kansas. I also want to thank William Alston, Albert Casullo, Wayne A. Davis, Risto Hilpinen, Leonard Schulte, Ernest Sosa, Wayne Wasserman, and the editors of the *Journal of Philosophy* for helpful comments.

Chapter 8

Belief, reason, and inference

If we are to know ourselves, then by and large we must know for what reasons we believe what we do. If we are rational, we want to avoid believing for bad reasons and to have good reasons for believing at least many of the things we do believe. If we are to understand others, and to know in general what to expect from them, we must grasp not only what some of their important beliefs are, but for what reasons, or at least what sorts of reasons, they hold them. There are, then, ideals of self-knowledge, rationality, and mutual understanding which cannot be explicated apart from the notion of believing for a reason. The notion is also important in relation to both epistemic justification and knowledge. But how are we to understand this notion? Is a belief for a reason equivalent to one based on *inference?* And how does a belief for a reason differ from one rooted in prejudice but backed up by a plausible *rationalization?* What is it to believe *partly* for a reason and partly on the basis of, say, wishful thinking? And how is believing for a reason related to believing on the *basis* of something, such as another belief? A good account of believing for a reason should help us solve these and other problems. The account that follows is framed with such problems in mind and intended to clarify certain issues in the philosophy of mind as well as several that are important in epistemology.

I
BELIEFS, REASONS, AND INFERENCES

Our vocabulary for speaking about reasons is extremely rich. If the related parlance concerning inference is added to our discussion of believing for a reason, the dangers of confusion mount. This section will attempt to distinguish different sorts of reasons, to connect reasons with beliefs, and to relate both to inference.

REASONS AND REASON STATES

Consider a case in which a person, S (Sam, let us say), believes that his brakes are worn and believes it entirely for one reason: that they squeak. If asked for what reason he believes this, he would be disposed to say simply that they squeak; and others might say of him that the reason for which he believes that his brakes are worn is that they squeak. Notice, however, that someone might describe the reason for which he believes his brakes are worn as his *believing* that they squeak. This sort of reference to his beliefs might be appropriate if one had some doubt oneself about whether they did squeak. Moreover, even if they did not, ascribing to S the belief that they did would serve to express his reason. Similarly, even when S says only that they squeak, he *expresses* a belief that they do; and if he does not believe that they do, it is not at all clear that their squeaking can be a reason for which he believes they are worn. There is, then, some diversity of usage regarding 'reason for which' in the relevant contexts, and to avoid confusion we must establish a way of speaking about reasons. What I shall do is take a reason, r, for which S believes a proposition, p, to be a proposition S believes. We can then refer to S's believing that r as a *reason state*. While very commonly, in expressing a reason, r, for which we believe something, or in ascribing such a reason to someone else, we presuppose that r is true, or at least do not take it to be false, I shall not assume that r must be true. After all, one kind of bad reason for which someone might believe something is a proposition that is (and can fairly readily be seen to be) false.

This terminology seems both natural and clarifying. For instance, when we talk of good reasons for a *proposition*, we can conceptualize the attribution in terms of relations between propositions. If, on the other hand, someone speaks of a reason's causing a belief, we can both account for the slight oddity of so speaking, and make literal sense of the relevant locutions, by supposing that what is intended is ascription of a causal relation between a (concrete) belief *state* and the belief for which the proposition expressed by that state is the reason. Similarly, since we sometimes talk of a belief –

e.g., of the belief that there is life elsewhere in the universe – being *true*, when we mean that the proposition believed is true, it is not surprising that reason states, when conceived as beliefs, are sometimes referred to as reasons. The terminology I suggest, then, should be clarifying and should beg no questions.

SOME MAIN VARIETIES OF REASONS

There are many kinds of reasons relevant to believing, and we should distinguish them if we are to understand believing for a reason.[1] Let me briefly illustrate (without offering definitions) what are perhaps the most important kinds.

Reasons to believe p are normative, in the sense that they have at least some justificatory weight, and impersonal, in the sense that they imply nothing about any particular person. There can be reasons to believe there is life elsewhere in the universe even if no one actually believes there is, or even believes the propositions constituting those reasons. In this connection, we talk of *discovering* (good) reasons. I leave open whether *every* truth is such that there are good reasons to believe it, but I doubt that. It may be that affirming the existence of good reasons to believe something is implicitly relative to persons (or at least to possible rational beings) and presupposes their having some degree of *access* to the reasons in question.

Related to reasons to believe are *reasons for S to believe,* which are normative, but personal, in the minimal sense that S believes, or at least, by virtue of information available to him, epistemically ought to believe, the propositions expressing them. If *S has* evidence for life elsewhere in the universe, then there is at least one reason *for him* to believe it exists, whether he does or not, and even whether or not he has any notion that the evidence does support that conclusion.

By contrast, *a reason S has for believing* is personal, but not necessarily normative. Thus, that Ann has, in S's hearing, given testimony that there is life elsewhere in the universe might be a reason S has to believe there is. A reason of this sort is usually personal by virtue of S's believing both the proposition in question (in this

---

1. I have indicated these sorts of reasons, and discussed some of their interconnections, in Chapter 3, this volume.

case, that there is life elsewhere in the universe) and the proposition(s) expressing what, typically at least, he in some sense takes to support it (that Ann has given testimony in favor of it). But such a reason need not be normative; it might have no justificatory force, e.g. because the testifier is quite obviously unreliable. There are cases, moreover, in which a reason S has for believing p, whether normative or not, is personal only in a weaker sense. S may have a reason to believe p, yet either *not* believe p, say because he finds the mere thought that p disturbing, or not believe the proposition constituting the reason, e.g. because he has not seen that this proposition readily follows from other things he believes.

Usually, but by no means necessarily, a reason S has for believing a proposition which he believes will also be *a reason why S believes* it, i.e., one that at least partly explains why he does, in the sense, strictly speaking, that his *believing* the proposition constituting the reason explains this. Typically, a reason S has for believing is readily available for such an explanatory role in a way a reason for S to believe it need not be, since, I take it, typically a reason S has for believing p is one that in some sense he *does* take to support p. If S believes something he takes to support the proposition that there is life elsewhere in the universe, then even if his believing this is not part of what explains why he believes there is life elsewhere, it is ready to become such an explainer: e.g., should his other basis for the latter belief collapse, this (subjectively) evidential belief might be "invoked" for a supporting role, whether automatically or, more likely, in his attempting to assemble evidence or protect conviction; and in being so invoked it is very likely to become a reason why S believes there is life elsewhere in the universe.

We can now locate *a reason for which S believes p:* it must at least be a reason he has for believing p *and* an actual basis of his belief that p, in a sense implying that it is a reason why he believes it. Reports in scientific journals cannot be a reason for which S believes there is life elsewhere in the universe unless his believing those reports is at least part of the reason why he believes that there is such life. It may or may not be a reason *to* believe this. (There *may* be a secondary, non-epistemic use: perhaps one may say such things as that the reason for which she believes that her child is normal is simply her passionate fear of deviance in the family. But if such talk is permissible and does not turn out, when contextually interpreted, to meet the conditions this paper suggests to explicate reasons for which, then I suspect it employs 'reason for which' equivalently with 'reason why'.)

If this sketch of reasons is approximately correct, then to do justice to the notion of S's believing a proposition, p, for a reason, r, which I take to be equivalent to r's being a reason for which S believes p, we must capture the sense in which r is also a reason S *has* to believe, and a reason *why* S believes, p. Certainly r can also be a (normative) reason to believe p, but our account must not assume that it is. We should also be wary of phrases of the form of 'S's reason for believing p'. They may be used to express *either* a reason for which S believes it, or a reason he merely has to believe it – or used ambiguously. More positively, I suggest that if r is a reason for which S believes p, S must take some *connection* to hold between r and p, and his belief that r must play an explanatory (and presumably in some sense causal) role with respect to his belief that p. One way to see that these conditions are fundamental is to note that believing for a reason is not just having a belief that is an *effect* of a reason (strictly, of a reason state), though it is believing *on account of* a reason. It is, in a way, belief that *takes* some account of, in the sense that it is guided by, a reason. (Again, it is strictly the reason state that guides, on the assumption I am making here that abstract entities are not causal elements.) We might even say that a belief *for* a reason is to some degree under the control *of* reason. The account I shall develop, then, will construe beliefs for reasons as responses to reasons, and not mere effects; as held in the light of reasons, and not merely explainable in terms of them; and as, in a special way, under the control of reasons.

INFERENTIAL BELIEFS

A belief for a reason is quite naturally conceived as inferential, and sometimes philosophers have so characterized beliefs for a reason without discussing possible differences between being for a reason and being inferential. Consider S's believing that his brakes are worn, for the reason that they squeak. Unlike, say, the belief that there is something rectangular before me, this belief might be called inferential. But if we call it that, we must not assume that it is produced by *inference*, understood generically as a process of passing from one or more premises to a conclusion.[2] S might simply

2. In "A Theory of Practical Reasoning," *American Philosophical Quarterly* 19

note the squeak and, having a standing belief that squeaky brakes are worn, form the belief that his brakes are worn. This could even happen in a flash while S is mainly occupied with conversation. One may of course insist that there was a rapid or largely unconscious inference; but I believe that to do so is not necessary since the crucial epistemological and psychological point is just that his belief that the brakes are worn is due to a reason and not, say, grounded directly in perception.

In any event, we can make a distinction here that may help all parties to the dispute. If we take seriously the point that for every case of believing p for reason, r, there *is* an inference, in the sense of an abstract argumental structure – possibly enthymematic – from r to p, we may conceive every belief for a reason as *structurally inferential:* some argument underlies any such belief, at least in the sense that there is an argument whose premise(s) indicate the structure of the belief(s) causally grounding the belief that p, and is such that S is disposed in effect to appeal to the argument should he try to explain or justify his believing p. On the other hand, a belief for a reason need not arise from, or be sustained by, any tokening, e.g. internal recitation, of that structure which deserves the name 'inferring p from r'. Thus, a belief for a reason need not be *episodically inferential*. If it is, then it must also be structurally inferential, but the converse does not follow.

The distinction between structurally and episodically inferential beliefs is not sharp, but it is real. Moreover, a belief that is episodically inferential at a given time, say just as S is inferring its propositional object from premises he holds, or is entertaining the belief as true explicitly in the light of them, may be structurally inferential from then on, being simply grounded in an appropriate way on the underlying argument. Indeed, unless there are long-term unconscious inference processes, beliefs are not normally episodically inferential for any length of time. Even if they arise through inference and their propositional objects are periodically reinferred, through most of the time S holds them they will be structurally inferential. They may in fact cease to be inferential at all, as where S forgets the relevant reason(s) yet retains the beliefs in question. Perhaps, then, we may conceive a belief for a reason as inferential in one or the other of these two senses. This should help us – so far as we under-

(1982), I have argued for a similar thesis as applied to actions, and also made a number of related points about inference.

stand the notion of inference. But it will turn out, I think, that to understand how a belief may be *based on inference*, as where it arises from or is sustained by either an inference process or one or more reasons, we must solve the problems to which I now turn in developing an account of believing for a reason.

II
BELIEVING FOR A REASON

This section will explain and defend conditions that seem individually necessary and jointly sufficient for S's believing p for a reason, r. The account developed is meant to preserve the distinctions made above, and in Section III it will be applied to some important problems.

EXPLANATORY SUSTENANCE

It seems plain that if r is a reason for which S believes p, then S's believing r is part of what explains why S believes p – at least if it is granted that S must believe the proposition constituting his reason. If we do not suppose there is such an explanatory relation, it is at best difficult to interpret the 'for' in 'believes for (on account of) a reason'. This is not to imply that the *formation* of S's belief that p, say, that his brakes are worn, must be explainable in terms of his believing that r. He might have first believed this through testimony and later, on getting his own auditory evidence, also – or instead – come to believe it for the more direct reason constituted by the proposition that they squeak. Believing for a reason does not entail having *come* to believe for that reason, or for any reason.

This example indicates something else of importance: believing p for a reason, r, is consistent with the belief's being *overdetermined*, in the sense that another reason belief, that s, adequately explains why S holds that r. Indeed, there may even be a non-belief, such as a perceptual cue, which also adequately explains this. Moreover, a belief for a reason may be merely *potentially* overdetermined, as where S merely *has* another reason belief, say that s, which is (i) sufficient to sustain the belief, but, because S has not seen any connection between s and p, is (ii) not doing any sustaining work though it *would* do that work if, other things equal, S were to cease

239

to believe *r*. Compare two pillars beneath a bridge, one bearing weight, the other placed against the first with its top just tangent to the bridge's underside, ready to bear weight should the first pillar crumble. A belief for a reason may also be *partly* sustained by other sorts of factors, such as biases. But surely if the belief is unqualifiedly for a reason, *r* – and not just partly for it – then *S* satisfies an *explanatory sustaining requirement:* his believing *r*, given contextually presupposed features such as the normal functioning of the brain, (a) in part explains (even if other factors also in part explain) why *S* believes *p*, and (b) actually sustains this belief, in the sense that, if any other sustaining factors, including potentially sustaining ones (such as other reason beliefs) were eliminated, then, other things equal, *S* would still believe that *p*.

This explanatory sustaining requirement seems intuitive and has rarely been questioned. But occasionally philosophers have been inclined to think that a sufficient condition for a belief to be for a reason is *S*'s being disposed to appeal to that reason in justifying the belief.[3] Now I grant that *normally* this is sufficient. But it is possible to have this disposition when one only thinks that *r* is a reason for which one believes *p*. Just this appears to happen in certain cases of rationalization, and if we accept a condition like the suggested one as sufficient we shall be hard pressed to make a plausible distinction between real reasons and rationalizations.[4] Surely even having a reason, seeing that it is one, and using it in defense of *p* is not sufficient for believing *for* that reason. One might be merely rationalizing one's belief.

CONNECTING BELIEFS

It has been suggested above that when *S* believes *p* for a reason, *r*, he believes *p* in the light of *r*, not merely because of it, and that

---

3. Keith Lehrer, e.g., has suggested that something roughly equivalent to this is sufficient for one belief to be based on another: "What I mean by saying that a person's belief is not based on certain evidence is that he would not appeal to that evidence to justify his belief." See "Knowledge, Truth and Evidence," in Michael Roth and Leon Galis, eds., *Knowledge* (New York: Random House, 1970), p. 56.
4. The notion of rationalization is difficult to explicate, and there are complicated issues here. I have tried to deal with the major ones in Chapter 14, this volume, and in "Self-Deception and Rationality," in Mike W. Martin, ed., *Self-Deception and Self-Understanding* (Lawrence: University Press of Kansas, 1985).

he must in some way see *r* as supporting *p*. In part, the idea is that otherwise his belief that *p* is *cognitively unmotivated;* the reason *S* has for it, *r*, figures in the reason *why* he believes *p*, but his believing it is not *on account of r*, where this suggests, not his explicitly taking *r* into account, but his belief system's somehow reflecting *r*'s subjectively registered support for *p*. Or so I shall argue, beginning with an explicit formulation of the idea.

To capture the appropriate kind of connection, we must avoid not only positing beliefs *S* need not have, but also attributing to *S* concepts beyond the grasp of the least conceptually developed creatures capable of believing for a reason. On both counts, we may *not* claim that *S* believes *r* is a *reason* for *p*, or evidence for it or grounds for it; nor should we assume that *S* must have any epistemic concepts at all, since we should leave open that children can believe for a reason before they acquire epistemic concepts. My suggestion is that while such *de dicto* beliefs may play the required connecting role, we need a condition that recognizes *de re* beliefs as well. I propose, then, a disjunctive *connecting belief requirement:* where *r* is a reason for which *S* believes *p*, there is a connecting relation, specifically, a *support* relation, *C*, such that either *S* believes *C* to hold between *r* and *p*, or *S* believes something to the effect that *r* bears *C* to *p*. Now this relation may be as conceptually elementary as implication (though presumably not material implication); *S* may believe implication to hold between *r* and *p* by simply taking *r* to be such that if *r*, then *p* (if taking is not a kind of believing, I regard it as sufficient, in this sort of case, for the kind of believing in question). *S* need not conceptualize the relation of implication here, nor believe *that r* implies *p*. *C* may also be confirmation, justification, probabilistic implication, entailment, explanation, evidencing, indicating, and so on. There is room, then, for a huge variety of both *de re* and *de dicto* beliefs to make the appropriate connection, for *S*, between *r* and *p*.[5]

---

5. This conception of connecting beliefs stakes out a ground in between the sort of view suggested by Judith Jarvis Thomson, on which one may reason from a set of premises to a conclusion only if one believes this set "is reason for" the conclusion, and the modified Armstrongian view of Barbara Winters, on which "for me to base my belief *q* on my belief *p* I must conclude *q* from *p*, infer it, reason to it," where "*A* infers *q* from other beliefs *p* only if the set of beliefs [*p, q*] instantiates an inference pattern and *A*'s transition from *p* to *q* is a result of *A*'s general disposition to make transitions that exhibit that form." See Barbara Winters, "Reasonable Believing," *Dialectica* 34 (1980), p. 14; Judith Jarvis Thomson, "Reasons and Reasoning," in Max Black, ed., *Philosophy in America* (Ithaca: Cornell University Press, 1980), p. 298; and, for the second

The concept of believing for a reason is not without vagueness, and that is partly why we cannot precisely specify what counts as a support relation. Those relations all have this much in common, however: they make r relevant, for S, to p, and his taking one or more to hold between r and p tends to lead him to, or to confirm him in, the belief that p. This point in part underlies plausible versions of the view that reasons (reason states) are not causes.

By virtue of connecting relations, S believes p *in the light of a reason*, and not simply because of a reason (state). They are in this respect essential in accounting for an important property of believing for a reason: it is *discriminative*. There are two broad aspects of this: first, the belief that r does not, *qua* reason belief, or *basis belief*, as we might call it, tend to give rise to or sustain just any belief, but only those S takes r to support; secondly, where r is the *only* reason for which S believes p, so far as S is disposed to explain or justify his belief that p (e.g., on being asked why he believes it), he (i) spontaneously tends to appeal to r, and (ii) does not spontaneously tend to appeal to other beliefs, in the explanatory or justificatory attempt. This holds even if – by some direct route involving no support relation – other beliefs *are* part of what sustains his belief that p (there can be other beliefs satisfying this sustaining condition, but other beliefs doing so is not implicit in our *concept* of believing for a reason). Thus, the belief that his brakes squeak quite naturally sustains (or generates) the belief that his brakes are worn, but does not tend to sustain (or give rise to) the belief that he is being a nuisance – unless he takes making such noises to be, e.g., sufficient for being a nuisance, in which case he has an appropriate connecting belief. And if asked why he thinks his (recently purchased) brakes are worn, then if he is disposed to give an explanation at all, he immediately tends to cite his reason and to explain its relevance in terms of some support relation; he does not first form a connecting belief and then follow it to a reason: that is a way of rationalization, not of real reasons. On the view that believing for a reason is structurally inferential, we might say that the connecting belief is the line that leads one from the reason to that for which it is a reason, or from the conclusion back to its inferential ground.

Believing for a reason is discriminative in still another way: con-

quotation from Winters, her "Inferring," *Philosophical Studies* 44 (1983), p. 216. Even assuming that, as I have argued, inferring is not entailed by believing for a reason, both views are plausibly taken to apply to the latter relation as well.

cerning choice or acceptance of formulations of both p and r. Suppose r is the reason for which S believes p, and S cites r in explanation or justification of his believing p. Now imagine someone's altering S's words and saying, "Why should their squeaking indicate that they are frayed?" If S does not believe, say, that their being worn is (or implies) their being frayed, and thus has no connecting belief making this formulation of his belief relevant to his reason, then he will not tend to take his reason – that the brakes squeak – to indicate fraying and will – on that basis, at least – not tend to feel challenged, as he would likely feel if someone asked why the brakes' squeaking should indicate their being *worn*. His connecting belief helps to discriminate among formulations and, in suitable contexts, sorts out the (subjectively) relevant from the irrelevant. Now compare someone's saying to him, "That high-pitched hum does not mean wear." His connecting belief makes *squeaking* relevant to wear and, other things equal (e.g., if he does not form a new belief which provides a connection), it will lead him not to tend to regard his as an objection, since it does not capture his reason. Even if he believes that such a high-pitched hum is equivalent to the relevant squeak, if he did not conceptualize the squeak as such a hum originally, he must *connect* the hum with the squeak if he is to feel the point as a denial that his reason is good. Again, the discrimination among formulations seems due largely to a connecting belief.

We can clarify the connecting belief requirement further by addressing some objections. I want to consider two problems: whether the connecting belief requirement leads to a vicious regress, and whether it need be objectionable to a naturalistic epistemology.

One might think that if S's believing p for reason r requires S at least to believe some support relation, C, to hold between r and p, then S must also believe an appropriate relation to hold between C and r (or C and p), e.g. to believe that if r bears C to p, then p is warranted by r. I suspect that this objection is rooted in a tendency to think (rightly) of believing for a reason as in some sense inferential and (wrongly) to conceive the propositional object of the connecting belief as necessarily a *premise* in the corresponding argument. Then, if the entire premise set of that argument is identified with the reason for which S believes p, there must indeed be a further connecting belief. But this line of thought is mistaken. Leaving aside that when the connecting belief is *de re*, S need have

no belief whose propositional object is suitable to serve as a premise, note that having a connecting belief, say believing *C* to hold
between *r* and *p*, *implies* (and perhaps even constitutes) grasping
an appropriate connection between *C* and both *r* and *p*. No higher-
order connecting belief is needed on that score. Moreover, if a
connecting belief does have the same content as, say, the major
premise in a mixed hypothetical syllogism (e.g. the premise that
if Socrates is human, he is mortal), then the minor may be taken
– as it typically is on independent grounds – to be *S's* reason for
the conclusion, for instance the conclusion that Socrates is mortal.
To be sure, if one is seeking to represent *S's* reason so that its
justificatory role is as explicit as possible, it may then be appropriate
to take the whole premise set as the reason. But in that case it is
plausible to suppose that *S has* a suitable connecting belief. In any
event, we apparently need never treat believing for a reason as
subject to a requirement that the belief that *p* be grounded in an
inference in which (i) the propositional object of a connecting belief
is a premise and (ii) the entire premise set is the reason for which
S believes *p*. Certainly many connecting beliefs will themselves be
grounded on reasons; but some may also be both non-inferentially
held and non-inferentially justified, and surely no regress can be
generated by pursuing their basis.

Some philosophers might also object that the connecting belief
requirement is not naturalistic, e.g. because the notion of support
is clarified partly in terms of concepts like justification, and that
since believing for a reason seems itself to be a psychological concept the requirement is mistaken. The notion of justification is
indeed used in explicating support, and clearly the concept of believing for a reason is largely psychological; but we need not assume
that no naturalistic analysis of justification (and similar concepts)
can be given. On the other hand, while *S* may believe for a bad
reason, the concept of a reason for believing simpliciter may have
an irreducibly normative (or at least non-naturalistic) component,
if only in the form of an objective requirement that the reason not
be wholly *irrelevant* to what it is *S's* reason for. There may be an
epistemic nadir from which one could not descend to even worse
reasons, but would begin to adduce "considerations" that are not
reasons at all. I suspect there is, but our account is neutral on this
matter. The notion of believing for a reason is not obviously subject
to a relevance requirement of the kind imagined, and in any case
there may be no harm in allowing epistemically irrelevant consid-

erations to count as reasons for which someone believes p, so long as we have ample resources for substantive and logical criticism.

A naturalistic epistemologist may be inclined to avoid this entire issue by dispensing with connecting beliefs. For Armstrong, e.g., q is a reason for which S believes p if and only if

> There exists some general proposition (x) (if Fx, then Gx), such that q has the form Fb and p has the form Gb, and such that A [S] is disposed so that: if A believes something of the form Fx, then this belief-state will both create (if necessary) and weakly causally sustain [roughly, sustain compatibly with other factors' doing so as well] within A's mind the belief that the corresponding proposition of the form Gx is true.[6]

On this view, that the brakes squeak could be the reason for which S believes the brakes are worn even if S had no connecting belief, so long as (in its place) there is a general proposition, e.g. that squeaky brakes are worn, such that (for whatever reason) S's coming to believe an instance of its antecedent will create or sustain S's believing an instance of its consequent.

Let us explore this. Consider a doting husband whose belief that his wife no longer loves him causes him to believe that he is no good, that he will lose his job, and even that human life is ultimately futile. He might satisfy Armstrong's condition. There might be a suitable generalization *causally* linking, in minds like his, believed loss of love of one's spouse to belief that human life is ultimately futile. Thus, all minds of a certain sort (uxorious, we might imagine) are such that if a male with such a mind believes that (human) life has come to lack (its great value of) his wife's loving him, then that belief produces in him the belief that (human) life is ultimately futile. But surely such a man, however *colored* his beliefs are by his sad realization, need not believe that human life is ultimately futile, *for* a reason, let alone for the reason that his wife no longer loves him. He can believe the former *because* he believes the latter, without its being a reason for which he believes it: it is simply a reason why he does. If, on the other hand, he took her no longer loving him to support that conclusion (e.g., because if *he* is not lovable to a woman like her, then human life is ultimately futile), he would believe, for a reason, that human life is ultimately futile.

---

6. See D.M. Armstrong, *Belief, Truth and Knowledge* (Cambridge: Cambridge University Press, 1973), p. 85.

There is a difficulty with this argument. The facts might arguably be explained on the weaker assumption that S is simply not *disposed* to believe, of the proposition that his wife no longer loves him, that it supports the proposition that human life is ultimately futile. This kind of disposition might then be held to be all that is needed to secure, for S, the connection between the reason and the proposition for which it is a reason. But this is surely too weak; it allows that S might be, on balance, much more strongly disposed to *deny* that there is such a support relation. If so, it is far from clear how the disposition would suffice to make the connection. The natural response is to make the disposition *overriding*, where this implies both that S does not disbelieve that there is a support relation and that whatever inclines him to believe there is outweighs anything that inclines him to believe there is not.

Even this emendation will not solve our problem, however; for there are too many inappropriate sources of the relevant disposition, including a desire to appear to be rational. Thus, the depressed husband might be overridingly disposed to form the connecting belief only because he wants to see his beliefs as rationally grounded. His being so disposed would not show that he believes, for a reason, that human life is ultimately futile. We could add that the disposition is, e.g., purely epistemic; but then we might not be able to do justice to cases in which S believes for a bad reason, say owing to a disposition to form a connecting belief that is irrational in a way that renders it unclear whether the disposition is epistemic at all. Moreover, how much do we gain in simplicity in going from the minimal connecting belief condition sketched above to a complex disposition condition? Very little, at best, particularly when it is appreciated that the connecting belief condition does not require S to have the *thought* that r supports p, or any thought explicitly connecting the two propositions. Connecting beliefs need not be *occurrent*.

One may now wonder, of course, how much difference there is between a *dispositional belief*, such as I am describing, and a *disposition to believe*. The difference is not sharp, but it is important.[7] In broad terms, the former is a belief- and behavior-guiding state; the latter is a readiness to enter into such a state given certain eliciting conditions. The former is capable of explaining other beliefs one

---

7. In "Believing and Affirming," *Mind* XCI (1982) I have argued for this distinction and suggested its importance.

already has; the latter can explain belief *formation*, but apparently explains one's existing beliefs at best derivatively, by virtue of its being realized in the formation of the explaining belief(s). For instance, suppose S is being merely disposed to believe his brakes squeak, since he has grounds for this but has not put them together so as to form the belief. This will not explain why he believes they are worn except by virtue of manifesting itself in the belief that they squeak (or in some other kind of explainer). This difference in explanatory power is one reason why beliefs are more suitable than mere dispositions to believe for making the connection between a reason and what it is a reason for, and in explaining the sense in which believing for a reason is discriminative. Granted, nothing said here proves the connecting belief condition, and a connecting disposition requirement would probably accomplish much of the relevant task; but the connecting belief condition does seem more plausible than alternatives, and other reasons for its plausibility should emerge in the next subsection.

EXPLANATORY CONNECTEDNESS

If we reflect on the intuitive idea that where *r* is a reason for which S believes *p*, S believes in the light of a reason, it should not be surprising if the connecting belief also plays an explanatory (and broadly causal) role regarding S's belief that *p*. I think, indeed, that it has much the same kind of explanatory importance as S's basis belief (that *r*). Recall the case in which, because S believes his wife no longer loves him, he believes that human life is ultimately futile. Now suppose that he does (foolishly) hold the connecting belief that if she no longer loves him, then human life is ultimately futile. Can the proposition that she no longer loves him be the reason for which he believes human life is ultimately futile, even if, other things equal, he would have believed this *without* taking the former to support the latter, or having any other connecting belief? If we suppose so, we allow the possibility that his connecting belief *does no connecting:* it might be, e.g., that his belief that his wife no longer loves him depresses him and, via his depression, causes him to believe that human life is ultimately futile. This is not a case of believing *for* a reason; his connecting belief is not something in the light of which he believes what he does. The reason could, for instance, just as easily have led to some quite different belief so far as the influence of the connecting belief goes; he only happens to have a belief with a content suitable for enabling him to grasp the connection, but his belief that she no longer loves him might have caused anger and, thereby, a belief that the world should be destroyed. His causally idle "connecting" belief need not have interfered at all. It would be a retrospective basis for being surprised at oneself if one noticed the origin of one's belief that the world should be destroyed; but it would have exercised no influence over what further beliefs the "basis" belief produced.

It appears, then, that believing for a reason is subject to an *explanatory connectedness requirement*: if *r* is a reason for which *S* believes *p*, then *S*'s believing some support relation to hold between *r* and *p* (or his believing something to the effect that *r* does support *p*, or his having both beliefs) is part of what sustains *S*'s believing *p*. (Only one connecting belief *need* play an explanatory role, though it would seem at least unusual if *S* had one which played none at all, and this is a possibility I shall generally ignore.) It will help in assessing this condition if we again consider believing for a reason as structurally inferential. There is wide, though perhaps not universal, agreement among philosophers that inference is a causal process. To be sure, philosophers like Armstrong, who reject the connecting belief condition, would also reject this one, both as a requirement on believing for a reason and as a condition on coming to believe *p* on the basis of inferring it from *r*. Harman even goes so far as to say, regarding the "suggestion that, when *S* infers *P* from [presumptive evidence] *E*, *S* believes *P* partly because *S* believes that *E* confirms *P*."

> I suspect that the truth is the other way around: *S* can suppose that *E* confirms *P* only because *S* finds himself able to infer *P* from *E*.[8]

One reaction to this is that it puts epistemology at the mercy of psychology: what we can see as evidence is a matter of what we discover already evidentially moves us. But that is hardly a refutation, and Harman may intend to suggest precisely this. So let us explore the issue on its merits.

Certainly one *can* come to believe that *r* supports *p*, because one's believing that *r* causes one to believe that *p*, or because of one's

---

8. See Gilbert Harman, "Inferential Justification," *Journal of Philosophy*, LXXIII (1976), p. 570.

discovering this causal connection. Such a connecting belief may, but need not, be formed in relation to a rationalization: there may really be a support relation, the grasping of which figures in the relevant belief's (or discovery's) causing the formation of the connecting belief, which in turn sustains the belief that p. Indeed, it is reasonable, in considering whether r does support (confirm, entail, etc.) p, to ask oneself whether one can (intuitively) infer p from r. This question, however, is not simply psychological. For one thing, surely r supports p if and only if it is, to some degree, *reasonable* (for some possible being, at least) to infer the latter from the former, and perhaps we intuitively tend to find it easier to see whether the right side of the equivalence is satisfied than to see whether the left is. This point may be part of what makes Harman's apparently psychologistic claim plausible.

It is also crucial to see that, virtually instantaneously, S can both (i) come to believe that r and that r supports p, and (ii) infer p from r. S need not consider each proposition separately. Indeed, I doubt that they need even be entertained, though perhaps if S *infers* p, he must at least have the passing thought that p (this would not preclude the inference's being unconscious, since, for one thing, the rest of the process could be unconscious, and S need not realize he believes or has inferred p). My claim is only the minimal one that where, in inferring p, S comes to believe it on the basis of r, from which he infers it, he must not only believe a support relation to hold between r and p (or something to the effect that r supports p), but the latter belief must be part of what explains his coming to believe p. Again, I suggest that without some such requirement we cannot distinguish between (a) p's being adopted by S through inference from r, and (b) S's belief that r merely causing his believing p, in the presence of his believing r to support p. In the latter instances, S believes because of, but not in the light of, and hence not for, a reason. His belief formation is not *guided* by his taking a support relation to hold between r and p. The difference is somewhat like that between *following* and merely acting in accord with a rule. In following a rule, S must not only in some sense take his behavior to accord with the rule, but so behave in part because he does take it to accord with the rule, or at least takes the rule to apply to it.

It may be that Harman is influenced by perception of the following kind of case. Suppose S has a standing, unarticulated (perhaps never entertained) belief that if r, then p, e.g. that if the branches of the trees are swaying, then there is a wind. *S* then "instantly" comes to believe there is a wind, if he comes to believe (through seeing it) that the branches are swaying. Here it may look as though the connecting belief (that if the branches are swaying, there is a wind) plays no role, and that belief itself, if expressed by *S* – say, in explaining why he thinks there is a wind – can appear to be a product of a natural tendency to rationalize his adopting the belief that there is a wind on the basis of his belief that the branches are swaying. After all, given the instantaneous genesis of the former belief, one is even inclined to say that *S* just "saw" that there was a wind. The term 'infer' is not natural here, and thus, if one later finds *S* drawing the inference in the course of explaining why he believes there is a wind, it may easily seem that he is only then "making the connection" between the two propositions, and that previously his belief of the first simply caused his belief of the second, quite apart from the influence of the connecting belief. But once we recall that a belief for a reason need be only structurally inferential, this sort of case looks less troublesome for the explanatory connectedness requirement. Recall, too, that there is no sharp distinction between believing for a reason and having a belief "directly" produced by a perceptual cue, where, in retrospect, one can formulate the cue and appeal to it as a reason for one's belief. *There* one need have no connecting belief; and typically such a belief arises only later as one makes the inference from the perceptual proposition to the one believed on the basis of it. But that is not, initially, a case of believing for a reason. On balance, then, close scrutiny of the relevant cases supports the explanatory connectedness requirement.

SUBJECTIVE GROUNDING

Mature, reflective people who attend closely to the question for what reason(s) they believe something are rather good at telling for what reason(s) they believe it *if* they believe it for one or more reasons. People are certainly fallible in this, as in telling *whether* they believe for a reason at all. Error is particularly likely where one has two reasons for believing something but disapproves of one and wants to see oneself as believing only for the other: the cognitive counterpart of Kantian cases in which a moral person whose inclinations are aligned with duty wishes to act only *from* duty. Still, our access to the reasons for which we believe is in some sense privileged, and we often know such reasons without self-observation or inference from introspective data. Why should this be? It may be in part due to a natural tendency for the bases, at least the inferential bases, of our beliefs to manifest themselves to us, at least if we consider carefully why we hold the belief(s) in question, and for the guiding influence of a connecting belief to leave a trace by which, on suitable introspection, that belief can be identified by S. The evolutionary value of this is obvious: if we cannot in general readily find out why we believe what we do believe, we cannot effectively monitor and correct our own inferential tendencies; and the more readily we can come to know our reasons – and connecting beliefs – the more easily we can correct our erroneous beliefs and improve our inferential tendencies.

Whatever the explanation for the measure of privileged access we have, it may well be that our having it is not a contingent matter. Imagine someone saying, e.g., that although the reason for which S believes his brakes are worn is that they squeak, he neither knows that this is his reason nor has any tendency to make the appropriate connection between the former belief and the latter, for instance to see the latter as the basis of the former. We can certainly imagine his reason's being obscured by other reasons or somehow repressed; but we would demand an explanation of why he apparently cannot make the connection: we would want to know what is inhibiting the natural disposition, and once we found that and cleared it away we would expect him to see the connection readily. Far from being hard to discern, reasons for which we believe are usually what we first blurt out if asked, by someone with whom we are not guarded, why we believe whatever it is. (Freud may have held similar views even about repressed elements: for him, that ultimately patients should be able to see them for themselves, directly, was apparently a criterion he adhered to in attributing repression.)

If there is a conceptual requirement lurking here, what is it? The case of the wind and branches is instructive: if we ask S his reason for believing there is a wind, he is disposed, without inference or self-observation, to say that his reason is that the branches are swaying. The case contrasts markedly with that of rationalization of a belief one holds, in which S may have to make an effort to conceal his real reason for believing p and may have to seek reasons he has (or can be thought to have had) for believing p. But when the (real) reason for which S believes *p* is *r*, S has, I think, a natural tendency to regard his belief that *p* is in some way grounded in (his belief that) *r*. I suggest, then, a *subjective grounding requirement*: independently of seeking reasons he has or might have, for believing *p*, S is non-inferentially disposed to attribute his belief that *p* to his belief that *r*. This disposition may of course be inhibited, say by self-deception. But it is natural and pervasive; it is part of what makes us the kinds of rational, self-conscious, self-monitoring, self-corrective beings we are.

Two aspects of this non-inferential disposition must be further clarified: the sense in which it is built in, and the sorts of attribution in which it manifests itself. To say that the disposition is built in is in part to say this: S would have it even if he did not believe, or indeed disbelieved, that *r* is a good reason for *p*. If, e.g., S's belief that Joe is stealthy is based on his belief that Joe has a certain national origin, then there is a special causal relation between the two beliefs such that even if S realized that the former belief does not express a good reason for the latter, he would still be disposed to appeal to the former to explain his holding the latter. If it *is* a reason for which he believes, it exercises – when S thinks about why he believes *p* – a pressure for recognition. Its recognition can be obscured by other reasons, by repression, even by pigheaded disavowal; but our conception of believing for a reason seems to require that if S does not, given appropriate opportunity (such as an unthreatening person's asking him why he believes *p*) tend to attribute his belief that *p* to the belief expressing his real reason for it, then there must be an explanation of that.

This case contrasts both with rationalization of a belief one holds and with seeking, for a belief one has, a justification or explanation one does not yet have. In those cases S's disposition to cite reasons *for p* – reasons which do not include his real reason(s) for believing it – does not arise independently of his seeking reasons, even if he already believes the propositions in question. *It* also lacks the spontaneity of the disposition to attribute a belief to one's real reason for it. It depends on S's search for reasons, or on his considering why he believes *p*, and not on, say, the sustaining connections affirmed by the sustaining and explanatory connectedness conditions.

One kind of attribution has already been illustrated: it often occurs when S appeals to his believing that *r* in answer to the question why he believes *p*. Call this kind of attribution *explanatory*.

In the context of such a question, he may make an explanatory attribution simply by *citing r*, e.g. saying simply that his brakes squeak, provided he does so in a way that *expresses* his believing r – something generally implied by citing r in explanation, since we normally do not offer as explanations statements we do not believe. Attribution may also be *causal*, as where S appeals to his believing that r in answering the question what caused him to believe p; and these two sorts of attribution may overlap, particularly if S thinks of explaining as offering a cause, or of offering a cause as explaining. Similarly, either certain why-questions or certain requests for evidence or justification may evoke a *justificatory* attribution. Asked her evidence for believing that there has recently been little rain, Ann might say that she believes the grass has lacked water for at least a month.

Regarding the manner in which attributions occur, those so far cited are behavioral. But we may speak of Jan's attributing a property, e.g. jealousy, to Joan in virtue of Jan's *believing* something of Joan, and I shall suppose that any of the kinds of attribution described above can be cognitive rather than behavioral. A minimal case of attribution might occur when S simply takes his belief that p to come from (be caused by, be due to, or the like) his belief that r. Since taking is *de re*, this may not even require his having a concept of belief. Indeed, there may be one such case not even requiring doxastic or causal concepts: S's taking a suitable causal relation to hold between his belief that r and his belief that p, and taking r to imply p, where he in some sense sees both propositions as belonging to his view (e.g., regards them assentingly, or with a sense of approval), without conceiving them strictly as believed, or conceptualizing them in relation to any causal connections. But even if this case is not possible, surely quite small children are capable of elementary doxastic and causal attribution, and it is arguable that, prior to developing this minimal capacity, they may have reasons for believing (by virtue of having beliefs that express reasons for further beliefs), and believe because of them, but not yet believe for reasons.

The non-inferential disposition in question need not be manifested. This may be because the belief that r is unconscious (indeed, the requirement even allows that the belief that p be unconscious). This is a case of the disposition's being inhibited by, say, repressive factors. The disposition may also not be manifested because the two beliefs in question are insignificant to S and they arise, and pass, in moments. But normally the disposition is quite likely to be manifested when queries by others, or occasions for self-examination, lead to considering why one believes *p*. When it is manifested, it may express itself in behavior, e.g. in giving an explanation, in thought, or simply in belief. This may seem to rarefy the disposition to a point of little significance. But it does not: the beliefs in question tend to be knowledge; and even when they are not, they play an important role in self-understanding and self-direction, as well as a social role in making ourselves intelligible to others. It may be impossible to give an exhaustive list of inhibitors; but if we try to imagine *S* believing that *p* for a reason where he has no such disposition whatever – rather than one inhibited by some competing factor – we have a belief so cut off from the reason why *S* holds it that *S* in some sense *cannot* make the connection. He can *create* a connection, for instance by forming new beliefs concerning the relation of *r* to *p*. But if, given his present beliefs, he cannot make the connection, we do not conceive the putative reason as capable of the appropriate guiding role, and the case becomes one of believing because of, but not for, a reason.

ACCIDENTALITY

We have now articulated conditions sufficiently strong to cover the normal cases. But there are strange possibilities against which the concept of believing for a reason is armed, and by exploring them we can learn a good deal more about its contours. The first problem concerns accidental connections.

Imagine that, in the presence of a machine which has the capacity to influence the brain so as to produce beliefs, *S* happens to form the beliefs that *r*, and that *r* warrants *p*. It might also just happen that the machine is so adjusted that the formation of these beliefs causes it to produce in *S* a belief that *p*. The machine might at the same time suppress the normal causative processes by which the first two beliefs would produce the third, so that the third is not overdetermined, but generated by the first two only through the accidental activation of the machine. We can even imagine that the machine also produces the non-inferential attribution disposition characteristic of believing for a reason. Our previous four conditions are now satisfied. But do we have a belief for a reason? I think not. It would be one thing if the generative beliefs were

accidentally produced; for then it would simply be accidental that
S has the reason he does have, and that happens commonly, as
where one accidentally stumbles upon information. But if *r* is a
reason *in the light of* which S believes that *p*, guides S's belief formation (or retention), and is discriminative, then surely the explanatory relation between the belief that *p* and the basis and
connecting beliefs is not accidental.

The verdict is more difficult if we suppose that only *one* of the
relevant sustaining relations is accidentally mediated by the machine, or that only the attribution disposition is. Perhaps there is
no definite answer here apart from a detailed specification of the
individual case. Certainly in clear cases of believing for a reason
none of the three conditions is accidentally satisfied. The wisest
course may be to build non-accidentality into the account regarding
all three. But where accident intrudes in only one instance, particularly in the genesis of the disposition – whose *presence* is perhaps
more important to the concept of believing for a reason than is its
origin – the case may well be borderline. It is in a tentative spirit,
then, that I include the following *non-accidentality condition*: the basis
and connecting beliefs do not, singly or in combination, accidentally produce the belief that *p*. I am inclined to think that we should
also rule out these beliefs accidentally producing the disposition
to attribute the belief that *p* to them, and surely in actual cases this
connection is not accidental. But there may be insufficient reason
to extend the non-accidentality requirement to this disposition, and
I am not formally adding it to the conditions being developed.

Accidental connections are difficult to define. They typically contrast with reliable ones, but non-accidentality is not simply unreliability. If Sue intelligently guesses distances, yet is quite often
right, she makes unreliable, but not accidental, projections. The
connection between her guesses and the true distances can be
unreliable without being accidental; and if she is right, she may
not be justified, and likely does not know, but she is not just
accidentally correct. Nor can we say that a non-accidental causal
connection is one not backed by a *law*; for while it is true that we
do normally contrast accidental with nomic connections, we are
not entitled to rule out the deterministic view that for every accidental causal connection there are descriptions of the cause and
effect under which they instantiate a universal law.

One might think we could simply bypass the problem of accidental interventions by requiring that the basis and connecting

beliefs sustain or bring about the belief that *p directly*, i.e., without causal intermediaries. But believing for a reason is compatible with such intermediaries, and presumably there normally are some. It may help to note that accidental connections of the kind to be ruled out are typically conceived as abnormal. But perhaps the primary notion to keep in mind here is that of an intervention which is not only abnormal for *S*, but undermines the guiding role of connecting beliefs. If the reason for which *S* believes his brakes are worn is that they squeak, then in the context the latter belief, together with his taking their squeaking to imply their being worn, renders it expectable, and precludes its being accidental, that he believes they are worn.

An idea related to the view that the crucial connection must be direct is that if we take seriously our previous requirement that the basis and connecting beliefs (partly) *explain* why S believes *p*, we can see that they cannot accidentally produce or sustain that belief. Note, for instance, how misleading it would be in such accidental cases to say that *S* believes *p because* he believes *r*, or to offer simply his believing *r*, together with his believing it to support *p*, in explaining why he believes *p*. But suppose there are, as for all we know there may be, covering laws backing the relevant accidental connections. Would because-statements of the indicated kinds then be false? And would the suggested explanations be incorrect, as opposed to being misleading uses of explanatory terminology which *normally* presupposes that the explanation is grounded in the conceptual framework of reasons rather than that of other psychological factors and possibly abnormalities in the brain? These are difficult questions, and we are pulled in two directions: toward a positive answer by the normal presuppositions of the relevant explanatory terminology, toward a negative answer by the thought that accidental connections do not preclude a causal account that might, using our best neuropsychological theories, yield good scientific understanding. Fortunately, we need not settle this here. If there is a notion of explanation that will do the work of the accidentality condition, it is certainly not ready to hand; it will have to be explicated, and surely in clarifying it we shall have to make clear that its application rules out the sorts of accidental connections considered here, as well as the kinds of intermediaries to be discussed shortly. Thus, if there is, say, a sense of 'because' such that if *S* believes *p* because he believes *r* then *r* is a reason for which he believes *p*, that sense will be no easier to explicate than the relation of believing for a reason itself. For this and other reasons, I prefer to presuppose only a weaker notion of explanation than such a use would express and to rule out certain inappropriate causal connections directly.

In discussing accidental intervention, we saw how a machine could be a causal intermediary in the generation of a belief for a reason from S's basis and connecting beliefs. It turns out that some *non-accidental* intermediaries are also *alien*, in a sense implying that they prevent a belief which meets our first four conditions from being properly said to be held for a reason. The notion of an alien intermediary suggests that the primary such case would be the intervention of another person, e.g. one operating the neurological machine described above. For instance, someone might, as a result of (discovering) S's basis and connecting beliefs, want to assure his doxastic virtue (since S does not always put two and two together) and might thereby cause him to form the belief that p. Even on the assumption that S's having the basis and connecting beliefs sustains the person's manipulation, there seems to be a cognitive short circuit here: the distant causes are as they should be, but our sense is that S's belief that p is not connected with its cognitive basis in the way it should be; it is, for one thing, not guided in the normal way.

Someone might conclude from such examples that *any* intervention by another person is alien. But suppose Ann helps Tom overcome an abnormality, e.g. holds open a switch that enables impulses to travel as they would have before an injury severed a neural connection. This seems a friendly, enabling intervention, not a supplantive one. Moreover, an intermediary taking the causal chain far outside the body can be friendly. Owing to an injury to S, a machine in his home might be required to enable his basis beliefs to produce his beliefs for reasons; but since this electrical intermediary is normal *for* him (even the first time the machine is properly hooked up for him), and could preserve the control of his beliefs for reasons by the reasons for which he holds them, the machine need not preclude his believing for a reason even when he is far from home. On the other hand, imagine that everything is normal, except that a friend, eager to make sure that one forms the belief one should given one's premises, uses a neurological machine to produce another (operative) sufficient condition for the belief that p. The friend would not have done this if one had not had the basis and connecting beliefs; and they do play their normal causative and guiding role (so far as that is possible given the overdetermination). What, then, is the effect of the uninvited aid? This may simply be a borderline case; in any event, I am disinclined to call the intervention alien. It is, however, potentially alien.

We can understand believing for a reason better if we consider possible interventions in relation to the sense in which beliefs for a reason are under the *control* of reason, i.e., of one's cognitive system conceived as embodying some minimal degree of rationality: for instance, as tending to instantiate such elementary logical principles as modus ponens and the laws of the syllogism. One aspect of this control is implicit in the idea, stressed above, that believing for a reason is discriminative. Another aspect might be expressed by calling such beliefs *contrastive:* believing p for r contrasts both with believing other things and with believing for other reasons. Let us take up these two contrasts in turn.

Imagine an intermediary that satisfies all the conditions so far set out (e.g., one that operates non-accidentally and is sustained by the basis and connecting beliefs), but has one peculiar effect: it renders S's belief that p so deeply rooted and firm that even if he (a) believed not-p with the greatest conviction of which he is capable apart from the intermediary (and on the basis of confident beliefs expressing good reasons for believing not-p), and (b) wanted unreservedly and very strongly to be consistent, he would still believe p and indeed believe it more firmly than not-p. (If one supposes that S cannot believe both p and not-p, we can substitute, for not-p, a different proposition q which, like not-p, S believes to be inconsistent with p.) It would seem that S's belief that p is now "implanted" in such a way that it cannot be said to be a belief for a reason. For one thing, it has more strength than it could normally get from the basis belief, which should be his ground for holding it, and that in itself suggests a cognitive imbalance. For another, there is no rational cognitive influence, in the sense of one rooted in a set of reasons (even subjective reasons), sufficient to overturn the belief. The belief is, we might say, *cognitively irreversible*. In holding it S has ceased to be open to rational dissuasion no matter how firm or (subjectively) cogent his opposing reasons. In this sense, then, it is (arguably) not under the control of reason.

It is plausible to hold, then, that an intermediary which imposes irreversibility is alien. But that may be going too far. What if the belief is of a very fundamental kind, e.g. that something exists? (This is probably not normally based on reasons; but it could be, e.g. perhaps on the ground that one exists oneself, and it will serve for the point in any case.) Must this be irreversible to be under the control of reason, or even to be simply for a reason (including a good reason which justifies it)? That is not entirely clear. It may still be thought that a machine's *imposing* irreversibility would prevent the irreversible belief's being suitably under the control of reason; but that is not clear either. However, if, as I am inclined to think, reversibility falls just short of a necessary condition on believing for a reason, there is a related requirement that is necessary.

Part of what makes the reversibility condition plausible is that apparently, if a belief is under the control of reason, and particularly if it is held for a reason, then it should be *susceptible to counterinfluence by opposing reasons*. The reversibility view gives a strong interpretation of this susceptibility: roughly, S must be capable of believing something else instead given sufficient counterreason. On the reversibility view, believing for a reason entails a kind of *cognitive freedom*. Particularly for those inclined toward doxastic voluntarism, which conceives beliefs as under voluntary control and assesses them on principles parallel to the principles applicable to actions, such freedom is likely to seem necessary for believing for a reason, which, after all, is, given that the reason is good enough, a case of justified belief. But there is a weaker interpretation of the essential susceptibility: perhaps S's belief that p need only be under the control of reason in the sense that it is *integrated* into his cognitive system, where this requires mainly that the strength of one's belief is appropriately responsive to opposing reasons. Thus, while one's belief that one exists may be psychologically overwhelming, in the sense that no opposing beliefs can overturn it, it cannot – at least if it is held for a reason – be entirely immune to the influence of opposing reasons: some beliefs would not be altogether psychologically impotent against it, and can at least reduce its strength. The contrast here, then, is not between the belief that p and other beliefs, but between r and other reasons.

On the integration view, then, a kind of *cognitive autonomy* is crucial for believing for a reason: in part, this means that while counterevidence cannot be brought to bear so as to uproot a belief

for a reason, and one may be unable to believe otherwise, counterreasons can be brought to bear with some effect, so that one is
at least more nearly open to believing otherwise and can seriously
consider alternative propositions. Now it does seem that, however
firmly rooted a belief, if it is for a reason then it is integrated into
the cognitive system in a way that opens it to some degree of
influence to beliefs expressing (what S takes to be) counterreasons.
(Something like this *may* apply even to beliefs that are not for a
reason, such as direct introspective beliefs; but it is not clear that
that is so, and no such claim is implied here.) Believing for a reason,
then, is contrastive not in the sense that opposing reasons must
be capable of leading S to hold *different beliefs* instead, but in the
sense that he is capable of being influenced, in the way he holds
that belief, by *different reasons*.

One other kind of intermediary deserves mention. A basis belief
(that r) and connecting belief could produce S's believing that p
only given the cooperation of a motivational intermediary, paradigmatically S's *wanting* to believe p. If all our other conditions are
satisfied – in which case the normal cognitive sustainers are *necessary* for his believing p – does S believe p for a reason? Surely the
most we can say is that he believes it in part for a reason; for his
wanting to believe it is also necessary for his belief, and its being
necessary indicates that the belief's basis in reason, specifically in
his belief that r, is far less extensive than usual. This applies even
if the want is itself somehow (perhaps waywardly) produced by
the basis and connecting beliefs, so long as it is not a mere by-
product of them which is not necessary in its own right for the
belief that p. In cases like this the motivational influence dilutes,
though it does not eliminate, the rational one. Degree of dilution
may vary, and the next section will suggest how to weigh the
degree of influence of a reason relative to other factors producing
or sustaining the belief that p. But where such motivational influence rises to a necessary condition, we have believing only in part
for a reason.

What emerges in this subsection, then, is a *normal intermediaries
condition:* S believes p for r only if his basis and connecting beliefs
do not sustain or produce his believing that p via an alien intermediary. The same probably holds for the disposition to attribute
the belief that p to those beliefs, but I shall not make that a strict
requirement. I offer no analysis of such intermediaries, but we have

noted what may be the main kinds: certain interventions by other persons; causal factors that undermine the integration of the belief that p in S's cognitive system; and motivational factors that dilute the influence of the basis and connecting beliefs to the point that they can produce or sustain the belief that p only with the aid of one or more wants of S's. As in the case of intermediaries rendering the connection between the basis and connecting beliefs accidental, one might think that alien intermediaries are ruled out by the explanatory connection between those beliefs and the belief that p. But if we recall that the alien intermediaries are produced or sustained by those beliefs and are factors *by virtue of which* the beliefs produce or sustain the belief that p, this is not clear. In any event, if it is so, we must still rule out such intermediaries to specify the relevant sense of 'explain': the sense such that believing for a reason can be explicated simply in terms of explainability by, and subjective grounding in, that reason.

There may be other kinds of alien intermediaries; if so, they can perhaps be understood on the basis of the notions of control and cognitive integration as developed above. We may also be aided by functional characterizations. We might say, e.g., that an alien intermediary occurs when and only when the relevant beliefs bring about (or sustain) the belief in a manner different from the way, whatever it is, in which they bring it about when it arises from them through an ordinary inference. Functional characterizations have been common in recent literature,[9] but I shall put limited weight on them. They often leave too much unspecified, though their heuristic value may be quite significant.

In the light of the requirements that have emerged, we can construct a general account of believing for a reason. We must do more than combine the requirements, however. If S believes p for a reason r, then the associated basis and connecting beliefs are sufficient to explain why he believes p; indeed, together they fully explain it, in the sense that citing them (given appropriate contextually presupposed information) is *sufficient* to provide an under-

---

9. For functional characterizations of various notions involving causal chains, see Gilbert Harman, *Thought* (Princeton: Princeton University Press, 1973), pp. 43–46; Raimo Tuomela, *Human Action and its Explanation* (Dordrecht and Boston: D. Reidel, 1975), e.g. ch. 4, sects. 1 and 2, and ch. 9, pp. 256–258; and Lawrence Davis, *Theory of Action* (Englewood Cliffs: Prentice-Hall, 1979), esp. pp. 18–22.

standing of why S believes p, even if some other reason state is also sufficient. Adding this (and some minor points) to the conditions developed above, the account we arrive at is this:

I. S believes that p, for a reason, r, at time t, if and only if, at t, there is a support relation, C, such that (1) S believes that p and that r; (2) S believes C to hold between r and p (or believes something to the effect that r bears C to p); (3) S's basis belief, that r, and at least one connecting belief, i.e., his believing C to hold between r and p, or his believing something to the effect that r bears C to p, are part of what explains why S believes p, and, together, fully explain this; (4) S is non-inferentially disposed, independently of seeking reasons he has, had, or might have had, at or before t, for believing p, to attribute his belief that p to the explaining beliefs specified in (3); (5) those explaining beliefs do not (singly or together) accidentally sustain or produce S's belief that p; and (6) those beliefs do not (singly or together) sustain or produce it via an alien intermediary.

Some of the materials used in this account need further clarification. Some of that clarification will come in the next two sections. But, as one would expect given the vagueness of the concept being explicated, elements of vagueness will remain.

III
MULTIPLE REASONS, SUPPORTING
REASONS, AND RATIONAL INFLUENCE

People often believe for a variety of reasons, and sometimes they believe only in part for a reason, their main reason being something else. As this suggests, reasons for which we believe have different degrees of influence on us. All these notions are important both in assessing people's justification and in understanding them. Let us consider some ways in which the account developed above can help us understand these and related notions.

MULTIPLE REASONS

We should first note how the account accommodates the distinction between believing for just one psychologically sufficient reason and

– what formulation I explicates – believing for at least one such reason. To capture the notion of believing p for exactly one such reason, r, we need a uniqueness requirement. What we may say is that if S satisfies formulation I *and* has no reason besides r which meets its conditions, then S believes that p for just one psychologically sufficient reason: roughly, one powerful enough to sustain S's believing that p (assuming normal functioning of S's cognitive system). But S might still believe p *in part*, even in good part, for another reason. That reason would not satisfy clause (3), being insufficient to explain why S believes p. Still, we should find a way of ruling such reasons out: of capturing the notion of believing that p *wholly for one reason*, as opposed to believing it *for only one wholly sufficient reason* (where the kind of sufficiency in question is psychological, not evidential). To say that S believes p "wholly" for one reason is of course not to imply that nothing but the basis and connecting belief(s) explains it; what is excluded in the relevant sort of context is simply that any other reason plays a significant role (and, in some contexts, perhaps also that such non-reasons as wishful thinking are significant aspects of what explains the belief).

To capture the notion of believing wholly for one reason, at least where only further *reasons for* believing are to be ruled out, we need an *explanatory uniqueness requirement*: we simply add to the conditions that if S has any other reason for believing p, then, taken together, his beliefs of the propositions expressing it and connecting it with p do not, *even in part*, explain or sustain his believing p. Thus,

II. S believes that p wholly for reason r, at t, if and only if, at t, r satisfies I, and if S has any other reason, r_i, for believing p, r_i does not satisfy I, nor does S's believing r_i, together with an associated connecting belief, explain, even in part, why he believes p.

The idea is that if any other reasons S has do not play the relevant explanatory role, then they are merely reasons he has, not reasons for which, even in part, he believes. They might still be potential overdeterminers, in the sense that they each would fully explain his believing p if he ceased to believe that r: this is particularly likely if *one* of the two kinds of beliefs, the connecting and basis beliefs, plays an explanatory part. But that is quite another matter.

If we need a stronger characterization of believing wholly for one reason, we may add a clause specifying that there is no want (or other cognitively alien factor) which in part explains why S believes p. But this condition would be difficult to explicate: we must not rule out the influence of a want in the special case in which p is to the effect that one has that very want; and there are influences *dependent on,* or *causative of* the belief that r, which must also be allowed an explanatory role with respect to the belief that p. Fortunately, believing wholly for one reason is normally contrasted with believing at least partly for one or more other *reasons,* and we have captured that sort of exclusiveness.

We are now in a good position to explicate believing for multiple psychologically sufficient reasons. The idea is this:

III. S believes that p, for reasons $r_1, r_2, \ldots, r_n$, at t, if and only if, at t, (1) each r_i satisfies I, and (2) each is such that S may be truly said to believe that p because he believes it, or to believe p on the basis of it.

Clause (2) is apparently entailed by (1), but it serves to make explicit that each reason (by virtue of the relevant beliefs) plays a significant enough role to explain fully why S believes p, in the sense (indicated above) that *it* supplies enough information to enable us to understand why S believes p. Each reason, however, is still only *part of what explains* that, since the other reasons do so also; and it might be best to use phrases like 'because, for one thing, he believes it' and 'in part on the basis of it'. But each reason, being psychologically sufficient to carry conviction and produce the belief that p, is not a *merely partial explainer* of that belief, since it *sufficiently* explains it: it enables one to understand why S believes p. Fully explaining, then, does not entail completely explaining, which I take to imply explaining in the way the totality of full *and* partial explainers would; nor does it entail exclusively explaining, which I take to be fully explaining in a way that implies that nothing else explains the thing in question, even in part. (The notions of complete and exclusive explanation may both be idealizations, but they are surely intelligible.)

SUPPORTING REASONS

From what we have noted about differences in explanatory power, it is clear that reasons may have different degrees of psychological (as well as evidential) weight. One important category of reasons,

psychologically characterized, is what I shall call *merely (partially)*
supporting reasons: each contributes to producing or sustaining S's
belief that p, but none is a main reason for which he believes it
and hence (as I am using 'main') each is only a partial explainer:

IV. A reason, r, which S has, at t, for believing that p, is, at t,
a merely supporting reason for which, at t, he believes p, if and
only if, at t, (1) r satisfies clauses (1), (2), (4), (5), and (6) of I; (2)
the basis belief and at least one connecting belief partially sustain,
and partially explain, S's believing p; and (3) S has the disposition
specified in (3), except that normally he is disposed to attribute his
belief that p only in part to the explaining beliefs just specified
in (2).

A number of merely supporting reasons can *collectively* explain why
S believes p: each would partially explain it, and jointly they would
explain it sufficiently to yield understanding of why S believes p.

While it may be uncommon for S to believe something only on
the basis of reasons none of which is psychologically sufficient,
this is possible. Then merely supporting reasons would be the only
reasons that explain why S believes p. Surely one can believe something simply for a number of minor reasons, no one of which is
(psychologically) sufficient; and that can be so even if no one of
them is necessary. None could be psychologically sufficient, however cogent it might be evidentially, or it would not be merely a
partial explainer. Granted, a conjunction of minor reasons might
easily be joined together through S's believing their conjunction,
which then might be quite sufficient to produce or sustain the belief
that p; and in practice it may be difficult to distinguish a conjunction
of reasons from a conjunctive reason built out of them. But the
conjunction case is possible, and is a distinct kind of believing for
reasons.

RATIONAL INFLUENCE

We have noted that beliefs expressing reasons may differ in their
psychological influence as well as their evidential force. This applies
to both merely supporting reasons and main reasons. The intuitive
notion is that one may believe something *more for* one reason than
for another. Using the materials developed so far, we might express
the general idea as follows:

V. Where r_1 and r_2 are reasons for which (in part) S believes p at t, r_1 is, at t, a more influential reason than r_2, relative to S's believing p, if and only if, at t, S's believing that r_1, together with the associated connecting belief(s), contributes more to sustaining or bringing about his believing that p than does his believing r_2, together with the connecting belief(s) associated with it.

The relevant contribution is in some sense causal, and the central idea, for merely supporting reasons, is giving a more nearly sufficient explanation, and, for main (thus fully explaining) reasons, giving a more nearly complete explanation. A related "measure" is how much a reason (via the relevant beliefs) contributes to the strength of S's tendency to believe p. That in turn is mainly a matter of the degree to which the belief will resist being uprooted by countervailing factors, perhaps most notably opposing beliefs of S's, e.g. beliefs of propositions he takes to disconfirm p.

We might now try to explicate the notion of the *difference in influence* between r_1 and r_2 being greater than that between r_2 and r_3, where these are reasons for which S believes p. For we can now say that two such reasons have the same degree of influence provided neither is more influential than the other; and using that notion we may compare the magnitude of the relevant disparities. But developing such comparisons turns out to be quite complicated and will not be attempted here. There are many other aspects of the influence of reasons which we must also leave aside, including the ways in which it may change over time, and how one reason may be more influential than a second in producing a belief yet less influential than the second in sustaining it later on. It is sufficient for our purposes that many of the materials needed to clarify these notions have now been laid out.

IV
SOME EPISTEMOLOGICAL IMPLICATIONS
OF THE ACCOUNT

Our account of believing for reasons has now been developed in sufficient detail to enable us to indicate its significance for some epistemologically important topics. This section will briefly do this.

Belief, reason, and inference

Since believing for a good reason is believing for a reason (one that is good), the account clarifies believing for a good reason. We have, to be sure, said nothing about when a reason is objectively good; but the epistemological tasks concerning good reasons go far beyond that, and our results bear on some of them. One issue, for instance, is how to evaluate a belief held for both good *and* bad reasons. This will be in part a matter of how good and how bad they are. Another factor is how influential the good reasons are relative to the bad ones. In clarifying that comparison, our account can help considerably. It would guide us in finding out, e.g., whether all the main reasons are among the good ones, whether any of the bad ones is necessary for S's believing *p*, and whether the collective influence of the good reasons is greater than that of the bad.

A second important point is that so far as believing for good reasons is an ideal we want to realize, we cannot effectively pursue it, nor know how nearly we have fulfilled it, without a clear understanding of what it is to believe for a reason. The account provides not only a conceptual explication, but a set of conditions which, to some extent, one can apply to oneself, and, with their cooperation, to others, in everyday situations. Indeed, *if* an indirectly (prima facie) justified belief is simply a belief held *for* at least one good reason, then if our conditions are supplemented with an account of what constitutes a good reason, we shall have all the materials we need to understand one of the main kinds of justified belief and, in good part, one of the main kinds of knowledge: (structurally) inferential knowledge. The account has further implications for understanding and assessing good reasons, but let us pass on to a related topic.

JUSTIFICATION AND KNOWLEDGE

May we say that, in order for S's belief that *p* to be objectively justified by virtue of his (believed) reason or evidence, *r*, for *p*, or to be knowledge by virtue of his possessing *r*, S's belief that *p* must be based on his belief that *r*? Elsewhere I have argued for part of this thesis: for a sustaining requirement to the effect that the evidential (basis) belief must play a causal sustaining role.[10] It is a further question whether S must believe *p for* the reason which the evidential belief expresses; but I suspect that this is controversial at least mainly because it is taken to imply the sustaining requirement[11] (as I believe it does). If so, then what is usually called inferential knowledge can be conceived, at least in part, as true belief *for* the (objectively sufficient) reason(s) constituting its inferential basis.

Similar issues arise for subjective justification, by which I mean, very roughly, justification from S's own point of view, not in the sense of his actual or likely *opinion* whether he is justified, but in relation to what he believes and epistemically ought to believe given the information accessible to him. One important question here is this: supposing S is a generally rational person, is he justified by *r*, even from his own point of view, in believing *p*, if his belief of *r* is not a reason for which he believes *p*, but only (say) one to which he is disposed to appeal in rationalizing his belief that *p*? This is a problem which the account developed above can help us pursue. For to answer the question it is essential that we be able to distinguish (real) reasons for which one believes from rationalizations, which are (in part) reasons one has for believing which play no appropriate explanatory role. One way we can make the distinction in self-critical reflection is by ascertaining whether or not we have the spontaneous non-inferential disposition to attribute a belief to a reason.

EPISTEMIC BASIS RELATIONS

Epistemologists have often made use of the notion of one belief's being *based* on another, and a number hold that one cannot know

10. In "The Causal Structure of Indirect Justification" (Chapter 7, this volume). Notice that the point here concerns S's *justifiably believing p*; for *p* may be *justified for* S even if he does not justifiably believe it (or does not believe it at all). In the light of this one could, like Richard Feldman and Earl Conee, call a belief that *p* which is not based on S's evidence for *p* (nor otherwise justifiably held), yet is justified *for* S in virtue of that evidence, *ill-founded* rather than unjustified. See their "Evidentialism," *Philosophical Studies* 48 (1985).

11. In, e.g., Keith Lehrer's *Knowledge* (Oxford: Oxford University Press, 1974), some of the other requirements are granted and the sustaining requirement attacked (pp. 122–126). I have assessed this attack in Chapter 7, this volume. For other accounts of how beliefs are based on others and how this basis relation is relevant to indirect justification, see George S. Pappas, "Basing Relations," in George S. Pappas, ed., *Justification and Knowledge* (Dordrecht and Boston: D. Reidel, 1979), and Joseph Tolliver, "Basing Beliefs on Reasons," *Grazer Philosophische Studien* 15 (1982).

that p on the basis of evidence r unless one's belief of p is based on one's belief of r.[12] Does our account also yield an account of this evidential basis relation? *I* believe so. To begin with, if r is a reason for which S believes p, then surely S's belief that p is based on his belief that r. Granted, sometimes 'reason for which' may be used differently, as where one says that the reason for which one believes the car is moving is that one *sees* it moving.[13] But perhaps the seeing is thought to imply believing; and certainly in *saying* this one is expressing a *belief* that one sees the movement. Note that in such cases of perceptual grounds 'reason for which', as opposed to 'reason why', is awkward in the third person. S believes it is moving simply because he sees it moving; this is probably not believing for a reason at all, and that may account for the strain in 'the reason for which he believes it is moving is that he sees it moving'. Seeing this is the reason *why* he believes that, and might also be considered a *ground* of the belief, but those are different matters.

Supposing, however, that believing for a reason entails believing on the basis of a belief expressing that reason, does believing on the basis of another belief entail believing for a reason – the proposition that belief expresses? There is at least one exception: a non-inferential second-order belief that one believes p, e.g. believing that one believes Tom is a real friend, may apparently be based on

12. See, e.g., Armstrong, op. cit., p. 205, and Fred Dretske, for whom S's having a conclusive reason, R, for believing that P (a condition necessary for knowing that P), requires that S believe P "on the basis of R." See "Conclusive Reasons," in George S. Pappas and Marshall Swain, eds., *Essays on Knowledge and Justification* (Ithaca and London: Cornell University Press, 1978), p. 56. Jonathan L. Kvanvig, in "Swain on the Basing Relation," *Analysis* 45 (1985), also seems to hold a version of this. For him, however, the crucial basis is *not* causal. He says, e.g., that "The context of this discussion [of how beliefs expressing one's evidence for p must be related to one's belief that p if it is to be knowledge] is the context of determining what sorts of conditions a belief must meet in order to meet the justification condition for knowledge," p. 153. Kvanvig thus apparently conceives the basis relation functionally in terms of the role he takes it to have in the concept of knowledge based on evidence. This is an interesting strategy, but it seems to underestimate the independent work done by the notion of one belief's being (evidentially) based on another, and it may prejudice the account of basing as a result of preconceptions about knowledge.

13. See, e.g., Marshall Swain, *Reasons and Knowledge* (Ithaca and London: Cornell University Press, 1981), esp. pp. 75–76, for an even broader use of 'reason'. I use 'reason why' at least as broadly, but I suspect that in speaking of reasons as something beliefs are based on, Swain's terminology may tempt one to conflate reasons why with other kinds.

that first-order belief even if S does not have a connecting belief, say a second-order belief, of the proposition that Tom is a real friend, to the effect that it supports the proposition that one believes that he is. The basis relation here might be considered a non-inferential kind. There may be a cognitively direct connection between the two beliefs, hence no connecting belief. Perhaps, e.g., if a belief that p is introspectively sought, say by one's attentively asking oneself whether one believes p, then normally it just "directly" produces the belief that one has it. Even here, however, most of the elements in our account apply to the relation between the "basis belief" and the second-order belief that one has it: the explanatory sustaining requirement, the disposition condition, and the non-accidentality and normal intermediaries conditions. In any event, apart from this case and a few others, such as certain kinds of believing "on the basis of" wishful thinking (where the relation may not be epistemic at all), believing p on the basis of believing r does entail that r is a reason for which one believes p. This is confirmed by various parallels between believing for a reason and believing on the basis of a further proposition. There is, for instance, believing wholly on the basis of; partly on the basis of; on the basis of multiple beliefs; and on the basis of merely supporting beliefs.

Thus, our account of believing for a reason can, with at most minor qualifications, at least explicate the inferential epistemic basis relation. Where the basis of belief is simply another belief or a non-belief state, such as a perceptual one, all the conditions except the connecting belief condition hold, and it is arguable that an analogue of it obtains too: S's believing, *of* the state in question, of a suitable support relation, and of p, something to the effect that the former bears that relation to the latter. But it is not clear that this analogue holds, and I leave the matter open.

INFERENTIAL BELIEF

No account of inference has been given; indeed, the notion of inference has been used at points to help motivate and clarify the account of believing for a reason, which may be conceived as structurally inferential. Often, this structural property is all philosophers have had in mind in calling a belief inferential: that it is *indirect*, i.e., not based on another belief expressing a reason for which S holds it. For this sense of 'inferential belief' we have given an account. But what about episodically inferential beliefs, those actually arising on the basis of a process of inference? Regarding them, the account partially explicates the complicated notion of their "arising on the basis of" inference. For this surely implies their being in some way grounded on the relevant inference, and an important aspect of that is their being based on the premise(s) of the inference, in the sense that at least one premise is a reason for which S believes the conclusion. One cannot believe the brakes are worn on the basis of inferring this from the proposition that they squeak unless that proposition is a reason for which one believes this; and presumably one's connecting belief is the (perhaps tacit) one that if they squeak, they are worn. If this conditional is also a premise, then either (a) both premises are reasons, or a conjunctive reason, for which S believes the brakes are worn, and there is a connecting belief linking them to the proposition that the brakes squeak, or (b) only the minor is S's reason and his belief of the conditional is the connecting belief. We thus have a distinction between two ways in which an inference can supply reasons.

On the other hand, suppose one believes the brakes are worn on the basis of believing that they squeak, and believes that on the basis of Jan's testimony that they squeak. Does one then believe that they are worn on the basis of her testimony? Not necessarily: the basis relation is *non-transitive;* e.g., the third belief may not be suitably *connected* in one's mind with the first. Our account helps to explain this; for clearly one would not need to have formed the required connecting belief, particularly if one formed the other two connecting beliefs at different times, say, getting the testimony on Monday and coming to believe, only on Friday, that squeaky brakes are worn. We get similar results for the relations, being the (or a) reason for which one believes, and being inferred from, as our example shows. Suppose that (i) r is the (or a) reason for which one believes p, and p is inferred from r; and (ii) s is the (or a) reason for which one believes r, and r is inferred from s. It simply does not follow that (iii) s is the (or a) reason for which one believes p, or that p is inferred from s. This should not be surprising; after all, as our testimony case also shows, s can be (by itself) a good reason *to* believe r and r (by itself) a good reason to believe p, without s's being (by itself) a good reason to believe p. It would be unfortunate if our psychology did not accord with this epistemic fact.

DOXASTIC VOLUNTARISM

As I understand believing for a reason, it is strikingly parallel to acting for a reason.[14] Indeed, if one thinks of believing as even slightly under our control, e.g. in the sense that we can cultivate, resist, or sometimes uproot our beliefs, my account can perhaps be appreciated better than if one thinks of beliefs as states that simply come and go largely independently of what we think and do regarding them. This is not in the least to say that the account implies that believing *is* something we do, much less something generally under our voluntary control, and the point that believing for a reason is parallel to acting for a reason is quite neutral with respect to doxastic voluntarism. But it does bring out what makes such voluntarism plausible, and it can help us assess how far various kinds of voluntarism can be carried. Moreover, if there is a tendency to exaggerate how behavioral believing is, there may be an equally serious tendency to ignore the extent to which intentional action, while an event, is like a propositional attitude: it does, after all, in some sense embody intentionality even if not necessarily intention in particular. For these and other reasons, our account takes us some distance toward a more unified psychology, and toward connecting epistemology with the philosophy of mind. If the theory of cognition and the theory of motivation are significantly parallel, it may be because of something very general and quite basic in our makeup.

CONCLUSION

The notion of believing for a reason is both causal and epistemic. It is causal at least in the sense that a reason for which one believes plays an explanatory sustaining role with respect to the belief based on it. It is epistemic at least in the sense that, for S, the reason bears to that for which it is a reason a supporting relation in virtue of which the former is relevant to the latter. But a belief for a reason is not a mere effect of the reason; it is, by virtue of S's belief(s) connecting it to his reason, a discriminative response to that reason; and partly because it is such a response, S normally has a sense

---

14. These parallels are evident in my "Acting for Reasons," *Philosophical Review* XCV (1986).

of its resting on the reason for which he holds it, and is non-inferentially disposed to attribute it to that reason. A belief for a reason is non-accidentally produced by the belief expressing the reason and by at least one belief connecting it to the proposition *S* believes for that reason; and it is, in a special way, under the control of reason and thereby integrated into *S*'s cognitive system. Reasons for which a person believes come in many kinds, and they differ in both psychological strength and evidential cogency. They may work singly or in sets; they may produce beliefs which *S* need not even know he has, or may be unable to trace to their basis in his reasons; or they may generate beliefs through vividly conscious inferences. Our account is aimed at clarifying all of these concepts and patterns; and if it is sound, it can be used in both the epistemological appraisal of beliefs and the psychological assessment of cognition.[15]

15. Earlier versions of this paper were given at the University of Rochester and Virginia Commonwealth University, and I benefited from the discussions. For detailed comments I also want to thank Richard Feldman, John Boyce, and John Heil.

Chapter 9

Structural justification

Justification comes in many forms and is predicable of many kinds of things. Its primary bearers are actions and beliefs; but it may belong, globally, to entire outlooks on the world and, specifically, to individual propositions. It may also apply to persons, policies, and other complex entities which, unlike actions, are not events and, unlike propositions, do not have truth value. Even to catalogue and interconnect the bearers of justification would be a large task. My project here will not accomplish that, though it should lay some of the groundwork for doing it. My focus is on the forms of justification rather than its bearers, and I shall locate and clarify a kind which, though applicable to a great diversity of elements, is often left faceless in the crowd of justificatory notions that more often occupy philosophers. In doing this it is easiest to work with the cognitive domain; for even if we do not assume – as I certainly do not – that all justification is ultimately explicable in terms of justified belief, the domain of belief is at once central in epistemology and a good model for other territories in which justification resides. I begin with a sketch of justificatory attributions and from there proceed to explicate the notion central in this paper.

I. FOUR KINDS OF JUSTIFICATION

(1) When I justifiedly believe something, I have *doxastic justification* – or simply *belief justification:* to have this is simply to have justified belief.[1] (2) When I do not believe something, but have a ground

1. The term 'doxastic' in this use was suggested by Roderick Firth in "Are Epistemic Concepts Reducible to Ethical Concepts?" in A. I. Goldman and J. Kim, eds., *Values and Morals* (Dordrecht and Boston: D. Reidel, 1978; 'belief justifica-

for believing it such that, if (other things equal) I believed it *on* that ground, I would justifiedly believe it, I have *situational justification*. This is, roughly, the presence in one's epistemic situation of a justifying ground for p.[2] Thus, while I did not – until I thought of the matter – believe that the chair beneath me minutely sags from my weight, I was previously justified *in* believing this, by virtue of my justified beliefs about the material sustaining me in relation to my weight.[3] Since one also has justifying grounds when one justifiedly believes p, situational justification occurs with, as well as without, doxastic justification. (3) We may speak of justification for propositions: we can ask if there is any justification for the view, cited without attribution in a gossip column, that Jack is guilty, or for the conclusion that Jill has left town. Call this *propositional justification;* it may exist whether or not anyone believes the proposition so justified and whether or not anyone is situationally justified in believing it. It may be, e.g., that while no one now has evidence for concluding Jill has left town (and so no one has situational justification for it), a brief investigation would unearth some and thereby confirm that indeed there was justification. Propositional justification is, then, *relative* to potential believers – being something like (genuine) evidence that is available to one or more persons indicated in the relevant context – but it is not *predicated* of any actual person. Of these three sorts of justification, propositional justification has been given least attention, common though the notion is in standard parlance.

There is a fourth notion, related to propositional justification,

tion' is simply the standard English equivalent which I proposed in *Belief, Justification, and Knowledge* (Belmont, California: Wadsworth Publishing Co., 1988). The former is more common in the literature and I will use it more often.
2. This term comes from *Belief, Justification, and Knowledge*, cited in note 1. Firth used 'propositional justification' here, but it seems to me that the relevant notion is *person-relative* propositional justification – a proposition's being justified *for* a person. That term is cumbersome, but more important, 'situational' has the virtue of calling attention to the subject's epistemic situation, which contains the ground(s) of justification. There is also a phenomenon, described in the text, which I think is more properly called propositional justification.
3. That I did not believe this until the matter came up may be controversial; in "Believing and Affirming," *Mind* XCI (1982) and "Dispositional Beliefs and Dispositions to Believe" (in progress) I defend the implied distinction between dispositional (non-occurrent) beliefs and – what is illustrated here – mere dispositions to believe, where the disposition to have relevant belief is actualized by elicitors such as thinking about the grounds one has or may have.

to which philosophers have paid still less attention. Let me bring it out by example. Imagine that Gail is a student of mine about to embark on a job search. I believe her to be good in her main fields, a capable teacher, and something of a generalist as well; but I also know that the competition is stiff. Given all that I now know and justifiedly believe, I am not justified in believing (or in disbelieving) that she will get a job on the first round. I do not, then, have situational justification for believing this: in what I take to be roughly equivalent terminology, the proposition that she will get a job on the first round is not justified for me. But suppose I have heard of an opening in a department which I have good reason to believe would regard Gail very highly, though I have not thought about her in connection with it and have not drawn this conclusion. As I think about the school, I conclude that they need, and will likely realize that they need, a generalist; that they are men of good will who prefer not to remain an all male department; and they would take my recommendation very seriously. It also occurs to me that one of them has a degree from Tri-State College (which happens to be Gail's undergraduate school). Suppose further that there is an opening in a similar department, where the facts are different but reflection would also lead me, with equal warrant, to the same conclusion, though again I have not drawn it. Now imagine that the time for recommendations arrives and I am depressed as I say to Gail that I *hope* she will find something. I speak cautiously to her because I do not think I am justified in saying more, and I am suspending judgment. Suddenly, I search my memory, remember both the openings I heard about months before, and form the intention to recommend her for both. Now I may be justified in believing, and may justifiedly believe, that she will get a job on the first round. What this case shows is that while the proposition that she will get a job on the first round was initially not, on the basis of the total evidence contained in my beliefs (including my propositional knowledge), *justified* for me, it was *justifiable* for me. I want to call the kind of justification I had prior to recalling the openings and thinking about them *structural justification*.

The plausibility of calling such justification structural derives from its grounds being available to me, by reflection, *in* my cognitive structure – internally accessible to reflection, as some epistemologists would put it – though reflection may not be needed to bring it to mind – yet not organized or pulled together in such a way as to justify me, without further ado, in believing that Gail will get a job on the first round. I have the makings of a justification, but they are *unintegrated* and so do not amount to a justification as they stand in my cognitive system: roughly, in my body of beliefs, dispositions to believe, inferential tendencies, memory, and consciousness. Once I have recalled the openings and the facts about them, the proposition that Gail will get the job is justified for me: I now have, in my body of beliefs, grounds which adequately (if minimally) support that proposition. My epistemic situation now contains *cognitively registered* grounds for the belief. Prior to my recalling the openings and forming the intention to recommend Gail for them, the proposition is only *justifiable* for me: I in some sense *have* a justification, but it is buried in my cognitive inventory, not registered in premises I believe, or displayed in my perceptual consciousness, or in any other way ready to ground my believing the proposition.

We can sharpen the contrast between structural justification and its more familiar cousin, situational justification, if we connect both with the notion of believing a proposition on the basis of a ground. There are two cases of believing to be considered here: the inferential one just illustrated, in which one believes a proposition on the basis of one or more others, and the non-inferential one, in which the ground on the basis of which one believes is experiential, as in the case of believing the paper one is seeing to be white on the basis of visual impressions of white. Situational justification for believing p occurs where one's epistemic situation contains a ground, whether inferential or not, such that, should one (other things equal) believe p on the basis of that ground, one would justifiedly believe it.

Structural justification is, as it were, pre-situational: in order to get from structural to situational justification one must either form the appropriate belief(s) or have the relevant experience, say by recalling certain events or by introspecting. Thus, it is because I recall the openings that I have situational justification for forming the beliefs which express my (inferential) grounds for believing that Gail will get a job on the first round. When I do form these beliefs, I am situationally justified in believing that, in turn. Because I formed them as a result of accessing materials already in my cognitive system, as opposed to my making new observations or getting testimony on the subject, my original justification is properly called structural.

As this example indicates, I take the relevant structure to be not only cognitive but such that those of its aspects pertinent to the justification in question are available to the subject by reflection, including introspective reflection. If in some cases reflection, as opposed to, say, merely asking oneself a relevant question, is not needed, in others only extensive reflection will bring the justifying elements to mind. The sense in which structural justification for believing p is *had*, then, is not occurrent, but dispositional: under certain – highly variable – kinds of conditions, S can bring the justifying elements into consciousness and can form, or hold, the belief that p on the basis of them. There are, however, two ways in which reflection can bring the justifying elements into consciousness. With situational justification, the justifier is accessible through what we might call *revelatory reflection:* a belief or recollection or percept, say, is already present as a justifier of the propositional object of the belief that p – making p justified *for* S – and S need only reflect to become aware of this set of elements and, upon believing p on the basis of them, to acquire a justified belief that p. With structural justification, on the other hand, the justifiers are accessible only through *generative reflection* (or thought): the kind that, through such things as producing a belief not yet possessed, yields situational justification.[4] Generative reflection produces justification by producing new grounds, whether inferential, as in the case of newly formed beliefs expressing premises for p, or direct, as in the case of memory impressions of the state of affairs p expresses. These grounds provide situational justification, which in turn may lead to actually justified belief of p.

One might think that except in the case of doxastic justification we should not speak of justification at all, but only justifiability. It is true that a situationally justified belief that p is, if not already justified, justifiable – most notably by S's coming to hold it on the basis of the elements that justify p for S. Similarly, if S has structural justification for p, S can, by both reflection *and* coming to believe p on the basis of the justifying elements, achieve justified belief

---

4. These terms are drawn from my "Causalist Internalism" (Chapter 11, this volume), where they are associated with the distinction between justified and merely justifiable belief.

that *p*. In each case *believing p* is justifiable for *S* (whether the belief is already held or not); but in the former *p* itself is justified for *S*, whereas in the latter *p* is only justifi*able* for *S*. But neither situational nor structural justification is simply a "counterfactual property": granting that *S*'s having them *implies* counterfactuals, it is not equivalent to them. Both are actual properties that *S* has in virtue of perceptual states, memory impressions, beliefs, and certain other psychological attributes. Indeed, even propositional justification exists not just because the proposition is justifiable in the abstract, but because someone has actual properties that make the relevant evidence accessible.

The varieties of non-doxastic justification, then, though they correspond to different sorts of justifiability, are not reducible to it. And if they are all ultimately understandable by appeal to doxastic justification, they are not species of it; they each correspond to different locutions; and distinguishing them conceptually can clarify the overall theory of justification and the diverse ways in which we may be said to have evidence. If a kind of reduction is possible by virtue of all four kinds being analyzable in terms of one, say doxastic justification, it may still be best for epistemological theory to work with each independently. It is at best cumbersome, e.g., to say, not that *S* has structural justification for believing *p*, but instead that while *S* does not presently have grounds for *p* such that *S* is justified in believing it, still, by reflection *S* can acquire grounds for *p* such that, if he comes to believe it on those grounds, this belief will be justified.

It should be apparent from the centrality of accessibility through reflection that the notion of structural justification as I am developing it is internalist in the following sense. The justification in question is internally accessible to *S*: roughly, available to consciousness through reflection, including introspective reflection, as opposed to perceptual observation or testimony from someone else. It is not merely part of the subject's psychological or physical make-up, nor need it be a guarantor (or probabilizer) of truth independently of accessible elements. This is not to say that a counterpart notion of structural justification cannot be developed from an externalist perspective, but that is not my approach here.[5]

5. If structural justification is conceived as a kind of justifiability, an externalist construal is readily imagined: *p* is structurally justified for *S* provided (roughly) *S*'s reflecting in a suitable way would produce in *S* an externally sat-

II. SOME VARIETIES AND DEGREES OF STRUCTURAL JUSTIFICATION

The placement example can be used to bring out the broadest division among kinds of structural justification: that between inferential and non-inferential sorts, between the kind grounded in premises for p and the kind grounded directly in, say, sensory experience. The structural justification I have for believing that Gail will get a job on the first round is inferential. For my justification comes through at least one proposition such that it is only on the basis of *it* as a (justified) premise – whether I actually draw a conclusion from it or not – that the proposition is justifiable for me. Thus, the belief of this proposition, a belief in which my structural justification would culminate if fully realized in my cognitive system, would be inferential, in the broad sense that the belief would be based on one or more other beliefs of mine and would derive its justification therefrom.[6] By contrast, my structural justification for believing that there is a relevant job opening might be non-inferential; I might, e.g., have a disposition to recall a mention of the opening by a friend, and when my memory is jogged by my search for relevant information and I do recall the opening, the basis of my belief that it exists is not another proposition I believe, but rather my memorial impression of the conversation. The proposition that the opening exists is justified for me *by* memory, not by inference from anything I *believe about* my memory.[7]

It will be obvious that structural justification, like any other kind, admits of degree. Some grounds are better than others; some inferences from grounds to a conclusion are better justified than others; and some propositions for which one has justification are

isfactory justification for p. It might, e.g., result in calculating probabilities that in fact do render p probable and produce belief of it. The accessibility of the justifiers is still internal; but on this view they must in the context also be reliable belief-producers.

6. There need not be an actual *process* of inference for this to occur; the belief might arise, and remain, as structurally rather than episodically inferential. Nothing major in this paper hinges on this difference, but for those interested it is developed and defended in Chapter 8, this volume; and, for the case of action, it is more fully elaborated in my *Practical Reasoning* (London and New York: Routledge, 1989), esp. chs. 4–5.

7. I am sidestepping here the issue whether all non-inferential justification, even in the structural case, is ultimately grounded at least partly in non-inferential justification; but I hope it is clear that the reasons for (and against) saying this can be applied to structural justification as in other cases of justification.

also such that one has some degree of justification for their negations. For these and related reasons, structural justification may be weak as well as strong. A number of the elements of strength can be discerned as we consider some main kinds of structural justification. I shall begin with inferential cases and conclude with the remaining ones.

The first pair of cases to be noted have in common S's believing a set of adequate premises. Here 'premises' does not imply that an inference is drawn but only that an inference would be appropriate; and adequacy is simply sufficiency for justification: that is, the premise set – call it q – justifies the conclusion – call it p – for S. In the first case, S believes the premises but would need to reflect a moment to see *how* q supports p. By contrast with the case of situational justification, then, S is not epistemically ready to believe p on the basis of q until S registers the connection between them, say by making the connection through reflection. This is why p is only justif*iable* for S and not, until S, say, completes sufficient reflection, justif*ied* for S. Call this a case of *unrealized connection*, since what S needs to pass from structural to situational justification is simply an appropriate grasp of their evidential connection. None of this implies that a connection can be made *only* through reflection. It may be obvious to me, once I think of them together, that q implies p; or I may have a standing belief to the effect that propositions of the first kind support propositions of the second, as where the first, like a falling barometer, expresses a mark of the truth of the second.

In the second case, S has registered the connection but is not appropriately disposed to believe p on the basis of q, say because S mistakenly, but with ample warrant, thinks that q is inadequate evidence for p. Call this an instance of a *mistakenly defeated connection*. Here (or in some variants of this case, at least) this epistemic belief is consistent with S's in some way having a justification for p, yet the belief prevents S's being justified in believing p, since holding that belief would be against S's own best (and reasonable) evidential judgment. We would then have another case of structural justification without situational justification.

Once we understand these cases, it becomes clear how to single out certain others. Suppose, for instance, we substitute, for believing q, a disposition to believe it. This would put me a step further from actually focusing on my justification for p and forming a justified belief of it – where such belief-formation is the cognitive culmination of structural justification. For even upon registering the connection between q and p, I would not have q as a premise until I came to believe it. What we have here is a *doxastically un-realized premise*, since I have not formed (even "unconsciously") a belief expressing that premise. In the same way, we can get a variant of the second case, in which one mistakenly believes that q inadequately supports p. In this variant, in order to form a justified belief that p, one would need *both* to form the premise belief and to overcome the erroneous, and perhaps also unreasonable, epistemic belief. This case would combine unwarranted defeat with lack of doxastic realization.

Among the various possibilities that remain, at least one other deserves mention. It occurs where I am disposed to believe, but do not believe, q because I might mistakenly, yet with ample warrant, think I lack adequate ground for q, say because I have an argument that I quite reasonably (but wrongly) take to disprove it. Here we have a *mistakenly defeated premise*. While there would *be* an adequate ground for q, say a deeply buried but accessible memory of a proof of q, and, in virtue of that memory and my registering the proof's connection with p, I would have a justification for p, still I would not be justified in believing p (or so it would seem for at least some cases in which one quite reasonably thinks one lacks adequate justification for q or for p), and I could not (other things equal) form a justified belief of p without overcoming the mistaken tendency to resist believing q.[8]

This is not to imply that a disposition to believe, as opposed to actually believing, a proposition that is adequate evidence for p cannot itself justify one's belief of p. I leave this difficult question open; but a disposition at least cannot do so if its would-be justifying effect is defeated, as it seems to be, by the reasonable epistemic belief blocking acceptance of q. If the disposition did justify q, moreover, note that this would not in my terminology yield a

---

8. It is arguable that if one has ample warrant to believe one lacks adequate grounds for q, then even if this is false one lacks structural *as well as* situational justification for q. If this line is correct, we might then say that S's structural justification is only prima facie, the same status S's situational justification has. It is possible, however, that the structural justification is unaffected by the mistaken epistemic belief, e.g. because if S grasped the elements that structurally justify p then the error underlying the mistaken belief would immediately come to light, whereas the justification for q, which that belief specifically concerns, is defeated by this epistemic belief. There presumably are, then, cases of the kind described in the text.

case of inferential justification of the belief that p; one would be disposed to infer p from q but, not having formed a belief that q, one would not believe p on the basis of believing q.

The main cases so far described are variants of two kinds: first, those in which S believes q but lacks something that connects it with p and is required for being justified in believing p; and secondly, those in which S does not believe p but is disposed to believe q and would thereby – or at least upon suitably registering the connection between q and p – acquire situational justification for believing p. There are also cases exhibiting greater distance between the basis of S's structural justification and an actual justified belief that p. Imagine that I neither believe nor am disposed to believe that q, but am able, by reflection, to arrive at grounds for q and thereby at a disposition to believe it. Perhaps not every such case is one of having justification for p; if, e.g., I also had a much stronger tendency to arrive instead at grounds for not-q, we might think the evidence for q can merely be had by me. But we can imagine mathematical cases in which, although there is no conflicting evidence, justification is so to speak on my cognitive map, yet finding the right path requires my thinking about the various familiar routes and tracing them until an unfamiliar, implicit route comes into view. As this suggests, one possibility is that q is conjunctive and, even when one arrives at the conjuncts separately, one does not have them as premises for p until they somehow are combined in one's mind. The same distinction – between a disposition to believe q and a readiness to arrive at a belief by reflection – applies to S's relation to the connection between q and p. And there are many subcases which we need not even mention once the general grounds of classification are clear.

Before we move to the topic of non-inferential structural justification, we should extend what has been said to the case of second-order beliefs. Epistemic beliefs whose subject is *propositions* have already been mentioned. Epistemic beliefs can also be about other *beliefs* and can defeat justification in that instance too. Thus, I might in a special case have structural justification both for p and for the proposition that I am not justified in believing p. These instances of structural justification are in tension with one another and in different situations one or the other might dominate. Thus, whether or not I actually come to believe that I am not warranted in believing p, the structural justification I have for the proposition that I am not warranted could prevent such justification as I have for p from being adequate for, say, my knowing that p should I believe p on the relevant basis. On the other hand, if my justification for the second-order epistemic belief derives from an insufficiently considered skepticism and my justification for p is excellent, this justification for p may prevail despite my tendency to deny that I have it.

With this much before us, we can be brief about the non-inferential cases. Here a ground for p, say a visual experience, gives me a justification for p without doing so through my believing that that ground obtains. My memorial tendencies might justify me (structurally) in believing that John visited me once even if they supply me with no premises for this. For I might be able, by thinking about John in relation to my past visitors, to call up images, or remember events, such that they would non-inferentially ground my believing John visited. Again, I am not justified *in* believing this initially; but I have a justification in the sense that, by reflection, I can put myself into a position in which I am justified in believing it and can thereby come to form an actually justified belief of it. To be sure, once my reflection elicits the justificatory grounds, I can (in principle) always *formulate* them in a way that provides an inferential justification. But to conclude from this that my justification must be inferential in the first place would be a grave error. That what justifies us in believing p can be given inferentially in an argument for p does not imply that the original function of this justifier is inferential. Indeed, if there were no non-inferential justification prior to premises and formulable in them only by its retrospective (or second-order) grasp, it is at best unclear how there could be any justification at all.[9]

Similar examples can be drawn from the domains of perception, consciousness, and a priori reflection. In all of these one can have capacities whose exercise takes one to a ground for a proposition, where the distance one must reflectively traverse is such that, while one has a justification for p, one is not yet justified in believing it. One may need to scrutinize one's visual field and think about its contents; one may need to examine one's thoughts and feelings;

---

9. This is of course part of the classical regress problem. For an opposing point of view see Laurence BonJour, *The Structure of Empirical Knowledge* (Cambridge, MA: Harvard University Press, 1985), and for a brief reply see *Belief, Justification, and Knowledge*, cited in note 1, ch. 6. Further responses to BonJour and other coherentists are given by Paul K. Moser in *Knowledge and Evidence* (Cambridge and New York: Cambridge University Press, 1989).

one may need to draw inferences from propositions one believes. The task may be easy or difficult, long or short. But in each case there is at least one path one can take from some ground one has to a justified belief that *p*. The next section will examine these paths and their role in the cognitive structure.

III. COGNITIVE STRUCTURE AND JUSTIFICATORY PATHS

It is time to clarify the metaphor of a justificatory path. The basic idea is that of a relation, direct or indirect, between a ground – which is the origin of the path – and what that ground justifies – which is the destination of the path. This is not to paint a simple linear picture of justification; for all I am saying here, justificatory paths are only one route to justification and achieve it by producing coherence. Certainly a normal cognitive system exhibits an interlocking pattern of paths, and a ground can be undermined by leading to an unacceptable destination, just as, by contrast, traceability to a solid ground can underlie justification. What implies an obviously unjustified proposition, for instance, must itself be at least diminished in its justification, quite as what is implied by an obviously justified proposition must inherit at least some degree of justification.[10] A theory of justification in which paths are central need not, then, treat beliefs as isolated strands of cognition. That there are grounds provides a basis of justification, but does not imply that this basis cannot itself be altered by either lateral or vertical pressures: for instance, by apparent inconsistencies among grounds and by disconfirmation derived from what is inferentially built upon them.

Structural justification occurs when there is an appropriate justificatory path from the justified proposition to the ground(s) of its

10. There is no simple transmission principle that covers all the cases here. For much discussion of closure see Peter D. Klein, *Certainty: A Refutation of Scepticism* (Minneapolis: University of Minnesota Press, 1981); Fred I. Dretske, "Epistemic Operators," *Journal of Philosophy* LXVII (1970), which Klein discusses critically; and my "Justification, Deductive Closure, and Reasons to Believe," *Dialogue* xxx (1991), and "The Inferential Transmission of Justification and Knowledge" (in progress), which attempt to provide an account of justificatory transmission that does justice to the views of both. I offer no account of obviousness, but I take it to be relative to something like a reasonable person, to lie between self-evidence and dubiousness, and to be much closer to the former than the latter.

justification. If we can understand such paths, we can understand much of what is important about structural justification. My account takes these paths to be internal and requires that they be longer than those appropriate to situational justification: to repeat, there the proposition is *justified for S* and *S* will (other things remaining equal) justifiedly believe it by simply coming to believe it on the basis of the justifying ground; in the structural case, the proposition is only *justifiable for S,* and (other things remaining equal) in order for *S* to form a justified belief of it some cognitive change must occur which creates situational justification. To speak somewhat speculatively, structural justification at least normally implies a *capacity* to believe *p*, but does not imply an inclination to believe it upon considering whether it is so; situational justification at least normally implies both a capacity to believe *p* and some inclination to believe it upon considering whether it is so.[11] This difference is connected with the point that in the latter case reflection has further to go to reach ground level.

It should be noted that while the notion of structural justification contrasts with that of situational justification, one can have both for the same proposition so long as they reside in different grounds. One could have situational justification for believing *p*, by virtue of believing premises *q*, and structural justification for believing *p*, by virtue of a disposition to believe *r*, which also warrants *p*. Indeed, both of these possibilities are compatible with one's having doxastic justification as well, say because one believes *p* on the basis of *s*, which is an adequate ground for it and renders it propositionally justified. The kind of justification one has for a proposition, then, is relative both to the kind of ground that provides it and to one's cognitive relation to that ground.

It is implicit in what has been said so far that one important property of justificatory paths is *length.* Some of the factors that go into it have been illustrated. One is the number of inferential links which, in *S*'s mind, connect *q* with *p*, i.e., the number of inferences *S* would draw starting with *q* and ending with *p*, if, other things remaining equal, *S* wanted to justify *p*, began with *q* as a premise, and proceeded rationally. There would be only one link if *S* would infer *p* directly from *q*, two if the inference would go through *r* as an intermediate premise, three if it would go from *r* to *q* and then

---

11. The qualification 'normally' is needed because, for one thing, *S* may be unable to believe *p* because that would be highly damaging to *S*'s ego.

to p, etc. A parallel factor – where the justification is non-inferential – is the number of cognitive changes needed to put S into a position of justified belief that p, for instance the number of dispositions one must realize in order to have the requisite memory impressions to ground believing that one has visited Mark's home.

We might also speak of the *depth* of a path. This is mainly a matter of how far reflection must go into memory or the recesses of consciousness or the subject matter in question, in order to yield a ground from which S can trace a path to p, e.g. by a reasoning process. Depth tends to be proportional to length, but it need not be: I may need to bring a repressed event to consciousness in order to believe p justifiedly, yet the resulting path might go directly from the recollection I finally ferret out to the proposition I come to believe on the basis of it. I dig deep among associations until I get the crucial thing in consciousness, but I do not reach it by an inferential path. We might also single out a kind of depth that corresponds to how far down in S's evidential cognitive hierarchy the path goes, say to beliefs of what seems to S self-evident as opposed to merely true. This is (person-relative) *epistemic depth* – depth in the cognitive foundations – as opposed to *psychological depth* – depth measured by the difficulty of reflectively reaching the justifying ground for p, whether because of repression, length, or some other factor. The former is commonly a matter of the depth *of* the ground, the latter commonly a matter of the depth *to* it.

Still another variable is *embeddedness*. By this I mean the degree to which the path represents a stable cognitive feature of the agent. Some beliefs are psychologically basic in us and, in addition to being non-inferential, seem to us incapable of falsity, while others are held tentatively; some images we easily mistrust, while others are too vivid to attribute to anything but reality; and so on for other sources of belief. Even a deep path need not be highly embedded; a short path certainly may be. But there are probably no simple correlations here.

Length, (psychological) depth, and embeddedness are psychological as opposed to epistemic variables. They can be used in developing a theory of justification, but are not themselves grounds for attributing it or normative in the sense appropriate to epistemic concepts of appraisal. But there are also epistemic dimensions of justificatory paths. I shall mention four.

An important element in assessing the degree of structural justification is the *adequacy* of the crucial justificatory path(s). This notion can be given an externalist construal in terms of the objective likelihood of the truth of p relative to that of S's premises for it, q – roughly, the reliability of the connection between them; but I have in mind an internalist notion. On this showing, adequacy would be a function of the justificatory power of the original ground and the strength of the ensuing links. On an externalist construal, reliability would be a matter of the truth-conduciveness of these items; and where structural justification is of the kind likely to produce *knowledge,* reliability would seem to be a crucial factor.

To illustrate adequacy construed on internalist lines, imagine an inferential chain: if q is abundantly justifiable and is traceable to p by a deductively valid inferential chain, then (other things equal) p is abundantly justified for S. Inductive links would transmit less justification. A weaker ground would generate less to begin with. Similarly, where the path is non-inferential, we can still discern these two variables: roughly, the quality of the source and the preservation of the justification it supplies.

That two or more paths can lead to the same proposition has already been suggested. This is *convergence* of paths. It can lead to overdetermination: two or more independent sources of justification, each sufficient to justify p for S. This is common, and it yields not only justification stronger than S would have by any one of the paths, but also a degree of systematization of the cognitive structure, as where S can regard p as explaining, or helping to explain, propositions from several domains with features suggesting p as their most likely explainer. The overdetermination just illustrated is justificationally *homogeneous,* in the sense that each path originates in a structural justifier; overdetermination may also be *heterogeneous,* as where one path originates in a structural justifier and another in a situational justifier. If S believes p, the heterogeneity can be threefold: the third path may originate in a doxastic justifier – one in which the belief is actually grounded. The first kind of path is potential, since S does not believe p on the basis of the relevant ground; the second kind may be potential or actual, since S may or may not believe p on the basis of the ground, and so there may or may not be an appropriate (partly causal) connection; and the third kind must be actual, since in the case of doxastic justification S must believe p on the basis of the justifying ground.

If there can be convergence, we should also expect possible *divergence:* one ground leading, by way of different links, to different propositions. A single recollection of Gail's paper may readily justify the quite different beliefs that she was articulate and that she was tall. Here there may be sufficient justification for many propositions, and certainly they can be systematized to some degree by their traceability to a common ground. That ground may, but need not, constitute or suggest an explanation of them all.

The final case to be mentioned here is *obstruction*. There is obstruction in the psychological sense of a factor that prevents formation of the belief that *p*, but there is also obstruction in the justificatory sense of a defeater, as where *p* obviously conflicts (logically or probabilistically) with another proposition *S* is justified in believing or justifiedly believes. If the conflict is logical and obvious to *S*, then *S* is unlikely to come to believe *p*, at least where *S* already believes the competitor; but note that there can be such a conflict where *S* has better justification for *p* than for its competitor. Here we might have psychological, but not justificatory, defeat. Where *S*'s justification for the competitor is better, we would have justificatory even if not psychological defeat.

There are other dimensions of justificatory paths, but the beginnings of a theory of justificatory paths have been set out. The points made in this section should help in understanding structural justification and thereby the broad notion of having justification. I do not take this to be exactly equivalent to having evidence, but it is quite similar and structurally parallel. We also have, then, some of the basic materials for understanding the ways in which one may have evidence.[12] The remainder of this paper will simply bring out some general properties of structural justification and show its generalizability beyond the domain of belief.

IV. SOME EPISTEMOLOGICALLY SIGNIFICANT PROPERTIES OF STRUCTURAL JUSTIFICATION

Although the notion of structural justification is in some ways weaker than the other main normative notions applicable to belief,

---

12. The notion of having evidence is addressed in Richard Feldman's "Having Evidence," in David Austin, ed., *Philosophical Analysis* (Dordrecht: Kluwer, 1988) and by Moser, *op. cit.*

it has some of the same properties. Let me sketch two kinds, the first epistemic and the second causal and descriptive.

First, structural justification apparently has the capacity to justify other dispositions. While structural justification with respect to *p* does not justify – though it has the potential to justify – believing *p*, it can justify a disposition to believe *p*. Thus, I may be justified in my disposition to believe *p*, even though I am not justified, without further changes, *in* believing *p*.[13] Where I am justified in believing *p*, the justifying elements are such that (other things equal) if I come to believe *p* because of those elements, then my belief of it will be justified. Things are epistemically in order in me; what is lacking is only the normal causal connection that holds between a ground and a belief justified by it. In the case of a justified disposition to believe *p*, two things are needed for justified belief that *p:* one is the integration of the relevant ground(s), e.g. a grasp of their connection with *p*, which is often possible only through a grasp of their connection with one another; the second is the causal connection just mentioned. It may seem strange that one could be justified in the disposition to believe, yet not the belief, that *p*. But we must bear in mind that situational justification for *p* represents a stronger epistemic position: *S* is not justified in believing *p* unless there is some justifying ground for *p*, whether experiential – say, perceptual or memorial – or cognitive, such that *S* either has that ground or believes the relevant proposition, whereas *S* can have structural justification for *p* provided *S* is suitably disposed to *acquire* a ground.[14]

13. In taking dispositions to admit of justification, I mean to be taking them to be psychologically real, though non-occurrent and supervenient, properties of persons. Thus, to have a justified disposition is not equivalent to the truth of subjunctives like, 'If *S* should come to believe *p* on the basis of the relevant grounds, *S* would justifiedly believe it'. This sort of thing can hold of someone who does not, in the relevant sense, *have* the grounds; and it is having those grounds (reachable) in the cognitive system that grounds the justified disposition.

14. One might argue that *S* can have a justified disposition to believe *p*, without situational justification for it, because *S* can come to believe *p* other than *through* the actualization of the justified disposition, say on impulse. Suppose I do not recall John's visit (though I could if I properly searched my memory) but simply form the belief that he visited, because it facilitates thinking about him. Now I merely have, but have not "used," my structural justification (embedded in my memory) for *p*, and I am not justified in believing it. The belief lacks a ground, though I have a ground *for* a ground of it. The main trouble with this reasoning is that, even when I have a good justification for believing *p*, I can *still* come to believe it for some other, inadequate

Second, the notion of structural justification has causal import, at least in the sense that by virtue of the properties such justification supervenes on, appeals to it can be explanatory in a broadly causal sense (this is admittedly an indirect kind of causal import, since the actual causes seem to be the supervenience base properties). Suppose I refuse to grant John's claim that we know each other only through the telephone and correspondence. By way of explanation one might note that I have structural justification for believing that he visited me, and that we have some tendency not to believe what we have such justification for believing false. It need not be that I subliminally believe he visited (though that is possible here); rather, there are factors, such as buried memories I have not brought together, which, in ways I may not fully understand, make me resist holding the view against which I have an as yet unarticulated justification. Granted that these are the causal factors, noting my justification can serve to appeal to the operation of such factors even when we know only what sort of thing they are and not their exact identity.

A third property of structural justification is its descriptive power. Consider a rational outlook on the world, in the sense of a world view. This is a global notion which is best understood not as a group of beliefs but as a coherent set of beliefs *and* dispositions to believe, where the latter are elements of the kind rooted in or closely connected with structural justification. A rational outlook on the world is not just a matter of a set of warranted beliefs about it; it is in part a readiness to arrive at views about it, by reflection, when appropriate questions arise. This reserve from which justified views will emerge by (generative) reflection is in part what structural justification yields. Quite parallel points apply to the notion of a rational person; but here we have other propositional attitudes to consider as well as beliefs. Structural justification of the cognitive sort under discussion remains, however, an important part of the picture, and as we shall shortly see it has non-cognitive analogues.

Regarding epistemic properties of structural justification, there are just two cases to be mentioned here. First, structural justification observes only limited closure. If I have it for p, and p entails

---

reason. The important possibility pointed out in the reasoning, then, does not discriminate between structural and situational justification.

(even self-evidently entails) *r*, it does not follow that I have it for *r*. Too many factors can intervene; so, while the justificatory path may perhaps carry some justification, my relation to *r* may be such that I am not sufficiently justified with respect to it to acquire (without new grounds not available through reflection alone) a justified belief of it.[15] Second, structural justification typically implies a potential for knowledge, but does not imply actual knowledge, even when *p* is true and there are no untoward conditions of the kind specified in the literature in showing that justified true belief is not sufficient for knowledge. The obvious point here is that knowing entails believing, and structural justification, since it does not imply believing, cannot imply knowing. But an equally important point is that there are cases in which one has a perfectly good justification yet does not know, even when the proposition in question is true. Think of a justified belief that one's train will be about on time; one rarely knows such a thing, but may justifiedly believe it. On the other hand, when one's structural justification for a true proposition, *p*, is sufficiently strong, we may loosely speak of *p* as among the things *S* "knows." We might call this *virtual knowledge*. If you know a lot about a subject, you are commonly credited with knowing many propositions for which you would need to reflect at least briefly to discover a justificatory path. Structural justification that is accessible enough and concerns propositions one can explain and defend can generate a strong potential for knowledge even if, in strict usage, there is no knowledge without belief.

V. NON-EPISTEMIC STRUCTURAL JUSTIFICATION

The main work of this paper has been to clarify a notion of justification which is easily lost in the welter of epistemic terms. But the significance of the notion is by no means limited to epistemology. Indeed, while cognitive justification has been the domain of application of my account of the notion of structural justification,

---

15. Again, the issue is transmission of justification, and for reasons given in my "Justification, Deductive Closure, and Reasons to Believe" and "The Inferential Transmission of Justification and Knowledge" (both cited in note 10), I maintain that while some degree of justification does transmit, it may not be sufficient for overall justification at the end of the chain.

that notion is really far more general. Any propositional attitude admits of structural justification, and so does action. Let us briefly consider these cases in turn.

It should be easy to see how the account of structural justification applies to conative attitudes. While admittedly we do not often speak of justified wants, we do speak of rational desires and of what people should or should not want given what might be called their "basic nature" as understood in terms of their ideals, beliefs, and deepest desires. I can be justified *in* wanting my daughter to assert her independence, and I can simply have a structural justification for wanting this. In the former case the want is justified for me (whether I have it or not); in the second it is only justifiable for me. In the former case I presumably have basic, rational wants, say for her to have a good life, such that I believe her asserting independence will contribute to their realization. In the latter case, I presumably have dispositions to form such wants. Where we have justificatory cognitive paths in the case of justification for believing, we have justificatory motivational paths in the case of justification for wanting. And by and large the same distinctions apply in both domains. There is, e.g., embeddedness, psychological depth, and, opposite epistemic depth, a kind of normative depth, depending on how far the path goes into the foundations of S's system of rational desires. If the path ends in a merely instrumental desire, then (other things equal) it goes less deep normatively than one ending in an intrinsic one. This is plausible at least on the assumption that the rationality of an instrumental desire depends on that of an intrinsic one.

Actions, being events and not dispositions, are ontologically different from the propositional attitudes. But the notion of structural justification still applies. It may well be that (prospective) justification for actions is equivalent to justification for intending to perform them. If not, there is a relation near enough to equivalence to enable us to understand structural justification for actions by drawing a parallel between structural justification as applied to beliefs and structural justification as applied to intentions. Similarly, we get a counterpart fourfold distinction: there is (1) justifiedly doing, (2) being justified in doing, (3) an action (type) being justified for an agent, and (4) an agent's simply having a justification for doing something. If (as I hold) the justification (and indeed the rationality) of actions is determined largely by the justification (and rationality) of the wants and beliefs underlying them, then the full assessment of action will require not only elucidation of these four notions, but connecting them with their counterparts for the wants and beliefs underlying actions. The task is large, but at least it can be better understood in relation to the framework developed in this paper.

Let me illustrate the applicability of structural justification to one case: that of rationality in relation to self-interest. It has often seemed to philosophers that rational action is, ultimately, action justified (or at least justifiable) by considerations of self-interest.[16] One way to take this is to interpret self-interest in terms of self-regarding desires, such as those for one's own pleasure, and then to argue that for every rational action, the agent has at least situational justification for it in terms of one or more beliefs to the effect that it will contribute appropriately to satisfying some such desire. But we can accommodate a wider range of prima facie rational actions (at least action-types) if we substitute structural justification for situational justification here. For there may surely be things one is disposed to want whose achievement would be intuitively in one's interest, that one does not actually want and would come to want only upon some reflection on facts, experiences, concepts, etc., internally accessible to one (recall that if they are not internally accessible, then the potential justification, however significant it may be, is not structural in my sense). I omit considerations about the rationality of the relevant instrumental beliefs and the relative strengths (or rationality) of the self-interested wants in relation to one another and other wants. I also abstract from the issue of whether there are certain sorts of things which every self-interested person, or even every rational one, *should* want intrinsically. The notion of structural justification is neutral with respect to these issues and at the same time provides a broader conception of rationality to work with, whether in relation to self-interest or the foundations of ethics or the theory of rationality in general.

16. For some discussion of this see William K. Frankena, "Concepts of Rational Action in the History of Ethics," *Social Theory and Practice* (1983), in which he suggests that the Greeks tended to hold a version of egoism as a basis of ethics. For clarification of the difficult notion of self-interest, see Mark C. Overvold, "Self-Interest and the Concept of Self-Sacrifice," *Canadian Journal of Philosophy* X (1980) and "Morality, Self-Interest, and Reasons for Being Moral," *Philosophy and Phenomenological Research* XLIV (1984).

CONCLUSION

I conclude by simply listing the advantages of countenancing structural justification as a distinct kind (or form), as opposed to lumping it with what is ordinarily called being justified in believing or, sometimes, having reason to believe (or to want, or to do). First, we get a more perspicuous account of the nature and scope of justification, something particularly important given the widespread skeptical tendency to regard justification for belief as exhausted by what one can readily marshal as premises. Second, we clarify the issue of epistemic responsibility, though without a commitment to doxastic voluntarism, since we can now ask whether such responsibility should be ascribed – either in crediting or criticizing people – not only on the basis of their having grounds they can readily cite, but in terms of their possessing resources at a greater distance from consciousness. Should we, in effect, make more room for the inventory of justification by including what is not ready to hand? Responsibility may be possible not just on the basis of what one can readily say for oneself when relevantly challenged; it can be achieved even where one would need considerable reflection to meet the challenge, though perhaps only where one has at least situational justification for believing that such reflection would meet a relevant challenge. Third, countenancing structural justification also enables us to distinguish justified belief from various cases of justifiable belief, and similarly for the other propositional attitudes and for action. In making this distinction, we can clarify how the distance from the merely justifiable to the actually justified can be traveled along one or another kind of justificatory path. And fourth, by allowing so much justification to be built into the cognitive structure of the agent, we make it much easier to account for the justificatory role of experience and reason. From a single experience or a single piece of reasoning, many justificatory paths can radiate; similarly, a large range of propositions can be such that the agent could trace a path from them to a suitable ground in experience and reason. This makes it possible for the vast edifice of a person's justified beliefs, and the even more extensive network of propositions that are justified for an agent though not believed, to be seen as adequately grounded in the range of experiences, memories, and thoughts realistically attributable to normal people. Our justification goes much further than our readily accessible grounds for our actual justified beliefs; and

295

our reserve supply of justifying elements, even if it is not sufficient to satisfy skeptics, can bring far more than our beliefs, our current experiences, and our immediate memories into the framework of experiential and rational grounds that provide foundations of justification and knowledge.[17]

17. This chapter was written to honor the memory of Mark C. Overvold, with whom I spent many stimulating and profitable hours discussing philosophical problems related to it. For comments on earlier drafts I thank Frederick Adams – whose probing commentary raises valuable questions I have not had space to address here – Paul Moser, and Kevin Possin. Discussion at the Mark Overvold Conference was also helpful, and I am grateful for a thorough referee's report received after the paper was sent out for blind review.

PART III

EPISTEMIC PRINCIPLES
AND SKEPTICISM

Chapter 10

Justification, truth, and reliability

There are two quite different strands in the concept of justification, its normative character and its connection with truth. There is a tendency to take one of these as fundamental. That may explain why recent treatments of justification have often been dominated by one or the other of two contrasting views: epistemic deontologism,[1] which takes a belief to be justified provided the subject (S) meets his epistemic obligations relevant to that belief; and reliabilism, which conceives a belief's justification as determined by the reliability – roughly, the tendency to yield true beliefs – of the process(es) by which it is produced or sustained. This paper develops a third account of justification. The account has affinities to both views, but it aims at a better integration of the apparently disparate central strands in justification. My starting point is the relation between justification and truth.

I. JUSTIFICATION AND TRUTH

It is widely held that (epistemic) justification and truth are connected; but I believe that contemporary epistemologists have not adequately explicated this connection.[2] I want to clarify and account

---

1. The analogy to deontology regarding moral justification is intended and will be pursued. For illuminating treatments of the contrast between normative and reliabilist conceptions of justification, see William P. Alston, e.g. "Concepts of Epistemic Justification," *The Monist* 68 (1985), and "Epistemic Circularity," *Philosophy and Phenomenological Research* 46 (1986).
2. Philosophers have said that the process of justification aims at truth, but this needs clarification (to which I try to contribute below). Among the recent works that treat the connection between justification and truth in a way relevant to this paper are John L. Pollock, *Knowledge and Justification* (Princeton,

for it. At least two pitfalls must be avoided here. One mistake is excessive focus on the process of justification, particularly that of justifying beliefs in response to skepticism. This mistake is especially likely if one is preoccupied with the normative aspect of justification, which is very prominent in attempts to justify a belief by explicit appeal to a standard. The other mistake is excessive focus on the property of justification, justifiedness. That mistake is especially tempting for those preoccupied with the link between justification and truth, which may seem discernible simply by analyzing the notion of justified belief. We must not only avoid such mistakes, but also account for the relation between the process and the property. This relation has been somewhat neglected, perhaps because many philosophers have concentrated on the process or the property, or conflated the one with the other. I shall discuss the relation in some detail.

Whatever the connection between justification – whether as process or property – and truth, justification does not entail truth. Granted, there may well be strong axiomatic justification: a kind possessed by beliefs which are based simply on understanding the proposition believed and cannot be unjustified, e.g. beliefs of simple self-evident propositions, say that if some dogs are mammals, some mammals are dogs. Strong axiomatic justification apparently *does* connect the *concepts* of justification and truth; for it is a kind of justification whose possession seems to entail truth. Descartes apparently thought that (suitably reflective) beliefs that one now exists are so justified; and he sought to build truth into the entire ediface of justified beliefs by showing that they are all either so justified or deductively based on beliefs that are. But if any empirical beliefs (beliefs of empirical propositions) possess strong axiomatic justification, it is only certain beliefs about oneself; and unless – as is doubtful – all other justified beliefs are deductively based on these, we must still ask how, for beliefs about the external world, justification is connected with truth.

If entailment does not constitute the general connection between justification and truth, what weaker tie might? Consider a case.

1974), esp. chap. 1; Laurence BonJour, *The Structure of Empirical Knowledge* (Cambridge, Mass., 1985), esp. chap. 1; Ernest Sosa, "The Foundations of Foundationalism," *Noûs* 13 (1979); Roderick M. Chisholm, "A Version of Foundationalism," *Midwest Studies in Philosophy* 5 (1980); Keith Lehrer and Stewart Cohen, "Justification, Truth, and Coherence," *Synthese* 55 (1983); and the papers cited in note 1.

Judy and Jack are taking a train on a fall evening. His view is obscured and he asks what color the foliage is. She might say, "Green," to which he might reply, "Can it still be green this far north?" A natural answer would be, "I can see it clearly, and it certainly looks green." It is significant that this answer *both* responds to a challenge of the truth of her statement and expresses a justification for her believing it. Imagine, moreover, that Jack perversely rejoins: "I know your seeing it clearly and its looking green to you justifies your belief, but is that relevant to its *truth?*" What are we to make of this? It is not a skeptical response, such as noting that she could be wrong. He admits that she has a justification and questions whether it is relevant to the truth of her justified belief. So understood, his rejoinder seems unintelligible. I believe that it appears unintelligible precisely because of the conceptual connection between (epistemic) justification and truth: it seems to be at least partly constitutive of justification that, in *some* way, it *counts toward truth.*

It is difficult to explicate the idea that justification counts toward truth. There are at least two interpretations, one stressing the property of justification, the other the process. The first is ontological, the second teleological. On the ontological view, when something (such as what Judy cites) justifies a belief, then, in a suitable range of relevantly similar possible worlds, notably worlds like ours where the same sort of things is believed on the same sort of basis, this belief is true. One may perhaps equally well speak of relevantly similar circumstances; and there are other ways to express the basic idea.[3] On the teleological view, the conceptual connection between justification and truth is a matter of justification's "aiming" at truth, not in the consequentialist sense that what justifies produces or indicates true belief, but in the sense that the proper aim of giving a justification of a belief is to show (or argue for) its truth. The teleological view, then, ties justification to *seeking truth* and makes the *practice* of justification, above all the giving of justifications, fundamental in the connection between the concepts of justification and truth. The ontological view makes the *property* of justification,

---

3. One might, e.g., speak of prima facie truth, where S's belief that p is prima facie true provided it is either true or there is an appropriate single explanation both of why p seems true to S and why p is either false or in no way implied by what justifies S, e.g. a hallucination. This will not apply to all false belief; for it requires a restricted kind of explanation. But perhaps that kind cannot be fully specified, and perhaps there need not be such explanations for every justified false belief. I thus prefer the notion of truth-conduciveness.

justifiedness, fundamental in this. It ties justification to *indicating truth*. Clearly, the two views can agree on what properties are suitable in giving a justification; and both hold that justification admits of degree and that if one belief is better justified than a second, then what justifies the first counts more toward truth than what justifies the second. But as we shall see, the differences between the views are more important than their similarities.

On the ontological view, correct generation principles for justification exhibit it as grounded in a state of affairs somehow connected with the truth of the belief in question. The state of affairs may be said to be truth-conducive; to count toward the truth of the belief; or to entail its prima facie truth (or a tendency toward truth). All these terms suggest fallibility: that at least normally a justified belief can be false because of some untoward circumstance.[4] Propositions may also be said to be justified, e.g. where someone asks whether there is any justification for a conjectured mathematical claim. We may speak of propositional justification here.[5] One other case should be mentioned: that of *S*'s being justified relative to a proposition, as where *S* is justified *in* believing something obviously implied by propositions *S* believes. Here we may also speak of the relevant proposition, say *p*, being justified *for S*. This is person-relative propositional justification.[6] It does not entail *S*'s actually believing that *p*; it occurs when there is something about *S*, whether an evidential belief or something phenomenal, e.g. having a visual impression of green, such that his believing it would be justified if he believed it on that basis. Such justification may also be said to derive from something about *S*, on the basis of which he could believe *p*, which *does* justify *p*. A full account of justification should clarify all three kinds.

One reason that reliabilism is attractive as an account of justification should now be evident. It explains the connection between

4. A belief is indefeasibly justified if nothing could undermine its justification. Perhaps *S* could not unjustifiably believe a simple logical truth such as that if A = B, then B = A, even if *S* could believe it for bad reasons.
5. I have discussed such justification in Chapter 7, this volume.
6. Person-relative propositional justification is treated in Chapter 7, this volume. The notion is roughly equivalent to what Roderick Firth calls "propositional justification" in "Are Epistemic Concepts Reducible to Ethical Concepts?", in A. I. Goldman and J. Kim, eds., *Values and Morals* (Dordrecht, 1978). For criticism of Firth's paper and a case for construing epistemic principles differently than I do with respect to a causal element linking a belief to what justifies it, see Richard Foley, "Epistemic Luck and the Purely Epistemic," *American Philosophical Quarterly* 21 (1984).

justification and truth – at least if this connection is viewed ontologically. For if what justifies a belief is, say, production by a process
that tends to yield true beliefs, then a justified belief has a (causal)
basis that counts toward its truth. What justifies it will by its very
nature be truth-conducive. By contrast, deontologism cannot readily account for an ontological connection between justification and
truth. For – unless deontologists can find plausible principles of
obligation whose satisfaction *entails* a reliable basis for beliefs – one
could apparently meet one's intellectual obligations without one's
bases for one's beliefs counting toward their truth. My problem,
in part, is to explicate the relation between justification and truth
in a way that avoids various difficulties of each of these theories,
yet preserves some of their merits.

II. THE GENERATION OF JUSTIFICATION

A good way to explore the connection between justification and
truth is to consider what sorts of epistemic principles might account
for justification. First, however, some preliminary points. (1) I take
justification to be a supervenient property. It supervenes on non-
normative properties like being in a sensory state, having a memory
impression, and understanding a proposition. Let us also assume
the following two points, typically accepted by reliabilists and
deontologists alike. (2) Two beliefs cannot differ in justificatory
status without differing in the sorts of non-normative properties
cited: the relevant supervenience base properties. (3) As (2) suggests, the justifiedness of a belief is somehow determined by those
properties. If all this is so, then the most plausible generation
principles for direct (roughly, non-inferential) justification will exhibit it as grounded in non-normative properties.

My fourth preliminary point is that generation principles (like
other epistemic principles) differ in many dimensions. They may
be *momentary*, applying to justification at a single time, or *cross-
temporal*, applying to justification over time or at multiple times.
They may be *content-specific*, e.g. restricted to beliefs about percep-
tibles; or *content-neutral* say in applying to *any* proposition S seems
to remember. A principle might be called *empirical* if it applies only
to empirical beliefs, *a priori* if its scope is a priori beliefs, and *epistemically mixed* if it applies to both sorts. And a principle may of
course be *absolute* or *prima facie*.

There is a further distinction, specially significant for competing conceptions of justification. A generation principle may or may not exhibit *subjective accessibility:* roughly, the factors it represents as conferring justification may or may not be available to S's direct awareness[7] through ordinary (even if searching) reflection. Thus, if Judy's belief that the foliage is green is justified by its looking green to her, then a principle accounting for this justification would be an accessibility principle if, by ordinary reflection, she can become (directly) aware of how the foliage looks to her. Can she? That depends on whether, by ordinary reflection, she can become aware of (a) how *the foliage* looks to her, where this entails her having a perceptual relation to it; or only of (say) (b) *its looking to her as if the foliage is green,* where (b) is phenomenal: a matter of the content of her experience, say an impression of green foliage. Suppose that only (b) is available to her direct awareness. Then a different sort of generation principle is needed, one that represents a state like (b) as prima facie justifying her belief that the foliage is green.

It is evident that some potential justifiers are more readily accessible to awareness than others. Moreover, a generation principle can exhibit *mixed accessibility,* representing justification as arising from a combination of factors, some accessible and others, e.g. conditions of observation, not. If we assume that only the (mentally) internal is directly accessible, a theorist who holds that correct generation principles exhibit unmixed accessibility might be called a *pure internalist;* one who holds that they do not may be called an *externalist.*[8] Some views are more externalist than others; the degree of a view's externalism is proportional to the number and importance of the inaccessible justification generators it countenances relative to the number and importance of the accessible ones it countenances. It is doubtful that *pure* externalism, positing no subjectively accessible generators, has been seriously defended; pure

---

7. Direct awareness is unmediated; e.g., S is not directly aware of how something appears to him if it is only *through* his being aware of something else that he is aware of it. But time and introspection may be needed to become directly aware of certain kinds of things.

8. My use of 'externalism' and 'internalism' is at least close to one of their most common uses. For relevant discussions see D. M. Armstrong, *Belief, Truth and Knowledge* (Cambridge, 1973), esp. chap. 11; Laurence BonJour, "Externalist Theories of Empirical Knowledge," *Midwest Studies in Philosophy* 5 (1980); and William P. Alston, "Internalism and Externalism in Epistemology," *Philosophical Topics* 14 (1986).

internalism has been held and may indeed be entailed by certain kinds of coherentism.[9] Internalism and externalism are each associated with major epistemological drives. We should consider those drives before discussing particular epistemic principles.

I have spoken of the property and the process of justification. The two notions are systematically linked, and their relation is too little appreciated. A major connection is this: a belief is justified (has the property of justifiedness) if and only if it has one or more other, non-normative properties such that (i) in virtue of them it is justified, and (ii) *citing* them can, at least in principle, both show that it is justified and (conceptually) *constitute* justifying it. Call this *the process-property integration thesis*. Both epistemically and conceptually, it ties the properties on which justifiedness supervenes to the process of justifying the belief in question; and while it does not entail that S can readily cite them in justifying it, it does entail that the properties are so usable: that a property can confer justification only if citing it can constitute showing justification. One might think the property is more fundamental than the process; but we need not assume that, and my concern is with relations between the two that are independent of which, if either, is more fundamental to justification.

The process-property integration thesis, at least if it is (as it seems) conceptually true, helps to explain why it is natural to think of justification as generated by base properties S can adduce in response to a challenge. For if the thesis is a conceptual truth, then if we think of S's belief that *p* as justified, we should tend to think of it as having properties the citing of which *justifies* it; and, given how closely we associate the process and the property of justification, we should tend to think of these base properties as the sort S *can* cite, at least on reflection, in justifying it. Pure internalism entails that these points hold for all justified beliefs. Indeed, in part for this reason, the integration thesis helps to motivate at least a moderate internalism *independently* of deontologism: whether justification derives from meeting obligations or not, one cannot use only inaccessible justifiers in the process of (comprehendingly) jus-

9. This is suggested by a statement of Keith Lehrer's coherentism, in *Knowledge* (Oxford, 1974): "There is nothing other than one's belief to which one can appeal in the justification of belief. There is no exit from the circle of one's beliefs" (p. 188). But apparently not all the crucial properties of one's beliefs are accessible. If not, the view is internalist not in the accessibility sense, but only in the weaker sense that it bases justification on mental factors.

tifying one's beliefs, and it is at best difficult to see how the integration thesis could be conceptually true if all of the properties conferring justification were inaccessible. If, however, one reflects on the relation between justification and truth, it is also natural to expect generation principles to cite factors in virtue of which the beliefs which the principles count as justified are likely to be true. And for beliefs about the external world, the best candidates for such factors, e.g. production of the belief by *veridical* perception, do not seem directly accessible to awareness.

There is, then, a tension we must resolve: if we conceive justification as something one can give upon reflection, we tend to think of generators of justification as subjectively accessible; if we conceive justification as truth-conducive, we tend to think of its generators more objectively, as factors that render the beliefs they justify likely to be true. Granted, the tension perhaps need not arise for introspective beliefs; perhaps they are necessarily both grounded in subjectively accessible mental states and reliably produced. But with beliefs about the external world, the pure internalist is hard pressed to account for the apparently necessary connection between justification and truth, and the externalist is hard pressed to account for the apparently necessary availability of justifiers to the subject upon appropriate reflection.

If one conceives justification deontologically, this tension is reinforced. For if being justified consists in meeting epistemic obligations, then, by reflecting, one should be able to know one has met them. If, relative to my purview, my epistemic behavior is faultless, surely I have fulfilled my epistemic obligations. Granted, an epistemic deontologist, like an ethical one, *can* distinguish objective and subjective obligation and tie justification to the former. This may be an implausible move, but its possibility serves to bring out that it is the sense that justification must be available to S, and not a deontological view of justification as such, that generates the tension: it stems from basic properties of justification, not some special conception of it. One might posit two or more concepts of justification; but while I grant the plausibility of that view, I want to resolve the tension in a conceptually more economical way, and I assume there is a single, though complex, practice of justification, and an associated property of justifiedness, each discernible both in standard epistemic parlance and in the epistemological tradition since Plato.

III. SOME EPISTEMIC PRINCIPLES

Given the points made so far, we can explore some epistemic principles that may partly account for direct justification.[10] These will not be a *complete* set, one that accounts for all directly justified beliefs, nor can I take up indirect justification. Moreover, I discuss only momentary principles, and to minimize controversy the sample principles may not be the strongest warranted. Let us begin with *empirical grounding* – with principles concerning empirical beliefs – and explore introspective, perceptual, and memorial principles. A kind of *a priori grounding* will then be examined.

Take introspection first, and start with thinking, traditionally taken as a paradigmatic subject of directly justified beliefs. It is arguable that if S believes that S is thinking, this belief is justified. Granted, such beliefs may generate only strong prima facie justification, and hence may entail justification on balance only in the absence of certain overriders, e.g. S's having a well justified belief of an obvious contrary.[11] To simplify, let us use the prima facie formulation. If we do, we can presumably generalize to something like

P1   For any occurrent mental state *m*, if S believes, non-inferentially and attentively, that S is in *m*, then this belief is prima facie justified,

where an occurrent mental state is a mental process or phenomenal state, and attentively believing a proposition does not imply reflection, but only something like focusing carefully on it. Should P1 stipulate that *m*'s occurring is the *basis* of S's belief, since a brain manipulator could perhaps instill a false, groundless belief that one is, e.g., reasoning? I leave this open and assume that S's belief would still be prima facie justified.[12]

10. I have discussed direct justification in Chapters 1 and 2, this volume. Given the results of those studies and the supporting works they cite, I assume there *are* directly justified beliefs. I also assume that while there are different conceptions of justification, there is a univocal concept of it expressed in speaking, pretheoretically, of justified belief.
11. This idea is hard to make precise; clearly not just any incompatible proposition is such that one's believing it undermines one's justification for *p*. It might, e.g., take a sophisticated argument, which S cannot follow, to show the inconsistency. More important, the sources of undermining justification must also be explicable by our overall theory of justification.
12. There are counterparts of P1 for dispositional mental states, e.g. wanting; for

307

Now consider a perceptual principle. Take first something about visual experience: if S has a spontaneous visual experience in which it appears to him that there is an x which is F, and on this basis he believes this, then this belief is prima facie justified, where F is a visual property, such as a shape or color, 'x' ranges over physical objects of the sort that have such properties, and its appearing to him that there is an x which is F is a phenomenal state that does not entail his believing this, but only a disposition to believe it. I offer no characterization of visual properties, but make no controversial assumptions about them. It is more important to comment on the spontaneity requirement. Suppose Jack can induce visual experiences in himself at will. The induced visual experiences might well not yield prima facie justification; presumably, only spontaneous ones do. Spontaneous visual experiences are not, however, just those actually caused by a perceived object; and some non-veridical spontaneous experiences, such as an impression of water on the road ahead, can yield prima facie justification. If the suggested principle were not prima facie, the analysis of spontaneity would be a major concern; but since some of the slack can be taken up in setting out what overrides the prima facie justification, we can leave our formulation as it is for purposes of discussion. (Indeed, it might be enough to require only that S take the experience to be spontaneous, or at least *not* be disposed to take it to be otherwise.)

If our visual principle is a reasonable model, a plausible counterpart for perceptual experience in general, substituting the notion of an impression that x is F for its appearing to S that there is an x which is F, would be

P2   If S has a spontaneous perceptual experience in which S has the impression that x is F (an x-is-Fish impression), and on this basis attentively believes that x is F, then this belief is prima facie justified,

where F is a perceptual property, for instance a tactual one, x is some object (such as foliage) appropriate to the impression, and having a perceptual, e.g. visual, impression is a conscious, phenomenal state. P2 is like P1 in applying to *de dicto* beliefs; similar

person-relative propositional justification, e.g. for the proposition that S is thinking being justified *for him*; and for *de re* cases, such as one's justifiably believing, of one's desire, that it is intense. I cannot discuss such variants, even in perceptual cases.

principles can be framed for *de re* cases. Since the relevant notion of spontaneity may be plausibly taken to be phenomenal, I construe P2 as a subjective accessibility principle even on the strong assumption that this requires access to the spontaneity *as well as* the impression. If, however, the relevant notion is *genetic*, this must perhaps be left open, since it is not clear that one is ever directly aware of such genetic aspects of a perceptual experience.

The next case to be explored is that of memory beliefs. Consider

> P3   If *S* has a spontaneous, confident memorial impression that *p* (where *p* is internally consistent), then if *S* attentively believes *p* on this basis, this belief is prima facie justified.

A memory impression need not embody an image, but is a state of consciousness in which one has a sense of pastness regarding either the object(s) or event(s) which *p* is about or one's acquaintance with its subject matter; and the confidence of such an impression is not a matter of its actually producing belief, but of a tendency to produce confident belief that *p*. The sense of pastness is phenomenal, though often so unintrusive that it allows total concentration on what is remembered, as where, in writing a letter, one simply recalls and conveys remembered facts and events. This sense may be unanalyzable; but we can say that while it does not entail believing *p*, nor even having a correct memory regarding *p*, it does entail being disposed to believe *p*. Lewis held a principle like P3, but perhaps more permissive.[13] It may be impossible to account for our intuitions about memorial beliefs without some such principle. We could try a *de re* principle: if the *truth* of *p* produces *S*'s spontaneous, confident memorial impression that *p*, then if *S* believes it on the basis of that impression, this belief is prima facie justified. This is plausible, but to account for justified but false memorial beliefs we need a principle which, like P3, links memorial justification to suitable memory impressions.

In the kinds of empirical grounding of direct justification we have considered, then, there are recurring features. The relevant principles seem to apply only to prima facie justification; the generators need not be such that *S* has (or readily can have) *direct* awareness

---

13. C. I. Lewis, *An Analysis of Knowledge and Valuation* (LaSalle, 1946), chap. 11. He says, e.g., that "whatever is remembered, whether as explicit recollection or merely in the form of our sense of the past, is *prima facie* credible because so remembered."

of what it is *about* them that justifies him; and, though we have not discussed them, there are versions applicable to both personal and propositional justification, as well as *de dicto* and *de re* versions. Let us now turn to a priori grounding.

Consider the logical truth that if no men are women, no women are men. Surely one believes such truths simply on the basis of understanding them (which I take to entail understanding the concepts figuring essentially in them). The same holds for such apparently necessary truths as that nothing is red and green all over at once. These could be believed on the basis of other propositions; but that is not normal, nor does one need such further beliefs for justifiably believing either kind of necessary truth. Using the notion of believing a proposition simply on the basis of understanding it, we may plausibly hold at least this restricted principle:

P4   If *p* is a necessary truth which, simply on the basis of understanding it, *S* attentively believes, then *S*'s belief that *p* is prima facie justified.

It is appropriate to speak of a priori grounding in P4 because the justification is based on reason broadly conceived. Indeed, it may well be that *any* belief attentively held simply on the basis of understanding its content is prima facie justified. Neither that principle nor P4 entails that all necessary truths, even all "simple" ones, are knowable a priori. P4 does not even entail that where *S*'s prima facie justification is not overridden, *S* knows that *p*. Nor is that true: think of mathematical theorems for which justified belief seems undeniable given a proof sketch, yet knowledge requires stronger reasons (or a completed proof).

As applied to most people, P4 will not account for their justification in believing any but quite simple necessary truths; but in principle one could believe a fairly complicated proposition simply on the basis of understanding it, and could be prima facie justified by so believing it, since the belief could be grounded in understanding its content and not on experience or any evidence for it one might have. However, unqualified justification is not entailed by the antecedent of P4 because, e.g., *S* may simultaneously have sufficiently good reason to disbelieve *p*. Many more generation principles could be considered, and a great deal must be said to explicate even P1–P4. But our brief discussion of them is sufficient to prepare us for the very general questions I now want to pursue concerning both their status and justification in general.

IV. THE STATUS OF THE EPISTEMIC PRINCIPLES

The prima facie qualification in P1–P4 deserves special comment. To understand them, we must also consider their epistemological status and their modality. I shall address these three topics in turn.

Regarding the prima facie qualification, at least four points are important. First, I am using 'prima facie justified' not in the *conditional sense* of 'justified provided certain conditions are met and otherwise not at all justified', but in a certain *defeasibility sense*, namely, 'having some degree of justification and justified on balance if the justification is not defeated'. Second, the prima facie justified belief that *p* may fail to be justified on balance because *S* has a (sufficiently) justified belief of an incompatible or disconfirming proposition. (It must also be sufficiently obvious to *S*, or at least to a hypothetical person who is a standard of rationality, that the relevant proposition counts against *p*; for *S* may have other relevant beliefs, e.g. one which warrants his thinking *p* and *q* compatible.) A third factor is *S*'s simply being justified *in* believing an appropriately conflicting proposition, say *q*: even if *S* does not believe *q*, his being justified in believing it might override his justification for *p*; for he might be such that he "ought" to believe *q* and not to believe *p*. Fourth, consider circumstantial factors. Suppose that one's memory is very unreliable regarding a certain period in one's life. Or, suppose that when Judy forms the belief that the foliage is green, the sun is nearly down and her glance is hasty. Such factors might preclude the relevant memory and perceptual beliefs' having justification on balance: defeating though not overriding it.

There is an issue here. A pure internalist will argue that external circumstances are relevant only derivatively, through internal variables; e.g., that the justification of Judy's perceptual belief is defeated because she ought to *believe* her light insufficient to discern the color of the foliage. An externalist will argue that actual unreliability may directly undermine justification. We need not settle this: our question is the sorts of factors covered by the prima facie

311

qualification. It should now be clear both why the qualification is appropriate and that we have a good enough idea of its scope so that its use does not trivialize the principles. Whether, a priori, we can specify *all* the factors that defeat prima facie justification, and thus formulate principles generating justification on balance, I leave open.

We come now to the epistemological status of the principles. Our broadest question is whether they are knowable a priori, i.e., roughly, through reflecting on them and the concepts figuring in them, and independently of experiential evidence (I do not assume that they cannot *also* be known experientially, say through testimony). If they are knowable a priori, they might be analytic or, more likely, conceptual synthetic truths: non-analytic, yet true by virtue of ("synthetic") relations of the relevant concepts. If they are empirical, they are presumably nomic. For one thing, they seem to support counterfactuals and to have explanatory power. Let us focus on P2.

An instance of P2 would be: If Jack has a spontaneous visual impression of green foliage before him, and on this basis attentively believes that the foliage before him is green, then this belief is prima facie justified. How might we know this? It will not do to say that the principle was arrived at by reflection on justification and so is a priori; for one way a principle can be arrived at by reflection seems compatible with its being indirectly testable and nomic, rather than a priori.[14] Consider, on the other hand, what is relevant to assessing P2. Surely it is reflection, both on the principle itself and on the kind of hypothetical cases usually appealed to in assessing philosophical theses; and even if we do not sharply distinguish a priori from empirical propositions, it is plausible to distinguish among propositions in respect of their position in a spectrum from direct observational testability to highly indirect confirmability or disconfirmability through experience, and to place at least some philosophical theses very far toward the latter end.

If we take such considerations seriously, we are likely to conclude that P2 is a priori, at least *if* we think philosophical theses in general are. But let us be careful. A reliabilist might reply that what occurs to us is this: if it seems to S that the foliage is green and he thereby believes it is, then probably S's belief is produced by something in

14. This claim is defended (indirectly) in my paper "The Concept of Wanting," *Philosophical Studies* 21 (1973).

virtue of which it is true, here the green foliage; hence, we accept P2 because we accept the reliability of perceptual processes. If such thinking underlies acceptance of P2, then, since the reliability of the genesis of an empirical belief is not knowable a priori, epistemic principles based on reliability are not knowable a priori either. If we know P2, it is because we know empirically that a suitable proportion of (such) visually produced beliefs is true. Call this idea *subsumptivism:* the covering principle (a philosophical one) is that a reliably produced belief is justified, and the instantial premise is that spontaneously arising perceptual beliefs are reliably produced (since they tend to be true). P2, then, is true.

Leaving aside how, on this approach, we could know epistemic principles themselves without pulling ourselves up by our bootstraps (since we would apparently have to presuppose some to get the information about reliability needed in order to know the others),[15] does subsumptivism account for our acceptance of principles like P1–P4? Here are two relevant points. First, we simply cannot say what sorts of beliefs are directly justified except by referring to the kinds of generators and sustainers discussed in Section III – introspective, perceptual, memorial, and intuitive (or rational). Secondly, a challenge to principles expressing the justificatory force of these elements may properly be met, not only by pointing to a reliable connection, but, more importantly, by a response exhibiting the sense that a basic conceptual truth has been denied. If, e.g., someone said that the fact that S attentively believes he is imaging is no reason to regard his belief that he is imaging as justified, we are likely to wonder if he really means this, or understands the terms he uses. Notice that the issue is what counts toward justification, not what yields unqualified justification. This line of reasoning, then, is consistent with a skeptical denial that such beliefs are necessarily justified *on balance.*

To be sure, challenging certain deeply entrenched empirical propositions can elicit similar incredulity. But there is at least one difference: testability.[16] The epistemic principles we are discussing are not observationally testable. Even to begin to test one, we would

---

15. For assessments of the circularity problem described here, see Alston's "Epistemic Circularity" (cited in note 1); and James Van Cleve, "Foundationalism, Epistemic Principles, and the Cartesian Circle," *Philosophical Review* 88 (1979).
16. That even what seem to be analytic truths can be testable is argued in "The Concept of Wanting," cited in note 14; the principles under study here would not meet even the weak criterion of testability used there.

apparently have to presuppose its soundness, or that of some principle of empirical grounding; and in any case it is not clear what observable outcomes would confirm or disconfirm it. Perhaps our experience could alter in a way that leads us to cease using the concept of justification which the principles in part constitute, but that is another matter. Accountability to experience in *this* sense is different from testability. We might also come to use 'justify' and its relatives in new senses. But we assess the principles by reflection, not by observing actual cognitive behavior, e.g. by seeing how often beliefs grounded in a certain way are true. Being such that we might have used, or might come to use, others, the principles might be said to be *historically contingent*, but they are *conceptually necessary*. The indicated distinction is not sharp, but it is real.

V. JUSTIFICATION AND THE PRESUMPTION OF RELIABILITY

If P1–P4 are a priori, we face a serious difficulty: when a justification is offered, why is questioning the reliability of the generators, such as perceptual experience, *necessarily* relevant? If it is not a conceptual truth that these factors reliably indicate truth, why should reliability matter in the important way it does in assessing attempts to justify a belief? The answer, I think, is that because of the conceptual connection between justification and truth, an objection to the effect that what purportedly generates justification is not truth-conducive *is* relevant to a principle representing that generator as conceptually sufficient for justification. But if this is so, we face a serious problem, at least if the connection between justification and truth is ontological. The problem is to account for the relation between justification and reliability: if our epistemic generation principles are a priori and there is an a priori connection between justification and truth, then apparently some degree of reliability in the generating elements must be knowable a priori; yet their reliability seems a wholly empirical matter.

To see the issue more concretely, imagine a Cartesian demon who acts in such a way that our experience could be just as it is and yet at least the majority of our beliefs about the external world false. By P1–P4 we could have a great many justified beliefs. But would their justification count toward their truth in such a world? One would think not. But if P1–P4 are a priori, it is reasonable to consider them necessary, as I shall at least for the sake of argument (if some a priori propositions are contingent, these principles do not seem to be among them). Then, if one satisfies them, one must have justified beliefs. Apparently, however, justification is truth-conducive, and one's justified beliefs thus tend to be true. What, then, of the case where our justificatory experience is systematically misleading and at least the majority of our beliefs about the world false? Or, supposing that case is not possible, what of one in which, though we often have true beliefs about the world, we at least as often have false ones about it, and we have no way to tell the true from the false?

At least three historically important positions can be viewed as answering this problem. One is Cartesianism, which, on one interpretation, construes the connection between justification and truth as entailment and then secures the possibility of justified beliefs about the external world by proving God's existence from indubitable premises and appealing to the divine nature to provide a deductive path from beliefs justified by immediate experience to beliefs about the external world. The second view is phenomenalism, which, as often set out, is like Cartesianism in taking the connection between justification and truth as entailment, but instead secures that deductive path by constructing external objects out of experience. The third view is Kantian. It rejects the phenomenalist account of external objects, which it takes to be unknowable in themselves; but it may be interpreted as securing the connection between justification and truth for objects of experience by imposing a priori conditions on their nature which guarantee that (under appropriate conditions) they tend to be as they appear. I cannot accept these views; but the difficulty of the problem increases their appeal, and some of their claims are warranted. Perhaps Descartes was right in thinking that the only deductive path from justification to truth about the external world is theistic; phenomenalism may be correct in claiming that the only indefeasibly justified empirical beliefs are about mind-dependent objects; and Kant is apparently right in maintaining that experience provides no deductive justification for beliefs about external things in themselves. Can we understand the relation between justification and truth if we assume a realist rather than a phenomenalist or idealist conception of truth, the a priori and necessary status of correct epistemic principles, and the truth-conduciveness of justification? This problem is the concern of the next section.

VI. JUSTIFICATION AND THE EXTERNAL WORLD

Imagine that Jack is in a world rigged by a demon so that his perceptual experience is systematically misleading. Thus, if it seems to him that the foliage is green and he thereby believes it is, he is wrong; but he cannot acquire good reason to believe he is wrong because attempted confirmation will be manipulated. He will, e.g., tactually hallucinate foliage if he tries to touch it. Can his belief that the foliage is green still be prima facie justified? By P2, it can. What the demon does might preclude justification on balance, but it need not. To sharpen our problem, however, assume Jack's belief is justified on balance. Must we conclude that since, owing to the demon, its falsity is guaranteed, the sense in which it is justified is not the one we seek to capture? In answering, we should consider at least two defenses of the view that there is an ontological connection between justification and truth. One appeals to relevantly similar possible worlds, the other to the metaphysics of perceptual objects.

According to the first defense, Jack's manipulated but perceptually well grounded belief has truth-conducive properties because, in a suitable range of worlds similar to his, such perceptually grounded beliefs are true, since, for one thing, those worlds have no demon. To support the truth-conduciveness of the belief's grounds, one might note that it *would* be true if there were not a special reason for its falsity: demonic machinations. Demons cannot, then, utterly sever the connection between justification and truth, as if it were contingent. What they do is wrench Jack's justification from its usual ontological counterpart: veridicality. On this view, then, what P2 implies for all possible worlds is not that most of the relevant justified perceptual beliefs actually are true, but rather that they are all grounded in truth-conducive elements. Thus, there is enough of a connection between justification and truth to save a proponent of principles like P1–P4 from either endorsing an idealist conception of truth or granting that beliefs with no objective probability of truth can satisfy the principles.

316

This defense, however, is at best inconclusive. On what basis may we suppose that worlds relevantly similar to ours (or Jack's) have no demons (or other causes of systematic error)? Perhaps we do not *take* a world to be like ours if perceptually well grounded beliefs therein are usually false. But to call only worlds in which such beliefs are usually true relevantly similar seems to presuppose that most of our justified perceptual beliefs *are* true, and the defense may thus beg the question. Granted, given our concept of our world, it is plausible to say that our perceptually justified beliefs are true unless there is a special reason for their falsity; but if a demon *does* inhabit relevantly similar worlds, his machinations are no longer "special," or at least are too pervasive to permit our claiming that in relevantly similar worlds justified beliefs are usually true. Moreover, granting that certain of our justified empirical beliefs can be falsified only by a sufficiently *systematic* demon, this at most shows that if at least one sense yields true beliefs, the deceptiveness of the others might be discovered, not that all our justified beliefs rest on truth-conducive factors.

One might try to defend the ontological connection view about (empirical) justification and truth in a second way, one that might explain why principles like P1–P4 are natural for a realist. First, we shift direction: instead of looking from experience to external objects, we look from them toward experience. Next, we avoid not only separating the concept of truth from that of justification, but also separating that of reality from that of justification. We do not characterize reality independently of truth and then understand truth in terms of representing reality, or characterize truth independently of reality and then conceive reality as whatever truth represents. The two notions are inextricably connected; hence, if either is essentially related to justification, the other should be also. Perhaps, then, one way to think of reality, or at least of real things to which P1–P3 apply, is in terms of what *must* be true if such a priori principles of justification are truth-conducive.

Part of the suggested point is this: it is implicit in our concept of a real empirical object that it can impinge on our senses, that, under certain conditions, it tends to affect our senses, and that it is the sort of thing which best explains our spontaneous perceptual experiences. This is not idealism. It does not, e.g., imply that apart from perceivers there are no real objects. The point is rather that it is partly because of what reality is, and not only because of what justification is, that justified beliefs are truth-conducive. Call this view *epistemic realism*. Its central claim is that accessibility to the sorts of experiences that confer epistemic justification is implicit in the concepts of the kinds of things to which P1–P3 apply: tables and chairs, earth and water, colors and sounds, movements of trees, and flashes of light. Could a table be such that it (conceptually) could not be perceptually taken to be one? Could a flash of light be such that it could not be perceived or produce a memory impression? Certainly a table could be designed to cause us to hallucinate something else each time we approach it, and always to elude our touch. But tables are in principle perceptible, and by their very nature *tend* to be seen, touched, etc., when approached head-on by a normal observer in normal light. If these points are correct, then the sorts of things to which P1–P3 apply are intrinsically the kind about which the formation of justified beliefs is to be expected whenever normal perceivers are near them under appropriate conditions.

Here we must be careful, however. The view in question is that real objects are epistemically constituted: necessarily such that they *tend* to produce justified beliefs (and knowledge) about them. This does not entail that most of our perceptual beliefs *are* true. But the more modest view that justification is truth-conducive seems to be supported by epistemic realism. For, arguably the best explanation of, or at least a somewhat probable inference from, say, my perceptually taking there to be a table beneath my arms, is that there really is one there. If epistemic realism is correct, this is not simply an epistemic point about justifiable explanatory hypotheses: the concept of a table *is* in part the concept of something that has (and can explain) such effects as perceptual experiences of the sort underlying my belief; and apparently this applies to nothing else. Other real objects *can* produce the same experiences, but what else is conceptually fitted to this role? If an hallucinogenic machine plays the role, it presumably does so through something that inhibits or distorts its normal effects. It is intrinsically liable to be exposed as a fraud. These and other points implicit in epistemic realism suggest that the spontaneous perceptual belief that there is a table beneath my arms has a special status: if it is appropriately grounded in my experience, it is, to some degree, truth-conducive.

Unfortunately, the desired connection between justification and truth cannot be guaranteed by this line either. Granted, a table before one in normal light may be intrinsically fitted to produce a perceptual experience through which one truly believes that it *is*

318

before one. But if we assume only that one has an experience *as of* a table, what entails a likelihood that there is one there? Perhaps what in *fact* best explains such experiences is that there is a table before one. But this is uncontroversial only so far as it rests on the epistemic point that such experience *justifies* one in believing this. We may not say, *a priori*, that there being a table there best explains such experiences, in a sense implying an objective likelihood that there is one, nor that nothing else (e.g., demonic machinations) is as well fitted to the role of causing such experiences. We cannot, in this way at least, move from the ontology of perceivable objects to the epistemology of perception. Reason may tell us that no competing explanations we are aware of, including skeptical explanations, are better; and this may help us answer skepticism; but that explanations presupposing the general veridicality of sense experience tend to be true is not knowable a priori.

If the considerations we have examined are the most plausible kind favoring an ontological connection between justification and truth, then apparently we cannot establish any such connection a priori. What epistemic realism does do, however, is help to unify P1–P4 (and similar principles). For it implies not only that objects are epistemically constituted, but that their essential properties, such as shape and texture, include those corresponding to the very modalities through which we know them: perception, for external objects; introspection, for mental phenomena (in our own case); and reason, for abstract objects. Moreover, we have seen no reason to deny that there is an a priori teleological relation between justification and truth. Reflection alone shows that the process of justifying a belief has, as its appropriate – even intrinsic – aim, showing or arguing for its truth (or at least probable truth). This is why it is conceptually improper to say such things as that one is trying to justify one's belief that *p* but is not at all concerned to show *p* to be true or probable. So far as we understand this, we take the kind of justification to be non-epistemic, e.g. moral justification for *retaining* (or causing oneself to hold) the belief. One could satisfy the *behavioral* conditions for giving a justification without being motivated to show that *p*, though this would not be (fully) *engaging* in our practice of justification: the practice whose character I have been illustrating, in which the concept of justification of belief is anchored. (If there are other concepts of justification, I believe they derive from this one.) That the intrinsic aim of the process is to show truth is not a psychological claim: it is a

319

relevance requirement, and it largely determines what counts as an appropriate objection.

An equally important point is that the elements, such as perceptual states, that we cite in this process *can* be seen, a priori, to count toward that aim. This is not because, in engaging in the practice of justification, we must take them to entail truth or probable truth, but because the kinds of principles in which the elements figure, principles like P1–P3, are constitutive of the practice. Engaging in the practice entails that one takes such justifiers as perceptual experience normally to be in some way truth-conducive; it does not require taking them to be *necessarily* such. Their de facto reliability (and thereby truth-conduciveness) is necessarily a presupposition *of* the practice; their necessary reliability is not, nor is it presupposed *in* the practice. We cannot know that, in every possible world, conformity with the principles conduces to forming true beliefs; but we can know a priori that in any possible world they generate (prima facie) justified beliefs. For the concept of justified belief is in part constituted by the very principles that license our appeal to these elements.

VII. RELIABILITY AND JUSTIFICATION

In the light of the framework developed above, we can clarify the relation between (empirical) justification and reliability. I begin with negative points. While reliability is apparently not built into P1–P3 as a priori principles, they can be seen a priori to provide grounds for holding beliefs. While they are not, as on an idealist view, partly constitutive of truth, they are partly constitutive of epistemically permissible attempts to show truth. Thus, justification does not necessarily imply truth or (objective) probability of truth; yet it is necessary that the process of justification "aim" at truth. Truth is a teleological aim of the practice to which that process belongs, though it need not be a motivational aim of those engaging in the practice. The sorts of generative factors figuring in P1–P4 are intrinsically suited to this process: given a proper appeal to them, one aims right, in the sense of 'properly', whether or not one hits the target. Perhaps a Cartesian demon could falsify our belief that there is a world out there; but he could not leave our experience unchanged and deprive us of any good reason to think there is.

For all the importance of the connection between justification and reliability, however, reliability does not constitute justification as understood here (or in normal contexts in which we justify beliefs). Imagine a perfectly reliable process that generates true beliefs, but does so neither through the elements in P1–P4 nor by anything accessible to S, apart, say, from his making a scientific study of his beliefs to discover what explains their truth. Thus, Jan might simply find herself believing, of people she meets, that they were born on some particular day; and these beliefs might arise from an undiscovered process so connected with her and them as to guarantee her correctness. Surely such beliefs are not justified – at least before she learns of her success – though perhaps they can be knowledge.[17] Thus, their reliable production is not sufficient to justify them. (I bypass problems about how to specify precisely *what types* of belief-generating processes are reliable; it turns out that this is very difficult for reliabilism.[18])

It might be objected that one's *citing* the reliable production of Jan's beliefs *does* justify them. Suppose it does. That there *is* a justification for a belief does not entail that S justifiably *holds* it,[19] and indeed the justification here is of her "beliefs" only in the sense of their propositional objects (or perhaps belief-types). For the reliable production of her beliefs to justify them she must have access to it, which she can obtain only by using principles like P1–P3. The reason why her beliefs are not justified here is, then, not that she cannot *give* a justification for them. One may be unable (in practice, at least) to give a justification for one's quite justified belief that one is, say, imaging red. Yet this belief might be introspectively grounded and instantiate P1; and while the elements in P1–P3 that generate empirical justification do surely tend to yield true beliefs, I am aware of no sound epistemic principles that exhibit mere reliable production of a belief, unconnected with either accessible factors or epistemic principles like P1–P4, as sufficient for its justification. (The examples of generation principles which reliabilists tend to use are similar to P1–P3; none has to my knowledge

17. For a plausible account of knowledge that supports this see Frederick I. Dretske, *Knowledge and the Flow of Information* (Cambridge, Mass., 1981).
18. For plausible criticism of reliabilist accounts of justification, see John L. Pollock, "Reliability and Justified Belief," *Canadian Journal of Philosophy* 14 (1984); Richard Feldman, "Reliability and Justification," *The Monist* 68 (1985); Richard Foley, "What's Wrong with Reliabilism?," *The Monist* 68 (1985); and Paul K. Moser, *Empirical Justification* (Dordrecht, 1985), esp. chap. 4.
19. That there is no entailment here is argued in Chapter 7, this volume.

adopted principles grounding justification in any but very familiar processes.)

Recall the process-property integration thesis, which asserts a conceptual connection between the property of justification (justifiedness) and the process of justification, and implies that for every justified belief there is a possible process of justifying the belief by invoking certain properties of it. If this paper is correct, the integration, as applied to us, is not only between the justifiedness of our beliefs and *possible* justificatory processes, but between it and our *actual practice* of justification. It appears that the basic justificatory elements to which we have appealed are by their nature the sorts of things that S can cite, given a grasp of ordinary facts and ordinary epistemic principles, in offering a justification. This usability is crucial because the practice of justification is, if not more fundamental than the property, at least the place where that property is anchored.

This point does not presuppose, though it may support, a deontological view of justification. An underlying truth in that view is that unless justifiers were usable in giving justification, the process and the property of justification could not be integrated as they are: the property seems to be precisely the sort of thing the process, as normally practiced, can show a belief to have, and the process is judged largely by its success in showing the relevant belief to have an appropriate set of the properties (such as we have discussed) which confer justification. The process and the property of justification seem to be made for each other – or by each other. This integration can exist whether or not the property supervenes on fulfillment of duties.

VIII. JUSTIFICATION AND KNOWLEDGE

In the integration of process and property, justification differs from knowledge. There is no process of knowledge, as opposed to coming to know. And showing one knows is very different from showing one is justified: the former entails showing that one is in an *epistemically successful* state, and apparently does not entail that one's getting there meets, or is, even indirectly, guided by, any normative standards; the latter entails showing that one is in an *epistemically acceptable* state, which one cannot be in without meeting normative standards. One need not *do* anything in fulfillment of the appropriate standards, as on the paradigm deontological views, but one's cognitive state must meet them. Justification, we might say, is roughly a matter of a *right to believe,* and is anchored in a social practice; knowledge is roughly a matter of *being right* (in a suitable way), and is anchored to the world. If this contrast is sound, it helps to explain why generators of knowledge, unlike generators of justification, apparently need not be things one can de facto appeal to in showing that someone knows something.

The connection just stressed, between the property and the process of justification, is important both because, negatively, it helps us see that reliability does not constitute justification, and because, positively, it helps us see why reliability seems so prominent in generation principles like P1–P4. Since the property of justification is, teleologically speaking, truth-conducive, the sorts of factors we conceive as justifiers should also be factors we think of as tending to produce true beliefs. This is not because we have discovered the (contingent) reliability of these factors and subsumed them under the principle that reliable belief-generators confer justification; it is more nearly because, given the purposes of our justificatory practice, nothing could serve, in the basic way they do, as a justificatory element, unless we *conceived* it as (at least contingently) truth-conducive. If we are trying to show that a belief has a property which is truth-conducive, the base properties we cite will clearly be ones we take to conduce to truth. We may err about the reliability of a given factor; but as we come to believe that a type of factor does reliably indicate truth, we tend to count citing it as providing (at least indirect) justification. In this way, *justification appropriates reliability,* or, at least, sufficiently widely assumed reliability. Because of this appropriation, moreover, our concept of justification can evolve as certain of our beliefs about reliable cognitive generation become sufficiently deep.

An ethical analogy is useful here. Suppose that what constitutes the rightness of an act is its conforming to certain moral rules, such as principles that require keeping promises. If the teleological basis of our practice embodying these rules is largely to enhance human welfare, it is to be expected that rightness will supervene on (perhaps among other things) such properties of an act as its conformity with rules which, if followed, conduce to our welfare. Citing such properties will then provide reasons for the rightness of an act. Rightness might even be extensionally equivalent to some complicated property of this sort. But it would not follow that rightness is analyzable in terms of such a property. On the other hand, because of the purposes of our moral practices, citing considerations of welfare to justify ascriptions of rightness will be so natural that denying their relevance may seem to deny conceptual connections. Similarly for justifiedness: it may be constituted by a belief's conformity with epistemic principles like P_1–P_4; and because our justificatory practice is based largely on a concern to grasp truths, it is to be expected that justification will supervene on properties of a belief (such as perceptual generation) in virtue of which we conceive of it as likely to be true. But it does not follow that justification is analyzable in terms of such properties as production by a truth-conducive (or reliable) process. Still, we will justify beliefs in terms of properties we believe are truth-conducive; and when a property is so conceived, denying its relevance to the justification of a belief that has it will seem conceptually deviant.

The contrasts I have drawn are easily misinterpreted. While I have argued that justification is not analyzable in terms of reliability, I grant that reliability may be the basis of a kind of *theory* of justification, as utilitarianism – the ethical analogue of reliabilism, I think – gives us a kind of theory of the right. It is not only that justifiedness could be extensionally equivalent to some sort of truth-conduciveness. There is a sense in which reliability can explain justification, or at least explain why we conceive as justificatory the factors we do so conceive. Recall first how the concept of justification is linked to a practice whose underlying concern is (partly) to lead us to believe truth and avoid error. The conceptual connection between justification and truth is tied, at least teleologically, to this concern; and perhaps evolutionary factors partly explain why we have the conception we do have of what confers justification, and why we are correct in taking the basic elements, such as sensory experience, as reliable. Could we have survived if the beliefs we take to be justified, and on which we regularly stake our lives, were not, with sufficient frequency, true? If all this is so, it is to be expected that we regard generators of belief as justificatory only if we also consider them reliable. On the other hand, just as happiness *can* be maximized by an act that is not right and a right act can fail to maximize happiness, a belief can be reliably produced – as in our divination case – without being justified, or be justified without being so produced. That beliefs we take to be so produced are characteristically beliefs we also consider justified does not show that reliable generation constitutes justification.

IX. SOME IMPLICATIONS OF THE ACCOUNT: SECOND-ORDER BELIEFS AND EPISTEMOLOGICAL NATURALISM

Plainly, there *can* be directly justified beliefs if principles even close to P1–P4 are sound. But can we *show* that there are? Nothing said above precludes this. To be sure, in arguing that we have justified beliefs it may be impossible to satisfy skeptics. I do not claim that anything I say would impress skeptics. I simply want to suggest how far the position of this paper can take us in an anti-skeptical direction.

Suppose that one can know a priori that certain kinds of occurrent mental state beliefs are prima facie justified (P1). If so, and surely if one can, as may well be possible, also know this directly, then one may justifiably believe it. Now suppose one believes P1 *and* that one is now in the occurrent state of thinking about skepticism. Apparently one may thereby justifiably believe that one has a prima facie justified belief that one is thinking about skepticism. Thus, there is some reason to think that we may justifiably believe that we have justified beliefs.

Can this second-order belief be *shown* to be true? Would arguing from the premises that (a) such occurrent mental state beliefs are prima facie justified, and (b) one is now in the occurrent mental state of thinking about skepticism, to the conclusion that one justifiably believes that one is in that state, show that one justifiably believes this? Much depends on how showing is conceived. On a weak interpretation, if one is justified in believing one's (true) premises, and validly (and non-circularly) argues from them to a conclusion, one has shown it. But it might be claimed that unless one's premises are self-evident, one must be able to say something on their behalf. There may also be dialectical conditions for showing, e.g. that in asserting the premises one not "presuppose" anything denied by a plausible case against the conclusion. Skeptics tend to prefer stronger notions. This issue cannot be settled here, and I conclude that it may be only on a weak, though significant, notion of showing, that one can show that one has a justified belief.

Those preferring a stronger notion might deny that showing, in *this* way, that there are justified second-order beliefs cuts against a skeptical denial that there are.

What about beliefs regarding the external world? If one may assume that a perceptual experience one is having is spontaneous, P2 could be used, in the way just sketched, to show that one justifiably believes, say, that the foliage is green. Perhaps, however, one may not assume, without inductive evidence, that a perceptual experience is spontaneous. I think there is a sense of 'spontaneous', strong enough to sustain second-order use of P2, for which one may believe this without inductive evidence; but until this matter is settled, principles like P2 do not allow our confidently concluding that we may justifiably believe that we have justified beliefs about the world.

We may conclude here, then, only that principles like P1–P3 provide *some* basis for our justifiably believing that we have justified beliefs about the world, and that they are, for at least one plausible notion of showing, a basis for rejecting skepticism concerning these beliefs. Suppose, on the other hand, that we do not conceive epistemic principles as a priori, but rather as, e.g., knowable only by virtue of knowing the actual reliability of belief generators. Could we justifiably believe that we have justified (empirical) beliefs? Let us assume so, since such second-order beliefs *could* be reliably produced. Could we show that we have justified empirical beliefs? In the weak sense just sketched, we could, provided we could justifiably and correctly believe the epistemic principle that reliably produced beliefs are justified, and that some belief of ours is so produced. Suppose we could fulfill this condition. Dialectically, at least, such a reliabilism still seems worse off than the normativism of this paper, in showing that we have justified beliefs. For one apparently could not argue for the crucial reliabilist epistemic principle – say, that spontaneous perceptual beliefs tend to be true – without presupposing it as one's basis for picking out justified beliefs as confirming instances of it. P2, by contrast, would be supported a priori and could be identified intuitively and apart from empirical knowledge of reliable processes. It may be, of course, that neither view enables us to show, in a strong sense, that any significant skeptical thesis is false; but the contrast is still important in understanding how, for non-skeptics, each kind of view accounts for second-order justification.

With respect to skepticism about knowledge the case is similar. Even if knowledge does not entail justification, showing that S has it requires using some epistemic principle and some proposition about S, say that a belief of S's is produced in a certain way. There is the added difficulty that the belief must be true, so that showing it constitutes knowledge entails showing, in *some* sense of 'show', that it is true. Let us pursue this.

Some philosophers, and certainly most skeptics, believe that premises show something only if they *entail* it. If this is true, prospects for showing that there is knowledge of the external world are dim. For it is doubtful that any plausible epistemic principles license *deduction* of propositions about the world from premises one is obviously justified in assuming, e.g. that one has an impression of green. But surely showing, as opposed to proving, does not require entailing grounds. Thus, if certain epistemic principles can be known a priori, perhaps they may be used to show that there is knowledge of the external world. That attempt may not succeed, but I do not see that it must fail. Let me elaborate briefly.

Nothing I have said presupposes that there is direct knowledge of epistemic principles. Such knowledge, or justified belief, can be a priori without being direct. But perhaps we are directly justified in believing (and even directly know) some epistemic principles, e.g. that if S is thinking about skepticism and on this basis non-inferentially and attentively believes he is, then this belief is justified. Given P4, our believing this principle is at least prima facie justified, provided – what seems plausible – that the principle is a necessary truth which we attentively believe simply on the basis of understanding it. If one is justified, directly, in believing some epistemic principles, then the prospects for showing that one has justified (empirical) beliefs, or even (empirical) knowledge – say, that one is thinking about skepticism – are improved. For one thing, if our justification for believing such principles is direct, their truth should be apparent, perhaps even close to self-evident, other than by the often controversial route through prior premises. Surely we are at least more likely to succeed in any strong kind of showing than on the assumption that epistemic principles are known empirically and indirectly.[20]

20. Considerations showing how difficult it would be, on the assumption that epistemic principles are empirical, to show that we have justified beliefs, are set out in Alston's "Epistemic Circularity," cited in note 1.

Much less needs to be said here about beliefs of necessary truths. Skeptics have been far less concerned with beliefs of prima facie necessary truths, and the case for skepticism regarding them is weaker. Surely there are necessary truths, such as very simple logical ones, which we are directly justified in believing. Moreover, let us assume that we can justifiably believe (directly) some of the relevant epistemic principles, e.g. P4. If, in addition, we are justified in believing some simple logical truths to *be* necessary and to be believed by us on the basis of understanding them, then we can justifiably hold (and perhaps know and even show the truth of) second-order beliefs to the effect that we are prima facie justified in our belief of some necessary truth, say that if no men are women, no women are men.

The suggested apriorist view of epistemic principles has been constructed to take account of not only the relation between justification and reliability, but also possible relations between our justificatory practice and evolutionary considerations. Is the view, then, naturalistic? Let us distinguish between a *substantively naturalistic* epistemology and a *conceptually naturalistic* one.[21] The former takes epistemological propositions, such as P1–P4, to be empirical and the latter simply uses no irreducibly normative concepts. Then, while the view is not substantively naturalistic, it could be conceptually naturalistic, depending on how normative concepts are to be understood. I have argued that justification is not analyzable in terms of reliability, but have not ruled out its being a natural property. This seems doubtful, however, and the position of this paper seems best regarded as a *teleological normativism*. It has affinities to intuitionism, but is not a deontologism and differs from, e.g., W. D. Ross's view at least in providing a way to unify the constitutive principles, in conceiving the relevant practice as having an underlying teleological aim, and, of course, in taking (epistemic) justification, unlike rightness, to apply to beliefs rather than actions. Moreover, just as reliabilism is not the only naturalistic epistemology, deontologism, while a kind of normativism, is not the only kind. For justification can be constituted by a priori, normative standards which justified beliefs must satisfy, even if such satisfaction is not a matter of one's fulfilling obligations.

21. This distinction is introduced and developed in Chapter 3, this volume.

CONCLUSION

My main subject is justification, and I want to reiterate that, as irrational divination suggests, knowledge should not be simply assumed to entail justification. Even if it does not, problems beset attempts to analyze it naturalistically.[22] Still, if it does not entail justification, perhaps the problems facing a naturalistic analysis of justification need not preclude such an analysis of knowledge. On some conceptions of naturalism, of course, a naturalistic view cannot countenance the synthetic a priori. But to insist on this is surely to assimilate naturalism as a metaphysical and conceptual view to empiricism. The historical association between naturalism and empiricism is strong, but they are independent.

Our direct concern has been what is often called epistemic justification. We may call it epistemic without assuming that knowledge entails justification, because, for one thing, whether this entailment holds or not, the relevant sort of justification counts towards a belief's being knowledge. However, the generic notion of justification is connected both with all the other propositional attitudes and with actions, and our results bear on that notion. One might think the concept occurring in those cases is radically different; but this view should be resisted if we can frame a good general account of justification. If we take off from the truth-conduciveness of the justifiers of belief, the likely bridge between epistemic and non-epistemic justification is a non-epistemic analogue of truth. Suppose we adopt a realist conception of value, of desirability, and of the justification of actions. We might then conceive non-epistemic justification, say of valuing good conversation, as supervening on the sorts of properties that count (at least teleologically) toward possession – objective instantiation – of these normative characteristics, e.g. toward the actual intrinsic goodness of conversation.[23] There are, then, significant parallels to the epistemological case, both in the generation principles and in the justificatory practices.

Thus, if this paper is correct, its results can be incorporated into a wider theory of justification. Such a theory must not only lay out generation principles in more detail than has been possible here,

22. For an indication of some of these problems, see Chapter 6, this volume.
23. I have pursued this line of inquiry in some detail in Chapter 13, this volume.

but also formulate transmission principles. If, however, the account of direct justification explored here is a good starting point, we can readily extend it both to other cases of direct justification and to the transmission of justification. We should find generation principles whose modal and epistemic status is similar to those explored here; we should find analogues of truth, such as objective value; and we should find counterparts of reliability. What generates the direct justification of a valuation, e.g., should be the kind of property conducive to the relevant sort of thing's being objectively valuable.

I do not present the teleological normativist account of justification as clearly correct; but it may be a good foil for both reliabilism and deontologism, and one of its merits is its ready applicability to non-epistemic justification. The account also provides a basis for understanding both the nature of epistemic generation principles and their connection with truth. Epistemic justification is seen as inseparably tied to a justificatory practice whose proper aim is to foster true beliefs and avoid false ones. In part because the concept of justification is tied to this practice, it is subject to accessibility requirements. Inaccessible justifiers could hardly serve as the basis of our epistemic practice, which embodies readily applicable standards of criticism and judgment. These requirements, in turn, are reflected in the elements which the principles constitutive of the practice represent as conferring direct justification. Those elements apparently cannot be shown a priori to be truth-conducive, but we can show a priori that justification has a teleological connection with truth.

It is true that there may well be at least one sort of justification, the strong axiomatic kind, that does entail truth. This case illustrates the conceptual connection between the two notions, but it also offers a paradigm to which – unless we follow Descartes – we must not assimilate all justification. For justification in general does not entail truth; the ontological connection implicit in strong axiomatic justification belongs only to the a priori and perhaps a few kinds of empirical belief about the internal world. The justifiedness of beliefs in general may, however, be viewed as the actual or – more often – potential upshot of a process whose intrinsic *aim* is reaching truth: justifiedness need not arise from a process of justification, as only a small proportion of our justified beliefs do; but it must be attainable through that process. Precisely because of this aim, the elements we regard as justificatory, such as sensory and memorial experiences, are elements that we also normally take to be at least in fact reliable indicators of truth; and as our beliefs about reliability change, our conception of what justifies, and even of justification itself, can evolve. But our concept of justification does not appear analyzable in terms of reliability; it seems irreducibly normative and inextricably connected to a normative practice.[24]

24. This paper has benefited from comments by many people from discussions at Notre Dame, Syracuse, Texas Tech, Wayne State University, and an NEH Summer Seminar which I directed in 1987. For comments on a very early version I thank John Heil, Eric Russert Kraemer, George S. Pappas, and especially Albert Casullo. The incisive and extensive remarks of William P. Alston were of great help at several points. I have also benefited much from detailed critical comments, on two versions, by Jonathan Kvanvig, Paul Moser, and Bruce Russell. John Bender, Richard Foley, Andrew Naylor, Kevin Possin, and Thomas Vinci also made many helpful points, and the report of the Editor, Ernest Sosa, on the penultimate version led to many further improvements.

Chapter 11

Causalist internalism

In its most general form, internalism is the view that what justifies a person's belief, the ground of it's justification, is something internal to that person.[1] The "internal," in the relevant sense, is that to which one has introspective, thus internal, access; it includes beliefs, visual and other sensory impressions, and thoughts. To have such access to something is to be aware of it or to be able, through self-consciousness or at least by introspective reflection, to become aware of it. By contrast, the production of a belief by a reliable process, say one that more often than not yields true beliefs, is not introspectively accessible. Thus reliabilism, as the view that what justifies a belief is some such reliable basis, is externalist. This formulation of internalism covers a number of contemporary positions and leaves much unspecified. Section I will sketch a version of the view which is plausible and should be acceptable to many internalists.

I. INTERNALISM AND INTROSPECTIVE ACCESS

First, internalism does not imply that one can become aware of the justifier under any particular description, such as "my evidence." Indeed, a plausible internalism need not even require that the awareness be conceptual, in the sense that one is aware of the ground under any concept. Thus if, after a camera flash, a tiny

1. For accounts of internalism of one or another kind, see Roderick M. Chisholm, *Theory of Knowledge*, 3rd edn. (Englewood Cliffs: Prentice-Hall, 1989); Laurence BonJour, *The Structure of Empirical Knowledge* (Cambridge: Harvard University Press, 1985); William P. Alston, "Internalism and Externalism in Epistemol-

child is aware of a blue after-image in its visual field, this may suffice to justify believing there is something blue out there, even if the child has not yet developed any concept of an afterimage or of a sensory state. Being justified by a ground, even if it should imply *having* some concept instantiated by that ground, does not require awareness of the ground under any particular one, and certainly not under an epistemic concept.

Second, so long as the awareness is introspective as opposed to, say, observational (and thus dependent on the external world), it need not even be *direct*. The main notion of directness relevant here is *phenomenal directness:* phenomenally direct awareness is awareness not mediated by any other object of awareness. In this sense, we need not be directly aware even of our beliefs; indeed, it may be – though this is not a commitment of internalism – that by their very nature dispositional mental states become objects of awareness only through their manifestations in consciousness. Granted, in the *inferential* sense of "direct" we may know directly that we have beliefs; but that is consistent with our awareness of them being mediated by, say, direct awareness of our assentingly entertaining their propositional object. Mediation by an object would not imply mediation by a premise.

Third, the appropriate introspective reflection may be extended, so long as it reveals elements that already justify our belief and it does not introduce new justifiers, e.g. through inferentially extending our knowledge of premises for the belief by leading us to propositions we did not previously believe and might have even rejected on first considering them. The appropriate kind of reflection, then, is *revelatory*, not *generative:* it reveals a ground one has, it does not create a ground to which one was in some sense entitled. The former kind of reflection is appropriate to *justified belief*, the latter to merely *justifiable belief.* This distinction is not sharp, but plainly there are cases in which a person (*S*) can believe something, say that the butler committed the crime, for bad reasons, yet *have* good reasons for believing it that would come to mind given careful

ogy," *Philosophical Topics* XIV (1986); John Pollock, *Contemporary Theories of Knowledge* (Totowa: Rowman and Littlefield, 1986); and Paul K. Moser, *Knowledge and Evidence* (Cambridge and New York: Cambridge University Press, 1989). Internalism is not new; Descartes is often cited as an internalist, and recent versions of the view not so called are found in (to name just three sources) earlier work of Chisholm's; in Keith Lehrer, *Knowledge* (Oxford: Oxford University Press, 1974); and in Carl Ginet, *Knowledge, Perception, and Memory* (Dordrecht and Boston: D. Reidel, 1975).

reflection of the kind that generates discoveries through one's drawing inferences from what one believes. Here *S*'s belief has potential, not actual, justification. The same case shows that the internalist notion of justification is not expressible simply by such counterfactuals as: If *S* were to reflect on what grounds *S* has for believing *p*, *S* would become aware of at least one good one. Even for subjects with enough conceptual sophistication to do this kind of reflection, such counterfactuals fail to distinguish between revelatory and generative reflection. For that reason (among others), internal access to revelatory reflection does not imply justified, as opposed to merely justifiable, belief.

II. THE PROBLEM OF INTROSPECTIVE ACCESS TO CAUSAL CONNECTIONS

As formulated here, internalism is neutral regarding the question whether the internal elements that justify a belief must *also* stand in some causal relation to it. But this causal constraint is plausible to some internalists, and a *causalist internalism* – one that embodies this constraint – is the kind to be developed here. Consider first the sense in which this view is causal.

In general terms, what I call *the causal requirement on justified belief* is this: a justified belief must be at least in part causally based on, i.e., in part produced or sustained by, what justifies it, for instance a sensory experience or beliefs of premises *S* takes to warrant the belief. A major motivation for the causal requirement is the idea that a justified belief is both *grounded* in what justifies it and, at least if empirical, supported by that in a way that *connects* the belief to the world, in the sense, roughly, that the (ultimate) ground is produced or sustained by some feature of the world and, given the transitivity of causation, the belief it grounds is also connected with that feature. White paper produces my steadfast impression of white; this in turn (partly) produces my belief that there is white before me; and my belief is justified above all because it is based on this impression. This connection between my belief and the world is important in explaining why justification should be thought necessary for *knowledge;* for (at least in empirical cases) knowledge must register some fact about the world.

On this causal view of justified belief, it is not enough that the propositional object of the belief be evidentially supported by some

334

justificatory proposition to which S has access, say by virtue of S's remembering it. To speak in Kantian terms, just as an action has moral worth only if done from, and not merely in conformity with, duty, so a belief is justified only if based on, and not merely evidentially in line with, one's ground(s). Roughly, a belief is justified *by* a ground only if held *on* that ground; and a causalist internalism maintains that only beliefs held on an internal ground can manifest epistemic virtue: only beliefs causally rooted in oneself can redound to one's epistemic character. As one gets no moral credit for accidentally doing one's duty, or doing it for a bad reason, one gets no epistemic credit unless one believes *on the basis of* a (suitable) ground and not merely in line with it.

Internalism, on the other hand, is motivated quite differently than is the causal requirement, and there is some reason to doubt that the two are ultimately compatible. Internalism is motivated in part by the idea that what justifies a belief is somehow available to one to use in *justifying* it[2] and in part by the conviction that even if a Cartesian demon caused us to hold countless false beliefs, we would remain justified in holding those of them suitably based on internal grounds: such grounds, then, seem central in justification.

The problem to be resolved by a causalist internalism arises as follows. It is simply not clear how one can have introspective access to the relevant causal relations, and hence to what causalist views take as a crucial condition of one's justification. This applies particularly to causal sustaining relations; for, unlike causal production, these need not be manifested by experienceable marks, such as inferential processes or phenomenal events. Consider an (apparently) justified belief that one will go to the office tomorrow. Can one, by introspective reflection, become aware of the relevant kind of causal sustaining relation between one's grounds for this and one's believing it?

A negative answer finds support along these lines. First, there seems to be no standard set of ways that such causal connections manifest themselves in consciousness: one introspects at best a constant conjunction. Moreover, it appears that to know or justifiably believe that my belief that I will go to the office is causally sustained by, say, my belief that nothing will prevent realization of my intention to go, I must know such things as this: that if I

---

2. An indication of how and why grounds of justification must be available to S is provided in Chapter 10, this volume.

lacked the latter belief, I would not hold, or would less strongly hold, the former. Can one know or justifiably believe such counterfactuals through introspective reflection? This is far from obvious. Indeed, it is not even obvious that when believingly entertaining the premises of a valid syllogism produces one's belief of the conclusion, one can know or justifiedly believe, on the basis of introspection, that this production relation actually holds. One is especially unlikely to know this where the conclusion is something one *wants* to believe, and believing it is thus subject to non-evidential influences. It is no wonder, then, that the causal requirement has been taken to be reliabilist[3] or at least inimical to internalism.[4]

In discussing this problem, we should concentrate on causal sustaining relations rather than production relations, since the former present the harder case for a causalist internalism. Let us start with a brief examination of the range of internalist positions, particularly as bearing on direct (roughly, non-inferential) justification.

III. FIRST-ORDER AND SECOND-ORDER INTERNALISM

Much depends on the *scope* of the accessibility requirement central to internalism. The guiding idea is that justified belief requires access to *what justifies* the belief,[5] e.g. to a visual experience. Call this view *first-order internalism*. The counterpart condition on justification *for* believing, *situational justification* – which does not entail actually believing – simply requires access to a ground *S* has that would produce a justified belief that *p* if *S* came to hold this belief appropriately on the basis of the ground. Since this ground can, in that way, produce an actual justified belief, which requires the ground's accessibility to *S*, we may reasonably take internalism to entail the accessibility of grounds even of merely situational justification. Again, the analogy to action is apt. Situational justifi-

---

3. See, e.g., Jonathan Kvanvig, "Subjective Justification," *Mind*, vol. 93 (1984).
4. See, e.g., Carl Ginet, "*Contra* Reliabilism," *The Monist*, vol. 69 (1985), and Richard Foley, *The Theory of Epistemic Rationality* (Cambridge: Harvard University Press, 1987), esp. pp. 175–86. Foley says, e.g., that "any account of rational belief that requires an individual's belief to be caused in an appropriate way by his evidence is not an account of epistemically rational belief" (p. 186).
5. Paul Moser suggests such a view in *Empirical Justification* (Dordrecht and Boston: D. Reidel, 1985).

cation is like the justification one *has* for doing something, say insisting one be paid a debt on time: one need not do it, as one need not believe everything for which one has good evidence; but one's justifying ground – recalling the promised time – is accessible, and if one does it on the basis of that ground, then one does it justifiedly.

By contrast, a strong internalist might require introspective access to *how what justifies does so*, where this implies a capacity to know, introspectively, how the justifier does so, or at least a capacity, regarding some way it justifies, to form, introspectively, a justified belief that it does so in that way. Call this *second-order internalism,* since in effect it implies that one does or can know (or justifiedly believe) something *about* one's belief, say that it is sustained by one's impression of white, or that its truth is entailed by that of a premise one believes. Suppose it were claimed that one must also be capable of knowing or justifiedly believing that, say, the impression provides *evidence* for believing there is something white before one. We would then have an internalism that is both second-order and, since it requires S to have concepts like that of evidence, *epistemic.*

It may well seem that first-order internalism implies second-order internalism. Certainly if S is aware of what justifies S's belief, e.g. of an impression of variegated human shapes before S, S is in a good position to form second-order beliefs about how this justifies the belief. Still, S need not form any. Being aware of something makes possible, and even natural, formation of beliefs about it; but it surely does not entail that, as where one's mind is heavily occupied with unrelated matters. Hence, it would be a mistake to hold that if one has a justified first-order belief, one *must also* have second-order beliefs concerning what justifies it. But what about the view that one can, but need not, know or justifiably believe an appropriate range of things about one's internal grounds? This, too, seems too strong. Suppose S is a child with insufficient conceptual resources to form the relevant kind of belief, say that S's impression of human figures supports the proposition that there are people before S. Then first-order but not second-order internalism allows S to have justified beliefs.

The distinction between first- and second-order internalism turns out to be important. For one thing, if we hold the latter, it may easily seem that one does not justifiedly believe p unless one can show one does, since, after all, if you have access to both what justifies you and how it does, you should be able – on reflection – to articulate all this in a way that shows your belief that *p* to be justified. You can cite a basis of your justification and in some sense explain how it grounds the justified belief. Much depends, of course, on what is built into awareness of how a ground justifies and into the notion of showing. Even if you are aware of both a causal sustaining relation and a parallel relation of evidential support between your ground and the belief it justifies, you may not be able to show your justification to the satisfaction of a skeptic. Skeptics have very high standards of adequate evidence and so of showing something. In any event, it is a mistake to hold that one justifiedly believes *p* only if one can show that one does. This would for most people rule out justified beliefs that they are in pain, or seem to see red. Hence, if second-order internalism implies this capacity, it is mistaken. Granted, in giving a justification, as an internalist implies is typically possible for a normal adult who has it, one may be exhibiting, and thereby showing, *what* justifies one; but this is not showing *that* it does.

Thus, an internalist defending the causal requirement may plausibly argue as follows against being saddled with second-order internalism. First, it is the relevant experiential state, or one's evidence beliefs, that *do* justify the belief that *p*; their causally producing or sustaining this belief is in part *how* they do it. If I cite one of these grounds to justify my belief that *p*, I give a justification of that belief; I need indicate the causal role of my ground only if I am trying to show that I justifiedly believe *p*. *Giving a justification* is roughly offering a ground that justifies; it is appropriate to a request *for* one's justification. *Showing one is justified* is roughly producing an argument with the epistemic conclusion that the belief in question is justified; it is appropriate to a challenge *of* one's justification. Compare explaining an intentional action by citing the reason for which one performed it, and showing *that* it was intentional, which implies much more, including one's providing evidence for a causal connection between the want expressing one's reason and the action. Hence, I can *have* a justified belief, and even give my justification for it, without being warranted in attributing to my ground the causal role which, on the sustaining requirement, it must play. Causalist internalism, then, does not require knowledge or justified beliefs about such causal roles.

To be sure, if a justifying ground *is* a causal factor, then access to it *is* access to a causal condition, and if one gives one's justification, one in fact *cites* a cause; but this does not imply knowledge, or justification for beliefs, about the justifier *as* a causal factor, nor that in giving one's justification one is showing any causal connection. If this line of argument is sound, then the answer to our problem is just this: since first-order internalism is the only plausible kind, or at least the most important kind, and, even conjoined with the causal requirement, it does not require introspective access to causal truths about belief production or sustenance, our lacking such access would not seriously threaten a causalist internalism.

The points just made constitute a plausible response both to the charge that first-order internalism commits one to second-order internalism and to the problem of reconciling the causal requirement on justification with first-order internalism. The misguided desire to construe justification so that if one has it one can show – say, in the face of skeptical queries – that one does is a powerful motivation for holding second-order internalism; but internalists need not hold it. They also need not posit introspective access to causal connections between justifiers and the beliefs they justify, even if these connections are necessary for justification.

So far, so good. But this defense of a causalist internalism still appears to have two dubious implications: first, that justification supervenes on (roughly in the sense that it is necessarily determined by) only the justifying experiential states and *not* also on their producing or sustaining any belief they justify; and second, that the causal connections in question are only contingent conditions on justification. Both notions go against at least the spirit of the causal requirement. As normally interpreted, the requirement implies that it is a necessary truth partly constitutive of the concept of justification that it supervenes on the relevant grounds *as* having an appropriate causal connection with the belief they justify. Is the guarded internalism formulated here really causalist?

A good way to deal with this problem is to insist on distinguishing between the supervenience base *of* justification and what *S* must have access to in order to *have* justification. Why must an internalist identify these? If we refuse to assimilate giving justification to showing that one has it, and if we insist that access to what justifies one need not imply an ability to show that one is justified, much less a capacity to lay out the elements essential in an analysis of justification, an internalist may hold that not everything in the supervenience base of justification need be introspectively accessible to the justified subject. If this shows that internalism is not as internal as it may sound, that can be granted. Perhaps it is only confusions or preoccupations with answering skepticism that have made it sound so internal in the first place.

One may accept this line and still be dissatisfied with the account of self-knowledge it suggests and with the resources it allows an internalist for dealing with skepticism, e.g. for arguing that we actually have justified beliefs. One might thus go on to raise the question whether a causalist internalism *can* provide for a kind of introspective access to causal connections crucial for justification. The next section pursues this issue.

IV. INTROSPECTIVE ACCESS TO CAUSAL CONDITIONS OF DIRECT JUSTIFICATION

We should first clear away an obstacle. Even if a first-order internalism does provide for a kind of introspective access to the relevant causal connections, it still does not entail second-order internalism. For surely S can have such access to those connections *without* having the capacity to acquire second-order knowledge or justified beliefs that they obtain. This can hold in at least one case: where S is aware of the causal connections in some way, but lacks concepts, such as that of causal sustenance, required to understand, and so to believe, the relevant causal propositions.

Moreover, unrestricted second-order internalism has a defect serious enough to make internalists forswear it. Consider a plausible second-order version: that if S is a normal clear-headed adult, then if S has a justified belief that *p*, S has introspective access to some way in which what justifies this belief does so, if only to a causal sustaining relation between the justifier and the belief it justifies, where this implies the capacity to form a justified belief that the former produces or sustains the latter. If this second-order causal belief is to be itself justified, then it, too, must have an internal causal ground about whose causal relation to it S can form a justified belief. The same holds, however, for *that* causal belief, and so on. No virtuous circle seems available to solve the problem, and it would be ad hoc to restrict the second-order thesis just to causal relations between first-order beliefs and their justifiers. Thus, the imagined second-order internalism would imply that there is no limit to the order of justified beliefs we can form about relations between our grounds and our beliefs. Empirically, at least, this implication seems plainly false.

If there is no entailment between first- and second-order internalism, and if the latter is in any case beset by a regress, one might think that there is no good reason to pursue the question whether we do have introspective access to causal connections between our grounds and the beliefs they justify. But there is good reason. For one thing, this question bears on our ability, given internal resources, not only to show, but also to know or justifiedly believe, that we are justified. The question also bears on the scope of self-knowledge.

To focus the issue, let us explore what may be called *causal connectionist internalism:* the view that justified belief requires, in addition to introspective access to an adequate ground which *does* produce or sustain the belief, introspective access to the relevant kind of causal connection. This view is not as strong as second-order internalism; unlike the latter, it does not entail an ability to form justified beliefs about every such connection. It also does not imply ability to form epistemic beliefs about these connections, such as that they are necessary to a ground's justifying a belief warranted by it. One might hold causal connectionist internalism on the basis of the following plausible assumptions: (1) that epistemic principles are *a priori*; (2) that – provided one has the appropriate concepts and intellectual capacities – one has internal, though to be sure not introspective – access, to the *a priori*; and (3) that one must have introspective access to *all* those properties on which one's justification essentially supervenes, i.e., supervenes in such a way that some grasp of the relevant base relations is necessary for understanding the concept. Thus, as a normal adult speaker of a language like English, I might be able, by reflection, to ascertain an epistemic principle linking a sensory state, via a (partly causal) basis relation, to a perceptual belief, and thereby come to know *how* my belief that there is something white before me is justified. I might come to know, e.g., that when, on the basis of a visual experience of white, I believe there is something white here, this belief is prima facie justified, and I might thereby come to know how the belief is justified. This idea is in the anti-skeptical spirit of internalism; it may in fact be one way to focus a Cartesian light of nature.

Since (3) seems mistaken, I do not believe that causalist internalism as such is committed to causal connectionism. But it may still be true that by and large we do have introspective access to causal connections between our grounds and our beliefs justified by them, and that, at least often, we can form justified beliefs about these connections. This is in any case an important thesis about justification and self-knowledge. The rest of this section explores the case for it.

It is essential to grasp that while the causalist internalism developed here is closely connected with the doctrine of privileged access, it does not imply a strong form of such access. The classical form of that doctrine has two sides; roughly, one thesis is that we are omniscient about a certain range of our mental properties, the other that certain of our beliefs attributing such properties to ourselves are infallible or of some very high epistemic status.[6] The former thesis rules out a certain kind of ignorance, the latter certain sorts of errors. We must distinguish the kind of accessibility that goes with a qualified omniscience thesis – in implying a high degree of spontaneous cognitive receptivity to one's epistemic grounds – from the kind that goes with a qualified infallibility thesis – in implying that those beliefs (if any) which one forms about such grounds have a high degree of reliability.

Call the first kind of accessibility *occurrent accessibility*: something is accessible in this sense if it is luminous in a way that implies that one need at most be "looking" in the right direction to become aware of it; one need not search. Thus, as one looks at an audience, one's experience of a human expanse is either such that one cannot help being aware of it, or at least need only focus attention in the right way to become aware of it.[7] As this illustrates, there are two main cases. The awareness is *focal* provided, even without one's specially attending to it, the object in question, like a figure viewed in a portrait, is focused in consciousness. An awareness is *peripheral* provided it is like one's awareness of furnishings in the background of the portrait, in that one need only attend to them, as opposed to changing one's field of view, to achieve at least some degree of focus on them. If, for instance, a bookcase were suddenly illumi-

---

6. For a related, brief account of privileged access see my *Belief, Justification, and Knowledge* (Belmont, CA: Wadsworth, 1988), ch. 3.
7. Paul Moser's awareness internalism seems to be of this sort; see, e.g., *Knowledge and Evidence*, esp. ch. 3. For assessment of Moser's internalism and a valuable discussion of internalist *vs.* externalist views, see William P. Alston, "An Internalist Externalism," *Synthese*, vol. 74 (1988).

nated by a flashlight beam, one would be aware of that even if one kept looking at the person in the portrait's center.

By contrast, *dispositional accessibility* requires only that if, in the right introspective way, you search, you will find; and finding is both becoming aware of the object found and acquiring a *position* in which one can know or justifiedly believe certain truths about it. In contrast to the luminescence of what is occurrently accessible, only luminibility is possessed by objects that are just dispositionally accessible; they can become luminescent given an appropriate change in one's introspective activity. There are stronger and weaker forms of dispositional accessibility, depending on how easily acquired and well grounded the relevant knowledge or justification is taken to be. One need only think about the bookcase to become aware that there are few books in it; one might or might not be able to discern their height and the colors of their covers; and one might or might not need to reflect to ascertain whether they are placed in order of height. Access to memorial images might be variable in this way, whereas one's access to one's steady auditory impressions of a symphony might be as focal as one's visual image of the conductor's moving hands.

Let us sharpen the problem here. The issue is dispositional accessibility and thus dispositional as opposed to occurrent internalism; i.e., our focus is on an internalism that requires, as a condition of justified belief, only dispositional as opposed to occurrent introspective access to a ground of the justification. For our concern, like that of most epistemologists addressing the topic, is more with resources than with inventory: more with our capacity to become aware of what justifies us than with our actual awareness of what does. On the other hand, we are also interested mainly in conceptual access rather than mere phenomenal access, where the latter is simply access to experience of the relevant properties and the former is access to the experience of those properties conceived in some appropriate way, e.g. as musical sounds.

There are two important dispositional accessibility theses that connect *awareness* of justifiers with knowledge and beliefs about them. The first is the view that normally, on suitable reflection, one can know, with respect to what justifies one's belief, that it is the case (e.g., that one is visually experiencing white) – call this having *epistemic access* to justifiers. The second is the view that, in the same situation, one normally can justifiedly believe that it is the case – call this having *justificational access*. If we take as a guiding internalist idea that (at least some) justification can survive a Cartesian demon *and* – related to this – that one should be able, under appropriate queries, to adduce what justifies one, then justificational access is strong enough to serve as our main focus. Internalism is a view about – though not a complete theory of – justification, not knowledge; but even apart from that, there is no reason why even a moderately strong (first-order) internalism need hold (or deny) that grounds of justification can be *known* through introspection. It is enough that through introspection one can justifiedly believe the relevant ground to be present.

Applying these points to connectionist internalism, our question is this: Can *S* have justificational access to the sorts of causal relations posited, by the causal requirement, between directly justified beliefs and their justifying grounds? Consider perceptual and memorial cases. Can one in general justifiedly believe, on introspective grounds, that one's belief that there is something white here is at least in part sustained by one's impression of a white surface? We need "at least in part" to allow overdetermination: all that the causal requirement demands is that some justificationally *sufficient* basis of justification play a suitable productive or sustaining role; not *every* basis of justification one has need play that role. If I believe *p* for one good reason, this may justify my belief even if I have other good reasons that I fail to "use," in the sense that they play no actual productive or sustaining role. Certainly I am fallible even regarding a sufficient causal basis; I can be wrong about which of my reasons is my main one, and can even take a mere rationalization to be the real basis of my belief. I might also find it specially difficult to acquire justification for believing the relevant causal connection holds, e.g. because someone convinces me that a pill I took is really what sustains my belief. I might then need some reason to deny its pre-empting the causal role of my experience, if my believing there is something white here is to remain justified.

Granted, where *S* has a strong desire to believe *p* and has only what *S* takes to be minimally adequate evidence for *p*, it may be difficult for *S* to tell whether the belief of the evidence proposition is a sufficient causal basis. But even here, careful reflection *tends* to yield a correct result; and we are aided by a natural tendency for our justified beliefs to be in part causally based on what we take to be adequate evidence for them. This is what makes believing against one's assessment of the evidence – as where one believes p despite judging that the evidence favors not-p – prima facie inexplicable in much the way acting against one's better judgment is. Other things equal, if we believe both that q and that q is on balance adequate evidence for p, we tend to believe p, *and* our belief that q tends to play a strong enough causal role in producing or sustaining the belief that p to satisfy the causal requirement on justification.

A related point is that if one forms a justified belief to the effect that one's belief that p is based on an adequate reason, then if, as is natural, this second-order belief becomes part of what sustains the belief that p, that fact alone tends to justify, and may fully justify, the belief that p. Its tendency to justify the belief is especially strong where the content of the second-order belief appropriately refers to sufficient evidence for p, as when one believes that one's belief that p is justified by the independent, firsthand testimony of several credible friends. To be sure, where a second-order belief justifies in this way, it does not yield direct justification; but the point is simply that often indirect justification of this kind is available to support, or, sometimes, replace, threatened direct justification. This is *not* to say that the causal basis of the second-order, causal beliefs must be knowable, or an object of justifiable belief. In fact, it appears that introspective access tends to be less extensive as the order of the belief rises, if only because propositions about relations between grounds and beliefs are more complex, and so prima facie harder to grasp, than either the grounds or the propositional objects of the beliefs. But there is nothing intrinsically external about knowledge or justified belief about causal connections, and it is significant if causal connectionism is correct in the thesis that we can have them at least regarding first-order beliefs.

Similar points seem to hold for the other cases of direct justification. Consider a memorial belief that Ann phoned recently. The case is harder, for the phenomenal justificatory base is less luminous. Still, can one not directly, or at least introspectively, know or justifiedly believe that one's belief is sustained by one's recollective sense that she phoned, particularly if that sense is supported by memorial images? One is aware of recalling the conversation, takes this as the basis of one's believing she phoned, and is not aware of any conflicting basis of one's believing she did. Even if the belief that this recollective sense causally grounds the belief that she phoned is not direct, there is no reason to doubt that it might be justified.

V. INTROSPECTIVE ACCESS TO CAUSAL CONDITIONS OF INDIRECT JUSTIFICATION

Regarding our access to causal conditions of indirectly justified beliefs, there is apparently more difficulty. One problem is that a belief of an evidence proposition, unlike an experience of white, is not strictly introspectable – only certain of its manifestations are. So there may seem to be an inferential gap to be overcome even to achieve justified belief that one has the evidential belief, before one ever gets to the question of its causal sustaining role. For another thing, inferential beliefs often differ from perceptual beliefs in having many disparate causes, such as premise sets from different domains, say memory and testimony. Still another problem is that there is no phenomenally sharp distinction between a memorial and thus direct belief for which one is aware of evidence and, on the other hand, an inferential belief for which one is aware of evidence. This suggests that we may tend to confuse the one kind of basis with the other, and so causes trouble for the view that one can know the sustainer in the relevant range of phenomenally similar cases: a belief S thinks is sustained by a memory impression may really be due to a premise S does not now recall. Finally, sustaining relations imply counterfactuals which it is not plain one may justifiably believe, e.g. that one would not believe p if one did not believe q (and such counterfactuals may be crucial, since it may often be true that evidence beliefs justify a further belief only if they are, at the time, necessary for it).

These problems are far from decisive against causal connectionist internalism. First, what is not itself introspectable may be readily knowable *through* what is introspectable, as one may know one is worried through the imagery and agitation one notes in oneself. Nor need the mediation be inferential: I can know I believe p *through* my experience of assentingly considering the proposition that I do, even if I do not *infer* that I believe p from this second-order proposition that I am assentingly considering the first-order proposition. What is known *by* some mark need not be *inferred from* the premise that it has that mark. Second, all *S* need know is *one* appropriate sustainer of the belief (*S* need not even know that it *is* appropriate, since we are considering only first-order internalism). Third, again overdetermination may allow justification by combined inferential *and* memorial routes; and even where a belief is justified by only one of these routes, *S* need not know which route it is: all that is required is internal access to a causal connection between one ground that is a sufficient basis of justification and the belief it justifies. Fourth, as to the counterfactuals, (a) we surely do, on introspective grounds, justifiedly believe some of the relevant sort, e.g. that if one did not believe the bookstore reliable, one would not believe a certain book is on order. (b) Even if we do not justifiedly believe such counterfactuals, unrestricted closure for justification should not be assumed.[8] *S* might, for instance, be justified in believing *p* without being justified in believing certain things *S* can see to be entailed by it.

Even where *S* is wrong about causal bases of the belief in question, *S* will have access to data that could reveal the error. For there is no limit to the number of relevant considerations reflection can introduce. This suggests that introspective reflection is intrinsically, if imperfectly, *self-corrective*. A fallibilist internalism may thus be rectificationist: holding that while one can be mistaken about the relevant causal bases of one's belief, which are psychological factors, and can even be wrong in attributing certain psychological states to oneself, one can, by reflection, at least approach correction of these errors. Nor is such a view implausible; it is at least hard to imagine an error of this sort that *S* could not in principle discover. Supposing there can be such errors, however, perhaps it is a conceptual truth that *S tends* to be right about such matters, at least if rational. More speculatively still, perhaps persons can, assuming that they have the concept of rationality and reflect adequately on themselves, know or at least justifiedly believe, through introspective reflection, that they are (minimally) rational in the relevant sense. It is at least not clear that any *person* could be so dissociated as to fail here. The Cartesian demon can destroy our personhood, but perhaps not leave it intact and still sever us so thoroughly from our psychological states and motivating reasons. As to the question whether persons who are capable of reflection on such matters can

8. A case against unrestricted closure is made in my paper "The Inferential Transmission of Justification and Knowledge" (in progress) and, briefly, *Belief, Justification, and Knowledge*, ch. 5.

at least justifiedly believe, by reflection, that they *are* persons, it may be that they can. It is at least arguable that the reflection in question warrants regarding oneself *as* a person.

In concluding this exploration of causal connectionist internalism, it is instructive to widen our perspective to include action. Consider first a major parallel between epistemology and the theory of action. Rather as we do not believe *p* for a reason unless we both *have* a ground for it and believe it (causally) *on* that ground, we do not act (intentionally) unless we both *have* a reason for the action and act *for* that reason, in a sense of "for" implying causal production or sustenance.[9] Moreover, as the belief that *p* is not justified unless the reason is (adequately) good, so an intentional action is not rational unless the (or a) reason for which it is performed is (adequately) good. Causalist internalism requires introspective access to a sufficient (causative) ground for a justified belief; the action theory counterpart would require similar access to a sufficient (causative) reason. On this view, the notion of action, by contrast with that of mere behavior, is an internal concept in much the same way the notion of a belief for a reason is; and justified and rational actions are quite like justified beliefs in requiring special connections with supporting grounds.[10] To be sure, we must allow "unconscious" reasons, quite as we must allow unconscious evidential grounds. But surely where such grounds can justify or render rational either beliefs or actions, they are not completely inaccessible to introspection, but only veiled from consciousness in a sense allowing that sufficient self-scrutiny may reveal their presence under some appropriate description.[11] Thus, a causalist internalism is plausible in the theory of action as well as in epistemology.[12]

9. I argue for this – allowing for the possible exception (not relevant here) of actions performed for their own sake – in "Acting for Reasons," *The Philosophical Review*, vol. 95 (1986), and there refer to many others who take action to be similarly causally grounded in one or more reasons.

10. The causalist aspect of this view, particularly for actions, is defended in Chapter 14, this volume. Relevant papers of mine and others are also cited there. Chapter 15 develops further parallels between epistemology and action theory.

11. A sketch of what it is for a belief to be unconscious in this sense, and a case for our having a capacity to become aware of such beliefs by special self-scrutiny, are given in my article, "Self-Deception, Action, and Will," *Erkenntnis*, vol. 18 (1982).

12. An account of internalism in the theory of action is provided in my paper, "An Internalist Conception of Rational Action," a successor to this paper, *Philosophical Perspectives*, vol. 4 (1989).

The prospects for a connectionist version of internalism in action theory are at least as good as for such connectionism in epistemology and raise parallel issues. It may be argued that we never do know, or justifiedly believe, that we act, or at least never know or believe this on grounds accessible to introspective reflection. But this view seems even less plausible than its epistemic counterpart, just criticized: the view that we never know or justifiedly believe that we believe something on the basis of a (sustaining or productive) ground. In any case, even if connectionist internalism is mistaken (as it may be for all that has been said about it here), causalist internalism does not depend on it and is highly plausible. Moreover, if we are to be skeptical about a connectionist internalism in epistemology, we must either be skeptical about internally grounded justification of self-ascriptions of actions or show why one need not to be a skeptic there too. With this in mind, let us turn to the question of how our findings bear on epistemological skepticism.

VI. CAUSALIST INTERNALISM AS A BASIS FOR REBUTTING SKEPTICISM

If causalist internalism may be fallibilistic, and if it requires only dispositional accessibility of justifiers and not access to causal connections between them and the beliefs they justify, then the causal requirement on justified belief need not be externalist. For justification – that is, what justifies a belief, as opposed to the relation between this justifier and the belief it justifies – remains rooted in what is introspectively accessible to S. A stronger internalism may also hold. For at least normally one can introspectively acquire knowledge or justified belief about the causal connections between justifiers and the beliefs they justify. If so, then S can often justifiedly indicate *how* a ground justifies a belief – at least so far as specifying causal production or sustaining relations can show this. S can thereby go some distance toward establishing that the belief is justified. But even if one generally lacks introspective access to these causal connections, there is no reason to doubt that one has introspective, if fallible, access to the grounds of any justified belief one holds and so can give a good answer to the question what justifies that belief. Internalism of the basic and most important kind does not turn on access to causal connections, even if what justifies a belief does so in part by virtue of such connections.

It might be objected that a causalist internalism fails to provide the bulwark against skepticism which is a main advantage of internalism. For suppose that, leaving all else the same, a Cartesian demon severs the crucial causal connections – which are, after all, contingent – with the result that we merely *have* good grounds but do not believe on the *basis* of them, since they play no productive or sustaining role; then the causal requirement is violated, since our evidence beliefs would no longer play a causal role in supporting the beliefs for which they express evidence, yet, by internalist lights, we would surely still be justified by that evidence. We still have introspective access to our evidential grounds, give them when appropriate, and derive justification from them. Hence, even if knowledge requires a causal sustaining relation, justification does not.[13]

Let us look more carefully at the demon case. If we distinguish between justifiedly believing and simply being justified *in* believing – between doxastic and situational justification – then we may say that in the demonic world our justification would be – though significant – of only the latter kind: we would be justified *in* believing that there is something white before us. This is still important; and it may be enough to account for the pivotal intuitions: we *have* the crucial epistemic right, and, given our experiential bases of belief, may believe, in the sense that we have justification for believing, the propositions they warrant. We may even *cite* the grounds of this right in giving our justification; we simply do not *exercise* the right: our beliefs that accord with, but are not based on, our grounds are like an action that just fortuitously accords with, but is not an *execution of*, an intention to perform it. The demon, then, is like a tyrant who can prevent our exercising our freedom of action, but cannot nullify our right to have that freedom.

If there is such a demon, then while the grounds we sincerely give in justifying our beliefs are rationalizations of our beliefs and do not doxastically justify them, they are good rationalizations: such that (other things being equal) if we did believe *for* the reasons they express, we then would justifiedly believe the propositions in question. To be sure, we unintentionally rationalize in citing the

13. Kevin Possin has well expressed the view to which I am responding here in an excellent unpublished study of the connection between skepticism and the epistemic basis relation.

grounds we offer, since we are at least strongly disposed to believe our justificatory grounds to be causal supports as well, whereas in the most common cases of rationalization we tend instead to realize that the reason we offer is not motivating. But surely we do rationalize if a ground we offer for a belief is not among the real reasons *why* we hold the belief. This approach to answering the demon objection may seem to bite the bullet; if it does, the bullet is soft.

There are some who would protest that the imagined kind of rationalization does justify. Granted, it justifies the *proposition* that *p for* us; but this falls short of justifying our *belief* that *p*, quite as providing a good, but *non-motivating* reason for a deed justifies the action-type, doing of the deed, by us, but not, as Kant apparently saw, *our* doing of it. We are, to be sure, *epistemically excusable* for holding a situationally justified belief which has been demonically severed from its normal causal basis in experience. This is important. But to take the point to imply justified believing, as some deontological views may, owing to S's having violated no epistemic duties, is to assimilate justification to excusability.

This line of reply to the demon objection leaves open the view that the chief support of internalism is an intuition that justification can survive the most ingenious Cartesian demonic machinations. But that view is too narrow. Perhaps internalism is also largely inspired by something more positive: its providing *both* a route to a plausible response to skepticism and an account of our ability to answer normal queries that call for a justification of our beliefs. Such a response to skepticism has just been outlined. The account of our ability to give our justification consists above all in showing how our justificatory grounds are accessible to introspection and so do not depend on our having information about the external world, nor on knowledge of the objective reliability of belief-forming processes. This account is *aided* rather than impeded by the causal requirement, on the plausible assumption that we are more *likely* to have access to our grounds for a belief if they bear at least some causal responsibility for it. A causal path is often readily traceable. On the causalist internalism developed here, then, we can explain the importance of demon cases in motivating internalism, without taking those cases as primary. We might indeed take as primary the social practice of justification in which we exhibit our rationality by reference, ultimately, to the internal factors on which justification of belief supervenes.

The imagined response to skepticism might seem to require infallible access; for it may seem that we must know with certainty, or at least be infallible about, what it is that justifies us, say an impression of white, so that we can cite it in answering the question what justifies us. But internalists need not so respond to skepticism. Notice a crucial premise here: you can meet a skeptical query only with an infallible claim. That standard commits one to deductivism: the view that only by deduction can justification or knowledge be inferentially transmitted from premises to conclusions. It is a strong rationalist standard, and one on which skepticism thrives. It is surely mistaken.[14] Skeptics give no clearly cogent reason to deny knowledge of the external world, nor for the view that only beliefs exhibiting certainty constitute knowledge, or for the claim that only deduction transmits justification or knowledge. Thus, the prospect of rebutting, though perhaps not of refuting, skepticism on non-Cartesian, even if modestly rationalistic, assumptions is a major motivation for internalism. If strong, Cartesian internalism is distinguished from the more plausible dispositional internalism developed here, then we can retain a causalist internalism and use it as at least a partial basis for rebutting the most threatening forms of skepticism about justification.

Quite apart from the need to deal with skepticism, there is good reason to think that an internalist view need not construe the causal requirement on justification as the property of externalist theories. This enables internalism to accomplish four important objectives: to distinguish between justifiedly believing and only being justified in believing, to account for the role of justification in contributing to knowledge, to exhibit justified belief as causally rooted in the subject in a way that makes it a manifestation, and not simply an accompaniment, of epistemic virtue, and to explain our social practice of justification as a natural way to express grounds that motivate, and do not merely rationalize, the beliefs they justify.[15]

14. Some reasons to reject this strong standard are set out in *Belief, Justification, and Knowledge,* ch. 9. For related discussion of skepticism, with special attention to its connection to internalism, see Ernest Sosa, "Beyond Skepticism, to the Best of Our Knowledge," *Mind,* vol. 92 (1988).
15. Earlier versions of this paper were given in a symposium at the Illinois Philosophical Society in 1987 and at Indiana and Purdue Universities. I thank my co-symposiasts, John Barker and Paul Moser, for critical responses, and all three audiences for valuable discussion. I have also benefited from additional comments by Michael DePaul, Richard Foley, Kevin Possin, William Tolhurst, and, on more than one draft, Paul Moser.

Chapter 12

The old skepticism,
the new foundationalism,
and naturalized epistemology

There are many kinds of skepticism. Skeptical positions differ in scope, in modality, in order, in target, and in many other ways. The target may be justification or knowledge or both. It may be claimed that there *is* no justification or knowledge, or that there *cannot* be any. A skeptic might, however, grant that there *can* be justification or knowledge but deny that we can *know* or be justified in believing that there is any: even if we have first-order justification or knowledge, second-order justification and knowledge may be beyond our grasp. The issues surrounding skepticism are numerous and complex,[1] and I shall address only skepticism about justification.[2] Much (though not all) of what must be said in answering skepticism about knowledge can be discovered in examining skepticism about justification; but if it should turn out (as I think it might) that skepticism about justification could be answered in a way that does not eliminate skepticism about knowledge, that fact would still be significant. We would presumably establish that it is at least not unreasonable to believe propositions in the vindicated range. In addition to restricting discussion to skepticism about justification, I will leave aside *strong skepticism*, understood as the view that only beliefs of self-evident propositions, or of propositions self-evidently entailed by the former, can be justified (and I will ignore radical forms of skepticism, which are even stronger).

1. The literature is also immense. For a recent survey article see Ernest Sosa's wide-ranging study "Beyond Skepticism, to the Best of Our Knowledge," *Mind* IIIc (1988).
2. A number of philosophers think that justification is the more important concept. For an indication of why this might be so, and indeed of the stronger position that the notion of knowledge is not of great philosophical importance, see Mark Kaplan, "It's Not What You Know That Counts," *Journal of Philosophy* LXXXII (1985).

My interest will be in *moderate skepticism*, in particular a broadly Humean skepticism that allows not only the possibility of justified beliefs of logical truths and of certain propositions self-evidently entailed by them but also of justified beliefs about one's own mental states. It denies, however, that we are justified in believing anything about the external world.[3]

I. AN APPRAISAL OF A CARTESIAN CASE FOR SKEPTICISM ABOUT EXTERNAL WORLD BELIEFS

I have just referred, as many others have, to "answering" skepticism. But this notion can easily obscure a distinction fundamental in appraising skepticism: the distinction (introduced in Chapter 10 and elsewhere) between rebutting skepticism and refuting it. Let us speak of rebutting skepticism when we refer to simply showing that one or more skeptical arguments is not sound or that a skeptical conclusion has not been established, e.g. to showing the invalidity of an argument for the view that there is no justified belief (or, more broadly, to showing the absence of any good reason to believe that skeptical thesis). By contrast, refuting skepticism is showing that a skeptical thesis is *false*, where this implies (assuming the skeptical position is consistent) showing a positive result such as that there is (or at least can be) justification for beliefs about the external world. Rebuttal of a skeptical thesis would entitle us to withhold it, and a rebuttal based on successful criticism of a sufficiently wide range of skeptical arguments might warrant regarding skepticism as, say, probably false; refutation of a skeptical thesis would entitle us to deny it. Rebuttal is less difficult to achieve than the latter; and suspending judgment on a skeptical claim requires less justification than rejecting it. Both must be considered in appraising "answers" to skepticism.

If any one skeptical narrative epitomizes the challenge of skep-

---

3. A Humean skepticism, being empiricist, would deny that there are synthetic entailments, and even a non-Humean skepticism might deny that they are ever self-evident; but it is not obvious that a moderate skepticism, as such, need deny either point. By contrast, any moderate skeptic is likely to allow that simple analytic propositions are justifiably believable, at least on the assumption that we have a priori knowledge of the conceptual equivalences through which analytic propositions can be formally reduced to logical truths through the use of definitions.

ticism, it is probably Descartes's evil demon scenario. Some may feel its power more keenly in its new, naturalized version, the case of the brain in a vat. But the incubus on epistemology is essentially the same. We are still haunted by Descartes' nightmare. Here is one way to see why. Suppose, to take what seems a paradigm of perceptual justification, that

(1) I am justified in believing *p* – that there is a bespeckled black-and-white surface before me.

(2) The proposition that *p*, self-evidently entails that there is no demon causing me to have *just* the kind of sensory experience I am now having *without* there being such a surface before me. But

(3) Necessarily, if I am justified in believing *p*, I am justified in believing any proposition that self-evidently follows from *p*; and

(4) I am not justified in believing that there is no such demon. Hence,

(5) I am not justified in believing that *p*.

A key premise for (4) is that I cannot be justified in believing that there is no such demon when, if there should be one, my *evidence base* would be just what it is now. Nothing in my experience (or otherwise accessible to me) would discriminate between the veridical case in which I see the surface and the demonic case in which I merely hallucinate one.[4]

Skeptical arguments quite similar to this have been widely discussed.[5] Many philosophers have argued that we are of course justified in believing that there is no such demon. Fewer have argued that (3), the crucial epistemic principle – *the transmission principle*, for short – is false. I think both approaches are promising but will first pursue the latter. The transmission principle is open to prima facie counterexamples. In proposing such an example, I use a strategy of rebuttal; attacking (4) requires attempting a refutation of skepticism: showing that we actually have justification

---

4. This phenomenon seems equivalent to what Michael Williams has called the neutrality of experience. For some elaboration of his view developed in criticizing Davidson, see his "Skepticism and Charity," *Ratio* (New Series) 1 (1988).

5. Sosa, op. cit., gives many references. Particularly relevant are Fred Dretske's "Epistemic Operators," *Journal of Philosophy* 67 (1970), and Peter Klein's *Certainty* (Minneapolis: University of Minnesota Press, 1981). Crispin Wright's "Skepticism and Dreaming: Imploding the Demon," *Mind* C (1991) exhibits still another approach. For extensive criticism of that paper see Anthony Brueckner, "Problems with the Wright Route to Skepticism," *Mind* CI (1992).

for a belief we hold. I leave that more complicated strategy for Section III.

Consider this possibility. I prove *p*, a theorem in the propositional calculus, check my results, and thereby come to be justified in believing that *p*. Because I sometimes make mistakes and need *p* for my work, I plan to ask a colleague, who is a logician and whom I justifiably believe to be better at such deductions, to check my work. Suppose that, feeling both my need for *p* and my invigorating success in my deduction, I now think of *p* with a sense of surety about it and infer from *p* that if my colleague says it is false, he is wrong. From the proposition that *p*, it certainly follows that if he says *p* is false, he is wrong. If it *is* a theorem (as we are assuming), then if he denies it, he is wrong (i.e., states a falsehood). This indeed seems self-evident, in the sense (roughly speaking) that (a) understanding it is sufficient for being justified in believing it and (b) believing it on the basis of understanding it is sufficient for knowing it.[6] But even though I am justified in believing that *p*, am I *automatically* justified in believing the *further* proposition that if he says that it is false, he is wrong? Suppose my checking my proof to the extent I did is only enough to give me the *minimum* basis for justification in believing *p*. Surely I would then not have sufficient grounds for the further proposition that if he says *p* is false, he is wrong.[7] If I had done the proof in two quite different ways and triple-checked each procedure, things might be different.

This minimality assumption is essential: I do not claim that there is *no* degree or kind of justification for which the relevant sort of transmission principle will hold, only that it fails for justification in general, particularly as taken to be such that (a) having it "entitles" one to believe (or warrants one in believing) *p* and (b) be-

---

6. This formulation is taken from my "Moral Epistemology and the Supervenience of Ethical Concepts," *Southern Journal of Philosophy* XXIX Supplement (1991), where it is briefly elaborated. Notice that the characterization does not entail something usually associated with self-evident propositions: being very readily understood by normal adults. Some such requirement could be added here without affecting my arguments. Moreover, I am referring to "fully" understanding, as opposed to partially understanding, *p*; but full understanding does not require *perfect* understanding.

7. This example is styled after one I gave in *Belief, Justification, and Knowledge* (Belmont, Cal.: Wadsworth Publishing Co., 1988). The example has been widely discussed and is critically assessed in Catherine M. Canary and Douglas Odegard, "Deductive Justification," *Dialogue* XXVIII (1989). For further discussion, and my reply to them, see my "Justification, Deductive Closure, and Reasons to Believe," *Dialogue* XXX (1991).

lieving a true proposition with that degree of justification implies – apart from such untoward cases as the post-Gettier literature has unearthed – knowing it. That degree of justification, I maintain, is such that I can possess it on the basis of a careful deduction of *p* and yet not be justified in believing all of *p*'s self-evidently entailed consequences. This degree can be quite high; my case requires only that, whatever the appropriate standard, it be just minimally met. If I had begun with indefeasible justification, then perhaps I would be justified in believing any self-evidently entailed consequence – at least if I could see that it was entailed.[8]

A crucial point here – and one that may go some distance toward explaining why we should not expect unrestricted closure principles for justification – is that the preservation of truth need not be precisely paralleled by the preservation of justification. Truth is an ontic notion, justification an epistemic notion; and we may not simply assume that logical principles, which formulate conditions for carrying truth into truth (i.e., for validity), are mirrored by epistemic principles. It is possible that Descartes foresaw that epistemic transmission is not precisely parallel to validity. Wanting to build a "firm and permanent structure in the sciences," he insisted on an epistemic strength in the foundations so great that it could not be attenuated by deduction and would reach as far as valid inference might take us.

There is a great deal to be said about the epistemic principle in question: viz., that justification is automatically transmitted across self-evident entailments. There is no hope of doing justice to the topic here.[9] It should help, however, to set forth weaker transmission principles that may hold and may partly explain the appeal

8. I disallow maximal, in the sense of indefeasible, justification, because the failure of transmission illustrated poses some threat to the initial justification even on the assumption that transmission does not always occur. For as suggested below, since reasonhood apparently does transmit over the relevant entailments, if *S* can (as in my example) deduce consequences he has reason to believe false, it would seem possible that, given such reasons to believe *p* false, *S* might go on to deduce enough disconfirming consequences to yield collective reason sufficient to defeat the original justification for *p* – in which case it is not indefeasible. An even stronger qualification would be to require that the initial justification must not be *absolute*, where absolute justification for *p* implies the impossibility *both* of defeat and of there being a reason for believing not-*p*; but I see no reason to go this far.

9. In a paper in progress I discuss a wide range of the relevant issues; here I can stress only the holistic character of justification as a general explanation of the failure – indicated by the theorem example – of what might be called simple linear transmission.

of the strong one that so powerfully aids skepticism. Nothing I have said is inconsistent with the principle that

> I. If there is reason (in the form of one or more reasons) to believe *p*, then there is reason to believe any proposition self-evidently entailed by *p* (hence to believe false any proposition self-evidently entailing not-*p*) – call this *the closure of reasons principle*.

A relativized parallel would be this:

> II. If there is reason for *S* to believe *p*, and *p* self-evidently entails *q*, then there is reason for *S* to believe *q*.

It is of course *S*'s *having* reason to believe *p* that is closest to *S*'s being justified in believing it. A parallel principle for the former notion is this:

> III. If *S* *has* reason to believe *p*, *p* entails *q*, and *S* can understand both *q* and the entailment of *q* by *p*, then *S* has reason to believe *q* – call this the *principle of closure for having reasons.*[10]

By way of clarification, I want to make four points. First, it is possible to have a reason for believing *p* while at the same time having a reason, even a better reason, for believing not-*p*. Second, the principle of closure for having reasons implies that such reasons are *indefinitely extendable:* they reach as far as entailments one can understand. If, for instance, one has a reason for *q* in virtue of one's having a reason for *p* and understanding its entailment of *q*, and the same holds for *q* in relation to *r*, then one has a reason for *r*; and so on. We can thus distinguish between having an *immediate* reason for believing something, which occurs where one has a reason for it not transmitted from a prior reason, and having a *mediated* reason for believing, which is a reason one has for it that

---

10. The reference to understanding here avoids the implication that one can have a reason to believe a proposition one cannot understand or have a reason one does possess transmit over an entailment one cannot understand. One might reply that in either case one has a reason but simply cannot see it as one. Indeed, one could argue that *S* might fail to understand even a self-evident entailment and hence propose that principle II. should, like III., require understanding of the entailment. I leave this open. These points may simply show that (as shown in Chapter 9) there are different notions, or at least different degrees of implicitness, of "having" a reason. There are many problems in formulating transmission principles, and I believe that for different plausible principles we get different notions of what it is to have a reason.

does arise by transmission from a prior reason. However – and this is the third point – as the first two points imply, the strength of the reason that is transmitted across the entailment may diminish progressively and approach zero. Finally, although self-evident entailment will often be the connective tissue in transmission of reasonhood, indefinite extendability is neither equivalent to, nor necessarily due to, transitivity of self-evident entailment. It is in fact not clear whether that relation *is* transitive.[11]

Distinguishing the principle of closure for having reasons from the transmission principle is of the first importance for the transmission issue. The principles are quite different; but they are easily conflated, partly because having a reason for *p* implies having *some* degree of justification for it. I have not denied any of these closure principles for reasons; indeed, I think they are plausible. I suspect it is the plausibility of weaker principles like these that makes the stronger transmission principle look so plausible when it is not distinguished from the others.

To see the difference between the transmission principle and the principle of closure for having reasons, recall that one can have *some* degree of justification for believing *p* yet not be justified, on balance, in believing it. Similarly – and, on some views, equivalently – one can have *a reason* (or some reason) to believe *p*, without being justified, overall, in believing it: without, we might say, having *adequate* reason to believe it. To reduce the vagueness of this formulation, we can regard the crucial level of justification relevant in discussions of skepticism – which we might simply call *adequate justification* – as the degree such that, when there is no Gettier-type problem, then *p*, if true, is known.[12] Alternatively, but

11. It is arguable that if *p* self-evidently entails *q* and *q* self-evidently entails *r*, then a bit of reflection is all that is needed to see that the first entails the third, and hence the relation is transitive. But first, it is not clear that this follows. A person considering just *p* and *r* might need *imagination* to see the intermediate step. Second, even if mere reflection on the relevant propositions would yield a grasp of the intermediary, *much* reflection might be needed. At most, then, we could conclude that what might be called *mediate self-evidence* is transitive. For some discussion of that notion of self-evidence and its importance in metaethics, see my "Moral Epistemology and the Supervenience of Ethical Concepts," *Southern Journal of Philosophy* XXIX Supplement (1991).

12. At least one further qualification may be needed. Consider the lottery case in which *S* justifiedly believes that *S*'s ticket, being one of a million in a fair lottery, will lose. Arguably, there is neither a Gettier problem here nor a degree of justification that is achievable by simply increasing the number of tickets and sufficient to render *S*'s belief knowledge if it is true.

I think not equivalently,[13] we can speak of that degree of justification sufficient to entitle an epistemically rational agent to believe *p*.[14] People may differ concerning what degree (or kind) this is. My point is that it is scarcely controversial that this status is not achieved by merely having *some* degree of justification for believing *p*, or merely *some* reason to believe it, any more than a task with many parts is completed by finishing just one of them.

The overall view I presuppose here is that the degree of one's justification for *p*, like one's justification simpliciter for believing *p*, is determined by one's overall relevant epistemic situation at the time. Many factors are pertinent, and they include not only the number and strength of supporting grounds but also the number and strength of defeaters, both counterevidence and reasons to doubt the efficacy of one's justifiers. To suppose that my epistemic situation relative to *q* must be the same, or at least as good, as my epistemic situation relative to *p*, simply because *p* self-evidently entails *q* and I am justified in believing *p*, is a manifestation of a simple *linear* concept of justification. The picture has justification traversing a line from a belief that has that justification to one that as yet does not. This omits – for one thing – the relevance of *adding* *q* to my system of beliefs (or other cognitions). That addition provides a new epistemic context, and the offspring may quite surprise the parents.

How do these reflections bear on answering skepticism? Perhaps we have rebutted the evil demon argument (or one such argument), which apparently depends on some similarly defective transmission principle; but if the weaker transmission principle, for having reasons, should hold, do we not face another Cartesian nightmare? For is there any better ground for holding that I have *some* reason to believe no demon is deceiving me than for holding that I am (overall) justified in believing this? I think there is; at least, there is *if* I have *some* reason to believe that there is a bespeckled surface before me, which seems quite evident, and if I may also presuppose something like the principle of closure for having reasons. But certainly we may say this much: we are at least better off if the

13. Not equivalently because, in lottery cases, it is not the degree, but the kind, of one's justification that prevents one's belief that one will lose from constituting knowledge – at least this is plausible. I have defended it in ch. 7 of *Belief, Justification, and Knowledge*.
14. I have in mind belief simpliciter, as opposed to belief at a given level of confidence. Confidence levels are relevant and can be taken into account, but doing so here would take us too far afield.

task is to produce only some reason to believe *p* rather than overall justification for believing it. The incubus is not as heavy, however much we may still dislike the burden. But how might we escape that burden, and can foundationalist theories be of any special help?

II. FOUNDATIONALISM AS A BASIS FOR ANSWERING SKEPTICISM

Since foundationalism is so strongly associated both with Descartes and with a linear conception of justification, it is useful to ask whether, in order to deal adequately with skepticism, we must reject both foundationalism and the strong transmission principles often attributed to it. Granting that the attack just mounted against automatic transmission of justification is neutral between foundationalism and coherentism, is there any plausible foundationalism that can both ground the attack and provide a basis for rebutting, or perhaps even refuting, skepticism about beliefs concerning the external world?

Let me sketch the kind of foundationalism that seems the best candidate for such a role. I start with a very general formulation, neutral with respect to the various competing versions. Call *foundationalism simpliciter* (as applied to justification) the conditional thesis that if a person, *S*, has any justified beliefs, then *S* has at least some directly (non-inferentially) justified beliefs on which any other justified beliefs *S* has depend (in some appropriate way) for (some appropriate degree of) their justification.[15] To get a particular version of foundationalism one must specify a number of variables, particularly the sorts of beliefs appropriate for the foundations, the kind of thing that might justify them, the degree of their justification, and the transmission principles by which superstructure beliefs may be justified on the basis of foundational ones. This perspective enables us to see a number of important differences among foundationalist views.

Cartesian foundationalism is widely taken to imply (as for pres-

---

15. This is a rough formulation drawn from my previous work; we could use a similar formulation for knowledge and for simply *having* justification for believing, and there are various ways to explicate direct justification and the relevant kind of dependency. For relevant discussion and a number of references to helpful literature, see Chapters 4 and 15.

ent purposes I shall assume it does) the following three principles: that (i) only beliefs (or other cognitions) that, owing to, say, their basis in the clarity and distinctness of their propositional contents, achieve epistemic certainly are admissible for the foundational level – call this *axiomatism* about foundations; (ii) only deductive inferences can transmit justification to superstructure elements – call this *deductivism about transmission;* and (iii) if one has these strong foundations, one can (or even does) know that one has the relevant kind of certainty (whatever that is) – call this *second-order foundationalism.* This triad yields a very strong view; but, however famous, it is clearly not the only kind of foundationalism.

By contrast, the kind of foundationalism that seems most plausible to me is fallibilist about the status of foundational beliefs, contextualist about their contents, inductivist about the transmission of justification and knowledge, first order, and (to a significant degree) holistic about justification in general. Since plausible candidates for sources of direct justification, such as sensory experience, need not absolutely guarantee truth, foundational beliefs need not be infallible. Since their justification can be defeated by, e.g., disconfirmatory experiences, they are only defeasibly justified. Since defeasible non-inferential justification is countenanced as sufficient for foundational beliefs, beliefs about one's own mental states or of self-evident propositions are not the only candidates for foundational beliefs; nor are there other a priori restrictions on the content of foundational beliefs. Indeed, because beliefs can be *memorially justified,* and (I contend) in that way non-inferentially justified, then there can be – so far as content is concerned – as many sorts of non-inferentially justified beliefs as there are kinds of propositions that can be non-inferentially believed and retained in memory. This is indefinitely many.[16] For all foundationalism requires, my belief (formed as I speak to others) that there are people in the room can be non-inferentially justified. Since inductive transmission is possible, I may justifiedly believe propositions on the basis of believing that (for instance) they best explain (and,

16. I leave open whether there are any believable propositions that can*not* be non-inferentially believed. It would seem that there may be, e.g., propositions one finds implausible but believes because the evidence is so strong. Here, one might be unable to believe the original proposition if one ceased to have the evidence propositions as a basis for one's belief. There might also be some propositions that are non-inferentially believable yet too complex to be retained in memory in a way appropriate for preservation of their justification, but I think this is at best a contingent truth.

absolutely speaking, well explain) what I believe with direct justification. Since foundationalism countenances direct justification, I can be justified in believing *p* without having one or more further beliefs expressing premises that provide me with an inferential justification for believing it; hence, second-order justification (at least of the most common, inferential kind) is not required for first-order justification, and – a point crucial in rebutting skepticism – I can *have* justification for believing *p* even if I cannot bring forward premises or grounds to show that I have it.

There is, moreover, no bar to coherence contributing to justification or to incoherence leading to revision of my belief system, including even its foundations. If there are linear justifications running from foundations to superstructure, there can be an interacting set of them – as well as defeating chains running from justified superstructure beliefs to the *negations* of propositions believed non-inferentially. This suggests how linearity in the transmission of justification is compatible with a significant degree of holism about its ultimate constitution: the foundations may be altered from above, not just the superstructure from below; large and complex groups of beliefs may be confirmed, or disconfirmed, together; and, in the interest of maximizing justification of our whole body of beliefs, we may choose among many alternative resolutions of tensions arising from new experiences or new inferences. Although we do not have an extreme holism on which every belief I have is evidentially (or even causally) relevant to every other, no belief is precluded, a priori, from being relevant to any other in either of these ways; and, both epistemically and causally, large groups of beliefs may be relevant to one or more other beliefs.

There are several ways in which this holistic, fallibilist foundationalism may help in dealing with skepticism about justification. First, it casts the issue in terms of defeasible justification at the outset. Hence, skeptical arguments showing the defeasibility of a justification will not suffice to undermine it.[17] Second, because it countenances non-inferential justification – and indeed leads us to expect that many people will have no premises available in their belief system from which they can argue for their foundational beliefs – the view makes it perfectly acceptable that there be justified

---

17. Often defeasibility is taken to be entailed by the belief's fallibility; the inference here is not obviously valid, but I am willing to grant for the sake of argument that the skeptic can show, for many of our justified beliefs, that their justification *is* defeasible.

beliefs which the believer cannot show, at least by argument, to
be justified. Thus, unlike what seem the most plausible coherence
theories, which are both internalist and conceive justification as
arising above all from inferential relations among beliefs (or at least
their contents), this foundationalism does not invite us to think
that if we cannot (on reflection) show that we are justified by
indicating how the belief under scrutiny coheres with others, then
we are not justified.[18] Perhaps, of course, we can show this from
the perspective of coherence theory, but it is an advantage in dealing with skepticism not to be committed to the view that the mere
possession of justified belief implies being able to show its justification. In any case, if coherentism implies the possibility of showing any given justified belief to cohere with certain other beliefs,
I suspect it will be through making essential use of certain parts
of a strategy to which I now turn, one more naturally drawn from
a foundationalist perspective.[19]

III. AN APPROACH TO THE REFUTATION
OF SKEPTICISM

I have stressed that, at least if a foundationalist approach to justification is sound, an inability to show that one is justified in
believing something by no means entails that one is not justified
therein. Inability to produce a justification of a belief does not entail
that I lack one. Indeed, the objects in the two cases are different.

18. This does not imply that *no* coherentism can avoid inviting us to conceive the
    matter so; but if coherence is a matter of relations between beliefs and is ac-
    cessible to reflection, then, if it can be exhibited in inferential relations, e.g.
    between beliefs of premises for *p* and the belief that *p* – and perhaps even if
    it cannot be so exhibited – it would seem that S could show the justification
    of any justified belief S has by locating it in an appropriate way in the coher-
    ent system that justified it in the first place. The burden seems to me to be
    on coherentists to develop a theory that does not have this consequence. For
    a theory as qualified as that of Laurence BonJour's in *The Structure of Empirical
    Knowledge* (Cambridge, Mass., 1985), it is difficult to be sure to what extent S
    should be able to produce justificatory argumentation, but this is at least sug-
    gested by the appeal to metajustificatory arguments. See esp. chs. 5 through
    7. Cp. Keith Lehrer's *Theory of Knowledge* (Boulder and San Francisco, 1990),
    esp. chs. 5 through 6.
19. This strategy is suggested in Chapter 10. No effort is made there to show
    that the strategy cannot be adapted to a coherentist view, but I believe there
    are independent reasons to resist such a view and have given an overview of
    some of them in Chapter 4, this volume.

The justificatory process I would engage in would produce second-order justification, justification for the proposition that I am justified in believing p (or at least that p is justified); the justification skeptically doubted in the first place is simply *for believing the first-order proposition that p* (or, perhaps, for p). This is easy to forget in the dialectic with skepticism. For the skeptic challenges our common-sense belief that we have a great deal of justification; and we want not just to rebut the arguments to this effect but also to refute their conclusions: not just to show that the skeptic's case is unsound but also to show that various kinds of beliefs we have are justified. But even epistemologists who realize that one can be justified in believing p without one's being able to show that one is are not satisfied with this point; there would be a historical imperative to refute skepticism even if epistemology could be plausibly held to be purely theoretical and not to depend on existential propositions to the effect that anyone actually has justification. Can this imperative be satisfied for anything so substantive as fallible beliefs of contingent propositions?[20]

Much depends, of course, on what counts as showing something (a topic that deserves a full-scale study in itself). Skeptics will naturally hold that only *entailing* grounds for p will show it; and although I deny this – as begging the question against the cogency of inductive reasoning – I shall try to use only deductively valid arguments in assessing the case for showing that there is justification. We must distinguish at least two ways of showing that we have justified belief: (1) *dialectical showing*, the second-order process of showing, by subsumptive appeal to an epistemic principle, that we have a justified belief, as where one subsumes a kind of belief under a generalization to the effect that all beliefs of that kind are justified; and (2) *simple showing*, the first-order process of simply *giving* a justification for a belief, in the sense of laying out that justification by adducing an adequate justifying ground for p in a way that indicates that p is justified, but without making any second-order claim. To illustrate simple showing, suppose I am asked to show that I am justified in believing that there is a bespeckled white surface before me. I might say that I see it or, pushed a bit by reminders of possible hallucinations, that I have a clear visual impression of such a surface. If this impression *does* in fact

20. I refer just to fallible beliefs of contingent propositions, as opposed to infallible ones such as that I exist, because the latter are not really challenging cases for the skeptic.

justify me, then I have given a justification: I have laid it out in a way that in some sense shows that I am justified, as, by exhibiting my pen, I might show that I have one.

This demonstration might be claimed to be merely a case of *exhibitive showing*: showing *what* justifies, not of (propositionally) showing in any sense *that* one is justified. I prefer to say that it is showing *that* one is justified *by* showing *what* justifies one; but if one accomplished only the latter, it still provides the *basis* for showing, in some way, that one is justified, e.g. by reflecting on how the exhibited ground is related to *p,* and thereby discovering a crucial epistemic premise usable in dialectically showing that one is justified. I grant, however, that in the example imagined I certainly have not used a second-order concept or appealed to an epistemic principle. Even the moderate skeptic wants nothing less than this; and – rightly or wrongly – skeptics will not concede that one has in any sense shown a justification unless one has done so dialectically.

If we set out to do that, we might ask what sorts of epistemic principles we may use to back up the claim that a belief we hold is justified and how we might be justified in believing *them*. The principle suggested by my example is something like this, understood as applying to all the senses:

> IV. If S has a clear sensory impression of *x*'s being *F* (or that *x* is *F*) and on the basis of that impression believes that *x* is *F*, then this belief is (prima facie) justified – call this *the perceptual principle.*[21]

To see how this principle can be used against skepticism we need a further distinction: between *personal showing*, the kind done by people, and impersonal, *argumental showing,* the kind done by what we call cogent arguments; impersonal showing, in turn, can be either simple or dialectical. Personal showing is a process; imper-

---

21. Here 'has the impression that *x* is *F*' does not entail believing that *x* is *F* but only being disposed to believe that it is (it is also not entailed by believing that *x* is *F*, since that is quite possible without having any sensory impression); and in 'an impression of *x*'s being *F*' the position of '*x*' is not referential: there need be no such entity, even at the level of sense-data. There are problems about how the content of the impression must be related to the belief, but these need not be settled for our purposes here. Note also that the principle can account for the justification of a belief grounded in a mere hallucination, though such a belief is not perceptual in the strict sense presupposing the occurrence of a normal perception.

sonal showing is a kind of epistemic status of an argument. An argument impersonally shows that *p* when its premise set provides an adequate ground for *p*, where adequacy may be either relativized to evidence accessible in the context, for instance to mathematical or scientific or sensory information, or taken more broadly, as implying only that the appropriate grounds *exist*. (Adequacy needs further analysis, to be sure – e.g., there are different cases depending on whether or not the ground can be *seen* by some relevant person or procedure to be one.) A person, S, shows that *p* when S provides an adequate ground for *p;* and if S is justified in accepting that ground and in using it to try to show that *p*, we may say that S personally (in a sense, subjectively) shows *p*, since the result is to produce justification for S's believing it.[22] It is personal showing that is of greatest interest here: we want to know whether we can show certain important skeptical claims to be false, not just whether there are (or can be) arguments that show this.

If I am to show that my belief that there is a bespeckled white surface here is justified, how can I be warranted in believing an epistemic principle like the one in question? Let us first consider the possibility that one can know a priori that such sensory impressions yield prima facie justification for perceptual beliefs of the kind at issue. One argument for this would be that such principles are partly constitutive of the concept of justification; hence they are justifiably believable on the basis of conceptual reflection, e.g. reflection about what one has to count as a justifier in order to qualify as having the concept of justification. Granted, such reflection would presumably have to range over cases of belief in which justification can be concretely (and intuitively) seen; for instance, we might try to imagine how someone could (i) understand the concept of justification yet (ii) sincerely claim, of my belief that there is a bespeckled white surface before me, that even though it is based on my clear visual impression of such a surface, it is not prima facie justified. It is at best difficult to imagine how (i) and (ii) can jointly hold. This confirms the status of the perceptual principle as partly constitutive of the concept of justification. These concrete cases we use to illustrate such an epistemic principle might

---

22. Not necessarily a justified belief, however, since S could still believe that *p* for some other, inadequate reason, as opposed to the good reason adduced. Note also that we would allow that S can show that *p* without being justified on either count, though I think that on reflection we *might* then prefer to say only that S's argument showed that *p*.

be hypothetical products of a priori reflection itself; they need not be an inductive evidence base for the principle, as opposed to concrete applications of it. Roughly, it is largely because we grasp the principle that we can construct the cases in question; we do not acquire the principle – as opposed to a formulation of it – by first constructing the cases. If the cases do constitute a kind of inductive base, they need not function in the way observations do in enumerative arguments for contingent generalizations.[23]

To be sure, it could be argued that such principles are not only a priori, but analytic, roughly in the sense that we can arrive at them directly by analysis of an appropriate concept. Suppose that justified belief can be analyzed as, simply, belief that accords with at least one of a certain set of epistemic principles, where the set includes the perceptual principle. Then the principle will be true "by definition." This interesting possibility deserves more discussion than I can give it here. I have no need to reject it, but I will make just one point to suggest why I resist it. Even if we could find a set of epistemic principles comprehensive enough – and sufficiently free from even preanalytic disagreements – to constitute a plausible analysis, there would remain the question of the status of our warrant for accepting *it*. I do not think, e.g., that its truth could be known on the basis of empirical linguistic knowledge about 'justification.'[24] There might indeed be as good reason to think such an analysis synthetically true as to think this of its constituent epistemic principles.

It is a further question whether there can be *non-inferential* justification for such epistemic principles. It is not self-evident that inductive grounding is the only kind of inferential justifiedness they might have; hence, ruling that out leaves other kinds of inferential justification open. But notice that, for the foundationalism introduced here, the non-inferential justification of epistemic principles is consistent with the possibility that they are

23. Granted, one could take a more particularist approach on which the primary a priori intuitions concern particular instances of the concept of justification. One can also combine particularist and generalist strands and appeal to a strategy of integrating intuitions of general principles with those of relevant particular cases, with an eye to reflective equilibrium. In that case one would presumably argue directly against the skeptical attack on the perceptual beliefs in question. Note, however, that one might still argue a priori for epistemic principles, *provided* one could find a suitable premise, such as that the cases one is considering are representative, which would enable one to deduce such principles from what one intuits about these cases.
24. For some reasons to hold this, see *Belief, Justification, and Knowledge*, ch. 4.

(1) inferentially justifi*able*, (2) justifiedly believed only after considerable reflection, and (3) defeasibly justified even then. They may be inferentially justifiable because foundational status does not imply *ultimacy* in the epistemic order, in the Aristotelian sense that there is nothing "prior" to p.[25] They may be justifiably believable only after reflection because the required kind of self-evidence is a matter of the kind of non-inferential knowledge obtainable by understanding, not a matter of the ease or speed with which the understanding comes; and given the fallibilism of the approach in question, justified beliefs of these principles may be defeasible. Thus, one can have non-inferential justification for the relevant epistemic principles even if they are not self-evident in the way axioms are. They may in fact seem self-evident only after long reflection on appropriate examples; that helps to explain how they can be defeasibly justified, but it does not imply that their justification is inferential.

Now I think that I am justified in believing our perceptual principle, and I will assume that my justification is non-inferential (though that assumption is not essential to the argument so long as I could have an inferential justification of sufficient strength, as seems possible). Suppose that (a) I justifiedly believe both the principle *and* that I now have a clear impression of a bespeckled white surface before me and, (b) on that basis, believe there is such a surface before me. From these two propositions it self-evidently follows that I have a justified belief that there is a bespeckled white surface before me. May I not, then, justifiedly believe that I have a (prima facie) justified belief about the external world? And in so arguing, have I not shown, dialectically, that the relevant kind of skepticism is false? On one plausible interpretation of what it is to show something, if one is justified in believing one's (true) premises, and validly (and non-circularly) argues from them to a conclusion, one has shown it.

I have put my conclusion rhetorically for good reason: I am trying to *exhibit* my dialectical showing and not to *claim* it. Suppose I claim categorically that I have shown that I have a justified belief; the proposition at issue now, if the skeptic challenges me, is the *third-order* one just asserted: that I have shown (hence justified) the second-order proposition that I have a justified belief that p (the

---

25. See *Posterior Analytics* 72b. Descartes may well have been influenced by this strongly axiomatic picture.

first-order proposition). I have presumably not shown this third-order proposition; but surely I do not need to in order simply to *have* shown the second-order proposition that I have a justified belief. This point is crucial to understanding the dialectic with skepticism: because we imagine a dialogue, we are always anticipating the skeptic's questioning whether our responses to a given challenge succeed; and because skeptics have an iterative habit of mind, they tend to query the credentials of everything one asserts. But a reply that shows justification at one level – and in one context, we might say – need not show it at the next, which would indeed require epistemic argument at that higher level (and so in a different context). Giving a justification may answer a request for one but need not show that the request *has* been answered; showing that one has justification establishes that one does, but it need not show that one *has* established this, even if one can do so; and so forth. We must not allow the skeptic's hunger for ever higher levels of justification to undermine an argument for justification at any level. On my approach we can in principle always move to a higher level; e.g., using the (a priori) principle that if one subsumes a belief (justifiedly) under an appropriate epistemic principle which says that beliefs of this sort are justified, one can, for any justified belief, find an epistemic principle by appeal to which one shows that the belief is justified. Still, our achievements at any one level do not depend on our having already done so, or even on our being able to do so.

A skeptic who accepted all I have said so far might still claim that unless my premises are self-evident, I must be able to say something on their behalf. Are they? It is arguable that the epistemic principle is self-evident in some sense; and although the instantial premise, that I have a clear impression of a bespeckled white surface, is not, moderate skeptics have tended to allow that we are justified in such occurrent mental state beliefs. Perhaps, however, one may not assume, without inductive evidence, that an impression is *clear*. I think there is a sense of 'clear,' strong enough to sustain our epistemic principle, for which one may believe this without inductive evidence; but this point is admittedly not self-evident. Perhaps, however, the wider epistemic principle we get by deleting the requirement of a clear impression is also true – but simply generates less justification. Perhaps when a sensory impression of x's being F is not clear, it simply generates less justification for believing x is F than it would yield if it were clear. Granted, a sufficiently *unclear* impression of x's being F may fail to produce justified belief to that effect; but this may be because *un*clarity is a defeating feature and not because the presence of an impression of x's being F is in itself not sufficient for some degree of justification. In any case, I think we may conclude that principles like the perceptual one may provide some basis for our justifiably believing that we have justified beliefs about the world, and that such principles are, for at least one plausible notion of showing, a basis for rejecting skepticism concerning these beliefs.

At least one serious problem remains, however, on the plausible assumption that a belief not *based*, in a partly causal sense, *on* its justifying ground is not justified *by* that ground.[26] Am I justified in believing that my belief that there is a bespeckled white surface before me is *based* on my impression to that effect? This is, after all, a partly causal proposition, and, arguably, I need inductive grounds for the relevant justification. Again, we confront a Cartesian nightmare: the demon might sever the causal connection between my belief and its ground, leaving my experience just as it is.[27] What justification do I have, then, for believing that the connection holds? Note that this demonic possibility does not threaten the view that we can rebut the skeptic. Skeptical arguments can still be shown to be unsound. But the possibility does threaten the view that we can dialectically show that skepticism is false in ways we might like. Granting that if I have an adequate experiential ground for p, I *can* justifiedly believe p; still, if the demon can sever the crucial connection, the problem is to show that I *do* justifiedly believe it.

Here are two points in reply. First, while I am fallible about whether a perceptual belief of mine is based on a matching impression I have, there is no reason to think that I am generally unjustified in my self-ascriptions of this basis relation; and we surely need not accept any skeptical argument from mere fallibility about

---

26. Though controversial, this assumption is widely accepted. I have defended it in Chapters 7 and 14.
27. This, I take it, is the sort of worry that troubles Crispin Wright, op. cit., and it may be a reason why Chisholm and other internalists never impose any causal requirement on justified belief. He does not approach it in the same way, however. I have tried to allay the worry in Chapter 11 and here only very briefly sketch how I conceive the issue.

p to lack of justification for believing it.[28] Indeed, most skeptics are willing to allow that we are justified in believing that we *have* beliefs; raising the question of whether we have any justification for our beliefs in fact *presupposes* that we do. Granted, radical skeptics can conditionalize, formulating all their arguments on the supposition that we have beliefs. This strategy may, in the end, deprive them of some of the materials that make their view seem threatening (e.g. by calling attention to the disparity between what they pre-suppose themselves – that they are making a case – and what they allow others to presuppose), but let that pass. My second point is unaffected: even if my belief is not based on the ground I have for it, in having that ground I still *have* a justification for *p*. If I can show that I have it, and the skeptic cannot provide good reason to doubt that I believe *on* that ground, my dialectical position is at least tolerable. Although it would be better to be able to show not only that I have justification *for* my beliefs, but also justified beliefs – that I am not only justified *in* believing, but also *justifiedly believe* – it is still important to be able to show that I have justification *for* them. One might say that at least I don't believe more than I am entitled to, even though I can't show that I don't believe on a basis other than my entitlement.

IV. SKEPTICISM AND NATURALIZED EPISTEMOLOGY

The position taken so far is internalist. This is not because foun-dationalism cannot be externalist. Not only can a foundationalist be, e.g., a reliabilist; contrary to how it has seemed to many,[29] it is not clear how a reliabilist can avoid being a foundationalist of *some* kind. For one thing, reliabilism countenances non-inferential justification, as in the case of perceptually grounded beliefs; it also apparently requires that inferential justification depend essentially on non-inferential justification[30]; and certainly neither production

28. This may of course be questioned; for some points by way of justification for it see ch. 9 of *Belief, Justification, and Knowledge*.
29. E.g., apparently to Mark Kaplan in "Epistemology on Holiday," *Journal of Philosophy* LXXXVIII (1991). I agree with much that he says, however, particu-larly with the point that epistemologists must provide criteria that we may actually use in self-appraisal and not just theoretical definition.
30. This is suggested in, e.g., Alvin I. Goldman's "What Is Justified Belief?", in George Pappas, ed., *Justification and Knowledge* (Dordrecht: D. Reidel, 1986). I

nor sustenance by truth-conducive processes is a coherence concept. Nor are the reliabilist's sources of justification even plausibly
thought to *depend* on or imply coherence (as opposed to defeasibility
by *in*coherence, which is a quite different thing). Granted, these
sources might in fact tend to produce coherent sets of beliefs; but
this seems to hold for the basic sources of belief as foundationalism
has usually understood them. Perception and introspection, for
instance, tend to produce, not one isolated belief at a time, but
sets of related, coherent beliefs. The main reason I present an
internalist foundationalism here is that it seems to provide the best
chance for refuting certain forms of skepticism. Let me develop
this suggestion with respect to a form of reliabilism, which seems
the most plausible kind of externalism.

Suppose that we do not conceive epistemic principles as an internalist is likely (though not required) to do, i.e., as justifiable a
priori, but rather as, say, knowable only by virtue of knowing the
actual reliability of belief generators. Could we then justifiedly
believe that we have justified (empirical) beliefs? We could, because
such second-order beliefs could be reliably produced. Could we
show that we have justified empirical beliefs?

In one sense we could, provided we could justifiably and truly
believe both the epistemic principle that reliably produced beliefs
are justified, *and* that some belief of ours is so produced. Suppose
we may justifiably and truly believe this. Such a reliabilism still
seems dialectically at a disadvantage as compared with the internalism I have been developing. For on reliabilist assumptions,
indeed, on any plausible assumptions, one could not reasonably
claim to be non-inferentially justified in believing such principles.
One would presumably have to believe – and would be justified
in believing – that a *non*-inferential belief of such a principle is
*un*justified. After all, one needs a wide evidence base to know
that a belief source, such as perceptual experience, is reliable.
Thus, to be justified in appealing to such a principle in any attempt
to show, against the skeptic, that I have a justified belief, I would
need to argue for my epistemic principle.[31] Now I apparently

am speaking here of justified beliefs, but the distinction between inferential
and non-inferential justification can also be applied to justification for
believing.

31. It might be argued that the need here is only dialectical, not conceptual: for
at least some reliabilists (as for some internalists) perhaps one could justifiedly believe that *p* even if one had a justified belief that one is not justified
in believing *p*. But if justification implies an objective likelihood of truth, pre-

could not argue for the crucial reliabilist epistemic principles –
e.g. that perceptual beliefs tend to be justified – without presupposing the truth (or at least probable truth) of such beliefs,
whereas the suggested internalist view construes certain epistemic
principles as knowable a priori and non-inferentially.[32] Let me
develop this point.

A reliabilist apparently must count on just such perceptual
beliefs to determine that this very kind of belief tends to be true
(and hence tends to be justified).[33] I would, for instance, need
to check on the truth value of beliefs about the colors of surfaces,
using other perceptual beliefs – and quite likely other color beliefs
– in order to determine that the original color beliefs tend to be
true. I could justifiably believe that my belief that there is a
bespeckled surface before me is justified, only if I could justifiably
believe this belief is reliably produced, and I could justifiably
believe that, in turn, only if I had inductive evidence that beliefs
produced as it apparently is – by visual impressions – are generally
true. This, however, would require depending on still other beliefs
produced by visual impressions and on further beliefs whose
status is similarly dependent on taking as true the beliefs produced by sensory experience. So, if I am not justified in the first
place in taking certain beliefs about the world to be true, I would
not be justified in taking perceptually grounded beliefs about the
world to be *likely* to be true – roughly, true most of the time –
and hence to be justified.

Even if – as an empiricist reliabilism might perhaps claim – the

sumably reliabilist justification for believing one is unjustified (hence unreliable) in believing a principle would imply that there is not a sufficiently strong
tendency, on the part of what underlies one's belief of that principle, to imply *its* probable truth and hence its justification. Perhaps this difficulty can be
met; but even apart from this problem, it would at least be questionable
whether one is successfully showing something if one depends on a premise
that one's theory says one is unjustified in believing.

32. We need not take reliabilism as *by definition* precluded from construing its epistemic principles as a priori, but such a view would at least seem at odds
with the externalism of the theory. Justification is based on a broadly causal
property, tending to produce true beliefs; and although that proposition may
be a priori, it is hard to see how to construct a plausible a priori case for
attributing reliability to any particular process and hence to any specific epistemic principle usable against skepticism.

33. For a valuable study of such epistemic circularity – and one which argues
that it need not be fatal to reliabilism about perceptual belief – see William P.
Alston, "Epistemic Circularity," *Philosophy and Phenomenological Research* 47
(1986).

schematic principle that reliably produced beliefs are justified is "analytic," any substantive principle about a type of belief, say that beliefs based on color impressions are reliably produced, could be shown to be justified only by presupposing some other substantive principle. It might indeed have to be one of the same kind, since it is not clear that one could devise a valid check on color beliefs without ultimately depending on an epistemic principle about color. But this is just the kind of principle needed against the skeptic; the very general principle that reliably produced beliefs are justified is a thesis of conceptual epistemology that does no real work against skepticism. There may be a way to make such circularity palatable; but obviating the need for it is surely some advantage in the rationalist approach.[34] To be sure, if something like the perceptual principle could not be established by an extended process of simple showing, e.g. illustrating it, distinguishing it from similar but mistaken principles, and refuting erroneous objections to it, it would have to be shown from more general principles. I believe that this should not be dismissed as hopeless. If there is such a possibility, it is not clear that the perceptual principle would have to be presupposed in the relevant arguments for it.

There would be other problems for such an enterprise, but circularity, at least of the kind just described, might well be avoided. One would need to rely on the use of reason to show an a priori principle; but one would not in general need to rely on that very principle. To be sure, once we come to a general principle of a priori justification – say that if S believes a proposition solely on the basis of reflection on the concepts figuring in it, then that belief is prima facie justified – it may not be possible to justify the principle *dialectically* without a kind of circularity. But, if some such principles are not, as I am inclined to think, self-evident, they are at least presupposed by any skeptics willing to offer an argument to justify their position. And these are surely the kinds of skeptics we should be chiefly concerned with.

If the internalist view taken here is not reliabilist, might it still be naturalistic? Let us continue to distinguish between a substantively naturalistic epistemology and a conceptually naturalistic

34. There are other problems besides circularity besetting the attempt to meet skepticism from reliabilist, and more generally, empiricist, assumptions. For an indication of some of them see Laurence BonJour, "Radical Empiricism and A Priori Knowledge," in progress.

one.[35] The former takes epistemological propositions, such as epistemic principles, to be empirical; the latter simply uses no irreducibly normative concepts. The former is naturalistic in substance – taking epistemology (as Quine does) to be about the natural world in the same way empirical science is; the latter is naturalistic only in concept, allowing that not all the truths of epistemology are about the natural world. The inspiration for the first view is presumably the idea that the truths of nature are the only truths there are; the second view simply says that, ultimately, all truths are expressable without relying on normative concepts. Although my view is not substantively naturalistic, I have said nothing here that rules out its being conceptually naturalistic. I do not believe, however, that justification is analyzable in terms of reliability. But I have left open that, in some other way, it might turn out to be a natural property. I do think it supervenes on natural properties and is, in that sense, *rooted* in the natural world, but it is by no means clear to me either that justifiedness is a natural property or that the notion of justification is reducible to some set of naturalistic concepts.

My view may seem anti-empirical, but it is not and is indeed devised with an eye to understanding scientific justification. The view is, however, anti-empiricist, if empiricism is understood as denying that anything substantive can be known or justifiably believed a priori. There is no question that experience is crucial not only for concept formation but also for determining how fruitful a philosophical theory is. Even if an epistemic principle is a priori and necessary and hence not refutable by experience, the course of experience may be such that the principle ceases to hold interest for us, and we evolve toward a different framework using different concepts. Imagine, e.g., that we ceased to have sensory impressions; there would then be no point in working with perceptual epistemic principles. This is largely why, in Chapter 10, I called them historically contingent. The epistemic principles we rely on in our daily critical practice seem to me so general, however, and so rich in ways to accommodate ostensible disconfirmation, that I see no reason to expect any such outcome. On the other hand, if we posit only empirical principles, whose justification is at the mercy of contingent events, there is surely less hope of adequately

35. As I have done (initially) in discussing Quine's position in Chapter 3.

dealing with skepticism. Principles whose justification depends on the specific course of experience seem unlikely to enable us to show that we can have justification no matter how that experience goes and even if, unbeknownst to us, it is plagued by a Cartesian nightmare.[36]

36. A much earlier version of this chapter was given at the Central Division Meetings of the American Philosophical Association, where I benefited from discussion with my co-symposiasts Mark Kaplan and Michael Williams. I have also profited from discussions with audiences at Pacific Lutheran University, the University of Georgia, the University of San Diego, and Washington State University. For many helpful comments I also thank Albert Casullo and Paul Moser.

PART IV

RATIONALITY

Chapter 13

An epistemic conception of rationality

Rational action has been very commonly conceived as action that maximizes the agent's expected utility. This conception has been qualified in many ways, and rational action has also been characterized along altogether different lines, particularly in the past two decades. It has been uncommon, however, for philosophers to try to account for rational action epistemically, on the model of justified belief. This paper will attempt to do that and to develop, in outline, an epistemic conception of rationality, one sufficiently general to encompass and, to some degree, unify, rational action, rational desire, and other rational elements. This is not to imply that the epistemic justification of a belief is equivalent to its rationality, or that the notion of justified belief is necessarily easier to understand than that of rationality. But certainly "rational belief" is sometimes used equivalently with "justified belief," and the two phrases are commendatory in quite similar ways. Moreover, if rational action, rational desire, and other important notions can be explicated, at least in part, on the model of justified belief, we can unify our theories of rational action and rational motivation with our epistemology. The first three sections of this paper will explore the extent to which such unification is possible. The conception of rationality they develop will then be compared with some leading alternative conceptions.

1. BACKGROUND
EPISTEMOLOGICAL ASSUMPTIONS

The most general assumption I shall make is that we may explicate justified belief using the notion of well-groundedness. In outline, the idea is this. Some beliefs on the part of a person, *S*, such as certain introspective, perceptual, and a priori beliefs, may be conceived as directly justified by virtue of being well-grounded in something – such as an appropriate experience or a certain sort of apprehension – not in need of justification or even amenable to it. Any other justified beliefs of *S*'s may be conceived as indirectly justified (and indirectly grounded) in relation to the former, the directly justified beliefs. On one plausible view, indirectly justified beliefs need not derive all their justification from the directly justified ones, but will derive enough of it from them so that even if they ceased to have whatever justification they derive from other sources, they would remain justified, in the sense that they would still be epistemically reasonable, that is, it would be more reasonable for *S* to retain them than to withhold belief from the relevant propositions.

This view is a version of modest foundationalism, and because it is modest it does not imply that directly justified beliefs are, say, infallible or indubitable, nor that only through deductive inferences can they transmit justification to superstructure beliefs based on them. The view is controversial; but I have elaborated and defended it elsewhere,[1] as have others, and my purpose here is simply to suggest how it may illuminate rational action and the rationality of desires and other propositional attitudes that motivate action.

Clearly, a fully developed foundationalist theory of justified belief must provide accounts of direct justification and of the transmission of justification from foundational beliefs to superstructure beliefs, that is, beliefs that are appropriately based on the former. In both cases, there are many possibilities. For our purposes, just two sorts of account need be mentioned in each case. First, regarding the justification of foundational beliefs, one might hold that they are justified by virtue of being produced by a reliable process, such as the process by which the ring of one's telephone normally causes one to believe that one's telephone is ringing.[2]

---

1. See, for example, my "Psychological Foundationalism" (Chapter 1, this volume); D. M. Armstrong, *Belief, Truth and Knowledge* (Cambridge: Cambridge University Press, 1973), esp. chaps. 11–14; and William P. Alston, "Two Types of Foundationalism," *Journal of Philosophy* 73 (1976): 165–85.
2. For representative reliability theories of (empirical) knowledge and of justified belief, see Fred I. Dretske, "Conclusive Reasons," *Australasian Journal of Philosophy* 49 (1971): 1–22; and *Knowledge and the Flow of Information* (Cambridge: Bradford Books and MIT Press, 1981), esp. chaps. 4 and 5; and Alvin I. Gold-

Another possibility is to conceive direct justification as accruing to certain beliefs by virtue of their content, for example by virtue of their being a certain kind of belief about one's immediate experience.[3] Concerning the transmission of justification, a foundationalist might require that for a foundational belief, say, that p, to justify a superstructure belief, say, that q, the propositional object of the former must entail that of the latter (for example, p would have to entail q). A weaker view would countenance transmission of justification without such entailment, for example with a suitably strong probabilistic relation between p and q. Since most foundationalists hold the weaker view regarding transmission, that is the one we shall consider. It will be necessary, however, to discuss both of the above conceptions of direct justification.

The notion of a well-grounded action seems to presuppose that of well-grounded desire. We should first explore the epistemic conception of rational desire (which, for convenience, I shall treat as equivalent to rational wanting, though I do not think that desiring and wanting are equivalent). This will be the task of the next section.

2. RATIONAL DESIRE

It seems obvious that desires may be appropriately assessed as rational or not rational. I shall also assume (more controversially) that the objects of desires and wants are states of affairs, but nothing significant for our main purposes will turn on this. Desires and beliefs are the only propositional attitudes I shall consider, but much of what is said should apply to at least many other propositional attitudes. For instance, if we can use the notion of well-groundedness to explicate rational desire, quite parallel points will apply, I think, to rational values and to other propositional atti-

man, "What is Justified Belief?" in *Justification and Knowledge*, ed. George S. Pappas (Dordrecht: D. Reidel, 1980).

3. This characterization seems applicable to Descartes, and a highly qualified form of the view is illustrated by Chisholm in "A Version of Foundationalism," in his *The Foundations of Knowing* (Minneapolis: University of Minnesota Press, 1982). It is not necessary, however, for a proponent of the view to be a Cartesian.

tudes.[4] How might a desire be well-grounded? If we begin with intrinsic desires – desires for something for its own sake – and draw on the analogy with directly justified beliefs, we should find that some intrinsic desires are directly grounded, and well-grounded, in the experience (or apprehension) of the relevant kind of state of affairs, say, one's listening to music. This leaves open what it is for an intrinsic desire to be well-grounded. To begin to solve that problem we need to distinguish two cases.

First, there are cases in which *S* justifiably believes something appropriate about the desired state of affairs, such as his listening to music. *S* might believe that it is worthwhile, enriching, pleasant, or a beautiful experience. We might call such properties *desirability* characteristics, since (in the present scheme) they are conceived as the sorts of properties in virtue of which a state of affairs really is desirable. *S*'s belief might also be *de re;* for example, *S* might justifiably believe, of the listening and the property of being pleasant, that the former has the latter, in which case *S* (who may be a small child) need not conceptualize either music or pleasantness in the (presumably richer) way required for *de dicto* belief. Thus, a quite wide range of beliefs may serve here (depending on what restrictions are needed to enable the belief to ground the rationality of the relevant intrinsic desire). In either case, we may speak of *cognitive grounding,* since the relevant beliefs are the basis of the rationality of the desire.

There seems to be at least one other kind of grounding through which an intrinsic desire can be rational. Suppose that I simply enjoy listening to music in virtue of experiencing the desirability characteristics of such listening, such as the perception of harmony and the sense of melodic contrasts. Could this not render my intrinsic desire to listen to music rational, even if I form no belief to the effect that my listening to music has these qualities? It would seem so. Indeed, it may be that this second kind of grounding – *experiential grounding,* we might call it – is more basic than the first. Perhaps if one could not intrinsically want to listen to music directly for the desirable qualities of such listening, one's intrinsic desire to listen to it could not be rational because one *believes* one's listening to it to have those qualities.

How might an epistemic conception of the rationality of an in-

---

4. Some of the relevant points are made in my "Axiological Foundationalism" (Chapter 2, this volume).

trinsic desire account for its rationality? One possibility is to give well-groundedness for intrinsic desires a reliabilist interpretation analogous to a reliabilist interpretation of what justifies direct, that is (roughly), noninferential, empirical beliefs. Consider cognitive grounding first. Just as a belief, such as that there is paper before me, can apparently be justified by virtue of being causally generated, in a reliable way, by an experience of the paper which the belief is about and in virtue of whose presence it is true, so a belief that listening to a piece of music is a beautiful experience might be reliably produced by an experience of the melodic, harmonic, and other relevant properties of the music in question, and can, in turn, reliably produce an intrinsic desire to listen to the music *for* those qualities. The idea is roughly that just as the belief that there is paper before me is justified because it is produced, by that very paper, through a reliable process and is hence *likely to be true,* the desire is rational because it is produced, via the justified belief about the desirability characteristics of the experience, by a process reliable in the sense that desires generated, by something desirable, through that process, are likely to be, as I suggest we might put it, *sound,* that is, to correspond to (to be desires for) what actually is desirable.

For extrinsic desires, whose rationality depends on that of at least one instrumental belief, the suggested account must be complicated. (Some of the required criteria will be indicated shortly.) This is not to suggest an *analysis* of justified belief or rational desire. I am simply sketching a partial theory, available to an epistemic account of rationality, of what constitutes their rationality, at least for direct (empirical) beliefs and cognitively grounded intrinsic desires.

Experiential grounding also (and perhaps more readily) admits of a reliabilist interpretation. It appears that an intrinsic desire might be reliably produced by the relevant qualities of one's listening to music, without the mediation of a belief that it has these qualities. Such a desire would be a closer analogue of a directly justified perceptual belief than would a cognitively grounded intrinsic desire. Rather as the belief arises from perceptual experience, the desire arises, on this conception, in a similarly direct way, from aesthetic experience. When it is reliably produced by properties of the experience in virtue of which the experience is desirable, the intrinsic desire for the experience is likely to be sound and is rational.

In both the cognitive and the experiential cases, this conception of rational intrinsic desires anchors them "to the world." They are grounded in the world either directly, via experience of something, or indirectly, via a belief that is itself justified by virtue of being directly grounded in the world. Despite appearances, this conception of rational intrinsic desires does not entail a naturalistic conception of either rationality or desirability, though it does entail a realist, as opposed, for example, to an emotivist, notion of desirability, since if nothing really is desirable, intrinsic desires can hardly be rational through being reliably produced by properties in virtue of which the thing in question is desirable. Naturalism is not entailed, however, because desirability can be a real property even if it supervenes on natural properties but is not itself a natural property.[5] (These points presuppose, of course, that there is a distinction between natural and nonnatural – for example, normative – properties. I am inclined to believe that there is, but cannot try to show that here.)

If desirability is not a natural property, however, then there is a problem for the reliabilist interpretation. For it is by no means obvious that nonnatural properties can enter into causal relations, hence not clear that they can reliably produce an intrinsic desire for something for such properties. We do, to be sure, speak of being moved by the beauty of a piece of music, and perhaps such locutions can be taken at face value. But it may well be that what actually moves us is the relevant combination of melody, harmony, rhythm, dynamics, and so forth, and that is apparently a set of natural physical properties. Let us suppose this for the sake of argument. It is crucial to see that these are just the sorts of natural properties on which musical beauty supervenes, and that all the reliabilist needs here is the thesis that these properties appropriately produce our intrinsic desire to listen to the music. For one thing, if a piece of music is beautiful in virtue of them, then its having them is clearly a reliable indication of that beauty. Notice also that even in certain perceptual cases there is an analogue of this. When one perceptually believes, through sight, that there is a person before one, it is presumably not personhood, but some

---

5. For defense of a realist conception of value properties see Panayot Butchvarov, "That Simple, Indefinable, Nonnatural Property *Good*," *Review of Metaphysics* 36 (1982): 51–75; and for an account of supervenience relevant to our discussion here see Jaegwon Kim, "Psychophysical Supervenience as a Mind-Body Theory," *Cognition and Brain Theory* 5 (1982).

of the properties in virtue of which the individual one sees is a person, that produce one's belief. Thus, whatever the (admittedly substantial) difficulties in explicating the relevant kind of reliability, we need not conclude that reliabilism is simply inapplicable to relations between non-natural properties and intrinsic desires.

This is a good place to reiterate that the justification of foundational beliefs *need* not be construed along reliabilist lines. Thus, the motivational analogy can also be detached from reliabilism. Perhaps, for example, it is simply a constitutive principle of reason that it is rational to desire intrinsically pleasurable experiences. How might this be?

If the rationality of intrinsically wanting to have pleasurable experiences is not quite self-evident, it is at least plausible to take such desires as rational. The same holds for intrinsic desires for one's own happiness, as Aristotle apparently believed. Note, for instance, that we normally take S's enjoying something to explain why he desires it intrinsically, and to exhibit the desire as natural for him in a sense implying that it is at least prima facie rational. We may wonder *why* S enjoys whatever it is, or think he *ought* not enjoy it. But if he does, it seems prima facie rational for him to desire it intrinsically. Similarly, it might be held to be an a priori truth that if listening to a beautiful piece of music really is intrinsically desirable – say because it is a beautiful experience – then intrinsically wanting to listen to it for the properties in virtue of which it is beautiful is prima facie rational. There are other possible views a realist about desirability might take to preserve the epistemological analogy, but there is no need to outline them here. We should, however, ask whether the analogy can be made out on a noncognitivist interpretation of sentences of the form of 'S's intrinsic desire for x is rational,' where 'rational' is treated like 'morally good.' Let us proceed to this question.

The main problem here is that, for noncognitivism, there is no property of (intrinsic) desirability and thus no analogue of truth. If the noncognitivist thinks of the relevant sentences as, say, expressing attitudes, it will still be possible to distinguish between good and bad grounds for having (or expressing) these attitudes. Presumably beliefs could be crucial to these grounds. A kind of cognitive grounding would thus be possible. One might say that if I justifiably believe that listening to music gives me pleasure, I am prima facie rational in holding, on that ground, the positive attitude I would express by, for example, "My intrinsic desire to listen to it is rational." We would have, then, a structural but not a substantive epistemological analogy. This would be significant and would help to undermine the irrationalist interpretation sometimes given to noncognitivism. But however that may be, I shall not pursue noncognitivism further. If the epistemological analogy I am developing is plausible, we shall have less reason to give a noncognitivist interpretation to terms like "rational" in the first place.

We must now ask how the rationality of extrinsic, that is, instrumental, desires is to be understood on the well-groundedness conception. The basic idea is that their rationality (or at least enough of it to render them reasonable) is transmitted from well-grounded intrinsic desires. Consider a simple case in which S has only one relevant intrinsic desire, namely to play the piano well, and extrinsically wants to play scales (as a means to playing well). A paradigm of transmission of rationality from the former to the latter desire would occur where (a) the latter is wholly based on the former (for example, because playing scales is desired *only* as a *means* to playing the piano well) and (b) S *justifiably* believes that playing scales will lead to playing the piano well.

This transmission of rationality from foundational (hence intrinsic) desires to superstructure desires is of course analogous to the inferential justification of a belief, and as in that case there are many varieties and many subtleties. All I can add here is that the transmission of rationality from well-grounded intrinsic desires may pass through many elements. We then have a *motivational chain*. The length of such chains is theoretically unlimited, but in practice they often seem quite short. It is important to see, however, that only the first desire after the foundational one need be directly based on it, that is, such that S desires the relevant object on the basis of what S believes to be its contribution to realizing the intrinsic desire. The motivational basis relation is nontransitive: each element, except the foundational one, must be directly based on its predecessor; but none need be directly based on any other besides its predecessor. S could want to buy flowers wholly on the basis of wanting to please Tom, and want to please Tom wholly on the basis of wanting to curry favor with him, yet never form any belief to the effect that buying the flowers will curry favor with Tom. S's desire to buy flowers would thus not be (directly) based on the desire to curry favor with Tom.

To be sure, S may have two well-grounded intrinsic desires such that, given S's rational beliefs, incompatible extrinsic desires would be at least prima facie rational (where incompatible desires are desires that cannot be jointly satisfied). One might thus rationally want to practice one's tennis now as a means to playing well, and rationally want to weed one's garden now as a means to eating well. This possibility should not be surprising; analogues apply in the domain of belief, for example in certain cases where S has evidence for incompatible propositions each of which is prima facie justified for him. There are many ways of deciding which extrinsic desire, if either, is more rational. Other things being equal, the one grounded in the stronger intrinsic desire is more rational and, in action, should (and will tend to) prevail; for example, if S wants to eat well more than to play tennis well, we would expect, and approve of, S's weeding the garden rather than playing tennis if we expect either. But other things need not be equal; one of the intrinsic desires may be more rational, or more important to S's overall system of desires, than the other. The problems raised here are complicated; but they or their counterparts beset any plausible theory of rational desire, and there is no need to try to solve them here.

Rational desires, then, may be plausibly conceived as well-grounded desires understood along the lines suggested. There is much to be said to clarify this conception, but at least the core of the idea is now before us. Rather than go into a detailed discussion of rational desire, I want now to extend the suggested conception to actions.

3. RATIONAL ACTION

This section will concern only intentional actions. Some nonintentional actions, such as those knowingly performed in doing something intentionally – the sort Bentham called obliquely intentional – may also be rational; but they may presumably be accounted for on the basis of an adequate conception of rationality for intentional actions. In outlining a conception of rationality for intentional actions, I shall simply assume that they are explainable in terms of the agent's desires and beliefs, and that the rationality of desires can be understood along the lines just indicated. If so, then perhaps actions can be conceived as rational in relation to intrinsic desires rather as extrinsic desires are in relation to intrinsic ones (beliefs play a crucial part in both cases). A rational action, then, might be conceived as a well-grounded one. I refer, of course, to tokens, not types. Our subject is the rationality of particular actions, not that of a type for a person. *A*-ing, for example resigning, might be a rational (type of) thing for me to do even if I never do it or, when I do, I do it entirely for bad reasons, so that *my doing* it is not rational. It might be *rationalizable* in the light of the reasons in virtue of which it is a rational type of thing for me to do, but a rationalizable action need not be rational.[6]

Let us explore the suggested conception of rationality. Suppose first that the foundational rational desires are those that are directly grounded, and well-grounded, either in certain justified beliefs or in appropriate experiences. Some actions may be directly based on these, that is, performed in order to realize them. If *S* believes, with respect to an action he is considering and a basic rational desire of his, that the former is certain to satisfy the latter, and on this basis performs the action, the action is prima facie well-grounded. In this way, regularly practicing the piano could be well-grounded for *S* relative to his rational intrinsic desire to play well. Again, we have an analogue of inferential justification. Indeed, some writers have held that there is always a practical inference mediating between motivational wants (or other motivational elements) and the actions they explain.[7]

It may be, of course, that an action is only indirectly and distantly based on a foundational desire. We then have a *purposive chain,* analogous to a motivational chain: *S A*'s in order to realize *x*, wants to realize *x* in order to realize *y*, and so on, until we reach something *S* wants intrinsically. As in the case of the motivational basis relation, this in-order-to relation, which I shall call the *purposive connecting relation,* is nontransitive. I can jog to maintain my health, and maintain my health to enhance my chances of a good life, yet not – if I do not "make the connection" between the first and third elements – jog in order to enhance my chances of a good life. But

---

6. I have developed and defended these points in Chapter 4, this volume.
7. This view is not frequently stated, but there are some philosophers who conceive all intentional actions as arising from practical reasoning, and clearly at least the most important kinds of rational actions are intentional. See, for example, Donald Davidson, "How is Weakness of the Will Possible?" in *Moral Concepts,* ed. Joel Feinberg (London and New York: Oxford University Press, 1969), p. 110; and Gilbert Harman, "Practical Reasoning," *Review of Metaphysics* 29 (1976): 451 (cp. p. 442). I have assessed both views in "A Theory of Practical Reasoning," *American Philosophical Quarterly* 19 (1982): 25–39.

in both cases the terminal element is well-grounded only if rationality is adequately transmitted from the foundational element(s), and this presumably requires that every *connecting belief*, such as the belief that jogging will help maintain one's health, is justified. A single action may, of course, be grounded in *more* than one rational intrinsic desire, say a desire to enhance one's chances of a good life and a desire to complete marathons. It may thus be rational in virtue of coterminous purposive chains. Coherence criteria may also play a role, such as the overall appropriateness of the action to *S*'s total system of motivation and cognition. The conception being developed simply makes well-groundedness central; it need not be the only source of rationality.

It should also be stressed that, as in the case of rational extrinsic desires, an epistemic conception of rational action may employ varying sorts of transmission principles. An approach modeled on modest foundationalism is unlikely to allow any action to be indefeasibly rational, that is (roughly) rational in such a way that the agent could not have had a set of desires and beliefs in the light of which it would not have been rational. Certainly there should be room for an action to fail to be rational because, although it is grounded, by a purposive chain, in a rational desire, d, at least one of the following conditions occurs: (1) an alternative action would have been preferable for *S* because it would have been, and *S* could have readily seen that it would be, grounded in a stronger competing intrinsic desire, d' (or one which *S* believed to be, or, given *S*'s information, should have believed to be, more worthy of fulfillment); or (2) *S* has a belief, which *S* has temporarily forgotten, that an alternative would more readily satisfy d (or *S* should, given his information, believe this); or (3) *S* has an alternative which, given information available to *S*, would yield more overall satisfaction of *S*'s rational intrinsic desires, for example by virtue of satisfying a number of them no one of which is as strong as d, but all of which together have a greater combined strength and are such that *S* would on reflection prefer their collective fulfillment to satisfying d.

Alternatives (1)–(3) may each be further specified in varying ways, and there are other defeasibility conditions that simply cannot be discussed here. But something must be said about cases in which *S* mistakenly but justifiably believes that *A*-ing is rational in the relevant sense. It seems natural to call such an action subjectively rational. Beliefs may be subjectively rational (or subjectively justified) in a parallel sense. But just as such beliefs, if true, do not represent knowledge, subjectively rational actions lack something: from the point of view of rationality, they might be said not to be the right thing for S to do. Here, too, there are distinctions we cannot develop. Two common ways in which the rationality of an action is defeated are these: S might A on the basis of a *non*rational want which S justifiably believes his A-ing will realize, or on the basis of a rational want which S *un*justifiably believes S's A-ing will realize. In these cases S may not believe S's A-ing is rational, but we might still want to speak of a kind of subjectively rational action. An adequate epistemic account of rational action, then, will have to be complicated. I believe, however, that other plausible accounts of rational action are at least equally complicated. For comparison and contrast, the next section will consider two of the most important accounts currently in the field.

4. ALTERNATIVE VIEWS OF RATIONALITY

If any conception of rational action may be called the classical view, it is probably the maximization of expected utility conception. Certainly this has been the point of departure for a huge number of discussions of the topic, and it is important that we consider it briefly. The central idea seems to be that the crucial mark of a rational action is its appropriateness to the aim(s) of the agent at the time of action. The rationality of an action, on this view, is a matter of how good a means it is, judged in the light of the agent's beliefs, to realizing the aim(s). To be sure, a proponent of this view might still want to take account of whether the aim(s) and the belief(s) are themselves rational; but the view is not usually qualified in that way. After all, if what is really crucial to rational action is its success as a means to one or more of the agent's ends, then the character of these ends should be irrelevant, except insofar as fulfilling one may be at odds with fulfilling another or with maximum fulfillment of the overall set.[8]

On one standard interpretation of the maximization of expected utility conception of rational action, the expected utility of an action is computed as follows: one determines (a) the alternative courses

8. C. G. Hempel argues for a version of the maximization of expected utility view in his *Aspects of Scientific Explanation* (New York: The Free Press, 1965), chap. 12, sec. 10.

of action S supposes S has, (b) what S believes are their possible outcomes, and (c) the subjective value for S (using arbitrarily chosen numbers from negative to positive) of each outcome; one then multiplies the subjective value of each outcome by the subjective probability of that outcome, and adds these products for each alternative action. A rational action for S in such a situation is one with a score at least as high as that of any of the relevant alternatives.

There are various ways of interpreting subjective probability and subjective utility. For our purposes the former may be conceived in terms of beliefs and the latter in terms of desires. Let us assume, then, that to say that the subjective probability, for S, of an outcome's occurring is n, is to say that S believes the likelihood of its occurring to be n. Similarly, to say that the subjective utility of an outcome is n is to say that n is the degree to which S wants it, or, in the case of negative utility, wants to avoid it.

It has been widely recognized that this conception of rational action applies only in special cases. But there seems to have been a tendency, in some quarters, to exaggerate the frequency of such cases in ordinary human behavior, including problem-solving behavior generally considered prima facie rational. A main reason for this tendency may be the assumption that if, on considering the question of how probable a possible outcome of A-ing is, S *would* assign a probability, then S believes, at least dispositionally, that its occurrence has that probability. But as I have elsewhere argued, this assumption assimilates dispositionally believing to a disposition to believe.[9] To illustrate, one may be cognitively so constituted that if someone asked whether there were fewer than 20,205 books in one's office, one would immediately assent. It does not follow that, prior to entertaining this proposition, one believed it. An analogy may help: the difference is like that between a machine's being designed so that, immediately upon being "asked" the sum of 125 and 128, it calculates 253 and displays this, and, on the other hand, this sum's *already* being in its memory bank.

It is quite similar with probability beliefs. We are often so disposed that on contemplating a possible event we form a probability belief about its occurrence; but it does not follow that we had such a belief all along. Moreover, a reasonably cautious person may be

---

9. This distinction is developed in my "Believing and Affirming," *Mind* 91 (1982): 115–20.

very reluctant to make such probability assignments and is often forced to hypothesize instead a *range* of values, such as between .50 and .75. Consider Sue, a surgeon. Even if she has statistics on the incidence of death from a kind of surgery she is considering for Tom, each patient is different, and she might well form only the cautious belief that his chance of surviving the surgery is better than even. Somewhat paradoxically, it seems that the better one understands probability and the complexity of future possibilities, the less often one's behavior satisfies the maximization of expected utility conception of rational action (other things being equal).

A natural reply here would be that while it may be important to see that the applicability of this conception is severely limited, I have still shown no deficiency in it for those cases to which it does apply. Indeed, I have not, and I shall make no attempt to refute the maximization of expected utility view of rational action. My main purpose is to develop a quite different conception, and my concern with the maximization view is chiefly to bring out, by contrast, important features of the epistemic and other conceptions of rational action. Let me, then, just note what I take to be four serious defects of that view that should be overcome by any adequate account of rational action. First, as noted, the view seems inapplicable to many of our (intentional) actions because, for one thing, we simply do not have (and may not even be able in good conscience to form) the required probability beliefs. Second, the view puts no constraints on the rationality of the desires in terms of which the agent's utility is presumably determined. Third, it places no restrictions on the justification of the relevant probability beliefs. Fourth, it does not require that a rational action (token) be causally grounded in the cognitive or motivational elements in the light of which it is said to be rational (though some defenders of the view, such as Hempel,[10] have built this in).

From the perspective of an epistemic approach to rationality, one might say that on the maximization of expected utility conception of rational action the only appropriate criteria of assessment in the rationality dimension are a kind of *coherence criterion*. It does not matter what is the content of the agent's wants and beliefs, nor whether they are rational; the rationality of an action is entirely relative to them. This makes the view an especially good foil for the epistemic conception of rational action sketched above. There

---

10. See Hempel, *Aspects of Scientific Explanation*, p. 463.

is, however, another view that is a good foil for both and is liable to none of the four objections just voiced. I refer to the theory of rationality developed by Richard Brandt in *A Theory of the Good and the Right*. Let us consider this theory at some length.

Brandt has given us a powerful and useful action-guiding conception of rational action. His strategy is to develop what he calls reforming (as opposed to lexical) definitions:

> I shall call a person's action "rational" in the sense of being rational to a first approximation, if and only if it is what he would have done if all the mechanisms determining action except for his desires and aversions (which are taken as they are) – that is, the *cognitive* inputs influencing decision/ action – had been optimal as far as possible. . . . Second, I shall call a desire or aversion "rational" if and only if it is what it would have been had the person undergone *cognitive psycho-therapy*. . . . Finally, I shall say that an action is "rational" in the sense of fully rational if and only if the desires and aversions which are involved in the action are rational, and if the condition is met for rationality to a first approximation.[11]

Methodologically, this procedure is attractive. Brandt starts with a plausible strengthening of the maximization of expected utility view, and then argues that if a fully rational action is to represent the best thing one can do (or at least something to which no alternative is preferable), as surely it should, then even actions rational by the strengthened criterion are not fully rational. To be fully rational an action must not only be based on minimally adequate cognitive inputs; it must also be based on minimally adequate desires or aversions. Minimal adequacy occurs when the cognitive inputs (for example, beliefs) and the agent's desires and aversions would survive were "every item of *relevant available* information . . . present to awareness, vividly, at the focus of attention, or with an equal share of attention."[12] Now

> A piece of information is relevant if its presence to awareness would make a difference to the person's tendency to

11. Richard Brandt, *A Theory of the Good and the Right* (Oxford: Oxford University Press, 1979), p. 11. Presumably the sense in which Brandt takes the relevant wants and beliefs to be "involved in the action" is causal.
12. Ibid., p. 11.

perform a certain act, or to the attractiveness of some prospective outcome to him. Hence it is an essentially causal notion. . . . Second . . . I prefer to define "all available information" as the propositions accepted by the science of the agent's day, plus factual propositions justified by publicly accessible evidence (including testimony of others about themselves) and the principles of logic.[13]

These ideas are developed at length by Brandt, and I cannot do him justice here. My aim is simply to bring out some central features of his approach by examining three topics: available information, relevant information, and unextinguishability as a sufficient condition for rational desire.

Given Brandt's notion of available information, even his conception of action rational to a first approximation is quite strong. For there are surely many things we do that are well planned, and even quite efficient in accomplishing reasonable goals, which we would not have done if we had all the relevant information. Often, for example, there is an even more efficient procedure that we do not know of, though more experienced people do. But if little is lost, the action still seems, in a common and significant sense, rational. Brandt is doubtless aware of this, and my point is not that his proposed definition is somehow mistaken, but simply that it sets a high – perhaps idealized – standard of rational action. Doubtless this is appropriate *if* we think of a rational action as the *best* thing to do in the circumstances.

Brandt's notion of relevance is harder to assess. One would expect the relevance of information to a belief or desire to be at least mainly a matter of some semantic or epistemic relation to its content. Why does he characterize the relation causally? I would imagine there are at least three reasons: relevance is extremely hard to explicate semantically or epistemically; a causal criterion is naturalistic and thus avoids evaluative notions of the kind he wishes to explicate by using his definition of "rational"; and if information is not relevant in Brandt's causal sense, an agent can hardly be faulted for not taking account of it, and hence may still be said to have done the *best he could*. If these are not among Brandt's reasons for using a causal criterion of relevance, they are at least plausible reasons.

Let us start with a prima facie counterexample. Suppose that my

13. Ibid., pp. 12–13.

brain has been manipulated by a diabolical neurosurgeon in such a way that I am no longer moved by coming to believe certain propositions that seem clearly relevant to some intrinsic desire of mine. To take a consideration that Brandt himself views as highly relevant to the rationality of an intrinsic desire, suppose my brain is altered so that my realization that an intrinsic desire of mine is artificial has no tendency to extinguish the desire, where intrinsic wants or aversions are artificial if they "could not have been brought about by experience with actual situations which the desires are for and the aversions are against . . . for instance, a non-prestige occupation like garbage collection or marriage to a person of another race, religion, or nationality."[14] I agree with Brandt that if one realizes that, say, one's intrinsic desire to avoid marrying someone of another nationality could not have arisen from the relevant kind of experience, this should tend to extinguish the want and is relevant to its rationality. But would it be any less relevant if one could not react appropriately to it? That seems doubtful, at least if "rational" is commendatory. Surely a desire should never be commendable simply because the person cannot alter it.

The problem is this. The criterion of relevance seems too narrow, and even apart from that, it seems that a person could have a nonrational (even irrational) desire that would survive cognitive psychotherapy. Brandt must call it rational. He might reply that since the imagined surgery is surely not unalterable in a sense making it nomically impossible for me to react appropriately, it is not impossible for my desire to extinguish through cognitive psychotherapy. But even if Brandt has nomic impossibility in mind, we may still ask about the logically possible case in which I nomically cannot react appropriately. There, too, the information still appears relevant. My inability to respond to a relevant criticism surely does not make it irrelevant. My prejudice may be "wired in" and thereby evoke sympathy, but it still seems an irrational attitude.

In any event, I believe that Brandt's way of dealing with this problem does not depend on moves of this sort. He says at one point:

> If a desire will not extinguish, then it is not irrational. This result is consistent with the general view that a desire (etc.) is rational if it has been influenced by facts and logic as

14. Ibid., p. 117.

much as possible. Unextinguishable desires meet this condition.[15]

The central idea here seems to be that rationality results when facts and logic have done all they possibly (nomically?) can. Thus, to say than an unextinguishable want can be irrational is to demand more than is possible for S on the basis of using logic and grasping facts. If S cannot be moved to cease intrinsically wanting x by any amount of exposure to logic and facts, surely we should conclude that *for* S the want is rational.

This position is certainly defensible, but let me offer an alternative. Just as we can distinguish acting rationally from acting merely excusably, we can distinguish having a rational desire from having an excusable one. Now clearly an unextinguishable desire is (for S) excusable, since there is nothing S can do (using logic and facts) to uproot it. But why must we then use the commendatory, action-guiding term "rational"? For Brandt, the reasoning might run, in part, as follows: since "rational" is taken to mean "not irrational,"[16] and what is irrational in S is presumably such that S is criticizable for it, whereas one is presumably not criticizable for what is excusable, unextinguishable desires are not irrational, and hence are rational.

This raises the question whether "rational" and "irrational" should be regarded as contradictories. I think not. For one thing, one is commendatory, the other condemnatory, yet the things – such as actions and wants – to which they apply vary, in the relevant respects, along a continuum. There are more good reasons, for instance, for some of the things we do, and desire, than for others; and both our actions and our desires are *influenced* by reasons to different degrees. There should thus be cases to which neither term appropriately applies. This does not entail that Brandt is unjustified in using "rational" and "irrational" as contradictories; but if he does, we must at least conclude that in some possible cases, such as that of the diabolical surgery, "rational" is not commendatory. The victim ought to try to resist the influence of the artificial desire, even though he cannot extinguish it. If we must

15. Ibid., p. 113.
16. Ibid., p. 112. Brandt's position is not merely terminological. He seems to conceive rationality as occurring where one has not made (and would not make, upon appropriate reflection) certain mistakes. It then becomes natural to treat "rational" as equivalent to "not irrational," since "irrational" suggests mistakes or similar deficiencies.

say, with Brandt, that the desire is (fully) rational, we are at least hard pressed to explain why the victim ought to try to resist acting on it and, toward that end, to strengthen competing wants.[17]

We are now in a good position to see how the view that well-groundedness is what is central to the rationality of intrinsic desires differs from the Brandtian account of their rationality. First, Brandt does not require any close analogue of grounding. For him, rational intrinsic desires need not have any particular kind of content or type of origin in experience, for example being based on appropriate beliefs or appropriate experiences. They are rational if they would pass a certain test. Undoubtedly, Brandt would suppose that in fact few if any intrinsic desires are rational unless they *do* rest on such beliefs or experiences. My point is simply that his view contains no positive conceptual requirement corresponding to well-groundedness. Second, the notion of well-groundedness admits of degree; so, on the well-groundedness conception, a rational intrinsic desire need not be optimally grounded. Third, the well-groundedness conception is neutral with respect to naturalism, whereas Brandt's view, properly understood, is naturalistic.

Speaking more generally, it again seems useful to draw a contrast from an epistemic perspective. Unlike the maximization of expected utility view, Brandt's is not plausibly conceived as purely coherentist. For his criteria of rational desire and rational belief are by no means purely coherence criteria, and in addition he strongly restricts the sorts of desires and beliefs in virtue of which S's A-ing may be rational: roughly, S's desires must be capable of surviving cognitive psychotherapy, and S's beliefs must reflect adequate information. But if Brandt's view is foundationalist, it is, at least as regards desires, a *procedural foundationalism:* rational intrinsic desires, the foundational motivating elements, need not have any particular content or type of content, but they must be capable of surviving exposure to appropriate information. This in turn leaves open the sort of action that may be rational (even if Brandt's view of justified belief should be a version of foundationalism – a matter on which I offer no interpretation of him). The question of

17. Brandt is aware of this problem and speaks to it on p. 122 in relation to intrinsic desires for money caused by its perceived usefulness in realizing intrinsic wants. He seems to think that if a want is either wired in or is causally inevitable on the basis of a rational want (such as an extrinsic want for money), it is rational. "This is what I'm like," S might say to a critic of the intrinsic want. But would such inescapability imply rationality?

what desires will survive such exposure is empirical. In principle, they might be egoistic or altruistic, hedonistic or puritanical, democratic or oligarchical. On the other hand, while I have attributed to the epistemic conception of rationality no theses about the sorts of desires and beliefs that are rational, even a modest foundationalist conception of rationality will presuppose that some particular desires, for example intrinsic desires for one's own happiness, and some specific beliefs, such as those about certain aspects of one's current immediate experience, are, under appropriate conditions, rational. Different theories will give different accounts of such foundational rationality and will differ as to what is foundationally rational. But a fully worked-out epistemic theory of rationality will try to reflect certain plausible intuitions as to what sorts of elements are properly taken to be desirable. Perhaps this is in part what Rawls is doing in conceiving primary goods – for example, freedom of the person and health – as such that rational persons want these whatever else they want.[18] In any case, let us apply to some examples a few of the contrasts between Brandt's view and the epistemic view outlined in this paper.

Take first the question of what determines the relevance of a consideration to the rationality of intrinsic desires. Returning to our victim of diabolical surgery, regardless of whether his intrinsic desire concerning marriage will extinguish, it need not be well-grounded. He neither has a justified belief, nor any appropriate experience, in virtue of which the desire is rational. This can explain why it is not rational, whereas, if cognitive psychotherapy will not extinguish it, Brandt's view must, implausibly, I think, take it to be rational. The well-groundedness view can also explain why obviously contradictory states of affairs cannot be rationally desired intrinsically: S cannot have experienced them, nor (presumably) can he justifiably believe them to have desirability characteristics. Suppose, on the other hand, that S researches cars and buys a good one at a good price, yet overlooks available information which would have led to S's getting a slightly better price. On the well-groundedness view, one could explain why S did not act optimally, yet still conceive the action as well-grounded to a high degree and thus as rational. On Brandt's scheme, the action must be called

18. See John Rawls, *A Theory of Justice* (Cambridge: Harvard University Press, 1971), for example p. 62, and chap. 3, sec. 25. For interpretation and defense of some of Rawls's views on rationality see Allen E. Buchanan, "Revisability and Rational Choice," *Canadian Journal of Philosophy* 5 (1975): 395–405.

irrational (though it should be pointed out that some irrational actions are not far from rational). No doubt there are other cases of intrinsic desires and of actions whose rationality or lack of it would be differently characterized on the well-groundedness conception than on Brandt's theory, though extensionally I would expect the two views to be close. This is not to imply that we can establish precise, uncontroversial criteria of well-groundedness for all intrinsic desires. But for at least a great many we can give some account of their rationality, or lack of it, by appeal to cognitive or experiential grounding conceived in the ways suggested in this paper.

Moreover, while on a realist conception of desirability a desire may be in some objective sense unsound, a realist epistemic conception of rationality may grant that two people may have well-grounded intrinsic desires for mutually incompatible states of affairs, such as one for a predominance of classical music on the radio, and one for a predominance of popular music on the radio. Some proponents of the conception might argue that these desires cannot both be *maximally* well-grounded, but that view is not essential to the position, any more than the claim that a maximally justified belief must be true is essential to a realist conception of epistemic justification. The position certainly allows for the joint possibility that Sue, for example, has a fully rational intrinsic desire to listen (herself) to classical music, while Tom has a fully rational intrinsic desire to listen (himself) to popular music. They may, perhaps, have different response patterns and different capacities. Thus, a kind of relativity is compatible with the well-groundedness view. For Brandt, on the other hand, there is a stronger relativity: if the two incompatible desires imagined do not change under appropriate exposure to information – as it seems they might not – there is no room for the view that one may be better grounded and in a sense more rational.

From much of what has been said it will be apparent that the main variables determining rationality on the well-groundedness conception admit of degree. The belief that a kind of experience has a certain desirability characteristic may be more or less justified. How much one wants a kind of experience may result from differing intensities of one's experience of, or differing degrees of apprehension of, its desirability characteristics. Connecting beliefs, such as that *A*-ing will realize a desire, may be more or less justified. They may also be an inadequate basis for action even if justified:

if *S* justifiably believes *A*-ing will realize *S*'s desire, but should see that *B*-ing would realize it much more efficiently, *S* is overlooking a preferable and incompatible alternative, and *S*'s *A*-ing would be at best prima facie well-grounded. Thus, not only does well-groundedness admit of degrees; a desire or action may be sufficiently well-grounded to be rational, yet nowhere near maximally rational.

5. CONCLUSION

We have seen, in outline, how one may conceive rational desire and rational action on the model of justified belief; and it should be clear how the notion of well-groundedness can be extended to apply to the rationality of other propositional attitudes. It must be granted, however, that rationality cannot be precisely defined on the well-groundedness conception. This may, of course, apply to any plausible conception of rationality, as I think it does to Brandt's, for instance. On the other hand, the well-groundedness conception of rationality seems to help us in specifying the variables determining rationality, and perhaps we can do so with sufficient clarity to approach a precise comparative concept, roughly one such that for any two elements of which rationality is predicable, they are either equally rational or one is more so than the other. Being able to tell which, if either, is more rational is another matter and seems to be a problem for any plausible theory currently available. Perhaps, however, even if we do nothing to reduce the vagueness of "rational," we may still be able to say with some precision when one desire or action is more rational than another, and thus when one of these is, relative to *S*'s capacities, maximally rational: when, for example, *S* is not capable of one that is any more rational. If we can achieve this, then the well-groundedness conception can serve as a highly useful critical and descriptive tool. The conception also has the advantage (over many alternatives) of providing much of the basis of a comprehensive theory of rationality, applicable to beliefs, desires, actions, and the other items we assess in terms of rationality.

Much work is needed to develop the well-groundedness conception of rationality as a critical and descriptive tool in the theory of action and, particularly, in the social sciences. That project is impossible here, but I can point out some implications of the conception which suggest that the project is worth doing. For one thing, the well-groundedness conception of rationality is psychologically realistic, in the sense that it does not make idealized assumptions about thought or behavior nor construe rationality so that it is plausibly attributed to few if any actual desires and beliefs. Second, it connects the rationality of actions, values, and other elements, with psychological properties of persons – such as their beliefs and wants – that are of major importance for understanding human behavior in general, individual and social. Both points deserve brief comment.

The conception is psychologically realistic because (among other things) it does not make rationality something few if any persons can often achieve, or require that all rational actions or rational desires be backed by *actual* reasoning processes, such as episodes of practical reasoning, or even that all rational propositional attitudes be conscious. Often rational elements do emerge from such processes; and they may derive rationality from the relevant premises and other factors. But often rational actions are "automatic," and frequently rational desires are spontaneous. The well-groundedness conception makes this easy to understand. For neither motivational nor purposive chains need be constituted by explicitly inferential links, nor is self-consciousness or deliberation required for transmission of rationality from foundational to superstructure elements. It may be rational, for example, to do exercises because one has appropriate beliefs connecting one's exercising with a certain kind of life which one wants intrinsically and rationally, even if one has not connected exercising to that kind of life by a series of inferences, or self-consciously evaluated either the activity of exercising or the kind of life to which (however indirectly) the exercising is connected by one's instrumental beliefs.

Regarding the connection between the well-groundedness conception of rationality and the understanding of human behavior, if the conception has the psychological connections I have stressed, then rationality so conceived has explanatory power. The point is not that we can explain why certain events or states occur simply by saying that they are rational, but rather that the application of the well-groundedness conception of rationality to an action or propositional attitude entails that it *can* be explained in a certain way. For instance, if an action is rational in this sense, then there is a want-belief (intentionalistic) explanation for it; and if a desire is rational, it is explainable, at least in part, either in terms of a desire prior to it in a motivational chain or (when it is intrinsic) in terms of a well-grounded belief or an appropriate experience.

I have suggested that a maximization of expected utility conception of rationality is too narrow and that Brandt's full-information, optimality conception of rationality is superior to that view and embodies a number of ideas which any plausible conception of rationality should incorporate, including epistemic conceptions. But I have argued that his causal criterion of relevant information is inadequate and that we seem well advised not to take "rational" as an absolute term with such strong necessary conditions. The contrasting proposal I have been exploring conceives rationality as a kind of well-groundedness. The resulting view enables us to unify our concept of rational belief and, indeed, of rational propositional attitudes in general; and for all of these cases it provides a way to distinguish rationality, which requires causal grounding, from rationalizability, which requires only the availability of reasons, and to articulate a range of variables in terms of which we can develop a reasonably clear comparative concept of rationality. The view also enables us to conceive rationality in an explanatory framework that is important in the social sciences, and to provide an interpretation of historically important conceptions of rationality, such as Aristotle's and Mill's.[19] There are certainly important differences between justified beliefs and, on the other hand, rational desires and rational actions. But the parallels are important, and the epistemic conception of rationality represents a major alternative to other kinds of approach to the problem.[20]

19. I have made a case for this, referring to Aristotle's *Nicomachean Ethics* 1097a30-b21, in "Axiological Foundationalism" (Chapter 2, this volume), and with reference to Mill's *Utilitarianism,* esp. chap. 4, in "The Structure of Motivation," *Pacific Philosophical Quarterly* 61 (1980): 258–75.
20. For helpful comments on earlier versions of some of the material in this paper I want to thank William P. Alston, Richard B. Brandt, Michael Bratman, and John King-Farlow.

Chapter 14

Rationalization and rationality

We are frequently asked why we did something. In answering, we usually give a reason, or what we take to be a reason, for doing it. Sometimes we give a reason for an action of ours even without being asked for an explanation. We may, for instance, think that an explanation is needed because the deed is unconventional; or, an observer may simply look puzzled by what we do. On some occasions what we offer as an explanation is described – or dismissed – as a rationalization. One clear implication of this is that what we have said does not really explain why we did the thing in question. But why is a rationalization not regarded as explanatory? And what else is implied in calling a person's proffered explanation a rationalization? It is surely not implied that what the agent says does not exhibit the action as rational; for rationalizations are appropriately so called precisely because they do in some way exhibit the action as rational, even if only by the agent's standards. Minimally, they *represent* it as rational, in a sense we shall clarify shortly. Moreover, sometimes a rationalization succeeds in giving the action in question at least the appearance of rationality. This makes it natural to ask whether rational action can be understood as action for which a suitable rationalization can be given. That it can be so conceived is an important and plausible position to which a number of philosophers are committed, though few have expressed it in these terms.

A main task here will be to assess the view that rational action is a kind of rationalizable action. A prior issue, however, and one to which philosophers have paid too little attention, is what constitutes rationalization. That question will be my concern in sections 1 and 2. I shall begin by explicating rationalization in contrast to explanation, and then continue in sections 3 and 4 by exploring the connections between rationalization and rationality.

1. RATIONALIZATION OF ACTIONS

Many purported explanations of action fail because they are merely rationalizations, as where a person cites an altruistic reason he had for helping someone, when in fact he was motivated by selfish reasons. This sort of case is the most typical kind of rationalization. It is possible, however, to offer a rationalization of something one has done, such as adopting a new rule for one's children, with no concern to explain why one has done it; and here we might aim only at exhibiting the action as rational. One might succeed in this, and it would then be inappropriate to speak of *mere* rationalization. Moreover, the object of rationalization need not be something that actually occurs. One can rationalize a possible course of action, say a controversial strategy being considered for adoption as a policy. Such a rationalization may or may not succeed in showing that the relevant kind of action is rational. However, as in the case in which one offers a rationalization of an actual deed with no attempt to explain the deed, the success of a rationalization of a hypothetical action in establishing the rationality of the action does not depend on explaining it.

In some instances, then, rationalization would not be conceived as an unsuccessful attempt to provide an explanation. Such a failure is implicit in the most common use of the term, but it has other uses. Can this diversity of uses be explained by a univocal account of rationalization, or are there essentially different notions operating here? Philosophers have not yet fully explicated rationalization, and an account of it that answers these and other important questions is still needed.[1] My intention here is to develop an account of rationalization for actions, extend it to apply to other elements that admit of rationalization, and clarify its relation both to explanation and to rationality.

A special kind of rationalization is prominent in Freudian psychology, but the term (in the sense relevant to our inquiry) antedates Freud and has a fairly stable nontechnical use. Neither Freud's writings, nor (so far as I know) any others can be taken as a definitive source of the concept to be explicated here, though the nontechnical concept of rationalization overlaps the main Freudian

1. I have tried to fill this gap in part in "Rationalization and Justification," read at the International Congress of Philosophy in Montreal in August 1983. This in turn draws on a few paragraphs of "The Causal Structure of Indirect Justification," Chapter 7, this volume.

one, and the explication of the former may help us understand the latter. There is, to be sure, a reasonably clear stipulative use of 'rationalization' by Davidson, who proposes to call explanations of an action by appeal to the agent's reasons for it *"rationalizations,* and say that the reason *rationalizes* the action."[2] But perhaps because rationalizations of actions are normally contrasted with explanations of them, this use has not been generally adopted.[3] The best procedure to follow here, then, is to frame clear examples and formulate an account that does justice to them and is theoretically useful in action theory. Let us start with two rather different cases.

Suppose that Joe declines an invitation to comment on Sam's paper at a conference. When asked why he is declining, Joe might say that he does not have enough time to do the work. But imagine that while he is in fact short of time, his real reason for declining is that he wants to avoid exposing himself to a browbeating by Sam. His *real reason* for declining is, roughly, the reason which actually *motivated* his doing it, in a sense of 'motivated' that implies his doing it on account of that reason. Here it would seem that what Joe said in answering the question is a rationalization. Joe gave *a* reason for the action, but not his real reason for it nor, indeed, an explaining reason at all. Joe might of course have more than one real reason for doing something. He would then be motivated by, and act on account of, each real reason.

Now consider a different case, one in which a rationalization of an action is offered by someone other than the agent. Suppose that someone angrily asks why Ann voted for a certain plan. Even if one does not know why, one could, in answering, rationalize the vote by citing one or more reasons for it that Ann might have had. One might hit upon her real reason, in which case one did not *simply* rationalize the act; but such third-person rationalizing is consistent with giving the agent's real (i.e., motivating) reason. In this it is unlike first-person rationalization; it is more like defending than explaining or attempting to explain. Like defending another's action, it does not require, but is consistent with, giving a real reason of his. To be sure, we might reject as insufficient or incorrect

2. See Donald Davidson: 1963, "Actions, Reasons, and Causes," *The Journal of Philosophy* 60, 685. Perhaps one way to distinguish the notion sketched there from the one that concerns us is to note that there the *reason* rationalizes the action, whereas our concern is with agents' rationalizations.
3. In a recent treatment of reasons and causes, e.g., Andrew Oldenquist conceives rationalizations as appealing to a reason that actually does not explain why *S A*-ed. See *Normative Behavior*, Washington, D.C., 1983, esp. p. 155.

any answer to "Why did she vote for the plan?" which does not explain her action. But this would not show that answers which provide only reasons she might have had are not rationalizations, only that offering them is in a sense evasive if they fail to explain the act.

Something should also be said about explanation. As I use the term, an explanation of why *S* *A*-ed is a correct answer to the corresponding why-question, i.e., 'Why did *S* *A*?'. To explain *S*'s *A*-ing is (normally) to give such an answer (even if the question is not actually asked); and what I shall call an *explaining reason* for *S*'s *A*-ing – for example, a set of his wants and beliefs – is *what* explains (or, at least, *one* thing that explains) this action. Hence, citing the reason in answer to the relevant why-question would constitute correctly answering it. Granted, we sometimes describe people as explaining actions when they answer such questions, even if we are not implying or presupposing that their answer is correct. But perhaps this illustrates a second use of 'explain' – an attempt use. Even here, however, if the answer turns out to be wrong, we are inclined to say that the speaker just thought he had an explanation. Thus, while one might hold that explanations are simply answers to (actual or possible) why-questions, some correct and some not, I doubt that this reflects our most careful usage, and I prefer to use 'explain' without qualification only where a correct answer is implied or presupposed. This is too large a topic to pursue now, but nothing will turn on it here. The crucial point is simply that as I am using 'explain', a factor does not explain an action unless there is a real connection between it and the action, such that the action occurred because of it.[4]

Against the background of examples and points now before us, let us note the crucial features of first-person rationalizations. Most obviously, the agent, *S*, says something – often but not always in response to a request for explanation or for justification – that he regards as, or may in the context be plausibly taken to regard as, an account of the action in question (*A*). Let us say that he gives a *purported account* of it, i.e. (roughly), something he offers as constituting an explanation (or a justification) of it or as constituting a possible explanation (or possible justification) of it, or at least as constituting something that might be plausibly taken to be an ex-

4. For discussions of explanation in the relevant sense as applied to actions see, e.g., Alvin I. Goldman: 1970, *A Theory of Human Action*, Englewood Cliffs, and Raimo Tuomela: 1977, *Human Action and Its Explanation*, Dordrecht.

planation (or justification) of it. Moreover, if *S* is rationalizing (rather than, say, giving an excuse), he must give a reason (of some sort) *for A*-ing (even if not a good one), not merely a reason *why* he *A*-ed (or might have). If he merely offers a possible (or even actual) explanation in terms of something that is not a reason, such as post-hypnotic suggestion or manipulation of his brain by demonic Martians, then he does not rationalize the action. He may thereby provide an *excuse*, but not a rationalization. Some rationalizations are also excuses; but the former are not in general the latter, and excuses are not typically rationalizations.

The distinction between a rationalization and an excuse takes us to my third point: the reason(s) *S* offers must represent *A*-ing as at least prima facie rational, in the sense that they constitute at least some reason, whether selfish or unselfish, moral or nonmoral, conventional or unconventional, etc., for a person in the relevant context to *A*. Otherwise *S* could be said only to be trying to rationalize. The fourth point to be made here is negative: the reason(s) offered do not in fact explain why *S A*-ed; for none is a real reason of *S*'s i.e., one *for* which (on account of which) *S* actually *A*-ed. This does not entail that *A*-ing was performed for a reason; one can rationalize a quite unintentional action, e.g. omitting a name from a list, where this occurs because of a distraction due to noisy conversation. The point is that whatever actually explains *S*'s *A*-ing (such as a distraction), it is not part of a rationalization *S* gives of it, even if *S* should mention it in the course of setting out that rationalization. What actually explains *S*'s *A*-ing is not a rationalization of his having *A*-ed, nor a basis for such a rationalization. Thus, if one is accused of rationalizing in saying, e.g., that one skipped a meeting because one was too tired to contribute to it, one can decisively refute the claim by showing that fatigue (and not, say, indolence) explains one's absenting oneself.

The account of first-person rationalization suggested by these points is this:

I. A first-person rationalization, by *S*, of *S*'s *A*-ing, is a purported account of that *A*-ing, given by *S*, which (a) offers one or more reasons for *S*'s *A*-ing, (b) represents *S*'s *A*-ing as at least prima facie rational given the reason(s); but (c) does not explain why *S A*-ed.

This gives us an *illocutionary conception of rationalization*, since it describes a kind of linguistic act. Sometimes the content, and not the giving, of the account is referred to as a rationalization, as where S's rationalization is said to be that prior obligations prevented S's coming to the meeting. This might be called *rationalization in the propositional sense*. The former sense will be our main concern.

Since a purported account, as I conceive it, is offered as constituting an explanation or a justification, it is plausible to maintain that rationalizers must have some appropriate belief to the effect that they are giving an account (whether correct or not) of their A-ing. But the range of appropriate beliefs is large. One need not, but may, believe only that one is giving a possible explanation (or possible reasons for) one's A-ing. Perhaps, indeed, it is enough that one believes oneself to be answering a relevant kind of query, e.g. "Why did you A?" or "Do you really think your A-ing was reasonable?"[5]

Other-person (i.e., second- and third-person) rationalizations, as conceived here, are different in not necessarily failing to explain why S A-ed. But the most common ones, I believe, are those that are not also explanations, and there is some plausibility in saying that those which do explain are only prima facie rationalizations. In any event, let us ask whether other-person rationalizations which are not explanatory must appeal only to reasons S *had* for A-ing, but *for which S* did not A. Consider some examples. An example of such a reason would be a proposition S believed which makes S's A-ing prima facie rational in the sense that if one *believes* the proposition – say, that A-ing will bring one great pleasure – it is prima facie rational to A. Similarly, something I want may be a prima facie reason for my A-ing, in the sense that if I want it (say, want to get food), and A-ing will obviously realize it, then it is prima facie rational for me to A. There may be other sorts of reasons one can have to A, but the most important kind seem to be these sorts, involving suitable beliefs or wants one has or, typically, sets of related beliefs and wants, e.g. wanting food and believing one's A-ing will get it. In any case, it seems clear that an other-person rationalization *need* not appeal to a reason S actually had for A-ing, but may appeal simply to a reason for A-ing. One might rationalize Ann's voting for a plan by citing a great virtue of it even if she did not believe it had that virtue. Such a rationalization is in a sense

5. Here I disagree with Oldenquist's view that when S rationalizes he mistakenly believes, of the (non-explaining) reason he gives as his reason, that it is his real reason for the act. See *op. cit.*, pp. 155–156. S may or may not believe this.

refutable by the point that she did not believe this, but even then it can serve to show that A-ing was *a* rational thing to do in the circumstances. Thus, I do not think that other-person rationalizations *should* be construed as refutable by such a consideration, though no doubt they typically do appeal to reasons S had for A-ing (or at least reasons the speaker thinks S had).

We might now ask the counterpart question regarding first-person rationalizations. Must a rationalization, by me, for my A-ing, appeal only to reasons I had for A-ing, or can it appeal only to reasons *for* my A-ing (i.e., for me to A) which are not reasons I had? Consider again Joe's declining the invitation, rationalized by his saying he does not have much time to do the work. Would this not still be a rationalization even if Joe knew he did not have enough time? It would still exhibit the act as prima facie rational given the reason cited and would still contrast with explanation and with giving one's real reason. These points seem sufficient to warrant conceiving it as a rationalization, though doubtless in the typical cases the agent appeals to reasons he had.

It turns out, then, that we must distinguish *rationalization by appeal to alleged reasons* from *rationalizations by appeal to reasons one had*. The latter are the typical cases, but the former are not uncommon. The former are often *deceitful rationalizations*, since in many such cases S knows or believes that the reason(s) S appeals to were not reasons S had at the time. Deceit need not be involved, however: I might mistakenly think that I had the relevant reasons(s), e.g. believed a proposition that was a reason for me to A, or that I wanted something and thereby had a reason. This could result simply from a failure of memory, in which case I am giving an *unintentional rationalization*, but might also be associated with self-deception.[6] Such *self-deceptive rationalizations* are apparently an important and common kind. Note, too, that a rationalization (first- or other-person) might appeal to some reasons I had and to some I did not have. These we might call *heterogeneous rationalizations*.

One further problem must be addressed before we explore rationalization in a wider context. What are we to say where S gives a reason S had for A-ing such that S A-ed in part for that reason, but that reason is not a main reason for which S acted, or sufficient to enable us adequately to explain S's A-ing by appeal to it? Imagine

6. For an account of self-deception with an indication of how it may embody unconscious beliefs, see my "Self-Deception, Action, and Will," *Erkenntnis* 18, 1982.

that Jan stops in Baltimore on her way from Washington to New York, her main reason being to see Joe. Still, she might want Baltimore seafood, and this might be a minor reason for which she stops. Assume that although one could not explain her stopping in Baltimore as done in order to eat the seafood, whereas one could explain it as done in order to see Joe, the former desire is *part* of what motivates her going, i.e., expresses a reason she has such that she does the thing in question in part for that reason, and her doing it is partially explainable by appeal to the reason. This implies such things as the following: that if she had a conflicting desire as strong as her desire to see Joe, her wanting to eat Baltimore seafood would normally cause, and could be used to explain, why she stopped in Baltimore instead of doing what would fulfill the conflicting desire. Now if asked by a friend suspicious about her relation to Joe, why she stopped in Baltimore, Jan answered, "I wanted Baltimore seafood," would this be rationalization? Surely, there is a substantial element of rationalization in her answer, and her purported account is not (unqualifiedly) explanatory: she cites what I would call a merely supporting reason, not an (adequately) explanatory reason. The most reasonable view to take here seems to be to call such cases *partial rationalizations,* to be contrasted with pure rationalizations, or rationalizations simpliciter.

It is not easy to characterize partial rationalizations. We cannot say that they are purported accounts which adduce only merely supporting reasons. For a sufficient number of such reasons may, taken together, quite adequately explain S's A-ing. I might have a dozen minor reasons to make a trip, none sufficient, none expressing necessary conditions, but all taken together providing sufficient reason for, and explanation of, my going. Thus, if I appeal to such a set of reasons, I am not rationalizing, though I may still be deceitful, since I may omit one or more main reasons for which I A-ed. If we call this sort of explanation rationalization, however, we should presumably have to say the same where I give just *one* of two or more main reasons, each of which is fully sufficient to explain my A-ing. This point, in turn, shows that we may not conceive partial rationalizations as purported accounts which appeal to one or more reasons that are only part of what explains (part of the reason why) S A's. For where there is genuine overdetermination, e.g. where two independent motivating reasons are each operative in producing, and sufficient to explain, S's A-ing, each may be only *part of what explains* the action, though not merely a *partial explainer* of it.

The notion we need, I suggest, is that of a purported account which is only partly a rationalization because it is partially explanatory. We might call it partial rationalization, where

II. A *partial rationalization,* by S, of S's A-ing, is a purported account, by S, of that A-ing, which appeals to one or more reasons such that this set of reasons is only a partial explainer of S's A-ing, i.e., is sufficient by itself to explain the action only in part.[7]

To be sure, if I cite a number of reasons which together are almost sufficient to explain my A-ing, we may be inclined to speak of a virtual explanation with an element (perhaps a large element) of rationalization, rather than a partial rationalization. But for convenience we may still use 'partial rationalization' as just characterized, and simply note that such rationalizations range from explanatorily minimal accounts to virtual explanations. At one end of the continuum are cases where S cites only one motivating reason, and that so weak as to have had virtually no influence on the act; at the other are cases where S cites almost enough in the way of motivating reason to explain the act. Note also that a partial rationalization is partially explanatory, not necessarily only partially successful *as* a rationalization. A *partially successful rationalization,* then, may or may not be a partial rationalization.

2. GENERALIZATION OF THE ACCOUNT

Three ideas are central to the conception of rationalization offered in section 1. (1) Rationalizations are purported accounts; (2) they appeal to one or more reasons; and (3) they do not give S's real reason for the action in question, or at least do not give a set of reasons which, as a whole, adequately explains why S A-ed. Now points that are clearly analogous apply to other things besides actions. For instance, beliefs are also such that we try to account

7. In speaking of a factor as sufficient to explain an action I do not mean to imply that it is by itself sufficient for the occurrence of the action. The idea is roughly that, taken together with contextually implicit information, the factor makes clear why the event in question occurred.

for them, to give reasons for them, and to explain why we hold them. Moreover, we may be as motivated to hide (from ourselves or others) why we believe what we do as to hide why we do certain things we do. If all this is so, our account of rationalization should be generalizable to beliefs and other items to which analogues of the three ideas apply, and we should expect the term 'rationalize' also to apply nonmetaphorically in these other cases.

This is, I think, what we do find. Consider first the case of belief. Suppose Sam says he believes that Ann would not be a good person for a certain job. If asked to elaborate, he might say that her training is only indirectly relevant and she will not easily fit in with the existing staff. Imagine, however, that either he does not believe these things, or he believes them and is not (cognitively) motivated by them, i.e., roughly, they are no part of what explains why he in fact believes she is not good for the job (and hence are not reasons *for* which he believes this – his real reasons for believing it). Suppose further that what does explain why he believes she is not good for the job is that he thinks such an attractive young woman may "get involved" with one of the two unattached young men. Might we not say Sam is rationalizing here, rather than explaining his belief? Indeed, might he not later call this a rationalization himself if he realizes what his real reason was and that excluding Ann for that reason is unfair? Even if 'rationalization' is not commonly applied in this way to belief, the relevant use is not deviant, and it is theoretically fruitful to contrast rationalization with explanation in the domain of belief as well as in that of behavior.

There is indeed a strong connection between the two sorts of rationalization. At least typically, where I rationalize (or am even disposed to rationalize) an action of mine, *A*, I am disposed to rationalize my belief (if I hold it) that my *A*-ing was warranted (appropriate, in order, permissible, or the like). If I do not hold the belief (say, where I am merely disposed to rationalize an un-intentional action but have not thought much about the action), I may be disposed to form such a belief on considering the matter. But I need not be so disposed, since I may take it as obvious that the action is inexcusably wrong and requires (say) rectification. Even here, however, the disposition to rationalize an action seems to imply a disposition to rationalize some related belief, e.g. that one's doing the thing in question is excusable (or can be made to look excusable) given certain reasons one had for it. Moreover, it appears that rationalizations of beliefs, or dispositions to rationalize

414

them, are also associated with dispositions to give rationalizations of certain actions. If, for example, Sam rationalizes his belief about Ann, we would expect him to be disposed to rationalize certain acts appropriate to it, notably those it motivates, such as not hiring her. It turns out, I believe, that rationalizations and dispositions to frame them are not isolated elements in human psychology. They play a systematic part in both thought and action, and they seem intimately tied to a person's self-image.

Pursuing the analogy we have been drawing, we might characterize first-person rationalization of a belief as follows:

III. A first-person rationalization, by *S*, of *S*'s belief that *p*, is a purported account of this belief, given by *S*, which (a) offers one or more reasons for *S*'s belief that *p*, (b) represents the belief as prima facie rational given the reason(s); but (c) does not explain why *S* believes *p*.

Instances of this might be called *belief rationalizations*. The other-person cases of such rationalizations may also be characterized on analogy with that of other-person rationalization of action.

There are, to be sure, some disanalogies between rationalizations of actions and rationalizations of beliefs: most obviously, actions are events, and beliefs are not. But this poses no significant problem here. One might object that it is significant that unlike many actions, few if any beliefs are under direct voluntary control. It is arguable, e.g., that normally few if any propositions are believable at will. I grant that this point is plausible; but it is easy to underestimate the degree of a person's control over his beliefs, and in any event the disanalogy is not crucial. Note that *by* doing things we may bring about our believing certain propositions, rather as *by* doing things we may bring about our doing certain others. There are, moreover, some things we can do only by doing others (whether those others are our means of doing them or, so to speak, our *way* of doing them). Thus, some acts are like at least some beliefs in being only indirectly under voluntary control. But we need not pursue this complicated issue further; for rationalization surely does not depend on voluntariness in any case. If Tom wants to downplay his occasional involuntary hemming, he may, when asked whether he has a cold, say that he was about to speak and wanted to clear his throat.

If we again reflect on the three elements of rationalization I have been stressing, and if we think of rationalization, generically, as an attempt, or at least what appears to be an attempt, to exhibit something as rational, we should expect to be able to generalize further. I think we may. Surely one can rationalize in answering "Why do you want that?" Similarly, one might offer a rationalization of one's valuing something, intending it, fearing it, or having a pro attitude toward it. It appears that all the propositional attitudes admit of rationalization. This is what one would expect given, e.g., that we apply to them, as we do to actions, the distinction between reasons one merely has for them and one's real (explaining) reasons for them. The general case for propositional attitudes may be described thus:

IV. A first-person rationalization, by S, of a propositional attitude of S's, ϕ, is a purported account of S's ϕ-ing, given by S, which (a) offers one or more reasons for ϕ-ing, (b) represents S's ϕ-ing as prima facie rational given the reason(s), but (c) does not explain why S ϕ's.[8]

Clearly, we should distinguish partial from full rationalizations here as in the case of rationalizations of actions. The other main distinctions made above will also apply to these further cases. We may, on the other hand, find some significant differences among the rationalizations appropriate to different propositional attitudes. There is no need to pursue all that here. What I now want to do is explore the relation between rationalization and rationality, taking actions as our central case.

3. RATIONALIZABILITY AND RATIONALITY

We have seen how rationalizations may be generically conceived as attempts to exhibit something as rational. I now want to ascertain

8. In discussing rationalization I have been assuming that, by and large, our actions are explainable by *some* reason(s) of ours and that something similar holds for a great many propositional attitudes, including all "inferential" beliefs. But suppose it turned out that our reasons are never explanatory, and only physical states of the body unconnected with reasons explain our behavior and cognition. At least two responses seem plausible: (1) that then, despite appearances, there would *be* no (intentional) actions and no inferential beliefs; and (2) that, despite appearances, even when we give what we now would on careful investigation call our real reason, it is not a real, explaining, reason and we are therefore rationalizing. These are strange possibilities indeed, but so is the possibility that suggests them (that possibility was called to my attention by an example of Albert Casullo's).

the sense in which they may succeed in this. Consider a case in which a kind of success is apparently achieved. Ted is a teacher. He likes his student, Lynn, and finds her term paper enjoyable reading. Because of these two facts he gives the paper a good grade (B). Now imagine that Ted's assistant, Sue, also reads the paper and on the basis of its content concludes that it deserves a C. She asks Ted why he gave it a B, whereupon he rereads it and then tells her that it has some extremely instructive examples. Now let us suppose that it does have such examples, and that its having them (given minimal adequacy in other respects) is a good reason to give it a B; but suppose further that Ted is rationalizing, having given the B prior to noticing this about the examples and entirely because he likes Lynn and (for nonacademic reasons) enjoyed the paper. Our question is whether, in virtue of the rationalization, or the reason to which it appeals, Ted's giving Lynn a B is rational.

A quite plausible answer is that since the rationalization indicates a good reason for Ted's giving the B, it shows that his doing so is rational. But I believe that to say this without qualification is a serious mistake. We must surely distinguish two different sorts of things that may be rational: types, such as the action-type, or kind of action, giving Lynn's paper a B; and tokens, such as the action-token, or particular action, Ted's particular giving of a B to this paper.[9] One way to put the difference is to distinguish between the point that giving the paper a B is a rational thing to do in the circumstances and the point that Ted rationally gives a B in the circumstances.

A similar distinction applies to explanation. It is one thing to explain a particular action (token), say Ted's giving Lynn's paper a B. It is quite another to explain the action-type, the giving of a B to the paper, if (as I am assuming) we may speak of explaining types at all. Clearly rationalizations do not explain action-tokens (at least not more than partially), but there seems to be a sense in which a rationalization may – provided it offers good reason for the relevant type of action – explain that type. For such rationalizations explain why a type is an appropriate kind of thing to do

9. I here construe action-types as properties and action-tokens as particulars, but our purposes do not require specifying whether they are concrete particulars or something (apparently) more abstract, such as whatever is designated by phrases like "Joe's instantiating at nine o'clock the property of giving Ann's paper a B." Nor is the terminology of types and tokens essential for my purposes: we could speak of specifications (by an agent at a time) and kinds of actions, unrestricted as to agent and time.

in the circumstances, and they may certainly render it intelligible in the circumstances. The difference is very much like that between explaining why an action occurred and simply exhibiting it as appropriate. The first kind of explanation is directed toward something in the world and is empirical; the second is more like explication and seems nonempirical.

One might object that even a particular action can be shown to be rational by a rationalization where the rationalization cites a reason which is not only a good reason for the action, but one the agent actually *had* at the time. Thus, it might be claimed that if Ted had noticed how instructive Lynn's examples were before giving the B, then even if this was not part of his reason for actually giving it, his giving it was rational. (It may be hard to imagine his believing this of the examples and yet giving the B entirely because he likes her and finds the paper enjoyable reading; but this is surely possible, particularly if the examples come early in the paper and do not stand out in his mind when he finally scribbles the grade at the end.) After all, since he gives a grade rational in the light of one of his own reasons for it, surely he rationally gives it.

I believe this reasoning is invalid. Notice that here 'one of his own reasons for it' refers not to a reason for which he actually gave the grade but to a reason he merely had for giving it. Moreover, 'rational in the light of one of his own reasons for it' can apply to the type of action in question, whereas our question concerns the token. To see that its reference in the imagined context is the type, notice that Ted's actual giving of the grade is reprehensible, being primarily an expression of irrelevant reasons: his liking Lynn and finding the paper enjoyable reading. Moreover, assuming that Ted's beliefs about appropriate grading are more or less normal (which is perfectly consistent with the case), his giving the B is reprehensible from the point of view of rationality, not just morally wrong. But if it were rational, this would not be so.

One might reply that what is reprehensible is not the action, but Ted's performing it for those reasons. This is plausible if it is taken to mean (roughly): the type is not reprehensible, only the token is, when it occurs for those reasons. But it might be claimed that there is a further token, of the type, *A*-ing for reason *r*, and that it is only a token of this type, namely, giving a B for the reason that one likes the student and finds the paper enjoyable reading, that is not rational. Supposing that there are such tokens and that they are not rational, I do not think they are *action*-tokens. Surely the relevant description designates *both* an action and an explaining reason for the action.

More important, even if we do construe 'giving a B for the reason that one likes the student and finds the paper enjoyable reading' as designating an action-token, such phrases could designate types, and we could then distinguish rational from nonrational tokenings. On one occasion, *S* could instantiate the type, *A*-ing for *r*, say, giving a B for B-level work, and his reason could be to grade professionally. On another occasion, he could instantiate *A*-ing for *r'*, say, giving a B for aesthetic qualities, and his reason could be to treat a beautiful girl by standards of beauty. In this second case, it certainly appears that the relevant token fails to be rational because *S*'s motivating reason for it is a bad one. At best, then, the imagined move just pushes the problem back one level, even if we grant that there are actions of the form of '*A*-ing for *r*'. Let me suggest, however, some further reasons why we should not consider Ted's particular grading to be rational.

First, consider the plausible principle that where one is acting rationally, in the sense of doing something such that one's doing it at least meets minimum standards of rationality, one is not acting for bad reasons, e.g. reasons in the light of which the action in question is not even prima facie rational. Now a (pure) rationalization does not appeal to any reasons for which one acts, and even where one *has* good reasons it does not rule out that one acts entirely for bad ones. How, then, can it show that one acts rationally (or be the basis of the rationality of an action)? I shall not attempt to say what in general constitutes a good or bad reason; that is an important question, but for our purposes the examples given adequately suggest the sort of thing meant by 'bad reason' (another important case is that in which one acts on a belief which would, if true, render the action rational, but is obviously false and should be seen by the agent to be irrational for him to hold).

The view that actions performed (wholly) for bad reasons are not rational is supported by a further point. Typically, where *S A*'s for a bad reason, yet *A* turns out to be a rational kind of thing to do, it is merely good fortune that *S* did not instead do something which is not a rational kind of thing to do. Recall Ted: Since all that motivates his giving Lynn a B is his liking her and finding her paper enjoyable reading, presumably he would (other things being equal) have given her a B even if he had not noticed her instructive examples, or there had been none. It is fortunate that he did notice

419

them, for he can then cite them to rationalize his action. But nothing in the nature of rationalization rules out its being just good fortune that *S* did not do something that, in the circumstances, would be an irrational kind of thing to do, say giving the paper a D. This is not so for actions rational in the light of one or more reasons *for* which they are performed. Since they are brought about (or sustained) by a good reason,[10] it is to be expected that they instantiate a type rational in the circumstances. They are, after all, produced or sustained by something in virtue of which they are rational kinds of things to do in those circumstances.

One might object that the above points bear on the assessment of the rationality of the agent, not that of the action. Thus, if Ted acts for a bad reason, he deserves criticism for letting himself so act; but if he has, and realizes he has, good reasons for the action, *it* may be rational. I agree that he deserves criticism. But why must we stop there? Indeed, once we distinguish the assessment of types from that of tokens, the plausibility of this move, as applied to tokens, is greatly reduced. For while the type may be rational for Ted given his good reasons, the token in question is actually based on *other* reasons and does not arise from – but only by good fortune matches – the good reasons. Why, then, should we say that the good reasons make the action-token rational? Indeed, because of the reasons why he is actually doing the deed, it manifests his failure to get his behavior under the control of the reasons he acknowledges as good. This seems an additional ground for not calling the token rational. There is no doubt that agents like those we are imagining here are criticizable *as* agents; but it seems wrong to stop there and allow their rationalizable actions performed for bad reasons to pass as rational.

One further point should be mentioned. It is often held that intentional actions arise from *practical reasoning.*[11] Even if this is not

---

10. Sometimes 'reason' is used to refer to propositional attitudes, most notably wants and beliefs; and sometimes it is used to refer to their contents. The former are the causal factors referred to here, and sustaining is mentioned to cover cases in which a factor that plays the crucial role with respect to an action does not bring it about but, e.g., begins to operate in the appropriate way after the action (or activity) starts. Since an action extended over time can be sustained by an appropriate reason at one time and not another, the rationality of tokens is, strictly speaking, relative to time. For our purposes, however, temporal variables may be left implicit.
11. See, e.g., Donald Davidson: 1969, "How Is Weakness of the Will Possible?" in Joel Feinberg (ed.), *Moral Concepts,* London and New York, p. 110; and

true without exception, clearly for every intentional action there is a corresponding practical argument. In such an argument the major premise expresses the agent's motivation, and the minor expresses his belief(s) connecting the action with this motivation (such as a belief that the action in question would fulfill the motivating want). Now a very natural view about rational actions is that either they arise from sound practical reasoning or, at least taken together with what actually motivates them and with the beliefs guiding them, they instantiate a good practical argument, roughly, one whose premises provide good reason for its conclusion. Thus, giving a B to reflect the quality of the paper might arise from or at least correspond to

(i) I want, in my grading, to reflect the actual quality of papers submitted;
(ii) Giving this a B would reflect its actual quality; hence
(iii) I should give it a B,

whereas giving a B for the bad reasons imagined would arise from or at least correspond to something like this:

(a) I want to give good paper grades to students I like whose papers are (for nonacademic reasons) enjoyable reading;
(b) Giving this paper a B would accomplish that; hence
(c) I should give this paper a B.

The second argument is quite arguably not good, for it contains an unreasonable premise, one expressing a want which a rational, appropriately informed person would not have or approve of; and, more importantly, the goal it expresses is neither rational nor such as to render the action in question rational. But as we have seen, a rationalization does not rule out that a practical argument of this sort is what actually underlies the action. This is surely a good reason to conclude that a rationalization does not show the action to be rational. One could object that the relevant practical argument is the one corresponding to the reason(s) given in the rationalization. But this, I believe, conflates the rationality of types with that of tokens. What makes it plausible, I suspect, is that because the rationalizing reasons are available to S to use in arguing that his A-ing was rational, and they yield a good argument, it seems

Gilbert Harman: 1978, "Practical Reasoning," *Review of Metaphysics* 29, 441, 451.

natural to conclude that he rationally *A*-ed. But if I have been right, such arguments support the rationality only of the type of thing he did, not of his doing it.

A related problem should be considered here. Suppose that although Ted's reason for giving Lynn a B was as specified, he had a standing *policy* of not giving a grade different from the one deserved. Then, it might be argued, he does rationally give the B, nor is it just good fortune that his action is of a kind rational in the circumstances. This is an intriguing objection. It raises the question whether one can *A* simply for reason *r*, even though one has a policy that precludes *A*-ing unless *r'* also holds. That is possible, I think, provided one is speaking of merely *having* the policy. But surely if the policy is to prevent *S*'s *A*-ing from being nonrational, he must be *observing* the policy as he *A*'s. In that case, however, it seems to figure among his reasons, even if only as an unarticulated background one. If Ted is observing such a policy when he gives the B, his motivating reason is something like this: given that she has earned a B, to give it because I like her and found the paper enjoyable. What we have here is a *complex reason*. Ted's attention may be focused on the latter part of the reason; e.g., it may be what he thinks of most in giving the B. It may also be what provides most of his motivation for giving it. Moreover, he may also have a *complex of reasons:* roughly, two or more operating together. Here the policy reason is separate but still serves as a main reason for which he acts. In both cases he would not have given the grade (other things being equal) had he not thought it deserved; and thus, in both cases, this policy consideration is a main reason for which he gives it, or an essential part of his main reason.[12] The point is not that his policy reason in particular must be necessary for the action if the action is to be rational (though surely some good reason must be), but only that a background reason may be necessary and may thereby render rational an action for which the *precipitating reason* is not good.

It is arguable, moreover, that a reason in the light of which an action (token) is rational must, in the context, be sufficient to explain it. (I leave open whether this requires that it be more than a

---

12. It is not easy to distinguish between *S*'s *A*-ing for a conjunction of reasons, say for *r* and for *r'*, and on the other hand acting on the corresponding conjunctive reason, here *r* and *r'*. A reason constituting a necessary condition will either be a single main reason or a part of a conjunctive one which, without it, would not be sufficient to explain the action.

probabilistic sufficient condition.) Consider another example. If Ted's policy reason is not sufficient to explain his giving the B, then a rationalization which cites it does not clearly show that Ted gave the B rationally; for even if he would not have given it if he thought it undeserved, he might have thought it deserved and not given it. (He might have passed the paper on to someone else to grade.) His sense of desert plays too small a role in his action; and while it may not be just good fortune that he did not give a different grade, it may yet be just good fortune that he gave the right one (or one he thought deserved). For if he had not had the relevant subjective feelings, his sense of desert could well have been insufficient to get him to give any grade.

Granted, such an action would be not as far from being rational here as where the rationalizing reason is not even necessary for the relevant action. But it seems most reasonable overall to conceive rational actions as not only such that they would not have occurred without good motivating reason, but such that they are performed *for* one or more good reasons. If one should prefer the weaker conception, one could simply provide for the relevant exception in stating one's thesis about the connection between rationalization and rationality. For example, one might say that while a rationalization of an action (token) even in terms of a good reason the agent had, and even in terms of a reason necessary for the action does not entail that the action is fully rational, it does imply that it is minimally rational. My main point is simply that no degree of rationality of the token is implied by its rationalizability by appeal to good but nonexplaining reasons for it on the part of the agent. Whether good reason must be sufficient as well as necessary is a less important issue.

It should be plain that the points emerging in this section are generalizable to the propositional attitudes. For tokens of those, as for action tokens, we could put the main negative part of our general thesis thus: *rationalizability does not entail rationality*. The sorts of arguments used to show this for actions also apply to beliefs, desires, values, and the other propositional attitudes. Let me stress, however, that I have argued for the negation of an entailment, not the entailment of a negation. A rationalizable action may perfectly well be rational, and so for beliefs and other propositional attitudes. For sometimes an action (or belief) which one performs (or holds) *for* one good reason is both rational on the basis of that and rationalizable in the light of other reasons one had for it, which were not reasons for which one acted (or believed). It is even more common for there simply to *be* reasons for a rational action or rational belief in virtue of which, though they are not reasons S has, it can be rationalized.

It should also be stressed that the distinction between types and tokens is relevant not just to determining what a rationalization of a token shows, but also to understanding rationalization itself. Recall our example of rationalizing a policy being considered for adoption. Since the policy may never be adopted, there need be no token here to assess as rational or not rational. Surely, then, we may speak of rationalizations of types, as well as of rationalizations of tokens. Once we distinguish these, it is easier to see why it is so tempting to take rationalizations of tokens, by appeal to good reasons, as showing the rationality of the relevant action; for they contain the materials for successfully rationalizing the relevant type, i.e., showing that *it* is rational. But as I have argued, reasons one has that make *A*-ing (say, giving a B) rational, do not necessarily show that if one *A*'s, one does so rationally.

Parallel points apply to the propositional attitudes. For instance, we can distinguish between rationalizing S's belief that *p* (a belief token) and rationalizing *the belief* that *p* (a belief type). The latter might be illustrated by anthropologists' rationalizing a strange belief attributed to a culture whose reasons for the belief they do not know, where they are simply trying to rebut the prejudice that the culture has irrational beliefs. (The case makes sense even if it turns out that no one holds just the belief in question.) We have, then, not only *behavioral rationalizations,* directed to actions, *cognitive rationalizations,* directed to beliefs, and *conative rationalizations,* directed to wants, but a distinction cutting across all these kinds. Thus, we might say that, roughly speaking,

> V. *A type-specific (behavioral) rationalization* is an attempt to represent an action-type as rational, as justifiable, or as appropriate, by citing one or more reasons in favor of it.

For beliefs we might say that, roughly speaking,

> VI. *A type-specific (cognitive) rationalization* is an attempt to represent a belief-type as rational, or as justifiable, or as appropriate, by citing one or more reasons in favor of it.

One can, of course, rationalize a proposition, for example a premise in an argument by an imagined objector, quite independently of thinking that someone might actually believe it. Here we may speak of *propositional rationalization,* which can be characterized by putting 'proposition' for 'belief-type' in VI. Quite parallel points hold for the other propositional attitudes, and they need not be discussed separately.

4. RATIONAL ACTION

A central thesis argued so far is that the rationality of particular actions must not be assimilated to their rationalizability. Indeed, neither entails the other. No attempt has been made to provide an overall account of rational action, nor can such an account be given here. But our results do point to one major condition which a correct account must meet; it must require that rational actions be performed for appropriate reasons, not merely rationalizable in terms of such reasons. Broadly speaking, this is a causal condition. Its importance has often been overlooked, and even writers who have recognized it have not (so far as I know) adequately brought out why it is important or how it is connected with the distinction between types and tokens.[13]

It is clear that the classical maximization of expected utility conception of rational action (as well as most sophistications of it) does not incorporate a causal condition of the appropriate sort. For the heart of such conceptions is simply some requirement to the effect that the action in question be appropriate to the content of the agent's motivation and beliefs. (Different theories provide different ways of selecting the relevant motivation and beliefs.) As a recent

13. Carl G. Hempel, e.g., argues that a rational action must not only be appropriate in the light of the content of the explaining factors, but also explainable as motivated by them. See his "Rational Action," *Proceedings and Addresses of the American Philosophical Association* 35, 1962. He imposes the latter condition, however, because he regards the concept of rational action as explanatory. He does not, so far as I can see, explicitly distinguish the rationality of tokens from that of types (relative to persons and situations). Richard B. Brandt also seems to impose a causal requirement on rational action, e.g. when he says that "an action is 'rational' in the sense of fully rational only if the desires and aversions *involved in* the action are rational." See *A Theory of the Good and the Right,* Oxford, 1979, p. 11 (emphasis mine). He does not, however, argue for this causal requirement against the non-causalist view of rationality I have been criticizing.

article puts it, "Predicating rationality of an act says that an appropriateness relation holds between the events that constitute the agent's act on the one hand and, on the other, his reasons for acting and related beliefs and his sensory information about the acting situation . . . ,"[14] where an act is appropriate to a set of such things "*if and only if it conserves what is important in it.*"[15] We need not analyze this; my point is only that this view imposes no causal requirement. Let me add, however, that I find the view plausible as applied to action-types in relation to S, i.e., to the notion of a type, A, *being rational for* S in a situation. There are other current views of rational action, apparently intended to apply to particular actions, that are similar in imposing no causal requirement.[16]

Given my emphasis on actions being rational relative to reasons, one might protest that the very concept of rational action is relative; actions are never rational simpliciter, but only relative to reasons. If so, one might then simply argue that a token performed for a bad reason is not rational relative to that reason but is rational relative to the good reason S had for it which he might use to rationalize it. Now it may be that rational actions are always rational *in virtue of* reasons of the agent (though this is by no means self-evident, since, for one thing, it is arguable that things done for their own sake, such as humming a melody, may be rational though

14. See Graeme Marshall: 1981, "Action on the Rationality Principle," *Australasian Journal of Philosophy* 59, 58–59. The example given on p. 59 confirms that the relevant notion of appropriateness does not embody a causal requirement.

15. Ibid., p. 59. The notion of importance used here is relative to persons and in a sense subjective. My use of the related notion of a good reason leaves open whether, as I am inclined to think, an objective account of good reasons can be given: one based essentially on intersubjective criteria of rationality.

16. See, e.g., Don Locke: 1982, "Beliefs, Desires and Reasons for Actions," *American Philosophical Quarterly* 19, 244–245. Locke does speak as if reasons in virtue of which an action is rational must be explanatory, but the relevant notion of explanation seems noncausal (and non-nomic). See also Martin Hollis: 1979, "Rational Man and Social Science," in Ross Harrison (ed.), *Rational Action*, Cambridge, esp. pp. 10–14. The notion Hollis explicitly characterizes is expressed by "*S* acts rationally in doing *a*," but what he says seems more appropriate to (and often insightful as applied to) *S*'s *A*-ing being rational for *S* (in the relevant circumstances). Hollis's wording on p. 14 suggests a causal condition, but he repeatedly stops short of saying anything that commits him to one. Sometimes, on the other hand, locutions I conceive as in some sense causal are used as if they were not. Peter Alexander, e.g., says: "A piece of behavior was rational if it was done *for* reasons which constitute a sufficient reason, *that is,* if it was likely to achieve what was intended and unlikely to lead to other consequences whose undesirability outweighs the desirability of what it was intended to achieve." See "Rational Behaviour and Psychoanalytic Explanation," *Mind* 71, 1962 (emphasis mine).

they are not performed for a reason). But this does not entail that rationality is intrinsically relational in the way just sketched. It may *supervene* on other properties without being a relation of the indicated sort between actions (or other elements) and those properties. Even if the objection were correct, however, I would argue that the relation crucial for rationality of tokens is their relation to the reasons that actuate them, not to the reasons available to rationalize them. For this thesis, variants of the arguments already given can be used. Thus, the objection threatens at most to complicate, rather than refute, my case for distinguishing rationality from rationalizability.

What our results in section 3 imply is that an account of rational action should contain a causal condition in virtue of which the action can be seen to have an appropriate basis. More specifically, I have suggested that a rational action is rational in virtue of a reason only if it is performed at least in part for that reason, where, in addition, appeal to that reason is sufficient (in the context) to explain why S did the thing in question. If this is so, then a fully developed account of rational action will incorporate some account of acting for a reason. Providing the latter account is itself a difficult task; but I do not see how we can fully understand rational action without such an account, and in any case acting for a reason is a central notion in action theory and has considerable independent interest.

There is also an epistemological problem raised by the results of this paper. If acting rationally implies acting for an adequate reason, then contrary to what has been very widely supposed, to know that S acted rationally it is not sufficient to know that in the circumstances S had (or even knew S had) adequate reasons for it. That would at most enable one to show that the action was a rational type for S to perform, but not that S rationally performed it. Granted, one need not know just *why* S did the deed to know S acted rationally; for one might know that S acted for one of several good reasons, yet not know which. But (unless there are kinds of actions that can be rational even when not performed for any reason), one must know S acted for a reason. The same applies in one's own case, of course.

This conclusion complicates our assessments of rational action by comparison with what they would be if the rationality of an action were simply a matter of whether S has (and believes S has) good reasons for it. But this conclusion should not be unwelcome.

Surely, we often find that an assessment of an action turns on the sort of reason that explains it. This is common with moral assessments. In moral contexts it is often crucial to distinguish between simply acting as morality requires and so acting *for* moral reasons. An agent who does the thing morality requires, but for purely selfish reasons, deserves no moral credit. Why should a person doing the rational thing in the circumstances, but purely for bad reasons, deserve any rational credit? Just as the former behavior does not count toward, and tends to count against, being a moral person, the latter behavior does not count for, and tends to count against, being a rational person. One could contend that the rationality of an agent's actions need not count toward that of the agent, though the reasons for which the agent acts do. But this is not plausible for action-tokens. Performing rational actions is surely a main indication of being rational.

Associated with this analogy between moral and rational actions are two different sorts of ideals. According to one kind, the *behavioral ideal*, a truly moral person always performs or tries to perform the type of action morality requires in his circumstances, such as rendering aid and paying one's debts; and the truly rational person always does or tries to do the type of thing rationality requires in his circumstances (including his reasons), paradigmatically, maximizing expected utility. The other kind of ideal is more demanding; it is an *integrated ideal* which requires that moral agents do or try to do what is moral, that rational agents do or try to do what is rational, and that in both cases they do or try to do so for the right reasons. Roughly, such agents aim at an appropriate integration of the reasons for which they act in a given way, with reasons there *are* to act in that way. A person pursuing only the behavioral ideal, by contrast, is simply aiming at producing – by whatever means are best – the actions rationality and morality require.

One might think that the second ideal is utopian, since we can only try to perform actions and we have no control over the reasons for which we do them. But that is clearly not true. Suppose for the sake of argument that where we have two powerful reasons for *A*-ing, one selfish and one not, which of them we act on (if either alone), cannot be under our direct voluntary control. We can still, over time, profoundly affect our tending to act on one or another sort of reason. We can, for instance, put some things out of mind, or subject them to intense scrutiny. We can expose ourselves to good influences. We can wait until certain passions subside before acting. And there are other strategies.

The more rigorous ideal is by no means utopian. Indeed, it may well be that pursuit of this ideal is more likely to enable one to fulfill the behavioral ideal than direct pursuit of that ideal. Just as, relative to our capacities, we are more likely to believe a maximal number of significant truths and a minimal number of falsehoods if we seek not merely to believe truths but also to believe truths on good grounds and not otherwise, so we are likely to succeed best in performing rational actions if we try, not just to perform certain types of actions, but to act for adequate reasons. Something like the more rigorous ideal seems to be our considered preference, or at least seems to exert a greater influence on us in our reflective moments. Our tendency to rationalize may be precisely a reflection of this; for if all we cared about were conformity of our actions and beliefs to reasons for them, we would less often ask for explanations of them, as opposed to asking what reasons there were for them. Moreover, in giving an account of our actions or beliefs we would less often try, as we typically do when we rationalize, to give the impression that the reasons we offer are (or are at least among) our real reasons for the action or belief being queried.

As before, we can extend what has been said about actions to beliefs and other propositional attitudes. In the case of beliefs, however, the counterpart point – that a belief is rational in the light of a reason only if it is held at least in part for that reason – is even more in need of emphasis. Perhaps in part because 'belief' can be used to mean 'proposition', it has been especially natural for philosophers to overlook the difference between rationality of belief-types for a person – often expressed in terms of the belief that p (or the proposition that p) being rational (or justifiable) for S – and the rationality of S's belief-tokens. This makes it easy to assimilate the rationality of belief to its rationalizability.[17] Parallel distinctions apply to the other propositional attitudes, and for all of them we can distinguish the two sorts of ideals of rationality described for actions.

I have argued for a conception of rationalizations of action as purported accounts of it that offer one or more reasons for it and

17. The interpretation Keith Lehrer gives to his gypsy lawyer case illustrates this. See *Knowledge*, Oxford, 1974, pp. 122–126. I have critically assessed Lehrer's case in Chapter 7, this volume.

thereby represent it as prima facie rational, but do not provide the agent's real reason(s) for it and do not explain it. I have argued that this conception may be generalized to the propositional attitudes and that neither in the case of actions nor in that of the propositional attitudes does rationalization of a token, even by appeal to good reasons the agent had at the time, entail its rationality. There are, however, rationalizations of types, and these may show the rationality of the relevant kinds of actions, or kinds of propositional attitudes, and, in a sense, explain them. In much of what we say about rational actions and rational propositional attitudes it is easy to fail to distinguish types from tokens, and, correspondingly, rationality of an agent-neutral sort from rationality of an agent-specific kind. It is in part because of such failures and because rationalizations can show types to be rational, that rationalizability by good reasons the agent had for an action has been mistakenly thought to entail its rationality. My conclusions lead to a more complicated account of rational action (tokens) than is sometimes given, one requiring an adequate causal basis in one or more reasons. The same holds for propositional attitudes. What emerges, however, is a more adequate conception of rationality, unifying actions with propositional attitudes and connecting both to a plausible overall ideal for a rational person.[18]

18. For helpful comments on an earlier version of this paper I am grateful to Frederick Adams, William P. Alston, John A. Barker, George Pappas, Thomas Vinci, and especially, John King-Farlow, who wrote extensive comments on it. I have also benefited from discussing the issues with members of the National Endowment for the Humanities Summer Seminar on Reasons, Justification, and Knowledge which I directed in 1983, and from discussion of the paper at Northern Illinois University.

Chapter 15

The architecture of reason

THE PSYCHOLOGICAL STRUCTURE
OF COGNITION

Our experience of the world is an expanse of colors and shapes, a blend of sounds and silences, a texture of surfaces smooth and rough, yielding and resistant, supporting and opposing. Before me are reds and blues and greys, patterns of light and dark, furniture and carpeting, human figures, and the faces of philosophers. These dimensions of experience are not a mere sensory array. They tend to produce perceptual beliefs. I believe that there are reds and blues and greys before me, that I stand on a hard surface, that the room is furnished, and that there are philosophers here. These beliefs are grounded in different ways. My belief about the colors is based on my seeing them. It is direct: it does not stem inferentially from any other belief.[1] My belief that there are philosophers here has multiple roots. While I see philosophers, my belief that they are here is also partly grounded in memory – since I recognize many philosophers – and partly inferential, resting on my further belief that most people who have come to hear this are philosophers.

My inferential beliefs presuppose further beliefs. Nothing premised, nothing inferred. And no belief I have expresses a premise for my perceptual belief that there are reds and blues and greys

---

1. It is notoriously hard to explicate this perceptual basis relation. It must at least be non-waywardly causal. For an indication of how the relation may be explicated, see Chapter 8, this volume. I would also argue that the seeing is direct. Some of my grounds are given in my *Belief, Justification, and Knowledge* (Belmont, California: Wadsworth Publishing Co., 1988), ch. 1.

here. I could search out a premise. Grappling with skepticism, I might form the beliefs that it appears to me that there are these colors here, and that if it so appears, then there are. But can I find still further premises? There are limits to how far I can go in framing premises.[2] Our beliefs lie in no infinite chains of inference. If skeptics want to chase us along unending byways of argument – or to force us to rotate in inferential circles – they must first induce us to form the beliefs that lead us down these paths of retreat. For even a studied life produces no such doxastic labyrinths, nor do our beliefs ever naturally lie in inferential circles. Only in the arena of dialectic do we tend toward such circular motion.[3]

Our beliefs arise in experience: in our perceptions of events, in our awareness of thoughts and feelings, in reflection on ideas, in flights of imagination. Many beliefs are preserved in memory, many multiplied by inference. Many more come from association, compounding, and the visions and revisions wrought by new experiences. There may be no particular beliefs we must all have; but we all have some beliefs directly grounded in our experience. These are the basis of our inferential beliefs. These doxastic foundations may change: we acquire new foundations, and old ones may decay or be displaced. We are corrected by fresh perceptions, instructed by others, and reshaped by reflection. But at any one time, our body of beliefs contains some grounded in experience and others based on those. Psychologically, the structure of theoretical reason is foundational.[4]

2. A person surely cannot (at least in fact) have an infinite set of beliefs. I have argued for this in "Believing and Affirming," *Mind* XCI (1982). In any case, one tends to run out of *plausible* premises, or at least plausible arguments, after just a few moves, particularly if one tries to select from among propositions one *already* believes or can at least believe without as it were talking oneself into it.

3. It is not even clearly possible for a belief to be ultimately based on itself in the way apparently implied by an inferential circle. For a brief discussion of this problem – and an indication of why holistic, as opposed to linear, coherentism does not require such circles – see ch. 6 of *Belief, Justification, and Knowledge*.

4. There is of course much more to be said about psychological foundationalism. I have discussed it at length, and cited relevant literature, in Chapter 1, this volume. I here ignore cases in which inferential beliefs are based on beliefs not grounded in experience in the usual way but, e.g., produced by wishful thinking.

PART ONE:
THEORETICAL REASON

EPISTEMOLOGICAL FOUNDATIONALISM

We can adopt the psychological foundationalism just expressed, without embracing its epistemological cousin: the view that knowledge and justified belief have a foundational structure. My belief that there are people here may rest directly on perception without being directly – that is, non-inferentially – *justified*. But epistemological foundationalism can be developed in a way that avoids the main objections to it. Consider a structural foundationalism which, as applied to justification, says simply that if we have any justified beliefs, we have some beliefs that are directly justified, and any other justified beliefs we have are justified through being based on at least one of the former.[5] The foundations, then, are directly justified; the superstructure rests on them. Historically, foundationalism has been tied to ideas not implicit in this version. The view has also suffered from guilt by association. It cannot be assessed until we lift its unnecessary burdens. I want to cast off those burdens, develop the theory in new directions, take it as a model for an account of practical rationality, and use the resulting view of practical reason to clarify the basis of morality.

When Aristotle gave his famous regress argument in the *Posterior Analytics* 72b, he concluded that the ultimate premises of knowledge must be *indemonstrable*.[6] He apparently took them to have

5. There are various candidates for this inferential basis relation. My preference is expressed in Chapter 8, this volume, but there is no need to bring in the details, and here I do not even presuppose a causal connection, though it is implicit in any epistemological foundationalism which (as is natural) is combined with a plausible psychological foundationalism. Note that this formulation allows that coherence also contributes to justification, so long as foundations are necessary conditions on justification. A view of this kind is suggested by some of what Quine has said (both in his writings and in a conversation we once had on the topic), though he is sometimes taken to hold a coherentism incompatible with the kind of foundationalism being developed here. See, e.g., W.V. Quine and Joseph Ullian, *The Web of Belief* (New York: Random House, 1970), esp. ch. 2, where, in answering the question whether there is any stopping point in the probing of evidence, the reply is: "There is a bottom, not rock bottom perhaps, but bottom enough: the reports of observation" (p. 13). See also the second edition (1978), which calls them "the basic evidence for all beliefs" (p. 28).
6. See esp. 72b4-24. I refer to only *one* conclusion Aristotle drew. His conclusion concerned "scientific knowledge"; as he repeatedly said, "Since the object of pure scientific knowledge cannot be other than it is, the truth obtained by de-

something like axiomatic certainty. But a properly qualified regress argument permits foundations with a weaker epistemic status, even if it does require that, at any given time, the ultimate premises of knowledge be *undemonstrated*. Nonetheless, if one's driving conception of knowledge is axiomatic, one will crave self-evident foundations. One will at least want something than which nothing more basic can be conceived, something not knowable from prior, better-grounded premises. It will also seem that inferential knowledge (or justification) must be *deductively* based on a good foundation. In Descartes, the leading modern foundationalist, some such deductivism is just what we find.[7]

But a plausible regress argument no more requires deductivism about the transmission of justification than axiomatism regarding its foundations. Thus, foundationalism may allow inductive transmission. I may justifiably take the flowers in a crisp centerpiece to be real simply because I believe that this best explains the pervasive smell of roses. Similarly, a plausible regress argument need only countenance foundational beliefs which, being directly justified, can stop the regress.[8] This does not require certainty.[9]

A good foundation need not be indestructible; it need only sustain the weight it is meant to bear. Not all foundations rest on bedrock, and even those that do may be anchored more or less firmly. There are also different kinds of bedrock. Perception is one

---

monstrative knowledge will be necessary . . . demonstration is an inference from necessary premises" (73a20-24). Concerning such premises he says that "A 'basic truth' in a demonstration is an immediate proposition. An immediate proposition is one which has no other proposition prior to it" (72a7-8). But the force of his regress argument, particularly in ruling out the possibility of knowledge from circular or infinite patterns, applies to knowledge (and justification) in *general* and, so conceived, allows for weaker foundations. (The quotations are from Mure's translation.)

7. Having said, e.g., that "the first principles are given by intuition alone, while, on the contrary, the remote conclusions are furnished only by deduction," he immediately adds that "These two methods are the most certain routes to knowledge, and the mind should admit no others." See Rule III in *Rules for the Direction of the Mind*, trans. by Elizabeth Haldane and G.R.T. Ross.

8. Direct justification need not stop the regress in the sense that it makes skepticism about beliefs that have it impossible. Indeed, no epistemology should automatically rule out skepticism.

9. Here I speak of certainty in general. There are many kinds. I have discussed some in *Belief, Justification, and Knowledge*, chs. 7 and 9. See also Roderick M. Chisholm, *The Foundations of Knowing* (Minneapolis: University of Minnesota Press, 1982). Below, it will often be preferable to speak of strong foundations as indefeasible, roughly in the sense that their justification cannot be defeated. Only a high degree of (epistemic) certainty would imply this.

kind: we sense what is outside us. Introspection is another: we are aware of what is in us. Intuition can be still harder, and yields a grasp of simple logical truths. Memory provides residual ground whose firmness varies with the quality and preservation of the original material.[10] Working from what we erect on bedrock, we can alter the foundations; and just as we can infer deductively or inductively, we can build cautiously or daringly. We can encase a fortress halfway below ground or thrust a spire into the clouds.

EPISTEMOLOGICAL FOUNDATIONALISM AND CONCEPTUAL COHERENTISM

If foundationalism can forswear indubitable premises, if it can allow inductive extension of justification, if, as a view about the structure and not the specific content of justified belief, it can permit a plurality of foundational materials and their alteration by pressures from what we build on them, can it also account for the role of coherence in justification? Can it explain that special connectedness of beliefs that is more than consistency, less than mutual entailment, and most commonly exemplified by relations of explanatory relevance, evidential support, and probabilistic connection?

In everyday life, as in science, coherence tends to confirm, incoherence to disconfirm. Thus, when I look ahead, my visual impressions confirm, and cohere with, my expectation that I will see faces. If the impressions fade into shadows, my experience becomes incoherent with my beliefs. I might look toward the lights, hoping to restore coherence by finding them dimmed. If the lights seem normal, I may wonder if I really do see faces. And suppose I test that belief by walking toward them, and no one responds to my touch. I would cease to believe there are people before me. Under the pressure of incoherence, I would abandon a foundational belief. But this pressure is not a product of incoherence alone; it is exerted partly by at least one other foundational belief: that no one responds to my touch. Similarly, where coherence confirms,

10. As an epistemic faculty, memory may do more than this. A memorial impression can justify a belief even if the impression is not based on one's actually remembering, as where one has a false but strong steady impression of having done something, and no reason to doubt this. (Relevant discussion, and an indication of how memory is basic with respect to justification in a way it is not for knowledge, are given in ch. 2 of *Belief, Justification, and Knowledge*.)

it extends justification already possessed. I have a justified belief that if I look, I will see people; and, in part because I justifiably expect to, my seeing people both confirms and coheres with my belief that they are here. Why should we deny, then, that foundationalism can account for the major epistemic role of coherence?

Skeptics, at least, and the many non-skeptics whose conception of justification is shaped by skepticism, may deny this. Recall my belief that there are people here. My justification for believing this depends on my visual impressions' *not* fading. One might reason, then, that even a psychologically foundational belief *derives* its justification from coherence. This reasoning is unsound. The case does not show that perceptual warrant can derive from coherence; it simply illustrates *defeasibility* by *in*coherence. Such *negative* epistemic dependence need not be denied by foundationalism.

It might be objected that my justification for believing that there are people here does derive from the coherence of this belief with my further belief – or disposition to believe – that certain presuppositional grounds hold, say that my impression of faces will not fade. I reject this claim of *positive* epistemic dependence. Granted, to *show* the second-order thesis that my belief is justified, I should argue for the absence of defeaters such as fading visual impressions. But why must my original, first-order justification in believing there are people here meet a requirement appropriate to the second-order task of vindicating it? It is natural to impose a positive dependence requirement if we are trying to depict justification as sufficient to withstand skepticism; for then we always want to have some supporting argument available and we tend to see justification as depending on such support. These preoccupations have powerfully influenced epistemology. But a plausible foundationalism refuses to collapse questions about what justification *is* into questions about what it takes to show that we have it.

It is here that a foundationalism which gives due weight to coherence stops short of full-blooded coherentism: the view that coherence is the *source* of justification. Coherence of one or another kind is an element in justification: coherence can contribute to it; incoherence can defeat it. Coherence is not the ground of justified belief, but incoherence can topple the structure. Unlike experience, coherence is not a basic source of justification: beliefs that have no justification gain none merely by acquiring coherence.[11] If I enter

11. This allows coherence to be a conditionally basic source, i.e. (roughly), to in-

an unfamiliar garden with closed eyes, the most beautiful coherence among my beliefs about its flowers will give me no justification for thinking them purple or pink, yellow or blue, short or tall. It is utterly different when I open my eyes to the multicolored panoply.

We may still grant the important point that justification depends negatively on coherence. My bank account is the source of the funds that back my checks, but it negatively depends on the absence of explosions that destroy all the records. The skeptic may say my check is worthless without a guarantee against such hazards. I grant I have no absolute assurance, but deny my check is worthless. I utterly reject the *inference* from my lacking that guarantee to its worthlessness. Even a good source need not be absolute. And coherentists, too, want to live on credit. One can of course live too well on credit. Skepticism is good medicine for such profligacy; but it has no warrant to declare us bankrupt.

These points are consistent with one important kind of coherentism: a coherence theory of conceptual competence. We do not acquire concepts piecemeal. They come, and work, in families. We understand redness in relation to other colors, straight lines as against curved, happiness in comparison with sadness, affirmation by contrast with negation. But suppose I can have no concept of redness without having some other color concept. Indeed, suppose that unless I have a rudimentary theoretical understanding of color,[12] I cannot even have the belief that there is red here. Still, the *justification* of my believing this may be direct. This conceptual coherentism does not imply epistemological coherentism. The *epistemic* priority of experience over inference does not imply its *con-*

crease the justification of a belief *given* that it has some degree of justification from another source, and to play other important roles I cannot describe here but have discussed in Chapter 4, this volume.

12. This is not to suggest a *theory;* I am taking a theoretical understanding to be the sort implicit in having a set of related concepts and being disposed to form beliefs, and make inferences, involving them. A capacity for a kind of interpretation may be implied, but not an actual attempt to explain. Some of what I say in this paragraph may help in understanding Alfred North Whitehead's view that "thought is a factor in the fact of experience. Thus the immediate fact is what it is, partly by reason of the thought involved in it." See *The Function of Reason* (Princeton: Princeton University Press, 1929), p. 80. My points in this section also bear closely on some of Wilfrid Sellars' "The Myth of the Given," in his *Science, Perception, and Reality* (London: Routledge and Kegan Paul, 1963), and on some points in Donald Davidson's "A Coherence Theory of Truth and Knowledge," in Dieter Henrich, ed., *Kant oder Hegel* (Stuttgart: Klett-Cotta, 1983).

ceptual priority over inference. Experiences do not come to us labeled, nor do we categorize them using semantically isolated concepts; but my experience can still directly justify my believing that there are reds and blues and greys here, and a woody feel at my fingertips.

To be sure, if we understand concepts in families, it is to be expected that our justified beliefs embodying those concepts often form coherent sets. Our experience of a lilac tree is not a series of atomic perceptions in one sensory mode at a time, with matter abstracted from form, foliage from branch, scent from flower; and even if it were, we would tend to form enough beliefs about the tree to make sense of it. Our perceptual beliefs tend to be mutually supporting, if only because they naturally cluster round objects that explain our experience.

By virtue of this mutual support, even foundational beliefs may be theory-laden. Indeed, breakdown of doxastic alliances is often what leads us to revise our beliefs. Suppose my visual and auditory beliefs conflict: tapping a glassy desk top, I hear a distinctly metallic sound. I would cease to believe it is glass and would suspend judgment about its make-up. Again, incoherence defeats a foundational belief. But this does not imply that coherence is a basic source of justification. Far from it. At least some degree of coherence stems from the same experiential sources that yield foundational justification: the tapestry of color and shape, the interplay of sound and movement, the bulgy resistance of solid objects. Coherence and justification are not cause and effect; they are more nearly common effects of the same causes.

Foundationalism as I am developing it, then, is neither conceptually nor epistemically atomistic. It grants that justification may be enhanced by coherence and diminished by incoherence. It is fallibilistic, not indubitabilist. It is committed to unmoved movers, but not to unmovable movers. Rejecting axiomatism about foundations of justification and deductivism about its transmission, it countenances explanatory potential as a main basis of warranted inference.[13] Imposing no specific requirements on the content of a

13. I use 'warrant' in the most common way, as a rough equivalent of 'justification'. For a different notion, stressing warrant as that in virtue of which true belief can be knowledge, see Alvin Plantinga's "Positive Epistemic Status and Proper Function," *Philosophical Perspectives* II (1988). I am also using 'justification' in what seems the most common way; but the notion is broad enough to encompass many kinds. I hope that my overall position clarifies it and paves the way for distinguishing among – and unifying – the most important

body of justified beliefs, it provides for a pluralism of world views. It describes a structure that a body of justified beliefs must have, one which matches the pattern that psychological reflection seems to reveal in us. Experience is the ground of that structure, but does not dictate its content; those with differing experience may have disparate justified outlooks on the world. But experience remains the ground of our warrant. It gives us both our initial justification and much of our capacity to resolve the incoherences we encounter.

Reason and experience are often contrasted as sources of justification; but I speak broadly of experience, and include the kind of reflection that yields a priori justification. Hence, my subject has been what is often called theoretical reason: reason as (in part) a capacity to ascertain truth. If the holistic, fallibilist foundationalism I have described is sound, then epistemically as well as psychologically, the structure of theoretical reason is foundational.[14]

PART TWO:
PRACTICAL REASON

THE PRACTICAL COUNTERPARTS
OF PSYCHOLOGICAL AND
EPISTEMOLOGICAL FOUNDATIONALISM

The domain of practical reason is more difficult to characterize. It is above all that of action. But action is *based* on motivation, rather as inferential belief is based on further belief. This certainly applies to actions performed for a reason. I write a check in order to take a journal; my reason for this – what I want from it – is to subscribe;

kinds; but I cannot discuss these matters here. I would make quite parallel remarks on my use of 'rationality'. Further, while I am here thinking of *beliefs* about explanatory power as justifying beliefs based on them, I leave open that a belief might be *directly* justified in virtue of its truth's explaining, or at least through one's having justification to believe its truth explains, one's present experience.

14. Strictly, I have spoken more of the structure of belief than of theoretical reason conceived as a capacity; but in part because it is by forming beliefs that we exercise theoretical reason, the structure of the capacity has a close correspondence with that of our system of beliefs. This system expresses not only results of our exercises of the capacity, but also many of its tendencies to function in producing further beliefs. Analogous points hold for desires in relation to practical reason.

and I act on the basis of that desire.[15] To understand practical reason, then, we must consider the rationality of both motivation and action.

There may be no concept that is as representative of motivation as belief is of cognition. But wanting, in the widest sense, may be, and it is a constituent in intending, which is the other leading candidate.[16] Suppose I recommend a former colleague for a job. I do it because I want this philosopher to get the job and believe the recommendation may help. This belief links my recommending the colleague to what I want, and thereby grounds my action in my reason for it: to help in the job search. The action is based on my desire, rather as my belief that a concert is about to begin might be based on my belief that the lights are dimming. Moreover, just as I have direct beliefs as bases of other beliefs, I have intrinsic wants as bases of other wants.[17] I want my colleague to get the job because I intrinsically want this colleague to flourish: I want that for its own sake. Some may think I must have a deeper desire, say to fulfill an obligation to help. Suppose I do. Still, at some point my action is grounded in my wanting something intrinsically. There may *be*, and I may *have*, reasons for wanting that, just as there may be, and I may have, some wants – say for food and drink, conversation and reflection – that are not *based*, in any inferential way, on other wants.[18] But we have no infinite or circular

15. I have explicated acting for reasons in "Acting for Reasons," *The Philosophical Review* XCV (1986) and there argue that with the possible exception of intrinsically motivated actions, actions for reasons are based on motivation – on wants, in the widest sense, in which they include desires – by virtue of connecting beliefs. The mode of basing is quite parallel to that linking one belief to a second belief it is (inferentially) based on.

16. That there is a suitably broad sense of 'want' I have argued in "Intending," *The Journal of Philosophy* LXX (1973), and I have tried to explicate wanting in the relevant sense in "The Concept of Wanting," *Philosophical Studies* 21 (1973). In places I shall for stylistic purposes shift between 'want' and 'desire', though I do not take these terms to be equivalent; but nothing should turn on these shifts.

17. This does not imply that every intrinsic want has another want based on it; while foundations normally have something built on them, they need not. The superstructure may also crumble leaving the foundations intact (though this is not typical). It also seems possible for a kind of *motivational inertia* to keep a previously instrumental desire from extinguishing when, e.g., one has ceased to believe its realization would contribute to that of any intrinsic desire one has; but there is no need to consider this case here. I also leave open the possibility of wants that *cannot* be (inferentially) based on others, as arguably some beliefs cannot. It is an interesting question whether Aristotle so conceived the desire for happiness.

18. One want may be causally grounded in a second without being inferentially

440

chains of desire, for the same sorts of reasons that we have no such chains of inferential beliefs.[19]

If this is so, then the psychological structure of motivation is foundational: if we want anything at all, we want something or other intrinsically.[20] Call this view *motivational foundationalism*. Aristotle implied a form of it in Book One of the *Nicomachean Ethics*[21]; and Hume affirmed a hedonistic variant in the *Enquiry Concerning the Principles of Morals*.[22] A counterpart psychological thesis – *behavioral foundationalism* – may hold for action, assuming that every intentional action is performed in order to realize some want. Thus, if there is any intentional action, it is grounded (at least ultimately) in one or more intrinsic desires.[23]

Suppose that practical reason is like theoretical reason in having a psychologically foundational structure. It does not follow that practical reason has normative foundations analogous to directly justified beliefs. But many philosophers at least since Plato have

based on it (there might, e.g., be only a wayward causal chain connecting them). I have in mind the practical inferential relation present when one wants A as a means to B, and in *that* sense wants it on the basis of wanting B.

19. I have argued that circular inferential chains of the relevant kind are apparently impossible for beliefs, in *Belief, Justification, and Knowledge*, ch. 6; for desires, in "The Structure of Motivation," *Pacific Philosophical Quarterly* 61 (1980); and for valuations, in Chapter 2, this volume. I have tried to show that such causal chains are, however, crucial for justification and rationality, in Chapters 7 and 14. I think that even if circular inferential chains are possible, positing them would be bad epistemology and unrealistic psychology.

20. If, as I hold, intrinsic wanting is not merely wanting something other than as a means, perhaps there can be wants that are neither intrinsic nor extrinsic. I am ignoring this possibility here; there is certainly good reason to think that no normal or rational person could have only non-intrinsic wants.

21. For a discussion of motivational foundationalism in general and Aristotle's version in particular see my "The Structure of Motivation," *Pacific Philosophical Quarterly* 61 (1980).

22. In the *Enquiry Concerning the Principles of Morals* Hume says, "Ask a man *why he uses exercise;* he will answer *because he desires to keep his health.* If you then enquire, *why he desires health,* he will readily reply, *because sickness is painful.* If you push your enquiries further, and desire a reason *why he hates pain,* it is impossible he can ever give any. This is an ultimate end, and is never referred to any other object." See the edition edited by P. Nidditch (Oxford: Oxford University Press, 1975), p. 293.

23. I have discussed both kinds of foundationalism in "The Structure of Motivation," cited in note 21. The grounding may of course be indirect and may involve many links in the motivational chain. As with belief, the relevant basis relation (expressed by – among other phrases – 'in order to' in its main use) is *non-transitive:* one can A in order to B, which one wants to do, and B in order to C, say to enjoy oneself, without A-ing in order to C. For one might not appropriately connect A with C.

taken a view that implies this. Are there intrinsic rational wants, as there apparently are directly justified beliefs? Clearly, a want can be instrumentally rational when one believes its realization will achieve something else one wants. Relative to my wanting my colleague to get a job, my wanting to recommend that is rational. But can I rationally want something for its *own* sake, or are intrinsic desires brute conative givens, natural perhaps, but not properly considered rational?

A good foundationalist answer will *not* be modeled on the widely discussed, strong versions of epistemological foundationalism. There need be no analogue of certainty: no indefeasibly rational desires. And since the foundationalism I am developing concerns structure and not specific content, there need be no particular thing, even if there are kinds of things, which everyone wants for its own sake: a pluralism of rational ends is quite open.[24] Coherence, moreover, has a role: positively, the mutual coherence of one's intrinsic desires – say, the kind of coherence based on their being jointly satisfiable and directed toward one's happiness – can count towards their rationality; negatively, incoherence can warrant correcting them. There is even a parallel to the rejection of deductivism: rationality may be transmitted from a foundational to a superstructure desire when realizing the latter is just likely, and not certain, to satisfy the former. Thus, wanting to recommend someone can be rational even if it has only a slight chance of achieving the intrinsically desired result.

What sorts of intrinsic desires might be directly, as opposed to inferentially, rational? The least controversial examples concern one's own pleasure or pain. Intrinsically wanting the things that constitute one's happiness is also a good candidate, particularly if it is understood along Aristotelian lines and tied to activities whose performance (under certain conditions) yields the distinct kind of happiness sought: animated conversation, joyful singing, a vig-

24. As I construe foundationalism simpliciter, and as it is best construed if we are to see it, in historical perspective, as heavily bound to a plausible regress argument, it simply says that the structure of a body of justified beliefs (or other justified intentional elements) is foundational; it leaves to particular theorists how strong the foundations must be, beyond a capacity to stop the regress, what sorts of content they may have, how they uphold the superstructure, and other matters, such as the appropriate transmission principles. I am construing motivational foundationalism in the same way, and as allowing the same kind of latitude. My own version of it is developed, in part, below.

orous tennis game, a walk on a breezy mountain road. Is there any reason to deny that such desires are directly, rather than just instrumentally, rational? The view is not provincial, either in the diversity of its proponents or in the variety of agents whose behavior confirms it. It allows for a multitude of rational ends, given the unlimited range of experiences and activities that can yield happiness. And many of the desires that are directly rational on this view would gain approval from reflection both on their objects and on how they would fit one's life plans.

Can we even conceive rational persons who have no directly rational desires, or who are, say, indifferent to their own happiness or suffering?[25] It is far from clear that we can. Why is it, moreover, that it is at least prima facie irrational to want something noninstrumentally while rationally believing that it will be wholly unsatisfying and entirely without pleasure? A glutton might, from sheer gustatory momentum, so desire to eat more escargots; but such ravenous desire is not rational. Nor is its irrationality disguisedly instrumental: the glutton does not want to eat as a means to pleasure, but *for its own sake*, for the anticipated intrinsic qualities of the consumption. Perhaps the irrationality of the desire depends on the belief that eating more would not be enjoyable; but that would not show that there are no directly rational or irrational desires, only that practical rationality can depend, at least negatively, on theoretical rationality.[26] That possibility is consistent with

25. I mean this to apply to human persons. Moreover, I am not denying that, say for religious reasons, one might try to cultivate indifference to one's suffering and happiness as ordinarily understood. This counts against a crude hedonistic notion of rational desire, but it seems intelligible only on the supposition that there is a kind of happiness, here presumably a spiritual kind, in one's sense of succeeding. Paradoxically, perhaps, the success seems incomplete unless there remains a residual, perhaps fleshly, desire to avoid pain, or some desire to achieve material happiness, which one feels one has *overcome*. Similar points may apply to the possibility of, say, wanting *only* to create art; surely one might intrinsically want a kind of aesthetic satisfaction that amounts to one's own version of happiness. If not, I doubt such a person would be *fully* rational.

26. This dependence would not imply that rational desire is entirely a matter of rational belief; indeed, the case illustrates only defeasibility of a noninstrumental desire by a rational belief, not positive dependence of an intrinsic desire on the belief that its object has certain qualities. Moreover, I take my points here to be consistent with the view that practical and theoretical reason are two aspects of the same basic capacity, as I think Kant held. He says, e.g., that "in the final analysis there can be but one and the same reason which must be differentiated only in application." See *Foundations of the Metaphysics of Morals*, Lewis White Beck trans. (New York: The Liberal Arts

my view of both. Indeed, the point that intrinsic wants are like non-inferential beliefs in being open to a kind of defeasibility *supports* the view that such desires admit of rationality.

INSTRUMENTALISM AS A CANDIDATE FOR COHERENTISM IN THE PRACTICAL SPHERE

If practical and theoretical rationality are as closely parallel as I hold, is there a practical counterpart of epistemological coherentism? It is arguable that there is, though this possibility has not been widely recognized.[27] In the practical sphere, it is instrumentalism that is the most influential view plausibly considered a kind of coherentism. For instrumentalism, while there may be things we naturally desire intrinsically, there is nothing it is intrinsically rational to want, nor are there rational intrinsic desires. We do have rational extrinsic desires, and their rationality derives from how well their realization would, on our beliefs,[28] contribute to satisfying our intrinsic desires. The rationality of actions is similarly subordinate to sheer intrinsic desire, and is governed only (or chiefly) by coherence criteria. Above all, if I do something which, on my beliefs, yields less satisfaction of my intrinsic desires[29] than something I might have done instead, I act irrationally. My be-

Press, 1959), section 392. It might be argued that directly rational desires are different from directly rational beliefs in that, while both are, broadly speaking, non-inferential, the former may depend on the rationality of propositional attitudes in a way the latter may not. My overall purposes do not require denying this, but it seems too strong, for reasons suggested below. Relevant points are also made in Chapter 13, this volume.

27. I have discussed the counterpart briefly in Chapter 13, this volume. For valuable related discussion of a coherentist view of rational action, critical of the view on grounds overlapping mine, see Stephen L. Darwall, *Impartial Reason* (Ithaca and London, 1983), esp. ch. 4.

28. Hume might also have considered – as certainly an instrumentalist may – what agents ought to believe given their evidence, but I am not trying to explicate Hume here and will ignore this complication.

29. The notion of less satisfaction here is problematic. The notion is surely not additive, and in any case it is not clear whether number of desires as well as their combined strength should count. Is the goal just total quantity of satisfaction or, say, the satisfaction of the most desires, other things equal? If number counts, we may have an impure instrumentalism; if it does not (and indeed even if it does), would it be instrumentally rational to cause oneself to have as one's only desire a terrifically intense one for a single thing if that were the easiest strong desire to satisfy? This or a similar strategy might be the best way of getting the maximum quantity of desire satisfaction.

havior is incoherent with my desires, at least in the sense that given my beliefs, I would, on reflection, have preferred to do something else. Hume may be plausibly read as an instrumentalist in roughly this sense.

Pure instrumentalism is a kind of *functionalism about practical rationality*. My action is rational provided it appropriately[30] contributes to satisfying my intrinsic desires whatever they are.[31] To be rational is to serve desire. Some servants are better than others; those they serve are not good or bad, they are simply demanding brutes. Quantity of desire being equal, the most exquisitely rendered contrapuntal Bach is no more worthy of pursuit than the most crudely shouted monochromatic rock.

As a functionalist view, instrumentalism must deny that there are desires whose rationality is intrinsic to them, say by virtue of their content or even their grounding in enjoyment of the kinds of experiences they are directed toward, whether active, as in singing, or passive, as in sunbathing. This functionalism can, however, treat the rationality of action as *relative* to the psychologically foundational intrinsic desires one happens to have. Instrumentalism so viewed may be conceived as a kind of foundationalism. Granted, an instrumentally rational action would cohere with one's overall set of relevant desires and beliefs; but that might be simply because it is grounded in this framework quite as it would be on the kind of foundationalist view I have developed: after all, what serves one's system of ends thereby coheres with it, just as a belief supported by one's foundational beliefs coheres with them. Moreover, just as incoherence may override a prima facie justified belief by introducing an inconsistency between it and certain foundational beliefs, defeat by an incoherence might render an action irrational

30. The most common interpretation of appropriateness here is optimality, in the sense that the action is at least as good as any available alternative from the point of view of satisfying my intrinsic desires. Satisfaction itself may be construed quantitatively or in some other way, e.g. (more plausibly) in terms of quantity taken in relation to my beliefs, second-order desires (say for primacy of some of my desires over others), and perhaps other factors. The rationality of extrinsic desires is understood similarly, in terms of the contribution their realization would make to satisfying intrinsic desires.
31. The classical decision-theoretic view seems a case in point. Indeed, it is arguable (though I cannot explore the issue here) that a pure instrumentalist must hold a maximization view, since otherwise rational actions would not accord fully with intrinsic desires. I do not regard Hume as committed to pure instrumentalism, though a case can be made for this. I suggest some reasons to think Hume a more guarded instrumentalist, in ch. 2 of *Practical Reasoning* (London and New York: Routledge, 1989).

445

relative to one's intrinsic desires when it is performed instead of an alternative that would serve them better. The instrumentalist's foundations would be construed functionally rather than substantively; but until we have a sharper specification of what constitutes coherence, it may be at least as reasonable to regard instrumentalism as a subjective foundationalism as to consider it a kind of coherentism.

Some philosophers have qualified instrumentalism by imposing procedural constraints. On one such view, my rational actions are those that appropriately contribute to the intrinsic desires I would have if, in the light of relevant facts, I adequately reflected on my intrinsic desires.[32] This rules out some possible intrinsic desires and restricts the basis of rationality. There is no particular ground on which we must build, but we may not use materials we would ourselves reject. This view may be called a procedurally constrained instrumentalism or a procedural foundationalism, depending on what we want to emphasize. But it is not, like the view I prefer, a substantive foundationalism, since it specifies no particular kinds of objects appropriate to rational desire.

AN INTERNALIST
MOTIVATIONAL FOUNDATIONALISM

Even a substantive foundationalism may be largely neutral regarding the objects of rational desire. It specifies only *kinds* of appropriate objects and so may countenance a vast range of directly rational wants. My view is also *internalist;* it takes what is introspectively accessible[33] – above all, experiences and beliefs – to determine what in particular it is rational to desire intrinsically. If, for instance, I both enjoy silently reciting poetry and believe the experience to be valuable, then, in virtue of these internally ac-

32. R. B. Brandt holds a sophisticated theory of this sort. See *A Theory of the Good and the Right* (Oxford: Oxford University Press, 1979). An interesting foil – though developed mainly for epistemic rationality – is Richard Foley, *The Theory of Epistemic Rationality* (Cambridge: Harvard University Press, 1987); Foley also proposes a kind of reflectivity test, but is subjectivistic in a way Brandt is not, in denying a constitutive role to facts and logic. It is interesting to consider both views as first-person versions of ideal observer theories.
33. There are various kinds and degrees of access. For some discussion of this in the epistemological case – whose relevance should be direct – see William P. Alston, "An Internalist Externalism," *Synthese* 74 (1988) and Chapter 10, this volume.

cessible facts about me (and even apart from my forming a belief that they obtain), it is prima facie rational for me to want experiences of that kind. It would seem moreover, that fully rational agents must have some degree of intrinsic desire for their own happiness (including the avoidance of their own suffering); but the view is highly pluralistic about what constitutes happiness.[34] This latitude preserves what is most plausible in subjectivism without leaving us only coherence constraints on the rationality of desire. A normative motivational foundationalism does not entail that Aristotle and Michelangelo, Shakespeare and Mozart, Jane Austen and Henry James, are fertile ground for rational desire. But if we assume that the best happiness requires the exercise of our most distinctively human capacities, or at least that happiness is best, over a lifetime, where exercise of those capacities is a major part of one's experience, it is understandable that these giants should be richer sources of happiness than their lesser counterparts. No source, however, is flatly discounted. That the excellences of art and philosophy and science are better objects of rational desire than the giddy flutters of intoxication does not entail that the latter cannot be rationally wanted at all.

Practical rationality, then, is grounded, through beliefs, in rational intrinsic desires. These include at least certain desires for happiness, pleasure, and avoidance of pain. Extrinsic rational desires are rational by virtue of being well grounded in rational intrinsic desires. I want my colleague to get the job because I believe this would yield something I intrinsically want: the flourishing of a fine philosopher. If this intrinsic want is rational, and if my belief connecting it with the extrinsic want based on it is justified, then that want – to write the recommendation – is also rational: it is rational to want what I justifiably believe to be a means to what I intrinsically and rationally want.[35] Similarly, rational action is well-grounded action, quite as justified belief is well-grounded belief.

34. It might be argued that, since pains are merely kinds of sensations, it is rational to want (intrinsically) to avoid having pain only if one *dislikes* it, and that for this reason pain does not have the same status as pleasure in explicating happiness. I agree with the second conclusion, but leave the first open. It appears, however, that it is at least prima facie irrational not to want to avoid having pain when one clearly focuses on what it is, or at least when one *has* it.

35. For wanting on balance, other things must be equal; e.g., I must not have another intrinsic want stronger and more important to me such that I believe or should believe that some other action would realize it. It is difficult to specify the whole range of relevant factors, but a general account certainly

This motivational structure is not static, either psychologically or normatively. My intrinsic wants change over time; and perhaps some that are rational can remain intrinsic yet, faced with an incoherence, cease to be rational. If I should stop enjoying cool swims, yet somehow retained and inertial intrinsic desire to take one, that desire might no longer be rational. And just as self-scrutiny may expunge a directly justified belief, it may unseat a rational intrinsic desire: the thesis that seemed obvious may have been confused with a similar one; the prospect that appealed so keenly may, on reflection, repel me. But, as my visual experience of reds and blues and greys may justify my belief that those colors are here, my zesty enjoyment of cool swims may justify my intrinsically wanting to take them.[36] In different ways, experience is the ground of both rational desire and justified belief. Normatively as well as psychologically, the structure of practical reason is foundational.

INTERNALIST OBJECTIVISM AND THE EXPERIENTIAL GROUNDS OF ALTRUISM AND RATIONAL DESIRE

How does this conception of practical reason bear on the status of morality? Some of the rational desires I have considered may seem self-interested. If practical rationality is rooted wholly in self-interested desire, then showing that it is rational to be moral is bedeviled by the task of deriving morality from self-interest. From enlightened self-interest, some derivation of morality may be possible. But there is another aspect of the relation between reason and morality. Might we have rational altruistic desires? Are others just means to our own ends, or can we rationally and intrinsically want something for someone else? We can. To see this, we need

seems possible. I should add that the wanted thing need not be conceived *as* wanted.

36. The *belief* that such a swim is enjoyable may also render rational – and give rise to or sustain – an intrinsic desire for it. But I think that the experiential basis of such desire is in a way more fundamental: if one could not want it for its constitutive qualities that attract one, believing that it has those qualities could not render rational one's wanting it for those qualities. It is doubtful that one could even rationally believe that an experience has the relevant kinds of qualities if one has never experienced those qualities or something suitably similar.

an account of practical rationality which, in the right way, is both objectivist and internalist.

Imagine taking a walk in the country. You are not in a hurry. You just want to enjoy the scenery. Suddenly, you hear a child crying. It is a boy of five caught in a blackberry bush. As he struggles to escape, he gets scratched. Naturally, you want to free him. Is this only an empathy that depends on projecting oneself into his situation? Is it just the influence of the dove kneaded into our frame? Surely it is rational to want to free him on *his* account. Perhaps it is *because* we know what it is like to be caught in such a tangle that we want to free him. But this genetic point does not imply that we want to free him in order to relieve our own vicarious suffering. We need not have *any* emotional desire. Nor must our desire be instrumental. We can intrinsically and rationally want to free him; and if no competing concern takes priority, it is also rational to do it.

If altruistic desires can be rational, what accounts for this? Consider the phenomenology of what may be our psychologically most primitive intrinsic desires, those regarding pleasure or pain we are directly experiencing. What does the boy intrinsically want? For one thing, he wants the pain to stop. If the sun has beaten down on him, he may also want water. The former desire is focused on unpleasant qualities of his immediate, painful experience; the latter, on pleasant qualities of an envisaged experience: the refreshing wetness of cool water. Moreover, he wants each experience – ceasing of the pain and refreshment by the water – *for* its qualities. He does not want it as a *means* to experiencing those qualities; they are intrinsic to the experience, and he wants it on their account.[37] Intrinsic desire *is* wanting something for its own sake; but it is still *for* its qualities, or qualities one takes as intrinsic to it, that one wants it. Consider pleasure. If I want to play the piano for pleasure, I do not want this as a means to musical pleasure: I want the flow of arpeggios, the harmony of chords, the feel of ivory and ebony, the contrasts of bass and treble, loud and soft, major and minor.

We can view intrinsic desires as self-interested without conceiving them as truly egoistic. The entangled boy wants the pain to stop. He need not want that *he* be free of it. He might well have

37. I am ignoring certain differences between pleasure and pain. They differ in their phenomenology, and there are related differences between hedonic desires and hedonic aversions. But I doubt that anything in my argument turns on these differences.

449

that desire; but it is not the primitive case: neither conceptually nor psychologically. The primitive case is a kind of occurrently experiential desire, a desire for something that is being directly experienced. Granted, the realization of his wants is an experience *of his*. He is their referential anchor, and the qualities for which he wants what he does are encountered in his experience; but he himself need not enter into the content of those wants. The same holds for his desire for water. To be sure, if what he wants is *to drink*, then perhaps in *some* way he does figure in the content of his desire: perhaps he wants that *he* drink.[38] But this is not the primitive case of desire. Wanting to be is conceptually prior to wanting to do. Ends are conceptually prior to means.[39]

One might think that since the boy's wanting the pain to stop *is* just his wanting the cessation of what he conceives indexically as *this* pain, he does enter into the content of his want. For the indexical, 'this', may seem to mean 'the pain *I* now have'. I doubt it means precisely this. Nor must he conceive the pain under such an indexical notion, as opposed to simply disliking it because of its felt unpleasantness. *Ascription* of his desire may require an indexical; his *having* it does not. He can have such a desire even before he has a self-concept. But if some indexical notion is part of the content of his want, we should construe it referentially, not conceptually: the relevant indexical terms are not abbreviatory, but demonstrative. They serve to identify the desired object, not to build an individuating concept of it by projecting it into a special relation to oneself, as if to assign it coordinates on an egocentric grid of consciousness.

38. If one must in such cases have a self-concept in the content of the relevant desire, there is still no particular way one must conceive oneself. Deep difficulties beset explication of the relevant notion and the associated *de se* locutions, such as 'he himself'. For an extensive treatment of these problems see Hector-Neri Castañeda, e.g. "He*: On the Logic of Self-Consciousness," *Ratio* 8 (1966) and, for later statements, his contribution to James E. Tomberlin, ed., *Action, Language, and the Structure of the World* (Indianapolis: Hackett Publishing Co., 1983). If action-wants have objects embodying a self-concept, so does intending; indeed, there is perhaps more reason to attribute such content to intending, since, for one thing, it may imply a more definite (often reflective) focus on the object.

39. The first of these priority theses seemed to one reader close to Sartre's pronouncement that existence precedes essence. Neither claim implies the other, but both theses are consistent with a plausible reading of Sartre's claim. The former indeed suggests something that may be implicit in it: our *experience* of ourselves is conceptually (and in other ways) prior to our developing a *concept* of ourselves, or of what we ought to be.

In the primitive cases, then, what we intrinsically want, whether it concerns something experienced here and now, such as pain, or something quite distant, like conducting a seminar next year, need not be wanted egoistically.[40] We need not want such things *qua* our experiences, even if we see ourselves as their subject: I may want that I conduct the seminar, but its being mine is not what makes it desirable to me. I want it for the animated interchange, the tracking of narrative and argument, the pleasures of discovery. We *locate* desired experiences in relation to ourselves; we must in order to bring them about: I cannot conduct a seminar if I have no conception of a path from me to it. But this referential line from my present consciousness to what I want does not make the content of my desire egoistic.

It is not only in the primitive case that rational intrinsic desires are not essentially egoistic. In many complex instances, the content of rational desires is a possible object of the desires of *others*. Cessation of the entangled child's pain can be quite like cessation of mine and wanted for the same qualities: the restorative relief, the renewed feeling of well-being. An egoist might object that even if what I rationally desire need not have me in its content, it is rational for me to want intrinsically only things whose realization *I* experience.[41] How, then, does the objective internalist view of desire

40. What I say is very much in the spirit of Joseph Butler's view of desire in relation to selfishness. See esp. his Sermon IV, "Upon the Love of Our Neighbor," in *Five Sermons* (Indianapolis: Hackett Publishing Co., 1983), ed. by Stephen L. Darwall. He says, e.g., "That all particular appetites and passions are toward *external things themselves*, distinct from the *pleasure arising from them*, is manifested from hence – that there could not be this pleasure were it not for that prior suitableness between the object and the passion; there could be no enjoyment or delight from one thing more than another, from eating food more than from swallowing a stone, if there were not an affection or appetite to one thing more than another" (p. 47). His thrust, however, does not concern the exact content of the desire in the way mine does. One of his main points is that even when the object is external the desire is *one's own*: "Every particular affection, even the love of our neighbor, is as really our own affection as self-love; and the pleasure arising from its gratification is as much my own pleasure as the pleasure self-love would have from knowing I myself should be happy some time hence, would be my own pleasure" (ibid.). It is consistent with what he says that while, say, a passion for tennis is for *it* and not for my pleasure or even for an internal sense of the zesty athletic experience, *what* I want is that *I* play tennis (his example in the first quotation is in fact of an action). Nor does Butler emphasize the psychological or conceptual primitiveness of certain kinds of objects of desire. Still, what he says is compatible with, and I think well supports, the view I am proposing here.
41. This surely fails to account for rational desires expressed about, say, disposi-

451

do more than show that altruistic desire need not be *ir*rational.
Why should altruistic desire be rational, and can it ever be sufficiently so to make it rational for one to be moral?

Consider the basis of rational intrinsic desire. It is in our experience; it is above all those experiential qualities intrinsic to pleasure
and pain and to the happy exercise of our capacities, including
conscious states of rewarding contemplation, whether aesthetic,
intellectual, or religious.[42] There is no limit to the range of appropriate experiences; they may be active or passive, physical or mental, mundane or otherworldly. The parched boy wants water for
its refreshing qualities; you want to free him for the sense of comforting another; I want to play the sonata for the auditory and
performative experience. The rationality of such desires supervenes
on these qualities: the cool relieving wetness of water, the restored
comfort of the rescued child, the melodic resonances of Beethoven.
I encounter these qualities in my own experience, but the rationality
of wanting things *for* those qualities supervenes on the qualities
themselves, not on these qualities *conceived* as experienced by *me*.[43]

Even when the object of a want is realizable only *in me*, I need
not want it *for me*. Our experience is our route to discovering the
qualities that ground rational desires, and those desires are realized
in it. But the basis of their rationality is not egoistic, and may be
the same for us all. Once this point is fully grasped, the grip of
egoism on our conception of practical reason can be broken. It is
true that the experiential supervenience of practical rationality, as

tion of one's estate after one's death; nor does it seem that rational desires
about such things must be grounded in *imagining* one's experiencing what is
wanted, or even rooted in matters "directly" concerning oneself.

42. To be sure, a rational intrinsic desire can be *cognitively grounded*, i.e.
(roughly), grounded in a justified belief that realizing it would be, say, rewarding. But the justification of such a belief will itself be experientially
grounded. Moreover, it may well be that if one did not have some rational
desires that are directly grounded in one's experience, one could not justifiably believe that realizing some desire would be (say) rewarding. It is least
unclear how one would have justified beliefs about what it is like for something to be rewarding in the relevant sense.

43. I am conceiving supervenience as a kind of asymmetric relation of determina-
tion, but cannot explicate it here. For valuable discussion see Jaegwon Kim,
e.g. "Supervenience and Nomological Incommensurability," *American Philosophical Quarterly* 15 (1978). I leave open whether one can *know* that an intrinsic desire is rational other than by experience of its object (or something
similar), and there can be rational intrinsic wants for something not experienceable, such as the truth (as opposed to contemplating the truth) of a certain mathematical proposition.

we might call it, is internal; but it is not egocentric. It is communicable to others and repeatable in their experience.[44]

There is an epistemological analogy. Our visual experience is the ground of our justified visual beliefs. My experience contains reds and blues and greys, and I thus believe that these colors are here. It is true that I see the colors by virtue of *my* visual impressions; but this does not require me to experience *myself as* experiencing the colors. Doubtless, if asked why I believe these colors are here, I will say that I see (or visually experience) them. But I answer from a second-order perspective: I cite the basis of my belief, and my *citing* it requires self-ascription. Our original question concerns

---

44. Cp. G. E. Moore: "when I talk of a thing as 'my own good' all that I can mean is that something which will be exclusively mine, as my own pleasure is mine . . . is also *good absolutely*. The *good* of it can in no possible sense be 'private' or belong to me; any more than a thing can *exist* privately or *for* one person only. The only reason I can have for aiming at 'my own good,' is that it is *good absolutely* that what I so call should belong to me . . . But if it is *good absolutely* that I should have it, then everyone else has as much reason for aiming at *my* having it as I have myself." See *Principia Ethica* (Cambridge: Cambridge University Press, 1903), p. 99. Moore is talking mainly about the *value* of what one wants; I am more concerned with the content of what one wants. Even if the content of a want is essentially egoistic its realization might be good absolutely. But my view of content is also compatible with Moore's view of value and makes his general position here seem natural – particularly his point that others have as much reason as I to promote my good. For the more alike the bases of our respective goods, the more readily they can see reason to promote mine if – as even egoists would not doubt – they can see reason to promote theirs.

I believe my view is also consistent with the main points made on altruism by Thomas Nagel in *The Possibility of Altruism* (Princeton: Princeton University Press, 1970). His emphasis there, more than mine, is on how one conceives oneself and others; mine, more than his, is on the content of rational desires, and I include those whose rationality seems prior to any comparative grasp of oneself in relation to others. His more recent view, however (which I read only after essentially finishing this essay) overlaps mine at many points, and I find his treatment of desire quite illuminating. In *The View from Nowhere* (Oxford and New York: Oxford University Press, 1986), he maintains, e.g., that the sufferer's "awareness of how bad it [pain] is doesn't essentially involve a thought of it as his . . . if I lacked or lost the concept of myself as distinct from other possible or actual persons, I would still apprehend the badness of pain, immediately" (p. 161). His focus differs from mine in being on the *value* of what we desire as opposed to the *rationality* of the relevant desires, and correspondingly on the difference between apprehending goodness and, as in my examples, experiencing natural properties on which goodness supervenes. He may also be ruling out less than I regarding the relation of the person to the object of intrinsic desire (perhaps suggesting, e.g., that a *non-comparative* self-concept is required for intrinsic desire). I think, however, that my internalist account of the rationality of desire is compatible with his main claims.

what, prior to my citing that basis, justifies my belief; the question is not a request to defend the belief, and the self-reference necessary to citing its basis must not be imported into that basis. Many philosophers have conflated the question of what justifies a belief with the problem of defending it. That is understandable: both preoccupy us in trying to show, against a skeptical onslaught, that we do have justified beliefs; and in this context self-ascription of visual experience is easily taken to be a defense of the belief grounded in that experience. But we must not let skepticism make us assimilate consciousness of objects to a kind of self-consciousness. The basis of my justification is my visual experience, not my visual experience *as* mine: I am not part of the object of the experience that justifies my belief. That it *is* mine must be noted to show the second-order claim challenged by skepticism: that I justifiably believe there are colors here. But what justifies the first-order perceptual belief is my experience of those colors, not an experience of myself as seeing them.

It may be thought that our primary perceptual beliefs are that *we* see, hear, feel, taste, or smell the things about which experience gives us justified belief, and that we ourselves must therefore enter into the content of the grounding experience. This inference is invalid: my visual experience of a tree may justify beliefs *about* me – say, that *I* see a tree – without being an experience *of* me. But the more interesting mistake is in the premise. If, because I see them, I believe there are people here, I am certainly *disposed* to believe I see them. But I need not actually form this self-referential belief; and once we carry through the distinction between dispositional beliefs and mere dispositions to believe,[45] we can see that self-referential beliefs are not primary.

The epistemological analogy has a further dimension. Just as, when we see a house only partially, or merely glimpse it in passing, we can believe it to be green without conceiving it *as* a house or

---

45. I have developed this distinction in "Believing and Affirming," *Mind* XCI (1982) and illustrated it in *Belief, Justification, and Knowledge*, ch. 1, which also distinguishes ordinary perceptual beliefs from the self-referential ones sometimes thought basic. Both distinctions are commonly neglected, and I believe their neglect is serious, as I argue, regarding the first, in Chapter 4, this volume. For detailed discussion of the second distinction (or one much like it), which supports my approach here, see Paul K. Moser, *Knowledge and Evidence* (New York: Cambridge University Press, 1989). Note that normally, seeing precedes acquisition of a concept of it; hence, it is plainly possible to see without believing that one does.

indeed forming *any* specific conception of what it is, we can have a desire regarding an experience without conceiving it as any specific kind.[46] We can want a stabbing pain to cease even if we do not conceive it *as* a stabbing pain, or even as ours. To have a want regarding an experience does require that it discriminatively affect one, in a sense implying a capacity to identify discerned features of the experience in a certain way, just as believing a house to be green implies that it discriminatively affects one through some (normally identifiable) connection to its properties. But our capacity to identify what we want underlies our associated powers of both indexical reference and accurate conceptualization; it is not a product of prior, self-referential thought.[47]

Rather as skepticism about theoretical reason has shaped concepts of rational belief, skepticism about practical reason has influenced conceptions of rational desire. In both cases, the effort to vindicate reason in the skeptical tribunal promotes the tendency to posit the self in the content of the experiences that ground rationality. This *projectionism* is a mistake, and it gives undeserved plausibility to egoistic conceptions of rationality. The mistake is abetted because, as we learn to distinguish between appearance and reality, it is often natural to form beliefs about our experience *as* our own, such as the cautious belief that it appears to me that Shirley is here.[48] Similarly, in contrasting my experience with another's, I may conceptualize it as pleasant for *me*, or want it as *my* playing the piano as opposed to that of someone who wants to use the same piano. But these are not the primitive cases. If my visual experience itself could not justify, my sense of *my* having it could not either. If it could not be rational to want to hear music

46. Perhaps one must conceive it as, say, that green thing over there; but apparently no conceptualization is required beyond what is implicit in having the perceptual belief about it (this is not, of course, easy to specify). In the parallel case of desire, again nothing seems required beyond what is implicit in wanting the object *for* the relevant properties (or apparent properties).
47. It is interesting to compare with my view elements of Jean-Paul Sartre's in *The Transcendence of the Ego*, trans. by Forest Williams and Robert Kirkpatrick (New York: Simon and Schuster, 1957). He says, e.g., "Reflection 'poisons' desire. On the unreflected level I bring Peter help because 'Peter is having to be helped'. But if my state is suddenly transformed into a reflected state, there I am watching myself act . . . It is no longer Peter who attracts me, it is *my* helpful consciousness which appears to me as having to be perpetuated" (p. 59).
48. I mean Shirley F. Anderson. If the American Philosophical Association has had a(n executive) mother in the past one-and-a-half decades of its unprecedented growth, it is she.

for the qualities intrinsic to hearing it, it could not be rational to want, for those qualities, that *I* hear it. As a belief is justified by sensory experience, a desire may be rational on the basis of rewarding experience. If we choose to be thoroughgoing realists, we might say that – in some way – sensory experience points toward truth, rewarding experience toward goodness.

What holds for rational desire is generally also true of valuation. If it is rational to *value* what it is rational to want intrinsically, then my conclusion about rational desire implies that the rationality of values – of our valuations of things – also supervenes, in the primitive cases, on qualities of experience, and that altruistic values can be perfectly rational. Valuing, as a practical normative attitude, is quite analogous to desire in its structure and grounds: we value some things intrinsically if we value any at all, and it is rational to value things intrinsically for the same sorts of qualities that make them objects of rational intrinsic desire.

ALTRUISM AS A RATIONAL BASIS FOR
MORAL PRINCIPLES

Suppose, now, that purely altruistic desires can be rational. We are still far from even a partial account of the relation between reason and morality. But if the objectivist internalism I have presented is sound, we now have a basis for arguing that altruistic desires can be not only rational, but *as* rational as self-interested ones. Many are not only rational enough to make it (rationally) permissible to have them, but sufficiently rational to make it impermissible to lack them. If the rationality of desire is, in the primitive cases, based on certain qualities of experiences, and if – as I am assuming – others may be justifiably taken to have relevantly similar experiences, then it is as rational for me to want you to enjoy a cold drink as to want to enjoy one myself. Just as my experience is desirable for those refreshing qualities, yours is desirable in the same way: for while I come to know these qualities *in* my own experience, I need not, and in the primitive case do not, want them egoistically, *as belonging to* my experience.

The rationality of desire strengths is a different matter. It can be as rational to want one thing as another, yet also rational to want the former more. I might have reason to think you need a cool drink more than I; this may make it rational to want more that you have it. But if I know that I can ensure my having it, whereas it may spill before I can get it to you, it might be rational for me to want more that I have it. Depending on how such factors balance, it may be more rational for me to *act* on one of the rational wants rather than the other. Other things equal, it is more rational to act on the stronger of two equally rational competing wants. Neither self-interest nor altruism prevails automatically; and even where altruism does prevail normatively, it may not prevail behaviorally: as weakness of will reminds us, altruistic judgment may not prevent selfish action.[49]

At least two principles of rationality emerge here, one concerning rational desire, the other rational belief. First, at least for clear-headed agents who believe that there are others similarly constituted in cognition, motivation, and sentience, it is rational to want, intrinsically, the happiness of others. Second, all else being equal, it is rational for such clearheaded agents to believe the satisfaction of others' intrinsic desires to be as valuable as that of their own.[50] A clearheaded rational person who accepts these principles should hold moral counterparts: principles of utility and of justice, for instance that one should contribute to the happiness of others, and should treat relevantly similar persons equally.

I leave open the possibility of other rational grounds for holding such moral principles. Moreover, the proposed principles of practical reason may justify further moral standards. But these principles do not by themselves imply that the moral principles they justify always generate obligations which are *overriding* from the point of view of a rational agent not already committed to the supremacy of moral reasons.[51] Nor does this follow just from

49. Clearly, it is possible for one to fail to do what it is rational for one to do. Many cases of weakness of will seem to illustrate this. I have defended the possibility of weakness of will, and given an account of what it is, in "Weakness of Will and Practical Judgment," *Noûs* XIII (1979). Further discussions of weakness of will and many references to relevant literature are provided in my *Practical Reasoning,* cited in note 31.

50. My language here is realistic, but a non-cognitivist could maintain a reinterpretation of the principle which would have much the same effect if accepted as a guide to conduct. On a more specific matter, I am leaving open *how* valuable rational persons should take the satisfaction of their intrinsic desires to be. It is possible to take realization of an intrinsic desire to have both good and bad properties, e.g. to be both pleasurable and immoral; one could thus regard it as, on balance, not rational (or on balance bad) that an intrinsic desire be satisfied even if this would yield much pleasure.

51. It may be thought that since the function of moral principles is to override other sorts of reasons in cases of conflict, moral reasons must be overriding.

the rationality of holding the moral principles. For one thing, not all values, not even all altruistic values, are moral. Thus, while rational agents must, in human relations, give some weight to these or similar moral principles, they may not always discern their duties or (so far as they can) always act morally. The rationality of wanting others' happiness and of valuing it as much as one's own does not clearly entail that immoral action is never rational. For it is not self-evidently irrational, and is in fact sometimes natural, to want one's own happiness more than another's even if one believes one's own no more valuable. Still, it is far from obvious that such desire would be rational, and it certainly seems less than fully rational. Moreover, if, as I hold, self-interested reasons are not better from a rational point of view than altruistic reasons, then self-interest is not an overriding rational ground for violating a moral obligation. This is not to say that it must be *irrational* to act immorally. That would be at best difficult to show; for it can be intelligent, efficient, and richly self-serving so to act. But what is not irrational need not be rational; and even what is rational may be less so than alternatives.

There is reason to think, then, that it is rational both to hold certain moral principles and to act on them. Perhaps, for those who live among others they believe similar to themselves in cognition, motivation, and sentience, it is not rational not to hold them. Still, even if moral principles have this status *and* are overriding, a rational person may sometimes fail to act morally. We make mistakes that betray no irrationality, yet result in morally deficient conduct. Without a defect in rationality, we may culpably forget an obligation and so break a promise, or misjudge the likelihood of achieving something and, daunted by the dim prospect of success, fail in our duty to do it. Perhaps a *fully* rational, adequately informed person must be moral. I do not rule this out, but cannot try to show it. It remains significant that practical reason, though it develops from one's own point of view, does not depend on always seeing oneself in that point of view, that

But this argument seems invalid if we take 'function' in any of the senses needed to make the premise plausible, e.g. as meaning 'purpose'. It simply cannot be assumed that such a function must always (if ever) be fulfillable. This issue has been extensively discussed in a number of writings of Kurt Baier, including *The Moral Point of View* (Ithaca: Cornell University Press, 1957) and later works. Cp. James P. Sterba, *How To Make People Just* (Totowa, New Jersey: Rowman and Littlefield, 1988), esp. ch. 4.

it transcends self-interest, and that its experiential grounds accord us all the same status as sources of ultimate reasons for action.[52]

PART THREE:
EPISTEMOLOGICAL TRADITION AND
INTERNALIST REALISM

THE CARTESIAN AND LOCKEAN TRADITIONS:
INTERNALIST RATIONALISM AND
NATURALISTIC EMPIRICISM

I have spoken much about how reason is built, but little about how it builds or its capacity to withstand skepticism toward what it has built. Its paradigm constructions are often taken to be both inferential and theoretical. But reason is not just inferential or theoretical. It does not simply draw conclusions; it also provides premises. And it reveals worthwhile ends as well as efficient means: the desirable as well as the direction of the desired. In all these tasks, imagination aids reason. But there is no sharp distinction between their activities. Especially for making inferences to the best explanation, we need imagination both to find possible explanations and to assess their virtues. Reason is not an isolated capacity; it is (in ways I cannot begin to describe here) entwined with imagination, emotion, desire, and will.

My account of reason can be better understood by connecting it with two great traditions. They differ regarding both the capacities of reason and its modes of activity. The first is epitomized by Descartes. In one Cartesian picture, the paradigm of rationality is intuition. He stresses the intellect's insight into truth, its deductive power, and its active character. He seeks to build knowledge of the world from within – with the help of God, whose existence he takes to be demonstrable from an internal starting point.[53] The mind surveys the field of experience, and when it fixes an object in clear

---

52. Even if this view is wrong and intrinsic desire is egoistic in content, a rational person would still have the burden of showing, or at least having adequate ground for believing, that others are not relevantly similar. I believe that even on this basis altruistic intrinsic desires could be shown to be rational.

53. The *Meditations* confirms this reading. I have in mind such aspects of it as the project of reasoning one's way to discovery of a firm foundation, the strong claims made for clarity and distinctness, and the attribution of error to the will's exceeding the proper scope of assent laid down by the intellect.

and distinct focus the will elicits – or at least permits – one's natural assent to the manifest truth. Even knowledge acquired through perceiving a piece of wax in one's hand is "an intuition of the mind."[54] The other tradition is epitomized by Locke, and in some respects perhaps even more, by Reid.[55] For Locke, the paradigm of cognition, and the basis of rational beliefs about the world, is perception. He stresses the mind's receptivity and sees knowledge of the external as arising, not through inferential ascent from within to without, but from the myriad perceptions that reveal the world. Perceptual knowledge comes naturally to the attentive subject. We need not reach it through the deliberate pursuit of clear and distinct truth, nor does it depend on permission of the will: such knowledge is a normal product of our sensitivity to the causal powers of objects. Locke calls perception "the Inlet of all Materials of Knowledge" and holds that "in bare naked perception the mind is for the most part only passive."[56] Descartes' epistemology is a vol-

---

54. Meditation II, in *The Philosophical Works of Descartes*, trans. by Elizabeth S. Haldane and G.R.T. Ross (Cambridge: Cambridge University Press, 1970), p. 155. Cp. Locke's example of the manna: his emphasis is not on what the mind brings to it but on its power to affect the mind. He says, "A piece of manna of a sensible bulk is able to produce in us the idea of a round or square figure . . ." (*An Essay Concerning Human Understanding*, ch. VIII, Sec. 8). If, for Locke, the mind is a *tabula rasa* on which the hand of experience writes, for Descartes its physical metaphor is a beam of light that illuminates objects to ready them for the will's directing, or at least permitting, judgment about them. But Descartes' voluntarism is not unlimited, nor does Locke deny the will any influence on belief. Indeed, he seems to regard it as our duty to bring evidence to bear on our beliefs, thereby influencing their formation even if, given exposure to appropriate evidence, we form them involuntarily.
55. See, e.g., Thomas Reid, *Essay on the Intellectual Powers of Man*, Essay 2 and 4.
56. See the *Essay*, ch. X, Sections 1 and 15. It is interesting that in paragraph 1 he says, "for the most part passive"; still, if his involuntarism seems qualified by that, the very next phrase in the sentence tends the other way: he says of the mind that "what it perceives, it cannot avoid perceiving." Even when he speaks of reason he seems to view its powers somewhat on a perceptual model. In ch. XVII, "Of Reason," e.g., he says of reason that by its faculty of inference (as opposed to "sagacity") it draws "into *view* the truth sought for . . . and consists of nothing but the *perception* of the connexion there is between the ideas in each step of the deduction . . ." (paragraph 2, my emphasis). In the text I am to some extent idealizing both Descartes and Locke. Certainly Locke, so far as he was an evidentialist, thought we can at least indirectly influence our beliefs, and in places Descartes speaks as if the key role of the will is not to produce belief but to prevent its premature formation. For valuable discussion of Locke's evidentialism, in relation to Descartes and others, see Nicholas Wolterstorff, "The Migration of the Theistic Arguments: From Natural Theology to Evidentialist Apologetics," in Robert Audi

untaristic rationalism, Locke's a naturalistic, mainly involuntarist empiricism.[57]

The influence of both traditions is incalculable. Consider just Hume and Kant. Conceived in one way, Hume exhibits the effects of certain Cartesian epistemic standards combined with Lockean empiricist elements but cut off from God. Kant, too, may be seen as retaining certain Cartesian standards.[58] But, unable to find compelling argument for taking God to guarantee a bridge from experience to external reality, and unwilling to take perception, as Locke did, to be a natural source of knowledge of the external, Kant preferred a limited victory over skepticism to lower epistemic standards, and he restricted empirical knowledge to the phenomenal world.

Qualified and variously blended, the Cartesian and Lockean traditions are very much with us. Contemporary voluntaristic internalism tends to attribute to the will less control of belief than Descartes did; but it is like his view in grounding justification in elements accessible to introspection.[59] Contemporary reliabilism falls more in the Lockean tradition; it is non-voluntarist, resolutely naturalistic, and externalist, grounding justification and knowledge in the truth-conduciveness of the processes producing belief.[60]

Major modern moral theories may also be viewed in relation to these traditions. Kant's ethics, for instance, exhibits a rationalist

---

and William J. Wainwright, eds., *Rationality, Religious Belief, and Moral Commitment* (Ithaca and London: Cornell University Press, 1986).

57. These points are confirmed by the *Essay*, though to be sure there are voluntarist (as well as some rationalist) elements in Locke.

58. Consider, e.g., Kant's statement, in his Preface to the First Edition of *The Critique of Pure Reason*, that "As regards the *form* of our enquiry, *certainty* and *clearness* are two essential requirements . . . As to *certainty*, I have prescribed to myself the maxim, that in this kind of investigation it is in no wise permissible to hold *opinions*. Everything, therefore, which bears any manner of resemblance to an hypothesis is to be treated as contraband . . . " See Norman Kemp Smith's translation (London: Macmillan, 1963), p. 11. Granted that Kant is here not talking of empirical knowledge, there is a notable resemblance to some of Descartes' remarks in the *Meditations*.

59. Roderick Chisholm's epistemology in *Theory of Knowledge*, 2nd edition (Englewood Cliffs: Prentice-Hall, 1977) is an example of this.

60. There are different ways for a theory to be naturalistic, however; and while reliabilists tend to be empiricistic, it is not clear that empiricism is required for a plausible version of the basic reliabilist idea that justified beliefs are those produced or sustained by suitably reliable processes. For a detailed statement of reliabilism see Alvin I. Goldman, *Epistemology and Cognition* (Cambridge: Harvard University Press, 1986).

conception of moral knowledge and a voluntarist view of moral rightness. In the full-blooded sense in which it implies moral worth, rightness, like Cartesian justification, is internal: it does not arise from the consequences of an act; it belongs to acts properly grounded in the will conceived as practical reason, quite as justification accrues to beliefs arising from voluntary assent guided by clear and distinct perception. Mill's utilitarianism exhibits an empiricist conception of moral knowledge and a non-voluntaristic, naturalist conception of rightness. The rightness of an act is not internally grounded in good will, but externally based on the act's consequences; and morally right acts are those with optimal hedonic effects, rather as, for reliabilism, justified beliefs are those which, by virtue of the kind they are, are likely to be true.[61]

Both the Cartesian and the Lockean traditions contain indispensable ingredients of an account of reason. Although I reject Cartesian voluntarism, I propose an internalist account both of justified belief and of rationality in general. Beliefs are not under direct voluntary control, and there are severe limits even on indirect control of them. When I have the arboreal impressions so familiar in my backyard, I cannot help believing there is a tree there. We can, however, influence our beliefs. We should expose ourselves to relevant evidence and monitor our beliefs and inferences with an eye to applying such self-corrective processes as logical scrutiny. We should beware of manipulators, listen to critics, and stand ready to test beliefs by their consequences for observation and reflection. We need, then, a measure of critical indirect voluntarism.

If internalism is sound for justification and rationality in general, it does not fully account for knowledge. For one thing, the object of knowledge – apart from self-knowledge – *is* external.[62] I thus

61. Two qualifications are needed here. First, I am only sketching a reliabilist notion of justification. Second, I do not mean to attribute a self-conscious reliabilism to Mill. But if something like this is not implicit in his epistemology, it at least goes well with his ethics. For ease of exposition, I have used a utilitarian criterion of "objective rightness," but the parallel is clearer for "subjective rightness": roughly, an act is subjectively right provided, relative to the agent's justified beliefs, it is of a type that reliably conduces optimally to happiness, i.e., a suitably large proportion (and more than half) of such acts contribute at least as favorably to the "proportion" of happiness to unhappiness as any available alternative.

62. This is not to imply that an adequate naturalistic account of knowledge can be given, though I do not rule that out and believe that there are apparently

combine internalism and externalism. In ethics, too, I seek a theory that embodies different kinds of ideals.[63] Normatively, it unites Kantian and utilitarian elements in recognizing both the internal bases of rational action and the desirability of producing human happiness. Metaethically, its internalism about justification is compatible with externalism about moral knowledge. Its conception of the structure of reason is, like that of both Descartes and Locke, foundationalist; and it stresses both the activity of mind – as positing, inferring, and imaginatively extending belief – and its receptivity to the imprints of the external events that envelop us. Much of our knowledge and justification is a gift; we need not earn it by reasoning or even careful observation. But through the critical use of reason we can build on what we are given. What we can build, moreover, is not limited to the empirical truths confirmable directly in experience or by logical operations on the ideas arising from it. Hume's instrumentalism about practical reason and his skepticism about induction yield a far narrower account of the scope of reason than mine.[64]

THE SKEPTICAL CHALLENGE TO
INTERNALIST REALISM

I have been affirming the power of reason. But what about skepticism? If justified belief is internally grounded, skepticism may seem best answerable by giving up realism. If justification is based on internal states and events, why not construe truth as internally

cases of knowledge without justification. If so, justification could be an irreducibly nonnaturalistic concept without thereby preventing a naturalistic account of at least some kinds of knowledge.
63. What I have in mind is similar to what William K. Frankena calls a mixed deontological theory. See, e.g., his *Ethics*, 2nd edition (Englewood Cliffs: Prentice-Hall, 1973).
64. Bertrand Russell followed Hume, but he granted that empiricism could not solve the problem of induction; see, for instance, "The Limits of Empiricism," Part IV, ch. 10 of *Human Knowledge: Its Scope and Limits* (New York; Simon and Schuster, 1948). There is, to be sure, a non-skeptical strain in Hume, but his skepticism seems required by his particular brand of strong empiricism. My own inclination is to countenance synthetic a priori propositions, including the sorts of epistemic principles apparently needed to deal with the problem of induction. A partial statement of my position on this issue is given in Chapter 10, this volume.

warranted assertibility and real objects as what properly warranted assertion is about?[65]

There are many difficulties with this view. One is that justification does not in general entail truth; we lose the concept of true belief, and hence of knowledge, if we collapse truth into any kind of justifiable belief. Indeed, even if physical objects are construed phenomenally, their existence does not follow from that of any set of experiences which, on internal grounds alone, we can know we have. Phenomenalism cannot in the end relieve our skeptical agonies,[66] and skepticism provides no good reason for internalist foundationalism to give up realism. Much the same holds in the practical case. If the rationality of an intrinsic desire has internal experiential grounds, it does not follow that its object really *is* desirable; but we need not for this reason be skeptics about desirability, value, and goodness, or construe them as mere subjective posits that serve to rationalize our desires.

Realism is also threatened by a skeptically tinged coherentism. For coherentism, no belief is directly justified or has a presumption of truth independently of others. But if a justified body of beliefs is simply one with an appropriate coherence, if we cannot even approach a unique system of justified beliefs, and if we do not have even the prima facie experiential access to reality implicit in objectivistic foundationalism, why accept realism rather than an anti-realist instrumentalism combined with a coherence theory of truth?[67] A coherentist need not respond skeptically to these

65. The realism I am discussing is construed as internalist because it is combined with an internalist epistemology; I am not referring to Hilary Putnam's internal realism, though there seem to be some affinities between the two views. See, e.g., his *The Many Faces of Realism* (LaSalle: Open Court Publishing Co., 1987), esp. Lecture II.

66. This point has often been missed or underemphasized. I take it that even if, e.g., seeing a tree is phenomenalistically analyzed, a plausible account will distinguish seeing a tree from hallucinating one and so allow that one may have a vivid arboreal experience yet not see a tree. Even if hallucination is normally discoverable by other experiences, a Cartesian demon could surely wreak the same perceptual havoc in the internal world as in the physical domain.

67. Three points should be made here. (1) I have in mind an instrumentalism, epistemological and ontological, such as that held by some philosophers of science. (2) I am not describing a pure doxastic coherentism, since experience is here included in the set of items that determine justification. But pure doxastic coherentism is less plausible, and there may perhaps be a way to allow experience to play the required role without in effect granting a weak version of direct justification to beliefs grounded in it, e.g. perceptually. (3) A similar

points or reject realism on their account. One view is that there is a presumption of truth on the part of a coherent system of beliefs whose content best explains one's overall experience.[68] Indeed, the idea is common ground between foundationalism and coherentism. It seems, however, more consonant with the former. For while foundationalists need not take directly justified beliefs to give us prima facie access to reality, they can at least leave this view open and can regard the truth of such beliefs as typically explainable by causal connections between those beliefs and the world.

Reliabilists tend to build prima facie access to reality directly into their account of justification: justified beliefs simply are those whose genesis gives them a high probability of truth, and the non-inferential ones are foundational. This conception of justification is highly favorable to realism; but it helps little against skepticism. For the suggested basis of justification is external and thus seems unavailable to anti-skeptical reflection, which cannot *presuppose* external sources of belief. A plausible skepticism will allow us to assume that we have visual experience, and we may then argue that this experience justifies our visual beliefs. But no skeptic will grant that our visual beliefs are reliably produced, and so mostly true: that would give up far too much at the outset.

There is little I can say here about how my position stands with respect to skepticism. But let me contrast *rebutting* skepticism – showing that the case for it is not cogent – with *refuting* it – showing that it is wrong, say by establishing that we *do* have justified beliefs about the world. The most important kinds of skepticism can be rebutted.[69] But there is far less reason to believe they can be refuted. Perhaps some can be, particularly if the epistemic principles we

line helps to explain why instrumentalists of any kind tend to be anti-realists about desirability; that tendency is in turn a factor inclining them to hold that intrinsic desires do not admit of rationality (while realism is not required for that view, the view is more plausible on realist assumptions).

68. Laurence BonJour holds a view along these lines for what I call direct beliefs, at least where they arise in trying to observe what is around one. See *The Structure of Empirical Knowledge* (Cambridge: Harvard University Press, 1985). In imposing an observation requirement on his coherentist account of knowledge, he is, however (as he is aware), abandoning a pure coherentism; and it is an interesting question how close this takes him to a foundationalism of the kind outlined here.

69. I have tried to make a beginning on this task in *Belief, Justification, and Knowledge*, ch. 9.

use as main premises are justifiable a priori and thus need not be held on inductive grounds.[70] But I will not even sketch an approach to such a refutation. My point here is that if we conceive justification in accordance with a fallibilistic foundationalism, we are less vulnerable to skepticism. For it is far more difficult for skeptics to show that we lack the defeasible justification this implies than to establish that we lack the kind of certainty which foundationalism (and indeed coherentism as well) is often wrongly thought to require for justification.

Suppose that we cannot refute, but can only rebut, skepticism regarding our beliefs about the external world. Should we then concede that we have no knowledge or justified beliefs about it? We should not. Skepticism has too often bedimmed the noontide sun in philosophy, and it can be averted. If in the end it cannot be vanquished, it is wise to grant that we may not *know* skepticism to be false. Nonetheless, we do have prima facie reasons to believe that there is both knowledge and justified belief about the world.

CONCLUSION

Thinking back on what I have said, I look again at the colors and shapes here, and again am conscious of reds and blues and greys, of sound and movement, surface and texture. My experience, present and remembered, and what is built on my experience, are the base of a structure of belief with a great diversity of ever-changing content. The structure has foundations, but they are neither fixed nor indubitable. Sometimes they give way, and I rebuild. I seek coherence and explanation, and I build toward that end; I sometimes encounter incoherence, and I adjust my outlook to rectify it. I do this within a framework; I always have something to work with, even if my foundations gradually change. Perception connects us with the external world; introspection scans the internal domain; reflection examines the abstract; memory retains a remarkable store of the raw materials that these sources yield; and,

70. The problem is discussed by William P. Alston in "Epistemic Circularity," *Philosophy and Phenomenological Research* 46 (1986) and in Chapter 10, this volume. If the principles are not a priori, then our warrant for believing them seems to depend on perceptual evidence in a way that would lead skeptics to consider it question-begging to rely on the principles in arguing that we have justified beliefs.

through the joint work of reasoning and imagination, we can build with this inventory in countless ways.

Practical reason is similar. Motivation of certain elemental kinds has almost the inevitability of experience itself. We all have intrinsic desires, other desires based on them, and tendencies, strong and weak, to act to achieve what we want. Our desires change with time. We extend them in framing a coherent plan of life; we relinquish some when incoherence besets the effort to satisfy them together. Perception shows us prospects we may want; introspection helps us determine our true inclinations toward envisaged objects of desire; memory, or its motivational analogue, preserves many of our desires; and, by imaginative reflection, we try to decide which to satisfy, and how. Just as the most basic of our warranted perceptual beliefs are grounded in experiences whose objects do not include us in their content, our rational intrinsic desires are, in the primitive cases, grounded in experiences which do not contain us among their objects. In these foundational cases, what makes it rational for me to want what I intrinsically desire tends to make it equally rational to want the same kind of thing for you. In this sense, rationality is impersonal.

So, too, is its close cousin, justification. What justifies my perceptual beliefs is the same experiential qualities that justify yours, and I may not rationally suppose that, though yours are based on the same kind of sensory evidence as mine, mine are better justified. It is true that whereas there can be no competition for an object of true belief, sometimes we cannot all have the same desired material things. But important as this is in a world of scarcity, it shows nothing about the rationality of desire. Moreover, much of what we most want can be shared: consumables may be divided and multiplied; many of our devoutly desired experiences, like many aesthetic, intellectual, and spiritual activities, are sharable; and some of our greatest pleasures have, as their special object, the delight of others.

This picture is of reason in the individual. But individuals are part of their culture. Culture influences reason, as reason may suffuse culture. Reason would have us value what we enjoy, particularly those activities that yield pleasure by engaging our complex faculties. It is culture that supplies many of these activities and most of the social and educational conditions for achieving rationality. Reason can embrace indefinitely many cultures; it constrains, but does not constrict. It would have us pursue activities we find rewarding, but it provides no precise list of these, nor does it ever endorse as final the cherished list of any one culture.

My view of reason is internalist but not subjectivist, fallibilist but not relativist, and realist but not dogmatic. It forswears both the tyranny of mind to which voluntaristic rationalism is prey and the tyranny of nature which is a liability of naturalistic empiricism. Reason is a powerful and active faculty, but we need not use it to pare ourselves down to the Cartesian minimum and construct knowledge of the world from egocentric beginnings. We do not build the world from within; we build within from the world. Perception connects us with reality; we need not project our egos into our experience and infer an external world as the best explanation of the contents of self-consciousness. Such work may be needed to disperse the clouds of skepticism, but normally we are not in their shadow.

Like reason, which is its central character, philosophy is autonomous: it has both its own methods and its own standards.[71] But the autonomy is not absolute. Philosophy is bound, historically, by its own past and, culturally, by the tensions and crises, the insights and discoveries, the dreams and metaphors, of the art and science and daily life of its times. Its evidential standards overlap those of science, but they are more general. They apply to the abstract and the concrete, the normative and the factual, and the interpretation of experience in any culture. Philosophy is a limitless domain of rational activity: unrestrainedly curious, relentlessly penetrating, boundlessly speculative. There are no limits either to the kinds of theories it can create or to its ability to critize its own results. To regard philosophy as a mere child of its times, to deny it the capacity to reach toward truth, to take its fallibility to warrant skepticism about its objectivity, is a temptation no less to be resisted than the dogmatism it would combat. There is a rational structure that can guide our inquiries; there are rational methods we can use in conducting them; there is a

71. Philosophy has both a hard, conceptual, and a soft, sociological, autonomy, as I have contended in "Realism, Rationality, and Philosophical Method," *Proceedings and Addresses of the American Philosophical Association* 61 (1987). For related (and sometimes contrasting) conceptions of philosophy see J. R. Lucas, "Philosophy and Philosophy Of," *Proceedings of the British Academy* LXXII (1986), Ernest Sosa, "Serious Philosophy and Freedom of Spirit," *The Journal of Philosophy* LXXXIV (1987), and Alasdair MacIntyre, *Whose Justice? Which Rationality?* (Notre Dame: University of Notre Dame Press, 1988).

monumental array of inexhaustible philosophical texts, ancient, medieval, and modern, intellectual anchors which, though they lean with the currents of fashion, are never pulled up. And reason, the critical voice in human conversation, the authority that subverts authority, the fabric of our excellences, the form of our forms of life, endures as a vital force in building theories of the reality it enables us to know.[72]

72. This essay has benefited from my discussions with many people, and a number of colleagues have given me helpful comments on earlier drafts. There is no hope of acknowledging all the colleagues and students from whom I have learned something on one or another topic in this essay, but recent discussions on the subject with William Alston, Karl Ameriks, Richard Brandt, Hector-Neri Castañeda, Frederick Crosson, Stephen Darwall, Michael DePaul, Richard Foley, Jorge Garcia, Alan Gewirth, John Gill, Gary Gutting, Robert Kane, Jaegwon Kim, Christine Korsgaard, Ernan McMullin, George Mavrodes, Andrew Naylor, David O'Connor, Alvin Plantinga, Philip Quinn, Amelie Oksenberg Rorty, Bruce Russell, Kenneth Sayre, Aaron Snyder, James Sterba, and Howard Wettstein were especially valuable. Most of these discussions were made possible by a Distinguished Scholar Fellowship in the Center for Philosophy of Religion at the University of Notre Dame during 1987–88, and I am grateful for that opportunity, as well as for research – and collegial – support from the University of Nebraska. I also benefited much from detailed written comments given me by William Alston, Hugh McCann, Joseph Mendola, Paul Moser, Allison Nespor, and Paul Pines. It will be quite some time before I can respond to all the insightful comments and critical points made by these and other colleagues; the notes – which omit much I would like to have cited – are some indication of directions in which I hope responses lie.

Index

Index